FROM THE EAST

FROM THE EAST

THE HISTORY OF THE LATTER-DAY
SAINTS IN ASIA • 1851–1996

R. LANIER BRITSCH

DESERET BOOK COMPANY
SALT LAKE CITY, UTAH

Library of Congress Cataloging-in-Publication Data

Britsch, R. Lanier
  From the east : the history of the Latter-day Saints in Asia / by
R. Lanier Britsch.
    p.   cm.
  Includes bibliographical references and index.
  ISBN 1-57345-268-8
  1. Church of Jesus Christ of Latter-day Saints—Asia—History.
2. Mormon Church—Asia—History. I. Title.
BX8617.A78B75   1998
289.3'5—dc21   97-36785
                                                  CIP

Printed in the United States of America   49510

10 9 8 7 6 5 4 3 2 1

This book is dedicated to my teacher-mentor friends,
to whom I bear an eternal obligation.

Professor Emeritus Russell N. Horiuchi, Geographer
Professor Emeritus Paul V. Hyer, Historian
Professor Emeritus Spencer J. Palmer, World Religionist
Professor Emeritus John L. Sorenson, Anthropologist

And I say unto you, That many shall come
from the east and west, and shall sit down with Abraham,
and Isaac, and Jacob, in the kingdom of heaven.

MATTHEW 8:11

CONTENTS

PREFACE

Had I known in 1972 that the book I was commencing would not be published until 1998, twenty-six years later, I might have despaired and moved on to other things. As time would have it, I worked on many other projects during the ensuing years anyway. The original target publication date in 1980 was not realized, and for a variety of reasons I set it aside. Fifteen years passed before I could return to it with full dedication. The time lapse proved to be a blessing because many wonderful, interesting, and inspiring events transpired in Asia during those years. Chief among them is that the Church expanded tremendously as new lands were opened to missionary work and to the presence of Church members. This is a much more engaging and useful book now than it would have been earlier.

From the East: The History of the Latter-day Saints in Asia, 1851–1996 deals with the history of The Church of Jesus Christ of Latter-day Saints in Asia. To most people *Asia* means the nations or geographical regions from Pakistan and east through India and Southeast Asia to China, Korea, and Japan. These are the areas covered in this history. The term *Asia* can be misleading. It gives the impression that the area is a monolith culturally, linguistically, politically, and so on. But Asia is diverse—a multitude of nations, peoples, languages, cultures, histories, religions, and governments. More than half the world's population lives there. To simply say that someone is Asian or Oriental is to display little knowledge of the situation. Trying to understand Asia's distinct cultures and histories has been one of the greatest challenges I've faced while writing this book.

Although missionary work has claimed center stage, *From the East* is not intended to be only a history of missions and their notable full-time missionaries. I have included the efforts of many others to live the gospel and to help establish the Church in Asian lands. Latter-day Saint servicemen and their families have done much to plant and sustain the young growth of the Church in Asia. Government workers, educators, contractors, and business people have also done their part. And once the foundations were set, local members did the greater share of building up the Church in every place where the faith has taken hold. Recognizing this, I have tried to include all categories of contributors.

Many readers will recognize major deficiencies in two areas, secular history and the histories of other Christian denominations. The size of the present volume should serve as sufficient explanation for my decision not to say more in that regard. I encourage study of the many excellent histories of Asian political, cultural, and religious affairs. Because LDS Church history has not occurred in a vacuum, I have tried to say enough about secular and religious history to build a context for Latter-day Saint developments.

Although this volume is large, it contains only a brief introduction to the Church in each country. In all likelihood, what I've written about the Church in Taiwan, for instance, will seem meager to those who live there or who have served there. And the same will be true for everywhere else. Hopefully, I will have said enough about each country to satisfy readers' overall needs.

A Note Concerning Languages and Spelling

The spelling of Asian names is most confusing. Almost all Asian languages are written in characters that are unintelligible to users of English. Chinese and Japanese are written in pictographic or ideographic characters. However, Japanese also uses phonetic characters. Korean, too, is written in a phonetic syllabary. The languages of South and Southeast Asia are written in alphabets, scripts, and symbols that are not familiar to us. Some languages, notably Japanese, have been standardized and are consistent among users in transliterated form. However, others, for example Korean, have not been standardized in this way. In this book I have chosen to use the versions of names found in Spencer and Shirley Palmer's book, *Korean Saints,* but these usages are not always consistent with spellings found in the *Ensign* or *Church News.* In other instances I have followed the most frequently used English versions of names.

Chinese has presented several problems, the most critical being the general use of the Wade-Giles transliteration system in Taiwan, a system that is similar to it in Hong Kong (where Cantonese is spoken), and pinyin, the approved system in the People's Republic of China. When writing about Taiwan, I have, as needed, chosen to observe the language conventions in use there. Attempts to impose the mainland system on Taiwan create awkward and often unrecognizable usages. In the section dealing with the People's Republic of China, I have used pinyin spellings.

With only a few exceptions, family names come first in Asian usage. In most cases I have followed this pattern. The exceptions include several General Authorities who are so familiar that their names seem most natural following the Western pattern. Elder Yoshihiko Kikuchi (family name) is a case in point. Interestingly, in Church periodicals Elder Han (family name) In Sang's name follows the Asian convention as often as it does the Western way, Elder In Sang Han. I have generally commented in the body of the text regarding language customs and usages.

Attempts at spelling Asian names in English often fall short of accuracy and are only approximations. The spellings of place names on maps vary greatly. I have attempted to achieve consistency if not total accuracy.

Acknowledgments

Acknowledging everyone by name who has helped me in the research and writing of this book is not possible. Sadly, I cannot remember the names of all the secretaries and student assistants who helped me find materials or who typed early drafts of the manuscript in the 1970s. I am, nevertheless, grateful for their time and talents. Even during the past two years, when I took up the project again, many people have come to my aid whose names I do not know, but I am thankful for their help. Dozens of people have submitted to oral history interviews. Most of their names are listed in the bibliography.

Several General Authorities of the Church have rendered wonderful assistance to me. I am grateful to President Gordon B. Hinckley for allowing me to use his journals as a primary source. I thank Elder John K. Carmack for reading several chapters in their early stages and giving me honest and helpful responses to my work. His personal support and encouragement are greatly appreciated. Elders Yoshihiko Kikuchi, Sam K. Shimabukuro, Merrill J. Bateman, Augusto A. Lim, Ben B. Banks, John H. Groberg, and Tai Kwok Yuen assisted through interviews or in other ways.

I appreciate my many friends and colleagues who read parts of the manuscript, provided documents, and assisted with travel, housing, food, or in other ways. Among those who must be included are Mary Ellen Edmunds, Larry R. White, Effian Kadarusman, Melvin Thatcher, Hsieh Fan, Chen Mung Yu, Hu Wei-I, Liang Yun-Sheng, Richard Stamps, A. C. Ho, Ted and Nola Christensen, David Phelps, Stephen K. Iba, Virgil N. Kovalenko, Ronald G. Watt, Robert and Jeanne Griffiths, Jerry and Marsha McClain, Ira and Patricia Todd, G. S. and Vilo Gill, David Shuler, Richard and Doris Smith, Wendy Chang Shamo, J. Scott Miller, Paul V. Hyer, Jeff Ringer, Mark Peterson, Masakazu Watabe, Niiyama Yasuo, and Timothy Hunt. I am grateful for the secretaries and transcribers who assisted in this project, among them Diane Morita, Muriel Tuairau, Marilyn Webb, and Marilyn Reynolds. Graduate research assistants included but were not limited to Charles Seng, Michael W. Hale, Cory Turner, and Lafayette A. Smith.

Over the years the staff members at the LDS Church Archives have given me countless hours of personal assistance, particularly Ron Watt and Bill Slaughter. This book could not have been written without the Historical Department of the Church.

I thank the administration of Brigham Young University for granting me two professional development leaves during part of 1978 and part of 1995 to do research and writing on this book. Particularly I thank Dean Clayne L. Pope and Associate Vice President John S. Tanner for facilitating my latest leave. I'm grateful to the university for providing research support of several kinds. And I express gratitude to the David M. Kennedy Center for International Studies for providing a hideaway, computer support, and a research grant to have a number of interviews transcribed.

To various editors at the *Ensign* magazine I extend appreciation for publishing my work and now allowing parts to be used again. The *Ensign* and *Church News* have been of immense value in my research. I thankfully acknowledge the hundreds of articles in both periodicals that have made my work possible. I also want to specifically thank the staff of the Historical Department of the Church for assistance and friendship over many years.

Most likely I would not have walked this path if Leonard J. Arrington, James B. Allen, and Davis Bitton had not invited me in 1972 to write a book that was tentatively titled *A History of the Latter-day Saints in Asia and the Pacific*. With the publication of this volume, that project is finally completed. (*Unto the Islands of the Sea: A History of the Latter-day Saints in the Pacific* was published by Deseret Book Company in 1986.)

I'm grateful to Deseret Book for the pleasant working relationship we've had since 1983. In the present instance, I'm grateful that Sheri L. Dew, vice president of publishing, supported the concept of *From the East* many months before I was able to present her the manuscript. Most recently I've enjoyed working with my editor, Linda R. Gundry, and layout and artistic designer, Ron Stucki. Good people, all.

Two of my six children (one who is two-years returned from his mission and the other who has been in the mission field for over a year) cannot remember when Dad started writing this book. To my great satisfaction they, along with their older brothers and sisters, have matter-of-factly supported this long-term effort. And JoAnn, my wife, has nurtured me, prodded me, and listened to or read the whole manuscript several times. She's always assured me that the book is important and that I shouldn't let it die. I love her and appreciate the thousands of blessings she has brought to me.

Numerous friends have read parts of this book, but I've been left to decide what is important and how to describe and interpret events. At best history is but an approximation of truth. History is not the product of the writer's imagination, but often the historian has to use his or her imagination to complete the story. I'm sure my version of what has happened in the growth of the Church in Asia will differ in many points from the memories of those who were there. My hope has been to be as true to the facts as possible, but I suspect readers will uncover problems and inaccuracies here and there. I regret that it cannot be otherwise.

1

INTRODUCTION

The Church and Asia

At the end of the twentieth century, Asia not only poses a significant challenge to fulfilling the Lord's charge to take the restored gospel to every nation, kindred, tongue, and people, but also offers great opportunities for spreading the gospel in a vast area extending from Karachi, Pakistan, to Tokyo, Japan. The inhabitants of China, India, Pakistan, Japan, Indonesia, and South Korea number more than three billion people. For The Church of Jesus Christ of Latter-day Saints, the magnitude of bearing witness in these lands and in the rest of Asia—comprising 56 percent of the world's population all told—is staggering.

Asia is the seat of many great ancient cultures and religions. The world's five greatest religions were born there, including Judaism, Christianity, and Islam. Asia is also the oldest and greatest center of Christian missionary activity. Those of us who are steeped in Western tradition are surprised to learn that during the first few centuries of Christianity, the most successful dissemination of the gospel was to the East, not to the West. The Apostle Thomas evidently took the gospel to India, and by the third century a community of Syrian Christians was established along India's Malabar Coast. During the seventh century, Nestorian Christians established a thriving church in China. Since the age of discovery, Roman Catholic and, later, Protestant missions covered most of the lands of Asia. Latter-day Saints owe gratitude to the valiant men and women who have translated the Holy Bible and who have taken their versions of Christianity as well as literacy and medical and social services to many of Asia's peoples.

Asia has been the least fertile (with the exception of the Muslim areas) of all the major Christian missionary fields of the world. Africa, Europe, the Americas, and Oceania have all been more productive of Christian converts. Although the foregoing areas are all nominally Christian, in all of Asia only the Philippine Islands (more than 90 percent Christian) is a Christian nation. The other somewhat successful areas of Christian evangelization are South Korea (35 percent Christian), Indonesia (10–12 percent Christian), Taiwan (5 percent Christian), and Vietnam (9.8 percent Christian). Korea, Indonesia, and the Philippines, the three most fruitful areas of Christian success, were never fully converted to the so-called higher religions—Islam, Hinduism, and Buddhism—before Christian missionaries arrived there. Ten percent of the Korean people remain Shamanists (followers of diviners), but a much higher percentage are influenced by such thinking. In Indonesia the major pockets of Christian success have occurred where the people were still animists. Because the Roman Catholic Spanish subjugated the Philippines before Islam spread far into that land, most Filipinos moved directly from tribal religions to Catholicism. On the other hand, the people in lands where the great religions hold sway have not easily converted to Christianity. In China before 1949, there were more than four million Christians, but they totaled only 0.7 percent of the population. Between 1.4 and 2.5 percent of the Japanese, 1 percent of the Thais, and 2.61 percent of the Indian people are Christian today. The established higher religions of Asia have not easily yielded to Christianity in general nor to The Church of Jesus Christ of Latter-day Saints.[1]

The history of the Latter-day Saints in Asia relates primarily to the post–World War II era. Although the Latter-day Saints established missions in South and Southeast Asia in the 1850s and the Japanese Mission from 1901 to 1924, circumstances were not such that the Church could succeed during the prewar period. However, since 1945 Asia has changed in many ways. Colonialism has ended, and new nations have arisen that provide religious freedom. Japan's defeat created for a time a new and healthy religious environment. New constitutions and governmental systems have made the evangelization of the Asian world much more possible than in former times. Improved economic circumstances have helped alleviate suffering in some areas, and improved literacy rates have placed more people within reach of the gospel message. Although considerable economic and political strife has followed each great war, a positive result has been the planting of the restored gospel by LDS servicemen. In addition, since the 1960s the Church has grown large enough and financially capable enough to support a much greater missionary program than ever before.

Some have asked, Why take the restored gospel to Asia? This question has an odd ring in light of the Savior's commission in Matthew 28:19 to take the gospel to all nations of the earth. Moreover, President Gordon B. Hinckley has said, "These [Asian] people are as entitled to the gospel as any on this earth."[2] But three or four decades ago it was not so unusual to hear such questions raised. President Joseph Fielding Smith answered this query by referring to Jacob, chapter 5, in the Book of Mormon. Using that scripture, he explained that the House of Israel is spread throughout the earth and that in the final period of the world's history descendants of Israel must be gathered into the Lord's church from the far corners of his vineyard—including Asia.[3]

The position of the Church regarding the brotherhood of man is clear. All members of the human family are the spiritual offspring of God, our Heavenly Father. All humankind is born with innate goodness (the light of Christ) and the ability to grow spiritually and intellectually. Heavenly Father has graced all peoples with religious and philosophical teachers who have improved the human condition and raised the level of righteousness among the nations. Although there is much within the broad realm of religion that has not been uplifting or enriching, there is much good in the major religions of the world. The world is filled with good people. The motivation of the Latter-day Saints has been to help make them better and to provide ordinances and an order in people's lives that will lead them back into the presence of their Heavenly Father.

Missionary work is and always has been an incredibly brave and bold endeavor. To invite people to change their lives can be disruptive and painful. Many Christian missionary groups have stopped using the word *convert* because they believe it implies arrogance and superiority on the part of the missionary. Latter-day Saints, however, view the matter differently. Conversion implies acceptance of the life and teachings of Jesus Christ and the blessings of following him. What others may call arrogance, Latter-day Saints consider humble witness of the saving truth, the fulfillment of Christ's commandment to take the gospel to all the world.

Mormon missionaries usually have not worried much about whether their devotion, earnestness, and confidence in their position may be misperceived as arrogance. Rather, they have simply moved forward with the assumption that they are right, that their message is the saving truth, always expecting new members of the Church to leave their pasts behind, to join with a new group of associates whom they usually hardly know, and to literally become a new person with a new life in Christ. Often the members of the new group are themselves relatively new to the Church and unprepared (except for their shared convictions of the truth) to help integrate other new members. Even so, the Church grows and new members hold on because they feel the same convictions the missionaries felt and they know they must continue faithful and help build up the Church. Because of their faith and assurances that the restored gospel is true and that they are engaged in a supernally important work, new converts weather whatever personal and social storms their convictions bring.

Most Latter-day Saint missionaries are young and inexperienced and know relatively little about the people they have been sent to teach. As a result, they may have difficulty distinguishing between the principles and practices of the restored gospel and their own native cultures and preferences. American missionaries especially have been prone to forward—albeit innocently and unwittingly—their own social customs in the name of Mormonism. The miracle is that despite such obstacles, cultural and otherwise, the Church does grow and create groups, branches, and wards that fill converts' lives with meaning, direction, joy, and faith in the Lord Jesus Christ.

Since 1830, when Joseph Smith's brother Samuel placed copies of the Book of Mormon in his bag and set out to spread the message of the Restoration, the methods used to teach the gospel have been many and varied. Until the post–World War II era, there was not a unified system for teaching the gospel to investigators of the Church. Richard Lloyd Anderson and Reed Bankhead devised the first systematic, sequential method of explaining gospel concepts and moving contacts toward baptism. In 1960 the Church put forward the first unified plan to be used in missions worldwide. In Asia the use of the various unified plans has been a help and a hindrance. The various cultural and religious traditions have suggested the need for a variety of approaches to begin the teaching process on common ground, but few adaptations have been made in an effort to suit teaching methods to the circumstances of each nation. Perhaps as years pass, further adaptations will be made in continued recognition of the fact that approaches based on common Christian understandings are not ipso facto appropriate for people of all cultures, languages, and religious persuasions.

One of the most remarkable facts regarding Mormon missions in Asia is that Church leaders saw fit to send missionaries there at such an early date. Missionaries were sent from England to India in 1851, and from Salt Lake City to India, Siam, and Hong Kong in 1852. At that time the Church was very small (total membership in 1854 was 68,429). Between 1850 and 1854 the Brethren set apart 322 missionaries to serve in thirteen missions that included

859 mission branches. A high percentage of the Church's human resources were expended on missionary work. When it is remembered who these early missionaries were—mostly married men whose wives and children remained at home to continue the labor of subduing the wilderness—the meaning of missionary work to the Church takes on gigantic proportions. Sending missionaries to the British Isles and Europe in the 1830s, 1840s, and 1850s was a demanding proposition. Sending missionaries to India, Burma, Ceylon, Siam, and China at that time is difficult to imagine.

India in the 1850s was under British control, but life there at that time was difficult, especially for men who traveled without purse or scrip. China in the 1850s was embroiled in a civil war that ultimately took the lives of twenty million people. A decade before, in 1842, the British had forced the rulers of the Qing (Ch'ing) dynasty to open five ports to foreign trade. Protestant missionaries began entering Chinese ports, but by 1853, when the first LDS missionaries to China arrived, Hong Kong, the only available port, was not hospitable to men in their financial condition.

In 1853 Japan was still a closed country. Not until 1854 did Commodore Matthew C. Perry of the United States force open Japan to normal intercourse with the Western world. Although Protestant missionaries entered Japan in 1859, posters around the country in 1872 still proclaimed Christianity to be illegal. After that time, conditions became more favorable for foreign missionary work, but the Church's decision to enter Japan in 1901 was still quite early considering the resources of the Church and the religious situation in that country. By 1901 Church membership had reached 292,931, with members living in 50 stakes, 577 wards and 21 missions. There were 518 missionaries serving worldwide.

Considering where the Church stood in relation to Asia in 1901, or better, in 1945, its growth in that part of the world has been wonderful—a miracle. Our hindsight is sometimes better than our understanding of the present, and it is certainly better than our ability to see into the future. The history of the Church has been a steady process of expansion as its manpower resources have grown. The 322 missionaries of the early 1850s have now expanded to more than fifty thousand. The Church's ability to cover the earth with the message of the Restoration is daily becoming greater. Large population segments of the world remain virtually untouched—1.2 billion Chinese, 975 million Indians, a billion Muslims, and so on—but as the Church continues to grow, its power to fulfill the Lord's commission to carry the gospel to every nation, kindred, tongue, and people will be fulfilled. This study seeks to historically document the efforts of the Church to carry the word of the restored gospel to Asia from 1851 until 1996.

NOTES

1. For further information on Christian missionary history in Asia, see Stephen Neill, *A History of Christian Missions*, 2nd ed. (Harmondsworth, London: Penguin Books, 1984). Statistics in this chapter are taken from Patrick Johnstone, *Operation World* (Grand Rapids, Mich.: Zondervan Publishing House, 1993).

2. Quoted in Sheri L. Dew, *Go Forward with Faith: The Biography of Gordon B. Hinckley* (Salt Lake City: Deseret Book Co., 1996), 551.

3. See Joseph Fielding Smith, *Answers to Gospel Questions*, comp. Joseph Fielding Smith Jr., 5 vols. (Salt Lake City: Deseret Book Co., 1979), 4:201–7.

2

EARLY ASIAN
MISSIONS
1851–1856

The 1850s Missions to
India, Burma, Siam, and China

More than seven decades ago, Elder Brigham H. Roberts, a well-known Latter-day Saint Church authority and historian, said concerning the LDS missionaries to India that "there is nothing more heroic in our Church annals than the labors and sufferings of these brethren of the mission to India."[1] Considering the times in which Roberts lived and the knowledge he had of the trials and sufferings of the early members of the Church, this statement takes on great proportions.[2]

The mission to India began not in Utah, where Brigham Young had established the Saints, but in England. The need for missionaries in India was recognized when two persons in India, Private Thomas Metcalf of the British Army and William A. Sheppard of Calcutta, wrote asking for tracts, literature, and other information about the Church. Concurrent with these requests came word concerning missionary efforts of two sailors who, after being baptized in England on January 27, 1849, had undertaken a voyage that terminated at Calcutta, India. There they waited while their ship received needed repairs. These men, George

Barber and Benjamin Richey, were the first known members of the Church to teach the restored gospel on Indian soil. While they were in Calcutta, they became acquainted with a Protestant group known as the Plymouth Brethren. Barber and Richey did their best to explain Mormonism and received a warm response from several members of the congregation. These sailors were not well-informed regarding doctrines of the Church, nor did they hold priesthood authority; for this reason, when they arrived back in England they asked Church authorities there to send someone to baptize several of the Plymouth Brethren.[3]

In response, Elder Joseph Richards was ordained, set apart, and sent to Calcutta by G. B. Wallace, a Church authority in England. Richards arrived at Calcutta in June 1851. He did not stay there long on this first visit, however, because he had obtained passage under contract as a sail maker and could not find a replacement when the ship sailed back to England. But while there he baptized the first Mormon converts of India, ordained several men to the priesthood, and established the "Wanderer's Branch."[4]

More than six months later, on December 25, 1851, Elder William Willes, Richards's replacement, arrived in Calcutta. He had been called by Lorenzo Snow, president of the Italian Mission, who felt it his prerogative to include India in his area of authority.[5] Willes was called especially to go to Calcutta. Elder Snow sent another elder, Hugh Findlay, to Bombay at the same time.

Willes found only six members of the Church in Calcutta, and they were without leadership. Richards had returned to London, and Maurice White, who had been ordained an elder and set apart as branch president in Calcutta only a week after his baptism, had also departed for England with the intention of learning more about doctrines and operations of the Church. Willes soon organized the group and gave the male members responsibilities such as that of secretary, treasurer, and book agent. Plans were made to publish a tract in the Bengali and Hindustani languages. Within a few days after his arrival, Willes was informed by James Patric Meik, one of the first converts, that he intended to build a lecture hall on land he had leased for the Church. By the time Elder Willes had been in India for two weeks, he had lectured several times concerning the gospel, and he was sure that he would have success. He was elated by a report from a native Indian woman named Anna, who had been baptized by Maurice White, to the effect that a whole church of Indian Episcopalian Christians would desire baptism just as soon as matters could "be arranged in relation to their social position, etc."[6]

Matthew McCune and his family were among the first converts to the Church in India in 1851. He preached the restored gospel in Calcutta and in Burma while serving in the military. He immigrated to Utah in the 1850s. (Courtesy LDS Church Archives)

In his first letter home, Willes wrote: "Although I am writing in this cool, businesslike strain, my heart is abounding with grateful emotions of thanksgiving that he has made me and my brethren the instruments in His hands for spreading such glorious tidings in a land filled with 'darkness, selfishness and cruel habitations.'"[7]

January, February, and March 1852 brought continued success. Willes had obtained the services of an Indian who had set to work translating *Ancient Gospel Restored,* a tract by Lorenzo Snow. Willes was also presenting a series of twenty lectures that were well attended. The number of people baptized continued to mount, and opposition to his message was minimal. By March 24 there were twelve European and twenty Indian members. On April 6 Willes baptized eleven local men who had come from a distant village. Three of these men were soon ordained to the Aaronic Priesthood.[8]

During April some opposition began to arise from the Protestant ministers and missionaries in Calcutta. These men told the new members of the Church that they would become "Muslims" and "be obliged to have many wives, etc., and that Joe Smith bought three hundred thousand Mormons with the Gold that he found in California." But even with such rumors, by the beginning of May 1852 Church membership in and around Calcutta had increased to 150, with 3 elders, 8 priests, 9 teachers, 8 deacons, and 122 lay members. By adding to that number children belonging to the baptized families, there were more than 300 Indian Saints of all sizes, colors, and languages. On the previous Christmas (1851) there were only six members.[9] By mid-May the Church had grown by another 39 members. The total membership amounted to 189, of whom 170 were *ryots*, or native farmers.

Spreading the message beyond Calcutta was physically difficult. Willes reported that when he left the confines of the city, the people were "scattered over an immense district of ploughed fields and very bad or no regular roads."[10] He had no knowledge of Indian social patterns, no missionary plan to follow, and the climate was very difficult to adjust to.

In August 1852 Joseph Richards returned to Calcutta, having sailed all the way around the Cape of Good Hope to England and back. A few days later, Richards baptized William Sheppard and his son. Sheppard, it will be remembered, had been one of those who originally inquired for information regarding Mormonism. Following these baptisms, there was little activity for the next two months. The monsoon rains continued heavy until early November, and by that time, even though attendance at meetings was picking up, Willes and Richards had decided to set out for the Punjab, a distance of about one thousand miles northwest of Calcutta. They sustained James Patric Meik as branch president in Calcutta and set out on their journey.[11]

What followed over the next number of months was one of

the great missionary journeys of Church history. Willes and Richards traveled more than 620 miles on foot before they became convinced that it would be more economical to travel by ox-drawn wagon. Traveling the ancient route called the Grand Trunk Road, they visited many of the sacred places of the Hindu religion, as well as the famed Taj Mahal. As they made their way up the Ganges River basin, they preached and baptized a number of people.

By the time they reached Agra (approximately eight hundred miles from Calcutta), they had baptized sixteen people. At this point, however, Richards's health began to fail him and he decided that he should not continue on to the Punjab. Accordingly, he made his way back toward Calcutta. But Willes decided to go on alone. From Agra he went to a village called Dugshai and from there to Simla, which is directly north of New Delhi. (Dugshai and Simla are what the British called "hill towns," high in the Himalayan foothills.) Willes also traveled in the Punjab, but his success there was very limited. He reported that the military establishments were almost all "closed-up" against him; he believed that the chaplains had carefully written to one another warning of his coming.[12]

HUGH FINDLAY'S WORK IN BOMBAY

Willes and Richards were not the only LDS missionaries working in India. Hugh Findlay had by this time, late 1852 and early 1853, been in Bombay for more than a year. He did not have the success that Willes enjoyed, for he had been met almost from the day of his arrival by opposition from the established Protestant sects, the press, and military officers and chaplains.[13] Thus it was necessary from the beginning that Findlay publicly defend his position in Bombay.

It took him almost six months to baptize his first six converts. He was not allowed in any military areas in Bombay and was forbidden to preach to military personnel. Because he was not making much headway in Bombay, Findlay decided to move to what he hoped would be a more fruitful location. He selected Poona, about ninety miles from Bombay, and went there. Again he was greeted by a hostile press and by military officers who were at first not willing to let him preach. Permission to proselytize was finally given because the officer in charge felt that "the less these people are opposed the less harm they would do."[14]

Several kinds of trouble occurred, mostly because of a rumor that the Mormons would buy the "drafts" of the British soldiers and send them to California; another problem had to do with an anti-Mormon tract that was widely distributed. Notwithstanding these difficulties, Elder Findlay was successful in organizing a branch of twelve members in Poona by mid-September 1852. They were a "little company . . . of a mixed birth, European, Eurasian, and native."[15]

In October, Findlay was directed to leave the military cantonment. By that time it was evident to the officer in charge that Findlay was not a temporary visitor. Findlay found new quarters, which he described in these words: "This house is a little uncouth to the eye, bearing a resemblance to an English store-room, or a Bombay go-down, having a door, six feet by six feet at each end, and two windows, four by six feet, on each side, with iron bars, and the light of day is an apology for glass, indeed having such an edifice for bedroom, parlour, and sanctuary, it required considerable faith to convince one's self that imprisonment is not added to banishment. But we 'stoop to conquer,' and are thankful to the Lord for it."[16]

Findlay held Church meetings in this place in addition to living there. He did have plans to build a chapel directly across the street, though, and saw its completion several months later.

After his expulsion from the cantonments, Findlay turned more and more to the local population. He studied the Maratha language and spent a great deal of time with a group of Brahmin intellectuals who made it a practice to discuss religion with missionaries.

MISSIONARIES FROM UTAH CALLED
TO INDIA, SIAM, AND CHINA

During the time when Willes and Richards were preaching in northern India and Findlay was working in Bombay and Poona, events were taking place in Utah that were of great importance to the India Mission as well as to other areas considered in this book. On August 28 and 29, 1852, President Brigham Young called a special conference of the Church. This meeting, held specifically for the purpose of calling and sending out 108 missionaries, was an extra meeting in the Church's yearly schedule of conferences. It was held early (before the usual time in October) so that the missionaries could reach their fields with greater ease before winter. Although this was primarily a missionary conference, it is remembered today because on August 29, 1852, the Church officially announced the doctrine of plural marriage.[17]

Nine of the 108 missionaries chosen were to go to Calcutta, India; four were to go to Siam (Thailand); and four were selected to go to Hong Kong, China.

The next two months found the newly called missionaries busy in preparation. All of the missionaries met several times with Church leaders and were given instructions and strengthened in their testimonies. They also discussed potential problems relating to their missions and made several decisions, such as to travel in wagons, with each group carrying its own food, bedding, and equipment.

On October 16, the missionaries were set apart and given priesthood blessings. They reported that the Spirit of the Lord was strongly felt that day and during the next few days. The presiding authorities of the Church gave many priesthood blessings.[18]

The group that left Salt Lake Valley during those autumn days of late October consisted of thirty-eight missionaries called to Calcutta, Siam, China, the Sandwich Islands, and Australia. All of the groups gathered at Peteetnot Creek (Payson, Utah) on October 24 and organized the camp. Hosea Stout, a missionary bound for China, was made captain; Nathanial Vary Jones, who was headed for India, was made chaplain; Burr Frost, who was to serve in Australia, was appointed sergeant of the guard; and Amos Milton Musser, en route to India, was clerk for the company. As they renewed their journey, the course they followed lay southwestward, roughly over the present U.S. Interstate 15 highway. They traveled by the iron mines near Cedar City, Utah, through Mountain Meadows, and on down the steep gully to Santa Clara Creek. On November 12 they were joined by a group of emigrants going to California to dig gold. The next three days they followed the Rio Virgin and then began the ascent to the top of Mormon Mesa, in present-day Nevada. They were a full day getting the fourteen wagons up the last steep incline with "twenty men on the lead and four horses behind them, with two men to roll the hind wheels. A slight accident might precipitate wagons and animals into the abyss on either side of the backbone on which part of the ascent was made. Three cheers were given as the last wagon reached the summit of the precipice in safety."[19]

Ahead of them now lay the fifty-two-mile stretch to Las Vegas. It was during this section of the trip that Nathaniel V. Jones became very ill. He did not respond to any of the usual remedies or the blessing of the elders, so it was necessary for the company to lay over at Las Vegas in hope of his recovery. In two days he improved enough for the group to resume movement. Three days after leaving Las Vegas, the company reached Cajon Pass. Because the men and animals were exhausted, their food was gone, and snow had begun to fall, it was a task to make it across the mountain; but by pushing on they were able to get to San Bernardino, California, in the evening of December 3, 1852.[20]

The elders were happy to see once again a well-organized community of Saints. San Bernardino was a thriving community surrounded by many acres of rich and fertile farmland. Church members there were very kind to the missionaries; they took them into their homes, fed them, and gave them every comfort they could provide. For twelve days the group rested and wrote letters home. They also sold their wagons, horses and mules, and all else that was not needed for the journeys that lay ahead. The members in San Bernardino were also very generous in giving money to the missionaries. On December 17 the company moved on toward Los Angeles and San Pedro, California, where they would embark for San Francisco and hence to their various fields of labor.

The group stayed a night in Los Angeles and were shocked by the drinking, vulgar language, and debauchery of the lower element.[21] They then moved on to San Pedro, where they arrived on the twenty-second and waited for passage to San Francisco. On December 29 fares were arranged at $17.60 per person (a full $37.50 less than the usual fares on steam packets), and the brig *Fremont* sailed for San Francisco on January 13. Musser and several others were able to work on board to help defray expenses, for even at such low fares the cost for the group was around $700.[22]

Because of illness, Walter Thompson, one of the elders bound for Hong Kong, did not go on to San Francisco from southern California. He had been sick on the trip to San Bernardino and on to San Pedro, and because he did not improve, he returned home to the Salt Lake Valley.[23]

The elders landed in San Francisco on January 9, 1853. Their next problem was raising funds to pay for their passage to the various missions. Musser listed the approximate cost for transportation to the different missions as follows:

Australian Mission	$1,250
Calcutta	$1,800
Sandwich Islands	$1,000
China	$1,000
Siam	$1,200
Total	$6,250

After Church authorities consulted with leaders of the San Francisco Branch, it was decided that because of especially high recent demands on the Church it would be well if the missionaries

tried to solicit funds from outside the Church. So for three
weeks the elders attempted to
collect funds, but they were
able to gather only $150 from
nonmembers. The remainder
of the needed money was
donated by T. S. Williams, who
gave $500, and by John M.
Horner, a wealthy member
who donated the difference,
which must have been
between $5,000 and $6,000.[24]

On January 22 the missionaries received their passports
from Washington and were free
to secure passage to their various destinations. Only one
week later, on January 29,
1853, the thirteen men who
were bound for India and Siam
embarked from San Francisco

*Amos Milton Musser served as mission
clerk while in India. His journals provide
a fine record of the East India Mission
from 1853 to 1855. Like several of his
companions, Musser circumnavigated the
globe "without purse or scrip." (Courtesy
LDS Church Archives)*

on a clipper ship called the *Monsoon*. They arrived at Calcutta on
April 25, having covered 10,976 miles in eighty-six days.[25]

The elders were very excited about their arrival and were in
good health and spirits. For a number of days they had intensified
their study of the gospel and missionary techniques. Every day
they held classes in which Richard Ballantyne and Chauncy W.
West lectured on English grammar, and the elders gave practice
sermons to each other and freely criticized what they heard.

As they traveled up the Hooghly River, they were struck by
the beauty of the scenery. Musser recorded these words: "April 25
[the actual date was April 26] A.M. We arrived opposite Ft. William
about 6 o'clock. The beauty of scenery surpasses anything I ever
before beheld on both sides of the river as we passed along its

shores. About noon we took a customs house officer aboard, the tide has been in our favor. . . . My feelings while beholding the beautiful scenes as we passed along the muddy channel of the Hooghly, which presented themselves as I stated before is undescribable."[26]

The elders were met at the docks by twelve-year-old Henry Frederick McCune, son of Matthew and Sarah McCune and the only male member of the Church in Calcutta at that time. With him were servants to carry the missionaries' luggage. Young McCune led the newly arrived group to his parents' forty-room bungalow, where each man was assigned a room and servant. Such a comfortable beginning was not a portent of easy times to come. Matthew McCune was in Burma on a military assignment, and Elders Willes and Richards were still up-country. The branch was not in good condition: "of about 180 members, 170 natives, there were but 6 or 8 left."[27] The missionaries were pleased, however, to discover that James Patric Meik had built a chapel, undoubtedly the first LDS chapel in all of Asia. At least they had a place to preach.

On April 29 the elders and local members held a conference, but only four of those present were not missionaries. The pertinent business at hand was to decide who would lead the mission and who would be assigned to the various parts of India. Nathaniel V. Jones was selected as president of the mission and president of the Calcutta Branch. The remaining elders were assigned as follows: Amos Milton Musser was to remain in Calcutta; Truman Leonard and Samuel Amos Woolley were to go to Chinsura, a city 30 miles north of Calcutta; William Fotheringham and William F. Carter were assigned to Dinapore, 290 miles northwest from Calcutta; and Richard Ballantyne, Robert Skelton, and Robert Owens were to sail south to Madras. The four who had been sent to Siam found they could not obtain passage during the next few months. As a result, they agreed that Elam Luddington and Levi Savage should stay in Calcutta and look for a way to Burma and then to Siam, and that Chauncy

Walker West and Benjamin F. Dewey were to go to Ceylon (Sri Lanka) until fall, when they expected to obtain passage. They had originally planned to go by way of Burma, but that way was not open because of the Second Anglo-Burmese War. Even in the best of times, passage from Burma to Siam was extremely difficult.

The days and weeks that followed were filled with activity. The elders bound for Madras, Ceylon, and Burma all found passage and sailed by June 20. All six of these elders had experiences at sea that involved considerable danger. Because of a severe storm, the first attempted voyage of Elders Luddington and Savage to Burma nearly took the lives of all on board. Musser described the return of the elders to Calcutta in this way: "While at dinner Brother Luddington came in in an awful predicament, close [sic] dirty, hat reduced to 2/3 the size, etc., etc. The ship they started to Rangoon in, three days after they left here she sprung a leak and they have been bailing and pumping water night and day ever since. They throwed all their cargo overboard and gave themselves up to the Lord and resigned themselves for a watery grave. They throwed all of the stores overboard, but the Lord delivered them safe."[28]

Ballantyne and Skelton, who had found it necessary to go to Madras without Robert Owens, were caught in the same storm, and their ship nearly sank. In all, the elders experienced six storms and other mishaps at sea that were severe enough to cause them to fear for their lives. Fortunately, however, no missionaries were lost at sea.

When the missionaries separated and went to their various areas of labor, the East India Mission practically became several unconnected missions. For one thing, communications between missionaries were very inadequate. Moreover, travel was slow and relatively expensive. Because of these problems India, Burma, and Siam were not a well-integrated mission in the sense that England and other LDS missions were at that time.

Truman Leonard and Samuel A. Woolley established themselves at Chinsura, where they found Joseph Richards. He had assumed leadership of the Chinsura Saints when he returned from his journey toward the Punjab. By this time he was in good health and had decided to go to Calcutta and from there to Salt Lake Valley. He sailed from Calcutta, bound for California and Utah, on June 18, 1853.[29] Leonard and Woolley worked in Chinsura for three months but did not baptize anyone.

William Fotheringham and William F. Carter traveled to Dinapore and worked there and round about for a short time before returning to Calcutta on June 5. Carter became very ill, and it was decided that in order to preserve his life he should be released from his call and sent home. On July 7 he boarded the *John Gilpin* and sailed for Boston. After Carter left, Fotheringham worked in Calcutta with Elders Jones, Musser, and Owens for the next month and a half.

During July and August several letters arrived in Calcutta that had been sent from William Willes, who was working near Delhi. In each letter he asked for a companion and finally sent twenty-five rupees (perhaps the equivalent to twenty-five dollars) to assist with any travel expenses for another elder. By August 19, 1853, Elders Fotheringham and Woolley had both decided to join Willes. A few days later they took places on a "Government Bullock Train" and traveled day and night for almost a month. When they arrived at Sikandarabad, they left the train and traveled a little distance to meet Willes at Belespore. By this time Willes was quite discouraged, but he felt there was still some hope for the people of that region. He decided, however, after spending only a brief time with Woolley and Fotheringham, that he would return to Calcutta. After discussing the work in that area with Willes, the two men went to Meerut (thirty-eight miles northeast of Delhi) and Willes returned to Calcutta.[30]

Meerut had the largest number of Europeans in the area of the Upper Provinces, with 250 civilians, many officers, and two or three regiments.[31] But even though there seemed to be a large number of potential converts, the elders met with poor success. The commanding officer of the cantonment was antagonistic, and his treatment of the elders was typical of what they received in nearly every part of India. When Woolley and Fotheringham called upon Brigadier General Scott, the commanding officer, and asked for permission to teach, he told them that he had been informed of their work by the Bishop of Calcutta and that he would not consider it fair to his own chaplains to have Mormons preaching in the area. Fotheringham reported their interview in this way:

> We then asked him if we could lodge in the cantonments. He replied not without his permission and if he granted us two weeks stay in this place, as soon as the time was expired, we would be under necessity of having it renewed again and many other restrictions he laid upon us which would be too numerous to mention. Among some of the restrictions was if we should get a place outside of the boundary lines to preach in we were not allowed to send a circular amongst the soldiers to notify our meetings. If we did we should be marched out of the cantonments without a moment's notice. Or if we should be found preaching to the soldiers on the streets we should be marched out. This is like tying a man's hands and feet and throwing him into a river and making him swim.[32]

They then turned to the civilian population, but having no success for five weeks, they moved to Delhi.[33] Then seven weeks later they traveled seventy miles north to the city of Karnal, and after that area proved unsuccessful, they migrated south toward Agra, arriving there at Christmastime 1853. But because once again they were not allowed to teach any military personnel, the civilian population was their only hope. They obtained a hall and held meetings for several nights, but when the crowds dwindled from twenty-four down to one investigator on the fourth night, the meetings were discontinued. The elders were tired and discouraged by this time; one wrote: "It makes me almost sick at heart to read of the Elders in other countries doing such great works.... I hope the Lord will be pleased to let us go before long to some other place where we can do some good for the cause. But God's will be done, not mine, unless mine is His. It was necessary for somebody to come here, and it might as well be us as any others."[34]

Woolley and Fotheringham left Agra and worked their way toward Calcutta. They preached the gospel at Cawnpore, a major British cantonment and settlement, Allahabad, and other towns along the way and then returned to Calcutta on March 6, 1854. Their long journey had not produced any success, for not a baptism was performed on the entire expedition.[35]

The months that marked their absence from Calcutta brought little more success there. Jones, Musser, Owens, and later Leonard, who had been at Chinsura until he thought his labors there to be useless, worked diligently at spreading their message. They printed several tracts, handed them to people in the streets and in their homes, and held many meetings in which they delivered lectures; but none of their approaches seemed to succeed.

By March 1854 the major problems of preaching in India had become quite evident. Elder N. V. Jones, in a long letter to the editor of the *Millennial Star* in England, summarized the problems that he and other missionaries were having in India. Concerning the types of people and the clergy who lived in the area where Willes and Richards and Woolley and Fotheringham had worked, Jones wrote:

> The settlements in the upper provinces are chiefly composed of invalids from the lower provinces and soldiers, who have, in a manner, worn themselves out in the service and have settled down upon small pensions. Besides these there are a few public officers who are engaged in business for the government of the company (East India), or some military station. The inhabitants range generally from ten to one hundred in a place, except Agra, and one or two other places, which have about two hundred each, and as to soldiers, it is a hard matter to get access to them, although the law does not rule over the consciences of men, but the discretionary

power of the officers does effectually accomplish it, to the great satisfaction of the clergy. There are two kinds of priests who are allowed to be with the soldiers, viz., the Church of England and Catholic, and all others are excluded, and the most rigid measures are taken to prevent their introduction.[36]

Jones commented on the aristocratic nature of the Englishmen the missionaries were working with: "The Europeans of India are generally of the aristocracy at home, and entertain such an exalted opinion of themselves, and of human greatness, that it is impossible for a common man to speak to them. There is scarcely a man in this country whose fate is not linked with either the company or the government, and to come to our meetings, or independently investigate our principles, would jeopardize his office and salary. In fact, that class of people, amongst which the Gospel has been preached with such good success[,] is not in this country."[37]

Concerning this same problem—European elitism and social consciousness—A. Milton Musser wrote: "In going to preach to the inhabitants of India (Europeans), is like going to England and America and selecting none but the aristocracy or upper ten to preach to; as all the European inhabitants of this country are living in the greatest ease, having many servants to wait on them. They care nothing for the servants of God."[38]

Perhaps Elder Jones did not feel that he had put his point across well enough, because he went on to explain: "If Gabriel from the region of Bliss, the presence of God, should come, I do not believe that he would attract any curiosity or create any excitement whatever. They would not stop their carriages or look out of their windows to see him. They are so lost in their own folly that the Holy Ghost and the Bible, is of so little consequence that they have not got time to spend with them."[39]

Jones and Musser overestimated the importance of the social position that most officers of the East India Company and military would have held at home in England. For the most part, these self-important people had gone to India in quest of power, wealth, and social importance. Hypocrisy was among the major weaknesses of this class of people known as nabobs.

British snootiness was a great problem, but the elders might have accepted it more easily if there had been an alternative group to whom they could turn. Unfortunately, the elders were as disappointed with the local peoples as they were with the British. Consider what Jones had to say about the Indian people:

> It appears that they have great disregard to all principles of honesty and honor, from the highest Rajahs to the meanest Ryot. And the greatest breaches of fidelity and trust are looked upon by the injured party with a degree of complacency, as though it was expected. And in the same light, they look upon all schemes of deliberate, systematic fraud, perjury and all violations of truth, honor, honesty; these things are indeed not matters of conscience with them. And they are fully competent to do the meanest possible amount, and are not capable of forming any friendship or attachments that can be valued over one *pice* (which is equivalent to one quarter of a cent). There are many in government and individual employ, who have been for years carrying on a well-regulated system of fraud, and who are known to be such characters by their employers; and to exchange them or turn them off would be only making a bad matter worse. To all human appearance, there is scarcely a redeeming quality in the nation.[40]

Jones was not generous in his assessment of India, but it must be recognized that he knew that many members of the Church in England, Europe, and America were watching and hoping for great success in India. He wanted to make sure they knew the problems the missionaries were having. Jones's attitude toward the people of India was typical of the other LDS missionaries. The treatment they received in every part of India was similar to what Jones described. Circumstances differed somewhat in each locality, but as a whole, affairs were much the same.

L.D. Saints Chapel built by A. Milton Musser at
Kurrachee India 1855

The original caption in the 1908 Improvement Era *reads "L. D. Saints Chapel built by A. Musser at Kurrachee, India 1855." Musser and Truman Leonard were the first LDS missionaries to preach the restored gospel in the land now called Pakistan. (From the* Improvement Era, *1908)*

The elders showed considerable personal stamina and courage. In addition to the rather long journeys that have been mentioned, missionaries worked and traveled in and around Madras; Colombo, Ceylon (now Sri Lanka); Bombay and its environs, Karachi (in modern Pakistan), Hyderabad and the area near there; Rangoon, Burma, and some areas inland from Rangoon.

Several points concerning the missionary work deserve mention: There were in total nineteen missionaries who served in India, Burma, and Siam. Of that number, two were converted and baptized in India. The mission was most fully staffed from April 1853 to July 1854, when the elders started to become very discouraged and thought more and more of going home.

It is almost impossible to determine the total number of converts made in the mission. Elder Robert Skelton, who was the last man to leave India (May 2, 1856), said he thought there were around sixty-one members in India and Burma at the time of his departure.[41] There were also eleven Church members who had immigrated to Salt Lake Valley. This small number of converts was a great disappointment to the missionaries. Willes had baptized many more people than this during his first four months in India. But most of the Indians who were baptized during that time left the Church when it became evident that they were not going to receive any worldly gain. This phenomenon was caused in part by the missionary methods of the Roman Catholics and Protestants. Elder Chauncy West interpreted the situation this way:

> The English and American missionaries who have gone to that country have been furnished with plenty of money by missionary societies at home, and when they found that they could not win the native with their principles, they have hired them to join their churches, and have written back what great things they are doing in converting the poor heathen. I have had numbers of them come to me and offer to leave the churches whose names they were then acknowledging and come to ours, if I would only give them a few more cents than they were getting. At the same time they knew no more about the principles and faith of the Church to which they professed to belong, than the brute-beast, and these same people will bow down and worship sticks and stones, gods of their own make, when they think there is no Christian seeing them.[42]

West was not entirely fair or did not know the history of missionary work in India. The practice of supporting Indian converts to Christianity had started when the early Protestant missionaries observed what happened to converts who left their castes and became Christians. These people were expelled from their castes and were considered dead in the eyes of their people. Considering the plight of their new converts, the missionaries gave them employment as custodians, teachers, domestic servants, cooks, and so on, and in that way preserved their lives. As the numbers of Indian converts increased, the problem grew out of control. In some instances Indians did play one sect against another when seeking better wages. This was a problem to the LDS missionaries, and it discouraged them on a number of occasions. The problem of apostasy was also common among the European converts.

As has been mentioned, the missionaries had some serious problems with the clergy of other denominations. It appears that all of the Christian churches in India were against the Mormon movement. This prejudice grew out of the fact that Joseph Smith, the founder, claimed to have restored the gospel of Jesus Christ. A greater reason for their prejudice, however, was their dislike of polygamy. This was the major point of contention in all the cities of India where the elders preached.

Although some effort was made to work with the local peoples, the elders did not consider themselves called to preach to these people. It was their understanding that they had been sent to India to convert the European population. Only after they failed with those people did they turn to the Indians. But teaching the Indians had several inherent problems. The first difficulty was communication. The missionaries attempted to learn some of the native languages—Burmese, Hindustani, Tamil, Telugu, and Maratha—but were not able to gain a useful mastery in any instance.

The LDS missionaries also found no shared religious ground. Whereas the elders carried a message having to do with one God whom they described as an anthropomorphic being, most of the people of India believed in a great number of deities of all types and forms. Those few Hindus (generally Brahmins) who were capable of understanding the non-dualistic concept of Brahman were not accessible to the missionaries (and even if they had been, they would have shared few points in common). The missionaries did not understand Hindu, Muslim, Parsee (Zoroastrian), Jain, or Buddhist concepts any better than Asians believing in these religions understood Mormonism—and this has changed little in the late twentieth century. In addition to even the most general concepts of God, the Mormons differed greatly with the people of India on the subject of the application of religion. Hinduism, particularly, not only is capable of all-inclusiveness in religious matters but also exalts that principle. Hinduism has had as its greatest asset for survival the ability to accept many levels and ideas of truth. But although the Mormons believed that truth existed to some degree in other religions, their brand of inclusiveness did not allow for so much flexibility. To them only one religion was capable of bringing salvation to men, and that was, of course, The Church of Jesus Christ of Latter-day Saints.

It could be supposed that the Mormons and the Muslims would have found some common ground for discussion, but there is no evidence that this was so. A more similar concept of God, a more similar concept of salvation, a "true believer" psychology among the adherents, and even the common concept of polygamy could have brought some feelings of common trust between the two groups, but they did not. Few or no Muslims were converted to the Church by these early missionaries to India.

Another matter was the teaching methods the missionaries used. There was no clear-cut program or approach to teaching the gospel. The missionaries distributed tracts, pamphlets (some of which were translated), and other literature (particularly the Book of Mormon), held lecture meetings, and visited homes; but these approaches were not well organized. Although the LDS missionaries did construct chapels at Calcutta (the first on the Asian continent), Poona, and Karachi, they did not sponsor any schools, medical centers, or other institutions that would be classed as part of the social gospel movement. Such programs were not part of the general missionary approach of the Church. The missionaries had traveled to India without any financial support from the Church or from missionary societies, and so they were completely dependent upon the generosity of the people of India for their daily sustenance while they were there. (Two exceptions occurred when Willes and Musser, at different times and in different parts of India, decided they should take employment in order to stay alive.) The point is that the elders were more dependent upon India than India was dependent upon the elders. After a year or so they were free to change their stations and go to work anywhere they felt they could convert more people. When the situation in which the missionaries found themselves is considered, their lack of patience can be understood.

Sometimes surprising growth comes from gospel seeds dropped along the way. Late in their mission, Elders A. Milton Musser and Truman Leonard taught the gospel in Karachi and Hyderabad, in the Indus River area, which is now part of Pakistan. When they departed for home, they did so thinking they had accomplished little or nothing there. But Elder Leonard left some literature with a young man named Robert Marshall: a first edition of the Pearl of Great Price that included Joseph Smith's prophecy of the coming American Civil War, some copies of the *Millennial Star*, and the first volume of the *Journal of Discourses*. A decade later the actual occurrence of the Civil War brought the Mormon materials back to Marshall's mind, and he began reading all the materials he had on the Church. He was soon convinced that Joseph Smith was a true prophet and wanted to be baptized. He shared his newly acquired views with family, friends, and acquaintances and became known as a Mormon.

In the 1880s Marshall or a member of his family wrote to the European Mission in Liverpool and received a reply, but nothing came of the interchange. Years passed and Robert Marshall became old and blind. He wanted to be baptized before he died. In 1903 one of his sons again wrote to England and asked for missionaries to come and baptize his father and others. They were informed by mission president Francis M. Lyman that a Mormon elder named John H. Cooper was presently in Calcutta, soon to return home. Cooper stopped off in Karachi for three months, from June 26 to September 24, 1903, during which time he baptized thirteen persons—six members of Marshall's family and seven others, including Henry J. Lilley, the man who reported this information to the *Improvement Era* in 1908.[43] Elder Cooper ordained some of the men to the office of elder and organized the Karachi Branch—the result of missionary work done almost fifty years before. By 1908 the branch had dwindled to four, the others having moved away from Karachi or having fallen away. The end of the branch's history is not known.

Lilley's report states that missionaries had been sent to India following the mission of the 1850s. Word has it that William Willes visited India again in the 1880s. How many other missionaries might have served there during these decades is not known.

THE EARLY MISSIONS TO BURMA AND SIAM

The elders bound for Siam (now called Thailand) had gone to Calcutta with the India group because separate passage to Bangkok was not available. These four men, Elam Luddington, Levi Savage Jr., Chauncey Walker West, and Benjamin F. Dewey, set their minds on reaching their destination, but in the end only one of them ever set foot on Siamese soil. Their intention had been to travel overland across Burma to Siam. However, the Second Anglo-Burmese War was then under way, and that route was closed. Even if there had not been a war, the terrain and plant and animal life were so treacherous and threatening that the overland route would have been nearly impossible. West and Dewey tried several times to find sea passage, but in the end, after visiting Ceylon and Bombay, they were forced because of bad weather in Southeast Asian waters to give up on their attempts to reach Bangkok.

Elders Luddington and Savage decided that they would go to Rangoon to work. Rangoon had already been secured and was at peace. From there they hoped to find a ship to Siam. They were encouraged to go to Rangoon by reports sent to Church members in Calcutta from Sergeant Major Matthew McCune, who had been baptized in India. In August 1852, at the time when new missionaries were being called to Asia, McCune, who was by this time an elder in the Church, was sent by the British-Indian Army to Rangoon. He traveled with William Adams, also a sergeant, who was a member of the Church and held the office of teacher in the Aaronic Priesthood. They arrived in Rangoon on August 17.[44]

Eager to teach Mormonism to other members of their military unit, they decided to hold lecture meetings each Tuesday and Thursday evening. At first their meetings were well attended, but attendance dwindled quickly and soon the elders became interested in the Burmese people. Elder McCune felt that the gospel should be preached to all people, and knowing that he could not teach the Burmese without a knowledge of their language, he made arrangements with a native teacher and started learning the Burmese tongue. He also hoped the gospel could soon be preached to a group of hill people called the Karens. Through rumors, he incorrectly judged these people to be ready for the gospel.

From August 1852 until January 1853, McCune and Adams worked diligently at teaching the gospel. Although their meetings were poorly attended and their handbills and announcements were frequently destroyed, they managed by January 1853 to baptize eight soldiers.

Elder McCune was transferred with his unit from Rangoon to Martaban in late 1852, and by the first part of 1853, he was scheduled to move into the field of combat. From January to August 1853, he was on active duty, but he continued his missionary work while in the field with his company.[45]

When he arrived back in Rangoon in August 1853, he found that the little branch there had become inactive. Persecutions had been too great for the new convert who had been left in charge. McCune was, of course, disappointed to find affairs in this state, but he was soon given hope by the arrival of Elders Luddington and Savage.[46] When Luddington and Savage arrived in Rangoon, they began holding meetings on the same schedule that McCune and Adams had followed. Evidently they had good attendance at their meetings. Sometimes they preached in a hall near the great Shirah-dong Pagoda, and sometimes they lectured on the government wharf. In a letter to England, Elder Luddington wrote of their success. He told of one meeting in which he spoke "to

Burmese, Bengalese [sic], Malays, Brahmins of different castes, Mussulmen, Armenians, Jews, and gentiles."[47]

In the meantime, Elder Savage decided that he would branch out on his own. He thought he would be happier if he went to work preaching to the Burmese. On September 28, 1853, he left Rangoon and sailed to Moulmein, across the Gulf of Martaban, where he remained for some months attempting to learn the Burmese language.[48]

By January 1854, Luddington, with the assistance of Sergeant McCune, had been able to baptize two more soldiers into the Church. But the work was moving slowly, for in the year and a half that McCune had been in Rangoon, only ten persons had become members. None were Burmese. Because Luddington still had a desire to realize his mission call to Siam, he sailed from Rangoon for Singapore on February 3, 1854, arriving at Penang, or Prince of Wales Island, late that month. After a stay there of five days, during which he preached the gospel, he sailed again, this time to Singapore. From there he took passage on a ship bound for Bangkok, arriving there on April 6, 1854. A few weeks later he wrote to the Saints in England: "I am following my calling at this time in the jungles of Siam, far from a civilized nation, and surrounded on the one hand by wild savages, and by wild beasts on the other."[49] He obviously exaggerated his circumstances (Siam, after all, was a nation with a long and highly cultured history), but he did not have an easy time in Bangkok. His only converts were Captain James Trail and his wife. Trail had given Luddington passage to Bangkok on his ship *Serious*.

Luddington remained in Bangkok for a little over four months, having had some difficult experiences. He was stoned twice, rejected by most of the Westerners, and had no success attracting attention among the Siamese people. Although he tried to learn the language, he did not believe he could gain a useful ability in it in less than a year or two. On August 12, 1854, he left Bangkok on Captain Trail's ship. From Bangkok he went to Singapore and from there to Hong Kong, where he hoped to find the elders who had been sent there. He endured terrible storms at sea but finally arrived safely in Utah in 1855.[50]

In March 1854 Elder William Willes, the second LDS missionary to be sent to India and who by this time had been given his choice to go home or stay in India, decided to go to Rangoon to help Matthew McCune, who was now working there alone.[51] Elder Willes added a great deal of enthusiasm to the Burma mission during the six months he stayed there. He baptized twenty persons and opened a school to teach the English language. He used the money he earned teaching English to pay his passage home to England.

Before the Burma mission ran its course, Savage returned to Rangoon, where he worked until late 1855. He and McCune were joined briefly by President Jones. The McCune family remained in Rangoon until 1856, when he was discharged from the army. He then took his family to Salt Lake City. From the time the McCunes left Rangoon until 1968, the Church did not have an official mission in Burma or Siam.[52]

THE EARLY MISSION TO CHINA

The India-Siam group were fortunate to arrange passage from San Francisco to their destination within a week after they received their passports in late January 1853. The three remaining China-bound elders, Hosea Stout, James Lewis, and Chapman Duncan, were not so favored. They did not sail from San Francisco until March 9. But even though they left the United States much later than their cohorts, they arrived in Hong Kong on April 28, only two days after the India group reached Calcutta.

The missionaries had seen Chinese junks for several days before landing and found the atmosphere quite exciting even before they docked. Hosea Stout recorded their reception upon arrival in Hong Kong: "We had scarcely dropped anchor before the deck was covered with Chinees [sic] men and women as well as professional whites who were seeking for an opportunity to make a drive on the Green Horns. While the china men were seeking employment and the women were soliciting our washing patronage, while others came forward to bargain off their professional sex to the crew and all whom it concerned at the lowest possible rates, which seemed on board to range at about one dollar each."[53]

Hosea Stout was one of three elders sent to open missionary work in China. Their short-lived mission in Hong Kong lasted only fifty-six days but manifested the willingness of the elders of the Church to take the gospel to every nation. (Courtesy LDS Church Archives)

The following day Elders Duncan and Stout went ashore and spent the morning walking about the city. They became acquainted with a Mr. Emeny, a ship chandler, who shared with them a great amount of information concerning the city and offered to rent them one of his rooms. They accepted the offer and had temporary quarters. For the next few days they sought information concerning conditions in the city and also looked for someone who would "be willing to hear the message we have to this nation but as yet we find none."[54] They were discouraged because the cost of rent was too high. As yet they had not been able to do any better than about thirty dollars a month each. Stout felt that they had reached their darkest hour. Fortunately, within a day or two they had befriended a landlord by the name of Dudell, who, after listening to the purposes of the missionaries, offered free rent for three months.

On Wednesday, May 5, 1853, the missionaries moved into their own apartment. It was located at "Canton Bazaar," where they had an "excellent suit [sic] of rooms." The rooms were on the third story of the building. The men hired a "Chinese servant at six dollars and fifty cents per month, who does all the duties of cook, market man, and chamber maid."[55] Apparently, they were a little embarrassed to have a servant, for Hosea Stout wrote, "Such is the force of custom here that it is far cheaper to employ one than to do without for we cannot purchase in the markets if you do you will be cheated in both weight and measures and shaved in your change."[56]

On the evening of May 6 the elders, after spending most of the day indoors because of the oppressive heat, held their first preaching meeting. They taught the gospel to a small group of British soldiers. On May 11 they made their first contact with Chinese people, to whom these missionaries had been sent. The first two Chinese to investigate were a pair of curious Christians. One was a local tailor, the other a product of the London Missionary Society. He had spent eight years in England and was well educated. Although it looked promising, nothing came of the meetings between the missionaries and their Chinese acquaintances.

The elders received little encouragement. They didn't seem to have any contacts or an approach that permitted them to make any headway. Their spirits were lifted momentarily when they met the acting editor of the *China Mail*, a local paper. This man treated them kindly and suggested that it would be wise if they would hold their meetings on the "green," or parade ground. He also promised not only to attend but also to publish the meeting times free of charge.[57] They accepted this offer and published the time for their meeting on the green. Stout wrote in his diary that "there were about 100 citizens and as many soldiers present. Elder Lewis spoke on the first principles of the gospel, showing also the difference between our religion and the sects of the day. He delivered a powerful discourse, handling the sects quite unciremoniously [sic]."[58]

Noting the people's seeming interest in the message of the restored gospel, Stout said that he felt that "the ice of superstition is broken and a good work will follow." Meetings were subsequently held on May 19 and 20. On the twentieth there were about thirty citizens and two hundred soldiers moving in and out of the group "in swarms." Although Stout thought Duncan was in his usual good form, he noticed a change of attitude and wrote, "It is amusing to see how nice and reserved the people act with an assumed modesty of a ticklish coquette wanting to talk but not be seen."[59] The cause of this change turned out to be the spreading of the news that the Mormons were polygamists. Articles appeared in three newspapers publicizing this fact.

The days dragged on and nothing was accomplished. The elders spent a large part of their time indoors because the weather was hot, humid, and often very rainy. Stout recorded meetings with various newspaper editors who seem to have been reasonable men; nevertheless, they did not stop printing articles that upset the missionaries. The elders took consolation in telling themselves that when the opposition of the devil starts to howl, it is a sure sign that the Lord's servants are about to succeed. Unfortunately for them, the situation went from bad to worse.

Their last meeting on the green was held on May 31. The elders preached to a group of about fifty persons, but even though the missionaries felt they did a good job of proving various contending religions wrong, the crowd did not ask a single question and left almost immediately. Future meetings were attempted, but the weather caused problems. The elders tried to find ways to enter people's homes to preach to them, but this also proved to be futile. On June 7 Stout wrote that he felt that he and his companions had done all that God or man could require of them in Hong Kong. "We have preached publicly and privately as long as anyone would hear and often tried when no one would hear." On June 9 they decided to go home.[60]

Stout was disturbed that they were not able to find interested listeners or even overt opposition. He found that "no one will give heed to what we say, neither does anyone manifest any opposition or interest but treats us with the utmost civility, conversing freely on all subjects except the pure principles of the gospel. When we approach that[,] they have universally in the most polite manner declined by saying that they did not wish to hear anything on that subject for they are willing to extend the mantle of charity over all Christian believers and ourselves among the rest, not doubting that we were good men and all would be right with all."[61]

That same day, June 9, the elders went on board the *Rose of Sharron*, an English ship, and arranged cabin passage to San Francisco. From that day until June 22, the elders were busy clearing up their few affairs, such as selling their furniture and preparing for their voyage back to San Francisco.

The mission to China cannot be assessed as anything but a complete failure. The missionaries were as well aware of this as any later observer. Sources such as Stout's journal reveal that the missionaries were quite well apprised of the situation as it existed in China *while* they were there. However, before they arrived in Hong Kong they knew almost nothing about Hong Kong and the Chinese situation.

The missionaries realized many of the reasons for their failure. Two letters speak of the Tai-ping Rebellion, the general cultural situation, and problems relating to the Chinese language. Probably the greatest disappointment the elders faced was that there were so few Europeans in Hong Kong. According to their count, there were some 250 European civilians in Hong Kong, plus between one and two thousand soldiers. Stout wrote concerning this problem: "Here we find a people situated differently from others we have seen and less likely to receive the gospel. There are no common or middle class inhabitants here. There are few whites and these are merchants, traders, all deeply engrossed in business."[62]

Stout wrote further that the Europeans in Hong Kong were the "would be *nabobs*, of the world. . . . This class we found almost unapproachable, on account of their wealth and popularity, and look with contempt upon all who are not of the same grade with themselves; also a few lawyers, doctors, and a small sprinkling of missionaries also of the upper circles, luxuriating upon the proceeds of the cent societies at home, and the miseries of the people in that region."[63]

It is quite possible that this opinion would have been different if he had made contact with the soldiers, but they were not allowed out of their posts except from five to eight o'clock each evening. "They were," according to Stout, "so fond of the licensed privileges found among the Chinese women, that they are as corrupt as vicious habits can make them." According to the record of Elder James Lewis, however, the soldiers turned away from Mormonism because of their officers.[64] It would appear that the missionaries in China received about the same treatment from the military that the elders in India received.

After the first and seemingly easiest approach to teaching the gospel had been closed, the next alternative was to turn to the Chinese. Unfortunately for the elders, not many Chinese knew English, and the elders knew no Chinese. This problem ultimately came down to one of money, for it would have cost about thirty dollars a month for a language teacher. Furthermore, most of the Chinese who knew English worked either for the government or for missionaries of other faiths. Although the elders knew that the language had to be learned if they were to teach the gospel, they did not know how they could accomplish this task. The elders found the variations in class structure among the Chinese to be an additional problem.

Within six weeks of their arrival in Hong Kong, the elders realized that they were not going to succeed. One might ask why they did not turn to another port or go inland. The answer is that the mainland of China was at this time seized in a great revolution: the Tai-ping Rebellion. This religiously motivated uprising had started in July 1851 and lasted until 1864. The Mormon elders arrived in China in April 1853, the time of some of the greatest success of the rebel army. During one period or another, the movement engulfed a great portion of China, and allegedly a total of twenty million people died in its battles and the resulting famines.[65]

Foreigners in Shanghai had organized themselves for any problems that might arise. All the trading ports were anxiously awaiting the outcome of the rebellion. Stout wrote that "the troops here are held in readiness to act as occasion requires. Part of the American fleet has arrived and is reconnoitering at Shanghai in preparation for rendering philanthropic services to Japan."[66]

The voyage home to San Francisco was a long one of sixty-two days. The winds were contrary, and at times the ship sat in doldrums. The arrival of the elders in San Francisco on August 22, 1853, ended LDS missionary efforts in China until 1949.

In 1996, after the Church had been established in Hong Kong for almost half a century, the Church dedicated a temple there for the use of Latter-day Saints from Hong Kong and other nations nearby. In the dedicatory prayer, President Gordon B. Hinckley memorialized the labors and sacrifices of the early missionaries and provided a beautiful benedictory on their services. His words may as well be applied to their companions who labored in India, Burma, and Siam at the same time. He prayed: "We are grateful for the faith of those who, nearly a century and a half ago, first came to Hong Kong as missionaries of Thy Church. Their labors were difficult and largely without reward. But their coming was an evidence of the outreach of our people to all nations of the earth in harmony with the commandments of Thy Beloved Son that the gospel should be preached to every nation, kindred, tongue and people."[67]

NOTES

1. B. H. Roberts, *A Comprehensive History of the Church*, 4:72.

2. For a more complete study of the India Mission, see my "A History of the Missionary Activities of the Church . . . in India, 1849–1856" (master's thesis, Brigham Young University, 1964); and my "The Latter-day Saint Mission to India," *BYU Studies* 12 (spring 1972): 262–78.

3. See Benjamin Richey to George A. Smith, 2 December 1865, Historical Department, Archives Division, The Church of Jesus Christ of Latter-day Saints, Salt Lake City; hereafter cited as LDS Church Archives. See also Andrew Jenson, "Manuscript History of the East India Mission," LDS Church Archives.

4. "East India Mission," 26 December 1851.

5. See William Willis, letter, "Departure of Elder Willis for Calcutta," *Millennial Star* 13 (15 November 1851): 348, and 14 (15 March 1852): 91. See also David J. Whittaker, "Richard Ballantyne and the Defense of Mormonism in India in the 1850s," in *Supporting Saints: Life Stories of Nineteenth-Century Mormons,* ed. Donald Q. Cannon and David J. Whittaker (Provo, Utah: BYU Religious Studies Center, 1985), 178–79, 179 n.16. Whittaker's article provides insight regarding publication efforts of the India Mission.

6. *Millennial Star* 14 (15 March 1852): 91.

7. Ibid.

8. See William Willis, letter, "Rapid Spread of the Gospel in Hindoostan," *Millennial Star* 14 (26 June 1852): 287.

9. William Willis, letter, "Glorious Success of the Truth in Hindoostan," *Millennial Star* 14 (10 July 1852): 315.

10. William Willis, extract of letter to Lorenzo Snow, "Baptisms and Healings," *Millennial Star* 14 (21 August 1852): 413–14.

11. See William Willes and Joseph Richards, "The East India Mission," *Millennial Star* 15 (21 May 1853): 332. The publisher changed the spelling of Willis to Willes.

12. William Willes, "The East India Mission," *Millennial Star* 15 (15 October 1853): 686; and Amos Milton Musser, Journals, 3:16–17, copies in Special Collections, Harold B. Lee Library, Brigham Young University, Provo, Utah (hereafter cited as BYU Special Collections) and LDS Church Archives.

13. See "Catholic Tablet, Varieties," *Millennial Star* 14 (11 September 1852): 463.

14. Hugh Findlay, "Success of the Truth in Western Hindoostan," *Millennial Star* 14 (27 November 1852): 635–36.

15. Ibid.

16. Hugh Findlay, "Further Intelligence from Hindoostan," *Millennial Star* 14 (4 December 1852): 654–55. See also Ross and Linnie Findlay, comps., *Missionary Journals of Hugh Findlay: India-Scotland* (Ephraim, Utah: n.p., 1973), 114.

17. See Roberts, *Comprehensive History,* 4:55–56.

18. See Musser, Journals, 1:7.

19. Ibid., 1:62.

20. For further details concerning the journey to San Bernardino and San Francisco, see Conway B. Sonne, *Knight of the Kingdom: The Story of Richard Ballantyne* (Salt Lake City: Deseret Book Co., 1949), 57–69; and Karl Brooks, "The Life of Amos Milton Musser" (master's thesis, Brigham Young University, 1961), 28–33. A revised version of Brooks's thesis was published by the Musser family in 1980 in Provo, Utah, by Stevenson's Genealogical Center.

21. See Musser, Journals, 1:28–29.

22. See ibid., 2:9.

23. See Wayne Stout, *Hosea Stout: Utah's Pioneer Statesman* (Salt Lake City: n.p., 1953), 165.

24. See *The Alta* (San Francisco), 10 January 1853; Musser, Journals, 2:16; Andrew Jenson, *Church Chronology* (Salt Lake City: Deseret Book Co., 1899), 47.

25. See Musser, Journals, 2:51.

26. Ibid.

27. Ibid., 2:55.

28. Ibid., 2:71.

29. See *Deseret News,* 5:350.

30. See Hugh Findlay, "The East India Mission," *Millennial Star* 15 (24 September 1853): 638; Musser, Journals, 3:16–17, 21, 34.

31. See S. A. Woolley, "The East India Mission," *Millennial Star* 16 (25 February 1854): 124–26. Meerut was one of the most active points of fighting during the rebellion (or mutiny) of 1857.

32. William Fotheringham to Amos Milton Musser, 19 October 1853, LDS Church Archives.

33. See ibid., 3 November 1853.

34. S. A. Woolley, "The East India Mission," *Millennial Star* 16 (25 February 1854): 189–90.

35. See Jenson, *Church Chronology*, 50.

36. *Millennial Star* 15 (3 October 1853): 811. See also Journal History of the Church, N.V. Jones to F. D. Richards, 3 October 1853, LDS Church Archives.

37. Ibid.

38. Musser, Journals, 2:72. Percival Spear has written well on the topic of the English elite in India. See his book *The Nabobs* (London: Oxford University Press, 1963).

39. *Millennial Star* 15:211–12.

40. Ibid.

41. R. Skelton, "Hindostan," See *Millennial Star* 18 (16 August 1856): 523; and Jenson, *Church Chronology*, 56.

42. *Deseret News*, 5:206.

43. Henry J. Lilley, "From India's Coral Strand," *Improvement Era* 12 (1908–9): 423–34.

44. Matthew McCune, "The Burman Mission," See *Millennial Star* 15 (15 January 1853): 44.

45. See *Millennial Star* 15 (August 1853): 53, 78ff.

46. See Musser, Journals, 3:81–4.

47. *Millennial Star* 16:190–91.

48. See Musser, Journals, 3:81–84.

49. *Millennial Star* 16:540–41.

50. See Andrew Jenson, "Manuscript History of the Siam Mission," 7–8, LDS Church Archives.

51. See *Millennial Star* 16:540–41.

52. See the author's article "The Early Missions to Burma and Siam," *Improvement Era*, March 1970, pp. 35–44.

53. *On the Mormon Frontier: The Diary of Hosea Stout*, ed. Juanita Brooks, 2 vols. (Salt Lake City: University of Utah Press, 1964), 2:476.

54. Ibid.

55. Ibid.

56. Ibid.

57. See ibid., 2:479.

58. Ibid.

59. Ibid., 2:479–80.

60. See ibid., 2:484.

61. Ibid.

62. Stout, *Hosea Stout*, 170–71.

63. *Deseret News*, 3:26.

64. See *Deseret News*, 4 January, 1852.

65. The movement first emerged in the province of Kwangsi (modern Guangxi). The founder, Hung Hsiu-ch'uan (Hong Xiuquan, 1814–1864), and his chief collaborators were *Hakkas*, that is, members of a distinct minority linguistic group who were descended from north Chinese migrants. Hung was not only a mystic but also a frustrated scholar who had failed more than once in the Canton Civil Service examinations. He had a religious experience that convinced him that he was a messiah, a concept he borrowed from Christianity. Just two months before the elders arrived in Hong Kong, The T'ai-p'ings captured Nanking (Nanjing), the number-two city of the Ch'ing (Qing)

empire. See Eugene P. Boardman, *Christian Influence upon the Theology of the Taiping Rebellion* (Madison: University of Wisconsin Press, 1952).

66. Stout, *Hosea Stout*, 171–72. Whether or not Stout said this tongue in cheek cannot be known. The interest in this statement comes with the knowledge that just before this letter was written, Commodore Matthew Calbraith Perry and his small fleet had arrived in Hong Kong and were on course toward Shanghai and later to Japan to open that country to foreign relations. Perhaps Stout saw in that act a "philanthropic service."

67. "May Thy watch care be over it" [dedicatory prayer of the Hong Kong Temple], *Church News*, 1 June 1996, 4.

3

JAPAN

1901–1924

The Early Japanese Mission

President Lorenzo Snow, who had pursued a course of expansion since he became leader of the Church in 1898, announced plans on February 14, 1901, to open a mission in Japan.[1] He chose Elder Heber J. Grant of the Council of the Twelve Apostles to preside over the new mission.

More than four decades had passed since the Church had first attempted to expand into Asia. The years since the 1850s had been difficult for the Church. Doubtless the most serious problem had been polygamy, or plural marriage, as the Saints preferred to call it. Church leaders and members alike had endured physical and psychological harassment from the government and the general public. Not until 1896, years after Utah first applied for statehood, was statehood achieved. But by the turn of the century the Church was gaining acceptance among the American people (though there were yet many barriers to pass, such as the Reed Smoot hearings in the Senate), and its financial situation was somewhat improved over that of a few years before. Perhaps these and other improvements gave President Snow and the Council of the Twelve the courage to pursue once again the great commission to take the gospel to "every nation, and kindred, and tongue, and people" (D&C 133:37).

There were several reasons why the Brethren decided to open a mission in Japan rather than in China or some other Asian nation. China was at this time recovering from the disruption and shock of the Boxer uprising, in which Christian missionaries had been among the main targets of Chinese anti-foreignism. Southeast Asia seemed to be beyond the purview and experience of most Latter-day Saints at that time, and India had already proved a failure from the LDS point of view. Japan, on the other hand, had shown to the world through its victory in the Sino-Japanese War of 1894–95 that it had "made wonderful strides within a few years in the arts of civilization."[2] Japan's modernization encouraged Church leaders because they believed that any people who were progressive would also be open to the message of the Restoration. Moreover, President Snow and other Church authorities had met some of Japan's most distinguished leaders and had found them to be men of goodwill, men who they believed would help the Church succeed if it were introduced in Japan.

When President Snow announced the new mission, he explained that he had been thinking about such a mission for many years. In 1872 "a party of distinguished officials of the Japanese government [the Iwakura diplomatic mission] visited Salt Lake en route to Washington from their own country," reported President Snow in 1901. "During their stopover they called on the Legislature and were given an appropriate welcome. . . . They expressed a great deal of interest in Utah and the manner in which it had been settled by the Mormons. Our talk was altogether very pleasant and they expressed considerable wonderment as to why we had not sent missionaries to Japan. That, together with the knowledge that they are a progressive people has remained with me until the present time, and while it may not be the actuating motive in attempting to open a mission there now, it probably had something to do with it."[3]

In retrospect it is strange that members of the Iwakura Mission noted the absence of Mormon missionaries in Japan.

President Snow apparently took this as an invitation to open a mission there, though that was probably not the intent of the comment. What President Snow and the other Brethren evidently did not know in 1901 was how much Japan had changed and developed since the 1870s. Nor did they have much information concerning Japan's religious history, because the country was only opened to the Western world as recently as 1854. But more important than international affairs or the progress of one nation or another was the fact that the Lord had made it clear to President Snow that this was the time to open a mission in Japan. Consider the substance of his remarks of June 26, 1901:

> When the Lord first sent forth his Elders in this generation very little was known as to what their labors would be and what they could accomplish. They failed in some respects but they did not fail in one thing; they did their duty. Apostles Orson Pratt and others were sent to Austria to open a mission there, but by reason of the rejection of their testimony, they did not succeed. Nevertheless, they did their duty and were blessed. Noah preached 120 years, he was a grand man, he did his duty but failed and this because the people rejected him. However, by doing his duty he secured to himself exaltation and glory. . . .
>
> As to these brethren who will shortly leave for Japan the Lord has not revealed to me that they will succeed, but He has shown me that it is their duty to go. They need not worry concerning the results, only be careful to search the Spirit of the Lord to see what it indicates to them. Do not be governed by your own wisdom, but rather by the wisdom of God.[4]

THE INTRODUCTION OF CHRISTIANITY IN JAPAN

Quite by accident, Portuguese sailors discovered Japan in 1543. Six years later the great Catholic Jesuit priest Francis Xavier arrived at Japan's shores bearing the message of Christ. Although he did not remain long, he established a mission that by 1615 had claimed the devotion of about five hundred thousand Japanese. Unfortunately, from 1587 onward, the Japanese government pursued a course of repression—and finally one of calculated persecution—of Christians. As a result, the once-thriving Christian community was nearly destroyed. Many devout Japanese Christians died as martyrs, thousands denied the faith, and only a few practiced their religion secretly from then until the 1860s.

Because of anti-foreign fears and feelings, the *shogun* (military dictator and ruler) closed Japanese ports and cut off relations with the outside world in 1639. From then until 1853, when Commodore Matthew C. Perry forced the Japanese government to engage in more normal relations, Japan was a closed country. Once a year a Dutch ship was allowed at Nagasaki, and occasionally Chinese and Korean traders were accepted. But for the greater part, Japan remained in isolation. By the calculated use of Confucianism, the government enforced an ethic of strict compliance and regimentation. Shinto, Japan's indigenous religion, sustained a feeling of respect for Japan's rulers and for its historic past. Buddhism, a foreign religion but one that had been naturalized over more than a thousand years, received continuing patronage, largely because its priests provided much of the formal education during this era.

After Japan was opened to the West, only five years passed before Protestant missionaries arrived in 1859. They were not warmly received; in truth, they were forced to work quietly, operating schools and medical clinics lest they be deported. Not until the early 1870s did they have any real success, but even then the government was openly hostile to the foreign faith.

The last shogun resigned in 1867, and early in 1868 the Emperor Meiji assumed full control of the Japanese state. With Meiji's ascension, Japan entered a new era of conscious westernization. But the government also faced the problem of national consolidation at a time when the old order was passing and a new one was coming to be. Since Shinto was in a way the embodiment of the past, the government employed it to help bring solidity to the regime. Christianity, being foreign, was distrusted and proscribed. Wall posters and other legal notices informed villagers throughout Japan that Christianity was not acceptable. When a group of secret Christians, a remnant of those who had gone underground in the 1600s, was discovered in the late 1860s, the government openly repressed the movement and placed some members of the group in prison.

Word of this anti-Christian policy reached government leaders in the United States and Europe and caused a strong anti-Japanese reaction. As a result, members of the Iwakura Mission were brought to an abrupt realization that their efforts to establish normal relations with the so-called Christian nations would fail if they did not change the anti-Christian policy at home. On February 23, 1873, while the Iwakura Mission was still in Europe, the anti-Christian edicts were removed. Technically the laws were not changed until 1889, but through the removal of the edicts the government gave tacit consent to the presence of Christians and Christian missionaries. After that time the number of Protestant and Catholic missionaries grew rapidly.

Growth in numbers of missionaries and converts laid the groundwork for the rapid expansion of Protestant Christianity during the 1880s. By 1888 there were more than twenty-five thousand Japanese Christians and 450 missionaries, and the entire Bible had been translated into Japanese and published.

But 1889 and 1890 brought changes that set back Christianity until after World War II. In February 1889 Emperor Meiji gave a constitution to the Japanese people. Although it was progressive by Asian standards, it was authoritarian in structure and strongly weighted in favor of the aristocracy. Its position concerning freedom of religion was somewhat vague. Article 28 of the constitution reads: "Japanese subjects, within the limits not prejudicial to peace and order, and not antagonistic to their duties as subjects, shall enjoy freedom of religious belief." This article of the new constitution left considerable latitude of interpretation, and both

Japanese Christians and foreign missionaries considered it a charter of liberty.

The next year, however, the Ministry of Education promulgated the "Imperial Rescript on Education" (*kyoiku chokugo),* a document that one writer described as "the most damaging blow [that] ever struck the Christian cause in Japan."[5] The basic concept underlying the rescript was that Japan, having a divine origin and mission, was unique among the nations. At the head of the Japanese people was the emperor, a direct descendant of Jimmu Tenno, the first god-emperor of Japan. The ancestral gods of Japan, the Shinto *kami,* demanded and deserved the reverent obeisance of every Japanese student. On all public holidays, the principal of every school was to read the entire rescript to the students as they stood at attention with heads bowed before the portrait of the emperor. Over the years, the psychological conditioning effect of this simple ceremony was great. The rescript implied, among other things, that Christian views of God and morality were not acceptable.

The overwhelming Japanese victory in the Sino-Japanese War focused the Japanese mind on the greatness of the Japanese nation and people. Foreign religions now seemed to have little if any place. Although the years from 1895 to 1901 were peaceful, Christianity made relatively little headway.[6] It was at this time that the LDS Church found itself ready to move into Japan.

THE ESTABLISHMENT OF THE JAPANESE MISSION

President Heber J. Grant and his companions were the first to admit that they did not know much about Japan. In Elder Grant's words the new mission was an "unknown quality." But in spite of some misgivings and apprehensions, President Snow, mission president Grant, and the others all believed the new mission would succeed. Other Christian groups had done well, President Snow reasoned; why not the Latter-day Saints?

Before going to Japan, President Grant chose two mature and experienced missionaries, Louis A. Kelsch and Horace S. Ensign, to go with him. Then, on May 10, 1901, he called eighteen-year-old Alma O. Taylor. Even before the missionaries left Salt Lake City, Elder Taylor worked on the Japanese language, and later he demonstrated unusual linguistic ability.

The Japan-bound elders departed from Salt Lake City, Utah, on July 24, 1901, and traveled to Vancouver, British Columbia, where they boarded the *Empress of India*, which carried them to Japan. They arrived there on August 12.

Upon their arrival they found that even if they had desired to slip into the country unnoticed, they could not have done so. The foreign press in Yokohama had received word of their coming, and as became evident during the coming weeks, the Christian community was united together to drum the Mormons out of the country before they could gain a foothold. Almost before the four elders settled into the Grand Hotel in Yokohama, they found themselves in a verbal battle in the local newspapers that went on intermittently for several months. At least eight newspapers and many more writers became involved.

Somewhat surprisingly, in a land where Victorian morality had little or no place, the basic issue was whether the Mormons could be allowed within a reasonable distance of Christian women. When President Grant and his companions applied for permanent accommodations at a Western-style boardinghouse, the owner, Mr. Staniland, told them bluntly that he could not consider taking them in. When word of this action reached the press, it caused a heated debate between liberals who were willing to accept the elders in spite of the polygamy issue and those conservatives who claimed that polygamy was not dead and hence the missionaries could not be accepted. The most delightful piece relating to this matter was written by the Japanese intellectual Takahashi Goro. With tongue in cheek he wrote: "The enlightened people of Tokio have recently welcomed a sect from Thibet that preaches Lamanism, polyandry, a plurality of husbands, and scarce have they welcomed them with extraordinary enthusiasm and the huzzahs died away before they are condemning, with absolute ignorance, the 'Mormon' religion! And these people who are condemning the 'Mormons' and polygamy are believers in concubinage! Can there be under the sun a greater inconsistency than this? We might say something about the Emperor and his concubines, but perhaps it would be considered disloyal, and therefore we will keep quiet."[7]

Years passed before the Latter-day Saint missionaries developed any degree of mutuality with the established Christian missions. There is no evidence that the established Japanese religious denominations paid any attention to the Mormons.

THE DEDICATION OF JAPAN FOR
THE PREACHING OF THE GOSPEL

Having decided the previous Sunday that they would seek a wooded place, a place of solitude, on the next Thursday—September 1, 1901, fast day—and there dedicate the land of Japan to the preaching of the gospel, President Grant led his three companions to a secluded spot in a small grove situated on the slope of one of the rolling hills lying south of Yokohama. There they formed a small circle, sang, and prayed for the Spirit of the Lord to attend them. When they felt that they were in the proper spirit, President Grant offered the dedicatory prayer. According to Alma O. Taylor, "his tongue was loosed and the Spirit rested mightily upon him; so much that we felt the angels of God were near for our hearts burned within us as the words fell from his lips. I never experienced such a peaceful influence or heard such a powerful prayer before. Every word penetrated into my very bones and I could have wept for joy."[8]

President Grant's prayer covered fifteen major points. Possibly of greatest importance was his supplication that Israel might be gathered, that Satan would release his hold upon the minds of the people, and that the hearts of the people might be prepared to

This photograph, taken 19 February 1902, shows Elder Heber J. Grant, president of the Japanese Mission (third from left), and his three companions (left to right)—Horace S. Ensign, Alma O. Taylor, and Louis A. Kelsch—at the location where Grant, on 1 September 1901, had dedicated Japan for the preaching of the gospel. (Courtesy LDS Church Archives)

recognize the truth when it was declared to them. With this prayer the mission was officially opened.

LATE 1901 TO 1903: A PERIOD OF MANY FIRSTS

Probably in no other country have the first LDS missionaries had a harder time getting out among the people than in Japan. In India, Burma, and Siam the elders had begun preaching the gospel immediately upon arriving in those lands. This was also true throughout the Pacific. But the elders serving in Japan seem to have felt the weight of history and tradition against them. Possibly the most formidable obstacle, at least in the beginning, was the Japanese language. It is probably the most difficult language in the world to learn to read, write, and speak. The grammar is complex and very different from those of European languages. The Chinese characters must be memorized; they cannot be sounded out as can those of alphabetic languages.

Within a week or two of their arrival, the elders hired a language teacher, the first of several over the next year or so. They decided that because they were all neophytes, they would devote their full time to language study until the next spring; then they would split into pairs and move out among the people. But this method proved tedious and slow, and by December Elders Ensign and Taylor had decided to move from the Metropol Hotel in Tokyo to a completely Japanese area where they would have to use the language. On December 4, 1901, Ensign and Taylor moved into the Nakai Hotel, actually a Japanese-style *ryokan*, or hotel, where they were to live for the next fifteen months.

Use of the jinrickshaw, which appears today to be a slow and perhaps inhumane means of transportation, continued well into the twentieth century. Elder Heber J. Grant traveled in such conveyances frequently while presiding over the Japanese Mission from 1901 to 1903. (Courtesy LDS Church Archives)

The elders in Japan seem to have been more thwarted by local customs, culture, and mores than those who served in the Pacific missions. Perhaps this was because the Pacific peoples generally looked to the missionaries for leadership not only in religious matters but also in matters of modernity. The more primitive cultures of the Pacific were not a threat to the missionaries. In Japan, on the other hand, the local culture was both old and advanced. Japanese civilization was well developed in every way—in the arts, literature, religion, history, philosophy, architecture, and so on. Also, the Japanese had come technologically abreast of the modern countries of the world. Taken together, Japanese language and civilization presented a considerable barrier. The language alone was so difficult that the elders did not decide to go out among the people to teach the gospel until February 1903, eighteen months after the first group arrived in the country.[9]

During the early months of 1902, while Ensign and Taylor were adjusting to Japanese food, manners, bathing habits, and so forth, President Grant and Elder Kelsch occupied their time studying the language and working on written materials to present to the Japanese people. In February President Grant (who was also an apostle) proposed to his companions that it might be well for him to return to Utah for general conference in April. He had several purposes in mind, among them to give a full report to Church leaders on conditions in Japan, to propose that additional elders be called to Japan, and to perform the marriage of one of his daughters. The other elders of course supported him in his plans.

Before President Grant left for home, however, two men were baptized into the Church, an event that was totally unexpected, for the elders had not as yet sought converts. The first convert was a man named Nakazawa Hajime, a Shinto priest who seems to have been something of a firebrand. His visits with the LDS missionaries evidently caused his dismissal from his position as a Shinto priest. Concerning Nakazawa's expulsion from his faith, Elder Taylor wrote: "The first Japanese to be put to death in effigy for the cause of truth in this land! The first one to be ostracized from the company of his fellows for having anything to do with the 'damned Mormons!'"[10] Nakazawa, who considered himself a "small Luther," demanded baptism even though the missionaries did not believe he was ready. On the morning of March 8, the elders, Nakazawa, and an interpreter, Mr. Hiroi, traveled to the village of Omori on Tokyo Bay. Finding the tide low,

This building served as the first Tokyo, Japan, missionary home during the early years of the mission. (Courtesy LDS Church Archives)

they took a rowboat out far enough to immerse the candidate. Then President Grant and Nakazawa climbed over the side into the water and performed the ordinance. Mr. Hiroi translated the baptismal prayer as President Grant spoke it in English. Following the baptism, President Grant confirmed Nakazawa a member of the Church and ordained him to the office of elder in the Melchizedek Priesthood.

Two days after this first baptism, a second candidate, Kikuchi Gaboro, a man who had visited the missionaries, presented himself to President Grant early in the morning and pleaded for baptism. Although President Grant did not feel good about baptizing Kikuchi, he was so insistent—arguing that he would understand the gospel better after he was baptized, and even claiming a willingness to die as the first Latter-day Saint martyr in Japan if necessary—that his request was granted later the same morning. He too was ordained an elder.[11]

President Grant sailed for America the next day. He was elated with the progress of the mission and enthusiastically reported the two baptisms to the Saints at home. Unfortunately, Nakazawa and Kikuchi both proved to be dishonest in their intentions and were later excommunicated from the Church. Sadly, they seem to represent the whole history of the early mission. A few excellent and devoted converts were made among the Japanese, but for the most part the mission was a great disappointment to the missionaries themselves and to the Church at home.

When President Grant returned from Salt Lake City, he brought his wife, Augusta; their daughter Mary; Horace Ensign's wife, Mary; and six additional missionaries: Joseph E. and Marie S. Featherstone, Erastus L. Jarvis, John W. Stoker, Sanford W. Hedges, and Fred A. Caine. With the new missionaries, the mission was large enough to hold regular Sunday services. The missionaries started a Sunday School in the hope that prospective members would find it helpful in their quest for truth.

By March 1903 the elders had made considerable progress in the Japanese language. They had spoken to each other in Japanese in their Church services and had even translated some hymns ("We Thank Thee, O God, for a Prophet" was first) and some tracts. They also were quite comfortable in their surroundings. Therefore President Grant assigned pairs of companions and sent them into the field. During late April, Elders Featherstone and Hedges moved to Hojo, Jarvis and Stoker went to Naoetsu, (about a day's train ride from Tokyo), and Ensign and Caine relocated to Nagano, more than half a day's journey away from Tokyo. The mission had moved into the extended period that lasted until its closure in 1924.

As would be expected, new elders came into the field from time to time, transfers were made, and cities were opened and closed to missionary activity. President Grant established the general pattern of missionary work before he was released to go home. However, he was dissatisfied with his performance in Japan. He had not learned to speak Japanese, nor had he moved to Japanese-style accommodations or eaten Japanese food when he could avoid it. Furthermore, during his presidency very few converts came into the Church. When he received his release to return to Salt Lake City, his first impulse was to ask for a six-month extension. But when he questioned himself about his motives for wanting to stay, he concluded: "What good is there for you to stay here? How much more can you do than Brother Ensign? And I began to realize it was a desire to be able to come home and tell you [the members of the Church] I had done something which prompted my wish to stay there longer."[12]

President Grant was too hard on himself. His principal assignment had been to supervise the work of the other missionaries. He had done what was right with regard to them. He had encouraged them to live in the Japanese style and had supported and helped them in their efforts to master the language. He had also recognized that tracts and Church publications that had worked well in other parts of the world were not appropriate for Japan and that new ones were required to address the special needs of the Japanese. Three tracts had been published in Japanese while President Grant presided over the mission. Under his direction, other procedures had been started that gave the mission stability and regularity. On September 8, 1903, President Grant and his family sailed from Yokohama for home. He was replaced by Elder Horace Ensign, who was already in the mission.[13]

TRANSLATION OF THE BOOK OF MORMON

During Elder Ensign's presidency, important things were accomplished. One stride forward was the organization of Sunday Schools in Hojo and Tokyo. Most important, however, were his contributions in the area of publications. He directed the writing and printing of a number of tracts, published a hymnal in Japanese, and instigated the lengthy process of translating the Book of Mormon. President Ensign believed, as had President

Grant before him, that the Book of Mormon would be a great proselytizing tool, one that would significantly help the work.

On January 11, 1904, President Ensign asked all of the missionaries to begin translating different sections of the book. This procedure did not work out for a number of reasons, but it was a beginning. By September, however, President Ensign could see that the translation would have to be placed in the hands of no more than one or two men. By that time Elder Taylor was by far the most competent translator. In fact, he was writing in *kanji*, Chinese-style characters. Concerning his call to translate full-time, Taylor wrote that "it was the direct answer to the earnest desires of my heart and a fulfilling of the promises given me in blessings pronounced by President Grant during his sojourn in Japan."[14] By September 15 he had completed the first book of Nephi—forty-nine English pages. Neither Elder Taylor nor President Ensign knew at the outset how large a project it would prove to be.

Shortly before President Ensign received his release to return home, new elders arrived in Japan, making it possible to open the work in Sapporo (on the island of Hokkaido) and Sendai (in northern Honshu). Ensign's release came on July 27, 1905. Young Elder Taylor was to be his replacement. By the time of the Ensigns' departure, seven people had been baptized, but two had been excommunicated.

During President Taylor's term as president, 1905 to 1909, the work moved generally at a slow pace. The number of missionaries grew slightly and averaged thirteen during those five years. But convert baptisms were few—one in 1905, two in 1906, and two more in 1907—and people at home began raising questions concerning the practicality of the mission. In answer to these criticisms, President Taylor sent a blanket rebuff to the doubting members of the Church: "Is the Japan mission a failure? Is it premature? The shortest answer to both these questions is an emphatic 'NO!' It is the mission of 'Mormonism' to preach the gospel to all the world for a witness before the end shall come. Therefore, counting its success or failure by the number of converts made is a gross mistake." President Taylor believed that one of the mission's goals was to spread the truth so that the world would be left without an excuse at Christ's second coming. He said, "Our success or failure, then, must be determined by the answer to the question, 'What has the Japan Mission done, what is it doing for the spread of the truth?'"

Taylor went on to explain the difficulty of communicating with the Japanese until elders had been in the field for at least two years. He also complained that the number of laborers was too few to do the work effectively.[15]

President Taylor had enough problems in Japan without additional ones from home. His most time-consuming task at hand was the translation of the Book of Mormon. This took a great deal more time and effort than was originally anticipated. The translating involved two steps: changing the scripture to Japanese and putting the Japanese into characters. A translator needed a knowledge of at least two thousand characters to do this work, and in view of the fact that Taylor and Elder Fred Caine (who worked side by side with Taylor) were so new to Japan when they started, what they accomplished was remarkable.

The first translation of the book was completed on March 21, 1906, but the corrections and revisions took longer than the original work. Because he was dissatisfied with his early sections, Taylor revised the entire first translation, and this took from May 1906 until December. The finished product was off the press on October 6, 1909. Five thousand copies were printed.[16]

President Taylor and Elder Caine received their releases to return home on December 18, 1909. Taylor had served almost nine years, and Caine had devoted eight years. Elder Elbert D. Thomas was appointed the new mission president.

SEASON OF PROGRESS AND CHALLENGE

President Elbert D. Thomas, who following his mission became a professor at the University of Utah and then a United

States senator from Utah, had ideas about language learning and mission tenure that differed from those of President Taylor. Thomas believed it was unnecessary for missionaries to remain in Japan for five or six years. In his opinion, they could become proficient in speaking the language in a shorter time, and learning to read it was not necessary. Because the First Presidency agreed with him, mission terms seldom lasted more than four years from then until the mission's closure.

During the Thomas years, 1910 to 1912, the elders opened work among the Ainu, the indigenous people of Hokkaido, and started missionary work in Osaka, a large

Missionaries with Japanese members in Osaka, Japan, 13 May 1917. (Courtesy LDS Church Archives)

industrial and commercial city in the west. They also started using street meetings as a method of finding investigators and advertising their Church services. In early 1911 the elders in Kofu initiated English language classes at Kofu Commercial School. These regular English classes were part of the school's curriculum. During 1911 and 1912, some of the elders played baseball with the Tokyo American Baseball team. This was the most important effort of the entire mission to establish warm relations with representatives from other churches.

From 1910 until 1921, the missionaries never ceased working on one kind of translation project or another. They published several books and a number of tracts. They also worked steadily at enlarging the number of meetings that were held in the branches. The Mutual Improvement Association was started in 1916, and the first Relief Society was organized in Tokyo on May 30, 1917.

During President Joseph H. Stimpson's era, from 1915 until 1921, the Church grew faster than at any earlier time. Between 1915 and 1920, the elders performed sixty baptisms, sixteen children were blessed, thirty-seven men were ordained to the Aaronic Priesthood, and the total membership grew to 124. President Stimpson was proud of the mission's accomplishments, but he was concerned about the small number of missionaries in the field—only eight.

President Stimpson struggled with this handicap and sought the help of Elder David O. McKay of the Council of the Twelve. In March 1920 Stimpson wrote a letter to Elder McKay to invite him to an international Sunday School convention to be held in Tokyo that fall. In his letter he pleaded with Elder McKay to use whatever influence he could to have six more missionaries sent to Japan. Three new elders did arrive in May 1920, the first to come in two and a half years, but they merely replaced several others who were released. There were only two elders working in each conference, and Sendai had been closed for lack of missionaries. Stimpson wrote, "We have so few missionaries here in the mission at the present time that the devil has to look elsewhere for a workshop."[17]

From 1920 onward, the Japan Mission was on trial. There is no question that by this time Church leaders in Salt Lake City were harboring grave doubts concerning the value of continuing the mission. During Stimpson's era, the missionaries continually received rumors from home that Church authorities were thinking about closing the mission. Confirmation was never received by Stimpson from the Brethren, but when Elder David O. McKay visited Japan as part of his world mission tour, one of his purposes was to assess the situation and decide whether or not the mission should be continued.

Elder McKay arrived in Japan on December 20, 1920, and

stayed for a month. While there he visited all of the mission conferences except one in Sapporo, Hokkaido, where a blizzard prevented such a visit. He spent considerable time asking questions and seeking to learn more about the Japanese people. At the end of his visit he concluded that the mission was worth continuing and that if this was so, enough missionaries must be assigned to make it a success. "It is like trying to run a sixty horsepower machine with a one horsepower motor and that out of repair," said Elder McKay.[18] He decided that the mission would be much better if there were several married couples appointed and distributed to each of the conferences.[19] These couples were to have six or eight missionaries working under them, and they were to act as guardians and counselors for their missionaries. This idea began to be put into effect during the coming months but never became fully operational. In June 1921 Hilton A. and Hazel Robertson arrived in Tokyo, and in November 1922 three more couples arrived in the mission. At the end of the year there were twenty missionaries in the field, three more than in any other year.

In addition to the plan for more missionaries, Elder McKay also made some suggestions concerning improving the work. He stressed the need to turn every conversation into a gospel discussion. Missionaries were always to carry tracts and other literature. They were to spend more time in teaching the gospel in public places such as markets. Street meetings were to be continued. Evidently the visitor did not feel that the missionaries had been working hard enough. He told them to work at least as hard as if they were earning salaries.

The last official act of Elder McKay was to release the Stimpsons to return home. They left Japan on February 11, 1921. In March 1921, Lloyd O. Ivie, a former missionary to Japan, and his new bride, Nora, arrived in Japan to assume leadership. Ivie continued in the spirit of the reforms or innovations started by Elder McKay. He tried to expand the work. He sent missionaries to four new areas and introduced new methods of language study. For a brief period, total numbers of missionaries, Book of Mormon

In 1920 and 1921, Elder David O. McKay of the Quorum of the Twelve (back row, third man from left), with his traveling companion, Hugh J. Cannon (third man from right of photo), traveled around the world visiting the missions of the Church. They visited Japan in December 1920 and January 1921. Elder McKay is shown here with mission president Joseph Stimpson (back row between McKay and Cannon) and a group of Japanese members. Nachie Tsune (far left with arms around child) later immigrated to Hawaii, where she did temple work for many years. (Courtesy LDS Church Archives)

sales, and baptisms increased; but by the end of 1922 matters had returned to the old pattern. In January 1922 Kofu, after having been worked for fourteen consecutive years, was closed. This left only three conferences in the mission. Unfortunately, after the arrival of the couples, leaders in Salt Lake City did not continue to send the numbers of missionaries that had been suggested by Elder McKay. The result was a dampening of enthusiasm among the missionaries.

During 1923 and 1924 missionary activity varied little throughout the mission, and weekday schedules were quite similar in all areas. The missionaries spent most mornings studying, teaching English at local schools, and taking care of various menial tasks such as letter writing, picture taking, shopping, and visiting the doctor. Active proselytizing did not usually begin until afternoon. They filled their evenings with English classes, Mutual

Improvement Association lessons, and visits to friends and investigators. As a rule, they held three meetings on Sunday. Large numbers of children attended Sunday School. The missionaries hoped these children would be a successful avenue of approach to their parents. Only a few members and investigators usually attended sacrament meetings. The missionaries also frequently held evening preaching meetings that drew fairly good numbers. Attendance patterns in the individual branches of the mission were not encouraging.

In summary, the statistics for the mission were far from impressive. This is evident in the following table of statistics for the years 1918 through 1924.[20]

Date	Number of Members	Convert Baptisms	Ordinations: Aaronic and Melchizedek	Number of Missionaries
1918	105	10	11	11
1919	118	13	4	10
1920	127	10	6	9
1921	135	10	11	13
1922	154	18	7	17
1923	158	6	1	19
1924	164	8	2	14

Were the Latter-day Saints different from other missionary groups in their lack of success? It appears that they were no less successful than other missionaries, and they may have been more successful. It is difficult to accumulate statistics to prove this statement, but the ratio of effectiveness was about proportional to the number of man-years invested by any missionary group. Other Christian missionaries stayed in Japan much longer and still had few converts, especially during the early years.[21] Figuring in terms of man-years, the LDS missionaries actually gained converts a little faster than did the Protestants.

Elder Hilton A. Robertson was appointed president of the mission when the Ivies were released in October 1923. The period of his leadership, which ended with the closing of the mission, was short-lived for two principal reasons, among others that will be mentioned later. The more serious reason was a problem that arose in Japan resulting from passage of the Oriental exclusion laws (often referred to as the Japanese exclusion laws) in the United States. A second contributing factor was the great Tokyo earthquake of September 1, 1923.

The destruction that came in the wake of this terrible earthquake was very great. It is estimated that between 120,000 and 150,000 people died—many in the flames that engulfed Tokyo, some under falling debris, and others as a result of riots and disorders. Several missionaries, including the Robertsons, were in Tokyo at the time of the disaster and were fortunate to escape bodily harm or death. Through the entire disaster, Robertson reported, not one member of the Church was injured, nor were any of the missionaries. The mission home lost some tile from the roof and plaster from the walls, but aside from that the place fared very well.[22]

The earthquake caused the work of the missionaries in Tokyo to stop for a long time. However, they filled their days by helping some of the members repair their homes and others to relocate.

At home in Utah, gloomy reports were circulated, and in one instance an incorrect report of the death of President Robertson was published in one of the Utah papers. Not until September 11 did the friends and relatives of the missionaries know they were safe.[23] The earthquake had a lasting effect on the mission in that it started the leaders at home thinking more seriously about the work in Japan and reassessing the position of the Church there. Also, the parents of the missionaries felt the distance from their sons and daughters to be greater than ever before.

Except for the unavailability of missionaries during World War I, international matters had no major effect on the mission until 1924, when America's Japanese exclusion law caused the most serious problems. A long series of state and national issues concerning the immigration of Orientals into the United States and subsequent issues relating to their possession of land had begun in 1882. This culminated with Congress's enactment in 1924 of a new immigration law, the second Johnson Act (also called the Exclusion Act of 1924), containing a section forbidding "aliens ineligible for citizenship" admittance to the United States.[24] Because the Asians of China and Japan were the only aliens not eligible for citizenship, the law was a direct insult to the Japanese nation and was interpreted by the Japanese as such.

The law went into effect on July 1, 1924. That day was observed throughout Japan as a "day of humiliation," and Tokyo blazed with posters that read "Hate Everything American." The largest of sixteen meetings of protest lasted continuously from one o'clock in the afternoon until ten o'clock in the evening, with an audience ranging from five thousand to twelve thousand people.[25]

The situation became very tense for the missionaries after this law was passed. On one occasion, shortly after the 1924 exclusion law went into effect, President Robertson found two posters tacked to his door saying, "Bei-jin Haiseki"—"American go home."

THE CLOSING OF THE MISSION

On June 13, 1924, President Hilton A. Robertson received from Church headquarters in Salt Lake City a telegram advising that twelve thousand yen was being wired to him. There was no message of explanation,[26] but Robertson and his missionaries had a good idea why the money was being sent. For several years rumors had circulated among them concerning the possible closing of the mission.[27] Even during a missionary conference a month earlier, President Robertson had "touched upon the possibilities of the Japan Mission closing and said that under present conditions, with the current thought as it is, it is impossible for the missionaries to spend their best efforts in the work." He also told the missionaries "that he hoped to learn in the very near future the fate of the mission."[28]

He was free to make such a statement because he had been

corresponding with the First Presidency regarding the matter. On January 31 he sent them a very carefully written appraisal of the condition of the mission. This was done after President Robertson had consulted with all of his missionaries to learn how they appraised conditions in their areas. This five-page report was seriously considered by Church president Heber J. Grant and his counselors.

In answering this letter, the First Presidency gave several indications that they were seriously considering closing the mission. The words "if the work continues" were used in one instance, and elsewhere they said they had doubted "the wisdom of continuing the mission." The most direct reference to closing the mission said:

> When we stop to think that over twenty years of hard labor have been performed in Japan, it certainly looks as though the Lord would justify us if we saw fit to close that mission, when we read the words: "I feel perfectly safe in saying that we haven't over five or six real Saints in the mission who are willing and ready to help carry on the work." The Lord has said in Section 18 of the Doctrine and Covenants:
>
> "And if it so be that you should labor all your days in crying repentance unto this people, and bring, save it be one soul unto me, how great shall be your joy with him in the kingdom of my Father!"
>
> We do not wish to lose one soul in Japan, but if the same amount of labor in some other country was performed, the chances are we would have many times as many converts.[29]

Robertson's letter had indicated that all of the missionaries felt "the same amount of labor with some other people would bring better results." The only thing that appears to have kept the First Presidency from a final decision to close the mission at that time was "whether we have done our duty in warning the Japanese nation."[30]

Following the May 1924 conference, the missionaries in

Osaka, Sapporo, and Sendai, as well as those in Tokyo, found attendance at scheduled meetings dropping weekly. Furthermore, some of the elders were insulted by irate Japanese who were aroused by the recent passage of the Japanese exclusion laws in the United States. Notes telling them to go home had been left on their doors. To their surprise, on Sunday, June 15, a Tokyo newspaper "contained a short telegram message stating that the Mormon missionaries would be immediately withdrawn from Japan."[31]

Why an earlier telegram from President Heber J. Grant had been delayed is not known, but on Thursday, June 26, 1924, the following correspondence dated June 9 arrived at the mission office: "Have decided to withdraw all missionaries from Japan temporarily. Cabling you twelve thousand yen for that purpose. If more needed cable us. Arrange return immediately. Grant."[32] The man who had opened the mission in 1901 had made the decision to close it temporarily.

When the telegram arrived on June 26 instructing them to return, the missionaries promptly set about making arrangements for closing the mission. During the first three weeks of July, elders and sisters arrived at Tokyo from their various locations. They spent most of their last month or so in Japan visiting members, selling and giving away mission-owned goods, shipping books, and engaging in similar activities.

Then, on July 24, 1924, Elders William E. Davis and Milton B. Taylor, along with Elder and Sister F. Wallace Browning (who had visited China since the notice of closure came), boarded the S.S. *President Cleveland* and sailed for the United States.

After June 29, all meetings were canceled except sacrament meeting, which was held until the last Sunday before departure. Only two to four Japanese Saints attended during that time. The elders passed out thirty-seven hundred tracts during the final days of the mission. On August 2 President and Sister Robertson went to Osaka to encourage the Saints there to "live up to their duties." Then they boarded the S.S. *President Pierce* in Kobe, and all the remaining missionaries, Elder and Sister Elwood L. Christensen and Elders Rulon Esplin, Vinal G. Mauss, Lewis H. Moore, and Ernest B. Woodward, boarded the same ship in Yokohama. Sailing from Japan on August 7, 1924, their departure marked the closing of the early mission of The Church of Jesus Christ of Latter-day Saints to Japan.[33]

When the missionaries arrived in Salt Lake City on August 22, 1924, President Grant greeted them, saying, "Thank God you are home because I know what is in store for the people of that land and we are glad you are safely home."[34] President Robertson made a statement many years later that was similar in spirit to that of President Grant's greeting. He said: "I think that the mission was closed for a purpose in 1924 when we returned home. I feel that the Lord knew what was going to transpire [speaking of ultranationalism and World War II] and he called the missionaries home and ordered the mission closed temporarily. Later on we find that the other denominations throughout the world who were proselyting in Japan were forced to close their missions and return to America at great loss and sacrifice."[35]

Considering the number of problems the mission had faced through the years, the disruptions of the final two years, and the psychological distress suffered by the missionaries, it is easy to understand the decision of the First Presidency and the Council of the Twelve to close the mission. It was true that the results had been "almost negligible." Nevertheless, the mission did produce some lasting contributions, translation work in particular, and a few converts who were brought into the Church remained faithful through the years until the work was recommenced following World War II.

NOTES

1. For in-depth histories of the early mission in Japan, see my "Early Latter-day Saint Missions to South and East Asia," (Ph.D. diss., Claremont Graduate School and University Center, 1967); and Murray L. Nichols, "History of the Japan Mission of the Church . . . , 1901–1924" (master's thesis, Brigham Young University, 1958).

2. "A Future Mission Field," *The Contributor,* October 1895, pp. 764–65.

3. *Deseret News,* 6 April 1901, p. 9.

4. Heber J. Grant, *A Japanese Journal,* comp. Gordon A. Madsen (n.p., n.d.), pp. 12–13.

5. John M. L. Young, *The Two Empires in Japan* (Tokyo: The Bible Times Press, 1958), p. 44.

6. See J. Herbert Kane, *A Global View of Christian Missions,* rev. ed. (Grand Rapids, Mich.: William B. Eerdmans Publishing Co., 1971), 238–49; Stephen Neill, *A History of Christian Missions,* 2nd ed. rev. (London: Penguin Books, 1986), pp. 276–82.

7. As quoted by Heber J. Grant, in Conference Report, April 1902, p. 47.

8. *Deseret News,* 21 October 1901; Alma O. Taylor, Journal B, 1 September 1901, Harold B. Lee Library, Brigham Young University, Provo, Utah (hereafter cited as BYU Special Collections). For a summary of the prayer, see the Alma O. Taylor Papers, BYU Special Collections.

9. See Taylor, Journal B, 9 February to 19 March 1903, BYU Special Collections.

10. Ibid., 23 February 1902.

11. See ibid., 10 March 1902.

12. Heber J. Grant, address, in Conference Reports, 1901–1904, 4 October 1903, 7.

13. President Grant was home for only a little more than two months when the First Presidency (Joseph F. Smith, John R. Winder, and Anthon H. Lund) called him to preside over the European Mission of the Church. He felt that this was in a way a second opportunity for success in the mission field.

14. Alma O. Taylor, Journal E, 16 July 1904, BYU Special Collections.

15. Alma O. Taylor, "About Japan and the Japanese Mission," *Improvement Era* 10 (November 1906): 6.

16. See Taylor's journals for a complete record of the translation process. See also his typed recollections of the same, in Taylor Papers, BYU Special Collections.

17. Joseph H. Stimpson to David O. McKay, 18 March 1920, Copybook H, 359, LDS Church Archives.

18. Mission Financial and Statistical Reports, Japan Mission, 1921, LDS Church Archives; hereafter cited as MFSR.

19. See Joseph H. Stimpson to Alma O. Taylor, 19 January 1921, Copybook I, 10, LDS Church Archives.

20. See MFSR, Japan Mission, 1920–1924; and Andrew Jenson, "Manuscript History of the Japan Mission," 1918–1924, LDS Church Archives.

21. See Kenneth Scott Latourette, *A History of the Expansion of Christianity, The Great Century: North America and Asia, A.D. 1800–A.D. 1914,* (Grand Rapids: Zondervan Publishing House, 1970), 6:385ff.

22. See Hilton A. Robertson, in Conference Report, October 1924, pp. 123–24.

23. This information is based on an article in the scrapbook of Hilton A. Robertson, Provo, Utah. Brother Robertson has passed away since this manuscript was written, and the present location of the scrapbook is unknown to the author. See *Deseret News,* 11 September 1923.

24. See Edwin O. Reischauer, *The United States and Japan* (New York: Viking Press, 1963), pp. 16–17, for an evaluation of these events. See also his *Japan: The Story of a Nation,* 4th ed. (New York: McGraw-Hill Publishing Co., 1990), p. 155.

25. See Sidney L. Gulick, "American-Japanese Relations: The Logic of the Exclusionists," *Annals of the American Academy of Social and Political Sciences* 122 (November 1925): 181.

26. See Japan Mission Journals (1901–1924), 13 June 1924, LDS Church Archives; hereafter cited as JMJ.

27. See my "The Closing of the Early Japan Mission," *BYU Studies* 15 (winter 1975): 171–90.

28. Ibid., 14 May 1924.

29. Heber J. Grant, Letterbook (21 February–19 July 1924), 20 February 1924, p. 155, LDS Church Archives. In the same letter the First Presidency mentioned that Lloyd O. Ivie, the previous mission president, estimated that there were "only five or six real converts to the Gospel in that mission."

30. Ibid., 156.

31. JMJ, 15 June 1924. The LDS missionaries in Japan were not aware that a formal public announcement concerning the closing of the mission had been made in the *Deseret News* on June 12, 1924. It is not surprising that by June 15 international news-wire services had picked up this information.

32. Jenson, "Japan Mission"; see Grant, Letterbook, 19 June 1924, p. 752.

33. See Jenson, "Japan Mission," 7 August 1924. One of the final entries in this history states simply that in the first twenty-three years, eighty-eight missionaries had served in Japan. One died in the mission field, and seven were sent home sick. Nine elders had been sent home in varying degrees of dishonor. During that period 174 Japanese had been baptized—112 men and 62 women. Ten members had been excommunicated, nine had died, and eight had moved. Seven elders, twenty-two priests, fifteen teachers, and thirty deacons had been ordained.

34. Ibid., 22 August 1924.

35. Hilton A. Robertson, in Conference Report, April 1947, p. 53.

4

JAPAN AND HAWAII

1924–1945

The Interim

HOLDING ON THROUGH "THE ABSOLUTE DARK AGES"

With the mission closed, President Grant often brooded over the isolated Japanese Saints and looked for the time when the gospel could again be taught to those people. In the interim a faithful Latter-day Saint, Nara Fujiya, who later described the era as "the absolute dark ages," helped keep members unified by maintaining the Mutual Improvement Association (the only Church meeting they were authorized to hold) and publishing a newsletter called *Shuro* (The Palm), which appeared from 1925 through the fall of 1929. There were about two dozen Japanese members who wished to maintain activity in the Church, but they were spread from Sapporo in the north, to Tokyo and Kofu in the middle, and to Osaka in the west. From 1924 to 1927, the little flocks tried valiantly to sustain one another. Parties, especially at Christmastime, brought some warmth and fellowship. Some of these members eventually fell away, but most survived through their dedication to the Church.

In 1927 the First Presidency appointed twenty-eight-year-old

Brother Nara to be the presiding elder in Japan and permitted the Saints to act more fully in priesthood functions. The First Presidency asked former mission president Alma O. Taylor to correspond with some of the members. But from 1927 until 1934 the picture is not clear. When Brother Nara's railway job took him to Manchuria in 1933, Church leaders found his replacement in BYU-educated Fujiwara Takeo.[1]

In 1926 BYU president Franklin S. Harris had visited Japan in a professional capacity, but he also represented the Brethren in visiting the Japanese members and helping with organizational matters. While in Sapporo, he met Fujiwara and invited him to attend BYU. Brother Fujiwara became the first Japanese to graduate from BYU. In 1934, shortly after his graduation, he accepted the call to serve as presiding elder and as a special missionary in Japan. He shepherded the Japanese Saints faithfully, even performing two baptisms of member children and trying diligently to activate members and remain in touch until his early death from pleurisy in 1936.[2] The decade from 1936 to 1945 was a period of little or no communication between the Church and the members in Japan. In fact, the focus shifted to Hawaii.

HARVESTING THE JAPANESE FIELD IN HAWAII

Recognizing that years might pass before missionaries could again preach in Japan, Heber J. Grant, the man who had established the Japanese Mission in 1901 and closed it in 1924, decided to continue work among the only significant population of Japanese who were available to the missionaries, the Japanese in Hawaii.[3]

When President Grant arrived in Hawaii to organize the Oahu Stake in 1935, he was introduced to nine Japanese of Hawaii, generally called Americans of Japanese Ancestry (AJA), who had been baptized members of the Church the day before.[4]

President Grant's entire Hawaiian experience pointed him to the conclusion that work had to be seriously undertaken among the Japanese, Chinese, and other Asians in Hawaii. From President Castle H. Murphy, who had felt compelled to start missionary work among the Chinese and Japanese in 1932, he learned of the various ethnic Sunday Schools in Honolulu. But the Japanese organization, which held all of its meetings in the Japanese language, seemed to impress him most. For a year or two before this, Elwood L. Christensen, a former missionary to Japan, had conducted services with the small but growing Japanese congregation.[5] Both President Grant and his counselor President J. Reuben Clark Jr. related prophetic visions of the role Hawaii was to play in the expansion of the Church into Asia. President Clark wrote: "It would seem not improbable that Hawaii is the most favorable place for the Church to make its next effort to preach the Gospel to the Japanese people; and it would further appear that a strong colony of Japanese Saints in Hawaii could operate from there into their homeland in a way that might bring many Japanese to a knowledge not only of Christianity, but of the restored Gospel. There are evidences that the fields are ripening; if so, they will be ready sooner or later for the harvest to begin."[6] The same reasoning was applied to the Chinese, Filipinos, and Indians of Hawaii. This vision of things to come has been fulfilled to a remarkable degree.

While President Grant was in the islands, he talked with President Murphy and others about reopening the Japanese Mission, but in Hawaii rather than in Japan. More than a year passed, and then, in November 1936, Hilton A. Robertson, who had served as mission president in Japan at the time the mission closed, and his wife, Hazel, were called to open the Japanese Mission in Hawaii. They arrived in Honolulu on February 24, 1937.

On the following Sunday the Robertsons met with a little band of thirty-five Japanese Saints and investigators. Among them was Sister Isune Nachie, who was now very old. She had joined the Church in Japan before the mission's closure and came to Laie in 1923 to do temple work. Edward L. Clissold described her as a true Saint. Others who were there were Dr. Tomizo Katsunuma, who had been converted to the Church while attending Utah State University in Logan, Utah, and Kay Ikegami, who also proved to be a faithful leader.

The first three missionaries to the Japanese Mission in Hawaii arrived in October 1937. They were Preston D. Evans, Roy W. Spear, and Melvyn A. Weenig. Weenig was later called as president of this mission in 1946. By the end of the first year, the total membership of the mission was seventeen: nine males and eight females. Four converts had been baptized, and the mission was off to a good start.

J. Christopher Conkling has prepared the following table to show the growth of the Japanese/Central Pacific Mission:[7]

	1937	1938	1939	1940	1941	1942	1943	1944	1945	1946	1947	1948	1949
Missionaries	5	19	32	54	55	18	13	7	4	34	66	89	77
Baptisms Total	4	13	26	37	48	156	72	48	34	30	15	52	67
Membership	17	30	60	101	150	302	375	437	484	522	532	604	671

As can be seen in this table, the number of missionaries increased fairly rapidly after 1937, and the number of members began to rise steadily as well. During 1938 the work was expanded to the island of Hawaii, and in January and February 1939, missionaries of this mission were sent to Maui and Kauai, respectively. From the beginning, the greatest success came from among the young AJA. Sunday Schools, Primary classes, and MIA groups were organized wherever the missionaries worked.

During the lifetime of the mission, the elders and sisters were encouraged to learn the Japanese language. In retrospect this seems almost unnecessary, but it was considered wise at the time even though nearly all of the converts were among the English-speaking young people. The major concern was that when the youths had been influenced by the missionaries, they would want to introduce the missionaries to their parents. It was hoped that an ability to speak the Japanese language would help to influence

Following its closure in Japan in 1924, the Japanese Mission was reopened in Hawaii in 1937. Mission president Hilton A. Robertson and his wife, Hazel, are sitting near the middle of the second row, among American Japanese members, friends, and missionaries. (Courtesy LDS Church Archives)

the older people, if only to convince them that their children should become Latter-day Saints.

Another reason for learning the Japanese language was the hope that the Japanese Mission in Hawaii would someday be the base of operations for the reopening of Japan to LDS missionary efforts. Although affairs did not work out in precisely this way, a missionary in Hawaii did teach the Japanese language to the first missionaries called to reopen Japan. In 1948, while waiting for permission to enter Japan, the first five elders studied the language on Oahu under the tutelage of Paul V. Hyer, who had learned to speak Japanese while serving a mission in Hawaii.

An important tie between the Japanese Mission in Hawaii and the Saints in Japan was established in 1939 when the Church sent President Hilton A. Robertson to Japan to maintain contact with the members there. Conkling described the trip in these words:

> In April and May of 1939, Hilton A. Robertson made an official visit to Japan on behalf of the Church. With only inaccurate addresses, he began searching for Nami Suzuki, an old sister who had once lived in and cooked for the mission home. Of all the millions in the Tokyo-Yokohama area, a young girl emerged from a public bath, saw the foreigner and asked what he wanted. When Robertson told her, she said, "That's my mother." She took him right to Sister Suzuki's, and Robertson got other addresses from her. He visited the Tokyo, Sapporo, and Osaka Saints, and assured them that they had not been forgotten and that missionaries would return someday. While in Japan he baptized several new members—the two surviving children of Sister Suzuki (with Elder Watanabe confirming) and Elder Katsura's daughter (with Katsura confirming), among others.[8]

The Robertsons were released in September 1940, and President Jay C. Jensen and his wife were called to direct the work. President Jensen, who had been a missionary in Japan during the early mission, continued the patterns of proselytizing established by President Robertson.

The churches of Hawaii, LDS and non-LDS, grew in number during World War II. Many of the new members were AJA. They, like many others, found themselves turning to religion more than before. It is fortunate that the Church had developed an organization ready to benefit from this new interest in Christian religions. A glance at the preceding table reveals that the Japanese Mission membership more than doubled during 1942, the first year of the war.

Concurrent with the greater interest in religion among the AJA was another development that may have contributed to the rapid growth during 1942. The missionaries were going home, and no new elders were on their way to replace them. It is probable that the missionaries put more pressure on their prospective converts to make decisions to be baptized than they might have otherwise done. Whatever the reasons, the number of converts expanded rapidly during 1942 and continued to grow throughout the war even though the missionary force was greatly diminished.

Edward L. Clissold, who was first counselor in the Oahu Stake presidency, was called to replace President Jensen in December 1942. He served as acting president until 1944, when his assignment as a reserve naval officer took him away from Hawaii. He was also temple president during these years.

One of the first changes Clissold made was the name of the mission. Because the term *Japanese* was held in derision and contempt, President Clissold felt that a more innocuous name would be better for the image of the mission. The name he chose for the mission was the Central Pacific Mission (CPM). This name remained from 1943 until the mission was combined with the Hawaiian Mission in 1950.

As the number of full-time missionaries dropped, President Clissold had to encourage the Japanese members to join with the long-established wards and branches. In 1944 President Castle Murphy was again called to Hawaii, this time to act simultaneously as president of the Hawaiian Mission, the Central Pacific Mission, and the Hawaii Temple. He was also servicemen's coordinator.

The conclusion of the war brought marked changes to the mission. In 1946 Melvyn A. Weenig and his wife, Georgia, were called to preside over the CPM, and before the year was over forty-five missionaries were serving in it, a number that Weenig did not believe adequate to handle the work. Over the next two years the mission force increased, but the number of baptisms did not grow accordingly. The immediacy of the war was past, and the AJA turned back toward their Japanese heritage.

But even though numbers of converts did not grow rapidly after the war, the AJA converts of earlier times remained loyal. According to Conkling, they "were the most faithful [Saints] in the world."[9] Among those who were converted to the Church by the Japanese/CPM were Adney Y. Komatsu, later to be the first AJA to be a mission president and then a General Authority of the Church; Tomosue Abo; Kenji Akagi; Russell N. Horiuchi; Kotaro Koizumi; William Nako; Arthur K. Nishimoto; Edward Okazaki and his wife, Chieko, who until mid-1997 served in the general presidency of the Relief Society; Satoru Sato; Ralph Shino; Sam Shimabukuro, who served as mission president, temple president, and as a member of the Second Quorum of the Seventy; Walter Teruya; Roy I. Tsuya; and others, all of whom (with the exception of Sister Okazaki) have been called to serve as mission presidents to Japan, as Regional Representatives, or as temple presidents in Tokyo. Many other Japanese from the CPM in Hawaii have served in Japan as missionaries.

One of the aspirations of President Weenig and his missionaries was to extend their mission to Japan. This was not the destiny of the CPM. It did, however, produce many missionaries who were called to Japan. It was to Edward L. Clissold, not to President Weenig, that the responsibility of reopening the Japanese Mission was given.

President Clissold had been assigned to Japan as a member of the Occupation forces at the end of the war. While there, he participated with the LDS servicemen and reported their missionary activities to President McKay after he returned home. In 1948 the First Presidency decided that Clissold and Weenig should go to Japan together, but because of restrictions of the Occupation forces, only one man could be sent. Because Brother Clissold was already familiar with conditions in Japan and knew many important people there, he was sent to reopen the mission in Japan. He arrived there in the spring of 1948.

After the war, the efforts of the CPM were centered almost entirely upon young people who did not speak Japanese and who were part of the new Hawaiian Mission. For this reason Church leaders in Hawaii and Salt Lake City began to question the need for a separate mission for Japanese Americans. Finally, in 1950, the

First Presidency decided to combine the CPM and Hawaiian Missions.

NOTES

1. See J. Christopher Conkling, "Members without a Church: Japanese Mormons in Japan from 1924 to 1948," *BYU Studies* 15 (spring 1975): 191–214.

2. See my "The Blossoming of the Church in Japan," *Ensign* 22 (October 1992): 33–34.

3. This chapter has been only slightly revised from chapter 10 of the author's book *Unto the Islands of the Sea* (Salt Lake City: Deseret Book Co., 1986).

4. See Edward L. Clissold Oral History, interview by author, Salt Lake City, Utah,1976, James Moyle Oral History Program, LDS Church Archives, typescript, pp. 6–7.

5. See Elwood L. Christensen Oral History, interview by author, Honolulu, Hawaii, 1978, James Moyle Oral History Program, LDS Church Archives, typescript, pp. 17–20.

6. J. Reuben Clark Jr., "The Outpost in Mid-Pacific," *Improvement Era* 38 (September 1935): 533.

7. See Conkling, "Members without a Church," p. 210. Conkling's data is from Mission Financial and Statistical Reports, Central Pacific Mission, 1937–1948, LDS Church Archives. I have added the information for 1949.

8. Ibid., p. 208.

9. Ibid., p. 211.

5

JAPAN

1945–1962

The Reopening and Foundation Years

Most Americans think of the Japanese as a deeply religious people—indeed, saturated with religion for both national and personal reasons. In truth, however, this conception needs explanation and interpretation. Although most Japanese claim to have religious beliefs or affiliations, Japan is a secularized society, one wherein religion plays a minor role in the lives of most of the people. In his book *The Japanese*, Edwin O. Reischauer, highly regarded scholar of Japanese history, says: "If this book dealt with a South Asian or Middle Eastern people, it might well have started with a consideration of religion. Even for most Western nations, religion would have required earlier and fuller treatment. But religion occupies a more peripheral position in Japan. Before the seventeenth century it did play much the same role in Japan as in the West, but the trend toward secularism that has recently become marked in the West dates back at least three centuries in Japan."[1]

Reischauer then explains the role Confucianism has played in Japanese religious and social life. Confucianism stresses a rational natural order and a social system based on strict ethical rules. But it has no concept of a personal deity, no priesthood, and very little religious ritual. Although few, if any, contemporary Japanese would consider themselves Confucianists, most Japanese are more strongly influenced in the way they live their lives by Confucianism than by Buddhism, Shinto, or the so-called new religions *(Shinkō-Shūkyō)* of the postwar era.[2]

The Japanese, like the Chinese, have seen little conflict among religious persuasions. For hundreds of years it has been traditional for a Japanese to be blessed at birth and married by a Shinto priest, to live his or her life according to Confucian ethics, and to be buried or cremated by a Buddhist priest. Buddhism, it should be noted, is the only religion (or philosophy, in the case of Confucianism) of the three that has a well-developed concept of mankind's destiny after death. When asked regarding their religious affiliations, most Japanese answer that they are Buddhist.

The history of religions in Japan during the twentieth century has been one of general decline punctuated by periods of upheaval, suppression, government misuse, and spectacular growth. Though it is beyond the scope of this book to review all of the major developments during the past nine-plus decades, it is appropriate to touch on a few events and trends that have had an effect on the history of the LDS Church in Japan.

Following the closing of the early mission in 1924, Japan moved steadily into the period of ultranationalism that eventually resulted in the Sino-Japanese War and World War II. During the 1930s the Japanese government required all citizens to visit Shinto shrines and to worship the emperor. The government took the position that "bowing to the portrait of the emperor was simply a patriotic gesture and that attendance at the Shinto shrines was devoid of religious significance."[3] This was hard for the Christians to accept, but in 1936 the churches were forced to submit to the government's position.[4]

When Protestant and Roman Catholic ministers, missionaries, and priests left Japan on "furlough" during the late 1930s, they were not allowed to return. Christianity had always been considered a foreign religion, and at a time of ultranationalism, it and its proponents were automatically suspect. The situation was further exacerbated when the government passed the Religious Bodies

Law of 1939. This law brought all religion under state control. According to this measure, all Christian churches were supposed to unite in one body, the *Kyodan*—a religious party or association. Some religious denominations did unite, others operated secretly, and still others were forced to disband or leave the country. By 1941 most Americans and other foreign missionaries had returned to their own lands. During the war, Japanese Christians and their churches were subjected to many pressures. Compulsory emperor worship was introduced, all hymns referring to the lordship of Jesus Christ were removed, and Sunday school materials were used by the government as a potent vehicle for the dissemination of government propaganda. Although Christian church services continued throughout the war, conditions were depressingly difficult by the end of the war. Not only had many non-Christian lives been lost, but Christians and their property were lost to the bombings of almost all of Japan's major cities.

When the war finally ended on August 14, 1945, the Japanese nation was exhausted, prostrate before the Allied forces. Although the Japanese people had been told that the American and other Allied troops would be harsh overlords, such proved to be untrue. The Allied forces, in turn, were surprised to find that the Japanese people, a people who had fought bitterly, even ferociously, were submissive and cooperative subjects of the Occupation government.

On October 4, 1945, the Supreme Commander for the Allied Powers (SCAP), a designation that was applied not only to General Douglas MacArthur but also to his Occupation government, repealed the Religious Bodies Law. Two months later, on December 28, SCAP gave a directive that became part of the law of the land under the title of the Religious Juridical Persons Law. The freedom of religion implied in this law was given legal validity when it was accepted as Article Twenty of the new constitution, which went into effect in May 1947. Another step, one of great importance, was Emperor Hirohito's proclamation, on January 1, 1946, that he was not a divine or quasi-divine person and that the Japanese people were not superior in any way to other races and peoples. "By this statement," writes Richard H. Drummond, "the traditional spiritual basis of the Japanese government and society, the doctrine of the divinity of the emperor, which had been developed with increasing explicitness for over half a century, was at one stroke demolished. For many Japanese the act was psychically more shattering than military defeat and surrender, and it left literally millions to reconstruct their spiritual foundations and standards of value."[5]

It was in this spiritual vacuum that dedicated LDS servicemen first taught the restored gospel of Jesus Christ. The time was right for the growth of all Christian churches as well as for many new religious movements that sprang from the Japanese people themselves. Protestants and Roman Catholics frequently refer to the period from 1945 to 1951 as the "Christian Boom." Circumstances were definitely right for the establishment of the LDS Church during that period. Between 1945 and 1951, the year the Occupation ended, the Japanese people were excited about most things American, and they were grateful to have religious freedom. But after 1951, when the economic growth of the nation began to spiral upward and most Japanese became quite comfortable with their new postwar standard of living, interest in religion slackened and the difficulty of converting Japanese to Mormonism became greater. The present trend toward secularism—that is, the process whereby religious thought, practice, and institutions have lost social significance—has intensified ever since the early 1950s.

THE REESTABLISHMENT OF
THE LDS CHURCH IN JAPAN

In 1944 Edward L. Clissold, at that time a member of the Oahu Stake presidency, president of the Hawaii Temple and the Central Pacific Mission, and an active-duty Navy officer, was sent to military government school at the University of Chicago. While there he was trained as a government administrator, and he

President Edward "Vaun" Clissold stands between Church members W. Paul Merrill (left) and Guy A. Hart, who were with the army engineers in Japan during the Occupation. Merrill and Hart advised Clissold regarding the feasibility of reconstructing the building the Church had purchased as a mission home. (Courtesy LDS Church Archives)

expected to be assigned as a provincial governor in Japan when the war ended. As he had anticipated, Clissold was sent to Japan immediately after the conclusion of hostilities. But contrary to his expectations, he was assigned to work in the education and religion section of SCAP.

During his short tour of duty in Japan (only two months), Clissold became acquainted with a number of LDS servicemen and the operation of servicemen's groups. He also became thoroughly familiar with the officers within the section of SCAP that had greatest influence on the development of religious affairs in postwar Japan. In addition, Clissold did what he could to find the remaining Japanese Latter-day Saints from the previous mission era. On October 30, 1945, he placed a small ad in Japanese in a Tokyo newspaper, saying: "URGENT NOTICE—I would like any member of the Church of Jesus Christ of Near-Day Saints (Mormon Church) to contact me as soon as possible. Daiichi Hotel, Room 548. Lt. Col. Edward Clissold."[6] Brother Nara Fujiya, who had shepherded the Japanese Saints from 1924 until 1933, responded to Brother Clissold's notice. As a result, a few other Japanese members were located and integrated into the activities of the LDS servicemen.[7]

In February 1946, the Clissolds returned to Honolulu to resume their business and Church activities that had been curtailed by the war. Brother Clissold was soon called as both a stake high councilor and stake mission president. In the spring of 1947, the First Presidency called Melvyn A. Weenig, president of the Central Pacific Mission, and Brother Clissold to go to Japan to investigate the possibility of reopening the mission, and if appropriate, to do so. Since the mission had been closed for so long, however, the U.S. Department of War would allow only one representative of the Church to enter the country. Because he had been in Japan recently and knew how to deal with the military government, Clissold was selected to go. He received word of this appointment and was set apart as mission president on October 22, 1947.

The First Presidency instructed President Clissold to preside over the members, to organize the Church, to establish a mission headquarters, and to make arrangements for missionaries to enter the country. When he arrived in Japan on March 6, 1948, President Clissold almost immediately saw the reason for his previous appointment to the education and religion section of SCAP. For the next several months he had regular contact with many of the men he had worked with in his military assignment. Through this affiliation he found help and open doors that greatly facilitated the organization of the mission.[8]

Since missionaries were not permitted entrance into Japan until provision had been made for their maintenance, President Clissold began immediately to search for living and office quarters. In April he located a partly burned mansion in Azabu, Tokyo,

President Edward L. Clissold purchased this building soon after he arrived in Japan to reopen the mission in 1948. The mansion served as mission home and offices for nearly thirty years before being razed to make way for the Tokyo Temple, which was dedicated in 1980. (Courtesy LDS Church Archives)

and through the help of many influential people, even Prince Takamatsu, and after a series of extremely complex negotiations, he obtained permission to buy the property.[9] This mansion had served as the residence of the Japanese minister of welfare during the war. Although it had taken a direct hit from an incendiary bomb, the walls of the ferro-concrete structure were still solid.[10] Renovation of the building began in May, and by the twenty-second of that month President Clissold moved into the servants' quarters over the garage. Although Sister Clissold and other missionaries moved into the home in September, the remodeling work was not completed until November 25, 1948. A large addition came later, and in the late 1970s the building was razed to make way for the new Tokyo Temple. It was in an excellent part of the city and served the Church well as a mission home and

The mansion, which had housed the Japanese minister of welfare, had taken direct hits from an incendiary bomb during World War II. This picture shows the building as it appeared when purchased by the Church. (Courtesy LDS Church Archives)

office for almost thirty years. It is significant that within the first month of the new mission the Church bought property in Japan. None had been acquired between 1901 and 1924.

The initial group of missionaries arrived in Japan on June 26, 1948. The first of their number, Harrison Theodore "Ted" Price, was called to serve in late 1947. The other four were Paul C. Andrus, Wayne McDaniel, Koji Okauchi, a *nisei* (second-generation American of Japanese Ancestry), and Raymond C. Price, brother to Ted. (Elder Paul Andrus and Elder Ted Price both later served as mission presidents in Japan, and Ray Price served in the presidency of the Tokyo Temple.) At least two of these men had fought against the Japanese in the Pacific theater during World War II. Now they were returning to teach the gospel of peace. Between December 1947 and March 1948, these elders were assigned to the Central Pacific Mission in Hawaii for language training under Paul V. Hyer, an elder who had learned to speak Japanese well. They not only studied the Japanese language but also tracted and taught the gospel with companions from the Central Pacific Mission. Their experience in Hawaii prepared them to teach the gospel as somewhat experienced missionaries. Otherwise they would have entered the Japanese mission field as total "greenies."[11] They were allowed to enter Japan only after President Clissold had made arrangements for them to live with American Saints in the Occupation forces.[12] Between June and the end of 1948, the mission force grew to seventeen: President and Sister Clissold, thirteen elders (seven Caucasians and six nisei), and two sister missionaries (both nisei).

One of the early assignments President Clissold gave the first group of elders was to find any members from the former mission who were still alive. Some of the converts of the early mission, such as Brothers Nara, Shiraishi, and Takagi, as well as a few women, had already found the Church and were serving well in one or two small groups. But by no means had all of the old members found the Church. Paul C. Andrus and his companion, Ray Price, found some members in the Yokohama area who had been out of touch with the Church since the late 1930s but who had nevertheless remained faithful. One of those who was overjoyed to know that the Church had returned to Japan was Sister Suzuki Nami. According to Elder Andrus, "she remained faithful even though during the war and during the Japanese incident in Manchuria she lost two of her sons and one daughter. . . . Her very nice home in Yokohama was bombed and burned and destroyed completely. When Ray Price and I found her, she and her husband were living on two tatami straw mats. Each mat is six by three feet. Over these they had a corrugated iron lean-to. They cooked in there on a charcoal brazier, a hibachi, and they slept there. This was their property where they had had their restaurant, which had also been destroyed."[13]

In their search the elders found a few other Japanese Saints, and along with new investigators and new converts they began to build not only a new church but also new lives from the rubble of war.

As the missionaries went to work proselytizing among the Japanese, they found them much more willing to listen to the message of the restored gospel than had been true before the war. The elders had several advantages that the missionaries before 1924 had not enjoyed. Among these were translated materials to share with prospective converts. The most important item was of course the Japanese version of the Book of Mormon. A collection of hymns and a few tracts were also available. But more important than the literature were the people, both those members who remained faithful from the early mission and the U.S. military people who not only lived the gospel and taught it to their Japanese friends but also contributed time, money, and leadership to the newly established mission.

Even before the mission was officially opened in March 1948, some Japanese had been baptized into the Church. The first Japanese to join were Sato Tatsui and his wife, Chiyo, who were taught the gospel by Ray Hanks and C. Elliott Richards. Mel Arnold and Boyd K. Packer also became friends and gospel teachers. On July 7, 1946, the Satos were baptized in a swimming pool at Kansaigakuin University. Elliott Richards baptized Brother Sato, and Boyd K. Packer baptized Chiyo.[14] Brother Sato, who remained faithful to the Church until his death in Salt Lake City in 1996, organized a Sunday School in Nagoya in 1946 and conducted it almost single-handedly until missionaries were sent there in October 1948. He later became the official translator for the Church in Japan and eventually retranslated the Book of Mormon as well as produced new translations of the Doctrine and Covenants, the Pearl of Great Price, and a number of other Church books and publications.[15]

As had been true during the early mission, many Japanese were eager to learn the English language. President Clissold noted that he had almost daily requests for the elders and sisters to teach spoken English at schools from elementary to college level, as well as at clubs and businesses. The missionaries took advantage of many of these opportunities to teach, provided that the learners were willing to be taught from LDS materials. English classes were the foundation of the first Mutual Improvement Associations in Japan after the war.

The day after President Clissold arrived in Japan, he was taken to a Japanese Sunday School that was directed by his friend Nara Fujiya and conducted by Tsukayama Kiyoshi. Forty-three people were in attendance. Certainly the circumstances of the reestablishment were better than those that had prevailed during the early mission. Brother Nara's little group became the nucleus of the Ogikubo Branch, which was organized later that year. By the end of 1948, President Clissold had organized a branch and four Sunday Schools. And these organizations were separate from the servicemen's groups. At that time, President Clissold reported that nine hundred people were attending LDS services every week. Twenty-two converts' names were entered on the Church records in 1948.[16]

When President Clissold submitted his year-end report to the Presiding Bishopric, he expressed confidence that the missionaries would bring many converts into the Church during the coming year. "The great needs of the mission at this time," wrote Clissold, "are literature in Japanese and more missionaries." The missionaries were working on the literature problem, but the shortage of missionaries Clissold perceived could be alleviated only at Church headquarters. President Clissold repeatedly asked the First Presidency to supply ten missionaries each month, five Caucasians and five Japanese-speaking nisei. His plan was to put Japanese speakers together with the language learners. This would eliminate the need for lost time in language study. Eventually the Caucasian elders and sisters would be able to function well, but in the meantime the nisei could carry the load. Considering the worldwide missionary demands of the Church, it was difficult for the Church leaders to meet his requests. It is regrettable that more missionaries could not have been sent. Taking into account the dislocation, the upheaval, the changes in the family system, and the newfound freedom of religion in

Occupation Japan, 1948 through 1951 could have been the best possible years for the Church to expand rapidly in that land.

Although President Clissold was not satisfied with the number of missionaries assigned to Japan, he used those whom he had to expand the proselytizing area to Sapporo in the north and to Osaka-Kobe in west-central Honshu. By the time he was released to return home on August 31, 1949, elders and sisters were teaching the restored gospel in at least ten major cities, including Tokyo, the largest city in the world.

On June 11, 1949, Elder Matthew Cowley of the Quorum of the Twelve and his wife, Elva, arrived in Tokyo for a tour of the mission. He was at that time president of the Asian and Pacific missions of the Church. During his stay in Japan, he visited most of the branches and traveled as far west as Hiroshima. While in Japan, Elder Cowley prophetically promised "many Church buildings and even [LDS] temples in this land."[17]

President Clissold's term as mission president was short by normal standards, but considering his previous service to the Church in Hawaii and his years away from home while in the military, his arrangements with the First Presidency to remain in Japan for only eighteen months were understandable. By the time he departed for home, he had accomplished all of the tasks assigned him by the First Presidency. Vinal G. Mauss, who followed Clissold as mission president, gave him high praise when he said, "I don't see how any one man could accomplish what he did, in the time he was there, in getting the facilities and the organization that were necessary."[18]

THE PRESIDENCY OF VINAL G. MAUSS

When President Mauss arrived in Japan on August 20, 1949, he began a mission that lasted for more than four years. Mauss, a businessman and mortician from Oakland, California, had served as a missionary to Japan during the last year or two of the early mission. During the years of his presidency, he moved the work along well, especially considering the international developments that occurred while he was in Japan.

Between 1949 and 1953, Japanese membership grew from 211 to more than 800, the number of districts expanded from one to five, and the number of Japanese branches grew from twelve Sunday Schools and one or two branches to twenty-five branches. The number of missionaries also expanded to a high of eighty-four during this time.

President Mauss's greatest contributions, however, were not in numerical growth but in the areas of missionary training and expanded proselytizing, Church organization, acquisition of property, and work with LDS servicemen's groups. If President Clissold laid the foundation for the Japanese Mission, President Mauss can be credited with the erection of the walls. By the end of 1949, the missionary force was up to forty-four. During 1950 President Mauss was busy integrating still another thirty-six elders and sisters. With the added numbers of workers, he asked all branch leaders to expand the Sunday Schools and to begin holding sacrament meetings. It was at that time that many of the Sunday Schools in fact became branches. By the end of 1950 there were fifteen branches in the mission. Almost all of these units were presided over by missionaries.

THE IMPACT OF THE KOREAN WAR

Midway in that year, however, war broke out in Korea, and before the end of the year its effects were being felt by the Japanese Mission. The military draft greatly diminished the supply of new LDS missionaries. But because the missionary terms in Japan were for three years rather than two and one-half or two years, the number of missionaries did not drop as quickly or as low as in other missions before the cease-fire in 1953. But the mission was affected, and President Mauss took action to keep his missionary force from dropping too far. In 1950 Mauss's missionaries baptized 184 people into the Church, ten more than the total number of converts who had joined during the entire twenty-three-year history of the early mission. He was elated and wanted to see the work expand.

Another effect of the Korean War was the assignment by the U.S. military of thousands of servicemen not only to Korea but also to Japan (which was a major staging area), Guam, Okinawa, and the Philippines. Among these military people were hundreds of Latter-day Saints. On June 23, 1951, the First Presidency asked President Mauss to include in the Japanese Mission Guam, the Philippines, and Okinawa, as well as all other parts of East Asia where LDS service personnel were stationed. They also asked him to visit the major areas and supervise the LDS servicemen's groups and districts. By 1953 there were seven groups and two servicemen's districts in Japan. There were even larger numbers in Korea, as well as other groups elsewhere in East Asia and the Philippines. President Mauss supervised all of these units.

In 1953 President Mauss's son, Armand, who was serving as president of one of the servicemen's districts in Japan, compiled a manual of operations for servicemen's organizations. This manual, published and distributed widely among LDS military personnel, served to unify record keeping and to help leaders understand not only how to keep records but also why priesthood ordinances such as baptisms, blessings, and ordinations should be cleared with the proper authority and recorded.[19] The servicemen's organization was completely separate from the Japanese Mission organization.[20]

The service personnel supported the development of the Church in many ways, not the least of which was by way of example. When it became evident to President Mauss that the supply of American missionaries was going to be diminished, he decided to call local Japanese members on full-time missions. By the end of 1952, eleven young Japanese men and women were serving two-year missions, and by mid-1953 the number was up to twenty. Almost all of them were supported by money contributed by LDS servicemen. Years later President Mauss asserted that his most important contribution to the Church in Japan was the calling of local missionaries. With only one or two exceptions, all of the local missionaries became strong leaders in the Church.[21]

DEVELOPING JAPANESE LEADERSHIP

In September 1951, before he was able to initiate missionary calls for local Saints, President Mauss found it necessary to combine the four Tokyo branches into two. Only two foreign elders were used to supervise the two new branch presidencies. The Tokyo First Branch was presided over by Takagi Tomigoro and his counselors, Shiraishi Genkichi and Imai Kazuo. The president of the Tokyo Second Branch was Nara Fujiya, and his counselors were Sato Tatsui, who had moved to Tokyo from Nagoya to work for the mission as a full-time translator, and Nakahigashi Mikio.[22] Most of these early leaders have remained active in the Church to the present or until their deaths. Although it was the exception to have only local men in the branch presidencies, it was an indication that some Japanese were ready for leadership positions by this time.

The activity of the Japanese Saints was impressive. Many of the young members of the Church had influenced their parents to stop drinking tea as a measure to improve their health. Members were eager and willing to pay tithes and offerings. At the end of 1952 there was an average attendance of more than 50 percent at sacrament meetings and 75 percent activity among priesthood holders. There was little unemployment or need for welfare help. Japan was definitely well on the way to economic recovery by 1951, and this fact was reflected in the well-being of the members and investigators.[23]

EFFECTS OF JAPAN'S GROWING ECONOMY AND JAPANESE CULTURAL TRAITS

On the other hand, there were some negative effects of Japan's new economic prosperity. One of these was a growing apathy toward religion. Mauss noted, "There has developed that spirit of indifference which always seems to come when there is an abundance of material things."[24] This change was observed not only by the Latter-day Saints but also by other Christian groups. That the mission was actually having less success in converting new members is reflected in the steady decline in baptisms from 214 in 1951 to 55 in 1955.[25] Only in 1956 did the mission begin to have greater success, but some of that success was really achieved in Korea, which was a district of the mission.

Economic prosperity was not the only cause of the decline in convert baptisms. The missionaries gradually learned that they did not understand Japanese thinking or Japanese customs. There was a tremendous gap in communication between the Japanese people and the American missionaries, a gap much larger than simply that of language. For example, the Japanese people have a religious tradition of inclusion rather than exclusion. They hold that all religious truth is relative. Whereas Christians in general and Mormons in particular believe that God has provided only one way to salvation, the Japanese are willing to assimilate various religious beliefs and patterns. In accepting one religion, most Japanese see no reason to give up others.

Another example is the Japanese desire to avoid direct confrontation or uncomfortable situations. It is of higher social value in Japan to avoid an embarrassing situation than to make a commitment that one does not intend to keep. When LDS missionaries pressed Japanese for certain answers or commitments, or when they asked prospective converts how they felt about the teachings of the Church, Japanese often pretended to agree, simply to avoid confrontation. Some Japanese even joined the Church as a way of paying back the missionaries for English-language lessons.

Similar to this is the matter of *giri/ninjo*, duty versus human feelings, which is frequently portrayed in sharp contrast in Japanese literature. In Japan, *giri* (duty) almost always takes precedence over *ninjo*, one's true feelings, beliefs, or ideas. Thus social conventions rule individual lives. Failure to conform brings shame to the individual and one's family. This has been a problem for the Church when investigators have cooperated with missionaries because good manners demanded such behavior. On the other hand, when Japanese have truly developed testimonies of the gospel, it has helped to cement loyalties to the Church. A third result of giri has been the tendency of some Japanese to favor traditional beliefs and behavior even when their mind, spirit, and feelings have inclined them toward the restored gospel. Remaining a loyal part of the Japanese national family, one's own family, one's place of employment, one's club or interest group has been a strong deterrent to conversion to the Church.

Still another problem was the Japanese custom of *ōn*, or obligation. Americans usually feel that they should return favors that are given as acts of kindness, but generally the repayments are casual and sometimes even forgotten. In Japan, on the other hand, the people believe in a rigid system of reciprocal obligations. Favors and kindnesses *must* be repaid. It is a moral obligation. In some cases Japanese investigators have joined the Church because they have "carried" an ōn to the missionaries. In other instances, the missionaries acquired an ōn to people of influence who had done favors to the Church, such as lending space for meetings. These missionaries did not realize that they were bound by duty *(giri)* to repay the favor with something of equal value. Such oversights have resulted in loss of face for the Church.[26] These kinds of problems—customs, economics, obligations, duties, and religious relativity—were becoming evident to the foreign missionaries during President Mauss's period, and they remain significant challenges in the present.

Because prices were rising rapidly, President Mauss decided to raise money to buy property for meeting places as rapidly as possible. Before his release, he succeeded in securing four fine homes to be used as chapels. The mission did not construct any new buildings at that time. President Mauss and the Saints decided to raise money to build a chapel in Tokyo. Although they did not succeed in collecting enough to move ahead with the project, they did carry out some activities that welded the local Saints, the missionaries, and the military people together. Two of the most successful money-raising activities were a fashion show and a program called "Hawaii Calls." The latter was a natural because many of the missionaries were from Hawaii.

TWO MORE YEARS OF SERVICE
FOR HILTON A. ROBERTSON

Vinal G. Mauss served long and well. His release to return home came in October 1953. His replacement was Hilton A. Robertson, who had recently been released as president of the Chinese Mission, which had been terminated a few months before in California.[27] Robertson and his wife, Hazel, had also served previously in Japan, where he closed the early mission, and in Hawaii, where he organized and presided over the Japanese-Central Pacific Mission from 1937 to 1940. He was a dedicated worker, steady and faithful. His missionaries admired his good qualities, and the members respected his years of experience and his insight into their needs.

When President McKay set Hilton A. Robertson apart as mission president, he gave him unusually broad authority. He was to preside over not only the Japanese Mission but also the Chinese Mission. "Yours is now a distinct responsibility, a mighty one, in holding the Presidency of the Missions in the Orient, in Asia," said President McKay. He told him to "organize these missions" and to "expand in excellency, in permanency." He specifically told President Robertson to take care of the little group of Chinese Saints in Hong Kong.[28]

When President Robertson arrived in Japan, he found the demands of the mission and the servicemen's organization to be very time-consuming. In fact, he hardly had time to think about China or other areas such as Korea, Okinawa, the Philippines, and Guam. But Church leaders in Salt Lake City, particularly President McKay, had a larger vision of the world and the missionary responsibility of the Church. In the summer of 1954 President McKay sent Elder Harold B. Lee of the Council of the Twelve Apostles to Japan and Asia to survey the progress of the mission and to study the possibilities for growth. Elder and Sister Lee arrived in Japan on August 20. During their stay they visited all five mission districts and the servicemen's districts. Elder Lee and President Robertson went to Korea, where they visited with many servicemen and held several conferences. The five LDS chaplains in Korea all strongly encouraged Elder Lee to send missionaries into Korea. Although Elder Lee was favorably impressed by their positive attitude, President Robertson was concerned about possible problems of health, housing, and food.[29] After the visit to Korea, Elder Lee and President Robertson and their wives traveled to Okinawa, Hong Kong, the Philippines, and Guam. When Elder Lee reported his trip to Asia at general conference a week after he returned to Salt Lake City, he told the Church: "The signs of divinity are in the Far East. The work of the Almighty is increasing with a tremendous surge."[30] During his travels in East Asia, Elder Lee met with 1,563 LDS servicemen and servicewomen.

Elder Lee was obviously impressed with the missionary possibilities he saw. Only a year later, undoubtedly as a result of Elder Lee's recommendations,[31] President Joseph Fielding Smith, then President of the Council of the Twelve, visited Asia, made some significant changes in mission organization, and dedicated several new lands for the preaching of the restored gospel. President and Sister Smith arrived in Tokyo on July 25, 1955. Two days later President Smith met with the missionaries and service people at Karuizawa. He there proposed that the mission, which had sometimes been called the Far East Mission but was generally known as the Japanese Mission, should be divided into two missions. Japan, Korea, and Okinawa were renamed the Northern Far East Mission. Hong Kong, Taiwan, the Philippines, and Guam were named the Southern Far East Mission. President Smith sustained

Missionaries of the newly renamed Northern Far East Mission in Japan are gathered around President Joseph Fielding Smith (dark suit, center second row) and his wife, Jessie. Surrounding President and Sister Smith are (left to right) H. Grant Heaton and his wife, Luana (holding baby), on their way to Hong Kong to open the Southern Far East Mission; and Hazel and Hilton A. Robertson, who presided over the Northern Far East Mission. (Courtesy LDS Church Archives)

H. Grant Heaton, who accompanied him, as president of the southern mission.[32]

This division in the mission was highly significant. It was an indication from the leaders of the Church that even though the missionaries had been unsuccessful in establishing a permanent mission in Hong Kong in 1949, they were ready to move forward again. That President Smith, the President of the Council of the Twelve, was selected to make this move and to dedicate the lands of South Korea, Okinawa, the Philippines, and Guam was no accident. His coming made it clear that the First Presidency and the Twelve considered the actions he carried out to be highly important. At that time the LDS servicemen outnumbered the Asian members (1,600 servicemen in thirty-four groups compared to 1,050 Asian members in twenty-five branches), but the prospects among the Asian people were recognized as excellent.

President Robertson's missionaries, however, did not convert many Japanese. The principal reason was the tremendous turnover in missionaries. Most of the local Japanese missionaries completed their terms during 1954 and early 1955, and President Robertson did not see the need to replace them with more local missionaries. Had he done so, he could have largely eliminated the other part of the problem, that of having too many missionaries who did not speak Japanese well enough to be effective. President Andrus, who followed Robertson, almost immediately reinstituted the pattern of calling local missionaries, but that change was not made until early 1956.

President Robertson's leadership was important in three other areas. He supported and helped Sato Tatsui with his retranslation of the Book of Mormon—a project that Sato began while President Clissold was still in Japan—and with his translations of the Doctrine and Covenants and the Pearl of Great Price, which he worked on concurrently with the Book of Mormon. While President Joseph Fielding Smith was in Japan, he spent considerable time with Brother Sato, explaining difficult passages and helping with interpretation of meaning. Brother Sato had worked carefully on this large assignment. Since Presidents Robertson, Mauss, and Clissold all encouraged him to take whatever time was needed to do the job right, the books were not published until President Andrus presided over the mission.

Another contribution was in the acquisition of property. President Robertson purchased for the Church at least three homes that doubled as chapels and living quarters for missionaries. He noted that wherever the Church had buildings the work was "greatly facilitated."[33]

Finally, President Robertson did much to strengthen the auxiliaries: the MIA, which had held meetings throughout the mission since the early months; Sunday Schools, which had been started early, even before sacrament meetings in most instances; and Relief Societies, which had been organized during Mauss's time. Primaries had their beginning under Robertson's direction in 1954.

President Robertson's health began to fail during 1955. He mentioned his health problems, particularly trouble with his vision, to President Smith. He undoubtedly also mentioned his long years of service in the mission field. In late October, only a day or two after Robertson had it confirmed that he had cataracts in both eyes, he and his wife received their letter of release.[34] It was soon announced in Salt Lake City that Paul C. Andrus and his wife, Frances, of Honolulu, both of whom had formerly served as missionaries under Presidents Clissold and Mauss, had been called to lead the Northern Far East Mission. The Andruses arrived in Japan on December 9, eleven days after the Robertsons sailed for home.

THE LENGTHY PRESIDENCY
OF PAUL ANDRUS

"Japan is in a period of great transition, economically and politically," wrote President Robertson in his 1954 report, "and the Japanese mind and attitude toward life is quite unstable, as you may realize, since the war. We hope this condition will right itself more rapidly, that we might be able to impress the people more with the importance and need of the restored gospel."[35] President Robertson probably misinterpreted his opportunities. Research in the sociology of religion points to the link between instability and the growth of proselytizing religions. Thirty-one-year-old President Andrus, on the other hand, could see nothing but significant progress during the five years since his release from his first mission and magnificent opportunities for proselytizing in the future. He wrote:

> The growth and the progress of the Church in Japan seems striking indeed as I return after an absence of five years and compare our position now with our position at that time. Although the number of branches is approximately the same, they are organized and functioning much more completely; there are more good leaders serving in the branches; the Church owns more property, and meeting places in general have improved; our members generally have grown stronger in faith and in works as their experience has increased and their testimonies have congealed. The Japanese economy has made very good progress in the last five years, and the goods and services available to the missionaries have grown in number and improved in quality accordingly. The present position of the Church in Japan seems all the more marvelous when I recall that not quite eight years have elapsed since Pres. Edward L. Clissold, and subsequently the missionaries, arrived back in Japan to reopen the work.[36]

President Andrus's positive attitude sustained him during the six-plus years he presided over the mission. His term was a period of rapid growth on many fronts. The mission-member population grew from just over one thousand to more than sixty-six hundred. During these years (1955 to 1962), the Church in Korea grew so rapidly that it was made a separate mission in 1962 (there were only sixty-five members there in 1955). The missionary force also doubled during this time, growing from 82 to 179 foreign missionaries. It was during President Andrus's time that Elder Gordon B. Hinckley began his years as supervisor of the Asian missions of the Church.

DEVELOPING A UNIFORM PLAN
FOR TEACHING THE GOSPEL

Shortly after President Andrus arrived, he learned that there was no uniform teaching plan and that each pair of elders or sisters used whatever methods suited them best. During the Clissold era, the missionaries had concluded that because the Japanese people were not Christian it would be necessary to teach them first about Christianity and then about the restored gospel. Later, during Mauss's time, the mission used the Anderson-Bankhead Plan for a while. This plan was gradually laid aside, and by late 1955 every set of missionaries had created their own system. Another problem made this nonsystem still less effective. During the first year or two of the mission, a number of converts, perhaps more than 50 percent, dropped into inactivity. According to President Andrus, some observers criticized the mission for baptizing converts too soon. As a result, during the Mauss and Robertson years the mission philosophy was that the missionaries should teach investigators until they asked for baptism. The missionaries did not generally push for a decision. As a result, by the end of the Robertson years the missionaries were baptizing only 0.7 converts a year per missionary. Clearly something had to be done to improve the situation.

President Andrus met with his traveling elders (later called supervising elders or assistants to the president) and asked them to create a uniform plan for teaching the gospel. A suitable plan was not accepted by the mission until late in 1956. In the meantime President Andrus placed the missionaries on a strict work schedule and encouraged them to move toward uniformity in their teaching methods. These simple measures more than doubled the number of converts per missionary in 1956.

Toward the end of that year, President Andrus received a copy of Willard Aston's book *Teaching the Gospel with Prayer and Testimony*. One of the basic principles taught in that book was that one teaches the gospel, bears testimony, and then invites the investigator to be baptized. "At the end of 1956," said Andrus, "I called together our leading elders and talked about this. We came up with a six-lesson teaching plan that was geared for the Japanese. We incorporated into it these principles. We announced the introduction of this plan and began using it in 1957."[37]

For the first time, the missionaries realized that their former slow approach had been wrong. Moreover, there was no need to convert the Japanese investigators to Christianity. The important objective was to convert Japanese directly to the restored gospel and "and let them find out about so-called Christianity thereafter."[38] It was this idea that moved the mission forward and brought the great growth of the next five years.

TRANSLATION OF THE STANDARD WORKS OF THE CHURCH

The new missionary approach dovetailed perfectly with the publication of the standard works in Japanese. As was noted earlier, Brother Sato completed his retranslation of the Book of Mormon and his new translations of the Doctrine and Covenants and the Pearl of Great Price during the closing months of 1955. Because President Andrus had done a considerable amount of translating during his first mission and was unusually well prepared to work with the Japanese language, he obtained permission from the First Presidency to organize a translation review committee in Japan. This committee was given final authority to approve the translation of the standard works. It consisted of President Andrus, Sato Tatsui, Takagi Tomigoro, Elder Ben Oniki, and Elder Don Lundberg. For a number of months they met every day for three or four hours until they completed the review and revision of the manuscripts. Sanseido Printing

Company, a large dictionary firm, printed ten thousand copies of the Book of Mormon, which were delivered to the mission home a day or two before Christmas 1956. The Doctrine and Covenants and Pearl of Great Price came off the press about a year later.

The timing of the publication of the Book of Mormon and the creation of the new proselytizing plan were just right to move the mission forward on its new course. The missionaries were able to go into the homes of investigators and tell them the story of Joseph Smith, give or sell them a copy of the Book of Mormon, and invite them to be baptized. The missionaries implemented the new plan, and before long they were baptizing people whom they had known for months or even years but whom they had failed to invite to join the Church. Convert baptisms jumped from 129 in 1956 to 616 in 1957. The average number of baptisms per missionary climbed to 5.8.[39]

PLANNING FOR FUTURE GROWTH

When Elder Delbert L. Stapley of the Quorum of the Twelve set President Andrus apart in Hawaii, he gave him a charge from the Brethren to prepare the Saints in Japan for the organization of a stake and to open missionary work in Korea and Okinawa. A similar charge had been given to H. Grant Heaton earlier that year to expand the Church into the Philippines, Taiwan, and Guam. Expansion was definitely on the minds of the First Presidency and Council of the Twelve. When President Andrus arrived in Japan, he surveyed the branches and decided that creation of a stake would be a long way off unless he reorganized some of the branches and opened new ones.

In 1955 there were two branches in Tokyo (a city of nine million people), one in Yokohama, one in Osaka, and so on. The previous mission presidents had operated on two premises. At first they sent missionaries to the cities where there were members of the Church to work with and build upon. Later, President Mauss moved the missionaries into a number of small cities because he believed that people in the rural areas deserved to hear the gospel and were more willing to listen to that message. But although the people of smaller towns proved to be friendly and kind, they were as set in their ways as the urban Japanese and did not accept the gospel readily. In fact, the Japanese of smaller communities were more tightly woven together than those of the big cities and were thus more difficult to shake loose from their established social ties. Therefore, President Andrus concentrated on the large metropolitan areas. Tokyo was not only large enough for many branches but also, as was shown during 1978 when the mission was divided, large enough for two or more missions.

Whenever he felt it wise to do so, Andrus closed small, out-of-the-way branches. Then, as soon as possible, he built the number of branches to five each in Tokyo, Osaka-Kobe, and Seoul, Korea. These branches later became the nucleus for stakes in all three cities.

As the Church grew, President Andrus was able to make two other important changes that helped prepare Japan and Korea for stakes. For reasons that were more Japanese in origin than American, very few Japanese men were ordained to the priesthood during the pre-Andrus years. In fact, by the end of 1955 there were only forty-one Japanese Melchizedek Priesthood holders. According to Armand J. Mauss, many Japanese Church leaders did not understand the value of having many men hold the priesthood and share the leadership of the branches. Hence, they did not propose that new converts should receive advancements in the priesthood. This hesitation was partly a result of their deep respect for the priesthood. The idea seems to have been that a new convert should prove himself for three to five years before he received the priesthood. Thus it was impossible for mission leaders to turn many positions over to the local members. This may have been one reason why most branches and districts were led by missionaries.

As more members came into the Church, Andrus set up a two-year program for advancement in the priesthood that, over the years of his mission, brought the number of Japanese and Korean Melchizedek priesthood holders to more than 350. This enlarged number made it possible for mission leaders to place local men in almost all (75 to 80 percent) branch and district positions. This move, of course, released many elders from administrative duties and allowed them to proselytize full-time.[40]

Because Elder Stapley had asked President Andrus to expand missionary work into Korea and Okinawa, Andrus went to those places soon after he arrived in Japan. In both areas he found the people to be ready for the gospel, particularly in Korea, but found physical circumstances difficult in both places. Nevertheless, through the help and consideration of Kim Ho Jik (whose story, along with that of the opening of Korea, is told in chapter 8), a few other members, and the LDS servicemen in Korea, and with the assistance of Sister Nakamura Nobu and some LDS servicemen in Naha, Okinawa, President Andrus made arrangements to send the elders to those areas.

OPENING MISSIONARY WORK IN OKINAWA

The Lord provided help to the mission in a most unusual way. In 1955 a former missionary to Japan named Elder Ralph Bird, who was now in the service, was assigned to Guam. But for some unknown reason, he one day received orders to go to Okinawa. When he arrived there, his military superiors did not expect him, nor did they have a job for him. They gave him some time off until they figured out the situation. President Andrus told the remainder of the story this way:

> So, speaking Japanese, he was interested in the Okinawans. He walked out into the countryside, and as he was walking along the road, he came to a home and decided . . . he would go in and speak with the people to see if he could take a picture of their home. So he slid open the door and said, "Gomen kudasai." [Excuse me or pardon me.] He didn't realize that at this very moment

Sister Nakamura was in her home on her knees praying that the Lord would lead her to the true church. And here Elder Bird came, opened the door, and said, "Gomen kudasai."

She came out and was very impressed that here was an American who could speak Japanese. So she asked, "How is it that you speak Japanese so well?" He said, "Well, I was a missionary for the Mormon Church in Japan." She said, "Wouldn't you come in and tell me about your church?" This is how they came together. He taught her and she was converted and baptized.[41]

Sister Nakamura Nobu, her teenaged daughter Ayako, and a woman named Tamanaha Kuniko were baptized into the Church in the East China Sea on Christmas Day 1955.

When President Andrus went to Okinawa looking for a place for the missionaries to stay, Sister Nakamura offered her home—a comfortable one by Okinawan standards—and it was there that the elders lived when they first arrived in the country. The first elders, Clarence LeRoy B. Anderson and Sam K. Shimabukuro (the latter served in the Second Quorum of the Seventy from 1992 to 1997), traveled to Okinawa from Japan proper by boat and arrived there on April 17, 1956. They stayed at the home of Sister Nakamura for two or three months. Her home was a former castle. Before long they had established a small branch and built a Quonset hut chapel.

OTHER STRIDES FORWARD

In addition to his efforts to expand the mission, to prepare the Saints for stakes, and to improve proselytizing efforts, President Andrus also helped to make Church materials—even beyond the standard works—available in Japanese and Korean. He organized a staff of translators, typists, and printers and produced most of the priesthood and auxiliary manuals and handbooks. During this time the mission began publication of *Seito No Michi* (Way of the Saints), which developed into a fine monthly magazine that replaced an earlier Church magazine, the *Messenger and the Grapevine*. In addition, the mission translated and published a new book of hymns in Japanese and also a translation of *Recreational Songs*. Although there was need for materials to be translated into Korean, the list of materials needing to be translated into Japanese was much longer.[42]

During the Andrus years, the mission continued to serve the needs of a large servicemen's organization. Of greater long-range importance, the number of branches in Japan and Okinawa between 1955 and 1962 grew from 26 to 37, and the number of branches in Korea expanded to seven. This growth made it obvious to all concerned that chapels were sorely needed. To meet this need, President Andrus purchased twenty-three chapel sites. These properties, which were obtained at great expense and after considerable expenditure of time and effort, became the basis for a large building program during later years.[43]

Without question, the most important property purchase made during this time, and probably the most profitable in the history of the Church, was the acquisition of the Yoyogi Street property in Omote Sando, Tokyo. President Andrus described the background of the purchase in this way:

> As we organized our five branches in Tokyo we wanted a good central location not only for a stake center, but someplace that would be a showplace for the Church in all of the country and represent the Church in all of the Far East. After all, this is Tokyo. It's the largest city in the world.
>
> So for years I looked for a place and finally found one in Tokyo that we thought would fill the bill. . . . We found this property just at the time that Brother Hinckley was coming [to Japan as part of his first tour of Asia]. The interesting part of the story is that this property, which was about 30,000 square feet in size [186 feet along the street and an average depth of 138 feet], was selling for $670,000 [plus $12,000 in real estate commissions]. Of course that was a very expensive price, and we couldn't consider it except for one thing: when President Mauss

was president of the mission way back in 1952, he bought a piece of property that was serving as the Tokyo Branch meetinghouse site. It was an old residence, but it was about 30,000 square feet, and he paid $20,000 worth of yen to acquire it.

In the meantime we found this other property that was better located right on the entrance boulevard to the Meiji Shrine. Every person in Japan knows where it is. If you say Meiji Jingu, Omote Sando, they all know where it is. Just like saying it's on the boulevard that runs past the Washington Monument.[44]

When Elder Hinckley looked at the property, he was impressed with its potential but staggered by the price. But before he had a chance to reject the property, President Andrus told him that the land President Mauss had purchased for $20,000 was now worth $500,000. Upon hearing this, Elder Hinckley immediately saw the possibility of gaining approval for purchase of this land. After prayerfully considering the matter and discussing it by telephone with President Henry D. Moyle of the First Presidency, Elder Hinckley recommended that the Church buy it. President McKay approved,[45] and on June 3 Elder Hinckley and President Andrus completed the transaction.

Over the years, the house on the Omote Sando property served as the Central Branch meeting place. At the same time the land continued to appreciate in value. Various mission presidents and Elder Hinckley considered different possibilities for the site. It was too valuable for a meetinghouse alone. The Church considered building a six-story structure that would house not only a chapel but also apartments, offices, a distribution center, translating facilities, missionary quarters and offices, and so forth.[46] But these ideas were not to be realized. After receiving offers of 5 million dollars, then 13.5 million dollars, the Church finally sold the property in 1973 for $24,150,943.40. The remarkable fact was that the net outlay from the Church was $150,000. The principal and interest from the transaction became available to help with the acquisition of hundreds of other chapel sites throughout Japan or however the leaders of the Church were inspired to expend the funds.[47]

President Clissold laid the foundation, President Mauss constructed the walls, and President Robertson continued the project. But it was President Andrus who built the roof for the Japanese Church and peopled it. It remained for President Dwayne N. Andersen to educate and refine the new occupants.

NOTES

1. Edwin O. Reischauer, *The Japanese* (Cambridge, Mass.: Belknap Press of Harvard University Press, 1978), 213. The most recent history of Japan by a prominent writer is Mikiso Hane, *Eastern Phoenix: Japan since 1945* (Boulder, Colo: Westview Press, 1996). Hane handles the religion-secularism question in almost the same manner. The fascinating fact, however, is that people "may profess affiliation with two or three different religions. In 1990, the total number of people that religious organizations claimed as members came to 217 million, twice the size of the population" (p. 182). It is difficult to have all the facets of Japanese religion reflect a clear light for non-Japanese.

2. There is considerable debate among sociologists of Japanese religion regarding the state of secularism in Japan. Winston Davis, for example, finds Japanese cultural and religious traits different enough from those of the West to question the validity of international surveys that include Japan. Even within Japan he questions whether standard questions regarding religiosity uncover the true religious feelings of the Japanese. "While belief naturally seems to be an appropriate index of religiousness to the westerner (and to the Japanese sociologist trained in western sociology)," writes Davis, "by itself it tells us only part of the story. The reason for this is that religious praxis (shugyō) and feelings (kimochi) and not belief per se form the core of Japanese religion. The best way to understand the real genius of this religion (and its putative decline) is to turn from what Japanese *believe* or *think* about religion to what they *feel* and *do*. This, of course, takes us from statistics to a more humanistic examination of religious behavior" (Winston Davis, *Japanese Religion and Society: Paradigms of Structure and Change* [Albany: State University of New York Press, 1992], p. 236; emphasis added).

Mikiso Hane (see n. 1 above) writes: "People state their religious affiliations if asked, but most people do not have strong commitments to any religious institutions, as do Christians, Jews, and Muslims in other societies" (*Eastern Phoenix*, 182). Hane quotes Hayashi Chikio, who wrote: "It seems safe to say that perceptions of religion differ in Japan and the West. Westerners see religion as something objective that must be acquired through education or study. The Japanese, by contrast, think of religion as an internal state. It need not have the clear-cut contours of Christian or Buddhist doctrine; it can be simply a nebulous emotional predisposition lying undetected until the individual is made aware of it" (Hayashi Chikio, "The National Character in Transition," *Japan Echo* 15 [1988], pp. 8–9).

3. J. Herbert Kane, *A Global View of Christian Missions*, rev. ed. (Grand Rapids, Mich.: Baker Book House, 1975), p. 252.

4. See D. C. Holtom, *Modern Japan and Shinto Nationalism* (Chicago: University of Chicago Press, 1943), p. 97.

5. Richard H. Drummond, *A History of Christianity in Japan* (Grand Rapids, Mich.: William B. Eerdmans Publishing Co., 1971), pp. 272–73.

6. A photocopy of the original advertisement is in my possession.

7. See Yukiko Konno, "Fujiya Nara: Twice a Pioneer," *Ensign* 23 (April 1993): 31, 33.

8. Edward L. Clissold, interview by Kenneth Barnum and J. Christopher Conkling, November 8, 1973. Tape recording in my possession.

9. See Mission Financial and Statistical Records, Japanese Mission, 1948, LDS Church Archives (hereafter cited as MFSR).

10. See Paul C. Andrus Oral History, interview by author, Honolulu, Hawaii, 1974, Oral History Program, LDS Church Archives, typescript, p. 5.

11. Paul V. Hyer, "Preparations for a Mission in Postwar Japan: Paul Hyer's 'Mini-Mission Training Center,'" unpublished paper in possession of the author.

12. Ibid, 3; and MFSR, Japanese Mission, 1948.

13. Andrus Oral History, pp. 7–8.

14. See Lucile C. Tate, *Boyd K. Packer: A Watchman on the Tower* (Salt Lake City: Bookcraft, 1995), pp. 64–66.

15. See Harrison T. Price, "A Cup of Tea," *Improvement Era* 65 (March 1962): 161, 184, 186; Spencer J. Palmer, *The Church Encounters Asia* (Salt Lake City: Deseret Book Co., 1970), pp. 65–69.

16. See MFSR, Japanese Mission, 1948.

17. Kan Watanabe et al., "Japan: Land of the Rising Sun," *Ensign* 5 (August 1975): 41.

18. Vinal Grant Mauss Oral History, interviews by author, Provo, Utah, 1975, James Moyle Oral History Program, LDS Church Archives, typescript, p. 15.

19. See Armand L. Mauss Oral History, interviews by William G. Hartley, 1974, Oral History Program, LDS Church Archives, typescript, p. 14 (interview 2).

20. See Vinal G. Mauss Oral History, pp. 20–21.

21. See ibid., 27, 28 passim.

22. See MHJM, 30 September 1951.

23. See MFSR, Japanese Mission, 1951, 1952.

24. Ibid., 1951.

25. See ibid., 1951–1955.

26. See Armand J. Mauss Oral History, 29–32.

27. See chapter 10.

28. See Hilton A. Robertson, Diary of Japanese Mission, 1954–1955, p. 3; copy in possession of the author.

29. See ibid., 31 August 1954, p. 100.

30. Harold B. Lee, "Report on the Orient," *Improvement Era* 56 (December 1954): 926.

31. See Don W. Marsh, *The Light of the Sun* (n.p., n.d. [1969?]), p. 52.

32. See Joseph Fielding Smith, "Report From the Far East Missions," *Improvement Era* 58 (December 1955): 917.

33. MFSR, Japanese Mission, 1954.

34. For a fine tribute to the Robertsons, see Muriel Jenkins Heal, "'We Will Go': The Robertson Response," *Ensign* 12 (April 1982): 32–35.

35. MFSR, Japanese Mission, 1954.

36. Ibid., 1955.

37. Andrus Oral History, pp. 24–25.

38. Ibid.

39. The number of convert baptisms for the remaining years of Andrus's presidency was 735 in 1958, 596 in 1959, 896 in 1960, and 1290 in 1961. There were 1,622 baptisms

in 1962, but that number belonged to President Andersen as well as to President Andrus. See MFSR, Japanese Mission, for applicable years.

40. See Andrus Oral History, p. 51.

41. Ibid., p. 19.

42. See ibid., p. 52.

43. See ibid., pp. 50–51.

44. Ibid., p. 30.

45. Gordon B. Hinckley, Journals, 29–30 May 1960, in possession of President Hinckley.

46. See Ezra Taft Benson, "A World Message," *Improvement Era* 73 (June 1970): 97.

47. See Andrus Oral History, p. 32.

6

JAPAN

1 9 6 2 – 1 9 7 8

To the Building of the Tokyo Temple

When President Dwayne N. Andersen and his wife, Peggy, arrived in Japan to assume the reigns of leadership of the rapidly growing mission, he soon recognized that tremendous growth had taken place in the mission since he served there in the early 1950s. His first mission to Japan had been during the Mauss era. He had served as a counselor in the mission presidency and had directed the affairs of the LDS servicemen's organization. Because as a seventy he had accepted a call to serve as a special missionary for two years during the Korean conflict, he did not have enough time then to learn the Japanese language. Nevertheless, he had observed well the Japanese and the workings of the mission, and he had a good grasp of the responsibility held by the mission president.

When President Andersen reviewed the status of the mission with President Andrus, he learned that there were now close to seven thousand Japanese members, seven times the number when he left Japan in 1953. He also learned that although only ten or twelve branches had been added during that time, existing branches were much larger than before and were attempting to carry on the full program of the Church. The number of missionaries had grown, too, from 66 in 1953 to more than 180 in 1962.

The magnitude of the growth and progress of the mission impressed President Andersen, but the very growth had created new challenges that needed considerable attention. By the end of President Andrus's period, there were sufficient members of the Church in Japan for leaders in Salt Lake City as well as in Japan to begin seriously contemplating the creation of a stake or stakes. But much would have to be done on many fronts before a stake could be organized. New modern chapels were sorely needed; more and better-trained priesthood leaders were required; and a group of solid families, of whom the husband and wife had been to the temple, would be desirable before a stake could be organized. It fell on President Andersen to move the Church forward in these areas and a number of others.

President Andersen arrived in Japan at a time of transition. The Korean area was divided off and made a separate mission at that time. And during the preceding months, the Church Missionary Committee had introduced the first uniform proselytizing plan that was used worldwide. Though this new plan was in use, some missionaries, recognizing they would soon be released, preferred not to expend the energy needed to learn the new discussions. This recalcitrance, along with some other problems, created some difficulty for President Andersen during the early months of his mission. Nevertheless, he worked to create a new spirit of enthusiasm (he fostered a program called PMA, or Positive Mental Attitude) and a heightened level of spirituality (he did this by example, by teaching, and by selecting senior elders and having them help new missionaries make the best possible adjustment to the pattern of missionary life). When President Andersen discussed success with his missionaries, he emphasized conversions rather than baptisms. "I felt that we shouldn't expand," said Andersen, "but should try to consolidate and build a strong foundation, and if they wanted more missionaries in Japan they should divide the mission and get more help, because one man just couldn't do it all." His greatest contribution was in consolidation, but he also stimulated considerable expansion.[1]

BUILDING CONSTRUCTION

Elder Gordon B. Hinckley made his first visit to Asia and Japan in 1960. A year later he was officially appointed supervisor of the Asian missions. During his second visit to Japan, in May 1961, he noted the serious need for chapels. "This is most urgently true in Japan. I think we must go forward with one good building in Tokyo."[2] But he did not hold to that number. By the next spring, Elder Hinckley had arranged for Wendell B. Mendelhall, chairman of the Church Building Committee, to go to Japan and make arrangements to start a substantial building program.[3] The First Presidency and Council of the Twelve approved construction of five buildings under the building (or labor) missionary program.

When President Andersen arrived in Tokyo, he found Melvin Hales and Sam Kalama, who had arrived three days earlier, waiting to start on two chapels there. In August, President Andersen began calling labor missionaries, and the program was soon under way.

President Andersen found it difficult to find young Japanese members who would work as labor missionaries. One reason was the Japanese tradition that held that those who labor with their hands are of the lower classes. He noted that most of the Church members were white-collar workers, college or high school students, or business people. Because the members were not accustomed to working with their hands, they shied away from calls to service in the building program. This attitude was changed somewhat when Japanese members looked on as American servicemen and women gave freely of their time and energy to build chapels. It was not unusual to see colonels, captains, and other officers working side by side with young enlisted men.

The servicemen played another vital role in the construction program. Since the time of President Mauss, they had regularly contributed to the mission building fund. By the early 1960s they had donated thousands of dollars. These funds formed the financial foundation of the building program.

The building missionary program proved to be a success during the Andersen years and continued into the late 1970s. Many of the building missionaries in Japan have developed into fine leaders in the Church, including Elder Yoshihiko Kikuchi of the First Quorum of the Seventy.

While President Andersen was in Japan, nine chapels were started. Two of these, the Tokyo North and Tokyo West Branch buildings, were completed and dedicated, and the Naha (Okinawa) Branch and the Gunma Branch were completed. Two other buildings, the Tokyo East Branch and the Fukuoka Branch, were completely remodeled. Four other buildings were under construction—the Abeno, Tokyo South, Yokohama, and Sapporo Branches. President Andersen also purchased seven building sites.[4]

The new buildings did much to establish the Church as a permanent part of Japan. The Saints took new pride in their membership, for they now had physical proof of the Church's stability and respectability, which is important in Japanese culture. Moreover, the Japanese Saints were able to follow more completely the worship patterns of the Church in the new buildings.

ENLARGEMENT OF THE PRIESTHOOD
AND LEADERSHIP DEVELOPMENT

Japanese society is a closed society. No foreigners hold national political positions, and few foreigners hold positions of authority in other areas. Thus it would be incorrect to assume that the Japanese Saints would feel comfortable in their church for long if foreigners held the most important leadership positions. President Andersen quickly recognized this fact as well as the importance of building local leadership as soon as possible. With the large membership base created before his time, he was able to choose from among the best prospects and train them for later roles as stake and mission leaders. Only by developing a strong local priesthood corps and women of equal ability to lead the auxiliaries could the Church find a permanent place in Japanese society.

President Andersen chose Watanabe Kan and Yamada Goro as counselors. President Watanabe lived in Osaka, and President Yamada lived in the Tokyo area. Whenever he traveled west and south, Andersen took Watanabe along. Watanabe served as translator for President Andersen, but Andersen included him in almost everything he did. Andersen constantly explained Church policies, procedures, and organizations. But when he held conferences in Tokyo or places north, he always took Yamada along for the same reasons. It is important to note that both men have since served as mission presidents and in many other important capacities. Watanabe served as a Regional Representative over part of Japan.

At the other extreme, President Andersen saw the need to involve new male converts in meaningful Church activity soon after they were baptized. The missionaries developed several lessons for new converts that introduced the programs of the Church and explained the importance of the priesthood and its availability to worthy males. Within a month of a new male convert's baptism, his branch president was supposed to interview him and ordain him to the Aaronic Priesthood. During Andersen's three years, there was steady improvement. Six hundred and seventy males were baptized during 1964 and the first six months of 1965, and 67 percent of these people were ordained to the priesthood. This was a significant increase compared with earlier years. Between 1962 and 1965, the number of Melchizedek Priesthood holders rose from 355 to 584.[5]

But having sufficient numbers of priesthood bearers was not enough. They and their female counterparts needed training in the policies, procedures, and order of the Church. President

Andersen instituted many programs in leadership training, particularly at Saturday leadership meetings in conjunction with quarterly district conferences.

According to President Andersen, it was amazing to see the faith that some of the leaders developed. For example, "a district councilman would go to work on Saturday with a suitcase. As soon as he'd get off work he'd get on a train and travel all night to a district assignment, such as a branch conference or something. He would arrive at the branch Sunday morning, hold meetings all day Sunday, and take care of district business and matters, get on the train Sunday evening, travel all Sunday night, arrive back to his place of work Monday morning, work all day Monday and arrive home on Monday night. So he left home Saturday morning and didn't see his family again until Monday night. They were willing to make these kinds of sacrifices."[6]

President Andersen also soon realized that if he would break with his usual pattern of taking his wife, Peggy, and Watanabe Kan to Okinawa by air, he could save enough money to take twenty mission leaders there by boat from Tokyo. The various mission auxiliary leaders and priesthood leaders contributed much more to the conferences than the Andersens and Watanabe could have done alone.[7]

But although the Japanese Saints made considerable progress toward parity with the better-developed parts of the Church, there remained some problems that only time and growth could change. For example, shortly after the mission organized the first elders quorum in the Tokyo area, a decision was made to hold a social. It was announced that each elder was supposed to bring either his wife or a female friend. When the party took place, however, the only women present were Sister Andersen and a girl who was helping with the serving. It was not customary for Japanese married couples to go to social events together. On the contrary, it was traditional for men to go out together and leave their wives at home. Thus custom conflicted with a traditional American Mormon way of socializing. It was also not common for husbands and wives to sit by each other in Church meetings or to make much effort to be in the same vicinity.

Still another problem was home teaching, which was being introduced Churchwide at this time. Church procedure suggested that home teachers visit each family each month in their home. In the Japanese setting this did not work well, for at least two reasons. First, the typical male member was the only person in his family belonging to the Church (this pattern has changed somewhat since that time), and the other family members frequently did not want the home teachers bothering them. Second, home teachers had to travel far. Thus it worked best to have the home teachers visit their families at the chapel.

In spite of some difficulties and cultural adjustments, many Japanese Saints developed strong faith and became fine examples of the Mormon way of life. They kept the Sabbath day holy even though it was generally their only day off work. They followed the other commandments such as the Word of Wisdom. During the Andersen years, tithing, which was largely kept in the mission, rose high enough that the Northern Far East Mission no longer depended on funds from Church headquarters for operating expenses. This pattern has continued to the present. The Japanese Church is totally self-supporting.

THE FIRST TEMPLE EXCURSION TO HAWAII

For believing Saints, few earthly acts have more significance than participation in temple ordinances. The young leaders within Japan were no exception. They wanted to receive their own endowments or special blessings from the Lord and to be sealed to their wives or husbands and children for eternity. This hope notwithstanding, until 1964 no one had figured out a way to take a group of Japanese Saints to the temple.

The stimulus to organize a tour group to travel to Salt Lake City or to Hawaii came from Yamanaka Kenji, an older convert who, in addition to being a tour director, knew many people in influential places. He concluded that at least a small group of branch and district officers, thirty or forty people, could afford to go to Salt Lake City. At about the same time, early 1964, President Andersen learned that Flying Tiger Airlines would be willing to carry a charter of approximately 160 people for $300 each. With this possibility in mind, mission leaders sent word to all branches asking how many people would like to participate in an excursion to Hawaii during the summer of 1965, a year and a half away. One hundred and seventy people said they would make the financial and spiritual preparations for the trip. The mission sponsored a number of money-making projects to raise funds, such as selling pearl tie tacks and even recording a stereo record of Church music and Japanese songs. The musical endeavor is described in the following account.[8]

JAPANESE SAINTS SING
Dwayne N. Andersen

[A] project for fund raising was a stereo record called "Japanese Saints Sing." This was a chorus of about 24 people singing Japanese songs and Church hymns. Brother Yamanaka knew the "top" man in the music field in Japan. This man arranged for a fine orchestra and the best recording studio to make the stereo record. This little group of singers, which included Elder Yoshihiko Kikuchi (now of the Quorum of the Seventy), practiced for weeks to get ready. They were practicing at the Northern Far East Mission Home the night before the record was to be taped. They had not practiced with the orchestra yet and sounded quite poor. I wondered how they could ever make a successful record. The next morning the little chorus went to the recording studio early enough to prac-tice a few minutes with the orchestra. Later in the morn-ing I went to the studio to give them moral support.

Arriving just as they were going to start recording, I

asked the chorister, young Brother Sato, if they had held a prayer. He said that the chorus group had prayed, but not with the orchestra or studio workers. I suggested that they pray again with everyone present, and he asked me to pray. As the recording light came on, everyone quieted down, and over the loudspeaker came the words: "It is time for prayer." I then stepped forward and gave a prayer in English, while the engineers, orchestra, and singers all stood at attention. As "amen" was said, many of the Church members were in tears. Later, one of the chorus women remarked: "My voice was tight and tense all morning, but when you prayed a feeling of calm came over me and I sang without tension." Others felt the same calmness.

After recording one song, they played it back so we could hear it. I could not believe my ears! It was just beautiful and sounded like a large chorus. One member told us that they felt like angels were singing with them! It was the first time that an entire record had been taped in one single day. Since the orchestra could only put in an eight-hour day, they taped the last few selections; and the chorus had to sing their numbers with the taped music. Earlier in trying to record, the orchestra's rhythm was very "swingy" for "Oh, My Father." So the chorus sang it a cappella to first show the orchestra how the rhythm should be. For the other songs, the orchestra leader tried to have his people follow the chorus. The entire day was just one big miracle. We had many people, after hearing the record, ask us if it was the Tabernacle Choir.

After the mission had announced its intention to follow through with the excursion, numerous problems arose, the most serious ones related to the cost of fare. The Civil Aeronautics Board would not allow Flying Tiger Airlines to come into Japan to pick up passengers. The mission leaders turned to Japan Air

Lines. But Japan Air Lines was generally uncooperative until President Andersen pointed out that during 1964 the Church had done more than $70,000 business with them. The Church, in fact, was their largest single client. After that the airlines agreed to charter a jetliner for $273 per person, round trip.

Making charter arrangements was time-consuming, but more important and more time-consuming were the spiritual preparations. The participants studied the significance of temple work, made changes in their lives if necessary, and in every way prepared themselves to be morally and spiritually ready to enter the temple. When the First Presidency learned through Elder Hinckley that the trip was going to become a reality, they asked President Andersen to send a translator to the temple in Hawaii to prepare the entire temple ceremony in Japanese. Sato Tatsui was selected for this assignment. He also played one of the leading roles in the ceremony when it was recorded in Japanese.

When the jetliner was coming in over Pearl Harbor in July 1965, one of the 166 participants looked down and said to himself, "I wonder what kind of reception I will get since my fellow Japanese dropped bombs . . . on Pearl Harbor? How will I be treated?" When the plane landed, the Hawaiian Saints gave the Japanese Saints one of the greatest welcomes ever. They piled leis high on every neck and greeted the newcomers warmly. "I had heard about brotherly love," said the worried brother, "but I never really knew what it was. Now I know what brotherly love is. Now I want to share this brotherly love that I have felt among these people whom we tried to destroy, but in return they have shown kindness and love."[9]

Elder Hinckley joined the group in the temple and sealed some of the couples. Many of the visitors had deeply moving experiences. In the words of Watanabe Kan, "The spirit that was there was just indescribable and it burned so strong that those offering prayers were choked up for lengthy periods of time before continuing in the supplications to the Lord."[10] Of the 164

Japanese who went to Hawaii, 134 were adults who received their own endowments. The rest were their children.

An added benefit from this excursion was the opportunity for the Japanese Saints to participate in meetings of the wards and stakes of Oahu. Arrangements were made to have each Japanese member assigned to a person who was his or her counterpart in the Church. Branch presidents from Japan spent considerable time with bishops in Hawaii and attended all of their meetings. Likewise, district presidents went with stake presidents, district councilors with high councilors, and so on. The leadership training was of immeasurable worth to the Japanese Saints.[11]

The 1965 temple trip was the first of many. The next one came in 1967, and after that the charter groups went to Hawaii almost yearly until the last group flew to Hawaii in July 1979. The Tokyo Temple was completed by the time the next departure would have taken place.

Hardly a week passed after the first temple group returned to Japan before President Andersen and his family departed from Japan for Hawaii, where he would take a position at the Church College (now BYU—Hawaii). His replacement was Adney Yoshio Komatsu and his wife, Judy.

THE KOMATSU YEARS: A PERIOD OF DEVELOPMENT AND MATURITY

When President Andersen left Japan, the formative period of Church history there was essentially over. But the contemporary era of the proliferation of stakes and missions was not quite ready to begin. President Komatsu's mission can best be characterized as a time of final preparation for the growth of the 1970s and 1980s. He saw it that way when he was there. When he had been in the mission for a year he wrote: "The Japanese people need stakes and wards. They need a temple. The full force and impact of the gospel on the lives of the Japanese will not be realized until the Saints here have the opportunity to receive their endowments and to perform other temple ordinances. The main thing which stands in the way of the organization of stakes and wards and the building of a temple in Japan is the lack of real strength in the Church here; not only in number of members, but in priesthood holders and real leaders."[12]

President Komatsu devoted his major efforts to training local leaders and carrying on the programs that President Andersen had started. This is not to say that he did not bring changes and progress to the mission, for he did. It was during his era that Elder Hinckley first recommended that the Northern Far East Mission should be divided. It was also during this time that the Translation and Distribution Services program of the Church was introduced in Japan. And it was during this time that Elder Hinckley and President Komatsu began negotiations for the Mormon Exhibit at Expo '70, the Japan World Exposition. But his desire was to add stability to the Church, not to create new programs.

Adney Y. Komatsu was different from previous mission presidents in several ways. He was the first American of Japanese ancestry, or first nisei, to serve as mission president in Asia. He was also the first product of the Japanese Central Pacific Mission to serve in that capacity. Unlike any of his predecessors, he had not served a full-time mission as a young man. He had, however, served as a counterintelligence officer in the U.S. Occupation Forces in Japan and had some fluency in the language. He was a convert, having found the Church through a basketball program directed by CPM missionaries. When he joined the Church in January 1941, he promised his widowed Buddhist mother, who was strongly opposed to his becoming a member of the Church, that he would be a good son. "I've associated with the missionaries," he said to her, "for a whole year and I know that in this church there is nothing but goodness, cleanliness, and purity. I believe the Joseph Smith story. If you let me join the Mormon Church I promise you that if you ever hear from your lady friends in your church that your number two boy is playing around and not doing anything good, his reputation is bad, and he is bringing embarrassment upon you because of his association with the Mormon Church, all you need to do is ask me to quit the Church and I will stop going."[13] He joined the Church with her blessing and, in his words, "I think she saw me becoming a much better son, rather than the opposite."

Even before he was inducted into the military service in 1945, President Komatsu had served in a number of Church callings, including Honolulu District MIA superintendent and counselor in the Kalihi Branch. Following the war, he married Judy Nobue Fujitani on June 2,

Elder Adney Yoshio Komatsu from Hawaii was the first person of Asian ancestry to become a General Authority of the Church. (Courtesy LDS Church Archives)

1950, and in time they became the parents of four children. During the 1950s and early 1960s, President Komatsu held positions such as Honolulu Stake high councilor, ward clerk, and bishop, in which capacity he was serving when he received his call as mission president. Professionally, he was employed at Honolulu Savings and Loan Company, where he eventually rose to senior vice president and manager of the mortgage division. He held that position when he was called as an Assistant to the Quorum of the Twelve in April 1975. When his call as a General Authority came seven years after his mission, he became the first person of both Japanese and non-Caucasian ancestry to be called to that position.

In addition to supervising the growth of missionary numbers from approximately 200 in 1965 to more than 250 in 1968, completing and dedicating five chapels, starting three others, and guiding the labor missionary program, President Komatsu presided over or participated in other important developments and events, some of which follow.

REGARDING VISITS AND SUPERVISION FROM CHURCH HEADQUARTERS

Until 1967 very few Church leaders—that is, General Authorities and General Board members—had visited Japan and Asia. From 1960 until 1965, when Elder Marion D. Hanks was assigned to help supervise the Asian missions, Elder Hinckley handled that part of the world alone. In 1966 he recommended to the Council of the First Presidency and the Twelve that Japan should be divided into two missions. But this recommendation was not approved at that time. Nevertheless, in November 1966 Elder Hinckley asked President Komatsu to begin looking for suitable quarters for a new mission in Osaka-Kobe. Komatsu eventually found an appropriate building, but the mission was not divided until the time of his release in 1968.

Japan seems to have come into focus on the map at Church headquarters when President Hugh B. Brown, First Counselor in the First Presidency, toured Asia and Japan in April 1967. He was thrilled with the strength and numbers of members. The part of his visit that is most remembered by the Japanese Saints was his address at the dedication of Abeno Branch chapel in Osaka, Friday, April 21. He was deeply moved by the size and quality of the congregation and spoke of his amazement at the quiet but rapid growth of the Church throughout the world. He then made a prophecy that has been remembered by the Japanese Saints and others: "Now I want to tell you people here tonight something that I have not said before. Some of you who are listening to me tonight will live to see the day when there will be a Japanese man in the Council of the Twelve Apostles of the Church. And I do not know when it will be. I will not live to see it. But some of you young people will see it. Then you will realize that God loves the Japanese people. And you will join with other nations in forming a great united Church all over the world. . . . I feel it in my heart tonight and I dare to make this prediction in the name of the Lord."[14]

President Brown did not live to see the fulfillment of his prophecy, but in 1975 and 1977 President Komatsu and then Yoshihiko Kikuchi were called as General Authorities. Both men are (or were) members of the First Quorum of the Seventy. An extraordinary incident occurred in connection with this prophecy. The night President Brown spoke these words, he and Elder Hinckley discussed what had been said. In the solemnity of their conversation, President Brown said to Elder Hinckley, "You are the apostle to these people and will be until one of their own is named an apostle." Elder Hinckley later noted, "This has been a sobering experience."[15]

CREATION OF THE TRANSLATION AND DISTRIBUTION DEPARTMENT

Later in 1967 an important change was made in the operation of the mission. Until that time the mission had sole responsibility for the translation and publication of all Japanese language materials. In October, however, Bishop Victor L. Brown of the Presiding Bishopric and J. Thomas Fyans, then of the Translation and Distribution Department, visited the Northern Far East Mission and implemented the Church's new translation and distribution system. They hired Watanabe Kan, a counselor in the mission presidency, to be director of translation and distribution for all of Asia. This new system professionalized the translation process and also removed the responsibility for it from the mission president. It was more expensive than the previous program, but it was much better. The highly motivated employees of the new department produced more than four thousand pages of translated materials within five months of the opening of the facilities. Included were many priesthood, Relief Society, and auxiliary manuals, and the family home evening manual for that year.[16]

Among visits from leaders in Salt Lake City, the tour of Japan by Elder and Sister Spencer W. Kimball in February 1968 was a highlight. Elder Kimball stopped off in Japan in a nonofficial capacity. He had not been assigned to tour the mission or to hold any meetings; he came because of personal interest, choosing to return from an official visit to Australia and New Zealand by way of Asia. By that time President Komatsu was working hard to duplicate stake organization in the districts of the mission, especially in Tokyo. He had taught the leaders how to hold priesthood executive meetings and other necessary meetings to correlate the programs of the Church. Elder Kimball arrived in Japan at a time when these programs needed encouragement from outside. In Tokyo Elder Kimball met with all district and branch presidencies—in fact, with all of the leadership at a general meeting. He addressed the congregation in a warm and comfortable way, saying, "I'm Elder Kimball. I'm seventy-two years old. I want to introduce myself to you. . . . I have four children." And so forth. Then he had each leader stand and introduce himself. He then noted the ages of the leaders and said, "How many of you have been to the temple?" After counting the hands, he said, "I average the age of leadership here to be in the early thirties. And ninety-five percent of you have been to the temple. This is better than many stakes of Zion that I know of within comparable distance of a temple."

Elder Kimball then leaned over to President Komatsu and said: "President, let's talk stake now, not a year from now. Let's talk stake organization now. In the stake we do these things this way. What are we doing? How can we get closer to the stake program? How can we implement the program most closely with our best abilities?" Then he told President Komatsu that if he followed this procedure, a stake would probably be organized two or three years earlier than was usual.[17] From that time on, President Komatsu and President Bills, who succeeded him, constantly

The first division of Japan as a mission came on 1 September 1968. Here President Edward Okazaki and Sister Chieko Okazaki with President Walter Bills and Sister Elsie Bills symbolically cut the map of Japan in half, forming the two missions. (Courtesy Chieko Okazaki)

emphasized preparation for stakehood. Two years later, the Tokyo Saints were ready for Japan's first stake.

By mid-1968 Japan had nearly twelve thousand Japanese Mormons in fifty-one branches and ten districts. Missionary numbers were well over two hundred, and there was obviously too much for one mission president to handle. The First Presidency and Council of the Twelve decided to divide the mission. Shortly before President Komatsu was to return home, the First Presidency changed the General Authority supervision of the area. Elder Ezra Taft Benson of the Twelve and Elder Bruce R. McConkie of the First Council of the Seventy were assigned to lead the Asian Missions. On June 15, 1968, Elder Benson, in a letter to President Komatsu, asked him to begin preparing for a division of the mission by adding another set of assistants, another mission secretary, and a commissarian, and by moving the missionaries around so that both missions would have people of equal ability.

Walter R. Bills, a former CPM missionary, replaced President Komatsu in mid-July 1968. The next month Edward Y. Okazaki, and his wife, Chieko, both converts of the CPM who now lived in Denver, Colorado, arrived in response to Edward's call to preside over a new mission in Osaka. On September 1, 1968, the Northern Far East Mission was divided to become the Japan Mission, with headquarters in Tokyo, and the Japan-Okinawa Mission, with headquarters in Osaka. With the division of the mission, Japan entered a new era of Church history, the contemporary period of institutional development. Following 1968, the missions in Japan grew so rapidly and the stakes multiplied so quickly that it is not possible here to plot the course and development of all missions and stakes.

EXPO '70, TOKYO STAKE, AND THE JAPAN EAST AND JAPAN WEST MISSIONS

Although the Church announced its participation in Expo '70, the Japan World Exposition, in November 1968, by that time more than a year of planning and negotiations had taken place. On October 16, 1967, Elder Gordon B. Hinckley and President Komatsu went to the offices of the Osaka International World's Fair, where they discussed with officials the possibility of a Mormon exhibit. The officials told Elder Hinckley that they would sell space only on the outer perimeters, but he showed little interest in that idea.

Other meetings followed, with Komatsu and local leaders doing the legwork. Then, in April 1968, Elders Hinckley, Komatsu, Watanabe, Iami, and building supervisor Marvin Harding agreed upon a site, one thousand square meters, that was among the Japanese exhibits. Elder Hinckley was especially concerned that the Church would have a Japanese rather than an

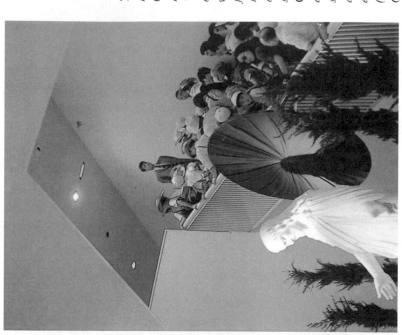

The Mormon Pavilion at the Osaka World's Fair—Expo '70—attracted over 6.6 million visitors during the fair's six-month run. The replica of Thorvaldsen's statue, The Christus, created a hallowed and sacred setting among the secular exhibits of the fair. (Courtesy Chieko Okazaki)

American image.[18] On May 2 the First Presidency and Council of the Twelve approved participation and allotted $300,000 for the project. Before long, final architectural drawings and plans were under way.

Emil B. Fetzer, Church architect, designed the pavilion, a modern Oriental building having two stories. Its main feature was its spire, capped with an eight-foot fiberglass replica of the angel Moroni statue that adorns the Salt Lake Temple and many other temples. The ground floor provided an assembly area, offices, and two displays, one on Japanese family life and the other a twelve-foot marble replica of Thorvaldsen's masterpiece, *The Christus*. On the second floor, visitors were conducted through rooms focusing on the Creation, the plan of salvation, the life of Christ, and the restoration of the gospel. They were then taken into one of two theaters that were showing the movie *Man's Search for Happiness*.[19]

The ground breaking for the pavilion took place in May 1969. Elder Ezra Taft Benson presided while important civic and Expo '70 officials, as well as three hundred members and friends, looked on. He told the assembled crowd that the Mormon pavilion would give the Church the opportunity to explain its history, doctrines, and programs and to make clear that the Mormon Church was a world church with a world message.[20] Nine months later the building, which was constructed largely of materials that could be reused in other LDS buildings, was ready for use. All that remained to be done was to install the displays and movable facilities. Everything was in readiness by March 13, one day before the official opening of the exposition. On that day President Hugh B. Brown offered the dedicatory prayer on the building. Other important Church leaders were also there: Elders Ezra Taft Benson and Gordon B. Hinckley of the Council of the Twelve and Bernard P. Brockbank, Assistant to the Twelve. Brockbank, who had directed previous exhibits in New York and Texas, was assigned to be commissioner for this pavilion. He was assisted by mission presidents Bills and Okazaki.

From a missionary point of view, the setting for the pavilion could not have been better. It was next door to the Japanese national exhibit and close to the Russian and United States exhibits. People thronged to the Mormon Pavilion. During the six months of the exposition 6,658,532 people went through the building and 780,000 left their names and addresses on the registers, expressing a willingness to have missionaries call at their homes. A total of 852,000 more people visited the Mormon exhibit in Japan in six months than visited the Mormon exhibit for the 1964–1965 World's Fair in New York in two years.[21]

The message of the pavilion was different from those of all other exhibits. While national and business pavilions centered their messages on the material and technical progress of mankind, the Church centered on the divinity of Jesus Christ, the reality of a living God, the importance of the Book of Mormon, the plan of salvation, and the role of the family in that eternal scheme. The guides were missionaries, generally American, and Japanese members. The American missionaries surprised many with their fluent Japanese (as well as Korean and Chinese) and impressed them with their cleanliness, courtesy, and obvious love for the Asian people. Concerning these guides, Elder Brockbank wrote: "Our most impressive exhibit was the spirit of the dedicated, loving, inspired missionaries. The missionaries radiated a great love for the Oriental people and the Oriental people had great respect for the missionaries. One Japanese gentleman said to me, 'I can hardly believe that such fine, clean young people would leave their homes, pay their own way, and learn a new language. They must truly love us.'

"All the missionaries serving in the four missions in Japan will have additional opportunities to reach and teach the people as a result of the fair."[22]

Beyond the attractiveness of the missionaries, the Church had gone to extra efforts to provide appropriate literature for the visitors from the major nations of Asia. Copies of the Book of Mormon were available not only in Japanese (fifty thousand copies sold) but also in Korean and Chinese. Tracts and pamphlets also were available, as were several other books. Undoubtedly the most impressive part of the pavilion tour was the showing of *Man's Search for Happiness*, a movie depicting man's journey through life and the meaning of that experience. W. O. Whitaker and the motion picture staff of Brigham Young University Studio traveled to Japan to produce the film in Japanese, with Japanese actors. After Expo '70 closed, the film became an important missionary tool in Japan.[23]

Elder Brockbank and other Church leaders who were connected with the Mormon Pavilion were greatly pleased with it as a missionary effort. The numbers of people who toured it were greater than expected at the outset, but more important were the warm responses from thousands of people who wrote of their appreciation for what the Church was teaching. Moreover, the missionaries all over Japan had thousands of names of friendly people who said they were willing to talk with them. This alone made the entire project worthwhile.

The week from March 13 to 18, 1970, was exhilarating. The Mormon Pavilion was dedicated on the thirteenth; the Tokyo Stake was organized on the fifteenth; the Japan East Mission, with headquarters at Sapporo, Hokkaido, was created on the sixteenth; and the Japan West Mission, with headquarters at Fukuoka, Kyushu, was founded on the eighteenth. From that time onward, most of the leaders in the missions and virtually all stake leaders were Japanese. During the 1970s most of the mission presidents were nisei who had originally joined the Church in Hawaii. Russell N. Horiuchi, who started the East Mission, was from Lahaina, Maui, but was called from a position as professor of geography at Brigham Young University. Many other nisei followed as presidents of the various missions. In 1935 President Heber J. Grant had a vision of a later time when Japanese from Hawaii would take the gospel to their people in Japan. During the 1970s that vision was fulfilled through the nisei mission presidents. But, of course, nisei had been serving in the Japanese missions since 1948.

More important than the contribution of the nisei from

Hawaii and the U.S. mainland was the coming-of-age of the Japanese Saints themselves. The first stake presidency was entirely Japanese. In most stakes throughout the Pacific, the first stake president or at least one of his counselors had been expatriate Americans; not so in Japan. Tanaka Kenji, who had joined the Church in 1952, was selected by Elders Benson, Brown, and Hinckley to be the first president. He chose Yoshihiko Kikuchi to be his first counselor and Sagara Kenichi as second counselor. The bishops of the six wards were all native Japanese. It is noteworthy that President Tanaka later served as president of the Japan Nagoya Mission.

Tanaka Kenji, first president of Tokyo Stake, has served the Church in many capacities, among them mission president and temple ordinance worker. (Photo by author)

At the same time, Watanabe Kan was called to serve as the first president of the Japan West Mission in Fukuoka. He was the first native Japanese to serve as mission president. Since that time the list of local Japanese mission presidents has become extensive. By the early 1970s the Church in Japan had come abreast of the Church in most other developed parts of the world.

Elder Ezra Taft Benson, who in his capacity as supervisor of all Asian missions visited that part of the world five times between 1968 and early 1970, was deeply impressed by the Church's progress throughout Asia. He was so impressed, in fact, that he wrote: "There has never been a time until now when the Church has had the strength and means to reach out effectively to the Asian nations. In the timetable of the Lord, the door is now open, and this is apparently the time for the work in Asia."[24]

THE JAPANESE CHURCH
BETWEEN 1970 AND 1978

In 1970 there were approximately 12,500 members of the Church in Japan. Although most of the stake and ward leaders were mature men and women, Church members in Japan were generally youthful. The feeling that the Church was a youth organization was fading by the mid-1970s, but a high percentage of converts came from the ranks of college-age students (83 percent between ages ten and thirty in 1972). This tendency has troubled many mission presidents. But it will probably never be overcome because of the natural inclination of youth to seek a better life through religious activity. Worldwide, with Japan being no exception, interest in religious values is highest among people between the ages of fourteen and twenty-three. Another reality is that college years present Japanese with their only opportunity to exercise agency regarding religion, politics, and other matters of choice. Earlier in life, parents usually closely control their children. Following college, companies, government offices and other employers, and coworkers usually control a person's options. At least until the 1970s, more women than men joined the Church (57.1 percent female to 42.9 percent male in 1972). This trend has generally been attributed to the elders' attractiveness to young girls. Although there is some truth to this assertion, the important fact is that Japanese women have more interest in religion than men and will probably continue to do so.[25]

Aside from the strong tendency toward youth conversions and female converts, the general membership in the 1970s was quite typical of the Japanese people as a whole. But it is a troublesome fact that the Japanese members were about 10 percent below the national high school and college educational level according to age (in 1972) and that the converts do not come out of the national religious background in equal proportion to the various other religious groups. Whereas 99 percent of the Japanese claim affiliation with either Buddhism, Shinto, new religions, or no religion, and only 1 percent of the population is Christian, more than 12 percent of the LDS membership in 1972 previously had an alignment with some Christian group. The education level is difficult to explain, but the high percentage of converts from a previous Christian background indicates at least two things: first, people who are already familiar with the Christian message have an easier time relating to and understanding Mormonism; and second, by the 1970s—and really the mid-1990s—the missionary message was not geared to the non-Christian Japanese population of Japan.

During the later 1960s the success ratio per missionary in gaining convert baptisms declined from 8.9 baptisms a year in 1962 to 1.9 baptisms per missionary in 1968. There was some improvement in the later 1970s, but the unfortunate truth is that although the number of missions grew significantly, the rate of missionary success did not increase much during the 1970s. In 1978 the 1,311 missionaries in Japan baptized 2,967 people, or 2.25 converts per missionary. In other words, the Church in Japan grew not because the missionaries had found a success formula that worked well or because the Japanese people were somehow naturally attracted to the Church, but because of the sheer numbers of missionaries.[26] It was encouraging, however, that whatever the cause, the Church was growing in Japan at a steady pace until 1978 and success was breeding success. The leaders of the Church were growing older (not just maturing in their callings), and as a result nonmembers who were older were finding it easier to accept the gospel. (In 1970 the average age of Japanese Mormons was 30.5 years. By 1992 the average age was 43.5.)[27] The social group (family, job, club, religious unit) is extremely important in Japan. Until recently it has not been easy for older Japanese to find a comfortable place, a place where they could gain the needed social support, in the LDS Church. But with the growing maturity of the Church in Japan, it was more attractive to all age groups.

GENERAL AUTHORITY SUPERVISION
AND CHURCH ADMINISTRATION

The creation of the Tokyo Stake helped the development of the Church in Japan in a number of ways. One of the most important was the regular visits General Authorities made to attend quarterly and, after the change, semiannual stake conferences. Whereas the number of General Authorities who had visited Japan until 1965 could be numbered on the fingers of one hand, with the interest in Expo '70 and the new stake, General Authority visits became not only frequent but almost commonplace.

Shortly after the founding of the Tokyo Stake, Adney Y. Komatsu was called to serve as Regional Representative over Hawaii and Japan. He held that position until April 1975, when he was called as an Assistant to the Council of the Twelve. Soon after, he was assigned by the First Presidency to live in Japan and supervise the Church in all of Asia. As the Church grew, Elder Komatsu's area was changed to include only Korea and Japan, and Elder Jacob de Jager was assigned to supervise the Philippines–Southeast Asia area.

Elder Komatsu supervised the Japan-Korea area until the summer of 1978, when he was replaced by Elder Yoshihiko Kikuchi. Elder Kikuchi, who was thirty-six years old at the time of his call as a member of the First Quorum of the Seventy, had previously served his fellow Japanese Saints in a number of important callings, the most recent of which was as president of the Tokyo Stake. The first Asian to serve as a General Authority of the Church, Elder Kikuchi received his call from President Spencer W. Kimball in a rather unusual way. A few days before general conference in October 1977, President Kimball phoned to ask Kikuchi if he was planning to attend conference. Kikuchi said he was not but that he was willing to come. He and his wife, Toshiko, had many frustrations to surmount, such as passport problems, traffic jams, a lost purse, and missed connections, but they finally arrived in Salt Lake City, late and exhausted. Nevertheless, the prophet extended a call for them to serve the Lord for the rest of their lives, and Elder Kikuchi was sustained as a member of the Seventy on October 1, 1977. After spending a few months in Salt Lake City at the Church offices, where he studied the workings of the Church in detail, Elder Kikuchi was ready to return to Japan to direct the work there. From the summer of 1978 until 1982, he presided over the Church in Japan and Korea.[28]

After arriving home in Japan, Elder Kikuchi worked closely with his friend President Tanaka Kenji of the Nagoya Mission on a new lesson plan for missionaries. But his greater attention soon focused on the ideas and missionary teaching methods of President Delbert H. "Dee" Groberg, who was the founding president of the Tokyo South Mission in July 1978.

In addition to the assignment of resident General Authorities, the Saints in Japan were blessed with visits by members of the First Presidency. President N. Eldon Tanner, a counselor in the First Presidency, came in the early 1970s; then President Harold B. Lee visited there and marveled at the tremendous progress of the Church since his first visit in 1954. The most significant visit by a General Authority to that time came in August 1975, when President Spencer W. Kimball presided at the first Japan Area Conference.

FAMILY HISTORY, SEMINARY AND INSTITUTE, AND PRESIDING BISHOPRIC SUPERVISION

A number of important changes and developments took place below the level of the General Authorities. For example, Japanese microfilmers were engaged, and continue to be, in photographing thousands of pages of records from registers at civic repositories and Buddhist temples throughout the land. This has led to a well-organized genealogy program. Also, since 1972 the Church Educational System has operated seminaries and institutes in

Japan. The home-study seminary was started by Robert T. Stout. The two programs grew quite rapidly: By 1978 there were 642 seminary students, 130 regular institute students, and 3,582 individual home-study institute students. These 4,354 pupils made up approximately 40 percent of all Asian seminary and institute students in 1978.[29]

In June 1977 the Presiding Bishopric announced the creation of a number of branch offices called Presiding Bishopric International Offices. In each office an area supervisor, later called the director of temporal affairs, was given responsibility for all departments under the Presiding Bishopric. The Presiding Bishopric appointed Arthur K. Nishimoto, a convert of the CPM in Hawaii and a former Japan mission president, as the first director of temporal affairs for Japan, Korea, Southeast Asia, and the Philippines. He worked closely with Elder Kikuchi, who had stewardship for the ecclesiastical side of the Church.

THE FIRST JAPAN AREA CONFERENCE AND THE ANNOUNCEMENT OF THE TOKYO TEMPLE

In 1971 the First Presidency recognized the great benefits that Saints in areas distant from Salt Lake City could realize from participation in conferences similar to general conference. Because Church members in Manchester, Mexico City, São Paulo, and Munich could generally not travel to Utah, President Joseph Fielding Smith and, later, President Harold B. Lee traveled to the people. They and President Spencer W. Kimball, who succeeded President Lee, followed an intensive program of visits with Church members worldwide. The area conferences, as these meetings were called, included many General Authorities and General Board members in each instance.

The seventh in the series of area conferences was held August 8–10, 1975, in the Budokan, a large cultural arts facility that had been built for the Tokyo Olympics. Saints from all over Japan, including Okinawa, gathered in Tokyo for the three days of meetings and activities. At the request of President Kimball, the Japanese members prepared an elaborate cultural program for Friday evening, August 8. Songs, drum playing, dances, and brief dramatic performances by more than two thousand participants delighted both local people and the foreign visitors.

Earlier that day, however, a much more significant though not widely known event had taken place. President Kimball, along with his counselor President Marion G. Romney, Elders Benson, Hinckley, and Ashton of the Twelve, and Elder Adney Y. Komatsu, met with the three stake presidents and six mission presidents from Japan. There President Kimball announced that the Church would construct a temple on the site of the Tokyo mission home. Elder Hinckley, chairman of the Church temple committee, spoke to the assembled leaders concerning monetary contributions and then presented President Kimball with a $100 bill. This was the first financial contribution toward construction of the new temple in Japan. Elder Hinckley explained that the building would cost approximately four million dollars (this figure was later raised to nine million dollars), 20 percent ($800,000) of which the Japanese Saints would be asked to contribute. The stake and mission presidents accepted the challenge to raise the money.[30]

The next morning, Saturday, August 9, at the first general session, President Kimball spoke to the 9,800 people in attendance. He laid a scriptural background for temple building and then dwelt on the sacrifices and hardships of those who built the Kirtland, Nauvoo, and Salt Lake Temples. He then said, "Now I bring to you a matter of great importance to all the people of the Asian world. We therefore propose to you that we build a temple in Tokyo for all the Church in Asia." There was applause from the congregation. Elder Hinckley noted that this was the first time he had been in a Church meeting when the people had broken into spontaneous applause. This was especially unusual considering the general restraint of the Japanese people. The announcement of the Church's eighteenth temple deeply moved the Japanese Saints. An observer wrote: "The few young people who understood English grasped their chests and held their breath waiting for the translation to affirm what they had heard.

"A few of the older Saints had been listening to the prophet's address with their eyes closed. When they heard the translation of the prophet's announcement, they slowly opened their eyes and then, as if suddenly realizing what they had heard was true, folded their arms, bowed their heads and cried."[31]

Elder Kikuchi, then president of the Tokyo Stake, held up a large framed architectural rendering of the temple. Though the building appeared large, it would be relatively small in comparison with other Mormon temples. The mission home lot was small but well situated in relation to public transportation facilities. It was in a fine section of the city.

On Sunday, a day free from employment, 12,300 people attended the last and largest session of the conference. The devoted and attentive audience deeply appreciated the counsel given by their leaders. Elder Hinckley, who had directed the work in Asia for eight years, told the people: "No one seeing what I have seen transpire in this land could deny the workings of the Almighty. He has laid His hand upon this nation; His spirit has brooded over the people. Their hearts have been touched as they have listened to the testimony of His witnesses."[32]

Japanese are sometimes characterized as stolid and unemotional people. This description does not apply to the Japanese Mormons. After the choir sang "God Be with You Till We Meet Again" and the closing prayer ended the conference, President Kimball observed the weeping people and was reluctant to leave. The Saints spontaneously sang the hymn "We Thank Thee, O God, for a Prophet." President Kimball and the General Authorities remained on the stand for about twenty minutes while the emotional congregation sang, smiled, and wept. The events of the conference had truly been historic.

Following 1975, the Church grew more rapidly in Japan. Five new stakes and two new missions were added in the next four years, and the membership increased by close to fifteen thousand.

Chapel construction continued in many cities. But of course the new temple received the main attention. The ground breaking was held on April 10, 1978. The local Saints had contributed many thousands of dollars more than what had been required of them. Not only Japanese Latter-day Saints but also members from many Asian lands had contributed to the building fund.

Some rather miraculous happenings occurred in regard to the temple grounds. For example, after President Kimball had announced that the temple would be built on the old mission home property, Elder Hinckley and others still considered some other sites. Elder Hinckley had been convinced for a long time that the mission home property was best, but it was so small that the architect and builders hoped for a larger lot on which to build. Better property could not be found elsewhere, but for unexplainable reasons the Church succeeded in acquiring land on both sides of the mission home. One property, owned by the Nomura Investment Company, was offered to the Church for 2.6 million dollars, even though the company had already been offered more than 3 million dollars for it. With the additional room, Emil B. Fetzer, Church architect, was able to make adjustments that provided a more beautiful and more functional building and adjoining annexes for worker apartments and rooms for visitors.

Construction of the new temple began in April 1978 and moved forward on schedule. The old building had to be razed, a tedious and demanding job in a very high-class neighborhood. Building codes in Tokyo required great attention to detail. Earthquake and typhoon precautions had to be structured into the 78,000-square-foot building. The Church architects were as concerned as anyone and designed the building to withstand the highest shocks on the Richter scale.

But more important than actual construction of the temple was the preparation of the members of the Church in Japan, in Asia, and in the United States. It was as though a great spotlight was trained on Japan, a spotlight that focused the eyes of the Church and its leaders on the accomplishments and potential of the Church in that land. The call of Elder Yoshihiko Kikuchi, a Japanese, as a member of the First Quorum of the Seventy and as Area Supervisor (and later Executive Administrator) of Japan and Korea symbolized the coming-of-age of the Church in Japan. But other developments kept Japan and its importance before the eyes of the Church. New stakes were organized in several cities. In May President Ezra Taft Benson, President of the Quorum of the Twelve, dedicated a new seven-story area administration headquarters of the Church two blocks from the temple site.[33] And the Japan Tokyo Mission was divided into the Japan Tokyo North and the Japan Tokyo South missions on July 1, 1978.[34] In December 1978 the Church announced that the Mormon Tabernacle Choir would perform in Japan and Korea the next September, a tour that was very successful from a musical and public relations standpoint.[35] In that same month, December 1978, the BYU football team played in Japan, an event that brought the Church recognition among a different Japanese audience.

During 1979 and 1980 Church members worldwide were kept abreast of the developments in Japan as reports on temple construction, the Tabernacle Choir visit, and other items appeared in the *Church News*, the *Ensign*, and in other Church periodicals. In February 1980 the Church announced that on July 1, 1980, the Japan Kobe Mission would be divided to create the Japan Osaka Mission, the sixth mission in Japan. A month later the Church announced that six area conferences would be held in the Philippines, Hong Kong, Taiwan, Korea, and concluding in Japan (Tokyo and Osaka) during October 1980. Four weeks later, on April 19, the dates for the Tokyo Temple open house and dedication were made public. In the same announcement the new temple president and matron, Dwayne N. Andersen and his wife, Peggy, were made known. The open house would be held from September 15 to October 18, with dedication services scheduled for October 27–29.[36] The stage was set. Only the final construction work and many local plans remained to be completed before the events of September and October 1980 could take place.

NOTES

1. See Dwayne N. Andersen Oral History, interviews by author, Provo, Utah, 1973, Oral History Program, LDS Church Archives, typescript, p. 47.

2. Gordon B. Hinckley, Journal, 20 May 1961; in possession of President Hinckley.

3. Ibid., March 1962.

4. See Andersen Oral History, p. 47.

5. See ibid., 45–47; see also Mission Financial and Statistical Reports, Japanese Mission, LDS Church Archives (hereafter cited as MFSR).

6. Andersen Oral History, p. 15.

7. Ibid., p. 34.

8. In Terry G. Nelson, "A History of the Church of Jesus Christ of Latter-day Saints in Japan from 1948 to 1980" (master's thesis, Brigham Young University, 1986), appendix B, pp. 158–59.

9. Ibid., p. 26.

10. Kan Watanabe et al., "Japan: Land of the Rising Sun," *Ensign* 5 (August 1975): 42.

11. Although the Andersen Oral History is the primary source for this section, see also Spencer J. Palmer, *The Church Encounters Asia* (Salt Lake City: Deseret Book Co., 1970), pp. 78–83.

12. *Success Messenger,* June 1966, p. 116, LDS Church Archives.

13. Adney Y. Komatsu Oral History, interviews by author, Honolulu, Hawaii, and Salt Lake City, Utah, 1974, James Moyle Oral History Program, LDS Church Archives, typescript, p. 4.

14. Hugh B. Brown, "Prophecies Regarding Japan," *BYU Studies* 10 (winter 1970): 159–60; see Hinckley, Journals, 21 April 1967.

15. Hinckley, Journals, 21 April 1967.

16. See Komatsu Oral History, pp. 33–34; Don W. Marsh, *The Light of the Sun: Japan and the Saints* (n.p., n.d. [1969?]), p. 66.

17. See Komatsu Oral History, pp. 20, 29–30.

18. Hinckley, Journal, 16 October 1967, 26 April 1968.

19. See Gerald Joseph Peterson, "History of Mormon Exhibits in World Expositions" (master's thesis, Brigham Young University, 1974), pp. 144–45.

20. See "Expo '70 Ground Breaking," *Church News,* 17 May 1969, p. 4.

21. See Peterson, "History of Mormon Exhibits," pp. 143, 146.

22. Bernard P. Brockbank, "The Mormon Pavilion at Expo '70," *Improvement Era* 73 (December 1970): 121.

23. For an extensive account of the production of the Japanese version of *Man's Search for Happiness,* see Palmer, *The Church Encounters Asia,* pp. 9–15.

24. Ezra Taft Benson, "The Future of the Church in Asia," *Improvement Era* 73 (March 1970): 14; see his "A World Message," *Improvement Era* 73 (June 1970): 96.

25. See Spencer J. Palmer et al., "Educational Needs of the Church of Jesus Christ of Latter-day Saints in Asia," report to the Church Commissioner of Education, 1972, LDS Church Archives, pp. 82–83.

26. See MFSR, Southern Far East Mission, 1962–1968, LDS Church Archives; see also Missionary Department Annual Report, 1978, p. 8, LDS Church Archives.

27. These statistics are according to Niiyama Yasuo, who formerly served as a Regional Representative in Japan.

28. See "Elder Yoshihiko Kikuchi," *Ensign* 7 (November 1977): 101–102; Gerry Avant, "War's Tragedies Lead to Gospel," *Church News,* 29 October 1977, p. 5.

29. "Church Educational System, Overview," pamphlet (Salt Lake City: The Church of Jesus Christ of Latter-day Saints, 1978), p. 38.

30. Hinckley, Journal, 8 August 1975.

31. Cherie Campbell, as quoted in "Temple to Be Built in Tokyo," *Ensign* 5 (October 1975): 86.

32. As quoted in "Japan Area General Conference," *Church News*, 16 August 1975, p. 5.

33. See "President Benson visits Asian countries," *Church News*, 10 June 1978, p. 4.

34. See "Three new missions formed," *Church News*, 4 March 1978, p. 3.

35. See "Choir to perform in Japan," *Church News*, 30 December 1978, p. 3; Dorothy Stowe, "Joy spans the Pacific as choir visits Orient," *Church News*, 22 September 1979, pp. 3, 8.

36. See "8 new missions formed," *Church News*, 16 February 1980, p. 3; "Area conferences in Far East planned," *Church News*, 22 March 1980, p. 3; and "Dedication dates set for temples in Tokyo, Seattle," *Church News*, 19 April 1980, p. 4.

7

JAPAN

1978–1996

From Temple Dedication Onward

By 1996 the LDS Church in Japan had grown to more than one hundred thousand members in twenty-five stakes and twenty districts. Although these numbers appear relatively large, they do not reveal the kind of growth that Church leaders projected in 1980.

Unquestionably the greatest statistical Church growth in Japan was the period from 1978 to 1982. During those years, official membership grew from around thirty thousand to near seventy thousand and the number of wards, branches, stakes, and districts more than doubled. But in the years that followed, baptismal rates have returned to previous levels and activity rates have been low.

Church growth in Japan since the late 1970s created many difficult questions. Leaders in Salt Lake City as well as in Japan struggled with the question of why Japanese join the Church in such small numbers and why so many of that small number fall away after baptism. Different proselytizing methods and programs were forwarded by mission presidents and Area Authorities, some with remarkable success and others with less favorable results; but in 1995 and 1996 the leaders of the Church in the Asia North Area pulled back, reducing the number of missions and missionaries, evidently because they did not believe anyone had answers to the problem of low baptism and retention rates.

THE TEMPLE OPENS

Five years passed between President Kimball's announcement of the temple and its completion. A high level of planning and preparing was required in order to be ready for the open house and dedication, but on September 13, 1980, ribbons were cut and "about 650 businessmen, politicians, university professors, ambassadors and media reporters" visited the temple as part of a VIP tour.[1] In the opening ceremony, David M. Kennedy, special representative of the First Presidency, gave a message from President Kimball. On September 15, the public phase of the open house began. Between that time and October 18, forty-eight thousand visitors walked through the ten-million-dollar edifice.

"On Monday Oct. 27 one of the most significant events of this dispensation will take place. It will be the dedication of the House of the Lord in Tokyo, Japan."[2] So began the editorial of the *Church News* issued in Salt Lake City only a few hours before President Spencer W. Kimball gave the prayer dedicating the first temple of the Church in an Asian country, the eighteenth operating temple of the Church. The editorial went on, asking, "When in world history has a temple of the Lord ever graced that part of the world? There is no record of such a thing."

In a way the editorial seemed to exclaim, "*This is a world church, a global church.* The Church is moving. Let's move forward with it!"

Many time zones ahead of Salt Lake City, the Saints in Japan and Asia gathered to hear words of counsel and the sacred prayer of dedication and sanctification that were offered by President Spencer W. Kimball. His counsel followed themes similar to those he spoke throughout the world—the importance of rearing good families, being sealed in the temple as couples and families, teaching the gospel to the children in regular family home evenings, attending the temple regularly, and so on. The 860 members who assembled in the temple for the first dedicatory session were deeply moved by the carefully worded prayer. In the first paragraph, President Kimball read: "We present to Thee this beautiful temple, provided by the sacrifice of Thy people in the Orient who love Thee and Thy Son."[3] As the prayer went on, he uttered many carefully selected phrases of affirmation and praise to Heavenly Father and His Son, Jesus Christ, words of gratitude for the Church, the priesthood, and for the thirty thousand missionaries who were then serving worldwide. He prayed for the rulers and governments of nations "that any barriers which

The Tokyo Temple, announced in 1975 and dedicated in 1980, was the first temple built by the Church in Asia. (Photo by author)

stand in the way of the spread of Thy gospel may be removed." He prayed that peace might "abide in the homes of all Thy saints. Bless the poor and the needy of Thy people. Let not the cry of the widow and the orphan, the lonely and oppressed go unheeded." President Kimball prayed for the youth of Zion in all the world. And he remembered the women of the Church: "Wilt Thou richly endow the sisters of the Church, our wives, our mothers, our daughters, with the spirit of their exalted callings and responsibilities." The prayer could have been spoken in England, in Canada, in South Africa, or in Sweden. In the eyes and mind of the prophet, the members of the Church in Japan and their new temple were as important as anywhere else.

Six additional dedicatory sessions were held during the next two days in the Tokyo Stake Center in order to accommodate larger audiences. A total of around seventy-five hundred people attended the seven sessions. President Kimball gave the same address and read the dedicatory prayer in each session. Other General Authorities and members of the temple presidency also spoke.[4]

The first president of the temple was Dwayne N. Andersen, former missionary and mission president in Japan. His wife, Peggy, was called as matron of the temple. Andersen was the mission president who helped so much in the effort to take the first group of Japanese Saints to the temple in Hawaii in 1965.

The entire dedication process was an exhilarating spiritual experience. The Japanese members were thrilled to be in the presence of the prophet and so many General Authorities of the Church. The temple served as the engine to move the Church forward at an increasing pace.

Over the years since the temple opened, President Andersen was the only president lacking a Japanese heritage. He was followed in 1982 by Elder Adney Y. Komatsu and several other converts from the Japanese-Central Pacific Mission in Hawaii. In 1994 Elder Yoshihiko Kikuchi of the Seventy was called home to Japan to preside at the temple.

Through the years the Japanese Saints have been steady in their temple and genealogy service. Not surprisingly, 1981, the year following the temple dedication, was the banner year for live endowments—1,247. The average per year since then has been 660. During the 1980s, as the total number of endowed members grew, the annual number of endowments for the dead rose steadily, topping out at 46,801 in 1988. Between that year and Elder Kikuchi's presidency, the numbers of participants dropped slowly to an average of 42,000 endowments per year. In 1995 enthusiasm picked up and the Japanese Saints performed over 50,000 endowments—no small feat for 7,300 recommend holders who were spread all over the country.[5] In 1993 the total number of endowments performed in the Tokyo Temple since it opened exceeded 500,000.

The Japanese members have been concerned for the salvation of their ancestors. Through the years since the opening of the temple, they have submitted significant numbers of names for temple ordinance work. As of 1993, the total number of family names submitted passed 300,000. The temple symbolizes the Japanese Saints' faith.

The annex to the Tokyo Temple, an important addition, was completed and put into use in July 1986. Through good fortune, the Church was able to acquire another lot

Elder Yoshihiko Kikuchi, called to the First Quorum of the Seventy in 1977, was the first Japanese to serve as a General Authority of the Church. Elder Kikuchi and his wife, Toshiko, served as president and matron of the Tokyo Temple during the 1990s. (Courtesy LDS Church Archives)

beside the temple. On this land the Church constructed a multipurpose building that included several apartments for temple missionaries and the Japan Missionary Training Center (JMTC) president and his wife, a small chapel and other facilities for a Tokyo ward, dorm rooms and classrooms for the JMTC, and dorm rooms for members from out of town who were there to do temple work. A small parking area was also added for Church employees and Sunday use.

Following the dedication services in Tokyo, the visiting authorities held area conferences in Tokyo (October 30–31, 1980) and Osaka (November 1). The crowds were not as large as the 18,000 who had attended in Manila, but the 10,000 in Tokyo's Budokan Hall and the 6,387 at the Matsushita Center in Osaka were enthusiastic and inspired by the messages from a large array of Church leaders. Elder Gordon B. Hinckley said, "This is a place where the Church has a tremendous future." The *Church News* reported that Elder Hinckley "then issued a challenge to the Japanese members to increase their number to 100,000 within the next five years." At that time there were 48,627 members in Japan. All fifteen hundred missionaries serving in Japan were blessed to meet with and hear from President Kimball and other leaders of the Church on the morning of the first day of the Tokyo conference. They too were encouraged to move the work forward more rapidly.[6]

MISSIONARY WORK IN JAPAN FROM 1978 TO 1996

During the 1970s baptismal rates for the Japanese missions were modest, reflecting growing difficulty among the missionaries in influencing a society that was becoming ever more materialistic and economically successful. The relatively short amount of time missionaries spent in the country (two years for elders, eighteen months for sisters) made it difficult for them to learn the Japanese language well enough to communicate effectively. For a time, from 1979 to 1982, new and unusual proselytizing methods raised the number of baptisms throughout Japan and Korea, but especially in the Tokyo South Mission, to new heights. Line graphs illustrating growth in baptismal numbers shot up like Mount Everest compared to the low and unimpressive foothills that preceded and followed from 1983 on to the present. Although the total number of members on record in Japan had grown to an impressive 106,000 by 1996, baptismal rates per missionary were not impressive and large numbers of less-active and lost members continue to cause headaches and heartaches for leaders in Japan.[7]

GENERAL AUTHORITY SUPERVISION
AND ADMINISTRATIVE ORGANIZATION

On July 1, 1984, the world was divided into thirteen administrative areas, of which three were outside the United States. The

Asia Area was created with Elder William R. Bradford, who had replaced Elder Kikuchi in 1982 and was already in charge in Tokyo, as the first Area President, with Elder Jack H Goaslind Jr. and Elder Robert B. Harbertson as counselors. A year later he and his new counselors, Elder Jacob de Jager and Elder Keith W. Wilcox, moved the headquarters for all of Asia to Hong Kong. Hong Kong remained the center of all Asian operations until 1987, when the Philippines/Micronesia Area was created with Elder George I. Cannon as its first president. The Asia Area was divided once again on September 1, 1992, when the Asia North Area Presidency was created to administer affairs in Japan and Korea. Elder W. Eugene Hansen was the new area's first president. His counselors were Elder Han In Sang, from Korea, and Elder Sam K. Shimabukuro, from Hawaii. A year later Elder Merrill J. Bateman replaced Elder Hansen as Area President, but he was soon called as Presiding Bishop of the Church and replaced by Elder David E. Sorensen. In 1996 the Area Presidency consisted of President Sorensen, and counselors Elder Rex D. Pinegar and Elder L. Edward Brown. Many Japanese members felt that the creation of the Asia North Area was a reaffirmation of the importance of their part of the world.

Since the 1970s, the Church in Japan has provided its own Regional Representatives. In August 1995 three men, two of whom are native Japanese, were called to serve as Area Authorities. They were Kashikura Hitoshi, Katanuma Seiji, and Gary Matsuda. Elder Kashikura, from Kanagawa-ken, was formerly a Regional Representative, stake president, and bishop. He was a department head at an engineering firm. Elder Katanuma had previously served as Regional Representative, stake president in Sapporo, mission president's counselor, and stake mission president. He was a professor at Hokkaido Kyoiku University. Elder Gary Matsuda was a U.S. Navy employee who was serving in Japan. In the Church he had formerly served as a Regional Representative, district president, bishop's counselor, and branch president.

Since the first stake was created in Tokyo in 1970, the Japanese Saints were blessed by frequent visits from General Authorities and general officers of the Church. The most important occasions for visits—area conferences—have been noted. But many regional and stake meetings have been important locally and, as is true throughout the Church, have kept the leaders and members in harmony with the movements, changes, and concerns of the leaders of the Church.

PHYSICAL FACILITIES AND TRANSLATION SERVICES

In 1995 the 106,000 Japanese Latter-day Saints were living in 300 wards and branches that were part of 25 stakes and 20 districts. Providing meetinghouses (building and maintaining them, or leasing them), furniture, teaching materials and leadership manuals, scriptures, and equipment for all of these units and members was the responsibility of the director of temporal affairs, who was also responsible for all Church finances. The temporal affairs operation began in 1977, with an office in Tokyo. Korea has a branch country office that carries out similar operations.

Providing meetinghouses and meeting places in Japan and East Asia has been a difficult and expensive proposition. By the mid-1990s the Church had constructed 160 meetinghouses in Japan. One hundred and eighty-four wards have their own buildings; in other words, 15 percent of the chapels are used by more than one ward. The remaining units meet in leased facilities.

Most of the wards and branches in Japan are in metropolitan areas. Meetinghouses are generally spaced forty minutes to one hour apart from each other. When members move to smaller cities or towns, they may find it necessary to travel up to two hours in order to attend Church meetings.

Many meetinghouses are freestanding, much like LDS chapels in North America. But most recent buildings have been constructed following what might be called an Asian model. Land

Although the Okamachi chapel is typical of many LDS chapels in Japan, newer structures are more vertical, with limited space demanding that chapels go up, not out. (Courtesy LDS Church Archives)

is so expensive in Japan that wisdom demands that buildings be built up more than out. The latest meetinghouses have parking on the ground floor and the chapel and classrooms and other facilities on two floors above. The main hall, usually thought of as the chapel, is now used as a multipurpose room. Folding chairs are used in place of permanent benches. The Church is well housed throughout Japan, and the necessary features of LDS buildings are present.[8]

The translation of Church materials has a long history in Japan. By the beginning of the period under consideration, a well-managed office of capable translators had been in operation for more than ten years. The most important project in recent years was the retranslation and publication of the Book of Mormon. It was done by a committee that operated under the supervision of the Quorum of the Twelve. Eugene M. Kitamura, director of temporal affairs, was chair of the committee during most of the process. It was necessary to create a more modern version because the older one by Brother Sato used language now considered a bit "too classic."[9] The new version brought consistency between Bible names that appear in the Book of Mormon and the standard biblical Japanese translations of those names. The Sato version used his own transliterations of biblical names along with his, or Alma O. Taylor's, transliterations of Book of Mormon names. (The standard Holy Bible used by the Church in Japan is the 1955 edition by the Japanese Bible Society. The Church is now the biggest buyer of this conservative version.) In addition to changes in expression, additional study helps were included, such as the Guide to the Scriptures. This guide "defines selected doctrines, principles, people, and places found in the Holy Bible, the Book of Mormon, the Doctrine and Covenants, and the Pearl of Great Price. It also provides key scriptural references" for study of each topic.[10] New second-edition translations of the Doctrine and Covenants and the Pearl of Great Price were also published in 1996. Other recent publications in Japanese include Elder M. Russell Ballard's *Our Search for Happiness* and President Hinckley's *Be Thou an Example.*

Japan and Korea are a Phase III translation area. This means that all materials that are provided to the Saints in North America are also translated into Japanese and Korean, including Church Educational System materials that are necessary for seminary and institute classes. In Japan, videos of CES firesides that originate in the Marriott Center at Brigham Young University, as well as other important events, are also dubbed with Japanese and distributed to the institutes around the country. The Church provides a magazine in Japanese, *Seito no Michi* (The Voice of the Saints), which, in addition to articles provided by the International Magazines office in Salt Lake City, contains sixteen pages of material dedicated to Japanese concerns and interests.

The seminary and institute program of the Church was begun in 1972. In Japan seminary courses were instituted that first year, and institute classes followed in Tokyo, Kobe, and Nagoya in 1973. Growth in the number of programs has continued since that time. The Church Educational System has leased some office space for institute directors in Hiroshima, Nagoya, and Sapporo; leased a building in Ikebukuro; and built special areas in meetinghouses in Tokyo, Shibuya (Tokyo), and Osaka. A number of Latter-day Saints are involved in seminary and institute as professionals and as volunteers. In 1995 fourteen coordinators were working full-time under a country director for CES. In addition, there were 575 volunteer teachers throughout the country. Of the potential seminary students in 1995, some 1,421 (55 percent) were enrolled. In that same year, 847 (85 percent) of 1,002 potential LDS college students were enrolled in institute classes. Because all Latter-day Saints between the ages of eighteen and thirty are encouraged to participate in institute courses, an additional 2,869 students took part.[11] The institute program did much to solidify the commitments and testimonies of the gospel of young Latter-day Saints. It also did much to bring LDS young people together in a wholesome environment that often led to temple marriages. The full-time CES personnel have set a strong example of service to the Church. Six of them have served as mission presidents in Japan as well as in other callings such as bishop and stake president.

MEDIA AND PUBLIC RELATIONS

Since the dedication of the Tokyo Temple, the Church and Church members in Japan have received a considerable amount of media attention. Kent Gilbert and Kent Derricott, missionaries who returned to Japan to work in law and business, respectively, attracted considerable attention. Both Kents surprised Japanese

TV audiences with their ability to speak Japanese and with their wit and understanding of Japan. Gilbert even published two or three books of his opinions about life and the world. Mormon missionaries in Japan received sporadic Japanese media attention during the 1970s and 1980s, but they also received notice from American news people who were stationed as foreign correspondents in Japan. In May 1988 James Fallows of *U.S. News and World Report* wrote about the growing number of former Mormon missionaries who were living in Japan (and elsewhere in Asia) and having success in Japanese business. Fallows wrote, "Of the Americans I've met in Asia who can operate deftly and successfully in the local language, a disproportionate number have been Mormons."[12] By 1996 there were three English-speaking wards in the Tokyo area, made up primarily of returned missionaries and their families.

In 1985 a Japanese television corporation traveled to Los Angeles to videotape footage on Mormon lifestyles, among other things. In that same year the Tabernacle Choir made its second tour of Japan and created a good deal of media attention. Other famous Mormons, for example Wally Joyner and Dale Murphy of major league baseball, were also recognized by the Japanese media. These two gave a fireside for the Church in November 1986 that generated considerable attention. In the 1990s the Church's own efforts to use media more effectively included a video about family home evening. More than five thousand copies were distributed to members of the Church, and another five hundred copies were distributed to nonmembers who wrote in asking for a copy.

But there was also a negative side to media attention. The Church was occasionally criticized from various quarters. Blatantly anti-Mormon materials were distributed by some other Christian churches in an effort to discredit the Church and its members.

Church member Numano Jiro of Tokuyama University has studied the Japanese media response to the Church. He calls the period from the 1980s to the present a "mixed media treatment of

Mormonism. While the same friendly treatment continued, news of a critical nature also began to appear."[13] Numano believes that increasing secularism and disregard for religion, which he says bears "a connotation of something negative," have damaged the Church. However, Brother Numano says that all things considered, the Church is tolerated if not positively heralded in the media.

THE KOBE EARTHQUAKE OF 1995

In 1923 Tokyo was struck by a massive earthquake that destroyed thousands of homes and other buildings and left between 120,000 and 150,000 people dead. Seventy-two years passed before the quake of January 17, 1995, struck Kobe. It was the second-largest earthquake in Japan, in terms of damage, in this century. Far fewer lives were lost in 1995, around 5,000, and fewer people were injured, 26,000, but the totals were staggering nonetheless. More than 20,000 homes were destroyed, and 56,000 buildings were damaged. Fortunately, even though the epicenter of the quake was only fifteen minutes' walking time from the Kobe Ward chapel and the Kobe Mission home, these buildings were not damaged. They were available to serve as a center for preparing meals, distributing food and supplies, and organizing relief efforts. One member, 76-year-old Nagai Kimiko, and her nonmember husband were killed. Two children of an investigator family also lost their lives. Considering the number of Latter-day Saints in Kobe, the Church was fortunate in not losing more lives. Among the 300,000 Kobe residents left homeless were thirty-five member families. The ward and stake moved quickly to provide shelter and to meet their other needs.

Stake president Donomoto Tsutumo and Kobe Ward bishop Takagi Kenji took charge of Latter-day Saint help and rescue operations. Kobe mission president Curtis P. Wilson was also very much involved. All three men were impressed with the untiring labors of the Japanese people, members and others, and their willingness to share and help each other.

Either working independently or in efforts organized by the Church, many Japanese members drove trucks supplied with water or other essentials such as food, blankets, and clothing. These services went on for many days after the quake. The Church also sent supplies of food into the distressed area. "Church volunteers," reported the *Ensign* magazine, "took shifts around the clock to unload trucks, inventory supplies, assess needs, and deliver the items. Most of those deliveries were done by bicycle, motorcycle, or on foot."[14]

Elder David E. Sorensen, Area President, paid special tribute to the women of the Church. He said: "The sisters were valiant in putting their hands to the plow. They carried water, prepared food, took care of the children. I just can't say enough. I must give praise to the sisters who have done so much to relieve the suffering not only of the Saints, but also of the neighbors in surrounding neighborhoods."[15]

When the crisis period was over, the Saints of Kobe and Japan had shown Christlike love to one another and to many others who were in need. Almost two years later, the Area Presidency summarized the efforts of the Japanese Saints this way: "Members helped set up temporary housing and soup kitchens, and food, clothing, and medical supplies poured in from members all over Japan. For three weeks, members filled five-gallon containers with water and brought them into the devastated areas. On the first Sunday in February 1995, members throughout the area held a special fast and earmarked their donations to help quake victims, including the sixty members who lost their homes."[16]

LIVING THE GOSPEL IN JAPAN

Japanese and Americans share many important values and customs. The human family is truly a family. No one understands this truth better than the members of the Church. But it is also true that cultures differ on many points that matter, not just on trivial or unimportant beliefs and ways of doing things. American Mormons and Japanese Mormons are different in a number of subtle ways and a few that are not so subtle. American English is much more casual than Japanese. The Japanese language reveals more concern for status and hierarchy than does English. Within the Church as well as without, Japanese people have more interest than Americans usually have in who is senior and who has been there for the shortest time, and who has held the most important positions and who is least experienced. New converts are sometimes not easily absorbed. A long period of "apprenticeship" seems to be expected for a person to be accepted into the LDS group.

American Mormons can be too casual regarding accepting the divorced into important positions such as a bishopric, while some Japanese Mormons, largely based on loss of face and shame, question a divorced person's right to hold a temple recommend, to say nothing of holding an important office in the Church. While most American members feel a sense of regret if their children seriously misbehave, some Japanese parents feel obligated to "resign" their Church positions in shame, as though they were the leader of a political party or a major corporation in which corruption has been discovered. According to Masakazu Watabe, there is frequent confusion among Japanese between the concepts of sin and shame. Too many members worry more about being shamed before the group or ward than being contrite and repentant because of sin. The atonement of Jesus Christ is to take away the effects of sin from those who repent and are baptized. Shame, on the other hand, is a social problem that can be put away by following socially prescribed solutions.[17]

Many Americans tend to expect all people in all cultures to follow American cultural norms. Some American Mormons expect all other Mormons worldwide to accept American mores as though they were commandments and part of the gospel. BYU professor Masakazu Watabe once asked, "Why should the priesthood brethren have to be taught to say 'I love you' to their wives in front of their children or in testimony meetings?"[18] Such an action is based on American preferences, not on gospel principles. The following excerpt from an essay[19] underscores this point.

THE UNSPOKEN WORDS
Masakazu Watabe

An old Japanese saying aptly characterizes the Japanese way of communication: "Ichi o kiite, Jūo shiru," meaning, "If you hear 'one,' you must know 'ten'" or "I do not say all that I feel." For example, in Japan one rarely, if ever, hears what one hears often and is encouraged to say in other parts of the world: "I love you." This is true even between husband and wife or parents and children.

I have been a member of the Church all my life, and my parents have been excellent members and examples for me in the gospel. Yet I cannot recall ever hearing my father or mother say to each other or to me, "I love you." Neither have I ever told either of them that I love them. But there is not a single doubt in my mind that they love me and know that I love them.

Here [is an example] of my [father] saying "one" and my understanding "ten." Just before I left on my mission, my whole family came to the United States and we visited Church historical sites and temples. After the tour across the United States, I said good-bye to them in Los Angeles to leave for the mission home in Salt Lake City. Much to [my] surprise, I had been called to go to Brazil, a distant and unknown country, rather than to Japan, my native land. The departure would have been less emotional had I received a call to Japan. As I said good-bye to my mother, my brothers, and my sisters, I saw that each of them was crying. When finally my father extended his hand and said, "Masakazu, gambatte" ("Son, try hard"), I noticed tears in his eyes, too. As if trying to hide them, he turned around, and I drove away, for I knew that, according to the customs of my country, I should not see my father's tears or show mine to him.

I could not stop crying, so I asked my brother to drive. As he drove, I reflected on my father's words and the tears in his eyes. I had never seen my father cry in public. But even with the cultural restraints, he felt he could not stop his tears because of the love and concern he had for me. I knew he meant more than he had said. I knew that in every one of his long prayers he would, as he had throughout my two older brothers' missions, plead for me and my success as a missionary. He would write me often and encourage me to be the best missionary there. And he would have complete confidence that I would do my very best for the Lord.

Mormon Japanese are caught up in the same tide of secularism, materialism, and economic growth that other Japanese are. And they are also having trouble rearing their children in a society that holds most of its school activities—athletics, clubs, special interest groups—on Sundays. Pornography is more available in Japan than in the United States, and parents and young members of the Church have to fight such influences. Sexual promiscuity, especially among males, is not considered an issue by most Japanese. Some members of the Church have expressed regret over "the failure of the Japanese moral system."[20] Following World War II, many Japanese discarded not only the questionable parts of their former moral and ethical system but also the good features, of which there were many. One observer called Japan a "moral wasteland" because the postwar generation does not have confidence in its moral, ethical, or spiritual roots. This situation has a bearing on the lives of all Japanese.

The Japanese quest for economic success has created strenuous demands on most husbands, but on other family members as well. It is typical to see trains and subways late in the evening filled with large numbers of white-collar workers in business suits riding home after a long day's work. Many Japanese live considerable distances from their places of work and spend several hours on public transportation going to and coming home from work. Mormon husbands and fathers are not exempt. Evening and Saturday work make fulfilling responsibilities in the home and in the Church difficult.

Hawaii native Elder Sam K. Shimabukuro was called to the Second Quorum of the Seventy in July 1991. Prior to that call, he served as bishop and stake president, mission president, and Tokyo Temple president. He served in the Asia North Area Presidency from 1991 to 1996. (Author photo)

Because travel was expensive and time-consuming, and in an effort to spend more time at home but still do their Church callings well, President Sakai Kiyoshi and his counselors in the Machida Stake in Tokyo experimented with stake presidency and high council meetings by conference call. They met together in person once a month, but on an appointed Wednesday at 10:00 P.M. they commenced their meeting by phone. Before they started, they sent by fax machine a copy of the agenda to all who were involved—up to twenty-nine people. They also used the Internet to share information. President Sakai's stake of thirty-six hundred members in five wards was typical of Japan in 1995. (Unfortunately, President Sakai had nearly one thousand members on his books as "lost" or "address unknown," making the actual total forty-six hundred.)[21] The Church was mature in his stake, the youngest bishop being just under forty years of age.

About 20 percent of his stake members attended sacrament meeting each week. Most of his active members held more than one calling in their wards or in the stake. The point, however, is that this group of leaders was trying to make the best of a difficult situation and seemed to be making a difference through the innovative use of technology.

Fortunately, in spite of the realities of contemporary life in Japan, at least twenty thousand people are solid members of the Church, and a number of others may yet return to full activity in the Church. Despite the high number of less-active and lost members, there has been real growth over the years. The Church in Japan is led by many priesthood leaders and sisters who are as knowledgeable, experienced, dedicated, and spiritual as members in any other land. Perhaps Elder Watanabe Kan, as a Regional Representative in 1975, said it best: "We in Japan haven't scratched the surface yet. As the great concepts of Mormonism become better known and more fully understood among the Japanese people as a whole, the potential of the Church in Japan, and likewise throughout Asia, will be of unlimited magnitude. Thousands of testimonies witness that the sun of faith has risen in the Land of the Rising Sun; and in these testimonies the promise of the future is sure!"[22]

NEW BEGINNINGS IN FAR-EAST RUSSIA

In 1995 a new geographical region, everything east of 126 degrees east longitude, was added to the Asia North Area of the Church, headquartered in Japan. Formerly called Eastern Siberia, Far-East Russia occupies a vast area bordering the Sea of Japan, the Sea of Okhotsk, and the Northern Pacific Ocean. In 1995 and 1996 several Latter-day Saint families and individuals were assigned to Vladivostok and Magadan by multinational corporations, and branches of the Church were created in each city. The first district of the Church was organized in Far-East Russia on March 8, 1996, with Michael Williams as president of the

Vladivostok District and Kevin Matthews as president of the Vladivostok Branch.[23]

Area President David E. Sorensen was actively involved with developments in this new area of the Church. In the fall of 1995 the city of Partizansk, which is about eighty miles east of Vladivostok, was hit by devastating floods that destroyed crop and fuel storage and created an extremely serious situation. Through President Sorensen's efforts, along with the Humanitarian Services Department of the Church (now called LDS Charities), the Church was able to send food, clothing, blankets, and medical aid to more than five thousand needy families. In total, the Church sent four large shipping containers of food and two containers of blankets and clothing. In addition to helping many needy people, Church leaders believed the gift "generated goodwill for the Church as well."[24]

As a result of relationships developed during the flood-relief effort, Russian government officials invited the Church to send humanitarian-services missionary couples "to teach English, business, law, and accounting at a university in Vladivostok."[25] Three American couples and a Korean couple were the first to go to Vladivostok to teach. Kim Ki Yong and his wife, Kim Kum Jae, arrived in early summer 1995, and the other three couples, after orientation at Church headquarters in Tokyo, arrived in September 1995. Brother Kim is an uncommonly talented linguist, speaking four languages, Korean, Japanese, Russian, and English. As a young man just out of high school, he was inducted into the Japanese army. While there he learned Japanese. When World War II ended, he was captured by the Russians and learned their language. After returning home to North Korea in 1949, he was forced to join the army of that nation. Being a Christian, Kim's father decided that in order to have religious freedom, they should flee to the south. His father said, "My sons, my sons! Even if we are punished for going to the south we must go, for only there will we be free to worship our Lord! We must go for your future and your children's future." So during the height of fighting of the

Korean War, they escaped by night and sailed to Pusan in a very small boat. Once there, Kim found work with the American military and had to learn English to succeed.[26] Twenty years later, in July 1970, Brother and Sister Kim joined the Church. His father had encouraged him to believe that the Lord's true church was on the earth. Since he found it, Kim has served well in many capacities. In 1995 he was called by the Lord to serve in Vladivostok, a place where both Russian and English are useful languages.

In addition to the humanitarian-services missionaries, by late 1996, ten full-time elders were serving in Vladivostok under the Asia North Area Mission. The future appeared to be bright when Elder Joseph B. Wirthlin of the Quorum of the Twelve visited there in November 1996. He was the first Apostle to visit Far-East Russia on official assignment in his calling. City by city, and nation by nation, the Church is being planted in the nations of the earth. The population of Far-Eastern Russia is not large in comparison with China, Japan, and the other great nations of Asia, but the millions who inhabit that part of the earth are now closer to hearing a witness of the restored gospel.

NOTES

1. "VIPs impressed by tour of Tokyo Temple," *Church News*, 20 September 1980, p. 3.

2. "A Temple in Japan," *Church News*, 25 October 1980, p. 16.

3. As quoted in "Dedication prayer for the temple," *Church News*, 8 November 1980, p. 12. President Spencer W. Kimball dedicated the Tokyo Temple on October 27, 1980.

4. See Jerry P. Cahill, "Times of Great Blessings: Witnessing the Miracles," *Ensign* 11 (January 1981): 72.

5. Yoshihiko Kikuchi, interview by the author, Tokyo, Japan, 21 September 1995, tape recording.

6. See Dell Van Orden, "'Tremendous' future for Church in Japan," *Church News*, 8 November 1980, pp. 4, 10.

7. For further study of missionary work in Japan between 1978 and 1996, see the following: Cyril I. A. Figuerres, "Demographic Study of Converts in Japan," research report of the Research and Evaluation Division of The Church of Jesus Christ of Latter-day Saints, 1987; Cyril I. A. Figuerres, "The Ammon Project: Establishing Real Growth and the First Generation Church in Japan," 1994, n.p., Japan and U.S. versions; Delbert H. Groberg, "Toward a Synoptic Model of Instructional Productivity," a study of missionary productivity during Groberg's years as mission president in Japan (Brigham Young University, Ph.D. dissertation, 1986); Todd S. Larkin, "The Tokyo South Mission

Miracle: Experiences and Methods," unpublished manuscript, copy in possession of the author; Terry G. Nelson, "A History of the Church of Jesus Christ of Latter-day Saints in Japan from 1948 to 1980" (Brigham Young University, master's thesis, 1986); and Masakazu Watabe, "Inner Unification and Outer Diversity," in *Proceedings of the Sixth Annual Conference of the International Society* (Provo: David M. Kennedy Center for International Studies, 1995), pp. 66–70. I am grateful for Niiyama Yasuo's help in providing articles in Japanese. Niiyama, a friend of many years, has been stake president, mission president, and Regional Representative in Japan.

8. Eugene M. Kitamura, interview by the author, Tokyo, Japan, 19 September 1995, tape recording.

9. Ibid.

10. *The Guide to the Scriptures,* English version (Salt Lake City: The Church of Jesus Christ of Latter-day Saints, 1993), p. 3.

11. This information was provided by CES administrative assistant "J" Stephen Jones, 25 October 1996.

12. James Fallows, "The World Beyond Salt Lake City: Mormons in Japan may lose the battle for converts—but they are helping to win the war for American competitiveness," *U.S. News and World Report,* 2 May 1988, p. 67.

13. Jiro Numano, "Transition in the Reception of the Mormon Church in Japan: An analysis in terms of newspaper and magazine articles," paper presented to the Mormon History Association, Park City, Utah, 20 May 1994.

14. "Saints in Kobe Rally after Quake," *Ensign* 25 (April 1995): 75. See also "Church assists victims of earthquake," *Church News,* 28 January 1995, p. 4.

15. "Church assists victims," p. 4.

16. David E. Sorensen, Rex D. Pinegar, and L. Edward Brown, "The Church in Japan, Korea, and Far-East Russia," *Ensign* 26 (November 1996): 111.

17. See Watabe, "Inner Unification and Outer Diversity," p. 68.

18. Ibid., p. 66.

19. Masakazu Watabe, "The Unspoken Words," *Ensign* 10 (December 1980): 23.

20. Kitamura interview.

21. Kiyoshi Sakai, interview by the author, Tokyo, Japan, 22 September 1995, tape recording.

22. Kan Watanabe et al., "Japan: Land of the Rising Sun," *Ensign* 5 (August 1975): 43.

23. See "Former 'closed city' visited by Elder Wirthlin," *Church News,* 7 December 1996, p. 5.

24. Mike Cannon, "Many families in Russia blessed by relief effort," *Church News,* 28 January 1995, pp. 3, 7.

25. Sorensen et al., "The Church in Japan," p. 110.

26. See "Kim Ki Yong," in Spencer J. and Shirley H. Palmer, *The Korean Saints: Personal Stories of Trial and Triumph, 1950–1980* (Provo, Utah: Religious Education, Brigham Young University, 1995), pp. 664–69.

8

KOREA

1950–1977

Pioneering in the Land of the Morning Calm

As was true in Japan following World War II, war with its miseries, sufferings, and heartaches was responsible for the introduction of Mormonism to the people of Korea. Because millions of soldiers and civilians died in the Korean conflict and untold damage and destruction ravaged the lives of the Korean people from 1950 to 1953, it is ironic that the message of the restored gospel, a message of peace, found its way into the lives of some Korean people at a time of so much woe.

The people of the Republic of (South) Korea (ROK), an anomaly created by the political ideologies of modern times, grieve for their own people who are now part of a Communist state. Although the Koreans had sought for isolation from the outside world (their country is often called the "Hermit Kingdom"), a sad fact is that the racially homogeneous Koreans, a people who share a common language and heritage, have been controlled by both the Chinese and the Japanese. The period of Japanese occupation lasted from 1910 to 1945 and is remembered as a time of national humiliation. Harsh Japanese army officers ruled with little concern for the antiquity and value of Korean culture. They imposed the Japanese language on Korean students. The bitter feelings generated during the Japanese era have waned somewhat, but they have not disappeared.

The dignified and conservative Korean people have created a unique culture and social system. Although Koreans are related racially to Chinese, Japanese, and other Mongoloid peoples, their culture, even though strongly influenced by Confucianism and Buddhism, is different from any other. Korea is not a replica of China or Japan. At the most basic level, Korean homes, foods, clothing, and language are different from those of China and Japan. The list of differences is long.

The religious history of Korea is also unique. At present, 70 to 80 percent of the people believe in Shamanism, although only about 10 percent list themselves as such. Shamanism, focusing on the power of mediums to contact spirits from the world of the dead, originated in unremembered times. Buddhism claims about one-fourth of the South Korean populace, although estimates vary between 19 and 47 percent. Confucianism, which is more a social and political philosophy than a religion, influences most Koreans, particularly in their personal interactions, family relations, and acts of protocol. Protestants and Roman Catholics constitute 27.1 percent and 6 percent of the populace, respectively—surprisingly large numbers considering that Korea is an Asian country.

Korea's first introduction to Christianity came in 1631, with a book written by a Jesuit missionary to China. About one hundred years later, a group of Korean scholars used that book and others for study and ultimately began practicing its teachings. The first Roman Catholic priest to enter Korea was astonished to find an established Catholic community of more than four thousand members. A number of noble Catholic workers taught their form of Christianity during the eighteenth and nineteenth centuries, and some died martyrs' deaths.

Protestants began proselytizing in 1832 but did not remain long. They did not obtain a permanent foothold until the 1880s. By then, however, working outside the country, they had already translated and published significant portions of the New

Testament in the Korean language. They published the entire Holy Bible in 1889.

In 1884, two years after the U.S.–Korea Treaty of 1882, Protestant workers began entering Korea, known as the "Land of the Morning Calm." Within two decades, they had converted large numbers of people. Christianity grew almost as much by word of mouth from Korean to Korean as through missionary efforts.

In 1910, however, the Japanese annexed Korea and imposed many restrictions on the people. A few Christian converts weakened under the Japanese yoke, but most became stronger and more devoted to the new religion. American missionary workers continued to serve by teaching Bible classes, opening hospitals, teaching schools, and offering other social services. Christianity continued to grow during the entire Japanese colonial period.

The Japanese may have unwittingly done Christianity a great favor in Korea. Whereas in Africa and other parts of Asia Christian missionaries were identified with colonialism, in Korea colonialism was instigated by Japan, a non-Christian, Asiatic power. "Not only were the missions not identified with colonialism," writes J. Herbert Kane, "they took their stand against it. The vast majority of the missionaries were Americans, and the United States was the only Western power that offered even token resistance to Japanese encroachments on the continent."[1] In short, the missionaries and Christianity were identified with nationalism, not colonialism.

Furthermore, as historian Stephen Neill points out, Korean Christians led the resistance movement: "In many countries the Christian, because of his association with the West, was suspect and in danger of being regarded as a second-class citizen. In Korea exactly the opposite was the case; to be a Christian was to be a patriot; the Churches were widely identified with the Korean national cause."[2]

This remained true after the Japanese annexation ended. When the Communists from North Korea invaded the south,

Christians were again identified with the war because they were persecuted by the Communists and because they were well represented in the ROK forces. Considering this, it is not surprising that American Mormon servicemen were well received by the Korean people. They were respected both as Americans and as Christians. Many of the early Korean converts to Mormonism were strongly affiliated with the Korean nationalist movement during the Japanese occupation as well as during the Korean War.

The Korean War was a terrible period. As the opposing forces fought their way back and forth, down and up the peninsula, thousands of Christian refugees fled from the north. Homeless and fearful people moved as far south as was possible. Pusan became the center for refugees. Here it was that many Koreans observed LDS servicemen as they lived lives of honor and devotion amid the generally loose circumstances of war; here some Koreans attended meetings with the servicemen and learned of the restored gospel.[3]

THE CONVERSION AND SERVICE OF KIM HO JIK

While the war continued in Korea, a man of unusual talent and prestige was attending Cornell University in New York. He was Kim Ho Jik, a high-ranking government and educational figure.[4] While at Cornell, Kim not only earned master's and doctoral degrees in nutritional science, but he also became acquainted with several Latter-day Saints who taught him the essentials of the restored gospel. He was baptized—the first native Korean to join the Church—on July 29, 1951, near the place where the Prophet Joseph was baptized in the Susquehanna River. As he came out of the baptismal waters, he reported hearing a voice saying to him, "Feed my sheep; feed my sheep." He followed this injunction until his death.

From the time he returned home to Korea in September 1951, he never hesitated to use his power or influence to benefit the

Church. Before his untimely death by a cerebral hemorrhage in 1959, he attained many high positions, including those of university president and vice-minister of education under President Syngman Rhee. Politically, he was undoubtedly the highest-ranked person the Church has had in Asia to the present.[5] A son and daughter of Brother Kim were among the first four Koreans to be baptized in their native land. This special event took place on August 3, 1952. By September 1953, more than twenty other Koreans had joined the Church in Pusan.

Between 1952 and 1955, Dr. Kim and many servicemen combined their efforts to establish the Church in Korea. Brother Kim was ordained an elder on May 17, 1953, and he was set apart as a special counselor in the Korea servicemen's group presidency at about the same time.[6] As Spencer J. Palmer, a professor of world religions at BYU has pointed out, they "attained success without the aid of any full-time missionaries or the benefit of Church literature of any kind in the native language."[7] Young men and women of quality came into the Church.

After the cease-fire brought stability to South Korea in 1953, the refugees in Pusan and the South went back to their homes farther north. The new members of the Church moved north too. Almost all members of the Pusan group, twenty-six of twenty-seven, returned to Seoul. This bombed-out city once again became the center of the government and the center of LDS Church activity.

From September until December 1953, the Korean Saints met with the servicemen's group at an air force base in Seoul. Then they had to move to the Eighth Army chapel in the Yong San area. Because of security problems (the Korean members had trouble entering the compound), the Korean Saints had to move their place of worship again. This time, however, the group leaders decided to create a Korean Sunday School, with Kim Ho Jik as superintendent. Thus in February 1954 the first truly Korean organization of the Church was created. By April more than sixty people were attending regularly.[8]

Dr. Kim Ho Jik (bottom right), who had just addressed the congregation, listens attentively while Elder Harold B. Lee of the Quorum of the Twelve speaks to LDS servicemen and Korean Saints assembled for conference at the 8th Army chapel in Seoul, 3 September 1954. Others pictured include (left to right) Chaplain Richard H. Henstrom, Northern Far East Mission president Hilton A. Robertson, Chaplain Spencer J. Palmer, and Chaplain Grant E. Mann. (Courtesy Spencer J. Palmer)

The early converts in Seoul were mostly young men, many of them students. Some of these members have since become less active, but others—among them Rhee Honam, Han In Sang, Oh Kehi, Park Jae Am, and Sister Kim Do Pil—remained faithful to the present or until death. They have served as stake presidents, mission presidents, Regional Representatives, and, in Han In Sang's case, as a General Authority of the Church. They and their families have been the foundation of the Church in Korea.[9]

In 1954 the Japanese Mission (or Far East Mission, as it was called for a short time) encompassed a vast amount of territory, including Japan, Korea, Okinawa, Guam, the Philippines, Taiwan, and Hong Kong. Although proselytizing missionaries were assigned only to Japan, servicemen's districts and groups were organized throughout the area. In Japan alone, more than fifteen hundred members of the Church were in servicemen's organizations. There were more servicemen's groups than Japanese branches.[10] Because of the heavy burden carried by the mission president in Japan, and because local people were coming into the Church in all areas, especially in Korea, the Council of the First Presidency and the Twelve assigned Elder Harold B. Lee to tour East Asia and recommend necessary changes and organizational divisions in that area. He spent almost two months, during August and September 1954, meeting with LDS servicemen, local members, and Church leaders in Asia.

Elder Lee visited with the Saints in Korea in September. As noted in chapter 5, when he returned home to Salt Lake City, he reported to the Church at large that "the signs of divinity are in the Far East. The work of the Almighty is increasing with a tremendous surge."[11] His positive report to the First Presidency and Council of the Twelve led to a similar visit to Asia the next summer by President Joseph Fielding Smith.

THE DEDICATION AND OPENING OF SOUTH KOREA TO FULL-TIME MISSIONARY WORK

In July and August 1955, President and Sister Joseph Fielding Smith visited East Asia. They were accompanied by H. Grant Heaton, who had been called to preside over the Southern Far East Mission, which was created at that time. Japan, Korea, and Okinawa were to be called the Northern Far East Mission. President Smith expressed to Robert H. Slover, LDS servicemen's coordinator, a strong desire to visit the Latter-day Saints in Korea. Because Korea was still totally under military administration, Slover arranged for President Smith to have a simulated rank of brigadier general, a move that enabled the two, along with President Hilton A. Robertson and H. Grant Heaton, to travel in Korea. President Smith flew to many places to meet with service-

Far East LDS servicemen's coordinator Col. Robert H. Slover, Northern Far East Mission president Hilton A. Robertson, Southern Far East Mission president H. Grant Heaton, and Korean LDS servicemen's supervisor Rodney W. Fye are shown here with President Joseph Fielding Smith (center) on their arrival at Kimpo Air Base in Seoul, Korea. On this visit President Smith dedicated Korea for the preaching of the gospel, 2 August 1955. (Courtesy LDS Church Archives)

men. In the process he also became acquainted with a number of local converts.

On the morning of August 2, 1955, President Smith told Robertson, Slover, and Heaton that he believed it was time to dedicate the land of Korea for the preaching of the restored gospel. These four men, together with Kim Ho Jik and three other servicemen, climbed a hill (behind what is now the national capitol building) overlooking the war-torn city of Seoul, and President Smith offered the prayer that turned the key to the preaching of the restored gospel in Korea. Korea servicemen's supervisor Rodney W. Fye, who was present, reported that "President Smith literally commanded Satan to free the land from his chains that it might become choice through the preaching of the gospel of Jesus Christ." President Smith further blessed the Korean members that they could prepare well for leadership responsibilities in the future. He also promised that stability would return to the country.[12] An interesting sidelight is that the first area conference in Korea (1975) was held in a large arena and activity center that was built at the bottom of the hill where the dedicatory prayer was said.

The Church was not then recognized by the government, and no official ecclesiastical organization had yet been created among the local Saints. On the day of dedication, however, President Smith set Kim Ho Jik apart as president of the Korean District of the Northern Far East Mission. He also suggested that the servicemen's district and the local Saints should be separated in preparation for the coming of full-time missionaries. Under Smith's direction, branches were organized in Seoul and Pusan. At the time of the dedication, there were sixty Korean members of the Church.

In December 1955 Paul C. Andrus, one of the first postwar missionaries in Japan, began his six-plus years as mission president over the Northern Far East Mission. Only two or three weeks passed after his arrival in Japan before he went to Korea to investigate the possibility of assigning full-time missionaries there. Dr. Kim, the local Saints, and the leaders of the LDS servicemen were strongly in favor of this idea. But several problems had to be solved before missionaries could come: obtaining the government's legal recognition of the Church, arranging for housing for the elders, and acquiring visas to enter the country. Dr. Kim helped President Andrus organize a religious corporation, leased a house, and demanded of bureaucrats that the missionary visas be approved. Without his influence, much more time would have passed before the Church could have sent missionaries to Korea.[13]

Two elders, Richard L. Detton and Don G. Powell, arrived in Korea in April 1956. During the following summer, they were joined by six other missionaries, and four of them moved to

President Paul C. Andrus of the Northern Far East Mission (center of back row) stands with the earliest elders assigned to proselytize in Korea. Back row, left to right: Gail E. Carr (who later served as the first mission president in Korea); Don G. Powell and Richard Detton (on both sides of Andrus), who were the first missionary companionship to serve in Korea; and Larry Orme. Front row: Newell E. Kimball, Clyde W. Newman, Karl C. Fletcher, and Dean M. Anderson. (Courtesy Spencer J. Palmer)

Pusan. Although the Korean Saints and the LDS servicemen did their best to make the missionaries' lives pleasant, conditions were difficult for them during the first few years. Korea was in a period of reconstruction. Food, clothing, building materials, and other supplies were hard to obtain, and health conditions were poor. During the summer of 1958, five of the ten elders in Korea were stricken with hepatitis, but they insisted that the missionary cause was worth the sacrifice and continued on.

Possibly more serious than health and housing problems was the difficulty of the language. Aside from the help that Brother Kim and other Korean Saints gave them, the missionaries were on their own in learning Korean, one of the world's most difficult tongues. They had no translated materials such as tracts, the Book of Mormon, and hymnbooks for more than a year after full-time missionary work began. Dr. Kim translated the Articles of Faith and the sacrament prayers, but communicating with nonmember

Koreans proved to be a strenuous task for the missionaries. Finally, in September 1957 the first missionary pamphlets printed in Korean came off the press. These seven new tracts and pamphlets replaced materials in the Japanese language. (One wonders how the elders convinced anyone that they should read the Japanese materials, considering the general feeling of animosity the Koreans held toward the Japanese.) Some of these anonymous translations were still in use in the late 1970s.

In spite of harsh living conditions and language difficulties, the Korean District of the Northern Far East Mission produced remarkable results. "In Korea," commented President Andrus, "we were getting about eighteen converts per missionary per year. If Korea had been a separate mission at that time they would have had the highest rate of conversion of any mission in the world."[14] This high rate of baptisms continued until about 1964 and then tapered off. By 1962, when Korea became an independent mission, there were more than sixteen hundred Korean Latter-day Saints.

A somewhat surprising fact, considering LDS missionary experience in other parts of the world, was that the vast majority, perhaps four out of five of those baptized, were male. In the late 1970s the conversion ratio was still 55 percent male to 45 percent female. During the early years, this anomaly could be explained on the basis of contacts between servicemen and young Korean men. But in the decades following the mid-1950s, the best explanation for this trend was the fact that society in Korea is male-oriented. As Robert H. Slover said, "You have to reach the men before you reach the women."[15] For this reason, it was mission policy to work with males rather than females.

Compared with other non-Christian areas of Asia, Korea was a land where the restored gospel was well accepted. The Latter-day Saints reaped the benefits accrued by other Christian missions. In addition, however, were several other reasons for LDS success. The Korean people, because of the influence of Confucianism, have maintained some of the best genealogies of any people in the world. Mormon doctrines concerning the eternal nature of the family, and especially concerning temple work, have had much appeal to Korean Saints. Education, too, is highly important to the Korean people. They prize education for its civilizing effects and also because of the obvious benefits it can bring financially.[16] But Korean members of the Church carry even further the importance of learning. They take literally the scriptural statement "It is impossible for a man to be saved in ignorance" (D&C 131:6).

Elder Han In Sang, who served as a member of the Second Quorum of the Seventy in the 1990s, suggests that Mormonism appeals to Koreans because of similarities between it and popular Korean beliefs. He feels that Mormonism is "the native" church. How far this should be carried is uncertain, but there is evidence that some popular Korean ideas about God correlate well with Mormon beliefs.[17]

Another reason for LDS success in Korea during the 1950s and early 1960s was the social, economic, and political situation in Korea during those years. Millions of people were displaced by the war. Families were disrupted, and some old norms were cast aside. Undoubtedly, in Korea as in Japan many people found themselves looking for new answers to the age-old problems of loneliness, sickness, old age, suffering, and death. LDS doctrines provided answers to the questions.

After about 1965, however, the ratio of baptisms per missionary per year began to drop. As the economy improved and misery became a distant memory, so did Korean interest in religion wane. Nevertheless, with the exception of the Philippines, a Christian nation, Korea has remained the Church's most fruitful Asian missionary field.

THE ESTABLISHMENT OF THE KOREAN MISSION

During the summer of 1962, President Andrus completed nearly seven years of service as mission president. At the time of his release, the First Presidency divided the mission and created the Korean Mission. They called Gail E. Carr, who had served as a missionary in Korea from 1956 to 1959, as mission president. He, along with his young wife, Gwyneth, and their new baby, arrived in Korea in July, and the new mission was created on the eighth. There were 1,603 Korean members, five branches, and nineteen missionaries at that time.

Obviously the Church in Korea was far more advanced than many new missions are at the time of their creation. For instance, the branches were almost entirely in the hands of local Saints. Even so, President and Sister Carr had many hardships to overcome and many problems to solve. The first was to find a mission office and a place to live. They stayed in a hotel for more than two months while President Carr searched for suitable real estate. He had one major disappointment when the seller of a fine piece of property in the Anam-dong area tried to impose some illegal stipulations in the final contract. Carr refused to deal on this basis, and the transaction fell through.

Before long, however, President Carr found another piece of property that was far better than the first, and by mid-October 1962, the mission was in its new headquarters. This property, called Paegun-jang, was situated in the Ch'ŏngun area, an excellent part of the city, only ten minutes from the heart of the business district and major government offices. The old original buildings were gradually razed, and in their place rose over time a mission home and office, a chapel, a translation and distribution building, and a missionary dormitory. The entire complex was an attractive credit to the Church.

In addition to the headquarters complex, President Carr also purchased land for chapels in Seoul, Pusan, and Taegu. In combination with Church construction supervisors Rex A. Cheney and Kenneth Roos, Carr had work well under way toward completion on one of the first LDS chapels on the Asian continent, the Seoul East Branch.[18]

During Carr's presidency, he organized two new branches, one of which was in Taegu, Korea's third-largest city. He also encouraged translation work. In 1963 the mission published a hymnal with 130 hymns, most of which were translated by a former Protestant seminary student, Chung Tai Pan. At about the same time, President Carr assigned Chung to translate the Book of Mormon. Later, Elder Bruce K. Grant and Elder Ronald K. Nielsen helped with the project, but these men did not complete the book. In 1964 President Carr assigned Han In Sang, the first Korean called to serve full-time in the new mission,[19] to revise the completed portions of the translation and to complete the work. Han reworked most of it and concluded his draft after his release in February 1966. The Book of Mormon in Korean was published in Seoul in March 1967, after Carr's release. During Carr's time, he also supervised the introduction of a new language study program.

Sister Carr, under priesthood direction, organized the first women's Relief Society in Korea. Initially, the sisters met together to discuss homemaking issues, but before long Kim Jung Sook, daughter of Kim Ho Jik, translated each lesson from English and taught them to the Korean sisters.[20]

Years later, Han In Sang paid the following tribute to his own mission president. He wrote:

"President Carr . . . was a man like John the Baptist in the wilderness. He was not a fancy man, but he was a real Christian. He was dynamic and hot-tempered. He made things happen. He suffered through tough living conditions. He was a great man who laid the early foundations of the Church in Korea. He exercised leadership in the purchase of initial properties at Yurak-ton, Samch'ŏng-dong, Ch'ongun-dong, and elsewhere. He was instrumental in establishing the first branches of the Church in Seoul, Taegu, and Pusan."[21]

When President Carr completed his mission in July 1965, the foundations of the Church in Korea had been suitably laid. The Church was a legal religious corporation, missionaries were in the country, the Church had acquired property, local Saints administered most organizations, and translation work was well under way.

Beginning in 1965, the Church in Korea entered a period of maturation and naturalization. Between then and March 1973, when the Seoul Stake was organized, the three mission presidents, the local leaders, and the missionaries did much to solidify and strengthen local organizations and to improve the public image of the Church.

In a land where education and academic accomplishment mean much, it was of great benefit to the progress of the Church that the three mission presidents after President Carr each had strong academic backgrounds. Spencer J. Palmer, who became mission president in August 1965, held a Ph.D. in history, with emphasis on Korean studies and world religions, from the University of California at Berkeley. Robert H. Slover, who took over the mission in the summer of 1968, held a Ph.D. in political science from Harvard University. Both men were on the faculty at Brigham Young University when they received their calls. L. Edward Brown, who became president in 1971 and who now serves in the Second Quorum of the Seventy, held an Ed.D. in educational administration and supervision from the University of Kansas and had served for a number of years as an LDS institute of religion teacher at Idaho State University. Palmer and Slover had both served in the military in Korea during the early 1950s, when the Church was newly established there. President Palmer was a chaplain; President Slover was an army officer and servicemen's coordinator for the Church. President Brown had been one of the early missionaries in Korea from 1957 until 1960.[22]

Each of these three mission presidents had their areas of strength. President Palmer emphasized public relations and interactions with people who had scholarly and political influence. Through his participation in the Korean Branch of the Royal Asiatic Society, he did much to enhance the image of the Church. He also hosted numerous social gatherings at the mission home in which government and academic leaders, as well as diplomatic officials from other countries, learned something of the goals, principles, and aspirations of the Church in Korea.

President Palmer also initiated contacts with the major radio

Elder Richard L. Evans of the Quorum of the Twelve Apostles visits Korea in 1965 as part of his around-the-world tour as president of Rotary Clubs International. He is shown here with district presidents (left to right) Song Jung Sup, Han In Sang, and Cha Jong Whan. Mission president Spencer J. Palmer completes the group.

and television stations and with the Korean press. Through personal appearances, interviews, missionary choir performances (especially around Christmastime), and weekly broadcasts of the Mormon Tabernacle Choir program with translations of Richard L. Evans's "Spoken Word" (begun in May 1968), the name of the Church became well known throughout the peninsula. After President Palmer left Korea, President Slover continued many of the public relations efforts, especially the Christmas broadcasts. In addition, he also gave many speeches to civic and social groups. President Slover also strengthened organizational and administrative aspects of the mission and the local Church structure, thus paving the way for the later creation of stakes and wards. From two districts he created four. He also supervised the growth of the number of missionaries from 75 to approximately 125.

Presidents Palmer, Slover, and Brown shared a concern for "naturalizing" the Church. They were uncomfortable about the Church's transplanted American tone and wanted to make it seem more truly Korean. This was a difficult task, but they did do much to help the local people learn how to lead their fellow members.

Expected goals for all mission presidents are to expand the faith through proselytizing and to establish new units of the Church wherever possible. During the Palmer years, the number of baptisms sagged below the level of the previous ten years. As mentioned, one probable cause for this drop was the growing Korean affluence of the mid-1960s. Another reason was the change in emphasis in the proselytizing procedure. President Palmer asked the missionaries to "seek out heads of families, older investigators, and friends of the Church." As a result, the average age of new converts rose by more than five years between 1965 and 1968. Before that time, the Church had some of the appearance of a youth movement. Now, as families came into the Church, it took on the feeling of a solid organization.[23] This solidity came, nevertheless, at the expense of a lower baptismal rate. During Carr's presidency the missionaries averaged 8.85 baptisms per missionary per year, but during the next three years the average dropped to 4.55 baptisms per missionary per year. Between 1968 and 1970, the average number of baptisms rose to 5.64, and in 1971 the number of baptisms per missionary rose to 8.5.

One reason that the number of baptisms began to increase in 1969 was the creation that year of the Language Training Mission at the Church College of Hawaii (the name changed to Brigham Young University—Hawaii Campus in 1974). This facility, which was established for the purpose of giving new missionaries training in languages, helped the incoming elders and sisters to enter Korea with the advantage of some language ability. Before that time, new missionaries had learned the Korean language from their companions in Korea. Another reason for increased success was President Slover's determination to organize the missionaries along standard lines, with missionary areas, districts, and zones. This procedure enhanced the quality of proselytizing because the elders were better trained, better supervised, and more highly motivated than before. President Slover also devoted much time to the improvement of missionary housing. "I found them [the elders] in very poor housing," recalled Slover, "very poor sanitary conditions."[24] He insisted, after nearly losing some missionaries to carbon monoxide asphyxiation, that all elders had to sleep in beds and not on the floor as Koreans do. Better organization and living conditions helped the missionaries to improve yearly.

Palmer, Slover, and Brown all pushed expansion into new areas. This was made possible by a steadily rising number of missionaries. Whereas President Carr had an average of thirty-five missionaries under him, by the end of President Brown's mission the number had risen to about 180. The additional missionaries were used to open new cities and towns during the Palmer-Slover years and to help advise local branch leaders. By 1968 the Church was established in every provincial capital and in all major cities throughout South Korea. President Brown, however, believed that concentrating the missionaries in the major cities and building larger, stronger branches and wards was wiser than sending elders to smaller towns where only weak branches could be organized.

The mission presidents made a conscious effort to call Korean men and women to leadership positions. President Palmer, for example, called Koreans to serve as counselors in the mission presidency and to lead the two districts and seven branches that existed in 1966. These Korean leaders were, according to Elder Gordon B. Hinckley, "men and women of genuine ability."[25] President Slover and President Brown further emphasized the move to use only Koreans in leadership positions. By mid-1970 President Slover had divided the two districts into four. During Brown's time, a stake was organized in Seoul.

THE TRANSLATION AND PUBLICATION PROGRAM

One of the most important ingredients in "Koreanizing" the Church was the production of language materials. The Book of Mormon, published in 1967, was by no means the only publication project during this era. Also of significance was the translation of the Doctrine and Covenants and the Pearl of Great Price. In March 1966 President Palmer called Chung Tai Pan, president of Shinch'un Branch, to retranslate a 1961 version that had been done by Hong Byung Sik. Because part of the old manuscript had been lost, Brother Chung had to start almost from the beginning. Although it required only six months for Brother Chung to do his initial work, it took until August 1968 for the manuscript to pass through revisions, editing, proofreading, and finally printing and binding. President Slover, who had just commenced his mission, presented one of the first copies of the Doctrine and Covenants to Elder Ezra Taft Benson on his first tour of the Korean Mission.

By the time the Doctrine and Covenants was published, the Church had created the Translation Services Department in Korea. Han In Sang, one of the translators of the Book of Mormon, was hired in 1967 to act as head of the new department. During the first four or five years of the department's existence, its mission was confined to translation and printing work. Later its purposes and responsibilities were expanded to handling and distributing many kinds of Church materials. Under Elder Han's coordination, but with the direction of the mission presidents, the Translation Services Department began producing manuals for auxiliary class work, a Relief Society magazine with all lessons translated into Korean, and a unified Church magazine, *Sung Do We Bot* (the *Saints' Friend*). In December 1970 the first complete translation of the family home evening manual came off the press in time for distribution to the members at Christmas. The publication of the standard works of the Church in Korean, along with the magazines and manuals, did much to strengthen the local members and to help the Church become a Korean institution.[26]

Koreans love music. When the small paperback songbook wore out during President Slover's era, he asked the Church Music Committee for permission to publish the full hymnal in Korean. Although the committee was not in favor of this suggestion, believing that the smaller book was adequate, Slover persisted and finally gained permission to publish the entire book. An impressive hymnal is of unusual importance in Korea. This is underscored by the fact that investigators often ask LDS missionaries to see the Church's hymnbook.

CHURCH CONSTRUCTION AND HOUSING

The extreme density of population in Korea has created high land values. As in Japan and Hong Kong, the Church has had great difficulty acquiring property in Korea. While he was a missionary district president, L. Edward Brown, after considerable difficulty, acquired the land on which the first chapels in Seoul and Pusan were built. President Carr acquired the mission compound land and several other properties. Presidents Palmer, Slover, and Brown each bought some property and supervised, under the direction of Church construction personnel, the building of several significant structures. Although the first four mission presidents worked regularly on the problem of construction, they had so many other responsibilities—and the Church's Korean real estate purchases sometimes took so long to complete—that fewer buildings were constructed than any of the presidents would have liked.

Throughout the years since the creation of the mission, money had been in short supply. Until 1971, only one Korean member of the Church, Dr. Kim Chang Sun, owned an automobile. Had it not been for the generosity of the LDS servicemen, the early chapels could not have been constructed. The servicemen contributed most of the local share required by the Church to undertake a building project. Only following the creation of the Seoul Stake in 1973 did the building program really come to life. All of the wards in the original Seoul Stake had separate, Church-constructed chapels by 1979. Additional buildings have been added almost continuously since. Although money was more readily available later on than in the early 1970s, the servicemen continued their contributions until the program was changed and headquarters paid for all construction costs.

Two or three buildings were unique when they were constructed. The mission home, although rather simple by the standards of many parts of the world, was constructed at a time (1966) when Korea was just getting back on its feet economically after the Korean War. In an effort to show the Church's loyalty to the Korean people and local industry, President Palmer insisted that to the extent possible every part of the mission home be made in Korea. This included carpets, attractive wall cover-

Seoul 4th Ward was among the first LDS chapels to be constructed on the Asian mainland.

ings, chandeliers (after a government official saw them and learned they were made in Korea, he had the same company man-ufacture some chandeliers for the Blue House, the Korean equiv-alent of the U.S. White House), furniture, draperies, roof tiles, and so forth.

President Palmer bought a property in Shinch'un (in Seoul) that he envisioned would one day be the site of Korea's first temple. It is situated on a hill overlooking Ehwa, Yonsei, and Sŏgang Universities to the south, east, and west and the Kimpo International Airport expressway to the north. It was like owning land overlooking Harvard, Yale, and Stanford Universities.[27] In 1975 and 1976 the Church Educational System constructed an LDS institute of religion building there, the first outside North America. And in 1985 the Church dedicated the Seoul Korea Temple there, a story that will be told in chapter nine. On the same property stood a modern chapel and missionary quarters. Between the time this land was bought and when the Church decided to build on it, a number of serious difficulties arose concerning the legality of the original contracts and regarding the property taxes on the land. The mission financial man, Koo Jung Shik, worked almost around-the-clock to resolve these problems. Through his efforts and the blessings of the Lord, the government capitulated to the Church's position and the buildings were constructed.[28]

Related to construction was the problem of missionary housing. Since the early days, the missionaries had lived in leased homes and generally had hired cooks and houseboys. This was a workable arrangement while the mission staff was small, but when the numbers grew to almost two hundred, the cost of leases mounted to close to five hundred thousand dollars and the problems of hiring and dismissing numerous domestic helpers became enormous. The financial involvement was so large because in the late 1960s and 1970s Korean landlords required between two and five thousand dollars for deposit. This *chŏnse*, or "key money," was invested by the landlord at a high rate of interest, then returned to the lessee (in this case the Church) when the lease expired. The landlord keeps the profits from the investment. This system was so complex that President Slover had a legal adviser, Brother Koo Jung Shik, on his mission staff full-time to handle lease arrangements. To reduce these problems, President Brown asked the missionaries to move in with families, eat at their tables, and rely on the woman of the house to do the necessary cleaning. Because of housing shortages, this would have been impossible earlier. This procedure reduced both costs and administrative difficulties for the mission.

TEMPLE EXCURSIONS TO HAWAII

For many of the Saints in the United States and other parts of the world, going to the temple is a relatively easy matter. But in Korea at that time, the late 1960s, going to the temple was fraught with difficulties. The matter of personal worthiness seems almost insignificant in comparison with the other walls that had to be scaled. More than a year of planning and preparation was required to get the first temple group ready. President Slover conducted a series of temple preparation seminars to help with personal preparation. The Korean Missionary Association, under Spencer Palmer at BYU, raised enough money to pay two-thirds of each participant's transportation costs. Great efforts were expended by Brother Palmer to have the temple ceremony translated into Korean. A basic translation was completed, and a group of Koreans were invited to the Los Angeles Temple to record the sacred script. Brother Hong Byung Sik flew to Hawaii with the tape recording in time to meet the group coming from Korea.[29] But the biggest obstacle was the Korean government. Immigration department policy did not allow couples to leave the country except in extremely unusual circumstances. For more than a year, President Slover and the Church legal advisor, Brother Koo, met with virtually everyone with any influence to beg for permission for the six temple-bound couples to leave the country. Finally, the restrictive policy was relaxed, and the couples flew to Hawaii on July 31, 1970. About a year later, shortly after President Brown arrived, a second group was allowed to go. To get a third group out of Korea, President Brown agreed to stop applying for passports. Only years later was the policy finally changed.

The six original temple couples were Brothers and Sisters Koo Jung Shik, Cha Jong Hwan, Choi Wook Hwan, Bae Young Chun, Kim Chang Sun, and Ho Choi. The six men were either branch presidents or district presidents. Doctor Kim and Brother Choi later served as stake presidents in Seoul; the others have been bishops, high councilors, or members of mission presidencies or mission presidents.[30]

THE FOUNDING OF THE SEMINARY
AND INSTITUTE PROGRAMS IN KOREA

The organization of the seminary and institute of religion programs in Korea is one of the grand successes of the Church in recent years. The idea of starting these programs was first brought to

President Slover by Dr. Joe J. Christensen, Associate Commissioner of Education for Seminaries and Institutes, in March 1971.[31] Even before President L. Edward Brown left the U.S. to take over the mission, Dr. Christensen contacted him concerning the proposed program. Once in Korea, President Brown pursued the concept and worked with CES officials to implement the program.

The initial CES plan was to send a returned missionary—one who had served his mission in Korea—to Korea to start the program. Brown objected to this proposal, contending that some Korean priesthood holders were capable of handling the program from the beginning. Because President Brown had had experience in the institute system, he felt confident that he could help the first local director administer the program as the CES head office desired. The leaders in Salt Lake City were not easily convinced but finally decided that Koreans should be able to do the job. Korea was a test case. Since then, most non-American institutes and seminaries have been placed in the hands of local administrators and teachers.

President Brown recommended Rhee Honam as institute director. Brother Rhee, who had joined the Church in the mid-1950s through the influence of his "Mormon buddies during the war" and who had by this time served as counselor to four mission presidents, was now a professor of English and Spanish at a university in Seoul. As President Brown said, "For Brother Rhee to resign his position was almost as difficult as Abraham taking Isaac to the mountain."[32] Because communications were slow between Seoul and Salt Lake City, Brother Rhee was not sure for some time whether or not he had a job with CES. Brown, seeing that something had to be done, assumed the CES leaders were going to move ahead with Rhee, and he opened an office at the mission home and gave Rhee a budget to run on. It all worked out well.

Brother Rhee hired Dr. Seo Hee Chul, Ph.D., who had been working for Church Translation and Distribution, as a teacher in Seoul. Years later Brother Seo described the development of the early team of institute teachers:

Brother Rhee Honam was called as the first area director of CES. I and Brother Kim Chong Gyun worked with him. Six months later Brother Pak Byung Kyu began lecturing in Kwangju, and another year and a half later Brother Do Gil Whoe in Pusan and Brother Kim Cha Bong in Seoul joined the staff and served diligently. At first there were 350 students and, in addition, over 500 students were enrolled in the seminary program which opened in each area. At first, because there weren't many people teaching, one would have to teach in Seoul during the day, then in the afternoon go to Inch'ŏn, Ch'unch'ŏn, Taejŏn, Kunsan, Chŏnju, or another outlying town, and teach a class, returning to Seoul around 1:00 or 2:00 A.M. and, if later, often staying the night and returning the next morning.[33]

In the beginning President Brown and Brother Rhee leased four rooms in a fine downtown building for classrooms. Both the students and teachers were happy to be associated with the "Mormon Institute." It was a prestigious institution from the start. In 1978 there were 1,504 regular and 112 individual-study students registered in classes in various cities of Korea. In addition to the institute students, 1,068 home-study seminary students were also enrolled in the program.[34]

Although institute classes are important to most young Latter-day Saints who enroll in the United States and elsewhere, many Koreans take their religion courses extremely seriously. For example, when the first institute graduation was held in Seoul in the mid-1970s, the valedictorian was Min Tong-Keun, a member who already held a Ph.D. and who was teaching philosophy at Ch'ungnam National University. Brother Min placed attendance at institute classes above all other priorities. His dedication to learning the gospel was not unlike many other Koreans.[35]

THE CREATION OF THE SEOUL STAKE

Whereas public relations were Spencer J. Palmer's greatest strength, and organization and administration were Robert H.

Slover's major contributions, L. Edward Brown emphasized family love within the priesthood framework. President Brown and his wife, Carol, worked tirelessly teaching the importance of family home evening, home teaching, priesthood executive committee meetings, and branch council meetings. He constantly taught the reasons for these programs and meetings and how they were supposed to function.

Brown, like his predecessors, was determined to make the Church a natural part of the Korean Saints' lives. However, he saw his purposes somewhat differently. He viewed the gospel as a third culture—a culture different from that of either America or Korea. He recognized the strength of the Korean family tradition but worked to re-create it along the love-centered lines of the gospel. Perceiving that Korean males, and especially husbands and fathers, tend to be quite dictatorial, President Brown taught the meaning of equal love and respect.

Sister Brown, too, taught the principle of love. The story is told of how she traveled from conference to conference with her husband, preaching at each meeting that Mormon husbands should tell their wives at least once a week that they love them. Doing such a thing would have been highly unusual for a Korean husband. Sister Brown's translator for each of her talks was President Park Jae Am, a counselor in the mission presidency. After hearing Sister Brown's admonition six times, he decided he would follow her counsel. On a beautiful spring day when the rice was coming up and the air was clean and fresh, Brother Park decided, as he walked home from work, that this was the day he would tell his wife he loved her. As he approached his house, Sister Park slid open the door and greeted him warmly. He tried to say the words but couldn't. Finally he said, "When I look at you, you remind me of spring." Needless to say, he startled her and moved her deeply. The next year he recounted this experience as he spoke at each conference.

In the Korean-Confucian order, not only are females considered inferior to males, but also, depending on education and wealth, males are stratified. An example of how one leader learned the Christian concept of God's equal love for his children occurred when President Brown suggested to district president Kim Chang Sun that a chapel custodian should be called as branch president. President Kim, a highly respected psychiatrist and professor of medicine, balked at the suggestion, reluctant because the candidate was only a custodian. President Brown suggested to Kim that they pray together about the matter. After their prayer, President Kim told President Brown that he knew the Lord wanted the custodian to be branch president. This experience had a remarkable impact on President Kim. President Kim became a powerful leader in the Church. He served as president of Seoul Korea West Stake, and the custodian served as stake patriarch. In the years that followed, Kim Chang Sun also served as a Regional Representative.[36]

Another concept that the Korean Saints have had to learn—a concept that troubles people everywhere—is the idea that all positions in the Church are important and that, in theory at least, one position is not superior to another. This problem is exaggerated in Korea by the concept of losing face. During the early years of the Church in Korea, it was sometimes the case for district and branch presidents to become less active when they were released and given less "prestigious" callings. President Slover said that he knew the Korean Saints were reaching maturity when after the release of Bae Soo Yul as district president, he remained strong in the faith even though he became "only" a Sunday School teacher. Brother Bae later served as a counselor in the Korea Pusan Mission.[37]

Perhaps even more important than making the Church a Korean institution was the molding of the Korean leaders into true Latter-day Saints. When this happened, Korea was ready for its first stake.

Stakehood was first seriously talked about in Korea during Robert H. Slover's brief return to Korea as Regional Representative in the area during 1972. He established a target date of 1974 for the organization of the Seoul Stake. Although President Brown

Seoul Stake, the first stake in Korea, was organized by Elder Spencer W. Kimball of the Quorum of the Twelve, 8 March 1973. Members of the stake presidency were (left to right) Kim Chang Sun, first counselor; Rhee Honam, president; and Choi Wook Hwan, second counselor. (Courtesy Rhee Honam)

was working steadily on matters of organization and administration, he did not know the stake would be created so soon. Nevertheless, in February 1973 President Brown received word from Church authorities in Salt Lake City that Elder Spencer W. Kimball, President of the Council of the Twelve, would be coming to Korea in early March to organize the stake.

After President Kimball interviewed a list of candidates, he selected Rhee Honam as stake president. The Seoul Stake was created on March 8, 1973. President Rhee, who had served as counselor to four mission presidents and who was seminary and institute director for Korea, chose Kim Chang Sun, a doctor of psychiatry, and Choi Wook Hwan, a dentist, as counselors. The new stake consisted of seven wards and two branches. Because of his years of apprenticeship under excellent leaders and because he knew the gospel well, President Rhee led the stake with vision, authority, and love.

THE ORGANIZATION OF
THE KOREA PUSAN MISSION

Korea is small geographically, but the population in the mid-1970s was approximately 33 million people. Because the Church was growing rapidly, the Church Missionary Committee sent increasing numbers of elders and sisters (lady missionaries first came to Korea in 1972, an indication that health conditions had improved greatly) to Korea during Brown's time and continued to do so after Eugene P. Till became president in July 1974. In April 1973 President Brown received notice that the mission was going to be divided. But because of visa problems (the Korean consulate in San Francisco refused to allow thirty visas at once) the plan to divide was suspended until the problems with the government could be worked out. The actual basis for the visa slowdown has never become known, but President Till assumed it was because of anti-government statements by members of other Christian churches at that time. He believed the LDS Church was lumped together with other Christians who were outspoken in their criticism of government.

Whatever the cause, President Till chose to counter the visa problem by using several public relations approaches to establish the image of the LDS Church as a family church, a concept that he rightly supposed would appeal to the government. He did this through the use of bumper stickers, a new device in Korea, and through performances by a missionary quintet, the New Horizons, and a choir of orphan girls, the Tender Apples. These singing groups performed frequently on radio and television and did much to enhance the image of the Church and to make the name of the Church familiar to the Korean people. (There is much more to the story of the Tender Apples Orphanage. It was owned and operated by Hwang Keun-Ok, a devout Latter-day Saint. Her story reveals a life of selfless service to Korea's poor, as well as to the orphans who lived with her and learned about the gospel and how to live useful, productive lives.)[38] After Till's public relations campaign of 1974–75, he had no more visa problems. Evidently personnel changes at the consulate in San Francisco also helped the Church get along better with the people there.[39] When President Till began his period of service, he found that about 10 percent of the people in Seoul recognized the name of the Church. At the end of his three years in Korea, "more than 70 percent of the people in Seoul recognized the Church's name."[40]

In the spring of 1975, the First Presidency called Han In Sang to be the first president of the soon-to-be-created Korea Pusan Mission. President Han was the first native Korean to serve as a mission president. On July 1, 1975, President Han officially opened the new mission. Under his leadership the districts and branches grew, and the missionaries brought many people into the Church. In the summer of 1978, President Han was succeeded by Rhee Honam.

GENERAL AUTHORITY SUPERVISION AND THE FIRST AREA CONFERENCE

Since Elder Harold B. Lee's 1954 visit to Korea, the General Authorities carefully watched over and supervised the progress of the Church there. During the 1960s and 1970s many General Authorities visited Korea, among them President Ezra Taft Benson, Elder Bruce R. McConkie, Elder Marion D. Hanks, and Elder Adney Y. Komatsu. But the man who was known as "Mr. Asia" to the people and friends of the Asian missions was Elder Gordon B. Hinckley. After his appointment as supervisor of the Asian missions in 1960, a position he held until the late 1960s and again in the 1970s, he never lost interest in or concern for the Asian Saints. Korea received parentlike attention from this great leader. Elder Hinckley visited Korea numerous times during those two decades and every leader in the country felt his personal concern.

Of great significance to the Korean Saints was the first area conference, held in Seoul on August 15 through August 17, 1975. Ko Won Yong, executive secretary in Seoul Stake, was assigned to organize the performance events to be held on Friday, August 15, in the Changch'ung Gymnasium. A thousand members participated in a

President Spencer W. Kimball was the first president of the Church to visit Korea. In August 1975, more than nine thousand members participated in the first Korean area conference. (Courtesy LDS Church Archives)

two-hour performance. According to Brother Ko, the program included a traditional Korean fan dance, a farmers' dance, and others.[41] The nine thousand people who attended the cultural program and other sessions were well taught by the thirteen General Authorities of the Church who were there. In one of his talks, President Spencer W. Kimball announced plans to build the Tokyo Temple. He had already revealed these plans while in Japan a week before, but his request for the Korean Saints to raise money to help build it met with mixed reactions. The reason for hesitation was the Korean government's policy of not allowing married couples to leave the country together. The question of their ever being able to go to the temple as husbands and wives coursed through many Korean minds. Knowing of the government's policy, however, President Kimball promised the Saints that if they would send their children on missions, pay their tithes, attend their meetings regularly, keep the commandments of the Lord, and contribute to the temple fund, the Lord would provide a way for them to go to the temple when it was completed. According to President Till, many Korean Saints talked about this promise and determined to follow President Kimball's counsel. In the summer of 1977 Park Chung-Hee, president of the Republic of Korea, announced that in 1980 Korea would open its doors and allow its people to leave as tourists. As a matter of course, couples would be allowed to leave the country together. Significantly, the Tokyo Temple, which was started in April 1978, was scheduled for completion in May 1980.[42]

According to Brother Park Byung Kyu, who was in attendance, on the final day of the area conference President Kimball stood at the door of Changch'ung Gymnasium and warmly greeted the audience members as they arrived. He shook hands until moments before the session was scheduled to begin. Such acts permanently endeared President Kimball to the Korean Saints.[43]

NOTES

1. J. Herbert Kane, *A Global View of Christian Missions*, rev. ed. (Grand Rapids, Mich.: Baker Book House, 1975), p. 268.

2. Stephen Neill, *Colonialism and Christian Missions* (New York: McGraw-Hill, 1966), p. 219.

3. Much of the research for this section, which covers the years 1951–61, was done by David K. Crook.

4. See Denny Roy, "Kim Ho Jik: Korean Pioneer," *Ensign* 18 (July 1988): 18–23. This article was reprinted in *Tambuli* 12 (February 1989): 8–13.

5. See Spencer J. Palmer, *The Church Encounters Asia* (Salt Lake City: Deseret Book Co., 1970), pp. 95–96; and Paul C. Andrus Oral History, interview by the author, Honolulu, Hawaii, Oral History Program, LDS Church Archives, typescript, pp. 15–16.

6. See Calvin R. Beck, "History of the Seoul LDS Group, August 1953 to May 1954," LDS Church Archives, typescript. See also Spencer J. Palmer and Shirley H. Palmer, eds, *The Korean Saints: Personal Stories of Trial and Triumph, 1950–1980* (Provo, Utah: Religious Education, Brigham Young University, 1995), pp. 23–25.

7. Palmer, *The Church Encounters Asia*, p. 93.

8. Beck, "History of the Seoul LDS Group."

9. Brief versions of Han's and Rhee's conversion stories are printed in *Ensign* 5 (August 1975): 44–50. See also "Han In Sang" and "Rhee Ho Nam" in Palmer and Palmer, *Korean Saints*, pp. 89–98, 184–89; and Robert H. Slover Oral History, interview by author, Provo, Utah, 1976, James Moyle Oral History Program, LDS Church Archives, typescript, pp. 5–6.

10. See Andrus Oral History, p. 14.

11. Harold B. Lee, as quoted in "Miraculous Power of Divine Intervention Present in Orient," *Church News*, 9 October 1954, p. 8.

12. See Palmer, *The Church Encounters Asia*, p. 100; Slover Oral History, pp. 7–8.

13. Andrus Oral History, pp. 15–16.

14. Ibid., p. 18.

15. Slover Oral History, p. 14.

16. In Shirley and Spencer Palmer's book *Korean Saints*, it is clear in biography after biography that Confucian respect for parents and tremendous respect for education are among the highest values of the Korean members of the Church.

17. See In Sang Han, "Encounter: The Korean Mind and the Gospel," *Ensign* 5 (August 1975): 47.

18. See Korean Mission Historical Reports, LDS Church Archives. See also Palmer, *The Church Encounters Asia*, pp. 103–4.

19. The first Korean to serve full-time was Lee Young Bum, who was called to replace one of the first foreign elders in 1956. Lee was originally called by President Andrus to serve for six months, but that call was extended to a year and a half. He was financially supported by donations from U.S. servicemen. See Palmer and Palmer, *Korean Saints*, p. 158.

20. See Dong Sull Choi, "A History of The Church of Jesus Christ of Latter-day Saints in Korea, 1950–1985" (Ph.D. diss., Brigham Young University, 1990), pp. 138–39.

21. As quoted in Palmer and Palmer, *Korean Saints*, p. 93.

22. Unless otherwise noted, the information in this section is derived from Spencer J. Palmer Oral History interview by S. Brad Jenkins, Provo, Utah, 1977, LDS Church Archives; Robert H. Slover Oral History; and Korean Mission (later called the Korea Seoul Mission) Historical Reports, LDS Church Archives. I am grateful for the research of S. Brad Jenkins.

23. Palmer, *The Church Encounters Asia*, p. 109.

24. Slover Oral History, p. 15.

25. Palmer, *The Church Encounters Asia*, p. 110.

26. See *Korean Mission: The White Field*, mission newsletter, September 1968, pp. 7–9, LDS Church Archives; Korean Mission Historical Reports, LDS Church Archives.

27. See *White Field*, January 1966, pp. 1–2.

28. See L. Edward Brown, interview by the author, Orem, Utah, and Pocatello, Idaho, 20 March 1979, taped telephone conversation.

29. See James B. Allen, "First Excursion: A Church for all lands—Korea," *Church News*, 7 April 1979, p. 24.

30. *The Saints' Friend*, September 1970, pp. 30–31, LDS Church Archives. I have also drawn on my personal knowledge of these developments.

31. See Korean Mission Historical Reports, 8 March 1971, LDS Church Archives.

32. Brown interview.

33. As quoted in Palmer and Palmer, *Korean Saints*, p. 502.

34. See "Church Educational System, Overview," unpublished CES report, 1978, p. 39. Copy in author's possession.

35. See "Top institute class graduate is Ph.D.," *Church News*, 29 January 1977, p. 15.

36. See Palmer and Palmer, *Korean Saints*, p. 341.

37. The three preceding examples are drawn from personal discussions with Robert H. Slover and the interview with L. Edward Brown.

38. See Shirleen Meek Saunders, "Whang Keun-Ok: Caring for Korea's Children," *Tambuli* 15 (October 1992): 32–41.

39. Eugene P. Till, interview by S. Brad Jenkins, October 1977, tape in possession of author.

40. Ibid.

41. See Palmer and Palmer, *Korean Saints*, 392–93.

42. Till interview.

43. See Choi, "History of the Church . . . in Korea," 202–3.

9

KOREA

1977–1996

Balancing Traditional Values with Gospel Service

THE LATE 1970s

The growth of the Church in Korea during the 1970s was impressive. Church membership at the end of 1978 stood at 12,971, up a thousand from the year before. Approximately three hundred missionaries were in the two missions. Membership growth in the Seoul area continued to be greater than anywhere else in Korea. Because of the growth of the Seoul Korea Stake, it was necessary in May 1977 to create the Seoul Korea West Stake from the original unit. President Kim Chang Sun was called as the new stake president. President Rhee remained president of the mother stake until 1978, when he was called to lead the Pusan Mission. He was replaced by Choi Wook Hwan, his first counselor.

By 1978 the local Saints occupied every major position in the Church with the exception of the presidency of the Korea Seoul Mission, which was held by F. Ray Hawkins. The Regional Representative, Han In Sang, was a native-born Korean. The Church in Korea continued to grow and mature in every way—more missions (the Seoul West Mission was created on July 1, 1979), more members, more wards and branches, more stakes (the

Seoul East Stake was formed April 18, 1979, with Ko Won Yong as president; the Pusan Stake was created on September 6, 1979, with Chang Jae Hwan as its first president; the Seoul North Stake was organized three days later, September 9, 1979, with Hong Moo Kwang as its leader; and the Kwangju Stake was constituted on October 25, 1980, presided over by Pak Byung Kyu—all between April 1979 and October 1980—and eight more stakes were created by 1986), and more buildings. But most important, the Korean Saints received the blessing of a temple in Seoul in 1985.

The Mormon Tabernacle Choir made its first visit to Japan and Korea in September 1979. The impressions left by this great musical organization were deep and lasting. Music is an important cultural tradition, and the quality of the music performed in the National Theater touched the hearts and lives of many nonmembers as well as Korean Latter-day Saints. When the choir returned a year or so later, the effect was equally positive.[1] The second tour came shortly before the second area conference.

THE AREA CONFERENCE OF 1980

In March 1980 the First Presidency announced a second series of conferences to be held in various Asian nations, including Korea. This tour started from the south and ended in Japan, where the new temple was dedicated. Korea was the penultimate stop. The area conference in Seoul was held on October 25 and 26, 1980. A hall large enough to hold the expected crowd could not be arranged, so the conference planners, hoping for good weather, opted to hold the general sessions outside at the Ch'ŏngun-dong church grounds.

Sheri L. Dew, author of President Gordon B. Hinckley's biography *Go Forward with Faith*, described the event in these words: "The temperature . . . plummeted to 28 degrees F., forcing the first session of conference inside the Seoul 4th Ward chapel. Thousands of members who couldn't find seats in the building sat outside and listened to the message over a public address system. The afternoon session was moved outdoors so that those who couldn't squeeze into the building could see President Kimball and the other visiting leaders, all of whom sat huddled on the stand in heavy coats and blankets."[2] A "cold and violently blowing wind"[3] raced through the six thousand conferencegoers, but the crowd was grateful and happy to be in the presence of the Lord's prophet and many other General Authorities and leaders of the Church.[4]

THE SEOUL KOREA TEMPLE

Immediately following the area conference, a number of Korean Church leaders traveled to Tokyo for the dedication of the temple the next day. Some Korean members had been asking for a temple since the early 1960s. Rhee Honam recalled when his friend Park Jae Am asked Elder Hinckley in 1960 or 1961 if there would ever be a temple in Korea. According to Brother Rhee, "Elder Hinckley just smiled and in a very encouraging tone promised us that if we stayed close to the Lord and were obedient to the Church there would one day be a temple in the Land of the Morning Calm."[5] During the area conference "many people were in great anticipation that the revelation for the building of the Seoul Temple would be given, [but] it was not."[6] Excited by the spirit of the event, the Korean Saints who traveled to the dedication in Tokyo became even more desirous of having their own temple. Elder Han In Sang, Regional Representative, gave the benediction at the first dedicatory session. In his prayer he asked the Lord for a temple in his land so that the Korean members might also be able to enjoy the blessings received therein.[7] In the months following the dedication in Tokyo, the stakes began conducting temple preparation classes and numerous articles appeared in the *Saints' Friend,* the Korean Church magazine, encouraging Korean members to prepare themselves spiritually for the day when they could have a temple in their own land.

They did not have to wait long. Less than six months later, a few days before general conference, on April 1, 1981, President Kimball announced plans for nine new temples, including one in Seoul, Korea. The *Church News* made an interesting observation regarding temple building in the Church: "The first nine temples of the Church took 97 years to construct, the second nine 47 years. The third nine were announced within seven years, and the last nine in one news conference."[8] The Korean priesthood brethren who were in Salt Lake City for the announcement and conference were deeply grateful to have their temple among the latest nine. Expressing the thoughts and feelings of other Regional Representatives and stake presidents who were there, Elder Han In Sang said: "We have more than 20,000 members of the Church in Korea. Only 100 have received their endowments; only 20 couples have been sealed." (It had been expected that the policy that restricted couples from traveling outside the country would be relaxed in 1980, but with the assassination of President Park Chung Hee in 1979, martial law was declared and the old policy remained in force until 1981.)

Ko Won Yong, president of the Seoul East Stake, and now an Area Authority, said he attended the Tokyo Temple dedication and heard President Kimball encourage priesthood leaders to tell their members to go to the temple. "I wondered," remembered President Ko, "how I could deliver the prophet's message to my people when we had no temple and they couldn't leave the country to be sealed as man and wife."[9] Joy and gratitude were the universal responses among the Korean Saints. When asked if the Korean Saints would contribute their share of the building's cost, the Korean leaders answered in the affirmative. Months later, they had given four times the amount asked by President Kimball.

Following the announcement, the Korean members began to fervently prepare to enter the temple. As General Authorities visited for stake and regional conferences and other training meetings, temple preparation became the common theme in their talks and lessons. The Korean members felt a renewed spirit as they strove to make themselves worthy to enter the house of the Lord. The rise in Church membership witnessed the increased dedication and spiritual growth.

The site chosen for the temple is known as the Shinch'on property. It had been acquired in 1965, during Spencer J. Palmer's mission presidency. Elder Paul Dredge and his companion had come across the property and encouraged Palmer to look into purchasing the land. President Palmer had moved quickly and incurred "the displeasure of the Church's real estate office." But as Sheri L. Dew recorded, "Elder Hinckley had intervened, and on a subsequent trip to Korea with President Hugh B. Brown he had inspected the property. President Brown had suggested that it would be a wonderful place to build a temple," and now, nineteen years later, his suggestion became a reality.[10] Since its purchase by the Church, the property had been well used for other Church purposes; a mission office and chapel had to be razed to make way for the new building. The temple's location is quite remarkable, being situated close to three of Korea's greatest universities. Over the years an added blessing was the construction of a major subway entrance only two blocks from the temple hill, making it convenient for members to travel there quickly and economically from throughout Seoul.

The architects and planners required a good deal of time to plan the new building and to make legal arrangements for constructing it. Zoning and building-code restrictions created a number of problems. For example, the Church was required to drill a well for water to aid in fire protection. Fortunately a seam found in the underlying granite 112 meters deep brought forth clear spring water. This water is used in the temple and does not require purification. Two years passed before ground-breaking services were held and the construction phase could begin. The Seoul Korea Temple was redesigned three times chiefly because the Korean Saints had given up their savings to build their temple. "Originally," said Han, "it was designed to be a very simple structure—just a couple of endowment rooms and one sealing room. Then it was expanded and expanded."[11]

Early in the morning of May 9, 1983, Elder Marvin J. Ashton of the Quorum of the Twelve conducted the ground-breaking ceremonies. In his prayer Elder Ashton asked, "May this temple be an ensign of truth, a beacon of peace and security."

Two years later the completed building was 12,000 square feet, with an 18,000-square-foot auxiliary building nearby. The architecture reflects distinctively Latter-day Saint lines and purposes while manifesting the beauty of Korean granite and a traditional 100-year black-tile roof. The temple has four ordinance rooms and three sealing rooms surrounding the celestial room. The completed edifice was appointed with furnishings built in Korea and reflected Korean traditional arts and culture. Similar to the annex beside the Tokyo Temple, the auxiliary building contained dorm space for twenty-two men and twenty-two women, as well as other working and mechanical space necessary to operate the temple. The auxiliary building is underground and may serve as a bomb shelter. It also provides parking space for sixteen cars. Shirley-June Younger, historical chairman for the Seoul Temple committee, described the setting in these words: "The grounds are so meticulously landscaped that the building seems to be nestled in a natural garden. Six shining white pillars circle the building; the pillar in front is topped by a statue of the angel Moroni.

"Despite the urban location of the temple, not far from downtown Seoul, those who visit the grounds enjoy a marked feeling of peace and serenity recognized by members of the Church as the influence of the Spirit of the Lord."[12]

The Seoul Temple was completed during the fall of 1985. While the final work was under way, preparations were completed for the open house and dedication. Members and missionaries were prepared to serve as tour guides, ushers, and hosts. More than thirteen thousand visitors toured the sacred structure between November 26 and December 7.

Another small but significant project was also under way that

Announced in April 1981, the Seoul Korea Temple was dedicated on December 14–15, 1985. It was the first temple of the Church to be constructed on the mainland of Asia. (Photo by Shin Jae Koo)

fall. Choi Dong Heon, first counselor in the Seoul West Stake presidency, was busy studying the Korean word for *temple*. The local temple committee decided to follow Choi's recommendation and change the word from *sinjŏn* to *sŏngjŏn*. The word *sŏngjŏn* better fit the meaning of "house of the Lord." *Sinjŏn*, which had been used for many years before that time, had a meaning closer to "house of the gods."[13]

December 14 and 15, 1985, had been planned for many months as the days for the dedication. During the previous month, however, President Spencer W. Kimball passed away and President Ezra Taft Benson was ordained as President of the Church. He selected Gordon B. Hinckley as his first counselor and Thomas S. Monson as his second counselor in the First Presidency. For about three years President Hinckley had been the only member of the First Presidency who was able to function in his office. Now, with President Benson as the Lord's prophet, there was a question whether President Hinckley would still be assigned to dedicate the new temple in Korea. But because the plans had been made, President Benson sent President Hinckley to Seoul to preside and conduct the ceremonies.

The weather was extremely cold, near zero degrees Fahrenheit, when he, Sister Hinckley, and other Church leaders arrived. President Hinckley recalled his first winter visit: "Snow was flying through the sky and the winds from Siberia were blowing across the land. . . . I walked the streets of this city and saw many people without housing, living in boxes trying to keep warm." In one of his addresses during the dedicatory services, he said he had "shed more tears for Korea than any other place in the world."[14] His love for the Korean Saints was open and obvious. He had been going to Korea for twenty-five years, and, as he said, had grown old while coming there.

In December 1985 there were more than forty-one thousand members of the Church in Korea. The number of missions had grown to three and the stakes to thirteen. Although the Church was relatively young, there were many leaders who had been seasoned well in Church service since the 1950s and 1960s. More than fifty-five hundred members participated in six dedicatory sessions—five sessions in Korean and one in English for American military people and others who were working in Korea. After the sixth session, President Hinckley was tired but satisfied that the Lord had accepted the new temple. In his journal he wrote: "We have experienced a great outpouring of the Spirit of the Lord.

There will never be another occasion like this in the history of the Church in Korea."[15]

Although President Hinckley disliked being the central figure at any event, his loving spirit, warm counsel, and historic remembrances made the dedicatory services as wonderful as they were. The words he fashioned for the dedicatory prayer reflected his deep love of Korea and his appreciation for the history of the Church there. In the dedicatory prayer, he said:

> Our hearts are filled with gratitude for this long awaited day. This is the first such house of the Lord ever constructed on the mainland of Asia. . . .
>
> The seeds of thy work were planted in Korea only a third of a century ago, when amidst the thunders of war, a few of thy faithful sons in military service exemplified the teachings of the gospel in their lives and shared them with a few of those they met. Then thou didst touch the heart of a great and good scholar and leader, Kim Ho Jik, while he was studying in the United States. When he returned to his native land, having experienced the inspiration of the Book of Mormon, and having received a testimony of the prophetic call of Joseph Smith, he shared with others the beauty of his newly found treasure. Missionaries were invited to Korea, and here they taught with faith and inspiration, finding one soul here, another there.
>
> From those times of small beginnings and serious privation thy work has moved forward, its numbers have increased many fold, and it has prospered under thy Church, even The Church of Jesus Christ of Latter-day Saints, and has become firmly rooted in the soil of this beautiful land, and become the spiritual home of many thousands of good people in Korea.
>
> Thou hast smiled with favor upon thy work here. The government of this nation has been hospitable to thy servants. Now, crowning all, is this beautiful edifice in which we meet and which we dedicate to thee.[16]

In addition to dedicating every part of the building to the Lord and for its sacred purposes, President Hinckley also prayed for the safety of the building—"May this, thy house, be preserved from the effects of storm and tempest, from the tremblings of the earth, from the desecration of enemies, from the destructive forces of war and civil strife"—for those who would enter therein, for the righteousness of the Korean Saints and their families, and so forth. In comparison with every historical event since that time, President Hinckley was right—no other occasion in the history of the Church in Korea compares with the temple dedication.

The first endowment session was held on December 17, 1985. The Seoul Korea Temple, unlike other temple districts, did not have adequate numbers of endowed members to officiate because so few couples had been allowed out of the country to obtain their endowments. Thus it was necessary to first endow couples who had been called to serve in the temple. Rhee Honam officiated as the first eleven couples received their temple blessings. Fortunately, a number of members in the servicemen's district were experienced in temple work and were able to assist in training the Korean workers. Regular sessions commenced in February 1986.[17]

TEMPLE PRESIDENCIES

The first president of the Seoul Korea Temple was Robert H. Slover, who had previously served as the third mission president in Korea. His wife, Rosemarie W. Slover was called to serve as temple matron. President Slover selected Huo Chae and Park Jae Am as counselors. Like Brother Slover, Huo and Park were men of long experience in the Church. Their interest in genealogy and temple work ranged back to their early years in the Church. Part of Brother Huo's biography[18] illustrates his depth.

THIRTY-THREE GENERATIONS
Huo Chea

In 1985, I was released as the Inch'ŏn stake president and called to serve in the first Seoul Temple presidency as Robert H. Slover's first counselor. I could not be lazy in a place as unique and holy as the temple, where the saving work for the dead and the living is performed. So I worked from early in the morning until eleven or twelve at night. As is emphasized in the temple, even though we do genealogy, without a temple we cannot receive the saving ordinances—these are all accomplished together.

My forefather's name is Huo Sun-mun. There are thirty-three generations between my son and him, which is approximately one thousand years. I have, from my forefather's time down, done four generations, and all have received their ordinances and have also been sealed in the temple. I have a future goal to bring salvation to the relatives of my direct family line by doing temple work for them. I have obtained twenty-seven of thirty-three volumes of genealogy and am extracting names from them. I have extracted about two thousand names so far [circa 1992].

In Inch'ōn I had a lot of interest in welfare work. When winter came I would buy about five hundred *yŏnt'an* [coal bricks used as fuel for heating] and stored it for distribution to poor people. When I visited families, I would give one or two hundred *yŏnt'an* to each, or I would pack one or two sacks of grain on my back to give to families that were struggling. At times the children would come out to greet me, as they were so happy to see me. When doing this type of work I would think, "Small works are the works of God," and keep working. Also, at times certain member families were faced with the dilemma of having to withdraw their children from school because the parents couldn't afford the registration fees. Without anyone knowing, I would pay the registration fees, and I did so on many occasions. And there was once a neighbor girl without any parents that was sentenced to life in prison. Seeing her unjustly accused, I helped her get acquitted through a retrial. For her, this was an act of great value.

Also, I have relatives with families of seven or eight children that live in the countryside, where making a living is difficult. I would choose one or two children from among each family and would make sure they received their education, from elementary all the way to high school. I took care of them even until they married. Up to now, I have helped eighteen or so family members. When I do things like this, I think that it is a small thing, but I get a great sense of joy knowing that I have done something valuable in behalf of God's work. We need to follow God's words, "Love thy neighbor as thyself," even if just a little. I have even provided for the treatment of members or of children with heart problems that were waiting in the hospital for surgery but could not afford it. I think I will continue doing things like this.

In the future, I think I will spend the remainder of my days focusing on God's work and serving as a steward in the temple.

As mentioned earlier, Park Jae Am, second counselor in the temple presidency, had asked Elder Hinckley many years before if Korea would have a temple. Over the years, Brother Park did not let this desire lie fallow. He was active in helping organize genealogy work in Korea, and he helped make arrangements for the Church Genealogical Department to do microfilming in Korea beginning in 1972.[19] He was also involved in having many rolls of microfilm placed in the Central National Library for the use of his fellow Church members. During the brief time he served in the temple presidency—he passed away in July 1988 at the age of fifty-four—he carried the normal duties of his office, but he especially loved work in the baptistry. "In the Seoul Temple he performed over twenty-thousand baptisms for the dead."[20] Brother Park was also the founder of LDS Social Services in Korea in 1977.

Spencer J. Palmer and his wife, Shirley, were the second couple to preside at the Seoul Korea Temple. He chose Lee Joon Taek and Park Nam Soo as counselors. Park Nam Soo "consecutively served as a temple sealer, a temple missionary, an assistant to the temple presidency, second counselor in the temple presidency, and first counselor in the temple presidency since the Seoul Temple first went into operation."[21] In August 1990 Pak Byung Kyu, who had served as countrywide director of CES since 1986, was the first Korean called to lead the Seoul Korea Temple. His wife, Rhee Young Ji, served as temple matron. In 1993 Pak returned to his former position with CES and was replaced by Bae Young Chun and his wife, Kim Soon Sung, who served by his side as matron of the temple. In the fall of 1996, following five years as a member of the Second Quorum of the Seventy, Han In Sang and his companion, Lee Kyu In, were called to be the president and matron of the temple.

Temple and genealogy work play a major role in the lives of many Korean members. In the book *Korean Saints*, a number of Korean members mention their love for the temple and their efforts to trace their genealogies and to submit names to the temple. Virtually every biography begins with genealogical information that places the writer in their family and gives some information regarding their forebears. A number have traced their roots back hundreds of years, and some, like Huo Chea, have records going back thirty-three or more generations. One well-known member, Brother Kim San, a great nationalist and freedom fighter, was reported to have family records going back sixty-six generations.[22]

CHURCH ADMINISTRATION
AND ORGANIZATION

Administratively, the Church in Korea has remained closely tied to Japan since the first missionaries entered Korea in 1956. Throughout the years, area supervision has come either from

A younger Han In Sang with three of his five children outside his home in Seoul in 1972. (Photo by author)

Japan or Hong Kong. Nevertheless, since 1978 Korea has had its own Regional Representatives, and in 1995, when Regional Representatives were discontinued and Area Authorities took their place, Koreans have held these positions. The first two Korean men to serve as Area Authorities were Kim Chong Youl and Ko Won Yong. They were men of considerable experience in Church administration. Elder Kim, a department head for the dental college at Yonsei University, had previously served as bishop, stake president's counselor, mission president's counselor, and Regional Representative. He is married to Hong Young Sook. Elder Ko had served in a bishopric when the Seoul Stake was first organized, then as executive secretary to stake president Rhee Honam, and so on. Over the years he served as a stake high councilor, stake president, and Regional Representative. His wife is Kim Eun Hee.

Many members of the Church in Korea were honored when one of their own, Han In Sang, was called as the first Korean to serve as a General Authority. His call, which became effective on

June 1, 1991, was to the Second Quorum of the Seventy. While in that calling he served in the Asia North Area Presidency, stationed in Tokyo, and in the temple department in Salt Lake City. He was released after the standard five years in October 1996. As noted before, his next assignment was president of the Seoul Korea Temple.

Elder Han has been blessed with unusual abilities as a translator and as an administrator. During his years of Church membership, among other callings, he has served as a missionary in Korea, as a branch president while on his mission, as a district president, mission president, and Regional Representative. Even before he became a General Authority, he had the opportunity of associating closely with many members of the First Presidency, the Quorum of the Twelve, and other General Authorities as he served as interpreter for them at area, regional, and stake conferences. Quick of mind, he has used his talents to translate for the Church in Korea, to manage the Church distribution center in Seoul, and to carry out his duties as regional manager for temporal affairs in Korea.[23]

MISSIONARY EXPANSION

The growth of the Church between 1979 and 1985, when the temple was dedicated, was impressive. The number of members grew from about eleven thousand in 1977 to more than forty thousand in 1985. Enthusiasm for the new temple was a significant impetus for the missionaries. They were able to refer to the new structure and explain gospel truths regarding the eternal nature of families and other principles related to temple worship. The year 1981 was the peak year in missionary productivity, with around 2,500 converts being brought into the Church. Eleven new stakes were created in Korea between 1979 and 1983. Subsequently, in 1986, another new stake was added. And two more stakes were created in 1992, bringing the total then (and in 1996) to sixteen. In 1986 the Korea Taejŏn Mission, Korea's fourth, was organized.

In 1986, as part of the growing pattern throughout the world, the Church organized a Missionary Training Center in Seoul. By 1989 an average of fifteen Korean elders and sisters were trained every month.[24] It is noteworthy that 94 percent of Koreans serving missions have either graduated from the CES institute program or participated in it.[25] Local missionaries have a tremendous advantage over American and other foreign elders and sisters because they understand the language, culture, beliefs, and persuasions of their own people.

Ever since President Kimball encouraged young priesthood holders throughout the world to serve missions, numbers of Korean missionaries have grown. In 1996 more than 25 percent of the missionary force in Korea were native Koreans. According to the Area Presidency, "In Korea, students who interrupt their university studies to serve a mission often face significant hurdles to resume their studies when they return, yet many choose to make this sacrifice."[26] All young Korean males also have a three-year military obligation that often delays their availability to serve a mission until they are twenty-five or twenty-six years of age. Nevertheless, many Korean Saints still serve missions.[27] A growing number of Koreans who serve missions are second-generation members of the Church. Since the 1970s, most of the presidents of Korean missions have been native members.

In October 1993 a young Latter-day Saint returned missionary, Kwon Young Joon, distinguished himself by placing first in the Korean National Judicial Examination, an examination that is taken by approximately 20,000 people annually and of which only 280 pass. Similar to the bar exam in the United States, the exam is used to select future judges and lawyers. Brother Kwon made some very difficult decisions before reaching this important place in his life. After being accepted in the law program at Seoul National University, Korea's most prestigious school, he received a call to serve a mission. Many teachers, fellow students, and even some Church members tried to dissuade him from accepting the prophet's call. But he had made up his mind while a seminary student to keep the Lord's commandments and had saved money to help support himself while on his mission. After serving a successful mission, he was readmitted at Seoul National University, went on to distinguish himself in the exam, and received legal schooling. After graduation he began three years of military service as a legal officer. Subsequently he married in the Seoul Korea Temple, and he and his wife, Lee Yeonshin, daughter of a stake president and herself a dentist, became the parents of a son, Kwon Jihyuck. It is expected that Brother Kwon will be appointed a judge when he leaves the navy.[28] The Korean media has given considerable notice to Brother Kwon's membership in the Church. He is striving to set the kind of example that will bring credit to the Church and glory to his Father in Heaven.

The place and importance of the Book of Mormon extends beyond the topic of missionary work and expansion of the Church, but it is also central to missionary work. The first three thousand Korean copies printed in 1967 were distributed, mostly to members, by 1970. Elder Han described the remarkable magnitude and distribution of the Korean Book of Mormon by the 1990s in these words: "Today, of course, the English edition of the Book of Mormon is largest by volume by far. Second is Spanish; third is Portuguese. But the fourth largest edition is Korean. This is surprising because membership in other countries is so much larger. There are 2.2 million English copies a year; in Spanish we are approaching a million; in Portuguese two hundred and thirty-five thousand; and in Korean two hundred and twenty-five thousand. At the end of 1991, the one millionth copy of the Korean-language Book of Mormon was sold at the distribution center in Seoul."[29]

Koreans are a book-loving and a book-reading people. Not only is the Book of Mormon deeply appreciated by the Korean Saints, but the other standard works of the Church are appreciated as well. The Korean Book of Mormon is an important tool in spreading the restored gospel.

PROGRESS IN THE CHURCH EDUCATIONAL SYSTEM

The seminary and institute programs of the Church Educational System in Korea have steadily grown in numbers of participants and in the quality of education that has been provided. Few places in the worldwide Church have been favored with so many stalwart, able, and dedicated seminary and institute teachers and administrators. Their lives have been wonderful examples of service to the Church as Regional Representatives, stake presidents, bishops, branch presidents, and in other priesthood callings. The present country director, Pak Byung Kyu, who replaced Rhee Honam in 1986, has served in these callings as well as temple president. Dr. Seo Hee Chul, who has twice been country director while colleagues have served as mission president and temple president, is also a man of great talent and dedication.

In 1995 the CES organization in Korea was staffed with a full-time country director and twelve full-time coordinators, all of whom teach seminary or institute classes or both. In addition, 190 volunteers teach around the country. The CES office is in Seoul. There are four institute buildings (some are part of chapels)—two in Seoul, one in Kwangju, and one in Pusan—but institute classes are offered in a number of other cities.

During the period since seminary and institute were started in 1972, seminary courses have been offered by home study. In recent years, however, a growing number of students (174 in 1995) have been able to participate in early-morning classes. In 1995 a total of 1,417 students were enrolled in seminary classes.

In 1993 the First Presidency asked the Church Educational System to include all members between the ages of eighteen and thirty in the institute program. CES in Korea has been very successful in including large numbers of members of this target age-group. In 1995 there were 1,687 nonstudents participating in the institute program, and 986 college students were enrolled, making a total of 2,673 young people who were engaged in formal weekday study of the gospel.[30] "The majority of Korean Church leaders today," wrote Seo Hee Chul, "or those people who have remained and served diligently in the Church, have participated in the Church institute program. . . . Also 87 percent of all stake leaders in Korea have had some special relationship with the institute programs."[31]

THE GOSPEL AND THE SAINTS OF KOREA

Of all the Asian people, the Koreans place the greatest emphasis on education. Korean members hold more higher degrees per capita than any comparable number of people in the entire Church. These highly educated, status-conscious people have chosen in significant numbers to submit themselves to the yoke of membership in the Church of Jesus Christ and are living lives of great devotion and sacrifice to the principles and expectations of the Church. In Korea, as in Japan, businesses and society apply immense pressure upon employees to work extremely long hours and to dedicate their lives almost completely to organizations outside of the family and church. Obeying the Word of Wisdom is also a big challenge. "Drinking and smoking is a way of life here, especially part of the business and social world," states government official Joo Duck Young. "After business hours, men go and drink together socially. It is an established and accepted part of work."[32] Yet many leaders and members have chosen to change jobs or to make other sacrifices in order to remain active in the Church.

In addition to leadership service in the Church, a number of Korean Saints have distinguished themselves in the world. Three examples of significant service or high attainment are Choi Hyun-Soo, Joo Duck Young, and Hwang Keun-Ok, who was noted in chapter 8.

Choi Hyun Soo, known in America and Europe as Hans Choi, has distinguished himself internationally as an opera singer. A baritone, he first emerged as a prominent singer when he was invited home from Italy, where he had been studying, to perform at the 1988 Olympics in Seoul. Two years later he won first prize in the Ninth International Tchaikovsky Competition in Moscow, Russia. "He [was] the first singer from Asia and the first non-Russian and first Latter-day Saint to win first place in the vocal competition." Among other places, he has since performed with the Tabernacle Choir, with the New York Opera, at the Teatro al Scala in Milan, Italy, and at Carnegie Hall in New York City. Brother Choi and his family are active members of the Korean Branch in New York City.[33]

Joo Duck Young is the highest-ranking government official in the Church in Korea, and perhaps throughout Asia. He joined the Church while in high school in Seoul in January 1960. Educated at Seoul National University, he has continued to use his talents to benefit his country and the Church. The following is an excerpt from his own story:[34]

> My life of faith over the more than thirty years that I have been a member of the Church attests to the fact that if we honestly make an effort, keep the commandments, and remain faithful the Lord will greatly bless us. In my case, I have been given an exceptional opportunity for service in the Ministry of Trade, first as Deputy Director of the Machinery and Industry Division. Later I was promoted to the position of Director General, which deals with the automobile, aircraft, and aerospace industries in Korea, and which is comparable to Deputy Assistant Secretary [of] the Department of State of the United States. . . .
>
> Korea has changed drastically during the past thirty to forty years, from one of the poorest countries in the world to a strong and modern industrial economy. The country has changed and so has the development of the Church. In the '50s and '60s and '70s the Church grew very rapidly in Korea. Until now, the growth has been marvelous and impressive. But now . . . with Korea's prosperity and secularization, we are having problems in retaining our members in full activity. For some, the attractions of the

material world are diverting them from full faithfulness in the Church. . . .

When I attended George Washington University [1979–1981] I learned for the first time that the Church had become an American [as opposed to a Utah] Church. . . . I began to realize that under the leadership of President Spencer W. Kimball, the Church was beginning to change from a national to a global organization. The internationalization of the Church was already under way. . . .

I realized as never before that the image and influence of the Church within Korea was lagging. . . . I decided that Church members in Korea should collect accurate information about the Church worldwide and bring this to the attention of the people of Korea. I decided that we must introduce the worldwide Church to the Korean public so that they may have clear and accurate information and photographs at their disposal to replace the deficient and inaccurate materials that have been heretofore available. . . .

In all of my Church positions, the one that has given me the most satisfying opportunity to further the cause of Zion in Korea has been my activity of recent years as Director of Public Affairs for the Church in Korea. It has allowed me and other Korean leaders to spread the light of the restored gospel with Korean Society, and to enhance the image of the Church in my native country.

As director of public affairs, Brother Joo has led out in the compilation of a book, intended for his own people, titled *Work of Miracles: Emergence of a New World Religion Seeking to Build Utopia on Earth,* which outlines the historical emergence of the Church, its missionary successes throughout the world, gospel doctrines, and the fruits of Mormonism.

Members with dedication like Brothers Kwon and Joo and Sister Hwang are helping to build the image of the Church in Korea. They are not alone. Thousands of Korean members are striving to overcome the world and live exemplary lives.

In 1996 the population of South Korea exceeded forty-five million, with 72 percent living in urban centers. Most of the populace was Korean, making it one of the most homogeneous countries in the world. In the American press, seldom a day went by without news of problems between North and South Korea, or regarding some other problem with unions, wages, education policies, public demonstrations, and so on. The Korea of the 1950s—with wars, suffering, poverty, and underdevelopment—was gone. South Korea had become one of the "little tigers," one of the small nations of East Asia with enormous ability to produce steel, ships, automobiles, electronics, and anything else the world market desired. South Korea's Human Economic Index placed it thirty-second among 173 countries.[35] But Korea was still Korea, and Koreans were still trying to be faithful to their heritage while they struggled to integrate the old conservative ways with those of a world economy and, to a great extent, a world culture.

In 1992 Shirley and Spencer Palmer published in Korea a book of biographies of Koreans who joined the Church between 1950 and 1980. Three years later a translated and revised edition was published in English under the title *The Korean Saints*.[36] Even a cursory reading reveals much regarding the heart and soul of the Church and Church members in Korea. Examples abound regarding filial sons and daughters who desire nothing more than to be a credit to their aged or dead parents and to be truly faithful to the restored gospel of the Lord Jesus Christ. Evidence is also abundant regarding the tremendous importance education plays in the lives of those who are featured in the Palmers' book, as well as in their hopes and dreams for their children. Also, seeming to go against Korean tradition, there are frequent statements by men regarding their love and respect for their wives and how much they have contributed to the success of their families, their service in the Church, and to their growth as human beings. Clearly, the gospel has had a positive effect in the lives of many Korean members.

At the end of 1996 there were approximately seventy thousand Korean members in Korea, plus a large but unknown number in the United States. The Church in Korea, along with Japan, is one of the few countries throughout the world that is financially self-supporting. The members have paid their share of the almost ninety buildings that serve 161 wards and branches and 22 stakes and districts.

Another lesson from *The Korean Saints* is the evidence that many Korean members have successfully amalgamated the best of their Confucian background with the teachings and life patterns of the restored gospel. Respect for ancestors and genealogy work has tied Korea's past traditions closely with temple work, family history, and genealogy as taught in the Church.

NOTES

1. See Dorothy Stowe, "Joy spans the Pacific as choir visits Orient," *Church News*, 22 September 1979, pp. 3, 8–9.

2. Sheri L. Dew, *Go Forward With Faith: The Biography of Gordon B. Hinckley* (Salt Lake City: Deseret Book Co., 1996), p. 376.

3. Palmer and Palmer, *Korean Saints*, p. 403.

4. See Dell Van Orden, "Saints throng to area meetings in the Far East," *Church News*, 1 November 1980, pp. 3–4, 9.

5. Dew, *Go Forward with Faith*, pp. 222–23.

6. Palmer and Palmer, *Korean Saints*, p. 403.

7. See *The Saints' Friend*, February/March 1986, p. 54. I am indebted to my former research assistant Cory Turner for reviewing this Korean periodical and providing a summary of important historical events.

8. "Plans announced for 9 new temples," *Church News*, 4 April 1981, p. 3.

9. Gerry Avant, "Their prayers are answered, a temple in their midsts," *Church News*, 11 April 1981, p. 23.

10. Dew, *Go Forward with Faith*, p. 437.

11. As quoted in Palmer and Palmer, *Korean Saints*, p. 97.

12. Shirley-June Younger, "Seoul Temple Dedicated," *Ensign* 16 (February 1986): 74–75.

13. *The Saints' Friend*, December 1985, p. 53.

14. As quoted in Gerry Avant, "'Land of Morning Calm' brightened by Korea temple," *Church News*, 22 December 1985, p. 6.

15. As quoted in Dew, *Go Forward with Faith*, p. 438.

16. "Dedicatory prayer recognizes small beginnings of work," *Church News*, 22 December 1985, p. 7.

17. See Shirley-Anne Younger, Gregg Newby, and Marylouise Le Cheminant, *For Those Who Dare to Dream* (Korea: n.p., n.d. [1990?]), pp. 59–60.

18. Palmer and Palmer, *Korean Saints*, p. 288.

19. See James B. Allen et al., *Hearts Turned to the Fathers* (Provo: BYU Studies, 1996), appendix 2, p. 348.

20. Palmer and Palmer, *Korean Saints*, pp. 178–79.

21. Palmer and Palmer, *Korean Saints*, p. 784.

22. See ibid., p. 370. Kim San's records dated to A.D. 927. The biographies men-

tioned in the prologue of *Korean Saints* are good samples of the kind of interest that Korean members have in genealogy. See the biographies of Choi Dong Sull, Cho Joong Hyun, Hwang Chung Youl, and Kim Jung Shik. Kim Jung Shik, for example, had submitted by 1991 "approximately 887 family group sheets, containing about 3,725 names" (p. 7).

23. The most available sources on Han In Sang are "Han In Sang," in Palmer and Palmer, *Korean Saints*, pp. 89–98; the somewhat adulatory article by Gerry Avant, "Korean is like a 'living treasure' among members," *Church News*, 2 February 1986, p. 6; "Two new General Authorities called," *Church News*, 1 June 1991, p. 3; Gerry Avant and John L. Hart, "His shoulders are used to heavy tasks," *Church News*, 6 July 1991, p. 6; "Han In Sang of the Seventy," *Ensign* 31 (August 1991): 75; and his first general conference address, "Take Up His Cross," *Ensign* 32 (May 1992): 81–82.

24. See Choi, "History of the Church," p. 316.

25. See Palmer and Palmer, *Korean Saints*, p. 503.

26. David E. Sorensen, Rex D. Pinegar, and L. Edward Brown, "The Church in Japan, Korea, and Far-East Russia," *Ensign* 26 (November 1996): 111.

27. See ibid. See also Merrill J. Bateman, Han In Sang, and Sam K. Shimabukuro, "Church Progress Continues in Japan and South Korea," *Ensign* 24 (May 1994): 112.

28. Information for this paragraph is derived from material supplied by Spencer J. Palmer. A longer version is part of a manuscript for a forthcoming article for the *Ensign* magazine, tentatively titled "Korean Pioneers Who Have Prepared the Way."

29. As quoted in Palmer and Palmer, *Korean Saints*, p. 94.

30. Information supplied by "J" Stephen Jones of the Church Educational System, 25 October 1996.

31. As quoted in Palmer and Palmer, *Korean Saints*, p. 503.

32. Kellene Ricks, "Korea, Land of the Morning Calm," *Ensign* 32 (July 1992): 36.

33. See John L. Hart, "Korean sings Italian opera: LDS baritone wins spot at Seoul Olympics," *Church News*, 27 August 1988, p. 14; Claudia L. Bushman, "Member wins Tchaikovsky prize," *Church News*, 6 October 1990, p. 13; and Sheridan Sheffield, "Gospel peace brings strength to opera singer," *Church News*, 22 August 1992, p. 5.

34. I have freely abridged Brother Joo's writing. A fuller account will appear in the *Ensign* in 1997 as part of an article by Spencer J. Palmer. Further information regarding Joo Duck Young is found in Ricks, "Korea, Land of the Morning Calm," pp. 36–37; and "Joo Duck Young," in Palmer and Palmer, *Korean Saints*, 297–99.

35. See "South Korea," vol. 2 of *Culturgrams: The Nations Around Us* (Provo, Utah: Publications Office of the David M. Kennedy Center for International Studies, 1995), pp. 138, 140.

36. For full publication information, see chapter 8, note 6.

10

THE CHINESE
REALM
1949–1959

Founding the Church in Hong Kong and Taiwan

Almost ten decades passed between the time when Elder Hosea Stout and his companions left Hong Kong in 1853 and the arrival in 1949 of the next group of LDS missionaries. The intervening years had not been kind to China and her people. Few parts of the world had endured more suffering, wars, rebellions, and revolutions than China. Foreign powers dismembered the once-glorious empire during the years following China's first treaty with a Western nation in 1842. From then until the turn of the century, the Ch'ing (Qing)[1] Dynasty steadily lost control. Token measures intended to bring China technologically abreast of the West failed, and the Boxer uprising in 1900 also fell short of its objective of driving all foreigners, especially Christian missionaries, from the country.

Continued degeneration finally brought the fall of the Manchu Ch'ing regime in the Chinese revolution of 1911. But the new government was unable to establish stability, and by 1916 the nation had fallen into the hands of warlords who ruled parts of the country for their own benefit. This situation continued until Chiang K'ai-shek consolidated most of the country under the

Kuomintang, the Nationalist government in the mid-1920s. By that time, the Chinese Communist party had been founded, and in the late 1920s it was a growing force. In the mid-1930s the Chinese Communists, with Mao Tse-tung (Mao Zedong) as leader, were established in the northwestern city of Yenan.

In 1937 war broke out between China and Japan. This protracted conflict finally ended in 1945, but it brought untold hardships to the Chinese people. Before China was on its feet, another war, this time between Mao's communist forces and the nationalist armies of Chiang K'ai-shek, ravaged the country. On October 1, 1949, the Communists established the People's Democratic Republic of China (PRC). Chiang and his followers retreated to the Island of Taiwan (Formosa), where they transplanted the Republic of China (ROC) government.

The history of Christianity in China largely parallels the foregoing political events. Protestant missions began in earnest after 1842, when five treaty ports were opened to Westerners. Although times were difficult and a number of missionaries died martyrs' deaths (the worst massacre took place during the Boxer uprising when 188 missionaries, missionary wives, and children were killed), thousands of Christians, both Protestant and Catholic, devoted their lives to the cause of Christ in China. The high watermark for the Protestants was 1925, when 8,158 missionaries and wives of missionaries were engaged in the work. Possibly as many Roman Catholics were there at the same time.

The Sino-Japanese War of 1937–1945 forced many missionaries to retreat to western China and some to leave the country. The missionaries who remained provided hospitals and medical centers and tried to help the Chinese people. Following the war, large numbers of Protestant and Catholic missionaries returned to China or entered for the first time; but before the Christian schools, hospitals, and teaching stations were fully organized again, the Communists defeated the Kuomintang forces. Christianity was in a grave situation. Some missionaries withdrew immediately when the Communists took over, but most decided to take the risk and see whether some kind of working relationship could be arranged. In 1951, however, the missionaries began leaving in large numbers. By 1953 most missionaries were out of the country. Christianity in Communist China was not dead, but it was in serious danger. Before "liberation" there were more than four million Chinese Christians.

When the LDS Church established its second mission in Hong Kong in July 1949, the Communists had not yet taken complete control of the mainland. No one knew that the end of the civil war would come so soon. At that time many informed observers believed that Chiang would somehow destroy Mao's forces. But history was not on the side of the Church, and the second mission was closed after only eighteen months. Taiwan was not a suitable alternative at that time because of the extreme difficulty the Kuomintang forces were having establishing their new government on that island.

But the LDS Chinese Mission of 1949 cannot be counted a failure in the sense of the 1853 experience. Much was accomplished that had lasting influence.

ELDER DAVID O. McKAY DEDICATES
THE CHINESE REALM

China was obviously on the minds of the leading Brethren of the Church when in 1920 they sent Elder David O. McKay on a world tour of missions. The First Presidency asked him to visit China and the surrounding countries and to evaluate these areas as possible mission fields. They also asked Elder McKay to dedicate China for the preaching of the gospel if he felt impressed to do so.

After visiting Japan during December 1920, Elder McKay and Hugh J. Cannon, his traveling companion, went to Korea, Manchuria, and Peking (Beijing), China, arriving there on January 8, 1921. They were disturbed by the poverty and chaos they encountered in China. Japan had impressed them as modern and promising; China was drab and depressing. Nevertheless, on the morning of Sunday, January 9, Elder McKay felt impressed to dedicate the land. He and Elder Cannon desired to offer the prayer in a tranquil place, preferably under the blue sky: "Placing themselves in the hands of the Lord to lead them as He saw fit, they walked almost directly to the walls of the 'Forbidden City,' the former home of emperors and nobility. Entering the gate they walked past shrines, pagodas and temples fast falling to decay . . . and came to a grove of what they took to be cypress trees. A hallowed and reverential feeling was upon them. It was one of those occasions which at rare intervals come to mortals when they are surrounded by a Presence so sacred that human words would be disturbing. The brethren were very sure unseen holy beings were directing their footsteps."[2]

Then, through the authority of the holy apostleship, Elder McKay dedicated, consecrated, and set apart the Chinese realm for the preaching of the restored gospel of Jesus Christ. He prayed that the Chinese government might be stabilized, that the message might be given in peace. "May the Elders and Sisters whom thou shalt call to this land as missionaries," he continued, "have keen insight into the mental and spiritual state of the Chinese mind. Give them special power and ability to approach this people in such a manner as will make the proper appeal to them. We beseech thee, O God, to reveal to thy servants the best methods to adopt and the best plans to follow in establishing thy work among this ancient, tradition-steeped people."[3] He pleaded for the suffering children and for China's young, and he prayed that the bonds of superstition, might be broken. He prayed: "Heavenly Father, . . . break the bands of superstition, and may the young men and young women come out of the darkness of the Past into the Glorious Light now shining among the children of men. Grant, our Father, that these young men and young women may through upright, virtuous lives and prayerful study, be prepared and inclined to declare this message of salvation in their own tongue to their fellowmen."[4] It was an inspired prayer, a dedication, and a prophecy.

Several weeks later, Elder Cannon wrote to the *Improvement Era* and reported this event. In the article he made it clear that Elder McKay did not expect China to be opened to LDS missionaries in the near future. Concerning the prayer, he wrote: "It was such a prayer and blessing as must be recognized in heaven, and though the effects may not be suddenly apparent, they will be none the less real."[5] But turbulent 1920s, 1930s, and 1940s, in China, combined with the problems of the depression and World War II, made it impossible for the Church to open missionary work there until after the war ended.

THE CHINESE MISSION FROM 1949 TO 1953

On July 14, 1949, Elder Matthew Cowley, a member of the Council of the Twelve and president of the Asian and Pacific missions of the Church, stood atop Victoria Peak on Hong Kong Island in the company of his wife, President Hilton A. and Sister Hazel Robertson, and Elder Henry and Sister SaiLang Aki. There he offered a prayer to officially open the Chinese Mission of the Church. Mindful of Elder McKay's dedicatory prayer of 1921, Elder Cowley once again "asked God to open up the way for the gospel to be brought to that great nation."[6]

The creation of the Chinese Mission[7] had been discussed among the First Presidency and Council of the Twelve Apostles for some time before they authorized President David O. McKay, second counselor in the First Presidency, to call Hilton A. Robertson, the man who they believed knew "more about the Oriental people than any other man in the Church," to open the new mission.[8] Robertson had presided over the closing of the early Japanese Mission, had opened and presided over the Japanese Mission in Hawaii from 1937 to 1940, and was currently a counselor in the East Provo Stake presidency.

After the Robertsons accepted the call to open China, President McKay telephoned Henry Wong Aki of the Oahu Stake high council and asked him and his wife, SaiLang, to accompany

In late June and early July 1949, Elder Matthew Cowley and his wife, Elva (top right), sailed to Hong Kong with newly called mission president Hilton A. Robertson (seated far left) and his wife, Hazel (center of back row). Henry Wong Aki, counselor in the mission presidency, his wife SaiLang (behind him), and Carolyn Robertson completed the mission group. The others pictured were LDS members in the employ of the USS President Cleveland.

the Robertsons to Hong Kong. Aki accepted the assignment and functioned as first counselor in the mission presidency.

When the missionary group (consisting of the Robertsons and their nineteen-year-old daughter, Carolyn, the Akis, and Elder and Sister Cowley) docked at Hong Kong on July 10, 1949, they found the weather hot and humid and the city overcrowded with refugees from the civil war in mainland China. Since the end of World War II, the population of the British Crown Colony had exploded from 600,000 to almost 2.5 million. The entire area under British control encompassed only four hundred square miles and consisted of Hong Kong Island, the Kowloon and Sai Kung Peninsulas, and the New Territories (a tract of land adjacent to the Chinese border that was leased by the British in 1898 for ninety-nine years). Most of the 1.7 million refugees were packed into slums where food and water were meager, sanitation was inadequate, and the danger of devastating fires was ever present. Longtime residents, both British and Chinese, lived in modern apartment buildings and worked in modern establishments. Everyone, however, was distressed about the immediate effects of the war as well as the possible long-term consequences of the Nationalist-Communist struggle.

From the day of their arrival, the missionaries had difficulty finding housing and chapel facilities. Only through the help of some of Elder Aki's relatives did the missionaries and the Cowleys find hotel rooms at the Kimberly Hotel, Kowloon. Permanent headquarters were even harder to find.

On July 12, Elders Cowley, Robertson, and Aki flew to Canton (Guangzhou) to investigate the possibility of doing missionary work there. They found Canton to be in even worse condition than Hong Kong and in greater danger because of the war. They returned to Hong Kong the same day, hoping the Church could at least gain a foothold there.[9]

Two days later the group met at Victoria Peak on Hong Kong Island, and Elder Cowley offered the prayer that officially opened the mission to the Chinese people. "Another outstanding day in the mission," wrote President Robertson at the end of the day. "We went to Hong Kong and to the Peak South side where prayers were offered by Brother Aki and myself and then Apostle Mathew Cowley prayed officially opening the mission. It was an inspirational hour of worship and thanksgiving to God, our Father in Heaven, for our safe arrival and for the blessings of employment in his Kingdom among the people of the populous nation so overridden by so many calamities of nature and man."[10] The following day, Elder and Sister Cowley left for Japan, and the little band of missionaries was on its own.

During the next eighteen months the missionaries accomplished much, considering the circumstances. The first two young missionaries were Elders H. Grant Heaton and William K. Paalani, who arrived on February 25, 1950. Six additional elders came to

Hong Kong and made significant progress in the Cantonese language and acquired a number of friends for the Church. Eighteen Chinese joined the Church. Three young girls, Nora Koot and her sisters, were the first Chinese to be baptized in Hong Kong. They were baptized in a temporarily dammed stream at the bottom of a waterfall at Diamond Hill on December 31, 1950. The next month, fifteen others, most of whom were relatives of the Akis, joined the Church. Progress was slow, but the elders started with no knowledge of the language, with no members of the Church, with no Mormon literature except the Bible in Chinese (and not even Elder Aki could read it), with a difficult British bureaucracy with which to deal (the missionaries had problems gaining permission to build a chapel on property they had an option to buy), and worst of all, with an international situation that was very unstable.

It was an international problem—the Korean War, which broke out in July 1950—that brought an end to the mission. By that time the Chinese Communists were totally in control of mainland China, and the border along the New Territories was tense. The Korean problem exacerbated the situation in Hong Kong, and no one was sure that the war would not spread throughout East Asia. On January 9, 1951, President Harry S. Truman asked the American people to unite behind an effort to block the conquest of the world by Communism. The following day, the U.S. consul general in Hong Kong advised all American dependents to leave the colony as soon as possible. Forty-five thousand Chinese troops were amassed along the borders, and the situation was dangerous.[11]

The First Presidency watched carefully, and then, on January 13, President McKay telephoned President Robertson to inquire concerning the safety of the missionaries. Upon hearing Robertson's assessment of conditions, President McKay asked him to take "all of the missionaries to the Hawaiian Islands for the time being."[12] On February 6, 1951, President Robertson and his companions sailed from Hong Kong. Elders Heaton and Paalani had not been in Hong Kong for even a year, and the other elders had been there a shorter time. Robertson considered the withdrawal to be a temporary move, motivated primarily by the tense international situation but also by the fact that the Church did not think it was wise to build a chapel and missionary quarters at that time; and without larger facilities (the living room of the mission home could accommodate only twenty-five people at a time) the Church could not grow.[13]

The mission operated in Honolulu until March 31, and then the missionaries were sent on to San Francisco. Until February 9, 1953, the missionaries of the Chinese Mission worked among the Chinese people of northern California, especially in San Francisco, Oakland, Fresno, Stockton, and Sacramento. The mission was then closed, primarily because of lack of interest among the American-Chinese people. Only a handful of persons had joined the Church.

THE OPENING OF THE
SOUTHERN FAR EAST MISSION

Only two months after President Robertson and his missionaries departed from Hong Kong, David O. McKay became President of the Church. Although he was strongly oriented toward missionary expansion, the Korean conflict and the conscription of young LDS men into the armed services curtailed missionary efforts throughout the world. The total missionary force dropped from a high of 5,164 in 1950 to 2,584 in 1953. The missions of the Church were hard-pressed to maintain their programs, and the opening of new fields was out of the question. But with the conclusion of open hostilities in Korea in 1953, the LDS missionary force climbed again; and by the end of 1955, 4,651 missionaries were in the field, a sufficient number for the First Presidency to again consider opening China.[14]

Only seven months after Robertson's release from the Chinese Mission in February 1953, he was called again into missionary service, this time as president of the Japanese Mission and the Chinese Mission. As president of the Japan Mission (which

was for a brief time called the Far East Mission), Robertson supervised all LDS activities in East Asia. Although full-time missionary work was limited to Japan, LDS servicemen's groups were
organized in Korea, Taiwan, Okinawa, Guam, and the Philippines.
Demands on the mission president and some of the older missionaries were heavy.

On May 23, 1955, President McKay called twenty-six-year-old
H. Grant Heaton to preside over a new mission, the Southern Far
East Mission, which was soon to be created. Heaton, who had
served as a missionary in Hong Kong during the earlier mission,
had learned Cantonese before being transferred to California.
During the Korean conflict he had served in military intelligence
as an interrogator of Chinese prisoners and had learned the
Mandarin language as well. He could read and write Chinese.
Supporting him in his new assignment was his wife, Luana, and
their six-month-old baby.

As had been true in 1949, a member of the Council of the
Twelve, this time Elder Joseph Fielding Smith, President of the
Quorum of the Twelve Apostles, accompanied the new mission
president to his post. En route, President Smith toured the Japan
Mission and also visited Korea and dedicated that land. While in
Japan, he held an important meeting with President Hilton A.
Robertson (who was now serving as president of the Japan
Mission), the LDS servicemen, the missionaries, and the Japanese
Saints. President Smith proposed that the mission be divided into
the Northern Far East Mission, which would consist of Japan,
Korea, and Okinawa, and the Southern Far East Mission, which
would consist of Hong Kong, Taiwan, the Philippines, Guam, and
other parts of South and Southeast Asia. Although it was not
accessible to missionary work, the People's Republic of China,
too, was part of the mission. The proposal was unanimously
accepted in Japan, as was the same proposal in Hong Kong on
August 16, 1955. Hence, on that day, the Church officially commenced its third and most successful effort to take the restored
gospel to China.[15]

Soon after, President Heaton, President Robertson, and President Smith flew to the Philippines. On August 21, at Clark Air Base, President Smith presided at a meeting with about fifty LDS servicemen. At that time he dedicated the Philippine Islands to the preaching of the gospel. While the three presidents were in Manila, they attempted to find a site for a chapel and mission home. Six years passed, however, before missionary work was opened there.

On August 23 the Smiths flew to Guam. Two days later they met in conference with the Guam Branch, which consisted primarily of service personnel. The Saints there, too, approved of the new Southern Far East Mission. President Smith then dedicated the Island of Guam for missionary work.[16]

Following the visit to the Philippines, President Heaton returned to Hong Kong. On August 23 eight charter missionaries arrived in Hong Kong on board the SS *President Wilson:* Garnet E. Birch, Gary L. Bradshaw, Duane W. Degn, Kenneth K. S. Fong, Malan R. Jackson, Keith A. Madsen, Ronald R. Ollis, and Jerry D. Wheat. Only Elders Degn, Ollis, and Wheat had been called to serve in Hong Kong; but on the long sea voyage to Japan, President Joseph Fielding Smith and President Heaton decided that three elders was a strange number to start a mission with, and so they assigned five Japan-bound elders to Hong Kong.[17] Six additional elders arrived on October 8. From the beginning the First Presidency and Church leaders supported the mission with sufficient manpower to accomplish the work.

On August 27 the Heatons and the eight missionary elders moved into a rented home on Argyle Street, Kowloon. The immediate task was to prepare the elders to do active missionary work. President Heaton was qualified to direct the language training program that was needed. He hired young Chinese men to teach the elders six hours a day, one teacher for every two elders. One of these teachers, a mattress salesman until then, was Ng Kat Hing. (Ng was later baptized by Elder Wheat and became a strong leader in the Church in Hong Kong. Over the years he has done translation work, run the distribution center, held almost every priesthood calling, and is now the first president of the Hong Kong Temple.) The initial training program consisted of twelve hours of study per day—six hours with a teacher, two hours with a tape recorder, two hours of scripture study, one hour of world religions, and one hour of group discussion.[18]

Within a few days, by early September, most of the converts from the earlier mission had been relocated. President Heaton soon organized a Sunday School, and even some of the investigators from the earlier period were studying the gospel. The elders used English classes to attract interest among nonmembers. The Book of Mormon and Bible were the basic texts. By September 18 the elders were out among the people two days a week tracting. The grueling study schedule was taking a toll among the missionaries, and they needed to get out. Because their ability to use Cantonese and Mandarin (some elders were assigned to study each language) was limited, they sought out English-speaking people—Chinese, Indians, Englishmen, and others.[19]

In contrast to the two earlier attempts to plant the Church on Chinese soil, in 1955 the people of Hong Kong were ready for the gospel. "Present conditions in Hong Kong," wrote President Heaton, "seem conducive to missionary work. This colony is a place of refuge for those who cannot find safety in the Communist-dominated country of their birth. Most of the Christian missions which have been expelled from China are trying to maintain an organization, and to do this they operate in Hong Kong with many limitations. The presence of so many missionaries representing so many different sects, has created a great deal of religious interest among the Chinese. These factions, combined with the natural tendency of people in distress to turn to a Divine source, make the preaching of the Restored Gospel very vital and also give great opportunities to the (LDS) missionaries to fill their assignment."[20]

President Heaton recognized the need for translated materials. One of his first acts was to advertise for professional translators. More than one hundred well-educated men applied for the job, and from them Heaton chose three who were the best qualified. Subsequently two of these men were dismissed, and Mr. Wang Kai-An became the Church translator. During the next few years Mr. Wang, who later became a member of the Church, translated many tracts and lesson materials for the mission.[21]

Missionary activity in Hong Kong Colony was intensive from the beginning. Before the year ended, President Heaton had leased three apartments and sent the missionaries into the field, created the Hong Kong-Kowloon District, organized three branches (the North Point Branch on October 23, and the Tsim Sha Tsui and Sham Shui Po Branches on November 17), and purchased the property at #2 Cornwall Street in Kowloon-Tong, which served as the mission home and office until the 1990s, when the site was used for the construction of the Hong Kong Temple. The leased apartments doubled as meeting halls for Church services. The new mission home required remodeling before it could be occupied. Before the year ended, Heaton had visited the LDS servicemen in the Philippines again. He had also made significant progress on a new missionary lesson plan that was designed especially for the Chinese people. After only four months, wrote Heaton, the elders were "well on their way to mastery of the language."[22]

BUYING THE CORNWALL STREET
PROPERTY AND OTHERS

The acquisition of the property on Cornwall Street was the most important real estate purchase the Church ever made in Hong Kong. Buying property in Hong Kong Colony has always been difficult. Costs have been unreasonably high, especially in comparison with prices in Utah. Heaton knew the Brethren intended to have the mission succeed and that to do so buildings were necessary for meetinghouses and a mission home and office. But as he searched for appropriate properties, he found that the turnaround time to get a positive reply from the Church bureaucracy in Salt Lake City was always too slow. The properties he chose were sold before he could buy them. Finally, President Heaton wrote directly to President David O. McKay and explained the problem. President McKay made a special arrangement with Heaton to wire funds to a bank in Hong Kong when the right properties were found. Heaton was to acquire properties in his name. The properties that Heaton bought were handled in this way and later deeded over to the Church.

BUYING #2 CORNWALL STREET
H. Grant Heaton

I had found the mission home that we were going to buy—a piece of property just up on Waterloo Road, just about four houses up on Boundary Street—and had wired for the money. The only thing it had going for it was that it was available. It wasn't very good at all. It was a house that we could live in and we thought that if we owned it we could probably control the termites. But it didn't have much to offer. Except it was available. And so I had gone in and negotiated a sound earnest money deposit on that property and had agreed that when the check came in from President McKay I was to go down and close the deal. In the meantime, a very good friend . . . called me and said, "Father Lee has a piece of property that is owned by some of his parishioners and he would like to get rid of it." Now, Father Lee . . . was the Abbot General of the Trappist Monastery over in Lantau Island. He happened to have been educated at the Trappist Monastery in Huntsville, Utah. He had been of a little service earlier, when I tried to open a bank account when we first came. The bank wasn't sure they wanted to convert a check written out for $20,000 into a Hong Kong bank account. They brought up several people to the teller's desk.

Pretty soon a voice from behind me spoke up. It said, "If that check is written by the Mormon Church, you can cash it. It doesn't matter how much it is." I turned around and here was this Catholic priest behind me. That was Father Lee. . . . But Father Lee had a piece of property that he insisted that I see. I said, "It is no good for me to look at it. We have already made a deposit and there is no way I can get out of this deposit." "But come look at it," he said. They dragged me kicking and screaming to #2 Cornwall Street. My opinion at that time was, in a ranking of 1 to 10, it was about a 15. It was the ideal place for us. It couldn't be better. As all of you well know.

And so I was troubled. I thought I had failed the Lord because I had chosen a piece of property and made a commitment on that piece of property and now here is one that we needed and we didn't have enough money for two. So I didn't know if President McKay would go for a blind deal like that or not. We obviously prayed a good deal about it. I decided I would go back to the old gentleman and see if there was some way I could talk him into keeping the deposit, but letting us out from the deal. I didn't want to be dishonorable with him and so, I went to his home. I had negotiated just with him prior to that time. When I went in, two of his sons were in the room. I think he was afraid that he hadn't really communicated to me well in Chinese. He and I spoke Cantonese together and I didn't have a great real estate vocabulary at the time. I thought he had his sons there to help translate, because they spoke English. And as we finished the small talk, one of his sons finally came to me and said, "Mr. Heaton, our father has sold, has made an agreement to sell you this place. He didn't consult us. We would prefer not selling it. Would you be willing to take back the deposit?" And, I was willing.

The Lord blessed us with Cornwall Street. It couldn't

have served us better under any circumstances over the years. For forty years it has served us well. I believe the Lord had a hand in directing Father Lee, although it wasn't his intent to magnify the Mormon Church in Hong Kong. He was a good, honest, sincere man.[23]

The new mission home was a beautiful colonial-style building with sixteen rooms, five bathrooms, and an attractive front yard.

THE CHURCH IN HONG KONG FROM 1956 TO 1959

Hong Kong is an unusual political entity.[24] Its very existence as a British colony was an anomaly. During the time when colonial powers were retreating from Asia, the British somehow held on there. Although few people find Hong Kong to be a desirable place from a social, economic, or political perspective, it continued, grew, and even prospered under difficult conditions. It is a city unique in all the world. It had and continues to have a pulse, a bustle that sets it apart.

Hong Kong was a chaotic place in the mid-1950s. As the population almost exploded with the influx of millions of refugees from mainland China, the British colonial government found itself faced with the difficult and costly task of housing these people. Efforts in this area have continued to the present. Refugees built shacks on hillsides, on rooftops, in alleys, and on city streets. Chinese with a variety of dialects competed with one another for jobs, food, and water. Social, medical, and welfare services were strained almost to the breaking point as former Chinese leaders and elites found themselves thrust to the bottom rung of Hong Kong's economic and social ladder. The high and the lowly mingled together as near equals. Sages and servants vied with each other for survival at least, and for economic and social betterment if possible.

Heaton and the missionaries may have overreacted to the

"Chineseness" of the situation. Having studied Chinese history and politics at the University of California at Berkeley, Heaton knew many of the problems of East-West relations. He was caught between his feelings of love for the Chinese and an educated distrust of their ability to turn situations to their own best advantage. So-called rice Christians, those who would claim to be Christians for an allotment of rice or some other benefit, were plentiful in Hong Kong. Many Christian churches distributed U.S. agricultural products to needy refugees, and unfortunately these products were sometimes used by the churches as a means of attracting members. President Heaton was fearful of the negative consequences of such situations and made every effort to avoid attracting people into the Church whose intentions were not sincere.

He was also concerned about bringing Chinese people into the Church who did not fully understand the teachings of the Church and the implications of membership. In an effort to teach the Chinese people well, Heaton and the missionaries developed a series of seventeen lessons that handled the basic tenets of the gospel from Jesus Christ to Joseph Smith and from the premortal existence to the last judgment. The original intention of the missionaries was to give investigators one lesson each week until they completed the series. After baptism, new converts were then required to listen to twenty more lessons that were designed to ground them solidly in the faith. The implications of this procedure were significant. The missionaries had to memorize the entire lesson plan—a large demand on any elder or sister. The amount of time the lesson plan required before the missionaries could consider their job done was great. Present-day missionaries can teach five or six times as many people in the same period of time. Nevertheless, the times and circumstances must be remembered. Because the new members of the Church did not have examples to follow in Church activity and because they did not have a deep knowledge of the restored gospel, the extended plan was undoubtedly desirable during the first several years of the mission. In addition to their proselyting work, the missionaries were also involved in branch and district leadership assignments.

The new mission celebrated its first success on May 31, 1956, when eleven Chinese were baptized, five of whom were refugees from Communist China. Two weeks later, four more Chinese were baptized into the Church. By the end of 1956, eighty-one converts had come into the Church in the Hong Kong area. In November two Chinese men, Lee Wing Foon and Ng Kat Hing, were called as counselors in a Sunday School superintendency. Other Chinese members were called as Sunday School teachers. The first Chinese to receive the Aaronic Priesthood were ordained on November 11.

In January 1957 the mission instituted regular sacrament meetings. Until then only a brief sacrament service had been held following Sunday School. In February President Heaton called Lee Nai Ken, a fairly new convert, to fill a mission. Elder Lee, the first Hong Kong Chinese to receive the Melchizedek Priesthood, served full-time from February until August 1957. In May 1957 Nora Koot, a convert of the 1949–51 mission, accepted a call to serve as a missionary. She was the first Chinese female to serve in that calling.

By the end of June there were forty missionaries and three hundred members in Hong Kong. The missionaries were having remarkable success in their proselyting efforts. President Heaton told the *Hong Kong Standard* that 30 percent of the people whom the elders and sisters contacted became members of the Church.[25]

Before the year ended, eighteen Chinese members of the Church were enrolled in a twenty-two-week missionary preparation course. Each class was to last two hours. Heaton expected some of the graduates to serve full-time missions if they could find money to finance themselves.

When President Heaton wrote his report of December 31, 1957, he made some unusual statements. In fact, he said some things that have seldom, if ever, been written by a mission president before or since. He complained that the missionaries had too many investigators and that they did not have time to meet with all the people who wanted to study the gospel. Since October, when a man named Chu Wan Yuen contacted the Church and then introduced his close friends to the missionaries, affairs had moved at a breathtaking pace. At about the same time, another influential Chinese named Wang Chih Tsao started introducing his friends to the missionaries in the Tsuen Wan area. Investigators became so numerous that the elders could not meet with each individual or family. To meet the need, they formed study groups and taught interested people in classes of 15 to 150. Seven nights a week they met with these groups and then raced through each day trying to meet every investigator at their home. The major weakness of this system, of course, was that the missionaries did not have enough time to establish meaningful relationships with and feel the spirit of their investigators. But there seemed to be no alternative.

Before the year ended, the missionaries had waiting lists of people who wanted to be taught the gospel. The first study group in Yuen Long multiplied from one to eleven between October and December. The elders had baptized thirty people, and fifty more were awaiting approval. President Heaton could see that by March 1958 there would be more than one hundred members of the Church in Yuen Long, and there was not even a place to meet. At that time the new branch was meeting in little wooden or rice straw houses, as was also often true in other parts of the New Territories, Kowloon, and Hong Kong.

The rapid influx of members placed a strain on the auxiliaries. There were very few experienced leaders. In January 1958 Heaton assigned ten elders to work full-time with baptized members. He expected to assign ten more missionaries to member work before midsummer and all of the missionaries to work with members by the end of the year. It worked out almost in that way. Because of the rapid growth during 1958 (904 baptisms), Heaton stopped all proselyting during January and February 1959. Even before that, however, he had put the damper on the group-study method of teaching the gospel. An unfortunately high attrition rate developed in late 1958, and President Heaton wisely counseled his missionaries to again teach only individuals and families. He reasoned that the honest in heart would be waiting when the missionaries had time to work with them.

It was difficult to explain what the sudden attraction of the Church was. Some sincere and lasting converts have reported that if they had remained in mainland China, where they had wealth and servants, they would have never seen the missionaries. Now that they were in humble circumstances, they were more teachable. A number of former provincial governors, generals, and highly educated men came into the Church. Many of them, however, fell away. Why they left so soon is a matter of speculation. Some missionaries of the time have suggested that these people hoped to better their social and economic position by joining the Church. Perhaps they thought the Church could help them leave Hong Kong and go to America. Another explanation is that President Heaton and his missionaries, who worked hard to appeal to the Chinese mind, seemed like sages. Whatever the cause, a high percentage of the converts through the group-study classes did not remain faithful to the Church.

On the other hand, observers familiar with the Hong Kong situation during the Heaton era have reported that only a few converts came into the Church hoping to gain immediate material advantage. The Church developed a reputation as a non-relief church. While other churches distributed rice and other foods, the people who joined the LDS Church found themselves confronted with the problem of giving up their aid from other churches. Many sincere converts to the Church were in serious financial difficulty and needed and deserved the assistance of the Church in overcoming their problems.

THE WELFARE OF THE HONG KONG SAINTS

The LDS mission in Hong Kong was faced with the problem of caring for its own. Though President Heaton knew well the doctrines of self-sufficiency, self-support, and self-reliance, he also knew that the leaders of the Church had preached from the early days that a church that could not save a man temporally could not save him spiritually. He found the responsibility of caring for the honest, needy poor while avoiding rice Christians to be a demanding task.

Heaton spearheaded a campaign in which the missionaries wrote home for old clothes and financial contributions for the poor. By Christmas 1957 two tons of clothes and $2,517 had arrived from the United States for distribution. Though this project was successful, it was evident to the mission staff that self-help projects would be much better in the long run. By March 1958, the mission was involved in several efforts to help the Chinese Saints improve their financial situations. The most important project was an arrangement that Heaton and some of the elders made with a few businesses in Utah to sell Chinese-Mormon handicrafts. Several thousands of dollars were earned by Hong Kong Saints before this project ran its course.

President Heaton called Wang Chih Tsao to coordinate a welfare committee of members from each branch. These members and the missionaries discussed ways to help the Saints. One branch, Sham Shui Po, enlisted the aid of two medical doctors—Kom Kwok, who employed traditional Chinese medical knowledge, and Sit Paak, who was trained in Western-style medicine—to treat branch members who were unable to pay for medical help elsewhere. The welfare committee also discussed the need for educational help, either elementary or secondary-technical study, and operated a scholarship fund for several years. Another need, or so it seemed for a while, was for vocational or on-the-job training. President Heaton involved the Church in two clothing factories. His intention was to run a training program in professional sewing. Unfortunately, the members did not want to learn to sew, and the project was a financial loss for the Church. In retrospect, it is evident that Heaton overreacted to the needs of the Saints. The economy of Hong Kong was improving rapidly by

1959. Furthermore, when Heaton surveyed the members of the Church in June 1959, he found that the Latter-day Saints were considerably better off than the average resident in Hong Kong. President Heaton and the welfare committee also considered establishing a chicken and pig farm on an island near Hong Kong and a brick factory in the New Territories. It is doubtful whether either undertaking would have succeeded. As Elder Mark E. Petersen concluded, the members of the Church were too well educated—that is, the older people—to be willing to work for either enterprise.

Concerning education for the young, President Heaton presented information to Elder Petersen that convinced him of the need for two elementary schools, one on the Hong Kong side and one in Kowloon, and a high school-vocational school. But Elder Petersen's positive recommendation to the First Presidency was not carried out. There were at that time 135 qualified schoolteachers in the mission who could have provided the complete staff of the elementary schools and part of the faculty for the secondary school. The issue of schools was discussed in Salt Lake and in Hong Kong for years to come, but beyond seminary and institute programs the Church did not undertake any education projects.

THE STRUGGLE TO ACQUIRE REAL ESTATE

Property for chapels was a challenging problem from the beginning. Hong Kong is densely populated, and land sells at a premium price. President Heaton and the missionaries entered the area with many preconceptions, among them the idea that chapels should spread over a large area and have parking, landscaping, and so forth. Although Heaton worked tirelessly at acquiring some government-held land, he found that without paying high black market prices, he could not acquire property. This he would not do. He finally settled for a different solution. In March 1957 he purchased for the Church four apartments at the top of a seven-story building in Tsim Sha Tsui in downtown Kowloon. Located at #2 Tak Shing Street, the completely remodeled apartments were converted to a chapel, seven classrooms, and missionary quarters. In September President Heaton bought apartment space on the eighth floor of an apartment house in Sham Shui Po and on the twelfth floor of a building in Happy Valley (Causeway Bay) on the Hong Kong Island side. Until the mid-1970s these three buildings serviced most LDS meetings in the downtown areas of Hong Kong and Kowloon.

To meet the needs of the rapidly growing Tsuen Wan Branch, which was situated ten miles north outside Kowloon, Heaton bought a complete four-story building in December 1957. It provided a chapel, classrooms, office space, and missionary quarters. Six months later he purchased a three-story building in Yuen Long. The building was not yet completed, and delays caused by government regulations put off use of the building for almost a year. In March 1959, the Church built a small chapel at Tui Geng Ling. The modest $4,500 structure was considered to be a first-phase building; nevertheless, it met the needs of the branch for a while. This was probably the first LDS-constructed chapel on the Asian mainland, at least the first built since the little chapels in Calcutta and Karachi, India, in the 1850s. When Elder Mark E. Petersen toured the mission in May and June 1959, he dedicated all five chapels in the Hong Kong area.

TRANSLATION AND PRINTING
OF CHURCH MATERIALS

In addition to President Heaton's struggle to acquire property, to care for the needy, and to develop new teaching plans, he and the missionaries were also deeply concerned with the responsibility to provide tracts, pamphlets, hymns, lesson manuals, and LDS scriptures in the Chinese language. Earlier it was mentioned that Heaton hired Wang Kai-An as a translator. Brother Wang published the first Chinese tracts, part of the "Rays of Living Light" series, in July 1956. Two months later the *Joseph Smith Tells His Own Story* pamphlet (later published worldwide as *Joseph Smith's Testimony*) was ready for distribution. By November Wang was translating Elder LeGrand Richards's *A Marvelous Work and a Wonder* for use as a Relief Society manual. Other translation projects were also completed and printed during this period.

In September 1957 Heaton formed a Book of Mormon translation committee. Parts of the book were assigned to a number of Chinese men for translation. The target date for its publication was June 1960, but for various reasons, the most significant ones being Heaton's release in the fall of 1959 and the problem of too much variation in style among different translators, the book was not published until 1966.

In March 1959 the mission started publication of a monthly magazine for the Saints. Titled *Voice of the Saints,* it contained translated articles and talks by General Authorities and items that were written in the mission.

By summer 1959 the Hong Kong part of the Southern Far East Mission was solidly established. Most of the branches were well housed by Hong Kong standards, and publications in Chinese were being printed in ever-increasing numbers. The temporal condition of the Saints was improving, and the spiritual condition of the members was generally healthy. There were problems in two branches because some of the members would not support and sustain Chinese Saints—their own people—in their callings as branch presidents, counselors, and so forth. But sacrament meeting attendance was 53 percent, better than the Church average, and almost 80 percent of the members could be considered active or semi-active.[26]

CHARACTERISTICS OF CHINESE MEMBERS

Who were these new Latter-day Saints? Although statistical information is not available, some of the missionaries and Elder Mark E. Petersen commented on this question. Elder Petersen reported to the First Presidency that the members were primarily refugees. Were the new members converts from Asian religions? Generally not. Wayne Bringhurst, missionary counselor to President Heaton, wrote: "We cannot underestimate the good the other (Christian) churches have done. . . . It is a rare occasion when a person with no previous knowledge of the Bible, Adam and Eve, or Jesus Christ comes into the Church."[27] But the new converts were Chinese, nevertheless. They brought with them many wonderful traits of character and seemingly inborn qualities for leadership.

By mid-1959 membership in Hong Kong was approaching 1,500. Among these members were 188 college graduates, 3 former provincial governors, 7 former generals in the Kuomintang Army, 5 people with Ph.D.s, and many skilled people. The new Chinese converts were proving their worth to the Church through missionary service. Chen Hsiao Hsin (David) baptized 114 converts during his first year in the mission field. He later served as president of the Hong Kong Mission from 1977 to 1980. His close friend, Tang Ching Nan (Jonathan), baptized 78 converts during his first year as a missionary. Their converts were as solid in the gospel as any in the mission.

During 1959, however, the number of converts was low. The missionaries made a conscious decision to require significant proof of conversion and devotion to the Church. From 1959 onward, the task of later mission presidents was basically one of building carefully on the solid foundation of the early years. To later mission presidents also fell the task of opening new areas such as the Philippines, South and Southeast Asia, and strengthening the work in Taiwan.

THE ESTABLISHMENT OF
THE CHURCH IN TAIWAN

When Elder Joseph Fielding Smith created the Southern Far East Mission in 1955 and toured the countries included in it, he was unable to visit Taiwan, the little Chinese island that the Portuguese named Formosa, "Beautiful Isle." Taiwan, which means "terraced bay" in Chinese, had been almost unknown to most Americans prior to the Nationalist retreat there in 1949 and 1950. Even in 1955 it was considered to be a temporary home by the more than one million soldiers and civilians of mainland China who were driven out by the Communists. Those native to the island, who spoke primarily a variation of Fukienese, were not happy to have the "aristocratic" mainlanders take over their island and control the more than seven million Taiwanese.

However, the Taiwanese were somewhat accustomed to domination from abroad. From 1895 until 1945, the Japanese controlled Taiwan as a colony. Before that, Taiwan was for two centuries part of China proper. Indeed, the mainlanders had some justification for their claimed right to direct the government in Taiwan.

When Protestant and Roman Catholic missionaries were forced to leave the mainland between 1949 and 1953, many of them moved to Taiwan. Before the 1950s, the Presbyterians were the dominant mission group. Since then the number of churches and missionary societies represented has grown greatly. At the end of World War II there were only thirty thousand Christians in Taiwan. By the mid-1970s the number had grown to more than six hundred thousand, and by the 1990s there were more than one million Christians there.

Taiwan is only a small place, but in comparison with Hong Kong's tiny area, its 13,808 square miles offer considerable space to the inhabitants. Taiwan is larger than Massachusetts and Connecticut combined and slightly smaller than the Netherlands.[28] By the late 1970s Taiwan had the second-highest standard of living in Asia, behind Japan. American-aid dollars helped greatly in developing Taiwan's economy. Aside from military assistance, the Republic of China has not received foreign aid from the United States since 1965.

When LDS missionaries first arrived in Taiwan in 1956, however, the economic situation was weak, religions were in flux, and the climate was one of government-promoted tension. Propaganda campaigns against the Communist Chinese were endless. In fact, the crusade to return to the mainland was so encompassing that the people hardly had time to think about other matters. It was into this environment that the first LDS missionaries came.

President Heaton, who had responsibility for Hong Kong, Guam, and the Philippines, also had the assignment to establish the Church in Taiwan. He made several visits there before he was ready to assign the first missionaries. It was fortunate that a few LDS servicemen and their families were stationed in Taipei. One stalwart convert to the Church was Captain Stanley Simiskey. He was the leader of the small band of Saints in Taiwan, all Americans. Heaton arranged for him to care for the elders when they arrived from Hong Kong on June 4, 1956.[29] Elders Duane W. Degn, Melvin C. Fish, Weldon J. Kitchen, and Keith A. Madsen expected to find a bleak, poverty-stricken land. To their delight they found the people of Taiwan to be well fed and well housed. Some luxuries were absent from their lives, but the comfort afforded by the greater space and the natural beauty of the island more than compensated for the missing elements of modernity.

By October 1956 the Taipei Branch had regular attendance of thirty-five people—missionaries, service personnel, and local Chinese investigators. The elders had studied Mandarin Chinese while in Hong Kong. But now that they were among the people, they found that a large majority did not use that language. Nevertheless, because Mandarin was the official language of Taiwan, they persisted in their effort to learn it. By March 1957 the number of elders had been doubled, and all of them were progressing well in the language.

The Taiwan elders realized their first success on April 27, 1957, when they baptized Ch'iu Hung-hsiang and Tseng I-Chang. Both men were educated, capable men. Brother Tseng, who was the first Chinese in Taiwan to be ordained an elder (April 1958), later served his nation as a consular officer in France, the

Philippines, and Saudi Arabia. He and Brother Ch'iu were called as counselors in the Taipei Branch Sunday School superintendency shortly after their baptisms. In April 1958 Elder Kitchen set Brother Tseng apart as a counselor in the branch presidency. He was the first Chinese in Taiwan to serve in that capacity.

By the end of 1957 the elders had baptized more than fifty Chinese, and by mid-1958 the work was moving ahead at a satisfactory pace. By then there were 286 local members, 184 of whom were in Taipei. In the first quarter of 1958, the elders extended the work to Tainan and Taichung, and soon after to Kaohsiung and other cities in the south.

But the Church did not take hold in Taiwan quite as quickly as it did in Hong Kong. There were several reasons for this. President Heaton did not assign as many missionaries there as in Hong Kong. He could not visit Taiwan very often—about quarterly—and did not feel comfortable having many elders and sisters away from his direct supervision. This led to feelings of separateness among many of the Taiwan workers. When Heaton or his counselors visited Taiwan, at least until September 1958, the missionaries treated them coolly, and when the leaders were gone, the Taiwan elders disregarded some mission rules and directions. But during the last part of 1958, President Heaton assigned his counselor, W. Brent Hardy, to live in Taiwan and act as president. This change brought the desired effect, and from then on the work progressed at a faster pace.

A change in local political conditions at about the same time also had a good effect. During August and September 1958, Communist China and the Republic of China almost went to war. Elder Hardy related that tensions were extremely high during this time and that the missionaries were not sure whether they could stay. At approximately the same time that the threat of war was at its height, the missionaries held an islandwide meeting in which they prayed that they could remain and pledged their loyalty to the Lord, the Church, the Chinese people, and each other. Within a few days the danger of war passed, and by the end of the year new investigators were studying the restored gospel. As the two powers settled into the uncomfortable peace that has endured to the present, the level of propaganda was reduced somewhat in Taiwan, and the people had an opportunity to think about matters other than war. From that time on, the LDS missionaries had better success.[30]

Evidently the missionaries did not encounter as much poverty in Taiwan as they had in Hong Kong. The mission records do not mention shortages of food, housing, or medical attention. Education, too, seems to have been adequate and steadily improving. President Heaton and the Taiwan elders did have a difficult time finding suitable property for chapels. By the time of Heaton's release, the Church had acquired no property. Meeting facilities were poor. Related to the property matter was official registration of the Church. The Church needed to own property before it could register. Hence, buying property took on additional importance.

Buddhism and Daoism (Taoism) were and are the dominant religions of the island. With the exception of the aboriginal tribes who were until recently animists but are now generally converted to Protestant Christianity, the people of Taiwan worship a number of folk deities. But they generally pattern their lives on Confucian ethical principles. Early LDS missionaries reported that their converts were almost never Buddhist or Roman Catholic. They found that their greatest success came "from those people who have studied in Christian schools and already have a good understanding of the Bible, but have never been baptized into any other church."[31]

The most important event in the Church in Taiwan from its founding in 1956 until 1959 was Elder Mark E. Petersen's visit from May 25 to June 1, 1959. He was the first General Authority to visit there. During that time, he and Sister Petersen visited with all of the missionaries and branches and also with high-ranking U.S. officials in the country to assess its political stability.

On June 1, shortly before leaving for Hong Kong, Elder and

Sister Petersen, President Heaton, and some missionaries and members gathered at the end of Chung Shan North Road, just below the Grand Hotel, for a special meeting. Elder Petersen then offered a prayer of rededication of the land and people of Taiwan. In his prayer he mentioned Elder McKay's dedication of the entire Chinese realm, but he asked for a special blessing on this particular part of it. He prayed "for all the freedoms that are necessary for the carrying on of the gospel."[32]

NOTES

1. Spellings of Chinese words vary greatly depending on the transliteration system used. Before the establishment of the People's Republic of China (PRC), the Wade-Giles system was the accepted means of transliteration. Today, however, the Pinyin system of the PRC has gained almost universal acceptance among scholars and in the print media. The major exceptions are found in Taiwan and Hong Kong. In this book the locally accepted spellings are used. From time to time the Pinyin spelling will be added in parentheses for the convenience of the reader. In this example the word *Ch'ing* in Wade-Giles is given in Pinyin in parentheses as *Qing*.

2. Hugh J. Cannon, as quoted in Palmer, *The Church Encounters Asia*, p. 35.

3. As quoted in ibid., p. 37.

4. As quoted in ibid.

5. Hugh J. Cannon, "The Chinese Realm Dedicated for the Preaching of the Gospel," *Improvement Era* 24 (February 1921): 445.

6. Matthew Cowley, as quoted in "The Language of Sincerity," *Improvement Era* 52 (November 1949): 715.

7. See Steven N. Talbot, "A History of the Chinese Mission of the Church . . . , 1949 to 1953," (unpublished paper, Brigham Young University, 1977).

8. See Hilton A. Robertson, Diary, 28 February 1949; copy in possession of the author.

9. See ibid., 12 July 1949.

10. Robertson, Diary, 14 July 1949.

11. See "Consul advises Americans to get out of Hong Kong," *Salt Lake Tribune*, 10 January 1951, p. 1.

12. As quoted in Chinese Mission Historical Reports, 31 March 1951, LDS Church Archives.

13. See Mission Financial and Statistical Reports, Chinese Mission, 1951, LDS Church Archives; hereafter cited as MFSR.

14. See Gordon Irving, "Numerical Strength and Geographical Distribution of the LDS Missionary Force, 1830–1974," *Task Papers in LDS History*, April 1975, LDS Church Archives, pp. 23, 26.

15. See Southern Far East Mission Historical Reports, 30 September 1955, LDS Church Archives; hereafter cited as SFEM.

16. See ibid.

17. Jerry D. Wheat, interview by the author, Hong Kong, 6 September 1995, tape recording.

18. See "Missionary System Set Up on Hong Kong," *Church News*, 29 October 1955;

see also "Mormon Church in H.K.," *South China Morning Post* (Hong Kong), 19 October 1955.

19. See SFEM, 30 September 1955.

20. H. Grant Heaton, "Missionary system set up in Hong Kong," *Church News*, 29 October 1955, p. 6.

21. See Diane E. Browning, "The Translation of Mormon Scriptures into Chinese" (unpublished paper, Brigham Young University, 1977), p. 2; in possession of the author.

22. SFEM, 31 December 1955, LDS Church Archives.

23. H. Grant Heaton delivered this testimony in the Ho Man Tin chapel, Kowloon-Tong, Hong Kong, 26 May 1996.

24. Unless otherwise noted, the basic source for this and the following section is SFEM, by date. President Heaton kept a thorough record of mission developments and activities.

25. See *Hong Kong Standard*, 1 September 1957.

26. A survey made while Elder Mark E. Petersen was in Hong Kong in June 1959 "indicated that only about 20 percent of the membership in this area is unemployed. Many have low wages, and low standard of living, but they are self-supporting. Those not employed are cared for by relatives and friends, not by the Church. The average income for our employed Saints is about $218 per month Hong Kong dollars. One American dollar is worth 5.85 Hong Kong dollars. Therefore in terms of American dollars the income would be about $27.40 per month. The average income for the people of the city generally is $130 per month, Hong Kong. Our people therefore are well above the average. The average size of L.D.S. family is 5.4 persons." See Mark E. Petersen to First Presidency, Tour of the Southern Far East Mission, General Observations, 6 July 1959, LDS Church Archives.

27. SFEM, 30 September 1958.

28. A useful introduction to Christianity in Taiwan is David Woodward's "Taiwan," in Donald E. Hoke, *The Church in Asia* (Chicago: Moody Press, 1975), pp. 609–21.

29. See "Mormon missionaries now labor in Formosa," *Church News*, 23 June 1956, p. 19.

30. W. Brent Hardy, interview by the author, Las Vegas, Nevada, 2 June 1975, tape recording.

31. SFEM, 30 September 1958.

32. Ibid., 30 June 1959.

11

THE CHINESE
REALM

1 9 5 9 – 1 9 7 8

Continuing Progress in Hong Kong and Taiwan

The development of the Church in the nations of the Southern Far East Mission from 1955 to 1978 was inspiring to those who witnessed it firsthand. Even outside observers who learn about the rise of the Church in those lands consider it an amazing phenomenon. Young President Heaton and those who served with him worked diligently to establish the Church not only in Hong Kong and Taiwan but also in Guam, the Philippines, and Singapore. Before 1970 ended, the Church was planted in the Philippines, Singapore, Vietnam, Thailand, and Indonesia, and representatives of the Church had visited with growing groups of Latter-day Saints in India and other parts of South and Southeast Asia. This chapter is devoted to the development of the Church in Hong Kong and Taiwan.

Robert Sherman Taylor, a businessman from Hawaii, assumed leadership of the Southern Far East Mission on September 15, 1959. He was not as well prepared for his new role in China as his predecessor had been, but he was a careful, well-organized man who had the ability to get things done. Though he had problems learning the Chinese languages, he was soon able to gain the loyalty of the Saints and missionaries.

To him fell a number of difficult tasks, not the least of which was the purchase of property and encouraging official recognition of the Church in Hong Kong, Taiwan, and the Philippines. As can be seen in the table below, President Taylor and the missionaries produced growing numbers of converts each year of his administration.

Southern Far East Mission Statistics, 1956–1968

Date	Total Members	Convert Baptisms	Melchizedek Priesthood	Branches/ Districts	Number of Missionaries
1956	212+	81	1		
1957	714	510	2	5	57+3
1958	1586	904	7	18/5	83+8
1959	1715	258	13	13/5	91+1
1960	2211	381	22	25/7	115+7
1961	3332	639	39	25/7	136+2
1962	3946	830	64	27/8	150+1
1963	5672	1430	*	28/3	170+1
1964	6981	1313		43/5	204+5
1965	7488	2548		41/6	203+11
1966	10524	1182	451	42/10	243+12
1967	7070**	583	369	30/9	130+14
1968	10337++	557		31/10	118+10

Hong Kong–Taiwan Mission Statistics, 1969–1970

Date	Total Members	Convert Baptisms	Melchizedek Priesthood	Branches/ Districts	Number of Missionaries
1969	8732	496	261	3/3	134+6
1970	9442	789		31/5	153+9

+ Mostly servicemen. The inclusion of servicemen has made this data less reliable.
* Melchizedek Priesthood numbers become unreliable at this point.
** The Philippines becomes a separate mission.
++ Add 1,450 servicemen in Vietnam and Thailand.

By April 1960 there were fewer than five hundred members of the Church in Taiwan, but through the challenge of Elder Gordon B. Hinckley and the continued encouragement of President Taylor, the Taiwan missionaries increased the total number of Chinese members in Taiwan to 831 by March 1962.[1]

It was during April 1960 that Elder Hinckley made his first tour of the Asian missions. He found conditions in Hong Kong and Taiwan less than desirable but marveled at the love the missionaries had for the Chinese people. Even in 1962 he described missionary living conditions in Taiwan as miserable but found the elders and sisters willing to accept them.

In September 1962 Jay A. Quealy Jr., former Oahu Stake president and a successful businessman, became president of the mission. He was a warm, well-organized, charismatic figure who received the respect of all who associated with him. The number of missionaries expanded rapidly between 1962 and 1965, largely because of the growth of the work in the Philippines, and the baptismal rate per missionary remained high. He was eager to see the local Saints in leadership positions and organized the districts of the mission so that the Chinese held the important posts. President Quealy pushed expansion of the Church into new nations. He and Elder Hinckley even visited India together, a story that is reported later. Although he did not know much Cantonese or Mandarin Chinese, President Quealy encouraged progress on the Book of Mormon translation and printing project. He had been released by the time it was published in late 1965, but he had the satisfaction of knowing that he had moved it toward completion.

Keith E. Garner, from Palo Alto, California, became president of the mission in August 1965. His previous contacts with the Chinese people had been as a missionary in Hawaii. He worked well with the missionaries, and the auxiliaries also received his attention. He emphasized the use of the Book of Mormon, which was first distributed during his time. President Garner devoted much time to work with servicemen in Vietnam.

While President Garner led the mission, the membership grew to more than 9,000, plus over 5,500 servicemen in Vietnam and Thailand. In 1967 the Philippines portion was divided off into a separate mission. More than 100 of the 243 missionaries and 3,000 of the members were transferred to the new mission. It was during 1966 that Elder Hinckley first recommended that Taiwan be made a separate mission, a move that was slow in coming.

W. Brent Hardy, fifth president of the mission, was also a businessman. He had served in Hong Kong and Taiwan during the early years of the mission and knew well the Mandarin and Cantonese languages and Chinese ways. His wife, too, spoke Cantonese. He worked closely with local leaders to strengthen the Chinese Saints. Virtually all programs of the Church were in use in Hong Kong and Taiwan by this time, and members were generally struggling with the same problems as the Saints elsewhere in the world. "President Hardy," said William S. Bradshaw, who followed him as mission president in Hong Kong, "had the mammoth responsibility of seeing the Church undergo organizational changes in many, many countries."[2] He was referring to the separation of Singapore, Indonesia, Thailand, and South Vietnam into the new Southeast Asia Mission in 1969, the reassimilation of South Vietnam a short time later, and the creation of the Taiwan Mission in January 1971. Being involved in these changes was time-consuming and taxing on his energies. President Hardy also worked at acquiring new property for chapels.

President William S. Bradshaw, who led the Hong Kong Mission from 1971 to 1974, also had a wife who knew Cantonese well. Bradshaw, a Harvard educated Ph.D. in zoology, spoke beautiful Chinese and came closer to the sagely Chinese ideal of a churchman than any president since H. Grant Heaton. President Bradshaw saw the need to move the Church toward a stake organization as rapidly as possible. He believed that leaders learned by doing, not merely by observing and reading. In addition to his work on properties, proselyting, and organizations, he also encouraged temple sealings and marriages, helped found seminary and institute programs, and spent a great deal of time working with missionaries in South Vietnam.

When Jerry D. Wheat, one of the first group of elders in Hong Kong in 1955, became mission president in 1974, the mission was on the verge of a number of great advancements, most notably the first area conference in August 1975 and the creation of the Hong Kong–Kowloon Stake in April 1976. Highly conscious of the Church's image, President Wheat demanded of his missionaries strict obedience to mission rules, immaculate apartments, and well-kept apparel. He was conscious of public relations and directed considerable media attention to visits by President Kimball and other General Authorities to the area conference. He also oversaw the construction of a new mission home at #2 Cornwall Street as well as a new district chapel (now a stake center) in Ho Man Tin, Kowloon-Tong. President Bradshaw had acquired this property following the continued efforts of his predecessors. President Wheat also initiated full-time missionary work in Macau, the tiny Portuguese colony only forty miles west from Hong Kong. David Hsiao Hsin Chen, one of the first Hong Kong Chinese to serve as a missionary for the Church and the first native-born Chinese to be a mission president, led the mission in Hong Kong from 1977 to 1980. President Chen's life of service to the Church, his devotion to personal improvement through hard work, his Ph.D. degree, and his position as a professor of political science at Brigham Young University—Hawaii Campus combined to make him a popular and effective leader with the missionaries and the local Saints.

THE HONG KONG AREA

By the end of 1977 there were only 4,256 members in Hong Kong, almost a fourth of whom were less-active or lost. Hong Kong, as we have said, is an anomaly: it is not truly Chinese, nor is it Western. Most of the people who live there are not citizens of the colony. The colony itself had a limited lifetime because it was scheduled to revert to the Chinese government in 1997 (which it did). Most residents of the colony live at a near-subsistence level and have little control over their work schedules.

A high percentage of members of the Church in Hong Kong are young. A 1972 survey found that 69.4 percent of Hong Kong converts joined the Church between the ages of twelve and twenty, and another 12.5 percent came into the Church between the ages of twenty-one and thirty. Only 5 percent of the members who joined were over age thirty.[3] At that time 72 percent of the active members had been in the Church four years or less, indicating a serious rate of member loss over the years. Where had they gone?

Between 1956 and 1962 (the last year such information was submitted on the annual mission reports to the Presiding Bishop's Office), 297 members from Hong Kong, 7 percent of the 1962 total, emigrated to other countries. During the 1970s there was no evidence that this emigration rate was higher or lower than at other times.[4] People leave Hong Kong for many reasons. Some go abroad for education. Others go to the United States, to the United Kingdom, Canada, Australia or elsewhere for work. Before the reversion of Hong Kong to the PRC, many Hong Kong residents left because of fear for the future of the colony. Other Church members experienced change in their work schedules, making it impossible for them to attend meetings. Particularly disturbing was that many of the best leaders in the Church had left the area. This is natural because they are capable and aggressive and have a desire to provide a good life for themselves and their families. Such people find ways to escape what has been called a "dead-end world." Although some visiting Church leaders asked the Chinese Saints to remain at home and build Zion there, the people of Hong Kong answered that they feel no sense of nationalism and have no ties, they want the kinds of opportunities Americans enjoy, and they want to rear their children in better circumstances. Although the Church suffers from this kind of thinking and action, no one should blame them for trying to improve their lives.

PROGRESS IN TAIWAN

Although the Church had a slower beginning in Taiwan than in Hong Kong, by the late 1970s, membership had passed that of

Hong Kong (7,933 members in 1977). This can be explained partially on the basis of population (17 million in Taiwan versus 4 million in Hong Kong), but other variables have had an influence on the situation. By the 1970s, Taiwan was much more stable than Hong Kong. Its economy was strong, and the people were generally satisfied with their lot in life. In December 1978 U.S. recognition of the People's Republic of China slowed LDS missionary work in Taiwan for a number of months, but by late 1979 feelings of animosity toward Americans were less evident.

The Church in Taiwan has attracted older members, 26 percent of them being over thirty in 1972. Whereas in 1972 only 2.1 percent of the Hong Kong members had a husband or wife in the Church, almost one-fourth of the Taiwan members had either a husband or a wife who was a member. The Church had a different image in Taiwan than in Hong Kong. In the former it was considered a family church; in the latter, it was considered a youth movement. In 1972, 45 percent of the Latter-day Saints in Taiwan were children of members, but only 15 percent of the Hong Kong members had their parents in the faith.[5]

In 1971 Taiwan became a separate mission. Under the direct leadership of President Malan R. Jackson (one of the first eight missionaries into Hong Kong), the Church developed greatly. The stepchild feeling of the Southern Far East Mission days was soon forgotten, and the Saints moved ahead with energy and enthusiasm.

The Taiwan Mission (its name was changed to the Taiwan Taipei Mission in 1974) did not long remain responsible for the entire island. In July 1976 it was divided, and the Taiwan Kaohsiung Mission was organized with P. Boyd Hales as its first president. In the spring of 1979 the First Presidency announced a further division, and the new Taiwan Taichung Mission was created with Frederick W. Crook as president.

During the late 1960s and 1970s the Chinese missions entered a new era. With the exception of Grant Heaton, before this time the Church did not have men available who had in-depth knowledge of the history and culture of the area. In 1949 Hilton A. Robertson, who had little education regarding Asian history, religions, or politics, was thought to be the most knowledgeable man in the Church on Asian matters. But now a new crop of scholars who had served in Hong Kong and Taiwan as missionaries came of age and provided a more sophisticated corps of leaders for this part of the world. First among these new leaders was Malan R. Jackson, an administrator at Arizona State University who was extremely energetic. He was followed in 1974 by Thomas P. Neilson, who was a professor of Chinese literature at Arizona State University when he received his call. In 1977 he was replaced by Frederick W. Crook, who holds a Ph.D. in economics and has special training in Asian affairs. Taiwan was led by these men who met the demand for academic or scholarly excellence that is admired—almost expected—by the Chinese. These leaders were nevertheless very American in their encouragement of their missionaries to teach the restored gospel with enthusiasm and courage. A number of men with similar qualifications have served since that time.

The methods used by the missionaries to teach the gospel in China have basically been the same as those that are used elsewhere in the world. In June 1961 the Church Missionary Committee announced a uniform plan of six lessons that were to be employed everywhere. These lessons replaced the seventeen-lesson plan that had been used in Hong Kong and Taiwan since 1955. As new improvements have been developed elsewhere in the Church since the early 1960s, particularly in Salt Lake City, the Chinese missions have put them to use. For example, President Thomas P. Neilson helped his missionaries develop some filmstrips that were intended to help Chinese Buddhists understand the Mormon concepts of families and temple work. The first filmstrip was titled *We Are Waiting*, referring to ancestors who are waiting for their temple work to be done.[6]

Of real significance in Hong Kong and Taiwan was the constant involvement of local Chinese missionaries. From the beginning in Hong Kong, young converts accepted calls to serve full-time missions. Although their numbers were not great during most years, in the early 1970s the number of Chinese missionaries grew. In 1971 twenty-eight Taiwan Chinese (ten elders and eighteen sisters) were serving. By the end of 1978, thirty-nine local missionaries were serving in Hong Kong and twenty-two in Taiwan.

THE TRANSLATION AND PUBLICATION OF THE STANDARD WORKS IN CHINESE

After President Heaton returned home, President Taylor encouraged the translation of the Book of Mormon. But it was not until President Quealy, at Elder Hinckley's instigation, became enthusiastic about the project that the work of translation got under way. In July 1963 Elder Hinckley called Larry K. Browning, then a student at National Taiwan University, to "supervise the translation of the Book of Mormon into Chinese."[7] He was asked to recommend a suitable Chinese translator to work with him on the project. Browning selected Hu Wei-I, who was serving as a counselor in the mission presidency. The two men worked together for almost two years. Unfortunately, they did not understand each other's assignments, and they disagreed on many points. Nevertheless, they knew that Elder Hinckley believed it was "the most important thing taking place in the Far East,"[8] and they finally put together what Brother Hu believed was a good translation. Browning did not agree. Hu thought the book should be translated literally, in a mid-level style that avoided elite and simple language. Browning thought some literary liberties should be taken in order to get the meaning of the book across. Hu's position eventually prevailed, and on December 20, 1965, one thousand copies of the book were published. A few months later, a second edition of 2,500 copies came off the press. Only typographical errors were corrected in the second printing. The book has been of great value to Chinese-speaking Saints. Elder

Hinckley was particularly pleased when he received the first copy. He took it to President McKay and explained that he had two major goals when he was assigned to supervise Church affairs in Asia. One was to see a Chinese translation of the Book of Mormon in print, and the other was to see the same in Korean, and at that time the Korean Book of Mormon was at press.[9]

The translation of the Doctrine and Covenants into Chinese was an unhappy experience for all concerned. In August 1966 President Garner called his counselor in Taiwan, President Ch'e Tsai Tien, to translate the Doctrine and Covenants and the Pearl of Great Price into Chinese. He was to be assisted by Thomas P. Neilson, then a student of Chinese literature. A year or two later Ch'e sent his translation of the Doctrine and Covenants to Hong Kong for review by Brothers Ng Kat Hing (head of translation projects in Hong Kong for almost a decade by that time) and Liu Nga Sang. In Hong Kong a number of other people became involved in the review and revision process, and a suitable product was not ready for printing until 1973. After the project was begun in 1966, the Translation and Distribution Department of the Church became involved.

The basic difficulty involved in completing a suitable translation grew out of two problems: too much nit-picking and too many personal preferences on the part of mission presidents and other reviewers and basic differences in structural preference between Cantonese and Mandarin speakers. The official version of the Doctrine and Covenants was published by Brother Ng in Hong Kong. However, the Taiwan Mission, under Malan R. Jackson, published its own version. Unfortunately, there are significant differences in text.[10] Diane E. Browning succinctly analyzes the problem in this way: "The great genius of the Chinese writing system, which has served to unify that nation for three thousand years, seems on the verge of being frustrated by competing versions of the same material by the Hong Kong and Taiwan translation offices. Since the publication of the Doctrine and Covenants, other translations, e.g. missionary discussions, the temple ceremony, and most recently, the names of Church General Authorities, have been translated differently, and these differences are not mere dialectical variants."[11]

The translation of the Pearl of Great Price did not go smoothly either. First, it is evident that Translation Services personnel in Asia did not expect careful, meticulous analysis of the style of Brother Ch'e's translation when they sent it to Salt Lake City for approval. They thought they had a satisfactory translation and wanted more or less unquestioning approval by the review committee. Second, even though the review com-

Hu Wei-I was the principal translator of the Book of Mormon into the Mandarin Chinese language. He also translated many other Latter-day Saint books and materials.

mittee suggested content and stylistic changes in almost every verse, when the Chinese version was printed, almost none of the reviewers' suggestions were incorporated into the printed text. Nevertheless, the Chinese version of the Pearl of Great Price was published in Taiwan in April 1976.

In less-developed parts of the world where the written word has not been cherished as it is in China, missionaries and members have been able to produce translations of the scriptures with greater ease. For example, it is evident that in Hawaii, Tonga, and other parts of Polynesia amateur but inspired translators have been able to provide excellent translations, translations that have stood the test of use and years. Chinese, however, is an immensely complex language, one that requires more than years of devoted Church service to master. To write well requires years of laborious training.

As this picture of the chapel illustrates, Kam Tong Hall has provided an elegant and useful setting for Church administration and activity in Hong Kong. It was purchased by Elder Gordon B. Hinckley and President Robert S. Taylor in May 1960.

In addition to the scriptures, the Church in Hong Kong and Taiwan published a wide variety of tracts, magazines, manuals, and books. Since 1966 these items have been produced through the general leadership of the Translation Department of the Church. Hu Wei-I personally translated James E. Talmage's *Jesus the Christ* and *Articles of Faith*, LeGrand Richards's *A Marvelous Work and a Wonder*, Joseph F. Smith's *Gospel Doctrine*, Joseph Smith's *Teachings of the Prophet Joseph Smith*, Joseph Fielding Smith's *Doctrines of Salvation*, and many other books.

THE DEVELOPMENT OF CHURCH PROPERTY

By the late 1970s a small number of chapels and other Church buildings were operating in Hong Kong and Taiwan. The mission acquired several apartment-style chapels in Hong Kong during Heaton's era ,and other chapels were added slowly. The only free-standing building owned by the Church on Hong Kong Island by the late 1970s was Kam Tong Hall, a beautifully remodeled mansion at #7 Castle Road, high on the hill overlooking Hong Kong Harbor. This hall was built by Sir Ho Kam (Robert) Tong, one of the few Chinese to be knighted. When Elder Gordon B. Hinckley and President Robert S. Taylor found the building on May 7, 1960, it was occupied by five or six families and was poorly kept. After the Church bought it, thirty thousand dollars (a large amount in those days) was required to make it a suitable Latter-day Saint meetinghouse. The four-story structure provided a chapel, cultural hall, classrooms, meetinghouse library, missionary quarters, and offices. In more recent

The Ho Man Tin chapel serves as a stake center. Located in Kowloon-Tong, this chapel was built on property that had been purchased after continuous efforts by several mission presidents. (Photo by author)

years it has served as the Asia Area offices and the Hong Kong Mission office.

In April 1967 President Hugh B. Brown, First Counselor in the First Presidency, dedicated the new Yuen Long chapel in the New Territories. It had been constructed by professional church builders, aided by member labor missionaries. It was the first chapel in the Southern Far East Mission area to have the appearance and facilities of a regular LDS chapel.

More recently, through the efforts of Presidents Hardy, Bradshaw, and Wheat, the Church constructed a four-story stake center in the Ho Man Tin area of mid-Kowloon. Located at the corner of Shek Ku and Sheung Shing Streets, the beautiful white

Taichung Stake Center in Taichung, Taiwan, is situated on a pie-shaped lot surrounded by busy streets next to the Taiwan Taichung Mission office and mission home. (Photo by author)

structure has a striking appearance. The first floor is used partially for parking but also provides classrooms, a baptismal font, and storage. On the second floor are found the Relief Society room, the Junior Sunday School room, a multipurpose room, and classrooms. The chapel and ward and stake offices are on the third floor, and the fourth floor is a fine cultural hall. By 1978 the Church had two other chapels on the Kowloon side: one at Kwun Tong and the other at #2 Cornwall Street, adjacent to the mission home.

The history of chapel building in Taiwan to 1978 is much briefer than in Hong Kong. As late as 1975 there were only three Church-owned chapels on the island. Every time Elder Hinckley visited Taiwan from 1960 onward, he looked for property. He regularly worked with government officials, real estate people, and others to try to help the cause along. President Taylor tried to buy land but was not too successful. Not until November 2, 1963, did the Church hold a ground-breaking ceremony for a chapel in Taipei. Almost three years passed before the structure, which was to serve the needs of two branches with nine hundred members and which had all the normal facilities of a modern LDS chapel, was dedicated by Elder Hinckley on October 16, 1966.[12] The second and third chapels were constructed at Kaohsiung and Taichung in the southern part of the island. By the late 1970s most branches and wards were still meeting in rented halls, apartments, and homes. The most important improvement was the addition of mission homes and mission offices in Taipei and Kaohsiung.

CHURCH EDUCATION EFFORTS

When Elder Mark E. Petersen returned from Hong Kong in 1959, he recommended to the First Presidency that the Church found two elementary schools (one in Hong Kong and one in Kowloon) and a secondary-vocational school. A year later, when Elder Hinckley visited the mission, the idea was evidently still alive. He wrote in his journal that the Church talked about establishing schools, but no commitment was made.[13] When he and President Taylor bought the Kam Tong Hall, they did so with the intention of using it for a school. Even though the school plan was being considered in 1961, it was evidently rejected in the upper councils of the Church at some later date.

In 1972 Neal A. Maxwell, commissioner of Church education, appointed a committee of Asian and international relations specialists from BYU to survey the educational needs of Latter-day Saints in Japan, Korea, Taiwan, Hong Kong, and the Philippines.[14] While in Hong Kong and Taiwan, the members of the Asia Educational Resources Project (AERP) visited with knowledgeable educational leaders, interviewed local Church leaders, and conducted a formal survey through the use of a questionnaire. The survey revealed that the Hong Kong Saints still perceived a need for educational help, most notably at the post-secondary level. They also strongly desired more religious education. Soon the home-study seminary program was implemented, and by 1978 some 208 students were participating in it. In addition, an individual-study institute program was serving 339 post-secondary young people by that time. Ed Andrus, a former Hong Kong missionary, returned there to help start these programs.

In Taiwan an even more active program of Church education was organized. Joseph Wan did much to create the seminary and institute program there. By 1975 as many as 420 young people were involved in the program in all three districts. The programs continued to blossom, and in 1978 there were 532 students participating, including 153 who were enrolled in a regular institute program in Taipei.[15] Although the AERP members suggested other programs, only religious education, the most requested and desired need, was addressed.[16]

WELFARE SERVICES MISSIONARIES

In keeping with their concern for the temporal welfare of members, Church leaders organized the health missionary program in 1971. In 1972 Sister Ira Gyllenbogel from Finland was sent to Taiwan as the first health services missionary. She, and others who followed, taught principles of health care and preventative medicine. In June 1972 Sister Mary Ellen Edmunds, who had been working as a health missionary in the Philippines, was joined by Molly Nutman from England and Rosalie Hacking from Idaho, when they arrived in Hong Kong as the first health missionaries in that mission. Sister Edmunds oriented the new missionaries by teaching them what had and had not worked in the Philippines. Health missionaries have been extremely successful in Hong Kong and Taiwan.

In about 1975 the program underwent a change of emphasis. Whereas the early health missionaries operated somewhat along the lines of the Peace Corps, after that time the name and purpose of their calling was modified. They were to be known as welfare services missionaries. Their purpose was to teach personal and family preparedness. Health was only one important part of a larger program. The new program was holistic, taking into consideration all areas of personal and family welfare.[17]

THE HONG KONG VISITORS' CENTER

On September 24, 1976, Elder Jacob de Jager of the First Quorum of the Seventy, then serving as supervisor of the Southeast Asia–Philippines Area of the Church, dedicated a new visitors' center in the city of Tsuen Wan, a suburb of Kowloon. The idea for the center was the result of a conversation between Elder A. Theodore Tuttle and President Jerry D. Wheat in October 1974. While visiting the Tsuen Wan chapel building, a four-story structure the Church purchased during the Heaton years, Elder Tuttle noted the large number of people who passed by. He suggested that this might be an appropriate place to establish a visitors' center. After the remodeling of the ground floor and the constructing of displays concerning the restored gospel, the idea became a reality.[18]

During the early months of its operation, the center attracted considerable attention. More than two thousand people toured the center during its first month. Between March and August 1977, forty-six people were baptized after a member or missionary took them to the center while they were having the missionary lessons. The center's approach emphasized traditional Chinese values, most notably the importance of the family and genealogy. The theme used during the initial months of operation was "God has given you many gifts. What is your gift to God?" The plan of salvation and the story of the restoration of the gospel are clearly depicted for visitors. Full-time missionaries and seventies (a stake calling at that time) operated the facility.[19]

The center served another important purpose: the Hong Kong Eighth Ward, which met in the same building, grew considerably because of the influence of the center. But there were also some problems. Tsuen Wan is an industrial city—neither a shopping center nor a tourist attraction—and most of the people who walked past the visitors' center were simply those who were on their way to and from work. The initial attraction of the center died down after the local people became acquainted with the building and its purposes.

THE OPENING OF MACAU
TO LDS MISSIONARY WORK

Over the years since the Southern Far East Mission was created, various mission presidents visited the Portuguese colony of Macau to investigate the possibility of teaching the gospel there. Macau is situated on a small peninsula on the south coast of China's Guangdong Province. It is only a two-hour boat trip away from Hong Kong. Until April 1976, when Elder Gordon B. Hinckley encouraged President Wheat to consider establishing the Church there, various problems had stood in the way of opening the work. On September 6, 1976, however, President Wheat sent four elders to Macau. They started proselyting that same day. With a population of fewer than one-half million in the 1990s, the city-colony was much smaller when the work commenced there. Membership growth has been slow, but by 1978 a branch of forty members had been established. Since that time growth has continued, and an average of ten elders and sisters have served there continuously. Though the English-speaking residents and the Portuguese people there have not been interested in the missionaries' message, the Chinese have displayed an interest in the gospel similar to that in Hong Kong.[20]

GENERAL AUTHORITY SUPERVISION
AND THE FIRST AREA CONFERENCE

Two Apostles have had extremely close relationships with the missions of Asia: Elder Gordon B. Hinckley and Elder Ezra Taft Benson. Elder Hinckley, as has been explained earlier, supervised the Asian areas from 1961 to 1968 and again from 1975 to 1976.

His warm yet decisive influence had a great impact on the leaders, Saints, and missionaries who served there. Elder Benson also taught the people well and did much to strengthen the organizations of the Church. Other General Authorities have had important roles to play in Asia. Elder Adney Y. Komatsu was the first General Authority to reside in Asia while supervising the area. He was followed by Elder Yoshihiko Kikuchi, who directed Church affairs in Japan and Korea, and Elder de Jager, who took over the southern part of the area. Before them, Elders Marion D. Hanks, Bruce R. McConkie, and James A. Cullimore worked with Elders Benson and Hinckley in the area.

The first area conferences of the Church in Hong Kong and Taiwan were held on August 13 and 14, 1975. President Spencer W. Kimball presided at both places, in Hong Kong on the thirteenth and in Taiwan the next day. He was accompanied by eleven other General Authorities; notable among them were Elders Benson, Hinckley, and Ashton, all of the Council of the Twelve.

The Hong Kong conference was more a city conference than an area conference. The small geographical size of Hong Kong has always encouraged conferences of all the Saints there. Two thousand members and friends filled the Lee Theatre as well as the ballroom of the nearby Lee Gardens Hotel (where they watched the proceedings on closed-circuit television) to participate in the event.

President Jerry D. Wheat went to great pains to have the best media coverage possible. As Elder Hinckley wrote in his journal, "We have had more favorable publicity in the last few days than I think we have had in all the years of the mission put together."[21] Approximately 44 percent of the Hong Kong membership attended the meetings.

The Taiwan meeting was a little larger and had more the feeling of an area conference. The Chinese Saints made all of the preparations for hotels, the meeting hall, bus transportation, choirs, public relations, and so forth. More than twenty-five hundred members and friends of the Church met in the Dr. Sun Yat-sen Memorial Hall in Taipei. During his brief stay in Taipei, President Kimball met for forty-five minutes with Yen Chia-Kan, president of the Republic of China. President Kimball explained the Church's teachings regarding genealogy, temple work, and welfare services. President Yen expressed interest in and support for the Church's programs. In the general session, President Kimball talked about temples and announced the Tokyo Temple, discussed missionary work, and set forth his vision of carrying the gospel to all the world. He also stressed the importance of service.

The Taiwan Saints joyously received President Kimball and the other General Authorities and visitors. One elder called the Saints' greeting of President Kimball a "gracious and respectful mobbing." Probably the most important result of the area conferences was the feeling that the Church is led by a living prophet of God and that the Lord loves all of his children.[22]

THE TAIPEI TAIWAN AND
HONG KONG–KOWLOON STAKES

Having prayerfully contemplated the matter for some time, on November 9, 1975, President Thomas P. Neilson submitted a proposal to the First Presidency asking that a stake be created in the Taiwan North District. On the following January 13, he received word back from Salt Lake City that the proposal had been approved. (January 1976 was an exciting month for Neilson and other leaders because only two weeks later he received word that the mission was to be divided.) On April 19 Elder Hinckley and Elder Komatsu arrived in Taipei, and the following day they selected Chang I-Ch'ing as the first Chinese to preside over a Chinese stake. The Taipei Taiwan Stake was created on April 22, 1976. The new stake had six wards and five branches comprising 4,497 members.

Three days later, on April 25, Elder Hinckley presented Poon Shui-tat (Sheldon) as president of the new Hong Kong–Kowloon

Stake. President Poon, age thirty, had previously served in many responsible positions. The stake consisted of six wards and two branches, totaling 3,410 members. In 1979 there were fourteen wards and branches in Hong Kong and fifty-one wards and branches in Taiwan.

There has been a tendency to view LDS growth in Hong Kong and Taiwan as insignificant in comparison with the total population of these areas or of the People's Republic of China. The 11,815 Saints (7,494 in Taiwan and 4,315 in Hong Kong in December 1978) were but a small percentage (.0000124) of China's estimated 950 million people. Nevertheless, considering the brief duration of LDS missionary work in these areas, the relatively small missionary force in the field during most years since the area was opened, the high standard of personal conduct and the high level of commitment demanded of new converts before and after baptism, the LDS missions in Hong Kong and Taiwan were quite successful. After the area was opened, only two decades passed before stakes were formed. The three missions, with 403 missionaries, brought 1,070 people into the Church (2.6 converts per missionary) in 1978. The baptismal rate compared well with that of Japan (2.7 converts per missionary) but fell well below that of the Philippines (8.3). The non-Christian nations of Asia remained difficult proselyting areas. They were, however, more productive than what some observers have labeled the "post-Christian" nations of Great Britain and Europe.

Relatively speaking, much had been accomplished in Hong Kong and Taiwan. But realistically the great task still remained. Hong Kong and Taiwan were only small training areas, places of preparation for the demanding challenges ahead.

NOTES

1. Gordon B. Hinckley, Journals, 1960–1962; in President Hinckley's possession.

2. William S. Bradshaw Oral History, interviews by author, Provo, Utah, 1974, James Moyle Oral History Program, LDS Church Archives, typescript, p. 17.

3. See Spencer J. Palmer et al., "Educational Needs of The Church of Jesus Christ

of Latter-day Saints in Asia: Final Report," Church Educational System, October 1972, p. 90.

4. See Jay A. Parry, "Hong Kong: Pearl of the Orient," *Ensign* 5 (August 1975): 54.

5. See Palmer et al., "Educational Needs," pp. 87–90.

6. See Taiwan Taipei Mission Historical Reports, 31 March 1976, LDS Church Archives.

7. Southern Far East Mission Historical Reports, 30 September 1963, LDS Church Archives.

8. Larry K. Browning, Diary, in his possession.

9. Hinckley, Journal, 1965.

10. See Diane E. Browning, "The Translation of Mormon Scriptures into Chinese" (unpublished paper, Brigham Young University, 1977), pp. 21–22; in possession of the author.

11. Ibid.

12. Hinckley, Journal, by date.

13. Ibid., 6 May 1960.

14. The present writer was part of that team.

15. See "Church Educational System, Overview," unpublished CES report, 1978, pp. 38–39. Copy in possession of author.

16. See Palmer et al., "Educational Needs." See the main report and the two supplements on Taiwan and Hong Kong.

17. See "Church's Health Team Teaches Maternal Care," *Church News*, 3 March 1979, p. 13.

18. See "Thousands Visit Hong Kong Center," *Church News*, 22 January 1977, p. 3.

19. See ibid.; and "Hong Kong Center Improves Attitudes Toward the Church, Baptisms Increase," *Church News*, 10 September 1977, p. 6.

20. See "Elders now preach in Macau, a Portuguese colony in China," *Church News*, 4 December 1976, p. 5; "Church flourishes in colony of Macao," *Church News*, 23 September 1978, p. 6.

21. Hinckley, Journal, 13 August 1975.

22. See Victoria Varley Hawkins, "Conference in Hong Kong"; and Kevin Moss, "Conference in Taiwan," *Ensign* 5 (October 1975): 91–93.

12

THE CHINESE
REALM

1978–1996

Taiwan and Hong Kong,
the People's Republic of China, and Mongolia

TAIWAN AND HONG KONG

By mid-1996 there were more than 22,000 members of the Church in Taiwan and almost 21,000 in Hong Kong. Although annual baptism rates varied somewhat in the two areas, an average of about 1,000 people joined the Church in each nation or colony from 1979 onward. Taiwan—largely because it had greater numbers of mature priesthood leaders, more territory, a larger populace (21 million versus 6.5 million in Hong Kong in 1996), more missionaries, and available land—received a temple in 1984. The two Taiwan missions, Kaohsiung and Taipei, were divided into three with the creation of the Taichung Mission in 1979, although the number was reduced to two in 1982. Additional stakes were created, bringing the number to five in 1994. There were also three districts. In the years since 1979, the Church acquired a number of properties and built almost thirty chapels. The seminary and institute programs grew steadily. In general, the Church reached a stage of maturity and solidity in Taiwan.

The same is true for the Church in Hong Kong. The small geographical size of the colony does not justify more than one mission even though the populace of around six million would do so in other parts of the world. In 1996 there were five stakes in Hong Kong and many wards. Some problems, such as the difficulty of acquiring land and the constant problem of leaders and members who move elsewhere, hindered Church growth there. But in May 1996 the Church dedicated the Hong Kong Temple and appeared to be as secure as any other denomination while the colony awaited reversion to the People's Republic of China in 1997.

In 1979 the People's Republic of China, under the leadership of Deng Xiaoping, opened its doors wider to foreigners. In the summer of that year Brigham Young University's Young Ambassadors performance group visited the PRC and initiated a multitude of relationships between China and the university, the Church, and many Church leaders. Although the Church is not legally recognized in China and proselyting is not allowed according to Chinese law and policy, branches of the Church are allowed for expatriates. As a result, many productive relationships and friendships abound between Church entities and Church members and Chinese officials and citizens.

Recently, in 1992, humanitarian services missionaries and regular proselyting elders entered Mongolia, now a free and independent nation. Long under the control of the Soviet Union, it is steadily leaving the realm of Communism and becoming part of the democratic world. More than six hundred Mongols are now (in 1996) baptized members of the Church.

Organization and Administration

In 1979 there was one stake in Taiwan and one in Hong Kong. On May 29, 1980, Elder Gordon B. Hinckley created the Hong Kong Kowloon Stake with twenty-nine-year-old Wong Chung-hei (Patrick) as the first president. President Wong, who had served as bishop and as a high councilor, was continuing a series of impor-

Liang Shih-An (Kent) (left), seated beside his father, Liang Yun-sheng, is the first Area Authority Seventy from Taiwan. The young Liang is among the few second-generation Latter-day Saints among the leaders of the Church in Asia. (Photo by author)

tant callings in the Church. Subsequently he served twice as a Regional Representative of the Twelve, and on August 15, 1995, he was called as an Area Authority of the Church. A year later, in 1996, he was called as second counselor in the Asia Area Presidency. Liang Shih-an (Kent) from Taipei was also called as an Area Authority at the same time. Liang, a professor and formerly a Regional Representative, stake president, high councilor, and bishop, is the son of Brother and Sister Liang Yun-sheng, who were converted to the Church in Taiwan in May 1958. Over the years, the older Liang served in many positions in the Church, including being in the first stake presidency. He was a patriarch, a counselor in the Southern Far East Mission presidency, and so on. His son, Elder Liang, grew up in a strong Mormon home and represents the strength of second-generation Mormon families in Asia.

On November 6, 1981, Taiwan gained its second stake, the Kaohsiung Stake, with Ho Tung-hai as president. Only four months later the Taipei Stake was divided into the Taipei East Stake (presided over by President Yen Yuan-hu) and the Taipei West Stake (with Liu Chu-hwa as president), bringing Taiwan's number of stakes to four. The Taichung Stake, the fifth and latest, was organized on December 18, 1994, with Chou Wen-tsung as president.

The Hong Kong Kowloon North Stake (later changed to the Hong Kong Talo Harbour Stake) and the New Territories Stake were organized on November 11, 1984, with Yau Fu-man and Johnson Ma as presidents, respectively. Ten years later, on March 20, 1994, the Hong Kong Kowloon West Stake was created with Poon Yin Sang (Peter) as president, thus bringing Hong Kong even with Taiwan in number of stakes. At the organizing stake conference meeting, Elder John K. Carmack, Area President, told the congregation: "These days of uncertainties and concerns in Hong Kong are also the most exciting days in the history of the Church in Hong Kong. We should all thank the Lord that we are permitted to be here to witness the history unfold."[1] Elder Carmack was referring to both the unrest that Hong Kong residents were facing as the uncertainties of 1997 drew nearer and to the joy that Hong Kong members were experiencing as they anticipated the completion of the Hong Kong Temple in 1996.

Unusual Mission Changes

The Hong Kong Mission has continued uninterrupted since Taiwan was divided off in 1971. But Taiwan provides a more varied history. After the initial creation of the Taiwan Mission in 1971, the mission was first divided in July 1976 with the creation of the Kaohsiung Mission in the south. Three years later the Brethren created the Taichung Mission, but three missions proved unnecessary, and the decision was made to close it, transferring parts of the mission to Taipei and Kaohsiung in July 1982. A year later the new mission president, finding that adequate educational facilities were not available for his children in Kaohsiung, sent his family to live in the mission facilities in Taichung. Upon learning of this situation, on September 28, 1983, Church authorities officially moved the mission headquarters to Taichung and changed the name of the mission to reflect the move.[2]

Church Growth and the Chinese Way

For the past two decades the dominant problem facing missionaries in Hong Kong and Taiwan has been materialism. This has not always been so, but with the rising pressure in Hong Kong to succeed temporally because of the crowded and intense conditions, and with the ever-rising standard of living in Taiwan, missionaries have had a growing problem finding individuals who have not made money and possessions their religion. During the decade from 1974 to 1984, Taiwan had the second-highest economic growth in the world. In earlier years, missionaries often wrote concerning the humble conditions in which most people lived. Such memories are largely missing from missionaries who have served in Taiwan since the mid-1970s.

Living conditions for most Chinese in Hong Kong remain extremely close. Privacy is difficult to find, and personal space for projects, study, hobbies, and the like is almost nonexistent. As mentioned several times before, most Hong Kong residents have been living with considerable uncertainty regarding how their lives will be affected by the change of government in 1997. Some Hong Kong residents, including Latter-day Saints, have chosen to immigrate to other countries if they have the means and the legal ability to do so. Most, however, have had to remain and wait for the unknown. The Church in Taiwan has also been affected by emigration. One student of the matter suggested that "it is relatively easier to find more qualified Chinese members available for a Church position in California or Salt Lake City than in Taiwan or Hong Kong."[3]

Typically, Chinese are not very religious in the Western sense of being conscious of membership in a particular church or a specific congregation. Nor are they accustomed to attending weekly worship services. Chinese religion is family-oriented and often home-centered. Local gods and spirits play major roles in most lives, as do fortune-telling, tea leaf reading, and reverence for the spirits of dead ancestors. Respect for dead ancestors and the rituals involved in paying honor to them is important to almost all Chinese, whether they call themselves Buddhists, Daoists, Confucianists, or some combination of the three. Most Chinese follow worship patterns that include parts of all three religions, but they seldom distinguish or know from which tradition these practices have come.

Respect for one's elders—filial piety, or *hsiao (xiao)*—living and dead, is important to most Chinese. Parents teach affection, obligation, and responsibility to other people, specifically to a child's parents and elders. Chinese children grow up with feelings of being connected, close, and interdependent. Decisions regarding religion are seldom made alone. They are family decisions, and most families would not consider leaving the customs of the past or fail to offer ritual respect for the dead on appointed days. Mormon missionaries, generally being young, have had a difficult time understanding why mature men and women insist on asking permission from their parents when desiring to join the Church. The missionaries do not understand that one is expected to respect and defer to the wishes of his elders until there is no family member older than himself.

Age and maleness have priority in the Chinese realm, but frequently Mormon missionaries have directed their proselyting attention to young women. The results have often been disruptive to the lives of these young people. Parents, particularly fathers, resent the influence of outsiders upon their children, even at ages that most Americans consider mature enough for people to make their own decisions. Traditionally, Chinese parents have strict control of their children's lives. When young people leave home to go away to college, the bonds of parental control are loosened, but not broken. It is during this stage that most converts to the Church are found.

TRACING MY ANCESTORS
Bai Tien

A couple of summers ago I was marching in the strong summer sunshine along the edge of the Mao Wushu Desert in Northwest China to visit my ancestral grave. I had never been there before and had been longing to go there ever since Father told me about it. And then I got the chance. I was on summer vacation and I was on a University-sponsored educational trip to Yanan, which was comparatively nearer to my hometown. [In China one's hometown is the town where one's father was born.] So I decided to take another all-day, bumpy bus ride from Yanan to my hometown county in the very northeast of Shanxi. As I was walking deeper into the desert, the sunshine was becoming stronger and stronger. And to step forward on the sands demanded a certain amount of efforts. Finally, after a two-hour walk in the hot summer sun, I reached my destination.

And now I was there, standing in front of my ancestors' graves, where they lay beneath the sands and the soil. There were four graves, two for my grandparents and another two for [no words here]. They were located in a square manner which looked like four piles of sand rather than formal and decent graves. And each one was very close to another so that they overlapped a little. It was a quiet place which was one side of a hill facing south. (The nearest village was almost a mile away.) Beyond this hill there was the mighty desert extending northwards, which was dotted with patches of green colour here and there, showing signs of afforestation. Everything was in silence. Time seemed to stop flowing. Only the warm desert wind was whistling away. The sun was shining brightly. I stood there motionless. Numerous senses of respect, love, gratefulness, loyalty, and the like were swarming inside me. A voice in my heart, perhaps it was my father's, was telling me again and again that this was my very origin, this is where I came from. I didn't and I couldn't labour my lips, but instead I was communicating with my ancestors. I said to them that I was one of their descendants, and that I came to see them for the first time in my life, and I came to be accepted by the "Bai" family; I said to them that I loved them, I worshiped them, I admired them and I thanked them for making "me" possible. I did not shed tears. I knew they didn't like it. They liked their boy to be strong-minded. I knelt down. It was a must. It was human. I knew they were pleased to see me and they agreed to accept me. They gave me their "blessings."

I did not stay long. Having sprinkled a bottle of wine over the graves in memory of my ancestors, I was prepared to leave. I stood there with my head bowing down for a few minutes. I said to my ancestors that I was ready to go and promised to do my best in the future. I looked my good-by at them and turned back and began to walk down the hill. When about a hundred yards apart, I turned back and looked up to that hill where my ancestors were buried. I said to myself: "This is a quiet place, and they rest in peace."[4]

Many Chinese believe Christianity is incompatible with Chinese traditions and values. Belief in the "Three Bonds" and "Five Virtues" of Confucianism continues to influence most Chinese.[5] Unfortunately, most people in Hong Kong and Taiwan have never heard of the Church, and those who have generally understand little of its history or doctrines. When Chinese understand the Church's teachings regarding the eternal nature of the family, temple sealings, and so forth, they find great compatibility between Chinese beliefs and the teachings of the restored gospel. But most never listen long enough to make the connection.

Among Church members in Hong Kong and Taiwan there

have been differences of opinion regarding the proper place of ancestor worship among members. Some have argued that the practice is pagan and totally inappropriate. Others have suggested that some elements of the practice are wholesome and not harmful if not carried to the extreme. Others have averred that ancestor worship is simply an early, perhaps apostate form of paying recognition and should be allowed if other parts of a believer's life are in order. And others have focused their attention on family history and genealogical research (which is amply supported in Hong Kong and Taiwan). Members in Taiwan continue to debate the matter. The most helpful guidance on the subject came from President Ezra Taft Benson, while he served as President of the Quorum of the Twelve. To the stake and mission presidents of Asia he wrote: "The important thing is that the person be taught, as part of his conversion to the gospel, that he no longer worships shrines and altars and ancestors, but he pays his devotions and offers his prayers to God, our Eternal Father, in the name of His Son, Jesus Christ. Converts so taught have not had serious difficulty in handling the problem."[6] A great difficulty for faithful Chinese members has been to manifest to loved family members who are non-Mormons that they honor their elders and dead ancestors while at the same time following the teachings of the Church.

General Authority Supervision and Administrative Offices

Since the mid-1970s various members of the Seventy have presided over Hong Kong and Taiwan. On July 1, 1984, the world was divided into thirteen administrative areas, of which three were outside the United States. The Asia Area was created with Elder William R. Bradford, who was already in charge in Tokyo, as the first Area President, with Elder Jack H Goaslind Jr. and Robert B. Harbertson as counselors. A year later President Bradford and his new counselors, Jacob de Jager and Keith W. Wilcox, moved the headquarters for all of Asia to Hong Kong. Hong Kong remained the center of all Asian operations until 1987, when the Philippines/Micronesia Area was created with Elder George I.

Cannon as president. The Asia Area was divided again on September 1, 1992, when the Asia North Area Presidency, presided over by Elder W. Eugene Hansen, was created to administer affairs in Japan and Korea.

The Asia Area Presidency in Hong Kong has had the enormous task of administering Church affairs not only in Hong Kong and Taiwan but also in all of South and Southeast Asia (except the Philippines). In addition, they have been responsible for Church affairs in the People's Republic of China and the establishment of new mission fields in Mongolia and countries of South and Southeast Asia.

Elder Tai Kwok Yuen, the first Chinese to serve as a General Authority, was called into the Second Quorum of the Seventy in June 1992. Prior to that calling, he had served as branch president, stake president's counselor, Regional Representative, and president of the Hong Kong Mission. As a Seventy he served in the Asia Area Presidency in Hong Kong. (Courtesy LDS Church)

Elder Tai Kwok Yuen, who served in the Asia Area Presidency from 1992 to the present, is the first Chinese to be called as a General Authority. He joined the Church in Hong Kong on June 9, 1959, at age seventeen. Through the encouragement of his illiterate aunt, who reared him, he gained an education, eventually graduating from the University of Sydney in Australia with a degree in chemical engineering. He also did graduate studies in management at the University of Hong Kong. In 1966 he married Lai Hui-hua, whom he had met in church after returning to Hong Kong from Australia. They are the parents of two sons and a daughter. Over the years, the Tais have lived in Hong Kong, England, and America. Elder Tai has served in a variety of Church leadership capacities, including branch president, high councilor, stake president's counselor, and Regional Representative. In 1989 they were called while living in California to lead the Hong Kong Mission. At the end of that period of service, President Gordon B. Hinckley in June 1992 called President Tai to be a member of the Second Quorum of the Seventy and to serve as second counselor in the Asia Area Presidency in Hong Kong. In 1995 he became president of that area.[7]

Administrative offices for the Area Presidency in Hong Kong have been located in Kam Tong Hall on Hong Kong Island. The lovely old building provides a warm and classy environment for visitors, members, and those of other faiths alike. As the Church grew in Taiwan, a similar headquarters building became more and more necessary. Fortunately,

The Taipei Church administration building houses a number of functions, including a distribution center, temporal affairs office, and Taipei Taiwan Mission offices and mission president's apartment, and the temple president's apartment. It has been a Church facility since early 1983. (Photo by author)

the first property purchased by the Church in Taipei, a small city block, was large enough to hold the original Taipei chapel (which later became the stake center) and new facilities (a home and a separate office) for the Taiwan Mission when it was created in 1971. But on March 31, 1982, the First Presidency announced the forthcoming construction of a new temple for Taiwan. The decision was made to build the temple on the land occupied by the mission home and office. This meant that a new mission home or apartment for the mission president and a new mission office were needed. But that was not all. The temple president also would need a residence. In addition, various other operations—the Presiding Bishopric area office, Translation Services, the distribution center, the islandwide construction offices—also needed office space. Fortunately, while these decisions were being pondered, a seven-story office building was under construction directly across the lane from the entrances to the stake center and proposed temple. Paul V. Hyer, the mission president, helped negotiate the purchase of the building, moved his family and mission office staff into the building in early 1983, and watched the temple go up from his new office.[8] The administration building, the stake center, and temple make up an efficient Church complex in a fine Taipei neighborhood. The Church Educational System offices are located in the stake center, as is a genealogy service center. Property costs in Taipei have inflated so much that the original price of the Church block would now purchase only one parking space. The Church is greatly blessed to have such a property.

The Taipei Taiwan Temple

From the early history of the Restoration, Latter-day Saints have viewed temples as the highest symbol of their spiritual aspirations. Missionaries often consider their work done only after people they have taught and baptized also attend the temple and receive the blessings of the Lord's holy house. Since the 1960s, mission records refer to plans for temple excursions to Hawaii or Salt Lake City. But because transportation costs were high, with only one exception, such plans never materialized. Nevertheless, Church leaders from the missions and the stakes, as well as visiting authorities, regularly encouraged members to save money and go to the temple. When President Spencer W. Kimball spoke at the first area conference in 1975, he announced plans for the Tokyo Temple and explained its purposes. Encouraging those present, he promised, "You, too, can have one."[9] At that time Taiwan was yet to have its first stake.

But the Church in Taiwan and Hong Kong grew in leadership strength and numbers, and only seven years passed before the Brethren decided to build the first temple in the Chinese realm in Taipei. On March 31, 1982, the First Presidency announced new temples for four cities, including Taipei. The Taipei Taiwan Temple was projected to be a small temple of ten thousand square feet. The completed structure was to have a capacity of ninety thousand endowments per year, featuring four ordinance rooms, three sealing rooms, a celestial room, a baptistry, and various offices.

The ground-breaking ceremonies were conducted on August 26, 1982, by President Gordon B. Hinckley, Second Counselor in the First Presidency, accompanied by Area Executive Administrator Marion D. Hanks. But construction did not begin until early 1983, and then it proceeded slowly. Completion was projected for early 1984, but not until October 30 did the twelve-day open house begin. Although slow, construction of the temple was "tremendously exhilarating for members," reported Paul Hyer. In addition to the beauty of the white tiles on the walls and the blue-tiled roof of the temple, the stake center next door was painted white and retiled with matching blue tile. The entire effect was one of considerable beauty.[10]

The new temple was dedicated in five sessions held on November 17 and 18, 1984. President Hinckley presided at three sessions, and Elder Howard W. Hunter conducted two sessions. Four sessions were held in Mandarin and one in Cantonese for the 150 members who attended from Hong Kong. A number of other General Authorities were present.

In one of his addresses, President Hinckley mentioned his participation in the purchase of the property on which they met. The land had formerly been a prison and a farm worked by the prisoners. "This house, built on what was once prison property, will open the prison doors of the veil of death," spoke President

The Taipei Taiwan Temple was announced in March 1982 and dedicated on 17–18 November 1984 by President Gordon B. Hinckley, who was at that time second counselor to President Spencer W. Kimball. (Photo by author)

Hinckley. He also expressed concern for the small number of members in Taiwan and Hong Kong who held temple recommends. "There are only 500 to do the work of millions. . . . There is so much to be done. The laborers are relatively few. There is no other place where a temple has been built where so few are eligible to use it."[11] By 1995 the number of recommend holders had grown to 1,331 in Taiwan, still a small number.

In the dedicatory prayer, reference was made to Elder David O. McKay's prayer dedicating the Chinese realm for the preaching of the gospel. The prayer read in part: "We thank thee for the firm foundation on which thy Church is now established in this part of the earth. We thank thee for this day when those who will use this temple may turn their hearts to their fathers, participating in thy holy house in those ordinances which will make it possible for their deceased forebears to move forward on the way that leads to eternal life." The prayer continued: "We pray for the government of this nation which has been hospitable to thy servants and thy work. . . . May thy work spread from here to the vast numbers of thy Chinese sons and daughters wherever they may be found. Touch the hearts of those who govern that they may open the doors of their nations to thy messengers of eternal truth. May thy work grow in beauty and strength in the great Chinese realm."[12]

Although the number of persons holding temple recommends was initially small, the first two temple presidents, John W. Clifford and Paul V. Hyer, complimented those who could attend, saying they were among the most devoted temple participants in the Church.[13] When the temple opened there were thirteen thousand members in Taiwan and ten thousand in Hong Kong. Now this number has almost doubled, and a new temple has been constructed in Hong Kong, a fact that attests to the continued growth in numbers of temple-worthy members in both places.

The first Chinese member to preside at the Taipei Taiwan Temple was Wang Wei, with his wife, Wang Hsiao-feng, as matron. They were called in 1993.

The Church Educational System in Hong Kong and Taiwan

Having been founded in the early 1970s in both areas, CES programs have continued to make steady growth and improvement through the years. Seminary, almost always taught through home study in Hong Kong and Taiwan, has grown more slowly than the institute program because more college-age persons join the Church than high school students. Few families in the Church have children of high school age, although more are coming along now. By the late 1980s Hong Kong had about 150 seminary students (under 20 percent of potential) and more than 250 institute students (about 60 percent of potential). Taiwan's statistics were higher, with 32 percent of potential seminary students participating and 91 percent of potential institute students taking part. These figures have improved in the 1990s. In 1996 Kwok Kam-Tim was country director in Hong Kong, and Wang Lu-pao was country director in Taiwan.

The Hong Kong Temple

As momentous as the opening of the Taipei Taiwan Temple was, the building and dedication of the Hong Kong Temple was a more dramatic event. Two very different factors set the Hong Kong Temple apart: finding an appropriate site and the question of what might transpire in Hong Kong when the People's Republic of China took over on July 1, 1997. Finding any kind of property in Hong Kong is almost impossible. Finding land that is suitable for a temple is much more difficult. Prices are extremely high everywhere, and many areas are inappropriate.

After gaining the support and blessing of President Ezra Taft Benson for the proposal to build a temple in Hong Kong, President Gordon B. Hinckley, First Counselor in the First Presidency, visited Hong Kong twice for the purpose of finding a temple site. On July 25 through 27, 1992, following a long day of visits to ten potential sites, President Hinckley retired to bed feeling quite discouraged. He awoke between two and three o'clock in the morning with the clear impression that the temple should be built on the site of the mission home and office at #2 Cornwall Street in Kowloon Tong. In the night he sketched a possible plan for a building that would serve more than one purpose, something the Latter-day Saints never had done with a temple before. "It was clear to me we should have two separate buildings in one," said President Hinckley. In the morning he shared his ideas with Ted D. Simmons, managing director for physical facilities for the Church. After going over this plan with the Area Presidency and local leaders, Church leaders decided to build a multipurpose temple at #2 Cornwall Street. Speaking at the temple dedication regarding his thoughts to build the temple with such an unusual plan, President Hinckley said, "If ever in my life I felt the inspiration of the Lord, it was with this building."[14]

Plans to build the Hong Kong Temple were announced on October 3, 1992, at general conference in Salt Lake City. President Hinckley's original plan was to construct an eight-story building. In addition to the temple proper, which would take up the top three floors (the baptismal font would be below the plaza level), the building would also house offices for the Hong Kong Mission, apartments for the mission and temple presidents and their families, a small chapel and classroom facility for a branch, an outlet for the sale of temple clothing, the building engineer's office, and limited parking. Civil regulations and zoning restrictions required that the building not stand more than seven stories above ground, so the original plan had to be tightened. The building has eighteen thousand square feet, eight thousand more than the Taipei Taiwan Temple. The finished structure, faced with light-green granite, has a dome covered in gold leaf and a spire with a statue of the angel Moroni at the top.

From the ground-breaking ceremony to the dedication, the question of what might happen after July 1, 1997, was constantly on the minds of all with an interest in the temple. In his address at the ground breaking (January 22, 1994), Elder John K. Carmack, Area President, said: "The question everyone asks me, and I assume you get asked it too, is, 'What is going to happen after 1997?' I am not a prophet and don't know all that will happen in 1997, but part of the answer is that we are building a temple that will serve China for a long time and that is a statement of our faith and confidence in the future. We have all been promised the continuation of religious freedom under the *Basic Law* and we fully expect to enjoy the freedom to worship, learn, and receive ordinances under that freedom. We break ground today as an act of faith and confidence in the future."[15]

Through negotiations of the British, Hong Kong representatives, and the government of the People's Republic of China, Hong Kong was established as a Special Administrative Region. The *Basic Law,* a sort of constitution for Hong Kong, was adopted on April 4, 1990. Of special interest to the Church was Article 141, which provided that China would not restrict freedom of religious belief, interfere in the internal affairs of religious organizations, or restrict religious activities that do not contravene the laws of the Special Administrative Region. "Religious organizations," according to Elder John K. Carmack, "were to be given the right to acquire property, receive outside financial support, have ownership rights, operate seminaries, schools, hospitals, and welfare institutions, and provide other social services." Of special significance is the right of religious organizations and individuals to have relationships with religious organizations and believers elsewhere. The result should be the freedom of religious organizations and individuals to continue their present rights and practices.[16]

Religious law and policy within the PRC highly restrict the religious activities of all Chinese citizens and foreigners. Missionaries are not allowed. Roman Catholics within the PRC have been criticized harshly and sometimes persecuted because they have allegiance to the Pope, a leader outside China. Considering the similar organizational nature of The Church of Jesus Christ of Latter-day Saints with its Prophet-President, First Presidency, Quorum of Twelve Apostles, and other central officers, if the government of the People's Republic of China were to decide to implement similar rules in Hong Kong, the Church would be in great difficulty.[17]

Questions regarding the continuation of the status quo notwithstanding, the Church moved ahead with confidence in the

Probably the most unusual LDS temple in the world, the Hong Kong Temple was announced in October 1992 and dedicated by President Gordon B. Hinckley on 26–27 May 1996. In addition to standard temple facilities, the building houses a small chapel and branch meeting rooms, as well as apartments for the mission president and temple president. (Photo by author)

honor of the PRC government to stand by the *Basic Law* and provide for the continuation of present religious rights and practice.

Five hundred VIP guests, twenty-five ministers of religion,

and thirteen thousand others visited the completed temple during the open house, which was held from May 7 to May 21, 1996.[18] Following several days of intense cleaning, seven dedicatory sessions were held on May 26 and 27. Approximately five thousand Church members from many nations attended the sessions, which were presided over by President Hinckley and conducted by either himself or President Thomas S. Monson, First Counselor in the First Presidency. Other General Authorities included Elder Neal A. Maxwell and Elder Joseph B. Wirthlin of the Council of the Twelve and the Area Presidency, Elders Tai Kwok Yuen, John H. Groberg, and Rulon G. Craven. Members came from Singapore and Thailand, also part of the temple district, as well as from Taiwan. Temple president Ng Kat Hing and his wife, Pang Lai Har, temple matron, were also present.[19] President and Sister Ng were among the earliest converts to the Church in Hong Kong. The dedication gave cause for the greatest reunion of missionaries to Hong Kong and Taiwan and their families that has ever taken place. A past mission president commented, "This has got to be the biggest reunion we'll ever have until we meet for the dedication of the Beijing Temple."

Beijing and China seemed to be ever on the minds of those who spoke and those who listened. Before reading the dedicatory prayer in one of the sessions, President Hinckley spoke for a moment about the nature of such prayers. He pointed out that dedicatory prayers are very specific, that they are read, word for word, in each session. Then he in a sense revealed his concern for the future of the temple. He invited all who were present to listen carefully to the specific words of the prayer as they related to the future of the Church in Hong Kong. In part the prayer reads: "We thank Thee for the freedom granted by this government in permitting Thy servants to labor here. . . . We pray that this harvest of souls may continue, that in the future as in the present, Thy people may be free and secure in their worship and that none shall hinder the service of missionaries called to this area. Bless all who befriend Thy Church, all who defend Thy people, and all who assist those called to teach the everlasting gospel. We pray that Thy work may grow and prosper in the great Chinese realm, and may those who govern be ever receptive to those called and sent as messengers of revealed truth."[20]

The Hong Kong Temple opened for regular endowment sessions on May 28, 1996, one day following the last dedication session.

THE CHURCH AND THE PEOPLE'S REPUBLIC OF CHINA

The day following the dedication of the Hong Kong Temple, President Gordon B. Hinckley, his wife, Marjorie, and others who were traveling with him crossed into China proper to visit the Chinese Folk Villages (patterned after the Polynesian Cultural Center in Hawaii) at Shenzhen Special Economic Zone, the newly created commercial and industrial city a short distance across the border. This was the first visit by a President of the Church to the PRC. President Hinckley had first visited China in 1980 while an Apostle. The red carpet was literally rolled out to greet President Hinckley and his party. According to a *Deseret News* report, "It seemed that a warmer welcome could not have been extended."[21] His May 1996 visit was acknowledged as important in the Church press, but it could be considered simply the latest visit to the PRC by a series of members of the Twelve and other General Authorities, beginning in the summer of 1979.

Not long after Deng Xiaoping assumed the reigns of government following the ouster of the "Gang of Four," he made clear China's intention to open its doors to foreign trade and greater diplomatic and cultural ties abroad. President Spencer W. Kimball, knowing that one-fourth of humanity lived within China's borders, asked in 1978 that China experts at Brigham Young University investigate the possibility of opening missionary work there. Although the report he received was not encouraging, President Kimball believed it was time to start preparing in earnest for closer relations with China. On September 29, 1978, at a meeting with the Regional Representatives of the Church, he emphasized the importance of China and asked, rhetorically, how many members of the Church could speak Mandarin Chinese. He encouraged more members to learn the language. BYU President Dallin H. Oaks, who was present at the meeting, soon thought of sending a BYU performing group to the PRC, but he learned that making arrangements for such a tour was impossible because the United States and China did not recognize each other diplomatically. But U.S.–Chinese relations changed quickly, and on January 1, 1979, diplomatic relations were normalized. BYU administrators and artistic directors decided to try to send the Young Ambassadors, a performance troupe, to China. Through various diplomatic channels and the efforts of Senator Frank Church of Idaho, who was chairman of the Senate Foreign Relations Committee, arrangements were made for two BYU representatives, Ed Blaser and Val Lindsey, to fly to Beijing through Romania. While in Beijing they enlisted the help of the China Youth Travel Service, which made arrangements for this tour and many others to follow.

In an address to the Regional Representatives at April general conference in 1979, President Kimball again pressed the China matter. He said, "It appears that the time is not too distant when the gospel might be preached" to the people of China. "The door to China is starting to open," the prophet said. "Rather than waiting to be asked, we should take affirmative action to obtain approval to enter."[22] The China tour was now more important than ever.

When the BYU group left for Asia, many questions remained unanswered. The tour and performance schedule for the Young Ambassadors was not firm even as they traveled from Hong Kong to Guangzhou by railroad in early July 1979. Chinese officials required the group to perform for a jury of cultural specialists before going on with the tour. The critics were impressed, and the tour proceeded to Beijing and then on to Shanghai and Hangzhou.

Before the tour was over, the Young Ambassadors had performed before seventeen thousand people in the major halls of four cities and had given at least forty-five impromptu performances at historic sites, such as the Great Wall and the Forbidden City, and at factories, nurseries, and other places. Randy Boothe, artistic director, reported, "We believe that was the first time a tour of this kind had ever been to China." Other individual performers such as comedian Bob Hope and violinist Isaac Stern had previously visited China, as had the Boston Symphony Orchestra, but this was likely the first "total show experience" to come from the United States.[23]

The young performers were excellent, but their ability to make friends was most impressive. They had studied the Mandarin language briefly and used it to introduce the various parts of the show. They also had learned some Chinese songs that the crowds appreciated. Everywhere they went they were on stage. They mingled freely with the Chinese people on trains, in hotels, and on the city streets.

Elder James E. Faust of the Quorum of the Twelve accompanied the Young Ambassadors during the part of their Asia tour that took them to China. While visiting the Forbidden City (the Palace Museum) in Beijing, the group gathered at a lovely pavilion in a beautiful garden and sang "I Am a Child of God." In the quiet of that spot, near the place where Elder David O. McKay dedicated the Chinese realm for the preaching of the gospel in 1921, Elder Faust voiced another prayer that the gospel might soon be taught in the People's Republic of China.

Over the years since that first tour, other BYU groups—the Folk Dance Ensemble, the Lamanite Generation, the Ballroom Dance Company, the Chamber Orchestra, and the Wind Symphony—have taken at least sixteen performance tours to China. General Authorities of the Church and BYU administrators have traveled with most of the groups. There is little question that BYU is among the two or three best-known and most highly respected foreign universities in China.

Through cultural exchanges, as the tours have been labeled, the Church has had a legitimate avenue for establishing contacts among China's highest officials. These relationships have developed in other areas, such as medicine, science, business, English teaching, and diplomacy. Chinese political leaders also visited Salt Lake City and the Polynesian Cultural Center in Laie, Hawaii, during the 1980s and 1990s. Vice Premier Geng Biao was the first such leader to visit the Polynesian Cultural Center in 1980, followed by Premier Zhao Ziyang in 1984 and President Li Xiannan in October 1985. In January 1981 Ambassador Chai Zemin was the first of several Chinese ambassadors to the United States to accept invitations to visit Church headquarters in Salt Lake City and Brigham Young University. The most recent visit was by Ambassador Li Daoyu in the spring of 1996.[24]

The Church has also provided humanitarian aid to the PRC on at least two occasions, and Church members have volunteered their medical knowledge and service many times. Most notable, Elder Russell M. Nelson, before and since his call as an Apostle in April 1984, has taught heart surgery at the Shandong Medical College in Jinan, Shandong Province. For his service in 1980 and 1984, he was named honorary professor in September 1984. His service and dedication to doing his teaching well were exceptional. He studied Mandarin Chinese and became proficient enough to communicate effectively, "particularly during surgery."[25] His ability to speak and understand Chinese has helped as he has visited China on several occasions since that time.

In February 1989 and again in August 1991, representatives of the Church, Elder Russell M. Nelson and Elder Merlin R. Lybbert, respectively, delivered checks for $25,000 and $25,600 to representatives of the Chinese government for earthquake damage reconstruction and to buy medical supplies for victims of a major flood.[26]

The distance between China and the Church has been closed through contacts of a number of kinds. BYU students have studied the Chinese language at Nanjing University every spring since the late 1980s. Faculty members have participated in a formal exchange program between Xian Foreign Languages University and the College of Humanities at BYU.[27] Hundreds of LDS business people, professors, and government employees have lived and served in various Chinese cities, most frequently Beijing, Shanghai, Guangzhou, and Xian. Three expatriate branches and several groups of the Church have operated in China since the late 1980s.

One of the most effective in-country initiatives has been the China Teachers Program of the David M. Kennedy Center for International Studies at Brigham Young University. In 1988 Ray C. Hillam, director of the Kennedy Center, and his colleagues implemented a system of teacher placement at various universities and institutes in China. The program started small but has expanded most years until during the 1995–96 school year eighty people were employed as English teachers in China. The purpose was at least twofold: to perform humanitarian service in the spirit suggested by President Kimball and to have a Latter-day Saint presence in China. By 1996 hundreds of teachers had participated in the placement program, and thousands of Chinese students had become acquainted with believing members of the Church. The teachers are not allowed to preach or teach about their religious beliefs, but their way of life has provided a good example for many who associate with them.[28]

In addition to the foreign Mormon involvement in China, thousands of Chinese students have left China to study at universities throughout the world. Since the mid-1980s hundreds of these students have studied at BYU and BYU—Hawaii. From 1985 until 1994 approximately $120,000 per year was allocated from PCC profits to support Chinese students at the two institutions.[29] Some of these students, as well as hundreds at other universities in the United States and the Western world, have learned about the restored gospel, become converted, and been baptized into the Church.

The status of these Chinese converts upon returning to China has been a problem. Chinese Mormons, of course, wish to associate with other members of the Church, but since the events at Tiananmen Square in May and June 1989, the government has strictly forbidden affiliation of Chinese citizens with expatriate religious groups and individuals. In short, American and other foreign Latter-day Saints are allowed to meet as religious organizations, but Chinese are not allowed to meet with them.

The missionary position of the Church has never varied; the Church will not enter a country under devious or illegal means. Leaders of the Church have been absolutely forthright with Chinese government officials regarding the Church's hopes and intentions in China. The hope of the Church is to take the restored gospel to every land and people, including China. Until June 4, 1989, various members of the Quorum of the Twelve, sometimes in company with BYU performance groups, sometimes alone, and sometimes in twos, have met with officers at the highest levels to convey the interests and commitments of the Church. Those who have been charged with primary responsibility for Asia, and thus China, for the past decade have been Elder Dallin H. Oaks, Elder Neal A. Maxwell, and Elder Joseph B. Wirthlin. During their periods as first contact for Asia, Elders Oaks and Maxwell made several trips to China to speak at such institutions as the Academy of Science, to negotiate with Chinese officials, and to survey the situation. Elder Oaks (along with Elder Nelson) shared the commitment of the Church to strictly adhere to Chinese religious law and policy, offered aid and gave promises of educational assistance, received encouragement, and were led to believe that Chinese members of the Church (those who joined outside China) would be free to practice their religious beliefs. But since the Tiananmen Incident, Chinese members have not been allowed to meet with other Chinese members or with expatriates. In spite of attempts by LDS representatives to gain modification of this position, the government has created an ever firmer legal and policy position against outside religions and teachers of religion.[30]

LDS China watchers have sometimes become frustrated with the slow pace of progress there. To those who have impatient thoughts, Elder Oaks gave some wise and sensitive counsel. On March 12, 1991, he delivered an important devotional address at BYU titled "Getting to Know China," in which he reviewed the relationships the Church and members of the Church have had with the People's Republic of China. Elder Oaks said:

> People sometimes ask me about what can be done to "open China." In response, I state my belief that China is already "open"—it is we who are closed. We are closed because we expect the Orient to be the same as the West, China to be the same as Canada or Chile. We must understand their way of thinking, their aspirations and their impressive accomplishments. We must observe their laws, and follow their example of patience. We must deserve to be their friends.
>
> As we become friends of China, and as we learn from them, our Father in Heaven, who has made "all nations of men . . . and [has] determined . . . the bounds of their habitation" (Acts 17:26), will bring His purposes to pass in that great nation "in his own time, and in his own way, and according to his own will" (D&C 88:68).[31]

When President Gordon B. Hinckley spoke to the missionaries of the Hong Kong Mission on May 25, 1996, he talked about China and the future growth of the Church there. He suggested, "Don't push it." It will come in the Lord's time. Considering present religious law and policy, Latter-day Saint missionary work will have to be in the Lord's time.

CHURCH BEGINNINGS IN MONGOLIA

The Mongols

During the thirteenth and fourteenth centuries no people in the world were more feared than the Mongols. Under the leadership of Chinggis (Genghis) Khan, the Mongols established an empire that stretched from Korea to Hungary. The Mongol Yüan dynasty (1280–1367) ruled China for almost a hundred years, and its influence lasted much longer. With the rise of the Manchu Qing (Ch'ing) dynasty in China in 1644, Mongolia fell under Chinese rule and was administered as a Chinese province called Inner and Outer Mongolia and remained under Chinese control until the revolution of 1911. By 1921 Russian Communists became predominant, and in 1924 Mongolia became the second Communist nation in the world—the first in Asia. For centuries Mongolia had been part of the Chinese sphere; from 1924 until the breakup of the Soviet Union beginning in 1989, Mongolia was under Russian dominance. A series of public protests in the capital, Ulaanbaatar (population 600,000), from December 1989 to March 1990, brought the resignation of Mongolia's third Communist leader, Dzhambiyn Batmunkh. Calls for political and economic reform have brought significant changes in government since that time. Until summer 1996, Communists of the Mongolian People's Revolutionary Party controlled the *Great Hura,* (parliament), at which time a coalition of democratic parties gained fifty of the seventy-six seats in the unicameral law-making body. The Democratic Union party supports religious freedom, making the situation for the LDS Church more comfortable than under the previous government. Religious freedom is a tenuous matter in many newly independent nations, including Mongolia. Formerly called Outer Mongolia and the People's Republic of Mongolia, it was renamed the Republic of Mongolia in 1992.

Mongolia is approximately the size of Alaska, with a population of 2.3 million. Its population density is the lowest of any nation in the world. Twenty-five percent of the people live in Ulaanbaatar, and another 35 percent live in Mongolia's other urban centers, such as Darkhan and Erdenet. Forty percent of the populous is rural, many of the people remaining seminomadic. According to *Culturgrams '96*, a publication of the David M. Kennedy Center for International Studies at BYU, "about 90 percent of the highly homogeneous population are Mongols," of whom the chief group is the Khalkhas. The Khalkha dialect is the standard language of the Mongols. During the years of Russian dominance the language was written in the Cyrillic alphabet, but in 1991 the parliament voted to restore the traditional script. Although an attempt was made to move back to the old cursive script, which is written vertically, the experiment proved unworkable, and in 1995 the decision was made to return to the Cyrillic alphabet because it was better understood throughout the world.

Before the Communist takeover, most Mongols believed in Tibetan Lamaist Buddhism and Shamanism,[32] but after 1929 all but one of the hundreds of monasteries were closed, most of the Buddhist priests and nuns having been brutally murdered. Since 1990 there has been a resurgence of Buddhism, with more than one hundred of the monasteries reopened. Many Mongols consider Buddhism the national religion, but a constitutional provision to make it official, proposed in 1991, failed. Since 1990, Mongolia has guaranteed freedom of religion, but assaults on religious liberty continue.

The Church in Mongolia

The spread of democracy and freedom of religion and the growth of free enterprise were preparatory steps in the establishment of the restored gospel in Mongolia. Before the fall of Communism, establishing missionary work was an impossibility. But on September 19, 1992, Elder Monte J. Brough, president of the Asia Area, announced that six missionary couples, "at the invitation of the Mongolian government, will be sent to the country to help improve Mongolia's higher education system." They would go as missionaries with permission to proselyte and hold Church meetings during hours when they were not engaged in teaching, consulting, advising, or otherwise helping with the reconstruction of Mongolia's higher education system.[33]

In a visit to the Mongolian Embassy in Washington, D.C., groundwork was laid by emeritus professors Paul V. Hyer and

Sechin Jagchid (a Mongol by birth) of Brigham Young University for a visit to BYU by the Mongolian Ambassador to the United States. Later, Elder Brough and Elder Merlin R. Lybbert traveled to Mongolia several times to meet with government officials and survey the areas where the Church might be of assistance. Because of the switch from a command economy and a Russian-language-centered education system, the new government faced many challenges. Education officials desired to move higher education toward a Western model; the Church offered to help.

The first six missionary couples were carefully selected. Every individual had talents and training to make a significant contribution. The team leaders were Kenneth H. Beesley and his wife, Donna. Formerly an associate commissioner of education for the Church and president of LDS Business College, Elder Beesley held seminars for the Ministry of Science and Education (MOSE) with universities, a technical university, and several business colleges. He also taught a class in English. Donna taught English classes at the Russian-Mongolian Secondary School No. 3 and tutored students outside class. Richard Harper taught psychology and English and consulted with the vice president of the Academy of Sciences. His wife, Anna, taught English and gave TOEFL (Test of English as a Foreign Language) review sessions. Stanley B. Smith taught English and business classes, and his wife, Marjorie, taught English at Russian-Mongolian Secondary School No. 3. Royce P. Flandro consulted regarding curriculum, faculty evaluation, and distance-learning. His wife, Jane, taught classes on how to start and manage small businesses. C. DuWayne Schmidt, M.D., lectured at the Medical University, rewrote a Mongolian textbook on pulmonary diseases, and donated medical books and journals and some medicines to the Medical University. His wife, Alice, taught English. Gary Carlson taught computer systems and donated a large library of computer books and journals, software, and hardware to the Technical University. His wife, Barbara, taught English classes, contributed a large library of books and teaching materials to the Otgon-Tenger Foreign

In the few years since the first Mongolian convert came into the Church in 1993, the Church in Mongolia has grown to around a thousand members. This picture, taken Christmas day 1993, shows a Church meeting in the State Central Library, which had been rented because investigators (there were only 23 members at this time) could not be accommodated in missionary apartments that had previously hosted meetings. (At this writing, September 1997, 42 Mongolians have served or are serving full-time missions for the Church.) (Courtesy Kenneth and Donna Beesley)

Language Institute, and established an ESL (English as a second language) library for LDS missionaries. All of these men had formerly been university professors.[34]

The couples arrived in Ulaanbaatar between September 16, 1992, and February 1993. In August 1993 they were joined by six young elders, fresh from the Missionary Training Center. They were assigned to teach English as a foreign language at various schools and universities. But their greatest contribution was their ability to teach the fundamentals of the restored gospel to the growing number of people, mostly students, who had become acquainted with the couple missionaries and who wanted to learn more about their religious beliefs.[35]

The first converts asked to be taught. Charlotte Lofgreen, a BYU English professor who was doing research and teaching

English in Mongolia, reported their conversions: "Since the missionaries had no scriptures or tracts in Mongolian, and therefore had to learn the language in the country, the teaching of English became an important key to opening the gospel door. Although Elder Stanley Smith taught business, he so impressed his students that they asked him to teach them English. After class one day, Purusuren and Batoolzi[36] inquired, 'Are you a Christian?' Receiving an affirmative reply, they asked to be taught about Jesus Christ. This was the beginning of the Church in Mongolia. Purusuren[37] and Batoolzi were baptized in February of 1993."[38] Three months later, on May 8, Gendenjamts Darrjargal became the first Mongolian woman and the third Mongolian person to be baptized.

The Dedication of Mongolia

On April 15, 1993, Elder Neal A. Maxwell visited Ulaanbaatar and dedicated Mongolia to the preaching of the gospel. He was accompanied by Elder Tai Kwok Yuen, a member of the Asia Area Presidency. Thirty-four people assembled on Zaysan, Monument Hill, overlooking Ulaanbaatar. The day was cold and windy, but the sky and air were clear. After humbly acknowledging God as the "Father of the whole human family," Elder Maxwell sought Heavenly Father's blessings on the "pioneering couples and all those missionaries who will follow." He asked for a blessing on "the new converts" and prayed that they would "be strong as they shape the future of the Church in Mongolia." Elder Maxwell prayed that the Mongolian people could be "happier and more prosperous." "Father," he prayed, "this is a wind-swept land. May it also be the case that the winds of freedom will never cease to blow in Mongolia. Preserve and protect the independence of Mongolia regardless of the moves made on the great checkerboard of the nations." He prayed that Mongolian members would be good citizens of the Church and of the nation. "I dedicate the land of Mongolia and bless its leaders and people, its soil, and its sky— all to the end that the nation may be blessed and that it will so respond to the gospel message so that Thy work may be firmly established here. May Mongolia even be as a beacon light to other nations."[39]

Continued Growth to 1996

Church meetings were initially held in the apartments of the missionary couples. But when the number grew to thirty-five, they had to move to a larger place. For six months the young branch met in the State Central Library with the assistance of the director, Mr. Otgon; but because of complaints regarding separation of church and state, the missionaries moved the meetings to another facility, the Peace and Friendship House. This government-owned building was very expensive. The rental contract there was not renewed in February 1996, making it necessary for the branch to move to another location. Finding and renting halls for Church services was particularly difficult in Mongolia because 95 percent of the buildings were still owned by the government and thus generally not available because of religious restrictions. The few private facilities that were available, like the government-owned facilities, were extremely expensive to rent.[40]

By December 1993, 110 members and investigators met together for sacrament meeting. By then two local members were serving as counselors in the branch presidency and a Mongolian sister led the Relief Society. Forty-four Mongolians entered the waters of baptism in 1993. By August 1994 there were 120 Mongolian members of the Church and growth continued steadily.

One of the most important matters for the Church when moving into new nations is to gain legal recognition. This is required so the Church can act as a legal corporation to rent, lease, or buy property and act legally in other transactions. The Church was registered with the Mongolian government in 1994. As has been expedient or required in other countries, legal status was also granted to one of the Church's legal entities, in this case Deseret

International Charities. This charitable organization was officially registered in Mongolia in May 1996.

Expansion has not been easy. The Church and individual members have been persecuted, rebuffed by unfavorable newspaper articles, forced out of employment, treated unkindly by other Christian groups, and so on. When young Mongolians join Christian churches, they are often accused of being disloyal to national values. Some Mongolians have a strong concern for the continuation of Mongolian culture and emphasize Buddhism in this context, and others fear dissonance and social chaos through the introduction of other religions, particularly Christianity. This has led to problems for the Church. Mission president Richard Cook and his wife, Mary, described these challenges:

> We faced a major roadblock when we opened the city of Darkhan in April [1996]. The city council refused to register the Church with the city and in fact ordered that the work be stopped. In a city council meeting the reason cited was "We have one Christian church in Darkhan. We only have one Buddhist church in Mongolia. We don't need another Christian church in this city." The missionaries stopped their work with investigators for one month in Darkhan. We met with our lawyer in Ulaanbaatar, and he challenged the city council's decision. He said that the fact that the Church was registered in the country gave us the right to practice in Darkhan. We continued our work in Darkhan as a dependent branch of the Selbe Branch in Ulaanbaatar and argued that we are not a "new" church. We have not been challenged.[41]

Interestingly, even though nationalistic Buddhists created problems for the Church, monks of the Dashchoiliin Monastery were "cooperative and respectful of our purposes and efforts."[42] Having been persecuted by the Communists, they were aware of the fragile nature of religious freedom. Their belief was that all religions should cooperate to protect religious liberty. In an effort to create and continue good relations, our missionaries taught English to the monks twice a week.

By July 1996 the branch in Ulaanbaatar had been divided into three branches (the Ulaanbaatar, Enkhtaivan, and Selbe Branches), and, as mentioned earlier, small branches had been established in Erdenet and Darkhan. Mongolia had more than six hundred Latter-day Saints. Branch members met separately in rented halls, and two of the branches had local branch presidents. Most of the branch organizations were staffed by Mongols, and nearly all teachers in branches were local. By that time, twenty Mongolian members had been called as missionaries to the United States, Canada, Russia, and Korea, with five more called to serve. Three of that number had been called to serve in their native Mongolia.

Without much fanfare, on July 1, 1995, Richard E. Cook, who was already serving with his wife, Mary, in Ulaanbaatar, began to serve as president of the new Mongolia Ulaanbaatar Mission. They were replaced on July 1, 1996, by Gary E. Cox and his wife, Joyce, who had served there previously. When the Coxes arrived in Mongolia, there were eight missionary couples, six sister missionaries, and eighteen elders serving, a total missionary force of forty.[43]

Over time the original assignments for couples to assist with the higher education system were expanded. By September 1995 missionaries with other talents had been sent to Mongolia. Among the specialists were accountants (of which President Cook was one) to help upgrade the country's accounting system and librarians to improve the library system. (The Church also donated appropriate books for faculty and student use.) In July 1996 a housing consultant was sent to assist officials of the Ministry of Infrastructure Development in evaluating low-cost methods of providing housing. In June 1995 Welfare Services shipped 289 boxes of math and science books to be distributed to schools throughout Ulaanbaatar. The missionaries helped distribute the books. In addition, young elders (five of the first six elders were Eagle Scouts) conducted workshops for the Boy Scouts organization in Mongolia.

As in many Asian nations, maintaining long-term visas for missionaries was a problem, in spite of the contributions made by the missionaries. Not everyone appreciated what the Church was doing, and some people in high government offices were influenced by groups who were opposed under any conditions to the Church's presence. Mongolian laws also demanded that long-term visa holders have formal letters of invitation from an appropriate individual or a recognized organization. To qualify for long-term visas, applicants had to have a contract to work or perform volunteer service in the country. To fulfill this requirement, LDS missionaries have willingly provided at least sixteen hours of English teaching per week. The Mongolian Higher Education Development Foundation acted as sponsor from the beginning. To extend the relationship between the Church and the Foundation, Elder John H. Groberg of the Asia Area Presidency negotiated a five-year contract in March 1996. The foundation was to "continue to issue letters of invitation to our missionaries. The Church, in turn, has agreed to conduct an annual seminar in Mongolia on an agreed-upon subject and to provide training abroad for selected professionals at BYU—Hawaii or BYU—Provo."[44] It is expected that the Church will continue to grow steadily in Mongolia for the foreseeable future.

NOTES

1. "Asia Area: Fifth stake organized," *Church News*, 23 April 1994, p. 12.

2. Monte Carlson, interview by Feng Xi, Provo, Utah, 18 February 1994, in Feng Xi, "A History of Mormon-Chinese Relations: 1849–1993" (Ph.D. diss., Brigham Young University, 1994), pp. 192–94.

3. Ibid., p. 202.

4. Bai Tien was an English language student in a class taught by George Bennion, teacher at Xian Foreign Languages University. This essay was written as an English class assignment.

5. The "Three Bonds" are the relationship of ruler and subject, father and son, and husband and wife. The "Five Virtues" are benevolence, righteousness, propriety, wisdom, and fidelity.

6. Ezra Taft Benson to All Stake and Mission Presidents in the Orient, 8 April 1975; copy in possession of the author.

7. See Mike Cannon, "'Lord's timetable' guides new leader," *Church News*, 19

September 1992, pp. 6–7; and "Tai Kwok Yuen of the Seventy," *Ensign* 22 (September 1992): 79.

8. Paul V. Hyer to Richard B. Stamps, 29 February 1996; copy in possession of the author.

9. As quoted in David C. H. Liu and Richard L. Jensen, "Taiwan Saints Eager for Temple Blessings," *Ensign* 14 (November 1984): 108.

10. See "LDS, others take pride in Taiwan temple at open house," *Church News*, 11 November 1984, p. 12.

11. Gerry Avant, "First temple in Chinese realm," *Church News*, 25 November 1984, p. 3.

12. David C. H. Liu, "Taipei Taiwan Temple Dedicated," *Ensign* 15 (February 1985): 75–76.

13. John L. Hart, "Temple Moments: Great is their joy," *Church News*, 10 December 1988, p. 16.

14. From notes taken by the author at the temple dedication, 27 May 1996, Hong Kong.

15. John K. Carmack, remarks at ground breaking of Hong Kong Temple, 22 January 1994; copy in possession of the author.

16. John K. Carmack, interview by the author, Salt Lake City, Utah, 30 November 1995.

17. See my "The Current Legal Status of Christianity in China," *Brigham Young University Law Review* 1995, no. 2: 347–99.

18. See "Hong Kong Temple visited by 13,000 during open house," *Church News*, 25 May 1996, pp. 4–5.

19. For more information regarding the life of President Ng, see Kellene Ricks, "Ng Kat Hing: Hong Kong Pioneer," *Ensign* 22 (August 1992): 50–52.

20. "Dedicatory Prayer of the Hong Kong Temple," *Church News*, 1 June 1996, p. 4.

21. Gerry Avant, "LDS leader pays visit to China's mainland," *Deseret News*, 28 May 1996, A1–A2.

22. As quoted in Dell Van Orden, "Door to China may be opening," *Church News*, 7 April 1979, p. 3; and "President Kimball Sees Missions in Communist China in Future," *Herald* (Provo, Utah), 1 April 1979, p. 24.

23. Lynne Hollstein Hansen, "Y students a success in China," *Church News*, 11 August 1979, p. 10.

24. See "Chinese leader visits center," *Church News*, 12 July 1980, p. 9; "Chinese ambassador visits Utah," *Church News*, 17 January 1981, p. 5; "Chinese Premier Visits BYU—Hawaii Campus, Polynesian Cultural Center," *Ensign* 14 (March 1984): 77–78; "Polynesian Cultural Center Hosts Chinese President," *Ensign* 15 (October 1985): 78. The author participated in hosting Ambassador Li Daoyu in 1996.

25. "Elder Nelson is named honorary professor by Chinese medical college," *Church News*, 29 September 1985, p. 6.

26. "Gift to help China rebuild after quake," *Church News*, 25 February 1989, p. 4; "Church donates Aid for Victims of Quake in China," *Ensign* 19 (May 1989): 109; and "Donation to help flood victims in China," *Church News*, 17 August 1991, p. 11.

27. See Carri P. Jenkins, "Bridging Barriers," *BYU Today* 40 (August 1986): 18–22, 25, 34–35.

28. The author, who served as director of the Kennedy Center, has firsthand knowledge of this program.

29. The same comment in n. 28 applies.

30. See note 16; and "China: Two apostles visit, assured that religious freedom exists and people are free to worship as they choose," *Church News*, 28 January 1989, pp. 3–4.

31. As quoted in "Open minds, hearts to people of China," *Church News*, 16 March 1991, p. 5.

32. Shamanism is a religion of northeastern Asia that emphasizes the spiritual and mystical powers of a priest (or priestess) called a Shaman (or Shamaness), who uses magic and trances to communicate with gods, ancestors, deceased family members, and so on.

33. See "Six missionary couples to help with Mongolia's higher education," *Church News*, 19 September 1992, pp. 3–4.

34. See Kenneth H. Beesley, "The LDS Church and Higher Education in Mongolia," *Proceedings of the Fifth Annual Conference of the International Society*, Brigham Young University, 15 August 1994, pp. 33–34.

35. See ibid., p. 32.

36. Spellings vary depending on the person writing the report. *Purusuren* is also given as *Lamjav Purevsuren*, and *Batoolzi* is also spelled *Tsendkhuu Bat-Ulzii*.

37. Mongolians have a patronymic and a given name. All people are called by their given names.

38. Charlotte D. Lofgreen, "Mongolia: The Morning Breaks," *Cameo: Latter-day Women in Profile* 2 (February 1994): 23–24.

39. Neal A. Maxwell, Official Dedicatory Prayer, 15 April 1993, Ulaanbaatar, Mongolia; copy in possession of the author. See also "Mongolia dedicated for preaching of the gospel," *Church News*, 19 June 1993, p. 3.

40. Richard E. and Mary N. Cook, "The Challenges of Sharing the Gospel in Countries with a Strong Secular Tradition: Mongolia," p. 7; copy in possession of the author. The Cooks described some of the problems they encountered acquiring property in these words:

"When we did find a suitable building to rent, costs were unreasonably high because our church was considered a 'foreign church.' The management often proved to be uncooperative. Rooms would be locked and unavailable for use, although we had paid for them. Finally, they refused to renew our lease in spite of the sizable income the rent brought their organization each year.

"The Enkhtaivan Branch was renting a movie theater in March 1996. One Sunday the manager of the theater approached our branch president and requested that during the months of May and June the Branch meet elsewhere. With the upcoming election to be held on June 30th, he did not want politicians who would be speaking at the theater to know that he was renting to a Christian group. We complied with his request and moved until after the election.

"The Church is attempting to buy a facility for permanent use by the members. This has been very difficult due to the inexperience of Mongolians with such transactions. All land is owned by the government and leased on a long-term basis by an interested buyer or builder. The major difficulty comes in trying to identify titles to property. There is no [institutionalized] system yet established in the country to identify liabilities against a property or who, in fact, owns the property. At one point we had found a privately owned, partially finished building in an ideal location. We felt that it was at a perfect stage to be finished to the Church's specifications. After weeks of negotiation with the owner, we made an offer. We were advised by our attorneys that before signing a contract we should advertise in the major newspapers, on television and radio to identify any liabilities that may be on the property. This process revealed many problems to a point where proceeding with the purchase would have been disastrous. The safest way to obtain a building is to build, but this is expensive and time-consuming."

41. Ibid., p. 6.

42. Ibid., pp. 7–8.

43. See ibid., p. 2.

44. Ibid., p. 5.

13

THE PHILIPPINES

1961–1980

Laying the Foundations

The area conference of the Church held in Manila, Republic of the Philippines, in August 1975 was a miracle to the early converts as well as to the visiting General Authorities of the Church. But one man, Elder Gordon B. Hinckley, was perhaps more moved and inspired than anyone else by the crowd of eighteen thousand members and friends. He remembered well his efforts and those of others to legally establish the Church in these islands. Only he and President Robert S. Taylor of the Southern Far East Mission knew the sorrow and sadness of the moment when they returned from a sacred meeting of rededication on the morning of April 28, 1961, and learned that their application for missionary visas had been denied. But they had overcome the obstacles of that time, and five weeks later four missionaries arrived in Manila from Hong Kong. On June 6, 1961, the elders tracted in the area of their newly rented home in Pasay City, a Manila suburb. They succeeded in entering every home they visited. Although there were discouraging times ahead, they had opened LDS missionary work in the Philippines.

Those four elders were not the first Latter-day Saints to teach the restored gospel in the Philippines. They were preceded by a faithful line of LDS servicemen and women, U.S. government employees, and businessmen and their families. The first LDS

Maxine Tate, American Red Cross worker, with LDS servicemen on Leyte, Philippines, toward the end of World War II. Sister Tate met and married E. M. "Pete" Grimm following the war. Manila became her principal residence for many years. (Courtesy Maxine Tate Grimm)

missionaries preached the gospel in Cortel de Mesic about August 30, 1898. They were Willard Call and George Seaman, members of the Utah artillery batteries that were sent to the Philippines during the Spanish-American War. Apostle John Henry Smith had set them apart as missionaries.[1]

Between that time and 1944, when numerous LDS servicemen and women were among General Douglas MacArthur's advancing forces, no known members were in the Philippines. Between 1944 and 1946 a number of LDS servicemen's groups functioned in various cities and bases, but as the islands returned to normal and gained their independence from the United States on July 4, 1946, the groups dwindled as quickly as they had come. A few Latter-day Saints, all Americans except Aniceta Fajardo, the first Filipino convert, remained. Most notable among the permanent residents was Maxine Tate Grimm.

From 1947 until 1951 few meetings were held. But because of the military buildup caused by the Korean War, LDS servicemen's groups again formed in 1951, and by February 13, 1953, Vinal G. Mauss, who as president of the Japanese Mission had responsibility for servicemen in all of Asia, found it advisable to organize the Luzon Servicemen's District. He called Major L. B. Davis as its first president. The new district consisted of groups at Manila–Sangley Point, Subic Bay, and Clark Air Force Base. The Clark Group was the largest and had the most auxiliaries, including the first Relief Society in the Philippines.[2]

The servicemen's groups remained under the Japanese (Far East) Mission until August 1955, when President Joseph Fielding Smith organized the Southern Far East Mission and dedicated the Philippines for the preaching of the gospel. This event took place between sessions of a servicemen's conference on Sunday, August 21, 1955, at a beautiful grove in Clark Air Force Base.[3] From then until 1961, when missionary work officially began, President H. Grant Heaton and then President Robert S. Taylor made regular visits to Luzon to hold conferences, make changes in district leadership, and register the Church with the government so that missionary work could begin. In June 1959 Elder Mark E. Petersen visited the Philippines for four days and concluded that missionary work could be done there. He recommended that the legal department in Salt Lake City "be requested to expedite papers for seeking registration of our Church in the Philippines."[4] Elder Gordon B. Hinckley entered the picture in May 1960, when he made his first visit to the Philippines. During this visit he became convinced that the Philippines could be as fruitful as many other fields. He recognized the advantage of having many LDS servicemen and their families there to support the elders when they arrived.[5]

Between May 1960 and April 1961, President Taylor arranged for legal recognition of the Church by the government and applied for visas for missionaries. On April 25, 1961, Elder Hinckley and President Taylor visited government offices and endured the discomforts of sultry air and sultry treatment from indifferent bureaucrats. It was necessary for Elder Hinckley and President Taylor to convince the officials that the elders and sisters would not be a burden on the economy or a problem for the government. On the twenty-seventh, President Taylor visited the Immigration Office and learned that the commissioners had recommended to their superiors that the missionaries be granted visas. Thus encouraged, President Taylor and Elder Hinckley arranged to hold a sunrise service the next morning at the Fort McKinley War Memorial Cemetery (now called the American War Memorial Cemetery).

Servicemen and their families, local American residents such as E. M. "Pete" and Maxine Grimm and one Filipino Saint gathered on the steps of the cemetery chapel. When Elder Hinckley told the approximately one hundred people that the Philippines had been dedicated six years before by President Smith, they were greatly surprised.[6] In that calm and beautiful setting, surrounded by the graves of thousands of American war dead, the group heard talks by Maxine Grimm, who outlined the history of Latter-day Saints in the Philippines since 1944, and by David Lagman, the first male Filipino to join the Church and the first Filipino to hold the office of an elder. Elder Hinckley then spoke: "This is an occasion you will never forget. What we begin here will affect the lives of thousands and thousands of people in this island republic, and its effects will go on from generation to generation for great and everlasting good."[7] Perhaps even Elder Hinckley did not realize the magnitude of the prophecy he was giving.

In his prayer of rededication, Elder Hinckley touched on many important things. One paragraph stands out as particularly prophetic and meaningful. He prayed:

> We invoke Thy blessings upon the people of this land, that they shall be friendly and hospitable, and kind and gracious to those who shall come here, and that many, yea, Lord, we pray that there shall be many thousands

The American War Memorial Cemetery is by its nature solemn and sacred. Thousands of American soldiers lie at eternal rest here. To Latter-day Saints it is additionally sacred because missionary work in the Philippines commenced here with a prayer of rededication offered by Elder Gordon B. Hinckley on 28 April 1961. Elder Hinckley and President Robert S. Taylor of the Southern Far East Mission are in the middle of the first standing row. Others include Maxine Tate Grimm (at organ, right); Ping Bachelor (standing at far left), the first person baptised after missionary work commenced; and David Lagman, the only Filipino member at the meeting. (Photo by author)

who shall receive this message and be blessed thereby. Wilt Thou bless them with receptive minds and understanding hearts, and with faith to receive, and with courage to live the principles of the Gospel, and with a desire to share with others the blessings which they shall receive. We pray that there shall be many men, faithful, good, virtuous, true men who shall join the Church and who shall accept and grow in leadership, that Thy work here shall be handled largely by local brethren, under the direction of those who hold the keys in this day and time, according to the law and order of Thy Church.[8]

Every blessing Elder Hinckley prayed for had been fulfilled in less than twenty years and has continued to expand since that time.

As mentioned before, later that day Elder Hinckley and President Taylor received word from the Office of Foreign Affairs that the missionary visas that they had been led to believe would be approved had been turned down. Fortunately, they appealed the decision and convinced the Minister of Foreign Affairs, who had ultimate jurisdiction in the matter, that the missionaries should be allowed in the country. By June the way was clear for missionaries to begin proselyting.

On June 5, 1961, President Taylor accompanied four elders— Raymond L. Goodson, Nester O. Ledesma, Kent C. Lowe, and Harry J. Murray—to Manila. The following day Taylor rented a large house, one that was big enough for small Church services, and the elders began preaching the gospel.[9]

THE PHILIPPINES, A UNIQUE
ASIAN MISSION FIELD

Considering the amazing success of the Church in the Philippines (approximately 20,000 members by 1975 and 370,000 by 1996), one wonders why the Church is doing so well there in comparison with Thailand, Japan, or areas in China. The explanation lies almost entirely in the historical development of the

Philippines. Ralph Tolliver, a Protestant missionary to the Philippines, presents the fundamental historical ingredients by means of an effective analogy:

> The Philippines are like an onion. The thin outside skin of the onion is American: the first things that impress the visitor to Manila are the Stars and Stripes that flew over the Philippines for forty-eight years, from 1898 to 1946 (interrupted by four years of Japanese occupation, from 1942–1945).
>
> Peel off the outside skin of the onion and the next layer is Spanish. He who delves into life in the Philippines soon discovers that its religion, music, social customs, and commercial systems of telling time, counting money, and weighing vegetables all come from . . . Spain's rule in the Philippines [1565–1898], the most important is the nominal Catholicism, which claims almost 85 percent of the people still today.
>
> Then peel off the Spanish layer and you come to the hard and durable core of Filipino life, which is Malayo-Indonesian. Proverbs and values, the family system, and personal relationships—the real game of life—is played by ancient tribal rules.
>
> But this make-believe onion is still an organic unit, for "Juan de la Cruz" (the Filipino "Joe Doe") functions during office hours as an American, goes to mass on Sunday morning like a Spaniard, and rules his home like a traditional Filipino. He is a mixture of East and West, old and new. Sometimes the conflict disturbs him, but most of the time he does not stop to think about the disparate influences which mold his life.[10]

Elements of all parts of this complex—American, Spanish, and Filipino—have combined to help the LDS Church succeed in the Philippines. Americans are generally respected and welcome there. They not only provided fair and equitable government from 1898 until 1946, but they also liberated the islands at the end of World War II. To the present, America is the Philippines' number-one trading partner, even though inequities there have recently caused problems. But more important than the legacy of efficient colonial government and U.S. trade are two other remnants of the colonial era: a feeling for democracy and the adoption of the English language.

When the Republic of the Philippines was created, its founders modeled its constitution on that of the United States. Along with other rights, freedom of religion was granted to the people. Although some observers have seen what they consider an overwhelming Roman Catholic influence in government—all of the presidents of the Philippines except the present leader have been Catholic—the existence of more than 350 different denominations is evidence that religious freedom exists. It is true that American democracy has not been duplicated there, but local inhabitants and foreigners are extended most liberties that Americans enjoy.

Estimates vary regarding the number of languages that are spoken in the Philippines. There are at least eighty-seven. The great majority of the people use one of four native languages: Tagalog, which is the basis for Filipino (the national language), Ilocano, Hiligaynon (Ilonggo), and Cebuano. But English is the real *lingua franca* of the nation. It is used in government, business, education, and communications. Half of Manila's newspapers are in English. More than half the population understands English, making the Philippines the third-largest English-speaking country in the world. The implications for missionary work are obvious.

The most important carryover from the Spanish era for LDS missionary work is Christianity. Before the Spanish conquest the Filipino people were generally animists. In 1565, when the Spanish conquest began, only the southwestern tip of Mindanao had been converted to Islam. The rule of the Roman Catholic Church had many negative features, but the people in general did become nominally Christian. It is much easier to convert an English-speaking Christian to the restored gospel than, for example, a Chinese-speaking Buddhist or Daoist.

The religious makeup of the nation is 83 percent Roman

Catholic, 9 percent Protestant (Protestant missionary work began in 1898 when the United States took control of the islands), 5 percent Muslim, and 3 percent other (Chinese faiths, animism, and so forth). Converts come into the Church in almost these same proportions, particularly from Catholicism and Protestantism.

The elements that are carried over from the pre-Spanish era, the native Filipino cultural traits, are many. Among those that have contributed to LDS success is the spirit of *bayanihan*, of working together. It is a willingness to extend one's heart to strangers as well as friends. This trait has helped the missionaries in their tracting. Another quality not to be overlooked is the importance of the family. All Asian peoples place high value on the family unit and its role in society. But in contrast to the Confucian areas (China, Korea, Japan, and Vietnam), where importance is placed on rigid familial propriety, in the Philippines the emphasis is on family life and solidarity. Hence the Church's position on families has met with considerable approval. The membership of the Church in the Philippines is closer to the "whole family" ideal than in any other part of Asia. At the end of the first decade of missionary work, more than 35 percent of all married members had mates who belonged to the Church, and almost 50 percent had brothers and sisters who were members.[11] This trend appears to have continued.

Another important contributor to the success of the Church, especially during the early years of the mission, was the influence and leadership of the LDS servicemen. Whereas in Taiwan the Chinese language caused problems and necessitated the organization of a separate English-speaking branch, in the Philippines the servicemen and their families were able to communicate with the local people, and they developed strong bonds of fellowship and love. In Manila near Clark Air Force Base and Subic Bay Naval Station there was no period of struggle while the Filipinos learned from the missionaries how to conduct meetings and organize the Church. Filipino leaders had the advantage of older role models to emulate, rather than youthful, inexperienced missionaries.

When the first four elders began work in June 1961, President Taylor made a significant administrative change. The Luzon Servicemen's District became the Luzon District, and the servicemen's groups were made regular branches. Thus, President Taylor created a normal ecclesiastical organization from the beginning. Theon Laney served as the first district president. He was followed by several other servicemen from Clark Air Force Base. In February 1964 President Jay A. Quealy Jr. reorganized the district presidency and called Harvey D. Brown as president. Brown, a U.S. government employee, was the first district president to reside in Manila. The Church was growing rapidly in the Manila area and needed closer supervision.

Though the missionaries did not meet with immediate success when they began teaching in earnest, they did make steady progress. By the end of 1961 they had baptized eight people. The first two converts were Jose Gutierrez Sr. and Lino Brocka. After that the work moved more rapidly ahead. "At the end of 1962," wrote district president Joseph V. Cook, "there were 8 missionaries, and 47 baptisms were recorded for the year [6 converts per missionary]. In [October] 1962, President Jay A. Quealy, Jr., became president of the Southern Far East Mission, and under his capable leadership the work continued to spread, with 232 baptisms in 1963 by 22 missionaries [10.5 converts per missionary]. In 1964 there were 263 baptisms with a total of 32 missionaries by the end of the year [8.2 converts per missionary]. As of May this year (1965) there were 42 missionaries and 115 baptisms were performed in the first four months of the year, making a total of 663 since the work began."[12] Most of these baptisms were performed in the small swimming pool at the home of E. M. and Maxine Grimm. Sister Grimm was a mainstay of the Church and a support to the missionaries from the beginning. In September 1965 President Cook shared his excitement about the work in the Philippines with the new mission president, Keith E. Garner.

Cook wrote: "I feel there is great room for growth and expansion. The Church has just begun to grow here, and we are going to have to make some very rapid adjustments to keep up with the rapid growth that is going to take place here in the Philippine Islands."[13]

Rapid adjustments *were* necessary. In 1966 Elder Hinckley recommended to the Council of the First Presidency and the Twelve that the Philippines become a separate mission. A year later, on June 28, 1967, Paul S. Rose became the first president of the newly created Philippines Mission. By the end of that year there were 3,193 members in the mission, 631 of whom had been converted that year. During the next three years, President Rose organized twenty-five new branches and groups, supervised the expansion of the missionary force from 100 to more than 150, and saw nearly 3,000 new converts come into the Church.

During President DeWitt C. Smith's era of mission leadership (1970 to 1973), the Church in the Philippines expanded from 6,400 to almost 13,000 members. Before his release as mission president, he helped Elder Ezra Taft Benson organize the Manila Philippines Stake on May 20, 1973, with Augusto A. Lim installed as president. What had taken many decades elsewhere to accomplish in growth and development of local leadership, the Filipino Saints had done in twelve busy years. The progress of the Church continued, and by 1979 membership was over 30,000, divided among three stakes in Metro Manila and three missions. With its nearly four million people (as of 1979) living in a sprawling area, Church leaders soon found it necessary to divide the original stake into three. (At that time a high percentage of members, probably more than 50 percent, lived in metro Manila.) This was done on May 29, 1977. Elder Gordon B. Hinckley called President Lim to become president of the new Quezon City Philippines Stake. Angel S. Pedroche, Lim's first counselor, became president of the Manila Philippines Stake, and Ruben M. Lacanienta, second counselor to President Lim, became president of the Makati Philippines Stake. The three stake presidents were among the most experienced leaders of the Church in the Philippines. All three men had joined the Church by 1964.[14] By 1979 there were about twenty wards and branches in the three stakes.

Expansion outside Manila and the Island of Luzon began when President Garner sent Elders Paul Wright and Thomas Pierce to Cebu City, in the Visayas Islands in the central Philippines. By 1972 there were thirteen groups and branches in that region. By the same time there were also ten thriving branches and groups in Mindanao. Two years later the First Presidency called Carl D. Jones, who had been serving for a year as president of the entire mission, to open the new Philippines Cebu City Mission. Progress was so rapid, however, that only three years later the First Presidency called Layton B. Jones to preside over the Philippines Davao Mission, which was created on July 1, 1977. The three Philippines missions were extremely productive, laying the foundation for the greater growth of the 1980s and 1990s. In 1978 the 456 missionaries baptized 3,805 converts, 8.34 per missionary.[15]

Mission presidents had difficulty directing the affairs of the large number of missionaries before the Cebu and Davao missions were organized; they also had an almost unmanageable amounts of territory to cover. The distance from northern Luzon to southern Mindanao is approximately 1,150 miles. Roads were poor by European or American standards, and travel by air was generally not so convenient as in more developed nations. Another reason to create new missions was the large population (44 or 45 million in 1979).

CHURCH PROPERTIES AND OTHER PROBLEMS

Rapid Church growth fostered an ongoing feeling of excitement. But growth also had a costly side, and in the Philippines annual incomes were and are generally low. In 1975 President Augusto A. Lim and his associates estimated "the average monthly income of a Latter-day Saint family in the Philippines to be about $60.00 (U.S.)."[16] In President Lim's words, "Probably less than 5 percent of the members come from either the upper or middle classes. The majority are from the working class, from the ordinary people of the country, and, in general, they are rather poor."[17] This shortage of funds created problems with building projects, maintenance, ward and branch budgets, individual subscriptions to Church magazines, and purchases of books, manuals, and teaching materials. Relatively speaking, Church expenses (aside from tithing) take a much greater percentage of the average Filipino's salary than the cost of similar requirements (family home evening manual, priesthood manual, lesson manuals, and so on) in the United States.

One wonders how the Church operated in a country where 65 percent of the average family income went for food, 25 percent went for housing, and only 10 percent was left for everything else—transportation, clothing, tithing, recreation, Church budget, building fund, temple fund, fast offerings, books, manuals, and other things. The new financial system based only on tithing, fast offerings, and missionary support (as decided upon by the members) that was introduced in the 1980s greatly benefited the average Filipino family.

The great disparity between the wealth of the Saints in America and the poverty of those in the Philippines has been most evident in the area of physical facilities. The story of the Makati chapel illustrates this point. The first LDS chapel constructed in the Philippines was built in the wealthy Makati subcity of Manila. The property was acquired by President Quealy after much searching by President Taylor, Elder Hinckley, and other local leaders. Mr. E. M. Grimm, then a nonmember but a solid friend of the Church, used his considerable influence to obtain the Makati land. Through the efforts of six local labor missionaries, combined with the efforts of local members and servicemen and their families who donated thousands of hours, the building was constructed between September 1964 and October 1966. Elder Hinckley dedicated the chapel in October 1966. The

The Buendia chapel in Makati, Metro Manila, was the first LDS meetinghouse constructed in the Philippines. It was dedicated 21 October 1966. Through the years it has played a major role in the development of the Church: it was the first Philippine stake center and had the first family history center in the Philippines. (Courtesy LDS Church Archives)

Makati chapel (usually referred to as the Buendia meetinghouse) stands today as a beautiful monument to the Church and is an outstanding example of LDS architecture. But the chapel's beauty and functional utility notwithstanding, it has taught local leaders and administrators in Salt Lake City many lessons. One was that even though Church leaders wanted to show the Filipino Saints they were equals with members elsewhere in the world and demonstrated this fact by building a large air-conditioned chapel, the local Saints could not afford to pay the electricity bill to run the air-conditioning system (approximately U.S. $500 to $1,000 per month). Moreover, they were not accustomed to air conditioning and found it too cold. In the 1980s the Church Building Committee approved the construction of much less expensive chapels that have louvered windows to allow the breezes to blow through.

While the Makati chapel was under construction, all of the branches were encouraged to donate hours of work on the build-

This chapel interior is typical of many in the Philippines. Over the years the Church has turned more and more frequently to the use of native materials in the construction of more numerous but smaller chapels. This is especially true in the more rural parts of the country. (Courtesy LDS Church Archives)

ing. One branch, Quezon City, which was supposed to share in the use of the chapel, failed to support the effort enthusiastically. When district president Cook asked the branch leaders what the problem was, he learned that the Quezon City members did not want to attend meetings in Makati. It had been necessary, in order to justify the building to the Salt Lake City office, to state that the new building would be used by both the Manila and Quezon City Branches. President Cook explained the reasons for the Quezon City members' lack of support: "If Quezon City Branch were to meet in the new chapel, this would mean almost all of them would have to travel by public transportation, since there is little private transportation in the branch. The fare from Quezon City to Buendia is 20 centavos per person. This means that for one person to go to church, both in the morning and evening, would cost 80 centavos. Some families, where there are six and seven members in the family [the average number of children per family in the Philippines was 7.7], find this to be as much money as the father makes in one day and almost two days. So it is easy to see why they are concerned about this."[18]

The problem was worked out so that the Quezon City Saints would not have to spend so much money on travel, but the lesson was there all the same. Even before the consolidated meeting schedule was introduced Churchwide in the early 1980s, in most branches and wards in the Philippines, leaders held as many meetings as possible on Sundays to reduce spending for transportation.

During the early years of the Church in the Philippines, many members were new in the Church and lacked leadership training and experience. According to the Asian Educational Resources Project in 1972, 81 percent of the members had been in the Church four years or fewer. This situation has improved statistically since then, but great challenges in the areas of teaching and training remain.

Although the high percentage of English speakers has been a great advantage, many members had only marginal facility in English. President Lim estimated in 1975 that only 25 percent of the Saints used English effectively. This meant that 75 percent of the members were really not available for important leadership positions in the Church. It also pointed to the need to begin teaching the gospel in the languages of the Filipino people.

The status of women is much higher in the Philippines than in other parts of Asia. Women are held in high esteem. In contrast to those in other Asian nations, Filipino women are often quite independent. The mother frequently dominates the family, creating what sociologists call a quasi-matriarchal society. In 1972 there were more females than males in the Church in the Philippines: 59 percent female, 41 percent male. Though not entirely bad, this shortage of male members occasionally led to a lack of priesthood leadership. Since 1970, however, the missionaries have concentrated on bringing whole families into the

Church. As a result, the numbers of male and female members are now nearly equal.

MISSIONARY WORK

In the early 1960s, when the missionaries in Hong Kong and Taiwan were struggling to learn the new six-lesson uniform proselyting plan, the elders in the Philippines were adapting easily to the new system. From the beginning the Philippines missionaries adopted proselyting methods that were similar to those used in the English language areas of the world. They tracted regularly and encouraged local members to provide them with names of friends and relatives who might be interested in the gospel message. It was not necessary to create new written materials, nor to spend years waiting for the scriptures to be put into a language the investigators and members could easily understand.

While the Church was still young in the Philippines, President Cook arranged for Elders Catalino Brocka and Emiliano Antonio Jr. to receive calls from the prophet to serve as full-time missionaries in Hawaii. They departed from Manila on February 28, 1965. During the same month President Quealy organized the first elders quorum in the Southern Far East Mission in the Manila area. This quorum provided partial monetary support for the two missionaries.

In January 1966 four additional Filipinos received calls to serve missions. Elder Moises Mabunga Jr. and Rodolfo Santos of the Quezon City Branch, Sister Rufina Salangad of the San Fernando Branch, and Sister Virginia Calica of the Manila Branch were called to serve in the Philippines Zone of the Southern Far East Mission. The two sister missionaries were the first Filipino women to serve full-time missions. These local missionaries were the first of thousands of Filipinos to serve missions in their home country. During the 1970s the number grew steadily.

As new techniques of attracting interest in the gospel were created elsewhere in the world, the missionaries adopted most of these methods to the Philippines. For example, during the 1970s the missionaries used media presentations such as movies, filmstrips, flip-charts, and flannel boards. During the mid-1970s President Raymond L. Goodson spearheaded the use of displays at fairs and other public occasions. Over the years such approaches have become common throughout the Philippines.

CHURCH EDUCATIONAL SYSTEM EFFORTS

When the members of the Asian Educational Resources Project team visited the Philippines in 1972, they learned that the Filipino Saints, like their fellow countrymen, had a great desire for education. Literacy was high in the Philippines, between 65 and 75 percent at that time (and estimated to be 90 percent in 1990)—higher than literacy rates in any other nation of Southeast Asia. But unemployment was also high (about 20 percent), and many Filipino Saints desired to improve themselves through technical and vocational training.

The Philippines had and continues to have an overabundance of college-educated people in proportion to the number of available jobs. Within the Church, however, the members lacked access to educational opportunities. They also lacked reading materials for Church use. The AERP team recommended that funds be allocated for chapel libraries and other kinds of educational assistance. However, because money was not then available for new schools and scholarship programs, CES administrators chose instead to emphasize religious education.

In July 1972 Stephen K. Iba, a former missionary to the Philippines, and his family arrived in Manila to initiate the seminary and institute programs of the Church Educational System. He introduced the home-study Book of Mormon program to 240 students. By 1978 the program had expanded to an enrollment of 1,210 home-study seminary students and 1,404 individual institute students. In 1974 Brother Iba returned to Brigham Young University for graduate studies and was replaced by Senen J.

Pineda, whom Iba had hired shortly after arriving in the Philippines. Incidentally, Brother Iba returned to Manila as mission president in July 1977.[19]

THE FIRST PHILIPPINES AREA CONFERENCE

On August 11 and 12, 1975, President Spencer W. Kimball and a dozen other General Authorities met with the Philippine Saints in one of the most successful of all area conferences. At that time there were slightly fewer than twenty thousand Latter-day Saints in the country, but more than eighteen thousand people filled the large Araneta Coliseum in Manila—the equivalent of 90 percent of the membership in the islands. Many of those in attendance were friends and investigators of the Church. Saints from all over the country had traveled long and far to be at the special gathering.

The cultural program given by the local Saints was colorful and representative of the traditions of the people from various parts of the country. In a mixture of Spanish and local dance traditions mingled with elements of modern music, the Saints performed beautifully in song and dance.

Of greater importance to the members was what the Church leaders brought to them. The talks, prayers, and musical numbers helped strengthen many testimonies. The Philippine members also warmly received the announcement of the forthcoming Tokyo Temple, not knowing that shortly after its dedication in October 1980 they would hear a similar announcement regarding their own temple in Manila. Although the cost of traveling to Japan from the Philippines to do temple work was expensive, it would be much less costly than going to Hawaii or the U.S. mainland.[20]

On Wednesday, August 13, 1975, Elder Gordon B. Hinckley, accompanied by President Kimball and the entire party of visiting leaders and their spouses, visited the American War Memorial Cemetery in Fort Bonifacio, Manila. There, in the sacred place

In 1975 and again in 1980, President Spencer W. Kimball met with Philippines President Ferdinand Marcos. They are accompanied by David M. Kennedy, special representative of the First Presidency. (Courtesy LDS Church Archives)

where he had opened the work only fourteen years before, Elder Hinckley spoke of what he later called the "miracle of Manila." He marveled at how much things had changed and at the contrast between his poor treatment from the lazy bureaucrats in April 1961 and the hospitable welcome President Kimball received from President Ferdinand E. Marcos at the presidential palace. They had breakfast together. All the visitors received warm treatment from the press, government agencies, and from high-ranking dignitaries. In his journal Elder Hinckley wrote: "I offered a prayer of thanksgiving to the Lord, expressing gratitude for the marvelous manner in which he had blessed us and brought a fulfillment of the prayer offered 14 years earlier. I expressed appreciation for the missionaries, for government officials who let them come, for the response of the people, for the marvelous harvest of thousands of souls, for the establishment of the firm basis of the Church in the Philippines. I spoke with gratitude of the sacrifice of the Savior of the World that we might have eternal life."[21]

NOTES

1. Willard Call, Diary, in possession of Adelaide W. Call, Spanish Fork, Utah. See Lowell E. Call, "Latter-day Saint Servicemen in the Philippine Islands: A Historical Study of Their Religious Activities and Influences Resulting in the Official Organization of The Church of Jesus Christ of Latter-day Saints in the Philippines" (master's thesis, Brigham Young University, 1955).

2. See Joseph V. Cook et al., comps., *A History of the Church of Jesus Christ of Latter-day Saints in the Philippines* (n.p., 1965), pp. 2–3.

3. See Joseph Fielding Smith, "Report from the Far East Missions," *Improvement Era* 58 (December 1955): 917.

4. Mark E. Petersen to the First Presidency, 6 July 1959, LDS Church Archives.

5. Gordon B. Hinckley, Journals, 14–15 May 1960.

6. Ibid., 25–28 April 1961.

7. Southern Far East Mission Historical Reports, 30 June 1961, LDS Church Archives; cited hereafter as SFEM.

8. Ibid.

9. Ibid.

10. Ralph Tolliver, "The Philippines," in Donald E. Hoke, *The Church in Asia* (Chicago: Moody Press, 1975), pp. 525–26.

11. See Spencer J. Palmer et al., "Educational Needs of The Church of Jesus Christ of Latter-day Saints in Asia: Final Report," Church Educational System, October 1972, pp. 83, 87, 90.

12. Cook et al., *History of the Church*, pp. 4–5; see also SFEM by date, particularly the December 31 report each year.

13. Joseph V. Cook to Keith E. Garner, 1 September 1965, LDS Church Archives.

14. See "3 Stakes formed from 1 in Philippines," *Church News*, 9 July 1977, p. 13.

15. See Missionary Department Annual Report, 1978, LDS Church Archives, p. 9.

16. Augusto A. Lim, "The Church in the Philippines," in *Mormonism: A Faith for All Cultures*, ed. F. LaMond Tullis (Provo: Brigham Young University Press, 1978), p. 160.

17. Ibid.

18. Cook to Garner, 1 September 1965.

19. See "Church Educational System, Overview," unpublished CES report, 1978, p. 39; copy in possession of author.

20. See "Conference in the Philippines," *Ensign* 5 (October 1975): 90–91.

21. Hinckley, Journals, 13 August 1975.

14

THE PHILIPPINES

1981–1996

A *Practical Church*

By 1996 Church membership in the Philippines had grown to nearly 370,000. There were forty-six stakes, ninety districts, and thirteen missions with just over one thousand wards and branches. Almost all leadership positions were held by Filipinos. One General Authority and three Area Authorities were Filipinos. A beautiful temple stood as a loved and heavily used symbol of the maturity of the Filipino Saints. Across the street and nearby, in what had become a complex of Church buildings, was the large Manila Philippines Area Church Administration Office, the Philippines Missionary Training Center, and housing (a two-story building with 150 beds) for temple patrons. Throughout the country chapels dotted the landscape. Many of those built most recently were simple and small, following the architectural preferences and needs of the Philippines and located in close proximity to the members. Some chapels were large, similar in appearance to LDS chapels in North America. Seminary classes were usually held in chapels, but the Church Educational System had also constructed a number of institute buildings near institutions of higher learning in different parts of the country. In short, the human and physical presence of the Church in the Philippines was substantial.

Now part of a Church complex consisting of the temple, a missionary training center, apartments for the temple presidency and temple missionaries, and patron housing, the Area Administration Building houses the Philippines/Micronesia Area Presidency, the director of temporal affairs for this area and the Asia Area, a welfare services office, translation services, and so on. (Photo by author)

The Church's greatest challenges in this land are not with outside forces and influences or intolerant governments and religions. Rather, poverty among members and all that relates to it is the greatest problem. Natural disasters are another serious difficulty, for the Philippines has the highest rate of natural disasters of any country in the world. But these challenges notwithstanding, the Church has moved forward. If one part of the restored gospel stands out in the Philippines it is the practicality of the faith. The Church has done much to help its members rise above their poverty and temporal difficulties.

A NEW ADMINISTRATIVE AREA

Until 1987 supervision of the Church in the Philippines was provided from Hong Kong and Tokyo. But in April 1987 the First Presidency announced the creation of the Philippines/Micronesia

Area.[1] It consisted of thirty-two stakes, twenty-two districts, and six missions, five of which were in the Philippines. A short time later the first Area Presidency was announced, consisting of Elders George I. Cannon, George R. Hill III, and Douglas J. Martin. Since then a number of the Seventy have been assigned to serve in this presidency. At this writing (summer 1996) the presidency is changing from Elders Ben B. Banks as president, with Elders Augusto A. Lim and Kenneth Johnson as counselors, to Elder Kenneth Johnson as president and Sheldon F. Child and Quentin L. Cook as counselors. Elder Lim, who was called as a member of the Second Quorum of the Seventy in June 1992 (a month before being released as mission president), was the first Filipino to be

Elder Augusto A. Lim, the first General Authority from the Philippines, was called to the Second Quorum of the Seventy in June 1992, a few weeks before his release as president of the Philippines Naga Mission. After his baptism in 1964, Elder Lim was almost immediately placed in leadership positions. He was the first stake president in the Philippines, then served as a Regional Representative, a mission president's counselor, and in other callings. In 1996 he and his wife, Myrna, were called to preside over the Manila Temple. (Courtesy LDS Church)

called as a General Authority. His call was unusual, an experiment, because he was asked to return to his regular profession as an attorney but to serve as a General Authority on weekends and as necessary. This pilot program led to the creation of Area Authorities. Their service is limited to the areas of the Church in which they reside, much like Elder Lim's call and authority. A week or two before Elder Lim's release from the Area Presidency, the First Presidency announced his call as president of the Philippines Manila Temple. He and his wife, Myrna, who was called as temple matron, were the first Filipinos to preside in that temple.

The creation of the Area Presidency has brought Church administration in the Philippines closer to the people, the challenges, and the opportunities of the country. The men serving in this presidency have been very busy. Since 1987 they have organized fifteen stakes (and then reorganized one stake as a district) and sixty-eight districts, reorganized numerous stakes and districts, supervised the creation of seven missions, and recommended the creation or reorganization of many wards and branches. They have also supervised public affairs, welfare, physical facilities (almost seven hundred meeting places are owned or rented for the wards and branches), seminary and institute, and so on. Chapel construction is constant. Leading the affairs of the Church in the Philippines during the great growth years has been a major task.

By the early 1990s the Philippines were divided into more than a dozen regions supervised by eight Regional Representatives until the creation of Area Authorities on August 15, 1995. Ambrosio C. Collado (attorney), Ruben G. Gapiz (director of the Church Welfare Services area office), and Remus G. Villarete (supervisor of the Church's area office in Cebu) were called to serve in this new position. All three were former Regional Representatives, stake presidents, and bishops; and Gapiz and Villarete have also served as mission presidents.

THE MANILA PHILIPPINES TEMPLE

At general conference in Salt Lake City on April 1, 1981, the First Presidency announced the Manila temple. A year earlier President Spencer W. Kimball had expressed his hope and the desire of Church leaders to provide temples in reasonable proximity to Church members worldwide. On August 25, 1982, President Gordon B. Hinckley, Second Counselor in the First Presidency, presided over the ground-breaking ceremony on a hilltop in the

Greenmeadows subdivision in Quezon City, metro Manila. A typhoon threatened, but through the prayers of members and missionaries the elements were tempered and the meeting went forward. More than two thousand members and friends from all over the islands, having traveled by boat, airplane, train and bus, crowded the temple site. "President Hinckley said the completion of the temple will bring the full Church program to this country. Members no longer have to think about going to Salt Lake City, Hawaii, Tokyo, or California. 'Now, right here in Manila, on this beautiful site, we will shortly have a sacred House of the Lord.'" Continuing, President Hinckley said: "We do something that has never been done in the history of this nation.

Construction of the Manila Temple took longer than planned because it was necessary to enlarge some areas even before the building was completed. Here, construction supervisor Wayne Tuttle reviews blueprints with his wife, Ruth. (Photo by author)

That which we do today is deep and wonderful, remarkable, and a significant and historic thing." And Elder Marion D. Hanks, added, "We now have the opportunity of preparing a home where we may through our faith grow up unto the Lord."[2]

Because of changes in design (the Church was growing so rapidly that enlargements were needed even before the temple was completed), late arrival of imported materials, and other delays, construction of the temple did not move forward as rapidly as was planned. Nevertheless, by July 1984, the Church announced the call of W. Garth Andrus as temple president and his wife, Eloise, as matron. At the same time, the First Presidency announced the open house and dedication to take place on September 3 through 15 and September 25 through 27, respectively.

Temple open houses offer the opportunity to bring nonmember friends and dignitaries closer to the most meaningful parts of the restored gospel. In Manila 26,522 individuals toured the beautiful new facility. In the Philippines, where getting acquainted with influential people is hard for missionaries to do, the temple helped break down the barriers. More than seventeen thousand tracts and four thousand copies of the Book of Mormon were placed with visitors during the open house.[3]

"The miracle of the Philippines," as President Hinckley referred to the wonderful growth of the Church there, became the theme of the dedicatory services. This expression was not an exaggeration. Between the announcement of the temple in 1981 and its dedication in 1984, membership had grown from almost 60,000 to nearly 100,000 members. (By the end of 1985, there were 115,656 members in the Philippines.) President Hinckley had been involved from the beginning in the Philippines and was thrilled with what had happened there.

President Hinckley was accompanied by Elders Marvin J. Ashton and L. Tom Perry of the Council of the Twelve and other General Authorities.[4] After the cornerstone was placed, nearly sixty-five hundred members attended the nine dedicatory sessions. Several paragraphs of the dedicatory prayer are particularly significant:

> This nation of the Philippines is a nation of many islands whose people love freedom and truth, whose hearts are sensitive to the testimony of thy servants, and who are responsive to the message of the eternal gospel. We thank thee for their faith. We thank thee for their spirit of sacrifice. We thank thee for the miracle of the progress of thy work in this land. In a few short years it

The Manila Philippines Temple was announced in 1981 and dedicated on 25–27 September 1984 by President Gordon B. Hinckley. It is the busiest of the small temples of the Church. This temple serves not only the Philippines but also Micronesia, Indonesia, Singapore, Thailand, and India.

has grown from small beginnings to its present stature with many established stakes of Zion.

We thank thee for the hospitality afforded thy servants by the government of the Republic of the Philippines. Bless the gracious officers of this nation, and preserve by thy mighty power peace and freedom in the land. Lift the blight of poverty from which so many suffer. Particularly bless thy faithful saints who live honestly with thee in the payment of their tithes and offerings. As was promised of old by thy prophet Malachi, open the windows of heaven and pour out blessings that there shall not be room enough to receive them. . . . Bless them that neither they nor their generations after them will go hungry, nor naked, nor without shelter from the storms that beat about them. Open their minds that they shall grow in wisdom in matters both spiritual and temporal.

May thy Church in this island nation grow and increase in numbers. . . .

May no unclean thing desecrate its sacred precincts. May it be preserved from the storms of nature, from vandalism, from trespass by those who are unworthy to enter it.[5]

President Hinckley's prayer that the temple would be "preserved from the storms of nature, from vandalism, from trespass by those who are unworthy to enter it" has been heard many times as typhoons, earthquakes, and other natural disturbances have ravaged the islands. Perhaps the most pointed manifestation of the Lord's protection came during a coup attempt. "In 1989," remembered Rabai B. Osumo, "the temple became the talk of the town. At the height of the failed coup, government soldiers using jets and helicopters bombarded rebel positions near the temple. Rebel soldiers sought cover in the temple grounds and tried to enter it. Their attempt was foiled. The aftermath of the conflict found the temple unscathed except a few bullet marks in its western wall."[6]

Two hours following completion of the last dedicatory session, the first endowment session began. It was for employees in the temple and temple workers. Since that time the temple has seen much use by the Philippine Saints.

Although the Manila temple has placed temple ordinances and blessings closer to the people, the cost of traveling there from the outer areas is still expensive by Filipino standards. To fly from Mindanao to Manila costs more than $150 (4,000 pesos), a sum equal to one month's wages for most members. So members usually travel by boat, which costs the equivalent of $15. The best time for boat travel is March, April, May, and part of June, when the seas are calm and less dangerous for small vessels. School is out during these months too.

Because many worthy members who hold leadership positions are too poor to afford the expense of traveling to the temple, the First Presidency has established a fund to supplement transportation, housing, and food costs for a single trip to the temple. In addition, each leader can use this fund to purchase three pairs of temple garments. Support levels vary depending on the amount of need, but many Filipinos have been helped to the temple through this program.[7]

FAMILY HISTORY AND GENEALOGY WORK

As is true throughout the Church, Saints in the Philippines are working to complete their four-generation family group sheets. During the year before the temple dedication, Church leaders throughout the Philippines encouraged members to complete this program. In 1984 the Manila Genealogical Service Center was established at the Church administrative offices in Makati. In addition to providing research facilities, this center was also established to support meetinghouse libraries throughout the country. Since that time every stake and many of the districts have founded and now operate family history centers. The temple and the family history centers have encouraged members to search for ancestors and to do temple work. Couple missionaries who are knowledgeable regarding family history research have been assigned to the Philippines to teach and encourage this work. Now located in the temporal affairs office, the center (now named the Family Service Center) collects family group sheets, inputs the information, and supplies the names to the temple.

Charles Brooks, manager of records acquisition for the Genealogical Society of Utah, and several technicians have been microfilming Filipino family records for a number of years. The available records will be completed in several more years. These records, mostly Roman Catholic parish and Spanish civil records, contain millions of baptismal, matrimonial, and burial records that date back to the sixteenth century. In 1995 the First Presidency approved implementation of the name extraction program. In this program members are called to type the names of the dead from the microfilmed records into a computer base that is used as the basis for temple work. Until recently all of the names used in the Manila temple, with the exception of family file names, have come from Salt Lake City. The extraction program will supply the Manila temple with local names.[8]

Because Filipino people have such close family ties, family history and temple work are of great interest to them. According to Elder Ben B. Banks, "Families are very important to Filipinos. That's one of the reasons why family history is progressing as fast as it is in the Philippines." Roland P. Arcansalin, temple recorder (manager of the temple), reports that the Manila temple is the "busiest of the smaller temples."

MISSIONARY WORK

In 1984 President Gordon B. Hinckley said: "I do not know of anyplace in the world where the harvest has been so great in such a short period. The Lord has touched this land in a miraculous and wonderful way. He has remembered His people on the isles of the sea."[9] Although President Hinckley was speaking at the dedication of the Manila temple, he was referring to the missionary miracle he had seen unfold since his visits of the early

1960s. That the people of the Philippines are primarily Christian goes far in explaining the wonderful success of the Church there, but other factors have also been important. For example, the remarkable role of local Filipino elders and sisters.

"On August 12, 1975, President Spencer W. Kimball came over to the Philippines and we had an Area Conference." So begins Roland Arcansalin's description of why he went on a mission. "I had just turned nineteen at that time, but when President Kimball said every young man should fill a mission, that woke me up and immediately, that night, I wrote a letter to my parents and I said, I won't be attending second semester of college this year because I am filling a mission."[10] Roland was among many young Filipinos who heard President Kimball's call to missionary service. Until then only a few locals were serving, but more than 20 Filipino elders entered the Philippines Manila Mission when he did. Since that time the number of local missionaries has continued to increase. In 1977 63 local missionaries were in the field, and in 1978 the number expanded to 134 local full-time missionaries, well over one-fourth of the missionaries in the country.

As noted earlier, the first division of the Philippines mission came on July 6, 1974, and the second division in 1977. Over the years these missions were divided many more times until there were thirteen missions when the Cabanatuan mission was created in 1992. As the missionary numbers grew, so did the convert baptisms. And, of course, the units of the Church increased. On November 15, 1981, the tenth stake, the Davao Stake, was created. By that time membership throughout the islands had risen to 56,985. More than 12,000 new converts joined in 1980 and nearly that number in 1981. But these almost incredible numbers soon paled in comparison with the growth that was yet to come. Membership crossed the 100,000 mark in 1985 and continued climbing. By 1990, there were 248,334 members in the Philippines. The year of greatest growth was 1988, with 38,907 people coming into the fold.

Again, many ingredients have contributed to the recipe that

produced such favorable results. Among the most important has been the Philippines Missionary Training Center. The Manila MTC, as it is often called, began operations in a house in Green Hills, San Juan, a quiet Manila suburb. That house and one next door that was rented for expansion served for almost ten years. The first group consisted of twenty-five elders and sisters. Capacity, a "batch," was forty missionaries. Two hundred batches of elders and sisters from the Philippines and seventeen other countries and territories in Asia and the Pacific were given training there.[11]

In December 1990 ground was broken for a new MTC to be situated across the street from the Manila temple. When the four-story structure was dedicated by Area President Vaughn J. Featherstone on September 20, 1992, it contained housing for eighty missionaries, nine classrooms, a multipurpose assembly hall, dining facilities, and a reception area.[12] The new facility and growing numbers of couple missionaries made it possible to organize a MTC couples district in 1994. (The first couples to receive MTC training in the Philippines were Elder and Sister Carmalino Cawit and Elder and Sister Ramon Mariano, who entered the old MTC on September 25, 1989.) Because couples have different teaching responsibilities than young missionaries—leadership, retention, reactivation, and special callings other than proselyting—the creation of the new district was desirable.[13] As of the second quarter of 1993, the old and new MTCs had trained 6,244 missionaries, most of whom were Filipinos.

The proportion of Filipino missionaries grew yearly, and by 1988 most of the mission force (82 percent) throughout the country was from the Philippines. Although there were advantages of having so many local missionaries, there were also some problems. Most of the missionaries and their families could not provide financial support while they served their missions. Therefore, it was necessary to obtain support from the general missionary fund of the Church. Most of the Filipino missionaries were living much better as missionaries than their families were. Some were sleeping on mattresses for the first time in their lives. Adjustments after their missions were often difficult. A second problem was that most of the local elders were from humble origins and shied away from interactions with middle- and upper-class Filipinos. (American missionaries, on the other hand, hardly worried about the social and economic status of those whom they taught.) The result has been the enlargement through conversions of the number of Filipino members below the poverty level. This has been magnified because most upper-class and professional Filipinos live in gated communities that make access almost impossible. This has been a concern to Church authorities because leaders rise most frequently from members with education and financial security.

Although the number of Filipino elders and sisters continued to grow during the 1990s, the number of foreign missionaries fell off. Visa difficulties arose that took several years to resolve. By 1996, the number of foreign missionaries was beginning to increase, and the ratio was improving.

Missionaries in the Philippines have probably used all of the methods and approaches for contacting and teaching the gospel that have been used elsewhere in the world. But they have also been part of at least two unusual programs, one that provided service in refugee camps and another that experimented with holding basic Church services in the home.

Mormon Christian Services

The beginnings and philosophy behind the welfare services missionaries in refugee camps is discussed more fully in chapter 15. Suffice it to say that in the aftermath of the Vietnam War, more than a million Indochinese (Vietnamese, Hmongs, Laos, and Cambodians) left their homelands and fled to friendly (or not-so-friendly) nations for refuge. Large camps were established in a number of countries, including the Philippines, where the Philippines Refugee Processing Center (PRPC) was established in 1980 at Morong, Bataan, site of the terrible concentration camp where thirty-nine thousand Allied servicemen were reportedly killed during World War II. Latter-day Saints became involved when Elder Marion D. Hanks, Executive Administrator of the Asia and Southeast Asia area, saw the opportunity for LDS missionaries to provide service at this camp and at one on Palauan Island.

After successfully serving in a camp in Thailand, in 1981 Sisters Lucinda Bateman and Mary Ann Meyers were asked by Elder Hanks to transfer to the PRPC at Bataan.[14] The agency title of the LDS humanitarian program was Mormon Christian Services (MCS). Sisters Bateman and Meyers were not warmly welcomed by the members of another church who were dominant at the camp, but they were allowed to teach English and American culture to groups of the handicapped and elderly. As they persisted and happily served, they came to be appreciated by the camp administrators. Over the months the administrators requested additional pairs of LDS sisters. They also improved the missionaries' teaching assignments, their housing, and other conditions. What began as an experiment in the eyes of the camp administrators eventually developed into a long-term arrangement lasting until 1994, when the camp at Bataan was closed. The number of missionaries assigned to the PRPC varied between four and ten.[15]

As was true in Thailand and Hong Kong, where sister missionaries performed similar service, the MCS program was based on an agreement that the Mormons would not preach their religion. But unlike the other two places, the agreement was modified in the Philippines and the sister missionaries were allowed to teach the restored gospel to refugees who asked to be taught. In late 1986 President Joel E. Leetham, president of the Philippines Quezon City Mission, met with Colonel Banzon, the deputy administrator of the PRPC, and together they worked out the agreement and also a plan to build a small LDS meetinghouse at the camp. They chose the site together. Construction began in August 1987, and the building was dedicated on January 3, 1988.

By that time there were five members in the camp, and forty others were being taught the missionary discussions.[16]

The PRPC was created to facilitate movement of Indochinese refugees to third countries for permanent residence. During the early 1980s large numbers of refugees filled the camp. But as conditions improved in Vietnam, Laos, and Cambodia, the number of refugees dwindled. By the 1990s only Vietnamese remained in the camp. They were of two classifications, those who were legal refugees and able to be resettled in a new country and those who would eventually have to return to Vietnam.

Six sisters were serving in the camp in 1994. By then there were twenty Vietnamese members and another twenty investigators. One of the most exciting experiences for all of these people was a trip from Bataan to the temple in Manila. The members were able to do baptisms for the dead, and the nonmembers visited the grounds, the administration building, and the MTC. The PRPC was closed in 1994, having outlived its original purpose.

The Family-Centered Church Experiment

Not long after Augusto A. Lim and his wife, Myrna, began their service as leaders of the new Philippines Naga Mission in 1989, they were informed by the Area Presidency that their mission was to conduct a carefully controlled missionary experiment. Members of the Quorum of the Twelve wanted to know if the Church could be operated well on a basic level among new members in Third World countries. Specifically, they wished to know if families could hold the basic meetings of the Church at home and grow in testimony and spirituality. The Area Presidency selected the Island of Marinduque for the experiment. Until that time the Island of Marinduque had been visited only briefly by LDS missionaries, and there were no members there. The initial twelve elders who were assigned to the island were carefully selected by the Area Presidency from among all of the missions in the Philippines. Their instructions were specific: teach only community leaders; teach couples; make no mention of branches, wards, or temples; baptize only couples; don't tell anyone at home or in other missions about the experiment. After converts had been made, meetings were to be held at home with the father presiding. Lesson materials for Church services were to be limited to the *Gospel Principles* manual—a series of forty-seven lessons on fundamental gospel knowledge—and the scriptures of the Church.

After a year of efforts to contact and teach community leaders, no success had been realized. It was difficult to teach husbands and wives together, and when one was interested the other usually was not. So the requirements were changed to include average families who were secure financially, that is, who had steady work. Being leaders, wealthy, or prominent was no longer required. With the target families expanded, the elders succeeded in bringing more converts into the Church. But the experiment was not successful. While it had been hoped that new members of the Church could operate on a very basic body of printed material, it was found that they, more than Church members in the established parts of the world, needed more commentaries, lesson materials, and books such as Talmage's *Jesus the Christ* or Richards's *A Marvelous Work and a Wonder.* Sunday meetings were repetitious and uninteresting. The smallness of the groups did not provide people with sufficient experience to enrich those who were present. The experiment was quietly ended. Regular missionary work was pursued, and the normal programs of the Church were established on Marinduque Island.[17] (Similar experiments with similar results were conducted in India and Latin America.)

A Missionary Problem Area

There have been some difficulties with radical Muslims on the Island of Mindanao that have required special attention. Since late 1993, no non-Filipinos have been allowed to serve as missionaries on Mindanao. The danger of kidnapping is too great because foreigners are sometimes thought to be wealthy. Even Filipino elders are restricted to proselyting during daylight hours. The Muslim separatist movement has been a problem for the central government for some time. Five percent of population in the Philippines is Muslim, and the greater part of that number lives on Mindanao. Most Muslims are not part of radical groups, but the few who are causing trouble are a serious threat to personal security in that part of the nation.

CHURCH WELFARE IN THE PHILIPPINES

In the Philippines the economic, health, and educational needs of the Saints have been a major concern for Church leaders since the early 1970s. Surveys reveal that Filipino Saints are "poorer than the general population. Twenty percent are squatters and 60 percent have no running water in their houses."[18] Unemployment and underemployment are serious problems among Filipino members. Very few members own automobiles, and only 5 to 15 percent own their own homes in the Manila area. Others rent their apartments or homes. Home ownership is somewhat higher outside metro Manila. Transportation costs are so high in proportion to income that many members go inactive because they cannot afford to travel to Church meetings.[19] Although literacy is relatively high and many members of the Church have post-high school education, too often training and degrees are in nontechnical areas that lead to educated unemployment.

Church members not only struggle with economic and educational challenges, but they also suffer with many health problems. Infant morbidity is relatively high in the Philippines, and Church members have not escaped this sorrow. Numerous other health problems exist that cause untold suffering among people of all ages. Missionaries too, Filipino and foreign, have been infected with hepatitis, tuberculosis, worms, and other parasites.

In 1971 President Harold B. Lee recognized the growing

health needs of the worldwide Church membership. He asked Dr. James O. Mason, Church health commissioner, to create a plan to address these needs. From his thinking, discussions with Church leaders, and consideration with other health professionals, Mason devised a plan that became the health missionary program. Missionaries with specialized training in medicine, nursing, nutrition, and related health fields were called by the Missionary Department to serve missions of eighteen months or two years. They were to teach disease prevention, guide members to use local health services, work through the existing programs of the Church, and assist mission presidents and their wives in the furtherance of missionary health.[20]

One of the earliest health missionaries called was Mary Ellen Edmunds, who had served a proselyting mission in the Philippines in 1963 and 1964. In 1972 she returned to the Philippines with the call to establish this new program. Her assignment was to help Filipino Saints take better care of their physical bodies. Years later she recalled her experience: "I felt the Holy Ghost bearing witness of the truths I taught about good nutrition, budgeting, and immunizing children. This witness was as clear and strong as the witness I had felt when I was teaching the First Vision, faith, and the importance of baptism."[21]

It soon became apparent that teaching about good health was related to teaching good nutrition, and nutrition to finances, and finances to education, and so on. Farmers, vocational specialists, skilled tradesmen, social workers, career counselors, and others were required to teach skills for temporal and spiritual success. Before long the health missionaries were made part of a wider group called welfare services missionaries, which included missionaries with a broader range of knowledge, skills, and experiences. By 1979 more than seven hundred welfare services missionaries were serving worldwide in sixty missions.[22] A variety of welfare services missionaries were assigned to the Philippines.

I DIDN'T KNOW I WASN'T
CARING FOR HER PROPERLY
Mary Ellen Edmunds

When I was in the Philippines in about 1972, one of the members of the Church approached us and said, "I want to ask for your help. We had our first baby after we were married. It was a little girl, and we loved her and were so excited. She grew to be eight months old and one day she died suddenly, unexpectedly. And when we asked the doctor why, he told us we hadn't cared for her properly." Even as she told me this, she wept again, saying, "I didn't know. I didn't know I wasn't caring for her properly." Then she dried her eyes and said, "I want to tell you sisters that another is coming. What can I do to have a healthy baby and to care for it properly?"

Well, it turned into a whole district project to have some classes on maternal and child health. This woman participated and did everything she possibly could. It meant changing a lot of traditions and going against some deeply ingrained customs, but she trusted us and was motivated by concern for her unborn child. She realized then that she was preparing an earthly body for one of Heavenly Father's spirit children.

Pretty soon her neighbors, most of whom weren't members of the Church, began to talk about "the Mormon baby." There was a great deal of anticipation about the birth; and when the baby was born, she was larger and healthier than any baby that neighborhood had ever seen. Those parents were so proud! You couldn't have persuaded them that the Word of Wisdom and proper sanitation weren't principles of the gospel when they saw the difference it made to their child. Last year I received photographs of her baptism. It was also a great experience to be in the Salt Lake Temple when her parents were sealed. Her father, the bishop, was able to come to Salt Lake City and they took advantage of the proximity to the temple. Their first little daughter, who had died, was also sealed to them, and she was there as well. We could all feel it. Now they've had two or three additional babies—babies who are strong, healthy, and born in the covenant. When I returned to the Philippines for a visit last year, this mother said, "You know, sister, I'm so happy because my children are very naughty in Church." Malnourished children, you know, are very listless and have no energy. It was a little signal that they were healthy. This mother also wrote to me: "I want to express my gratitude for the things I have learned which are making such a difference in my family. I realize now that some of the things my mother taught me—things her mother taught her—were not correct, but the truths I am learning will now be taught to my children, and their children, and the generations to come. We will not be damned any longer by ignorance. As they say, it is never too late to learn and change. God must love us dearly to allow us to have so much truth."[23]

Anecdotal evidence of success, such as the foregoing, indicated that the health missionaries and welfare services missionaries were remarkably successful as teachers of proper health practices. Fortunately, Professor John M. Hill and his colleagues statistically verified the results in a study of comparisons among twenty-two groups of Filipino Saints. Garth Mangum and Bruce Blumell summarized the study this way: "With three-quarters following the water purification instructions and two-thirds the kitchen sanitation and gardening techniques, the average incidence of diarrhea and fever among children was reduced 70.0 percent and eye, ear, lung, skin, and scalp infections by 53.2 percent. A subgroup with higher participation rates showed 92.9 percent and 85 percent reductions, respectively."[24]

Health matters continue to be a concern in the Philippines. Health fairs and clinics, often in conjunction with the Philippines Health Department or with local health organizations, have been held frequently in chapels, malls, parks, and community centers throughout the country. Health fairs usually have consisted of health awareness training (personal hygiene, obesity, smoking, stress, alcoholism, parasites, and prevention of AIDS, emphysema, and diabetes), displays, dental screenings, blood-pressure check-ups, immunization clinics, and similar undertakings. Often these events have been held with the help of proselyting missionaries.

In addition to Church-sponsored health programs, a private, not-for-profit organization called Mabuhay-Deseret Foundation (MDF) was founded in October 1988 with the encouragement and guidance of Dr. E. William Jackson, who was serving as president of the Philippines Manila Mission, and a group of humanitarian doctors. MDF specializes in providing surgeries to correct such conditions as cataracts, cross-eye, cleft lip, cleft palate, loss of limb, and burn contractures. Numerous non-Mormon Filipino physicians, nurses, and other specialists are part of the volunteer program. Services are provided to all people on the basis of need. In addition to medical services, MDF also provides postoperative and rehabilitative training. The philosophy of MDF is self-reliance. Those who receive help and their families are encouraged to raise as much money to pay for medical expenses as they are able. Making a financial contribution ensures self-esteem and involves a larger community. Since its inception, MDF has developed a broad group of affiliated medical practitioners and hospitals throughout the islands. By 1994 MDF had helped with 4,615 surgeries.[25]

The full teaching program of Church welfare has been carried out in the Philippines. Home food processing, gardening (even biointensive gardening), sewing, caring for the sick and the elderly, providing for one's family, and similar teachings have been important to the Philippine Saints. But more than in any other country, disaster relief has required major efforts locally and on a countrywide scale. The pages of "Dateline Philippines," a section of *Tambuli Magazine* (now *Liahona*), the Church magazine of the Philippines, frequently report the Church's involvement in preparedness and emergency-relief projects such as reconstructing a damaged house; providing typhoon, flood, volcano, or earthquake relief; training members in the principles of self-reliance, first aid, and emergency preparedness; sponsoring concerts to raise funds for disaster victims; and so on.

Typhoons and their massive destruction are so frequent that they hardly make the news in the Philippines. But two natural disasters took such heavy tolls that they demanded attention. On July 16, 1990, an earthquake that measured 7.7 on the Richter scale rocked northern Luzon Island, destroying nearly two thousand buildings, blocking roads, and damaging water, electric, and other utilities. When a full assessment of the damage had been made by civil and Church leaders, the results were severe. "Members in seven stakes and two districts were directly affected," wrote Marvin K. Gardner in the *Ensign*. "One hundred twenty homes of Church members were destroyed; another 340 were damaged. Several meetinghouses were also damaged—one severely. The Manila Temple was not affected. Of 1,666 casualties, 5 were members of the Church; all missionaries were safe."[26] Meetinghouses were used as places of refuge by hundreds of members and nonmembers. Church members rendered assistance to hundreds. The Baguio stake was selected by two national organizations to receive and distribute large amounts of donated commodities. Rice and vegetables were cooked into stew by Relief Society members and distributed to thirty-five tent cities. Over a two-week period Church members prepared and served more than thirty-four thousand meals.

But even though the members pulled together and relieved one another's suffering, many jobs were lost, homes were destroyed, and opportunities for education were hindered. Church members in other parts of the world contributed funds for humanitarian purposes. On September 21, 1990, Elder Richard G. Scott of the Council of the Twelve presented Emmanuel Pelaez, Philippines ambassador to the United States, a check for $25,000 for earthquake relief in the Philippines.[27] Through it all, the Filipino Saints put forth a positive, courageous face and moved forward the best they could.[28]

As if the 1990 earthquake was not enough, on June 9, 1991, Mount Pinatubo, which had been dormant for six hundred years, erupted and spewed ash over a vast area. About five thousand Church members were affected by the initial series of eruptions. About 80 percent of the homes of members in the Olongapo area were damaged or destroyed, and 40 percent of the homes in the Angeles stake. In total the damage and suffering caused by Mount Pinatubo was much greater than the earthquake of 1990. Millions of people had been displaced by 1992. Millions and millions of dollars in property values were destroyed. Vast areas of countryside and cities were covered by Pinatubo's ash.

Over time this great volcano has been a curse that keeps on cursing. When wet from heavy monsoon rains, the ash on Mount Pinatubo's sides turned into a continuous mud flow, called *lahar*, that goes on for miles. Everything in its path gets covered as it pushes through and around houses, gardens, offices, homes, and farm buildings. In 1993—two years after the initial eruptions—225,000 people were forced from their homes. In 1994 some 125,000 more people were left homeless. Among them were many members of the Church. In 1995, as in the previous years, Church welfare director Ruben Gapiz and his colleagues in Welfare Services spent much time supervising the evacuation and care of members as they were forced from their homes. Pinatubo is like a chronic disease that will not go away.

Twice the Church has made substantial contributions to the relief of those who were devastated by the volcano. On September 6, 1991, Elder M. Russell Ballard of the Council of the Twelve presented $25,000 to Deputy Ambassador Franklin Ebdalin in behalf of the Church.[29] And again, on June 25, 1992, the Area Presidency, Vaughn J. Featherstone, Ben B. Banks, and

Augusto A. Lim, met with newly elected President Fidel V. Ramos of the Philippines and presented him a check for one million pesos (U.S. $41,000) to help with the aftermath of Mount Pinatubo's eruption.

For reasons mentioned above—poverty especially—members can seldom put aside many provisions for hard times. Nevertheless, the Church has done much to prepare members before disasters strike. Bishops and branch presidents have kept stocks of food and other supplies for emergencies. The education and preparation process will never cease.

SELF-RELIANCE PROJECTS

During the past twenty years a number of projects have been undertaken to help Filipino members become financially stable. Commercial sewing machines were purchased during the 1980s to improve family clothing and to help women acquire employment. Marketing cooperatives, handicraft projects, a communal farming enterprise, and a small factory for making shell lampshades have achieved varying degrees of success.

One of the most successful projects has been a not-for-profit organization, the Philippines Enterprise Development Foundation (PEDF). Closely associated with Enterprise Mentors International (EMI), the group was established in the Philippines in 1989 to help small businesses and individuals "achieve greater productivity in their business endeavors, and thus an improved quality of life."[30] Two sister organizations, the Visayas Enterprise Foundation (VEF) and the Mindanao Enterprise Development Foundation (MEDF), have since been founded in central and southern Philippines. EMI works through local affiliated foundations that provide small business loans, training, and guidance. In 1995 EMI reported assisting "over 10,000 people to greater financial independence."[31] This assistance came through centers to train "street vendors, family firms, and small businesses to grow and become more productive."[32] Individuals and families who have received assistance run businesses as varied as pig farms, upholstery shops, bakeries, fruit stands, and slipper and other clothing industries.

Employment and underemployment are serious problems among Church members in the Philippines. Employment missionaries estimated in 1991 that thirteen thousand active members were unemployed. The employment program of the Church, as outlined in the *Welfare Services Resource Handbook*, has long been part of the Church program in the Philippines. But in November 1990 missionary couples from the United States arrived to encourage the full implementation of the Church employment system. Since then, working in conjunction with EMI and other state and private organizations, but primarily through the units of the Church, the welfare services missionaries assigned to employment have held many training sessions for local Church leaders, sponsored business and job fairs, counseled and taught hundreds of job seekers, helped members connect with potential employers, and so on. Seventy-five percent of jobs are never advertised. Church members have been encouraged to use the "hidden job market." Job networking—that is, following up on every friendship, association, family relationship, classmate, business associate, club relationship, and so on—has been taught as the most promising way of getting a job or improving employment through the hidden job market.

A variety of innovative seminars and training sessions have been held in different parts of the country. For example, in 1992 the Church welfare department in the Philippines, the Church Educational System, and Visayan Enterprise Foundation sponsored a business and job fair. VEF presented "a structured exercise to enable [participants] to identify business opportunities and investments. A Personnel Entrepreneurial Competency Test was administered to assess abilities in pursuing successful business ventures."[33] Those who scored high were encouraged to pursue careers in business. CES representatives detailed the process of applying for and receiving CES-sponsored education loans. And others outlined the process of getting a job.

The Philippines/Micronesia Area Presidency has been concerned and involved in the employment problem. They have regularly taught basic welfare principles, the need to pay a full tithing, to pray for the Lord's help, and to work hard at obtaining good employment.

CHURCH EDUCATION IN THE PHILIPPINES

Since its founding in 1972, the seminary and institute programs have flourished as in no other part of Asia. From the beginning, interest in religious education among the young Filipino members was high, but the size of these programs in terms of students, full-time and part-time faculty, and physical facilities has exceeded expectations. From the time when Stephen K. Iba returned to Utah in 1974 and Senen J. Pineda took over as CES area administrator for the Philippines, CES programs have been almost entirely in the hands of local administrators and teachers. The home-study seminary program grew to 4,000 students by 1979. Early-morning seminary was started in 1981. The Manila Institute of Religion was inaugurated in February 1982 and has grown steadily since then. In 1995 there were 11,848 institute students enrolled, and 11,282 daily and home-study seminary students were enrolled countrywide. The faculty and administration were large, consisting of 41 CES coordinators and institute directors, 21 paid secretaries, 470 volunteer institute teachers, and 897 volunteer seminary teachers. Various administrators have led Church education in the Philippines. From 1991 until 1996 Emmanuel Mascardo was the CES area director. By 1995 there were fifteen institute facilities, and two additional ones were under construction. Many of these facilities are attached to meetinghouses.[34]

The institutes have done much to bring Latter-day Saint young people together in a wholesome environment. As is true elsewhere in the world, the Latter-day Saints Student Association (LDSSA) organizes and sponsors a variety of activities. Temple marriages are encouraged in classes and as part of special meetings and services.

Through the Church Educational System, thousands of dollars of loan money is allocated to worthy college students to help support their higher education. The Philippines receives a large percentage of CES's budget for this purpose. The primary purpose of the loan program is to help returned missionaries afford to go to school. Some four hundred Filipino students receive this help each year. They are required to provide part of the cost of their own education. The program is working quite well in the Philippines.[35]

Beginning in 1993, a remarkable breakthrough occurred in Bacolod. Bishop Rufino A. Villanueva, CES coordinator for Negros Occidental, applied to the Department of Education, Culture and Sports and received permission for the Church to hold seminary classes during regular class periods in the three high schools in Bacolod City. Seminary students said that taking seminary at school helped them save time after school and also assured their safety when going home after classes. Clearly the notion of separation of church and state in the Philippines differs from that in the United States.[36] The arrangement in Bacolod City is unusual. Most seminary classes are held in meetinghouses anytime from early morning to after school. Institute classes, on the other hand, are offered throughout the day, like regular college courses.

TRANSLATION OF SCRIPTURES AND OTHER CHURCH MATERIALS

Since the early 1960s, discussions have addressed the question of which language or languages should be used in the Church in the Philippines. Early on, mission leaders opted for English. A relatively high percentage of Filipinos were reported to know

English, and the advantage of not having to translate scriptures and other Church materials into local languages appeared obvious. The widespread use of English has contributed much to the rapid growth and development of the Church in the Philippines. But the decision to use English also placed millions of people outside the circle of the restored gospel. The Savior commanded that his gospel should be taken to every nation, kindred, tongue, and people (see D&C 42:58; 90:11).

Even though all administrative and teaching manuals were distributed in English as early as 1963, in order to be more effective many missionaries were learning Tagalog and other Filipino languages on their own. Tagalog (or Filipino), the official language of the Philippines, is spoken by the majority of the people, but other languages are also of great importance. Ilocano is spoken in Northern and Central Luzon. Cebuano is the main dialect of Central and Eastern Visayas and Mindanao. Hiligaynon (Ilonggo) is spoken in the Western Visayas and some parts of Mindanao. Sunday School lessons and sacrament meeting talks were being given mostly in English, but with a significant admixture of Filipino languages. This practice has continued and grown to the present. When speakers wish to make their point clear in a talk or lesson, frequently they use Tag-English, a mixture of English sentences interspersed with Tagalog sentences. The same thing is done with English and other Filipino languages. In the provinces Filipino languages are often used more than English.

Leaders in the Philippines gradually recognized the need to provide scriptures, lesson manuals, and Church administration materials in local languages. By the 1980s articles were appearing in Tagalog in the Philippines Church magazine, *Tambuli*. In 1983 a local committee began translating parts of the Book of Mormon into Tagalog. Three years later the Church in the Philippines printed a few copies of the Tagalog translation for testing. In 1987, under direction of Kay Briggs of the Presiding Bishopric International Office and the Area Presidency, a committee under the leadership of Elder Ruben G. Gapiz, Regional Representative, was directed to complete an official translation of *Selections from the Book of Mormon*, "Mga Piniling Bahagi Mula sa Aklat ni Mormon." By working intensively, the last page was reviewed and approved for printing on June 10, 1988. Regarding the effort, Elder Gapiz said, "Our intention was to have a selection that is comprehensive and understandable to all levels without sacrificing its scriptural context."[37] The first copies arrived in Manila on January 6, 1989, and were distributed immediately to Church leaders around the country.

By then interest had grown in producing Book of Mormon selections in other dialects. And additional Church materials in local languages were also needed. During the 1990s, as part of the operations of the temporal affairs office, a full translation office was created and work proceeded rapidly in many languages. Book of Mormon selections were completed in Ilocano (1991), Cebuano (1992), Hiligaynon (1994), Pampango (1994), and Waray (1995).[38] In 1995 it was reported that the Church had printed *Selections from the Book of Mormon* in fifty world languages in 1994. "Of the 135,745 copies sold, 60.94% were in Tagalog, 19.56% Cebuano and 3.60% Ilocano—the top three in the list."[39] In the September 1995 issue of *Dateline Philippines*, a short article stated, "Salt Lake City Printing Office confirmed that the full complement of the Book of Mormon in Tagalog, Cebuano and Ilocano will be off the press soon." These complete translations were expected for distribution before the end of the year. Translations of the Doctrine and Covenants and the Pearl of Great Price were also well under way by that time.

On February 26, 1996, the number of Church members outside the United States outnumbered those in the United States. Among the ten languages most used in the worldwide Church, three were Filipino languages—Tagalog, Cebuano, and Ilocano. By 1995 the translation office was providing a variety of materials in eight Filipino languages. Although English is the official language of the Church in the Philippines, great effort is being expended to make gospel knowledge available to as many

Filipinos as possible. Missionaries, local and foreign, are learning and teaching the gospel in Filipino languages.[40] The scriptural injunction to take the gospel to people in their own tongue is being fulfilled.

VISITS BY THE LORD'S SERVANTS

Filipinos respond to visits by prophets and apostles much like Polynesians, with great warmth, enthusiasm, and gratitude. Each visit by a member of the Quorum of the Twelve or a President of the Church has been celebrated as an event of highest importance. When President Spencer W. Kimball visited Manila a second time on October 18 and 19, 1980, the local Saints were thrilled to be in his presence. President Kimball spoke three times, once to priesthood leaders and twice in area conference general sessions. More than eighteen thousand members and friends thronged Araneta Coliseum to participate.

Members came from distant points throughout the country. Maria Carmen Nunez's sacrifice to help her parents attend the conference illustrates the dedication of many Filipino Saints. They came from three hundred miles away in Cebu. The *Church News* related her experience: "'See,' she said as she touched her dress. 'I don't have a new dress or shoes for the conference, but it doesn't matter as long as my father is here.'

"She earned the money to bring her father, mother and sister to the conference by airplane. 'My father is 83 and he's had two heart attacks. He was baptized just last February.

"'It was really a sacrifice coming here. It's such a blessing to see the prophet and hear his voice, and the nicest thing is that both my mother and father could be here.'"[41]

As he had done in 1975, President Kimball met with President Ferdinand E. Marcos of the Philippines.

Members in the Philippines have been blessed to receive many visits by Apostles. Members of the Quorums of the Seventy, as they have presided in Area Presidencies, have visited district, stake, and regional conferences. When the Manila temple was built, President Gordon B. Hinckley presided over the ground-breaking and dedicatory services. Among other members of the Council of the Twelve who have visited the Philippines, Elder Neal A. Maxwell conducted a special service in 1991—attended by only a select few—at the American War Memorial Cemetery. That place has become especially sacred to the Church in the Philippines. Elder Maxwell gave an apostolic blessing there on January 23, 1991, in which he appealed to the Almighty to bless the land with greater and sufficient political tranquillity and economic stability since the Filipino people have already paid such a dear price for freedom.

When President Gordon B. Hinckley, now President of the Church, addressed one of the dedication sessions of the Hong Kong Temple on May 26, 1996, he mentioned that part of his schedule over the next few days included firesides with Church members in Manila and Cebu. He said he expected to meet with twenty thousand people in Manila. Several days later, on May 30, he spoke at the Amoranto Sports Complex to more than thirty-five thousand people, to that date probably the largest live audience to which a President of the Church had spoken anywhere in the world. "Initially, hundreds were turned away from the doors," wrote Gerry Avant in the *Church News*. "However, officials of the facility were so touched by the members' tears of disappointment that they relented and allowed them to enter." Sister Avant went on:

> Many of those who traveled long distances to Manila went to the grounds of the Manila Philippines Temple, where they spent hours, even days, until time to go to the fireside. Four LDS meetinghouses were used as sleeping accommodations for members to stay at night. The Church provided sleeping mats, which were spread on cultural hall and classroom floors, and portable cook stoves, which the travelers used outdoors to prepare their meals.
>
> A happy, almost surreal atmosphere seemed to settle on the temple grounds the evening before and the morn-

ing of the fireside. One could not help but think of the Book of Mormon account of the people who had gathered around the temple to listen to their beloved leader, King Benjamin. Here in Manila, members gathered around the temple in an exquisitely beautiful setting as they prepared to hear the words of today's prophet, a man they obviously love and revere.[42]

When President Hinckley spoke, he told the audience that he had been interviewed by the media three times that day. One of the questions he was asked was, "Why is this Church growing as it is in the Philippines?" "The answer," he said, "is simply this: This Church and this gospel fill a need in the lives of the people. We live in a world of shifting values. Moral values are crumbling throughout the world in nearly every nation, including this nation. And this Church stands as an anchor, a solid anchor of truth in a world of shifting values. Every man and every woman who joins this Church and clings to its teachings will live a better life, will be a happier man or woman, will carry in his or her heart a great love for the Lord and his ways.

"I've been asked another question, to the effect that people don't regard us as Christians. I'm sorry if that's the case. If that's the case, it comes of their ignorance of what we stand for. I don't know how anybody could stand stronger as witnesses of the Lord Jesus Christ than do the people of this Church."[43]

On the following day, May 31, President Hinckley traveled to Cebu, where he addressed another capacity crowd of 9,200 in the Cebu Coliseum. The response from members was equal to the meeting in Manila.

Before leaving Manila, President Hinckley visited the American War Memorial Cemetery, where he goes each time he travels to the Philippines. The cemetery and memorial hold deep feelings for the prophet. He considers it hallowed ground, not only because of the great sacrifices that were made for freedom by those whose remains lie there, but also for the place it holds in the history of the Church in the Philippines. Thirty-six years after he offered his prayer of rededication and commencement of missionary work in the Philippines, his joy in the growth of the Church must have been unbounded.

NOTES

1. "Four new areas will be created Aug. 15, bringing total to 17," *Church News*, 25 April 1987, p. 3.

2. "Jubilance at Asian temple ceremonies," *Church News*, 4 September 1982, pp. 3, 14.

3. See "Thousands attend temple open houses," *Church News*, 30 September 1984, p. 4.

4. Other General Authorities present were Elder William Grant Bangerter of the First Quorum of the Seventy, who was Executive Director of the Church Temple Department; the presidency of the Asia Area, Elders William R. Bradford, Jack H Goaslind Jr., and Robert B. Harbertson, all of the First Quorum of the Seventy; and Bishop H. Burke Peterson of the Presiding Bishopric. See Dell Van Orden, "Emotional rites note 'miracle of Philippines,'" *Church News*, 7 October 1984, p. 3.

5. "Temple brings Philippines all blessings," *Church News*, 30 September 1984, pp. 5, 10. This article contains a complete text of the dedicatory prayer.

6. Rabai B. Osumo, "The Church in the Philippines," *Tambuli* 15 (April 1991): Dateline Philippines, 12. This article is the most complete published to date regarding the history of the Church in the Philippines.

7. Roland P. Arcansalin, interview by the author, Manila, Philippines, 16 September 1995, tape recording.

8. Ben B. Banks, interview by the author, Manila, Philippines, 16 September 1995, tape recording; and Arcansalin interview.

9. Dell Van Orden, "Emotional rites note 'miracle of the Philippines,'" *Church News*, 7 October 1984, p. 10.

10. Arcansalin interview.

11. See Miles T. Tuason, "From 17 La Salle to Temple Drive: 10 Years of the MTC," *Tambuli* 17 (October 1993): Dateline Philippines, 1–2.

12. See "New Missionary Training Center Dedicated," *Tambuli* 15 (November 1992): Dateline Philippines, 3–4.

13. See Miles T. Tuason, "MTC Couples District Created," *Tambuli* 17 (March 1994): Dateline Philippines, 3.

14. Marion D. Hanks Oral History, interviews by Gordon Irving, Salt Lake City, Utah, 1983, James Moyle Oral History Program, LDS Church Archives, typescript, pp. 32–33.

15. See S. Calvert, "Our Trip to the Temple," *Tambuli* 18 (February 1994): Dateline Philippines, 3.

16. See "Gospel Flourishes in the Refugee Camp," *Tambuli* 11 (March 1988): Dateline Philippines, 6.

17. Augusto A. Lim, interview by the author, Manila, Philippines, 16 September 1995, tape recording.

18. Warner Woodworth, "Third World Strategies Toward Zion," *Sunstone* 14 (October 1990): 18. In *The Mormons' War on Poverty* (Salt Lake City: University of Utah Press, 1993), Garth Mangum and Bruce Blumell suggest that according to their personal observations "the poverty rate among LDS Filipinos is about 10 percent above the

national average" (p. 216). They go on as follows: "Nearly 60 percent of Filipinos are rural and, on average, experience more poverty than their urban counterparts. Because of LDS proselyting practices, 60 percent of LDS Filipinos are urban, heightening the contrast between LDS members and urban Filipinos. Approximately 100,000 adult Mormons are in the labor market, most already employed or self-employed; but the LDS unemployment rate, 15 percent in the late 1980s, was also above the national average. Compared to 16 percent of all urban Filipinos, close to half of the Mormons there are self-employed, which primarily means home manufacture, street huckstering, and operating independent 'jeepneys,' combination bus/taxis. Housing quality reflects those income and employment handicaps."

19. Arcansalin interview.

20. See James O. Mason, "The History of the Welfare Service Missionary Program," 12 August 1979 address at the Missionary Training Center, Provo, Utah, typescript, pp. 9, 11–12.

21. Mary Ellen Edmunds et al., "International Health and the Church," *The Journal of Collegium Aesculapium* 1 (December 1983): 10.

22. See James E. Faust, "Establishing the Church: Welfare Services Missionaries Are an Important Resource," *Ensign* 9 (November 1979): 91–93.

23. Edmunds et al., "International Health," p. 10.

24. Mangum and Blumell, *Mormons' War on Poverty*, p. 241. See also John M. Hill, M. E. Woods, and Steven D. Dorsey, "A Human Development Intervention in the Philippines: Effect on Child Morbidity," *Social Science Medicine* 27, no. 11 (1988): 1183–88.

25. See "Mabuhay-Deseret Foundation: dedicated to improve the quality of life," *Tambuli* 13 (March 1990): Dateline Philippines, 3–5; "Mabuhay-Deseret Foundation turns 2," *Tambuli* 13 (November 1990): Dateline Philippines, 6–7; Delmar Castel, "Mabuhay-Deseret Foundation conduct screening, clinic in Cebu," *Tambuli* 14 (September 1991): Dateline Philippines, 5; Grace May W. Teh, "Mabuhay-Deseret Foundation Is Still Around," *Tambuli* 17 (May 1994): Dateline Philippines, 4.

26. Marvin K. Gardner, "Philippine Saints Recover from Earthquake," *Ensign* 20 (October 1990): 74.

27. See "Funds help Philippine earthquake victims," *Church News*, 29 September 1990, p. 5.

28. For more details see "Quake jolts Philippines: 2 LDS missing," *Church News*, 21 July 1990, p. 10; Sheridan R. Sheffield, "Toll continues to rise in Philippines," *Church News*, 28 July 1990, p. 13; and Sheridan R. Sheffield, "Miracles found in Philippines quake," *Church News*, 4 August 1990, p. 3.

29. See "Church donates funds for Filipino relief," *Church News*, 28 September 1991, p. 4.

30. "Enterprise Development Program Established in the Philippines," *Tambuli* 13 (March 1990): Dateline Philippines, 9.

31. Warner Woodworth to Friends, Thanksgiving 1995, p. 2; in possession of author.

32. Woodworth, "Third World Strategies," p. 22.

33. J. Antonio T. San Gabriel, "Business and Job Fair," *Tambuli* 15 (December 1992): Dateline Philippines, 7–8. See also "The Church Employment System," *Tambuli* 14 (June 1991): Dateline Philippines, 7–9; "The Church Employment System Broadens Focus," *Tambuli* 16 (August 1993): Dateline Philippines, 4–6; and Duane and Jean Christensen, "Special Training and Counsel Given Manila Area Employment Specialists," *Tambuli* 16 (November 1993): Dateline Philippines, 1–2.

34. Emmanuel S. Mascardo, interview by the author, Orem, Utah, 24 September 1995, tape recording; "CES Philippines: Personnel, Location and Physical Facilities, 1995–1996," Friday, 8 September 1995, in possession of the author; "CES Philippines:

Program Report on Seminary and Institute, 1995–1996," Wednesday, 12 July 1995, in possession of the author.

35. Stephen K. Iba, interview by the author, Provo, Utah, 17 August 1995, tape recording.

36. Charrie R. Maquiran, "Seminary Classes Now Held in Bacolod City Public Schools," *Tambuli* 17 (February 1993): Dateline Philippines, 4.

37. "Tagalog Selection from the Book of Mormon," *Tambuli* 11 (August 1988): Dateline Philippines, 6–7.

38. See "Translated languages of the Book of Mormon," *Church News*, 6 January 1996, p. 7.

39. "Post Script: Para Sa Ating Kaalaman," *Liahona* 1 (November 1995): Dateline Philippines, 7. This article provides a chart with the titles of items available and the languages in which they are available from the Manila Distribution Center. The eight Filipino languages available were Tagalog, Cebuano, Ilocano, Bicol, Hilgaynon, Waray, Pangasinan, and Pampango. Titles available included (but not in all languages) *Gospel Principles, Joseph Smith's Testimony, Stories from the Book of Mormon, Stories from the Doctrine and Covenants, Stories from the Old Testament, Stories from the New Testament, Discussions for New Members, Missionary Discussions, Selections from the Book of Mormon*, and several Church videos dubbed in various languages. The sacrament prayer, *Priesthood Leader's Guidebook*, and the *Family Guidebook* have also been translated into several languages.

40. See Sheridan R. Sheffield, "From a tiny seed comes great growth," *Church News*, 11 May 1991, p. 12. On January 1, 1991, Tagalog was added to the languages taught at the Missionary Training Center in Provo, Utah.

41. Dell Van Orden, "Saints throng to area meetings in the Far East," *Church News*, 1 November 1980, p. 4.

42. Gerry Avant, "Tears flow, faith grows as Filipinos greet prophet," *Church News*, 8 June 1996, p. 4.

43. "Prophet testifies, reaffirms blessings," *Church News*, 8 June 1996, p. 7.

15

THAILAND AND CAMBODIA

1961 – 1996

A Foothold in the Shadow of the Buddha

In Southeast Asia every forward step for the Church has been hard won. Missionaries to this part of the world have known that they were pioneers who needed the same qualities of vision, courage, hard work, and faith that were required of the early Mormon pioneers to achieve dominion over the American frontier.

Thailand is a missionary frontier because Latter-day Saints have never confronted a people who are so completely devoted to their country, their king, their religion, and their local traditions. More than in China, Korea, or even Japan, the people of Thailand confront Christian missionaries with customs, beliefs, and cultural characteristics that are different from those of the Christian world. Although Roman Catholics have proselyted in Thailand for 400 years and Protestant missionaries have taught their form of Christianity for more than 160 years, Thai Christians comprise fewer than 1 percent of the total population. (In 1995 Thailand's population numbered some 60 million, including 226,500 Protestants and 236,000 Roman Catholics.) Between 93 and 95 percent of the people are Theravada (Orthodox) Buddhists; the remainder follow Islam or Chinese traditions. Most Thais are as much controlled by animism, a belief in local spirits, as by formal Buddhist beliefs.[1] Christian missionaries have had relatively few direct problems from the Thai government because local social pressure—whether Buddhist or animist—has been more than sufficient to convince all but the most determined students of Christianity that they do not wish to leave the local tradition. Most Thais believe it is not only anti-Buddhist to convert to Christianity but also unpatriotic and anti-Thai.

Nevertheless, even though the advantage has clearly been with the traditional culture, LDS missionaries have succeeded in winning a growing number of devoted converts to the restored gospel of Jesus Christ.

Formal LDS activities began in Bangkok in 1961. In June of that year, Max and Janet Berryessa and their four sons, from Brigham Young University, arrived on an assignment as education advisers to the Thai education department. Within days they met fellow Latter-day Saints Colonel Joseph Meacham and his wife, Shirley, and moved into a home next door to them. The two families held informal Church services together and soon invited another LDS family, Captain Robert and Virginia Liday, to join with them. In early 1962 President Robert S. Taylor of the Southern Far East Mission traveled to Bangkok to officially organize the first group of the Church. Berryessa was sustained as group leader with Brother Meacham as assistant. The group grew steadily as LDS military and technical advisers were assigned to the country in conjunction with the Vietnam conflict.

In May 1963 Elder Gordon B. Hinckley, supervisor of the Church in Asia and the Pacific, visited Thailand. While there he met with members of the Bangkok group and asked if Thailand was ready to receive missionaries. The response was positive but guarded because of the deep dedication the Thai people held for their Buddhist religion. In December 1964 Elder Hinckley again visited Thailand. In his journal he noted his positive impressions of the people, their relative prosperity, the general stability of the government, and the missionary-mindedness of the members.

Twice he observed that he thought the Church should have missionaries working there. He wrote: "When we come to this part of the world we are almost overwhelmed by a realization of the immensity of our task in preaching the restored gospel. Nevertheless, I feel that with the planning done by our American brothers and sisters who are living here, we could begin to do some missionary work."[2]

During this time the group was gaining in strength and the organization of the Church was becoming more complete. In September 1964 a modest Mutual Improvement Association was organized. In May 1965 the group outgrew the home in which they were meeting and arranged to meet in the private dining room of a restaurant. The American members had an active missionary program going. On January 21, 1966, Jim McElvee, a serviceman, became the first convert to be baptized in Thailand since 1854. Then, on September 11, 1966, Sister Nangnoi Thitapoora was baptized, the first Thai to join the Church. She worked for and lived with an American LDS family.

Several other important events occurred in 1966. On March 27 President Keith E. Garner organized the Thailand District of the Southern Far East Mission with Stirling Merrill as president. Because of the buildup of the Vietnam War, there were by this time a number of servicemen's groups, mostly in the northeast. By July the Bangkok group had more than two hundred members, and President Merrill saw fit to organize the Bangkok Branch, the first branch in the country, with Gordon M. Flammer as the first branch president.

TURNING THE KEY FOR
THE PREACHING OF THE GOSPEL

On November 1, 1966, Elder Hinckley and Elder Marion D. Hanks of the First Council of the Seventy, in company with mission president Garner and their wives, arrived in Bangkok after touring other areas of the Southern Far East Mission. That night they met with 145 members and investigators of the Church in a quarterly district conference. Elder Hanks noted that "a strong organization of the Church is now operating in Thailand."[3] The following morning Elder Hinckley dedicated Thailand and "turned the key" that opened the country for the preaching of the gospel. Elder Hanks described the occasion:

> Lumpini Park is a lovely oasis in the busy city of Bangkok, Thailand. Its beautiful lake and flower beds and trees and vast expanses of lawn draw many important visitors and have been the scene of many significant events. It is not likely, however, that the park has seen anything comparable to the event that occurred there at 6:30 A.M. on the morning of November 2, 1966.
>
> At that hour in this center spot of the ancient kingdom of Siam, Elder Gordon B. Hinckley of the Council of the Twelve . . . dedicated modern Thailand to the preaching of the Gospel of Jesus Christ. . . .
>
> The sweetness and solemnity of the sacred occasion touched and subdued the hearts of all who stood in the small circle on the slight prominence amidst the trees at lake side in Lumpini Park.[4]

In his prayer Elder Hinckley prayed that the Lord's Spirit might rest on the land, the people, and their nation. He prayed that the government officials would be kind to the missionaries. He also prayed that the tongues of the missionaries might be loosened so that they could speak the language of the people and "that they shall be effective in proclaiming Thy word; and may there be many, Father, yea, thousands and tens of thousands who will hearken to their message."[5]

Later the same day, Elders Hinckley and Hanks, along with others, visited Colonel Pin Muthukanta, director general of the Ministry of Religions. Colonel Pin (Thais use their first names almost exclusively) explained the procedure for registering the Church and offered to help them accomplish that task. Pin explained that although most Thais were Buddhists, there was religious freedom in Thailand.[6]

In December the process of legally incorporating and registering the Church in Thailand was begun by the leaders of the Bangkok Branch. Branch president Flammer was appointed president of the LDS legal entity. During their November visit, Elder Hinckley and Elder Hanks also selected a property, which by the time of Elder Hinckley's next visit to Bangkok in October 1967 had been purchased as a chapel site. The two-third-acre plot cost $77,000. The registration procedure was moving along well at that time, and Elder Hinckley expected missionaries to be in Thailand before long. On November 16 he announced to the Brethren in Salt Lake City that on November 1 the Church was officially incorporated and registered in Thailand.[7]

After two or three months of delays, the Church received permission to send missionaries into the country. But Thailand had strict limits on the number of aliens who could live in the country. Foreign missionaries, LDS and others, were required to leave the country every seventy-five days to renew their visas. Although Elder Hinckley and the mission president hoped that this regulation could be set aside by the government, it was not changed until 1978, when foreign missionaries were allowed to stay in the country on one-year visas. Even after that the Thai government would change its position several times.

FULL-TIME MISSIONARY WORK BEGINS

On February 2, 1968, President and Sister Garner and six missionaries, Peter W. Basker, Craig G. Christensen, L. Carl Hansen, Alan H. Hess, Larry R. White, and Robert W. Winegar, arrived in Bangkok to commence full-time missionary work. Elder Hess came from Hong Kong; the other five were transferred from Taiwan. International tensions were high at the moment because of the Tet Offensive of the Vietnam War. And "Due to the fighting in Vietnam," Elder White wrote later, "Bangkok's Don Muang Airport was crowded with troops when the missionaries and the mission president and his wife arrived. The troops could not return to their bases because they were under attack in Vietnam. This created a dramatic setting for the commencement of the work in Thailand."[8] President Garner soon found a residence for the missionaries that was also suitable for holding meetings. When the Garners left for Hong Kong three days later, he gave the missionaries rather terse directions: "Learn the Thai language and arrange to have the six missionary discussions translated."[9] They followed both instructions carefully.

Through intensive language study at a local school and through getting out among the people and using the language, they became conversant in a few months. All six missionaries had already learned either Mandarin or Cantonese. According to White, "On March 6, 1968, the six elders began full-time proselyting in the Thai language. On March 17, 1968, the first Thai meeting in the Thai language was held." The elders were helped greatly by the translation ability of Anan Eldredge, the first Thai male to join the Church. President Garner asked Anan to live with the elders, help them learn the Thai language, and help lay the foundation.[10] Anan had been adopted by an American LDS family.

Following instructions, the elders hired a translator, and by October 1968 the missionary discussions were printed in romanized Thai (i.e., using the Western alphabet rather than the Thai script), along with a Thai glossary. The next July, shortly after W. Brent Hardy replaced Garner as mission president in Hong Kong, Hardy asked the missionaries to revise and correct this translation of the six discussions. "This proved to be a ponderous task," said Craig G. Christensen, supervising elder, "for the native Thai translators who had been hired were faced with two major problems: (1) they were not familiar with the Church terminology and doctrine, and (2) the Thai language makes no provision for Christian concepts. For example, 'Savior' must be translated 'the Holy One who helps.' To date [1970], no suitable equivalent for 'priesthood' has been discovered or coined."[11] A month later, November 1968, *Joseph Smith's Testimony* was published in Thai, the first Latter-day Saint material to be printed in that language.

By that time, the elders had brought several Thais into the Church. Boonepluke and Rabiab Klaophin, who had been introduced to the missionaries by branch president Flammer, were baptized on May 15 in the first baptismal service held by the missionaries in Thailand. Regarding the cultural obstacles to Brother Boonepluke's baptism, Christensen commented: "A Thai man who rejects Buddhism is looked upon as somewhat of a traitor, because Buddhism and the Thai government are inextricably related historically, ceremonially, and philosophically. Such a person becomes a social outcast in many circles and is almost certain to bring disgrace upon his family."[12]

Nevertheless, he joined the Church. Unfortunately, pressures were too great and he soon fell away. Not long after, on July 4, 1968, Sister Srilaksana Suntarahut Gottsche and two of her daughters were baptized. By late 1968 Thai groups had been organized at Bangkok and Korat.

It was also during November 1968 that Elder Ezra Taft Benson of the Quorum of the Twelve visited Thailand on his first official visit since being assigned as supervisor of the Asia area. Prior to his visit for district conference, he informed President Hardy and the missionaries that he desired an audience with His Majesty, the King of Thailand, Bhumibol Adulyadej. When the elders in Bangkok began trying to make arrangements, they were discouraged by local officials. Nevertheless, on the eve of Elder Benson's visit, and after a special fast by the elders, permission was granted. Benson's former position as U.S. Secretary of Agriculture no doubt helped open the king's doors. Although an official told Elder Benson and his party that they could have no more than fifteen minutes with the king, the king was "so congenial and interested" in Elder Benson's message and purposes "that he didn't let them go for over 45 minutes." Elder Benson presented the king with copies of *Meet the Mormons*, a leather-bound English version of the Book of Mormon, and the Thai version of *Joseph Smith's Testimony*. The elders later learned that the king had kept a stadium full of people waiting while he conversed with Elder Benson.[13] According to Elder Benson, the interview was helpful because it brought the Church's presence in Thailand and the purposes of the Church to the attention of the king.

In the beginning, the missionary force was small. At the end of 1968 there were only eight elders in the country, and by the end of the next year the number had increased to only twenty-five. By then Thailand had become part of the new Southeast Asia Mission with headquarters in Singapore. Beginning in 1970, Thai was taught to missionaries at the Language Training Mission at the Church College of Hawaii in Laie. (During May 1975 all language training was consolidated at the LTM—the Language Training Mission, as it was then called—at Brigham Young University in Provo, Utah.)

When President G. Carlos Smith Jr. and his wife, Lavon, established the Southeast Asia Mission in November 1969, it was possible for him to devote much more time to Thailand than the presidents of the Southern Far East Mission had been able to do. During late 1969 and 1970 the work moved faster. In December 1969 translation work was started on the Book of Mormon. Church Translation Department leaders D'Monte W. Coombs and Watanabe Kan hired Mr. Prayoon Nanakorn, a non-Mormon, to be head translator. His work was reviewed by a small group of elders and a recent convert, Srilaksana Gottsche. Sister "Sri," however, ended up, along with elders and other members (there was always a committee involved), doing much of the final translation that was published in 1976.

Sister Sri's conversion to the gospel was something out of the ordinary. Elders Larry R. White and L. Carl Hansen found her at home on March 20, 1968, only six weeks after they arrived in Bangkok. When she entered the room, having been called by a maid, she greeted them in English. Years later, Elder White recounted: "It was my turn to give the introduction, and I began to tell her of the Book of Mormon in English. I had no sooner begun when the Spirit fell upon me and told me with great force that this lady would join the Church. This manifestation was so forceful that I was overcome by emotion and unable to continue speaking. (This had never happened to me before during an introduction. It has also never happened to me again since that time.) I passed the book to Elder Hansen to finish the introduction. He did so ably."[14]

Srilaksana Suntarahut Gottsche—Sister Sri—was the principal translator into Thai of the Book of Mormon, the Doctrine and Covenants, and the Pearl of Great Price. (Photo by author)

Thus began a series of meetings with Sister Sri. She says she was quite uninterested and didn't want them to come back. But White especially persisted, and eventually she accepted an English copy of the Book of Mormon. White continued: "In the middle of May, a transformation took place. I learned many years later what had happened. . . . She was waiting to go out with some of her friends when she noticed the Book of Mormon on the shelf. Because she had paid ten baht (about 50 cents) for it, she felt that she should at least read a little. She casually took the book off of the shelf and opened it at random. As soon as her eyes fell upon the first passage, she began to shake, and she felt something which she had never felt before. Immediately, she knew the book was true."[15]

Beginning at that moment, she read almost nonstop until she had completed every page. Sister Sri made a tremendous sacrifice to accept the gospel, and she has remained true to her testimony. She had been reared for much of her childhood as a companion to the queen. Her life had been filled with associations with Thailand's royalty and society's elite. Joining the Church ended these associations. She had learned English while in the best

The Asoke chapel was constructed with funds largely donated by American service personnel. It now serves as stake center and Church Educational System offices. (Photo by author)

Catholic schools. After attending Chulalongkorn University, she became the financial secretary for a group of high-level government officials. Her language skills were excellent.[16] Fortunately, she turned those skills to the service of the Lord as the principal translator of the Book of Mormon. Along with Anan Eldredge and other committee members, she also translated the Doctrine and Covenants and the Pearl of Great Price. When asked how she learned to be a translator, she replied, "By the gift of the language. By the Holy Ghost, by the Lord." She explained that when troubled with a word like *priesthood*, she would fast, pray, and talk to the Lord for many days. She finally received the answer to that word problem in a type of vision. She saw the word *thana purohit* ("in the air on the ceiling"). It does not have a literal meaning in Thai, but it became the word used for *priesthood* in all LDS publications in Thailand.[17]

In 1970 construction was started on what is called the Asoke chapel in downtown Bangkok. The property had been purchased in 1967. Most of the funds for construction were contributed by LDS servicemen stationed in Thailand. This project took much longer than local leaders hoped or expected. It was dedicated by Elder David B. Haight, then an Assistant to the Twelve, on August 28, 1974. For many years the Asoke chapel was the only LDS constructed building in Thailand. Having recently been remodeled (1995), it serves as the stake center and CES headquarters for the country.

Also during 1970, President Smith sent missionaries to Chiang Mai in the north and to Khon Kaen in the northeast. (Twelve other cities were opened during the next six years.) President Smith had started a missionary basketball program in 1969 as a means of increasing the visibility of the Church. During 1970 the elders' team played in tournaments in various parts of the country and brought favorable publicity. Later that year, in August, missionaries arranged to have *Music and the Spoken Word*, which originates from Temple Square in Salt Lake City, aired over Thai radio in Korat. At the same time, the elders initiated an open-house program in Chiang Mai. The purpose of this proselyting method was to introduce non-Mormons to the Church in a non-threatening, comfortable setting.

THE BUDDHA-IMAGE DEBACLE

Although President Smith and the missionaries worked earnestly to plant the gospel firmly and to create a good public image, notoriety came to the Church in an unexpected and unfortunate way. On June 22, 1972, a group of missionaries traveled to Sukhothai, the ancient capital of Thailand. This city, now in ruins, is important not only because of its historical significance but also because it contains many Buddhist relics and statues. While they were wandering through the area enjoying the lush vegetation and Thailand's ancient monuments, one of the elders climbed a statue of the Buddha (something akin to climbing the statue of Christ in the LDS visitors' center in Salt Lake City) and sat on the shoulders with his legs around the neck looking over and higher than the Buddha's head (for the Thai people, the head is the most sacred part of the body). Another elder took a picture. The Thais call this incident *khii Khss phra*, meaning "sitting on the neck of the Buddha." Although nothing malicious was intended, from the Thai point of view the two missionaries could not have committed a more disrespectful act of desecration.

The elder who took the picture took the film to a photo shop in Nakhon Sawan, the city where he was serving, for developing. An employee noticed the subject of the picture (a slide), made a copy, and sent it to a newspaper, the *Siam Rath*, where it appeared on Sunday, July 9, 1972. Other newspapers picked up the photograph and printed it, and the matter exploded into a national scandal. Seemingly every newspaper in the country became involved as the elders were accused in the newspapers and in court of conspiring to desecrate and insult the Buddhist religion and the Thai nation. The Thai Christian community, especially, made every effort to disassociate itself from the Mormons. Some of the articles that were written by members of other Christian faiths were the most vehement against the Church.

Three days after the picture first appeared in the *Siam Rath*, the two elders were arrested by the Nakhon Sawan police. The following day, before their lawyer could even prepare a case and before newly arrived mission president Miller F. Shurtleff could make the trip from Singapore to Nakhon Sawan, the elders were tried and found guilty of desecrating a Buddhist image and of committing contemptuous, insulting actions against the Buddhist religion. The judge sentenced them to six months in jail, the maximum the law allowed. They served the entire term. Following their release from jail, they were deported from the country, an event that was reported widely in the newspapers in Thailand and over Associated Press and other wire services.

There have been many consequences of this mistake. Nakhon Sawan had to be closed as a proselyting area, and only gradually did the furor die down elsewhere in the country. (At this date, 1996, there are still no missionaries in Nakhan Sawan.) Although some elders reported that more people had an interest in them and their purposes than before, the number of baptisms dropped throughout the country for the next two years. Fortunately, government officials handled the matter deftly. They simply warned the missionaries that such actions could not be tolerated. Two years later, however, President Paul D. Morris summarized the ongoing consequences of that innocent but thoughtless moment:

"The position of the Church in Thailand is still extremely tenuous. Everyone remembers our total foolishness in that serious insult to the Thai people and their religious beliefs. Thai members of the Church receive a great deal of very real persecution and abuse because of that mistake by two supposedly informed elders. The Thai people are extremely nationalistic. . . .

"It is most important that we do nothing at this time that may give people an excuse for further attacking the Church here."[18]

Perhaps no act by LDS missionaries during the past twenty-five years has more strongly emphasized the need for greater maturity, more cultural knowledge, and increased sensitivity everywhere in the Church than the Buddha-image problem in Thailand.[19] This incident has cast a dark shadow upon the Church in Thailand that affects relations with Thai bureaucrats to the present.

THAILAND BECOMES A MISSION

Because of the vastness of the area that the Southeast Asia Mission president had to supervise and because Thailand needed closer supervision, on August 6, 1973, the First Presidency created the Thailand Mission (the name was changed to the Thailand Bangkok Mission on June 20, 1974) and called Paul D. Morris as president, who was already residing in Bangkok. Morris and his wife, Betty, had served missions in Hong Kong. At the time of his call, Morris was employed as an economist by the U.S. Agency for International Development in Bangkok and was also serving as president of the Thailand District of the Southeast Asia Mission. Because of his long experience in Asia, President Morris was able to teach his missionaries many important concepts that improved Thai-LDS relations. The missionaries themselves were keenly aware of the need to adapt teaching materials, pictures, tracts, fliers, and the like to the Thai setting.[20]

Between 1973 and 1976 President Morris pressed the work forward on a number of fronts: many books and manuals were translated (between 1969 and 1980, about thirty different tracts were translated and printed in Thai), local leadership was strengthened, missionaries and members performed on radio and television, the family home evening program was expanded, and local members published articles about the Church in Thai newspapers. During that time sister missionaries were called to Thailand and were particularly helpful in the welfare services area.

A LATTER-DAY SAINT MUSICAL GROUP

In August 1976 Harvey D. Brown, another U.S. government employee who had many years of experience in Asia (he had held responsible positions in the Church in the Philippines and Vietnam) became the second president of the Thailand Bangkok Mission. His era is best remembered for the excellent progress made in building the image of the Church. In September, having received permission from Elder Hinckley, he announced to the missionaries his plan to re-form and enhance the usefulness of a singing group. Auditions were held, and six elders were selected to serve full-time in the *Sidthichon Yuk Sud Tai* ("the Latter-day Saints"). A few weeks later they gave their first performance. Their unique blend of Western and Thai sounds made them an instant success. By Christmastime 1976 they were touring the country and performing before thousands. They had already performed on television in Bangkok with positive reviews. The results were exactly what President Brown had hoped: interest in the Church increased markedly.

One of Brown's desires was to help various charities raise money. The group performed at many functions to benefit such organizations as the Thai International Red Cross, Bangkok Teachers College, various hospitals, and a fund-raising concert for a drug rehabilitation program. The *Sidthichon Yuk Sud Tai* received a special invitation to perform at a fund-raiser for one of the king's charities. One of the participants described the experience: "This concert proved to be a highlight in Church history in Thailand. After the music group finished its part of the show, which included songs written by the king, Queen Sirikit and King Bhumibol asked to meet the music group. The next day, the same newspaper which carried the picture five years earlier of a missionary desecrating a Buddha, carried a picture of the king receiving the formal bows of the music group members."[21]

Until this time, the group had been cautious about identifying their real purposes as missionaries of The Church of Jesus Christ of Latter-day Saints. Now, they decided to take the risk and let audiences, live and on TV, know who they were. Their popularity continued to grow. Referrals resulting from the group's activities kept the missionary force busy for more than a year. "In its twenty-eight months of existence," wrote Peter Ashman, one of the members of the group, "the music group appeared on TV over seventy times, recorded five albums, [gave] three royal performances, and did over 500 live performances for over one million people in every major city in Thailand."[22]

Believing that the purposes of the group had been fulfilled (the visa situation had improved considerably and many Thais viewed the Church more positively), President Brown discontinued the group in July 1979.

PROBLEMS WITH MISSIONARY VISAS AND NUMBERS

At the end of 1976 the missionary corps had grown to 170 missionaries, but in 1978, in spite of the success of the singing group, the government pressured the mission to drop its numbers to about 125 elders and sisters. In 1985 the number of missionaries was reduced to fewer than 100. And to make matters much more difficult, in 1986 the missionaries were required to leave the country to extend their visas every ninety days. The Cambodian border was closed because of internal warfare, and the missionaries were forced to make an expensive and time-consuming trip south across the border of Malaysia. The ninety-day renewal policy was not changed until 1992.

Under Presidents Morris and Brown, missionaries averaged one convert baptism each per year. In 1978 a total of 144 Thais joined the Church. There were ten local full-time missionaries serving, and membership exceeded 1,150 at the end of that year. One by one Elder Hinckley's dedicatory prayer that "thousands and tens of thousands" of people would join the Church was being fulfilled.

SERVICE TO THE DOWNTRODDEN

In May 1980 Elder Marion D. Hanks of the First Quorum of the Seventy was assigned as Executive Administrator over Southeast Asia. He had under his care eleven missions, including Thailand. Soon after assuming his responsibilities in Asia, two realities became clear to him. First, the Church was not perceived well by many influential people in Asia. The Church was known for its aggressive proselyting but not for Christian service, such as building hospitals and schools and caring for Asia's poor and downtrodden. "That, of course, was disappointing to me," Elder Hanks said later. "I felt and feel that we need to establish ourselves, not theologically according to their definition, but, at least in terms of behavior, we need to be able to identify with what we so earnestly pronounce ourselves to be, and that's Christian."[23]

Second, the effects of the Vietnam War and the horrors of the Pol Pot regime in Cambodia were still being felt in 1980, for more than one million Vietnamese, Cambodian, and Laotian refugees had sought asylum in new lands since 1975. Numerous refugee camps had sprung up along the Thai-Cambodian and Thai-Laotian borders, and other camps had been situated in other parts of the country.[24] (At one time there were twenty-one camps, including processing, holding, and transit centers.) In 1980 there were more than 250,000 refugees in Thailand, and by 1983 more than 600,000 refugees had crossed into the country.[25]

On a trip to Thailand, Bruce Opie, area director for temporal affairs, and a missionary couple took Elder Hanks to see Lumpini camp in Bangkok. Brother Opie had formerly served as mission president in Western Australia and had implemented extensive service projects among his missionaries. He was interested in seeing the Church pursue humanitarian service undertakings as a means of helping the helpless and building the reputation of the Church for Christian service. Elder Hanks was deeply moved by what he saw and experienced. As a consequence, the two matters—the way the Church was perceived and the problems of the refugees—came together in Elder Hanks's mind, and he conceived what he hoped would be a way of modestly helping some refugees while performing true Christian service in the name of the Church. He would involve the Church in service to refugees.

ESTABLISHING THE REFUGEE WELFARE SERVICES MISSIONARIES IN SOUTHEAST ASIA
Elder Marion D. Hanks

In April 1980 we learned we were going to Asia. I knew that in Asia there were enormous refugee problems, great concentrations of people who were in terrible trouble who were not being served adequately.

The Brethren were wonderfully cooperative. [Elder Gordon B. Hinckley gave special support.] A refugee fund was established by the Church. It was announced, the First Presidency gave their backing, and permission was given me to make some effort to intrude on the tremendous challenges that were out there—again, in a very modest way.

A new camp was contemplated out near the Gulf of Thailand, 100 miles out of Bangkok. I surveyed that setting, tried to make arrangements with the United Nations official, and was rejected. He told me that the mere mention of my coming—that is, a Mormon official—had aroused such antagonism and opposition in all the voluntary agencies that they had gone out of their way to foreclose any future for the Mormons in helping with refugee work in that area.

A miracle of sorts occurred. I was able to persuade—and I meant it—this wonderful young Swiss, who was giving his life to the work, spoke a dozen languages, and was a Christ-like person, that we could come in and give expert assistance without proselyting. I guaranteed it.

He said, "I am assured that Mormons are such aggressive proselyters that it is not possible for you to engage in this kind of work without your proselyting program."

"I am responsible for the Church in Asia," I replied, "I give you my personal assurance that it can and will happen and that we can give you something you are not getting from these other wonderful people. We will come with qualified people and will do a job for you that you will be grateful for."

Mario Howard later described his action as a great leap of faith, but he agreed to our coming. I was then notified that we were assigned the cultural orientation responsibility at this large camp in Phanat Nikhom, Chon Buri Province, Thailand. I telexed home: "I need now to back up my word. We need qualified teachers. We need materials to supply them."

While [a videotape] was being prepared, my wife and I took our first trip around the missions of Asia, our direct responsibility. First, we went to Kaohsiung in Southern Taiwan and held a missionary meeting just for get-acquainted purposes with those 150 missionaries. As part of the meeting, the mission president called on six missionaries to give us an idea about the place and the people.

When the sixth spoke, President [George A.] Baker leaned over to me and said, "Is that all you would like to hear from?"

I said, "Well, I am satisfied, but I would be happy to hear from any others if you have others you would like to call on." "Well, maybe one more, if I may." He called on a sister missionary.

She was a lovely looking young woman, and at the pulpit she said, "I joined the Church in Florida out of a very, very Catholic family. My joining was a great wrench to them and has been very disruptive to family unity. I am on this mission because I have a testimony of the gospel. I know the whisperings of the Spirit which brought me into the Church. Last night those whisperings came again. I was told I would speak today and what to say and so I prepared. When President Baker listed the six missionaries to speak, I began some serious self-examination. Had I mistaken the Spirit? Then I saw President Baker lean over to President Hanks, and I knew the word was getting through; and so, I was called and this is what I am to say to you." She then gave us the best two-and-a-half minute talk on love and forgetting ourselves and serving the Lord I have ever heard. She sat down.

The meeting ended and we stood up at the front shaking hands with the missionaries as they came by. But two didn't come; they went out the back door. Just as we were finishing shaking hands the two returned and came up to the front. I shook hands and said "Wait a minute."

A conversation ensued. The American was Rita Edmonds. I asked her a rather unusual question, three times, "What are you doing here?" Her first answer was that she was a welfare service missionary, her second was that she was trying to help the people, and her third answer, "I guess I don't know what you mean. I am here as a missionary trying to do the work."

I smiled and said, "What did you do before you came here?"

"I worked with a college president."

"What is your educational background?"

She mentioned a master's degree, and a doctor's degree from Columbia University.

"In what field?"

"In community education, family education."

I smiled again. "Shall I tell you what you are doing here? You are going to be the leader of the first organized team of Latter-day Saints moving into a refugee camp in Asia to help them get ready to go to their third country."

She began to cry. "Brother Hanks, for eight months I have been here pleading with the Lord to either help me get satisfied with what I am doing—which is very good work and which should satisfy me—or to fulfill the promises made in my blessing that I would be able to help some downtrodden refugee people in my lifetime." [Sister Edmonds had seen in her mind's eye the place where she was to serve. When she finally arrived in Phanat Nikom, Thailand, she felt that she was where she was supposed to be.]

My wife and I went to lunch with the Bakers. I asked President Baker, "How would you like to lose your finest sister missionary?"

Sister Baker said, "Oh, not Sister [Karen] Gerdes!" (She had given the talk on love.)

"Well," I said, "I really didn't have her in mind but that is a marvelous idea. How would you like to lose your *two* finest sister missionaries?" Those two with their credentials—one a social worker with university credentials, the other with a doctor's degree in community education—came to Thailand as forerunners of the team the Mormons were gathering to keep our promise.

I established three objectives for the Brethren as we began. The first was: we want to do it because it needs to be done. These are God's children. They are in terrible trouble. We're his disciples. We ought to be helping.

We have never, to my knowledge, breached the rule of the camp against teaching religion. We haven't had one single complaint. These wonderful young people have taught principles by the Spirit so that a Jesuit, a marvelous man and a Christ-like person, who watched them greet groups of arriving refugees, said, "There is something about these young women different from anybody else on earth. I have never seen refugee children leap into the arms of voluntary agency workers. Your people have something that is different and real."

Regarding the work which our LDS sisters performed in Hong Kong, [where the work was later extended], a letter came from Mr. Morgan, vice-president of Red Cross International, acknowledging that the camp would be closing and commending us:

"There is no doubt that the services your Church has provided have been enormously appreciated by the refugees. So often these poor people have been bewildered and overwhelmed by the mere act of survival in a hostile environment. Your Church members have given them the moment of respite, the instruction, and the hope for a future that will help them pick up the shattered threads of their lives. But your members have given something else too. There is a better understanding of your own objectives and ideals to the members of the other agencies and the people working in this center. Working together we have all moved closer and become ourselves much more understanding and tolerant. We are all going to miss you very much."

The second objective was to improve our institutional credibility, not because we wanted credit but because we wanted the credibility that comes when you do something worth being appreciated for.

[The third objective was to build the Kingdom.] I have told the Brethren I didn't know whether I would live to see it, but I had every confidence that we would see a strengthening of the kingdom if we just did the work of the Lord for those who came seeking, even though the initial result would be incidental to our purpose. We have seen that hope fulfilled in such measure as could be called miraculous. [26]

Rita Edmonds and Karen Gerdes flew from Taiwan to Hong Kong to begin their new assignment on September 17, 1980. While there they held numerous meetings with Bruce Opie and Elder Hanks and visited refugee camps and agencies that were involved with that service. Two weeks later they went on to Bangkok, where they received further orientation and sought inspiration regarding how they should proceed. On October 3, while sitting in an orientation meeting at the United Nations High Commissioner for Refugees Staff, Sister Edmonds had the plan fall into place in her mind. After spending a week filling out the details of how the Mormon refugee effort should operate, she called Elder Hanks, shared her thoughts, and asked for specific welfare services missionaries from several missions in Southeast Asia. Two Thai sisters who had previously served missions had been assigned by this time. Ten additional sisters were brought to Thailand by the end of October.[27] These were women of unusual ability—teachers, nurses, social workers, linguists. Regarding these sisters, Elder Hanks said:

"It is a miracle as large as any I ever heard of that these twelve were all there, all over cultural shock, they knew the languages of the Orient, and they were high quality, very attractive people, without exception. They were musically on a genius level. They could play everything. And they were, most importantly, filled with the Spirit. In almost every case . . . they were awaiting the fulfillment of their patriarchal blessings and their mission settings apart."[28]

In October 1980, when these sisters set up headquarters at a new refugee camp near Phanat Nikhom, Chon Buri Province, about one hundred miles south of Bangkok, their modest sign said simply "WSURT, Welfare Services Unit for Refugees in Thailand." Church media experts at Bonneville Productions in Salt Lake City had produced *A New Home*, a thirty-minute video-tape in English to help refugees understand the process of moving to a third country and a few basics regarding life in the United States. The welfare services sisters were ready when the first refugees arrived. Sixty thousand refugees were assigned to that camp at any time.[29]

The initial missionaries were replaced by others after about six months (with the exception of Sister Edmonds, who remained for a year), and a missionary couple from the Thailand Bangkok Mission was assigned to support and help. The refugee project went on in one form or another for ten years in Thailand and was instituted in Hong Kong and the Philippines as well. The missionaries taught no religion, for that was the original commitment. But they exemplified Christianity through their lives, and they taught some beautiful songs, such as "I Am a Child of God." Elder Hanks described service in action with these words:

"Here's a picture of this beautiful little black-haired missionary from Provo on her knees, totally unconscious of the fact that there were 500 refugees sitting there. She's got a little brown baby in her arms and there's a diaper on the floor. They had never seen a diaper. She holds this little brown child and smiles and warms him, and somehow he didn't cry. She kissed him on the cheek and then she laid him gently down—she had the diaper sitting on her sweater on the concrete floor—and put the diaper on him and then held him up. And the women crowded around. They treated her about like they would the Lord, if they had understood Him."[30]

They taught the refugees about the basic things of life in a modern country. With old equipment, such as a telephone, toilet, stove, chairs, table, bed, a refrigerator, and some paint purchased with a contribution from the LDS Refugee Fund, they set up a model home and helped the refugees understand how things worked.

"At Christmastime they put on a performance of the Nativity," recalled Elder Hanks. "Sister Edmonds was the mother with a little brown baby. I'm saying we didn't break any religious rules, but we were representing what we are. They put on this pageant and gave them a little Christmas party. The people came up after, and a lady said to Rita Edmonds, 'Jesus' story is a refugee story, isn't it? His parents had to leave their home. If those people in the restaurant—"the inn"—had known who He was, they'd have given Him their bed.' They'd never heard of Christ before. Well, this kind of thing was going on and people were being touched."

The hungry, the thirsty, the naked, the homeless, the sick, the friendless, were cared for by the refugee missionaries.[31] Many lives were changed, and after coming to America a number of refugees sought out the Church, learned of the restored gospel, and accepted baptism. In one form or another, the welfare services and the humanitarian services mission of the Church has continued since that time. Also, it is clear that the four hours of service that Mormon missionaries offer each week throughout the world had its inception, at least in concept, in the refugee missions of Thailand, Hong Kong, and the Philippines.

THE DEVELOPMENT OF SEMINARY AND INSTITUTE IN THAILAND

The first seminary classes in Thailand were offered to expatriate youth during the 1960s. Ten Thai members reportedly attended a seminary class in 1979. Suchat Chaichana, a missionary, was assigned to translate some seminary manuals into Thai in 1979 and 1980. Brother Suchat was asked to start the official CES program while serving on a Church-service basis from 1982 until 1984. In 1984 he was hired by CES as a full-time teacher and administrator. Since 1984 the seminary and institute program has gained numbers of students and faculty. In 1987 Brother Samart Kaivalvatana was hired as a second full-time teacher and administrator. He was assigned to the northeast and lived in Khon Kaen. Institute numbers have always been larger than seminary because of the common age of new converts; there are more members in the eighteen-to-thirty age bracket than in the younger group. Institute classes have played a major role in preparing and providing Thai missionaries. In 1987 thirty-five institute students entered the mission field. By the mid-1990s there were more than five hundred seminary and institute students in every branch in Thailand. Almost twenty teachers were involved and a number of daily seminary classes were being held.[32]

1988 TO 1995:
PERIOD OF REMARKABLE GROWTH

Mission president Anan Eldredge was born Anan Tubtimta and lived the early part of his life in a small village about five hundred kilometers north of Bangkok. When he was eight years old, his mother died, leaving him with lasting questions regarding life and death. His father was principal of a school and encouraged Anan to do well in his studies. "When I was sixteen," remembered Anan, "I left home and went to Bangkok, where I worked as a busboy in a hotel." He became friends with the youngest son of Louis and June Eldredge, Latter-day Saints who were working for the U.S. State Department in Thailand. They treated him like family, and when they were transferred north to a large military base, they invited Anan to come with them.

"I met two Latter-day Saint servicemen who discussed the

gospel with me. Through them, I finally found the answers I had on life and death. I discovered who I was, where I came from, and where I was going." He studied for six months and then asked for baptism. Anan was baptized on December 24, 1967.[33]

Along the way, the Eldredges invited Anan to be a permanent member of their family, and he was formally adopted. He changed his name to Eldredge and later moved to the United States with his new family.

As mentioned earlier, shortly after his baptism, Anan moved in with the first six mis-

Anan Eldredge was the first Thai member of the Church to serve as mission president. As a young missionary, he taught American elders the Thai language and translated many Church works. (Photo by author)

sionaries, taught them the Thai language, and helped with the first translations of LDS literature. From 1970 to 1973 Anan served a full-time mission in his homeland. After returning to California, marrying Margaret Brown (a convert from England) in the Los Angeles Temple, and earning a college degree, he served for five years as director of the new Church Translation and Distribution Center in Bangkok during the later 1970s.

In 1988, while living in Anchorage, Alaska, Anan was called to preside over the Thailand Bangkok Mission. He was the first Thai to serve in this capacity. During his tenure as mission president, President Anan (again, Thais use their first names almost exclusively) saw conversion rates increase considerably, and he and Margaret helped build up the Church in many ways. Anan constantly emphasized the need for members to fellowship and retain new converts and to activate less-active members. He also endured a period of personal suffering during which local newspapers, police, and courts harassed him for statements he had made regarding Thai traditions. During his time of difficulty, the members of the Church stood united behind him.[34]

The first Thai temple excursions happened because President Anan received inspiration to pursue that goal. Each year he called all of the district and branch presidents and their wives together to counsel with them, teach, share testimonies, and encourage them in their callings. While in a Sunday meeting, Anan began a major address, but the Spirit constrained him to change the subject. Remembering the moment, he said: "Sometimes you have a prepared talk and you want to go ahead with it. Then, after a couple of minutes, somehow—I don't know what happened—but I closed the book. I said, Brothers, do you know what we need? We need to sanctify ourselves. How long have you been a member of the Church? Twenty years? Eighteen years? Fifteen years? None of them had been to the temple. I finally said, we need to go to the temple. All of us."[35]

President Anan then challenged the leaders to sanctify themselves and to put aside the money necessary to take their families to the temple six months later. The leaders and their families made many sacrifices, but six months later 201 Thai Saints traveled in several groups to the Manila Philippines Temple to receive their endowments and be sealed as eternal families. CES country director Suchat Chaichana and his associate Samart Kaivalvatana traveled to each branch throughout the mission to teach the temple preparation course to the members.

President Kriangkrai Pithaphong of the Khon Kaen District listed the Manila temple excursion as one of several highlights of his life. "When we flew to Manila, it was a milestone in the history of the Church in Thailand. . . . We were all very excited," he recalled. "It was a trip we had planned for a long time. It was very expensive, approximately $350 per person. Everyone worked hard to raise the money to go. Even our ten-year-old daughter, Kesarin, made some money selling charcoal for cooking. It was a special time for us. . . . Being sealed together in the temple brought a special spirit to our family."[36] In January 1993 the next mission president, Larry R. White, wrote that the temple excursion "resulted in an unprecedented infusion of strength and dedication into the lives of Church member in Thailand."[37] Other smaller excursions have followed in subsequent years.

The years 1991 and 1992 brought political turmoil to all the people of Thailand. In February 1991 a military faction under the name of the National Peace-Keeping Council ousted the civilian government in a *coup d'ètat*. The council justified this move by claiming corruption in the civilian government. The pro-military faction appointed a civilian, the very popular and highly respected Anand Panyarachun, as prime minister. He served for a year with distinction and then graciously left office. He was replaced in March 1992 by General Suchinda Kraprayoon, one of the main leaders of the *coup*. But his appointment was not a popular one, because he had promised many times not to accept the office and also because he had not been elected to parliament, a legal requirement for election as prime minister. Soon the opposition parties began calling for his resignation and threatened to demonstrate in the streets.

On April 20, 1992, several weeks after Suchinda's appointment, fifty thousand people gathered in the Royal Plaza. For the next three weeks the calls for Suchinda's resignation became stronger and momentum increased. But he refused to step down. Demonstrations occurred nightly, with more than one hundred thousand people taking part. The movement also spread to other major Thai cities.

On May 18 the demonstrations became violent; at least six people were killed by riot police, and a state of emergency was declared. Missionaries were instructed to stay away from the demonstration areas and to use great care. The next day government forces fired at random on protesters, leaving many dead and wounded. President White instructed missionaries in Bangkok to stay in their apartments, and a district conference in Khon Kaen was canceled. David N. Phelps, a Latter-day Saint who had served his mission in Thailand and now worked as an attorney in Bangkok, was an eyewitness. He described these events this way:

> What ended up happening at that point, which was very, very dramatic, was that His Majesty, the King, intervened. His Majesty does not have any parliamentary power or any political power, but because he is a monarch that is so highly revered and loved, he has intense power because of the position he holds in Thai society. And he called before him this general [the prime minister], and also the man who had pretty much emerged as the leader of the pro-democracy movement. They came to his palace and on national television, they got, pardon the pun, a royal scolding. He was very stern. It was very apparent as we watched his face that he had not one bone of happiness in his body at that point. He looked at the two of them and he told them that he wanted the violence, the shooting, the killing, to stop immediately. He told them that the two of them were waging a major personal battle and those who were losing were all of the subjects of the Thai nation and he wanted it stopped immediately. That was all it took and the bloodshedding stopped.[38]

The king's intervention had a profound calming effect, but within a short time tensions increased. Although Suchinda resigned, the new candidate for prime minister from the military faction was not popular with most of the pro-democracy parties. Fears were high that more violence would erupt if he were elected prime minister.

This was the situation on June 7, 1992, when Elder Neal A. Maxwell and Elder Russell M. Nelson and their wives arrived in Bangkok for a district conference that day.

In the general session many profound and inspiring words were expressed by the Apostles and their wives, but the most meaningful moment came when Elder Maxwell pronounced an apostolic blessing. "Shortly before Elder Maxwell stood up to speak," President White recounted, "I expressed my desire to him that if possible he leave a special blessing on the King, the leaders and the people of Thailand because of the critical political situation." David Phelps, who acted as translator, added: "Elder Maxwell began his talk by greeting the members of the Church and by telling them that before he finished his talk he would pronounce a blessing. . . . He said, 'But the blessing that I will leave with you will not be an ordinary blessing, but under the office of the Holy Apostleship. I will leave an apostolic blessing.'" After giving an address on the Atonement of the Savior, Elder Maxwell said he wanted now to present an apostolic blessing. His words were eloquently simple, direct, and specific. In part, Elder Maxwell said:

"I leave a blessing on Thailand, the people, king, and leaders at this special hinge point in the history of this nation. I bless all those who have been named so there can be a spirit of reconciliation so what develops can be for the happiness and the good of the people of Thailand. Remember this blessing in your prayers to God today and tomorrow that these things will so occur. I bless you as a people that through your faithfulness, though your numbers are few, prayers and lives will be weighed in balance of this blessing. . . . I leave this blessing as an Apostle for myself and my colleague Elder Nelson."[39]

Responding to the blessing, President White wrote: "The Spirit bore witness to me in a profound way at the moment that apostolic power had been exercised in a manner I had not previously experienced in my life and that powers unseen would bring to pass and fulfill the words of the Lord's anointed servants."

From this time on, matters moved quickly and in a most unexpected way. On Wednesday, June 10, only three days after Elder Maxwell's blessing, to everyone's surprise, Anand Panyarachun, who had served so well as prime minister for a year and who was so well respected and loved, was appointed to serve as interim prime minister again. The *Bangkok Post* said this was "a move greeted by a spontaneous outpouring of jubilation and relief."[40] A feeling of peace came over the land.

Church leaders in Thailand were particularly pleased with Prime Minister Anand's appointment because they had worked well with his government while he was previously in office. Through the encouragement and assistance of political figures in Washington, D.C., the U.S. ambassador to Thailand (David F. Lambertson), and members of his staff, Prime Minister Anand's government created a new visa category that allowed Mormon missionaries to remain in Thailand for their entire missions and required them to renew their visas only once during that time. Mormon missionaries made their last trip to Malaysia in August 1992. At the same time, the government raised the number of missionary visas to one hundred. This allowed President White to send missionaries into a number of new areas to open branches. Convert baptisms rose to new highs in the wake of these stirring events. In 1993 the efforts of slightly more than one hundred missionaries resulted in more than four hundred baptisms.

By 1995 there were four districts and twenty-five branches in Thailand. Eleven chapels had been constructed, and others were under way. Church membership had surpassed the six thousand mark and was continuing to grow. Temple attendance, even at great cost and distance, was steadily increasing. New developments for the Church in Vietnam and Cambodia also came shortly after Elders Maxwell and Nelson left their blessings on Thailand.

The creation of the first stake in any nation is a signal event for Church members. Bangkok had been near the critical mass, so to speak, for some time. Shortly after Troy L. Corriveau, accompanied by his wife, Lynn, became mission president on July 5, 1994, he recognized that the Bangkok District was operating very much like a stake and, in his opinion, should be one. Not many changes and advances were required to be ready. In April 1995 President Corriveau submitted forms recommending that a stake be organized. Soon, he received word that the stake had been approved and that Elder Neal A. Maxwell would be returning along with Elder Tai of the Asia Area Presidency to organize the new stake on June 17 and 18, 1995. After interviewing potential candidates for stake president and other offices, Elder Maxwell told President Corriveau that there were many strong men to choose from.[41] Thipparat Kitsaward, who served previously as Bangkok District president, was sustained as the first president of the Bangkok Thailand Stake. He chose Suchat Chaichana, country CES director, as first counselor and Seksan Siriphan as second couselor. The stake consisted of 2,260 members in five wards and three branches.

Of special significance was the selection of Brother Pornchai Juntratip as Thailand's first stake patriarch. Brother Pornchai has been blind since his teenage years. He met the missionaries when he was in his late twenties.

When Thailand's first stake was organized in June 1995 by Elder Neal A. Maxwell of the Quorum of the Twelve, he selected Thipparat Kitsaward, formerly district president, to lead the Bangkok Stake. He is shown here with his wife, Buathong. (Photo by author)

They asked him if he had heard of Joseph Smith or the Church, and he responded that he had not. They told him of Joseph Smith's first vision and invited him to kneel and pray and ask Heavenly Father if what they had said was true. Brother Pornchai said, "When I got up from my knees, I had this soft, warm feeling down my spine."[42]

The elders brought him braille editions of the Book of Mormon and a copy of James E. Talmage's book *The Articles of Faith*—both in English. Fortunately, his father had helped him learn English when he was a boy. Later, Brother Pornchai com-

Pornchai Juntratip, Thailand's first patriarch, is blind, yet he holds a master's degree in English from BYU. (Courtesy David Mitchell/LDS International Magazines)

pleted a home-study course and received an American high school diploma. He believed he had been prepared for the elders' visit. Pornchai was baptized on December 6, 1976, at the age of twenty-eight.

Subsequently, Brother Pornchai studied English literature at BYU—Hawaii and BYU in Provo, where he received a bachelor's degree in 1983 and his master's degree in 1986. After he returned to Bangkok, the Church hired him as a translator of seminary and institute manuals. At first the process was cumbersome because he used tape recorders to record his translations, but he taught himself to use a Thai-language typewriter, which he soon replaced with a computer.

A couple years after returning home, Pornchai married Kwanjai, a returned missionary. Their marriage was sealed in the Manila temple in June 1990, when the large group went there. Their first son was born in August 1991. His name, Pituporn, means "patriarchal blessing," which can also be interpreted to mean "blessing to his father."

When Elder Maxwell began the interview process to select new stake and ward officers, he told the individuals who were involved that it would not be necessary to select a stake patriarch if a spiritually prepared person were not available. After interviewing Brother Pornchai, Elder Maxwell said, "Brother Pornchai is a patriarch." Brother Pornchai, though young at forty-two years of age, has a spiritually mature soul. He is, said a colleague, "a man without guile, untouched by worldly influences."[43]

ESTABLISHING THE CHURCH IN CAMBODIA

Since the days of the Vietnam War, when many LDS servicemen served in Cambodia, Church leaders in Southeast Asia have looked forward to the time when the restored gospel could be established there. Groups of Latter-day Saints, usually hardly more than families or a couple of members, held Church services together in Phnom Penh in the late 1960s and early 1970s. Many missionaries from Thailand also crossed into Cambodia to renew their visas during that time.

The 1990s have proven to be the moment in the Lord's timetable to allow the Church to take hold there. The following section[44] is the record President Larry R. White kept of developments leading to the establishment of the Church in Cambodia.

> ### STEP BY STEP TOWARD THE OPENING OF CAMBODIA
> *Larry R. White*
>
> March 1993—Arrangements have been made to visit Phnom Penh, Cambodia, with Elder John K. Carmack in April. If conditions remain stable in Cambodia, it should not be difficult to gain permission for welfare missionaries to work there. We have some excellent contacts with the Cambodian government.
> April 1993—From April 2 to May 1, Elder John K.

Carmack and I, and our wives, together with a Cambodian member, Vichit Ith, visited Phnom Penh, Cambodia, and had very encouraging talks with the Vice Minister for Foreign Affairs who reported to us that his country has religious freedom. Elder Carmack left a blessing on the land. After elections on May 23 through May 28, it will be clearer whether we can do anything in the country; however, we had informal invitations to send English teachers. If peace can be established in Cambodia, I see no reason why welfare missionaries could not be sent there.

May 1993—The blessing left by Elder Carmack on the nation of Cambodia on April 30 seems to have had a very beneficial and even miraculous result. The elections were accompanied by much less violence than expected with the Khmer Rouge having little influence. If, after the new government is installed, the situation remains stable, there should be no reason why we cannot send welfare missionaries to Phnom Penh, the capital of Cambodia.

June 1993—I have noted with interest the dramatic changes in Cambodia, and how events there seem to be moving towards a peaceful solution after 23 years of war. In my opinion, this will lead to the introduction of missionaries into that country in the not-too-distant future.

July 1993—Conditions in Cambodia continue to improve, and our sole Cambodian member in Thailand is serving as an advisor to Cambodia's prime minister-elect, Prince Ranariddh. The Area Presidency is fully involved and is directing efforts toward opening the country for the work.

August 1993—The situation in Cambodia looks even better than the one in Laos.

September 1993—On September 24, an auspicious event took place when King Norodom Sihanonk promulgated the new Cambodian constitution. A Cambodian member in attendance at the ceremony expressed surprise at the remarkable spirit of harmony, unity, and reconciliation that was present among the various factions. He felt that this was a direct realization of the blessing left on the land by Elder Carmack on April 30. One particularly touching moment was when the Prime Minister, Prince Ranariddh, publicly embraced young members of the royal guard who formerly had been members of the Khmer Rouge.

The establishment of a permanent government in Cambodia clears the way for the Church to begin preparations to send welfare missionaries there.

December 1993—December was also noteworthy in that on December 8, the Area President, Elder Carmack, and I met with the Secretary of State for the Ministry of Religion in Cambodia, who assured us that if the Church submitted its application for recognition, that recognition would be quickly forthcoming. A trip to submit that application is planned for January 11.

January 1994—Work on opening Cambodia and Laos is progressing apace with special progress occurring on January 11. Translation into Cambodian of application documents was completed on January 21 with plans made to present them on February 8.

February 1994—On February 15, Brother Vic Ith lodged the Cambodian language application with the Ministry of Religion for recognition of the Church, and on February 28, I received word that recognition had been granted, although I have not yet seen any documentation. (Recognition was actually granted on February 26.)

March 1994—On March 23, I accompanied Elder Donald C. Dobson and his wife, Sister Sharlene Dobson [who were transferred from the India Bangalore Mission], to Phnom Penh as we opened Cambodia for missionary work. Sunday, March 27, marked the first Church services. They were held at the Hawaii Hotel and nine Cambodian investigators were present together with some other members. The Joseph Smith story and the message of the restored gospel of Jesus Christ were preached in the Cambodian language as translated by Wayne Wright, a returned missionary living in Phnom Penh.

Commencing on March 23, we visited various government and educational authorities exploring the welfare project which is to be established there by the Dobsons. A feeling of joy, excitement, and optimism prevailed as another country is opened in partial fulfillment of the Prophet Joseph's prophecy contained in the Wentworth Letter and reiterated in President Kimball's prophetic address in 1974. It is a great privilege to be a witness to and a participant in the events which mark the expansion of the work in Southeast Asia, which is moving forward with increasing rapidity. I am grateful for the foresight and vision of the Area Presidency which have permitted these things to happen.

May 1994—On May 9, I accompanied Elder and Sister Tai to Cambodia and on that day we witnessed the first convert baptism in Phnom Penh, Sister Pahl Mao. We also established an English teaching program for the missionary couple with the Ministry of Religion. On May 10, the welfare service project application document was submitted to the Ministry of Foreign Affairs, and on May 27, a missionary couple, Elder Ronald E. Oswald and Sister Dawn Oswald, was transferred from Bangkok to Cambodia.

June 1994—I was thrilled to hear that four Cambodian-speaking missionaries will be transferred from the United States to Phnom Penh, Cambodia.

President White's monthly descriptions of the steps followed to take the Church to Cambodia make clear the processes that are generally undertaken by Church leaders when the Church enters a new country. Since White's record ended, the process has continued in a most promising way.

On August 8, 1994, four Cambodian-speaking elders—Richard W. Henderson (California Anaheim Mission), Jamie T. Hipwell (Massachusetts Boston Mission), John T. Smith (California Fresno Mission), and Brian W. Strong (Washington D.C. South Mission)—were transferred to Phnom Penh. They hardly had their bags unpacked when they began teaching Cambodians. Forty investigators were waiting for them, and they baptized seven during their first month. Subsequently other elders were brought in, and by April 1995 eight Cambodian-speaking elders and four Vietnamese-speaking elders were serving in Phnom Penh. In March 1995 Cambodia was officially made part of the Thailand Bangkok Mission. Until then it had been part of the Asia Area Mission.[45]

By summer 1995 four couples, retired college and CES teachers, had also been sent to Phnom Penh to set up seminary and institute classes and to work with the Royal Agricultural University in setting up a prototype feed mill and a model cannery. The wives were engaged teaching English as a foreign language at the university and in other locations. To show its goodwill, the Church shipped forty thousand pounds of rice to Cambodia to help relieve the suffering of drought victims. A similar amount of used clothing was also sent and distributed to rural villagers. More help of this kind arrived later.

The missionaries have been restricted to working during daylight hours because security is questionable. They cannot work outside Phnom Penh, but its population of more than one hundred thousand provides enough to do. In June 1995 the Phnom Penh Branch was under the leadership of branch president Oya Shigeyuki, a Japanese member. At that time the branch began meeting in two different groups consisting of Cambodian speakers and Vietnamese speakers. President Oya presided over both groups.[46] On November 19, 1995, President Troy Corriveau of the Thailand Bangkok Mission organized the Phnom Penh First,

Second, and Third Branches—two for Cambodians and one for Vietnamese. With the creation of the second Cambodian-speaking branch, the Church procured a new French-style villa to serve as a meetinghouse. The building is large enough to serve a number of functions: the first floor contains the chapel, meeting hall and classroom; the second floor houses the service couple missionaries; the third floor is home to the proselyting elders; and the fourth floor is open for further expansion.

On January 21, 1996, President Corriveau organized the Phnom Penh District of the Church, the first district in that country. The first Cambodian branch president, Ohm Borin, was sustained the following March. His willingness to accept this important calling was typical of many in the developing countries of the world. Brother Borin was serving as a counselor in the Second Branch when he arrived at branch correlation meeting and learned that the humanitarian service missionary who had been branch president (and his wife) had suddenly departed the country for medical reasons. The district president asked Elder Ohm Borin if he would accept the responsibility of being branch president. Ohm Borin asked if there was not someone more qualified. The district president said he felt that Ohm Borin should be branch president and asked if he would accept the call. "He paused a moment, took a deep breath, straightened himself as the mantle fell on him, and said yes, and immediately and commandingly took charge of the correlation meeting."[47]

By the end of that year there were close to three hundred members in three branches. The number of proselyting missionaries rose to twelve by 1996.

To date the most important event in Cambodian Church history was the visit to Phnom Penh and dedication of that land for the preaching of the gospel by President Gordon B. Hinckley. On May 28, 1996, following the dedication of the Hong Kong Temple on May 26 and 27 and in company with his wife, Marjorie, Elder Joseph B. Wirthlin of the Quorum of the Twelve (who at that time was responsible for Church work in Asia) and his wife, Elisa, and

Elder John H. Groberg of the Asia Area Presidency and his wife, Jean, President Hinckley met with 439 members and investigators at a fireside at the Cambodiana Hotel. The next morning a much smaller group, mostly missionaries and Church leaders, gathered on grassy banks of the watery intersection of the Mekong, Tonle Sap, and Bassac Rivers, and President Hinckley offered a prayer upon Cambodia and dedicated that land for missionary work and the establishment of the restored gospel.[48]

In the months following President Hinckley's visit and prayer, the number of convert baptisms grew more rapidly (111 people were baptized in August, September, and October). And the added numbers made necessary the creation of the Phnom Penh Fourth Branch. A third building was procured, located centrally about halfway between the other two buildings. President Oya was called to lead the new branch and Elder Chea Pyden, a young and able local convert was called to preside over the first branch. At the end of 1996, missionaries and leaders were hoping that continued political stability would allow the Church to expand outside the capital city.

Since completion of this manuscript, the dual–prime minister system that temporarily sustained peace in Cambodia was ended when Hun Sen, one of the prime ministers, overthrew Prince Ranariddh, the other prime minister, and ousted him from government. During the upheaval and violence that accompanied those events, the president of the new Cambodia Phnom Penh Mission and all of the foreign missionaries were forced to flee from the country. At this date, August 1997, the situation has not been resolved, although it is anticipated that missionary work will resume as soon as political matters are stable.

THE CHURCH IN MYANMAR AND LAOS

Myanmar (Burma) and Laos are also within the purview of the Thailand Bangkok mission president's responsibility. Through the years, a number of missionaries have gone into Burma from

Thailand. For a time a branch was organized there, but because of inaccessibility from outside and dissension inside, the branch was dissolved and no official activities were reported in late 1995. President Gordon B. Hinckley dedicated Burma for the preaching of the gospel on September 8, 1987, on the shore of Lake Inya in Rangoon. Elder Jacob de Jager, Asia Area President, and Sister Hinckley, were present.[49]

Laos, on the other hand, promises a situation similar to Cambodia. Forty tons each of rice and clothes were contributed to the Laotian government's efforts to alleviate suffering caused by a drought. By late 1996 formal arrangements to send in humanitarian missionaries have not been completed.

NOTES

1. See Leon B. Gold, "Thailand," in Donald E. Hoke, *The Church in Asia* (Chicago: Moody Press, 1975), p. 636; see also "Thailand," in Patrick Johnstone, *Operation World* (Grand Rapids, Mich.: Zondervan Publishing House, 1993), pp. 530–33.

2. Gordon B. Hinckley, Journals, 9 December 1964.

3. As quoted in Hinckley, Journals, 2 November 1966.

4. As quoted in ibid.

5. Hinckley, Journal, 2 November 1966. The entire prayer is printed in: Spencer J. Palmer, *The Church Encounters Asia* (Salt Lake City: Deseret Book Co., 1970), pp. 129–31.

6. See ibid.

7. See ibid., by date.

8. Larry R. White, "A Short History of the Church in Thailand," Thailand Bangkok Mission Manual, 1993; copy in possession of the author.

9. Craig B. Christensen, "The Beginnings in Thailand," *Improvement Era* 73 (March 1970): 32.

10. Anan Eldredge, interview by the author, Bangkok, Thailand, 8 September 1995, tape recording.

11. Christensen, "Beginnings in Thailand," pp. 33–34.

12. Ibid., p. 33.

13. See Alan H, Hess, Journal, 30 November 1968, LDS Church Archives.

14. Larry R. White, "A Conversion Story: Srilaksana Gottsche," Bangkok, Thailand, September 1993; copy in possession of the author.

15. Ibid.

16. See Joan Porter Ford and LaRene Porter Gaunt, "Raised by a Queen," in "The Gospel Dawning in Thailand," *Ensign* 25 (September 1995): 55. See also Srilaksana Suntarahut Gottsche, interview by the author, Bangkok, Thailand, 8 September 1995, tape recording.

17. Srilaksana interview.

18. Paul D. Morris to Dale Patterson, 19 October 1974, quoted in Dale Patterson, "One Thoughtless Moment" (Research paper, Brigham Young University, 1974), p. 15, in possession of the author.

19. See Manoth Suksabjarern, "Roman Catholic, Protestant, and Latter-day Saints Missions in Thailand: An Historical Survey" (master's thesis, Brigham Young University, 1977), pp. 89–90 and most of chapter 6.

Even in the 1990s, the Buddha-head issue remains a problem in Thailand. That one moment has not been forgotten by Thai bureaucrats or visa officers. When problems occur, the details of the affair are dredged up again as though it had happened yesterday. That only two young individuals were involved has seldom been remembered.

20. Bart Seliger, interview by the author, Bangkok, Thailand, 8 September 1995, tape recording.

21. Peter Ashman, "Thailand: An Example of Mass Media Utilization in the Mission Field" (research paper, Brigham Young University, 1980), pp. 6–7; copy in posession of the author.

22. Ibid., p. 8.

23. Marion D. Hanks Oral History, interviews by Gordon Irving, 1983, James Moyle Oral History Program, LDS Church Archives, typescript, p. 9.

24. See Lynellyn D. Long, *Ban Vinai, The Refugee Camp* (New York: Columbia University Press, 1993), chapter 3.

25. In April 1983, *Gist*, a U.S. State Department periodical, reported: "Since the fall of the noncommunist governments of Laos, Kampuchea (Cambodia), and Vietnam in 1975, more than 1.5 million refugees have fled from Indochina. More than 600,000 of them have sought asylum in Thailand; 500,000 have sought asylum in nine other first-asylum destinations (Hong Kong, Macau, Indonesia, Malaysia, Philippines, Singapore, Japan, South Korea, and Taiwan); and approximately 410,000 have left Vietnam directly for resettlement elsewhere. Since 1975, the US has resettled 629,000 refugees."

26. Abridged from Marion D. Hanks et al., "International Health," pp. 13–17.

27. Rita Edmonds, telephone interview by the author, Provo, Utah, 28 December 1995.

28. Hanks Oral History, p. 14.

29. Only one or two articles on the Mormon refugee effort were printed in Church periodicals. Elder Hanks did not want wide publicity for the project. The best article was "Helping refugees begin new life," *Church News*, 21 March 1981, pp. 7–10.

30. Ibid., p. 16.

31. Mary Ellen Edmunds, who has been influential in welfare services work, captures well the feeling of the work at the camp near Phanat Nikom in her chapter titled "Are We Not All Refugees?" in *Love Is a Verb* (Salt Lake City: Deseret Book Co., 1995).

32. See Ford and Gaunt, "Gospel Dawning in Thailand," p. 54; and Suchat Chaichana, "Church Education System, Thailand Historical Report, 1993"; copy in possession of the author.

33. See David Mitchell, "The Saints of Thailand," *Tambuli* 17 (May 1993): 44–45; and Anan Eldredge interview.

34. David N. Phelps, interview by the author, Bangkok, Thailand, 7 September 1995, tape recording.

35. Anan Eldredge interview.

36. Mitchell, "Saints of Thailand," p. 42.

37. White, "Short History," 4.

38. Phelps interview; and Larry R. White, "An Apostolic Blessing in Bangkok, June 1992," typescript in possession of the author. I have drawn on both sources for this section.

39. White, "Apostolic Blessing."

40. See "Anand appointed premier," *Bangkok Post*,11 June 1992, p. 1.

41. Troy Corriveau, interview by the author, Bangkok, Thailand, 7 September 1995, tape recording.

42. David Mitchell, "Pornchai Juntratip, Spiritually Prepared," *Tambuli* 17 (February 1993): 44.

43. Ibid., p. 43.

44. Larry R. White, Personal Writings, by date, copy in possession of the author. Another source for this section is White's "The Opening of Cambodia," December 1994, copy in possession of the author. Brother Vichit Ith, who is mentioned below, was living in Thailand when these events first began. His relationship to several persons in influential positions helped in the establishment of the Church in Cambodia. In late 1996 he was living in Phnom Penh, where he held an appointment as a special adviser to the new prime minister. He also works as president of the national airlines of Cambodia.

45. Corriveau interview.

46. See Shane H. Harrison, "Brief History of The Church of Jesus Christ of Latter-day Saints in Cambodia, June 1995–December 1996," correspondence with the author, 18 December 1996.

47. Ibid.

48. See "President Hinckley dedicates Cambodia," *Church News*, 8 June 1996, pp. 3, 5; and Leland D. and Joyce B. White, "Gospel Gains Foothold in Cambodia," *Ensign* 27 (January 1997): 77–78.

49. See Sheri L. Dew, *Go Forward with Faith: The Biography of Gordon B. Hinckley* (Salt Lake City: Deseret Book Co., 1996), pp. 452–53.

16

VIETNAM

1962–1996

A Silver Thread Shining Through

Speaking in general conference in 1962, Elder Gordon B. Hinckley drew the analogy of a tapestry to illustrate the growth of the Church in Asia. He said, "The Lord is weaving the tapestry of his grand design in those foreign parts." Six years later, after seeing the Vietnam War escalate and following a number of visits to Vietnam, he borrowed from the same analogy. He called attention "to that silver thread, small but radiant with hope, shining through the dark tapestry of war." He was speaking of the "bridgehead," small and weak, that would one day grow and "spring forth a great work affecting for good the lives of large numbers of our Father's children who live in that part of the world. Of that I have certain faith."[1] Spoken at the height of the Vietnam War, these were words of faith and courage.

Even at the end of the twentieth century, to most Americans the word *Vietnam* recalls unhappy memories that are best forgotten. The decade of the 1960s, during which the Vietnam War was at its height, was a time of domestic turmoil and discontent in the United States as well as in Vietnam. The spiral of economic inflation that continued into the 1980s had its beginning during the Vietnam War. Other problems in America and abroad also had their origins at that time. Never in the history of the United

States, with the exception of the Civil War, had the American populace been so divided regarding an issue. Never before had so many Americans refused to serve in the armed forces during a time of war. Debate and argumentation were abundant wherever people met. The nation was almost rent apart by strong disagreements among honest people. In addition to these problems, the war brought brutality, pain, and suffering in Vietnam.

But while the war in Vietnam grew in intensity during the early 1960s, among those who were sent there was a small number of LDS servicemen who acted as advisers to the South Vietnamese forces. On June 30, 1962, President Robert S. Taylor of the Southern Far East Mission organized the first LDS servicemen's group in Saigon, with Cecil L. "Bud" Cavender as group leader, Reed A. Prestgard as first counselor, and Maurice H. Lee as second counselor. Cavender, along with five other men, had held what was probably the first LDS Church service in Vietnam at Tan Son Nhut Air Base on February 25, 1962.

The group had grown since then. The work of this small group of fewer than fifty Saints was impressive. They not only taught the gospel to American service personnel but also shared the message with their Vietnamese associates. On November 3, 1962, Captain John T. Mullennex of the U.S. Air Force was baptized. He was baptized by his friend, Captain Maurice H. Lee.[2] Soon after, on February 3, 1963, two Vietnamese women, Duong Thuy Van and Nguyen Thi Thuy, joined the Church.[3] They, as well as Mullennex, were baptized in a font made from a five-hundred-gallon water purification tank.

Several LDS families were living in Saigon at that time. Sister Patricia Bean had taught them English at the Vietnamese-American Association, but she also taught them the gospel. She was the first missionary to the Vietnamese people in their own country. Sisters Van and Thuy are believed to be the first Vietnamese to join the Church in Vietnam. Sister Van later translated *Joseph Smith's Testimony*, the first Church publication in the Vietnamese language.[4] In September 1962, the group added a

The "Bien Hoa LDS Servicemen's Group" chapel was constructed in 1965 under Captain Ray Young's supervision. This picture was taken in 1971 while Virgil N. Kovalenko was group leader. Included in the picture are Nguyen N. Thach and three of his nine living children. Thach's plight following the fall of Saigon was the impetus for the creation of VASAA, an international humanitarian organization to assist with refugee and other causes. (Courtesy Virgil N. Kovalenko)

Sunday School, and in November they also organized a Primary, with Bud's wife, Kay, as president.

The buildup of American and other troops (Latter-day Saints from Taiwan, South Korea, the Philippines, Australia, and Europe also participated in the war) continued during the next three years, and by the end of 1965 several changes had been made in local Church organization. In May 1965 President Jay A. Quealy set apart Harper K. Morris as LDS servicemen's coordinator in South Vietnam. Soon after his appointment, Harper organized a servicemen's group at Bien Hoa Air Base, fifteen miles from Saigon. The Bien Hoa group was the first of many similar groups outside Saigon. It is noteworthy that by acquiring surplus materials and exchanging labor with an Italian contractor, this group constructed its own chapel before that year ended. No Church funds were used. It was a humble building with backless benches in the main meeting room, but it was a place of spiritual retreat for many servicemen. The Bien Hoa chapel was the only LDS chapel ever constructed in Vietnam. It was not unusual for servicemen to meet in small groups (sometimes as few as two) to renew their covenants and strengthen one another in the faith. The following report from the *Church News* in July 1966 illustrates this point:

> The following meeting of the Ban Me Thout group was held at 1300 hours on Sunday, July 10:
>
> Meeting: Sacrament
> Opening song: Redeemer of Israel
> Opening prayer: Nicholas Dereta
> Sacrament song: I Know That My Redeemer Lives
> Sacrament administered by James Hatfield and Nicholas Dereta
> Speaker: James Hatfield, Nicholas Dereta
> Closing song: I Need Thee Every Hour
> Closing prayer: James Hatfield
> Members present, two—members absent, none[5]

After February 1965 the buildup of American troops was rapid. By December 1965 there were fifteen hundred LDS servicemen in Vietnam, and President Keith E. Garner made South Vietnam one of four zones of the Southern Far East Mission. The South Vietnam Zone was further divided into three districts: the Northern District with headquarters at Da Nang; the Central District at Nha Trang, near Cam Rahn Bay; and the Southern District in Saigon. By May 1966 the estimated number of LDS military people had grown to twenty-two hundred. Seeing missionary opportunities, the president of the Southern District called six men to act as district missionaries. This number later reached as many as fifteen part-time missionaries. They had success with Americans as well as among the Vietnamese. In 1966, there were more than thirty Vietnamese numbered among the Saints.

Although the number of Vietnamese Saints was growing,

more Vietnamese women than men were in the Church. Vietnamese women worked for the U.S. military or the U.S. government as secretaries, receptionists, cooks, housekeepers, and so forth. Many of these converts were brought into the Church by LDS personnel for whom they worked. Vietnamese men, on the other hand, were frequently tied up in work away from home or in the Vietnamese armed forces and were not easily available to those who carried the gospel message.

During the buildup years and throughout the war, a number of nonmilitary Latter-day Saints were in Saigon. Among them were an architect named Robert J. Lewis and his family. He served in Vietnam for seven years, and Church services were held at his home for much of that time. Other civilian contractors and academics remained in Saigon for shorter periods.

Nguyen Cao Minh, the first Vietnamese elder, was ordained on October 2, 1966. Minh had been converted to the Church in Biloxi, Mississippi, while training for a military assignment in 1963. According to Richard C. Holloman Jr., who served as a missionary in Saigon and who studied the history of the Latter-day Saints in Vietnam, Minh "had the most far-reaching good effect on the Church in Vietnam of any Vietnamese member of the Church. In spite of military assignments that often kept him away from Saigon, Brother Minh gave over ten years of leadership to the Vietnamese priesthood holders and continually encouraged the translation and missionary work."[6]

THE DEDICATION OF SOUTH VIETNAM FOR MISSIONARY WORK

Church leaders in Salt Lake City and Hong Kong kept a watchful eye on the LDS service people in Vietnam. As their numbers grew, General Authorities, particularly Elders Gordon B. Hinckley, Marion D. Hanks, Ezra Taft Benson, and Bishop Victor L. Brown, visited South Vietnam to encourage them to remain faithful to their families and the Church. On such a visit in October 1966 Elders

Hinckley and Hanks came to Vietnam with instructions from President David O. McKay to dedicate South Vietnam for the preaching of the restored gospel, if they were impressed by the Spirit to do so.

After visiting with servicemen at conferences in Da Nang and Nha Trang, on October 30 the visiting authorities met with 205 civilian workers and servicemen and women on the top floor of the Caravelle Hotel in downtown Saigon. Elder Hanks encouraged the fighting men to remember both battles they were waging, the one against the enemy in Vietnam and the "battle everyone is fighting; the battle to return to our Father in Heaven."[7] (The Church was particularly concerned with "the danger of physical injury and death from [enemy] insurgency, and infringement of personal chastity." The home teaching program was designed so that every member would have regular contact with the Church, although finding all of the members was an ongoing task of considerable difficulty.)[8]

Elder Gordon B. Hinckley dedicated South Vietnam for the preaching of the gospel on Sunday, October 30, 1966, in the roof garden room of the Caravelle Hotel in Saigon. Navy Chief Lou Pollister is shown here with Elder Hinckley following the service. (Courtesy Lou Pollister)

Elder Hinckley then spoke at length. When he concluded, he paused and then informed the congregation that President David O. McKay had authorized him to dedicate South Vietnam. He offered a beautifully worded, exceptionally appropriate dedicatory prayer. He thanked the Lord for America and the U.S. Constitution and the freedoms it guaranteed. "We have seen in other parts of Asia," he prayed, "the manner in which Thou hast turned the hand and the work of the adversary to the good and the blessing of many of Thy children. And now we call upon Thee at this time that Thou wilt similarly pour out Thy spirit upon this land." He pleaded with the Lord that there might be peace and that freedom-loving men might be allowed their agency. He asked that an added measure of the Lord's Spirit might be poured out upon both the nonmembers and those who already had the gospel, so that the people might be more willing to listen to the message of the Savior and so that the members would be more eager to share the gospel. He also asked the Lord to "open the way for the coming of missionaries and make their labors fruitful of great and everlasting good in the lives of the people."[9]

One might question the wisdom of dedicating a land for the preaching of the gospel at a time of war. Traditionally, the Church dedicates countries when missionary work is about to commence or shortly after it has started. The usual pattern has been to remove missionaries from areas of active warfare, not to send them in. Nevertheless, Elder Hinckley, Elder Hanks, the mission president over the area, and the servicemen who led the Church in Vietnam all believed this was a different situation. Somehow, notwithstanding the grim horror of war, they expected the gospel to be established in Vietnam. In Elder Hinckley's conference address of April 1968, he said: "I make no defense of . . . war from this pulpit. . . . I seek only to call your attention to that silver thread, small but radiant with hope, shining through the dark tapestry of war—namely, the establishment of a bridgehead, small and frail now; but which somehow, under the mysterious ways of God, will be strengthened, and from which someday shall spring forth a great work affecting for good the lives of large numbers of our Father's children who live in that part of the world. Of that I have certain faith."[10]

Theirs was not a naive hope. Particularly in 1966, when Elder Hinckley dedicated the land, there was still a widespread belief that South Vietnam and the United States would win the war. Furthermore, many LDS servicemen and women were teaching the gospel to Vietnamese friends, and thirty or more had already joined the Church. All groups—military missionaries, new members, and potential investigators—needed the Lord's special blessings. Elder Hinckley said in his dedicatory prayer, "And so we feel it expedient at this time . . . to dedicate this land and invoke Thy blessings upon it."

There were other reasons for the hope held for Vietnam as a potential mission field. Most important was that Roman Catholics and Protestants had long been established in the nation and claimed 10 or 11 percent of the populace—possibly the highest percentage of Christians in any Asian nation except the Philippines and South Korea. Catholic missionary work began in the sixteenth century, and by the middle of the seventeenth century there were three hundred thousand baptized persons. Father Rhodes, the outstanding figure of the time, transliterated the Vietnamese (Chinese) characters into a script that is still in use today. When the Communists took control of the north, more than eight hundred thousand Catholic refugees came to South Vietnam from the north. Protestant missionary work began in 1911. Over the years they translated the Bible, which was of course helpful to Latter-day Saint proselyting efforts. A high percentage of the people were not followers of Buddhism or other Asian religions. Animism was common, and although LDS Church leaders were probably not aware of the fact, animists have come into Christianity in reasonable numbers and in all likelihood would have been attracted to Mormonism.

Whatever the justifications for dedicating Vietnam, to faithful Latter-day Saints only one reason really mattered: Elder Hinckley was told by President McKay to dedicate Vietnam if he felt impressed by the Spirit to do so. As it turned out, this Apostle of the Lord did receive a spiritual impression to dedicate the land, and he acted on it. Time is telling the full story.

Elder Hinckley had first visited Vietnam in April 1963, but he returned in 1966, 1967, and 1968. He was torn inside by the pain and suffering he observed. But he observed true manhood amid the misery. In 1966 he said, "No more faithful members are found anywhere in the world than among our servicemen."

A BROKEN SALTINE CRACKER
Joseph McPhie

I was asked to be president of the Southern Vietnam District, headquartered in Saigon. We had about twenty small Church units in the southern area, and every weekend we'd visit a few of them. My counselor and I went one Sunday morning to meet with members in one of these barren little outposts. We tried to contact the group leader and several other members, but they were all out on patrol. We were ready to leave but at the last minute decided to check the base chapel to see if anyone had shown up.

It was quite dark as we stood at the entrance of the chapel looking down toward the pulpit area. At first we thought nobody was there; then we saw a movement. As we walked down we saw two young men—one was a priest, one an elder. These two kids were standing there in their combat outfits with their guns set aside. Their group leader hadn't shown up and the elder was going to go ahead and hold the meeting.

[As part of the sacrament service] they had broken a saltine cracker in two and they had a canteen; one was going to drink out of the canteen, the other out of the cup. I've often thought what a beautiful picture that was of "where two are met in my name" (Doctrine and Covenants 6:32). We broke the cracker one more time. I drank out of the cup and my counselor drank out of the canteen. Here were these young kids, ten thousand miles from home, nobody knowing where they were. But even without leadership, they went ahead with a meeting. We had one of the most beautiful spiritual meetings I've ever had in my life—just the four of us.[11]

Elder Hanks, too, had direct responsibility for this area, and he, along with President Garner, visited Vietnam on many occasions. On military aircraft of some variety, they traveled to many stations in and near the battlefields. Concerning that period he later recalled: "It was a sobering and terrible time. We met men on Sunday or some other day of the week who would go out and be killed. I wrote many letters home. . . . I had so many sad experiences. When I'd get home I'd get a letter from a wife or a mother who would say, 'We thank you for telling us about our boy. Before your letter arrived, we had had no word from the Defense Department.'"[12] Elder Hanks' words provided a measure of solace in times of grief.

American involvement in the Vietnam War reached its peak in 1968, when more than fifty-five hundred LDS servicemen and servicewomen were assigned to Vietnam. (Statistics show that Latter-day Saints were consistently 1 percent of the total number of American forces throughout the war.) Numbers were constantly changing, but by 1969 the Southern District had twenty branches and groups, "each presided over by a president, two counselors, and clerk, under the direction of the Vietnam Southern District Presidency and twelve District High Councilmen. The district is similar to a stake in the built-up areas of Zion and the branches and groups are similar to wards. A program of priesthood, Sunday School, Relief Society, MIA, home teaching, missionary activities, and sacrament meeting is carried on in some of these branches and groups; priesthood and sacrament meetings, home teaching, and missionary work are carried on in all of them."[13]

In addition to the Saigon Branch, there were sixty groups throughout South Vietnam. For record purposes, all Vietnamese members were part of the Saigon Branch. Six LDS chaplains were assigned to Vietnam. In order to help and supervise Church activities, President Garner, and later Presidents W. Brent Hardy, G. Carlos Smith (of the Southeast Asia Mission), William S. Bradshaw, and Jerry D. Wheat visited the war zone at least every other month and usually monthly but sometimes more often. All five men found the work exhausting because of the intense pace that was required, but it was also highly rewarding as they met and counseled with servicemen, local Saints, and investigators. For a little less than a year, from November 1, 1969, until October 20, 1970, the Vietnam Church Zone was transferred to the Southeast Asia Mission. But because of transportation problems and unequal burdens on mission presidents, this arrangement proved unworkable. Hence, Vietnam was transferred back to the Hong Kong–Taiwan Mission.

In his study of the Church in South Vietnam, Richard C. Holloman summarized the extent of the Church's efforts to serve the members in Vietnam: "There were many evidences of deep concern for the Saints among the leaders of the Church on all levels. Elder Hinckley arranged for special Church films and films of conference sessions to be sent regularly to the servicemen. KSL conducted special interviews with LDS servicemen geared specifically for Utah audiences. The zone presidency arranged for a special Christmas message to come from the First Presidency of the Church to the servicemen. District meetings were often held to plan ways to incorporate Vietnamese members into the full workings of the branch. There was a continual concern for helping the Vietnamese Saints become more capable of leading themselves."[14]

In 1971 the U.S. government began removing troops from Vietnam. President Richard M. Nixon had campaigned for president on a promise to get America out of the war. The withdrawal of troops signaled to Church officials to prepare local leaders to operate the Church in Vietnam. With this in mind, on May 24, 1971, Southern District president Myrne R. Riley called Nguyen Cao Minh to be the first Vietnamese president of the Saigon Branch. Minh was released several months later because of a new military assignment, but his successor, Ralph Kurihara, selected two other Vietnamese elders, Nguyen Van The (pronounced "Tay") and Dang Thong Nhat, as his counselors. Brother The later replaced Kurihara and served as the last branch president until the 1990s.

William S. Bradshaw became president of the Hong Kong Mission, which included South Vietnam, during the summer of 1971. Since his first visit to Vietnam, he recognized the growing need to bring full-time missionaries into the country, largely to take the place of the departing servicemen. The Americans who were in Vietnam then "had a sense of destiny and a sense of the importance of building the Church among the local Vietnamese."[15] From that time onward, President Bradshaw made preparations for the entry of elders from Hong Kong.

He met with Phan The Ngoc, an attorney who had obtained legal recognition for the Church in 1967, and obtained documents assuring that the Church still had the right to exist and own property. On obtaining this assurance, Bradshaw wrote to U.S. ambassador Ellsworth Bunker to ascertain whether there were any problems or obstacles from an American point of view. At the same time, March 1972, President Bradshaw discussed the question of sending elders to Saigon with Elder James A. Cullimore, an Assistant to the Council of the Twelve. On receiving encouragement from him, Bradshaw wrote to Elder Marion G. Romney and explained his feelings and justifications for wanting to move missionaries into Saigon. This letter turned out to be poorly timed. It arrived on Elder Romney's desk at about the same time as did some grim news concerning the war and delayed the process for a time.

Finally, in November 1972 President Bradshaw received a reply to his March letter to Ambassador Bunker. It contained much legal information of worth, but more important was its positive tone, which led Bradshaw to believe that there was nothing in particular to worry about. Saigon was quite secure even though sometimes there were battles only fifteen or twenty miles away. Military advisers such as William R. Heaton Jr., a former Hong Kong missionary but now a Ph.D. in political science and an officer in the air force, had access to intelligence reports, all of which were favorable with respect to what the Church could anticipate in the near future.

Contrary to the situation in Indonesia, where the elders entered the country and then began work on the translation of Church books and literature, in Vietnam local members and American personnel who had formerly served missions in Hong Kong but who had learned the Vietnamese language had begun translating Church materials into Vietnamese as early as 1963. By the early 1970s a number of tracts, pamphlets, and other items were in print in Vietnamese. In 1970 W. Brent Hardy, President Bradshaw's predecessor, had established an official translation committee and set apart Sister Cong Ton Nu Tuong-Vy as head translator. Sister Vy, as she is known, a former high school teacher and a person of royal heritage (the word *Cong* in her name means "countess" in Vietnamese), led out in the translation of the Book of Mormon into Vietnamese, a project that was well under way by 1972.

Mrs. Vy was introduced to the gospel by Robert J. Lewis, who had met her in her successful real estate office in Saigon. Elder Hinckley had authorized raising funds for a possible future chapel, and Brother Lewis, an architect, thought he would survey possible land for a building. He asked a trusted Vietnamese friend who the most honest real estate person in Saigon was. He sent Lewis to SVP (from the French *s'il vous plait*), where he met Mrs. Vy. She later described SVP as an "information and travel service," but she evidently also handled real estate. In Lewis's words, "I could not know at the time that I was looking at the person whom the Lord had chosen to translate the Book of Mormon, the Doctrine and Covenants, and the Pearl of Great Price into Vietnamese. I thought I was there to buy real estate." She drove him around Saigon as they looked for potential building sites. In the process she asked which church he represented, what its members believed, and so on. Her interest was sincere, and she asked to be taught the gospel. Brother Lewis and a returned missionary,

Cong Ton Nu Tuong-Vy, Sister "Vy," was the principal translator of the Standard Works into Vietnamese. Beside her is Nguyen Van The, Saigon Branch president at the time of the fall in 1975. (Courtesy Virgil N. Kovalenko)

Captain William Shumate, taught her the discussions in her home in Saigon. Like many others, she was baptized at the "villa" where the Saigon Branch met, in a baptismal font constructed out of a cistern for water storage. A member had welded steel steps leading up onto the cistern and down into it. Brother Lewis baptized Sister Vy, and Brother Shumate confirmed her.[16]

Brother Lewis, who was branch president at the time, asked Sister Vy to help with the translation of the *Joseph Smith's Testimony* pamphlet. (Evidently the earlier translation had fallen into disuse.) When another translator failed to produce a satisfactory translation, she decided to attempt the job herself. "I took the pamphlet home," remembered Sister Vy, "and stayed up all night reading it. As I read, something strange happened to me. It was as if someone unseen was helping me understand. The first translator translated word for word; but as I finally understood part of the testimony, I put it aside and wrote my translation in my own words. I translated according to the thoughts and feelings impressed upon me. I did not know it at the time, but I was translating by the Spirit."[17]

The Vietnamese members read the new translation and said they understood what it meant. Sister Vy was then asked to translate four or five other tracts and pamphlets. As she worked on those pamphlets, she "began to love the Church and the doctrines and teachings of the gospel."

When Sister Vy was asked to help with the translation of the Book of Mormon, she sold her very successful business, secluded herself in a cottage she had built on a betel nut farm outside of Saigon, and devoted her full time to the work of translation. "When trying to translate the difficult parts," she later wrote, "I pondered and prayed. I would often dream at night about the parts and see where I could find help in my library. So I began to write. And as I translated, I pondered. I forgot myself. It was almost as if someone else was helping me write."[18] The undertaking took two years, but before it could be published, Saigon fell. She, along with the committee, also translated the Doctrine and Covenants and the Pearl of Great Price. These products too were not published until after the fall of Saigon. Sister Vy did not see the published versions of her work until 1985. She was brought out of Vietnam to Canada by VASAA (the Veterans Association for Service Activities Abroad) in early 1987. In April 1988, again through the help of VASAA, Sister Vy attended general conference, did her own temple work, and had an emotional reunion with President Gordon B. Hinckley, whom she had known from his many visits to Vietnam.

On January 27, 1973, the warring powers announced a cease-fire, the forthcoming withdrawal of all American military personnel, and the release of American prisoners of war from Hanoi. (Among the POWs who were released were a number of Latter-day Saints. Best known were Jay R. Jensen and Larry Chesley, who wrote books about their prison experiences, but there were others, such as Jay Hess and David "Jack" Rollins, who were introduced at general priesthood meeting in April 1973 and whose stories became known within the Church.) Withdrawal of American troops from South Vietnam was swift; the last troops left on March 29. Before that date President Bradshaw began receiving notes from Church leaders in Salt Lake City, among them Elder Gordon B. Hinckley, who asked about the status of the Church in Vietnam and particularly about what plans were being made for the Saigon Branch when the withdrawal of the LDS servicemen was complete.

With these questions on his mind, in late February 1973 President Bradshaw went to Vietnam. He asked again the questions he had been asking for more than a year: What's the prognosis for the war? Are the Vietnamese forces going to be strong enough to hold? What are the prospects for good missionary housing? What about medical care? How many LDS American government people will be on hand to lend stability to the branch and the work of the missionaries? What about missionary security? Anticipating the assignment of missionaries to Saigon, President Bradshaw asked members in Saigon to translate the six-lesson missionary plan before the elders entered the country.

Before President Bradshaw left Saigon on February 26, he was satisfied that all conditions were positive or at least satisfactory. Before leaving for Hong Kong, he pleaded with the Lord for a confirmation of his positive feelings. "What came," President Bradshaw said, "was an affirmation of our feelings and a very sweet peace concerning the future of the Church in South Vietnam."[19] This feeling removed all reservations from Bradshaw's mind. He wrote to Elder Hinckley the day after he returned to Hong Kong and firmly recommended that missionaries be sent. He also mentioned the high quality of the branch facilities and the housing that was available for the elders, and he described the brethren who would be remaining in Saigon, men such as Dr. Lester Bush, a physician who was connected with the U.S. Embassy, and several others.

President Bradshaw described the events of the next two weeks: "A few days intervened . . . and then I wrote on March 7 a formal letter to the Missionary Committee restating all the things that I had written Elder Hinckley privately. On March 13 I received this letter from the Missionary Committee over the signature of Elder Hinckley: 'Dear President Bradshaw, Your letter of February 27'—this was my letter to him, not the formal letter to the Committee—'concerning the work in Saigon was read to the First Presidency and the Twelve. After consideration of the matter, it was determined that you might be permitted to send four missionaries to Saigon.' That's as far as I got in the letter when I literally shouted for joy. I really did, and the missionaries who were in the office came running to see who had shot me."[20]

After President Bradshaw calmed down, he read the rest of the letter, which included some precautions. Among other requirements, the Brethren suggested that Bradshaw should obtain the written approval of the parents of the missionaries who were to go to Saigon.

The letters from the parents were obtained, and on April 6, 1973, President Bradshaw, in company with Elders James L. Christensen, Richard C. Holloman Jr., David T. Posey, and Colin B. Van Orman, flew to Saigon. They immediately established themselves at the branch headquarters, a villa at #253 Thanh Thai, in a lovely area near Cholon, the Chinese sector of the city.

The elders began formal study of Vietnamese on April 7, and on the following day they looked on as President Bradshaw reorganized the Saigon Branch presidency. Nguyen Van The was set apart as branch president, with Dang Thong Nhat and Lester Bush as counselors. The membership was around ninety-five, including four active Melchizedek Priesthood holders and six or seven Aaronic Priesthood bearers.

With only a few exceptions, the elders followed the normal proselyting procedures of LDS missions. Going door-to-door was neither wise nor necessary, so they did no tracting. The missionaries had many referrals from local members and from servicemen who had returned to the United States. They had no trouble meeting people in public places, on buses, or in English-language classes that they organized and taught. They taught the gospel not only in Vietnamese but also in English, French, and Chinese.

They learned the language quickly and associated freely with the people. The evidence of war was ever present in the form of rolls of barbed wire along most streets and armed guards at every corner of the city. Occasionally they heard sniper fire, and acts of sabotage destroyed buildings. The sky was sometimes black with the smoke of burning oil and other material, but the elders were not hampered much in their work.

The elders recognized a need to adapt the standard missionary lessons to the Vietnamese audience. Not having a Judeo-Christian background, most Vietnamese could not understand references to prophets, Apostles, revelations, angels, God, and Christ, all of which are referred to in the first discussion. The elders created special lessons or explanations to supplement the regular lessons. Until they mastered the Vietnamese language, however, it took the elders three or four hours to deliver each lesson. At first they needed six months to teach the full set of discussions.

During 1973 and 1974 Sister Vy, as part of the translation committee, completed the translation of the Book of Mormon. The translation committee, consisting of branch president The (chairman), Nguyen Cao Minh, and some nonmembers who were paid to assist in review, approved the final manuscript. President Bradshaw photocopied fifty copies of the manuscript and distributed them to the members and missionaries in May 1974. This was an unusual procedure, but it proved to be wise in the long run. During 1974 the translation committee also completed Vietnamese versions of LeGrand Richards's *A Marvelous Work and a Wonder,* the Doctrine and Covenants, and the Pearl of Great Price.[21]

In July 1974 Jerry D. Wheat, new president of the Hong Kong Mission, toured Vietnam for the first time. More than 150 members attended a conference at that time. By then, adults outnumbered youths, and males and females were nearly equal in number. A year before, when the missionaries were first in Saigon, youths and females had considerably outnumbered adults and males. The emphasis the elders had placed on working with families had borne fruit.

Tension in the war began to mount during the fall of 1974. The South Vietnamese government regularly reminded Saigon residents of the atrocities committed by the Viet Cong and North Vietnamese forces. The evidences of war came ever closer as rocket fire seriously damaged Bien Hoa Air Base and word of skirmishes in the countryside reached the elders and members. On November 1 the U.S. Embassy issued a warning to all Americans to stay off the streets of Saigon because of large demonstrations, violence, and political disturbances. But the elders knew the streets of the city better than most Americans, and by avoiding large crowds and trouble spots they were able to continue their work. They were fortunate that a number of American Latter-day Saints who held government or contracting jobs were still living in Saigon. One such person was Melvin L. Madsen, who worked for the U.S. State Department. His home became a refuge for the elders. His door was always open; cake and milk were in good supply. He also helped if problems arose with civilian authorities. When Saigon fell, Madsen not only helped the missionaries leave the country but also gathered Vietnamese members and assisted them with the evacuation process.

In mid-January 1975 three new elders arrived in Saigon. They brought to fifteen the total number of missionaries to serve in Vietnam. About the same time, however, the public transportation system began to fail. This made proselyting more difficult, but by giving more lessons at the branch chapel the elders increased the number of people they were teaching. As the threat of a Communist takeover grew, the number of Vietnamese who desired to learn of the restored gospel also grew rapidly. During February and March 1975, proselyting success was at its height.

New converts were joining the Church each month. There were close to 250 Vietnamese members in Saigon by the end of March.

On March 31, however, Louis Eldredge, an active and helpful Latter-day Saint who worked for the U.S. government in Saigon, called President Wheat and strongly suggested that the missionaries should begin exit procedures from Vietnam and apply for reentry visas into Hong Kong. President Wheat, who had plotted the movements of the Communist forces on a map, had made a previous decision to remove the elders from Vietnam as soon as the Communists were within one hundred miles of Saigon. Two days later, after considerable difficulty, he was able to make airline reservations for seven of the elders on April 3 and reservations for the other two on the following day. Concerning these events, President Wheat wrote: "If I was not on the phone, I was on my knees, giving deep consideration to what this would do to the morale of the missionaries, to the members, and everyone concerned. I felt very sick inside to think that we would have to move our missionaries out when they had thirty or forty people ready to be baptized in the next three weeks. The missionary work had never prospered as it had the last three or four weeks. Yet I knew the feelings of the parents having their missionaries there under such conditions."[22]

In Saigon the elders had, in a sense, become immune to the seriousness of their circumstances. They believed that the current problems would blow over and that they would be able to continue their work. Had it not been for the visit of Paul Bennion, an LDS civilian who ran into the chapel and yelled hysterically, "Elders, get out of here!" and a call from Sister June Eldredge, saying, "You had better prepare your visas and get out of here," the elders might have questioned President Wheat when he called and ordered them to leave the country. Almost miraculously they all completed the necessary paperwork in time to leave the country on their scheduled flights. The last two elders to leave, Elders Richard T. Bowman and Dee Oviatt, together with some Vietnamese members, destroyed all American-influenced materials and brought the branch records with them to Hong Kong. The evacuation of the elders may have taken place a few days earlier than absolutely necessary.[23]

From April 4 onward, President The devoted himself almost full-time to the needs and concerns of the members. President Wheat and Elder Bowman kept him informed by phone about changes in U.S. policy and plans for the evacuation of the Vietnamese members. On April 16 Wheat and Bowman flew back to Saigon and held a brief conference with the branch. More than 150 members showed up on short notice, verifying the effectiveness of a communications network President The had initiated among them. President Wheat and Elder Bowman did not know how dangerous the situation was in Saigon until they arrived at the airport. Church member Harrison Ted Price was shocked that they had returned to the country, but he met them at the airport and drove them around. The first night they were there they watched the firefights and heard the explosions of bombs all night. When they left for Hong Kong, they were fortunate to get on the last civilian flight out of Saigon.[24]

President Wheat's visit was hard on him and the members. He was under strict orders from the U.S. Embassy not to discuss evacuation plans with anyone but President The. Some members thought the mission president was trying to make them feel overly secure. Others asked why the elders had not stayed and risked their lives to save them as other Americans appeared to be doing for their friends and congregations. (Virtually all Americans were evacuated within a few days, leaving the local people on their own.) Although their actions were largely unknown to the members, President Wheat, along with Elder Bowman and President The, had been spending almost every waking hour working on membership lists and lists of investigators closely aligned with the Church. Through the influence of Latter-day Saint David C. Hoopes, who was well placed at the White House in Washington, D.C., the member lists were accepted by the U.S. government and became the basis for evacuation priority ratings. Government priorities were, first, U.S. citizens and their families; second, high-echelon officers in the Vietnamese military and government; third, U.S. government and U.S. contractors' employees; and fourth, individuals who had been working with any U.S. organization and could obtain affidavits for evacuation. Most of the Saigon Branch members fell into the fourth category.[25] But having a priority rating was one thing and getting out of the country was another.

A few members got out of the country during the week before April 27, the last Sunday when LDS worship services were held in Saigon. Through the efforts of Roger Shields of the U.S. Department of Defense in Washington, a Colonel Madison at Tan Son Nhut Air Base in Saigon had come to the aid of some Church members and placed them on C-130 Hercules transport aircraft that departed the country. But most of the Saints gathered on that day to receive instructions and make plans for leaving their native land. Years later, President The recalled the events of that painful hour:

> So it was that on Sunday, April 27, 1975, with the enemy at our very gates, members of the Saigon Branch met to discuss our collective fates. Cut off by the war from our lines of Church authority, we were afraid and felt utterly helpless. We reverently and humbly bowed our heads for opening prayer and then sang, "Come, Come Ye Saints" from the depths of our souls. Our tiny branch, so far away from the main body of the Church, conducted its own funeral. We knew that some of us might escape to freedom and others might be left behind. Some of us were not sure which would be worse. Either way, we would have to endure many difficult things we were not prepared to face. As we drew together at this perilous moment, we only knew that each of us, in addition to the gospel, had one thing in common: life as we knew it was over. "All is well, all is well."
> But all was not well. . . . [26]

President The hoped for calm, but the confusion caused by several desperate members finally caused Nguyen Cao Minh to stand and chastise the congregation and to plead with them to humbly support President The.

Several families went directly to the airport after the meeting. Another sixty members had been camped there for a few days, ready to take any means of escape. Spaces on the planes and helicopters were extremely limited because of the low priority assigned to the members of the Church. At least five more LDS families made their way into the airport just before the massive April 28 Communist shelling of the air base and the resultant twenty-four-hour curfew. President The's wife and children were flown to safety on one of the last airplanes out. A few other Church members were shuttled by helicopter to boats waiting offshore. But President The, Nguyen Cao Minh, Dr. Nghia, Sister Vy, Le Van Kha (second counselor in the branch presidency), Brother Pho and his family, Nguyen Hai Chau and his family, Nguyen Ngoc Thach and his family, and several other prominent LDS families were trapped in the city because of the unexpected rapidity of the Communist takeover. Saigon fell to the Communists on April 30. "Just over one hundred members of the Church are known to have left Vietnam" during the evacuation.[27] This left approximately 150 who were not able to escape. Brother Thinh, one who escaped, asserted that among the group of trapped Latter-day Saints were faithful Vietnamese members who were most deserving of blessings.

Those Saints who were evacuated were taken to refugee camps in Guam and the United States, generally to Camp Pendleton, California, where the Church established a branch. Before many months passed, they found their way into the stream of American life by obtaining new jobs and places to live. The Church found sponsors for eighty-three Vietnamese members, and other agencies helped the remaining few.

But what of those who remained behind? After April 30, 1975, it was as though a light went out, leaving everyone in near total darkness. Following unsuccessful attempts to leave the country by boat, several of the brethren returned to Saigon. They found that Saigon had been renamed Ho Chi Minh City and that new administration and laws were being implemented. Although branch members gathered once after the Communist takeover, when three or more people met they were required to fill out a report. The restrictions were too great, so no further meetings of the branch were held. The chapel was confiscated, and the membership was scattered. "The Saigon Branch, for all intents and purposes had ceased to exist, except in our hearts."[28] Before long, Brothers The, Thach, Nghia, and others were imprisoned in "reeducation camps." Their experiences were always difficult and sometimes brutal. By April 1977 Sister The, who settled in Provo, Utah, had received only one letter from her husband. Although Sister Vy was more successful in getting letters out of Vietnam, she was unable to say much that cast light on the situation.

But later some remarkable things happened. Following many months of inhumane suffering, political indoctrination, and "reeducation," President The (who spent twenty-seven months in prison), Brother Minh (who hid out until he fled), and many other Saints managed to escape from Vietnam. Like hundreds of thousands of other Vietnamese who could not endure life in Communist Vietnam, they took to the sea in overloaded and unreliable boats and became part of the "boat people" who caused so much concern for the international community. By 1980 most of the 150 members who were not evacuated before the Communist takeover had left Vietnam. By 1985 all but eighteen LDS families had escaped.[29]

THE CHURCH AND VIETNAM FROM THE FALL OF SAIGON TO THE 1990s

This history does not include the story of the growth of the Church among the various populations of Asians who live in the United States, Canada, Australia, or Western Europe, where many Koreans, Vietnamese, Laotians, Chinese, and other Asians have found the Church and become Latter-day Saints. Many wards and branches now serve one ethnic group or combined groups in non-Asian nations. And since the late 1970s, missionaries have been called to serve among the various refugee populations as well as among other Asian populations in many cities in the United States, Canada, Australia, and Western Europe. But the effects of the Vietnam War have had a much greater and more lasting influence on the Church and its members than the war itself.

The pages of the *Church News*, the *Ensign*, the *New Era*, *Tambuli*, and various other official and unofficial periodicals of the Church have frequently included stories of inspiration and blessing written by ex-servicemen who had their testimonies strengthened through battle or other experiences in Vietnam or Indochina. And stories of ordeals and miraculous escapes from Communist prisons, reeducation camps, or difficult situations have been told by Vietnamese or other Indochinese members of the Church. A brief example of the latter appeared in the *Church News* on August 4, 1985, ten years after the fall of Saigon. In part it read:

> [Tien Van] Pham escaped from Laos with four other boys, ages 12–14. They journeyed through the jungle by night to avoid patrols, and hid in trees by day. After three nights, they reached the turbulent waters of the Mekong River. When they could not find the man who was to take them across the river, they tried to cross by themselves. None of them could swim, so they clung to empty gas cans or plastic bags as they crossed. Floating branches punctured the plastic bags, and only three of the five survived.
>
> After crossing the river, they were taken to a refugee camp. Pham endured two years in the camp, and then emigrated after locating an older brother who lived in Salt Lake City. Pham met LDS welfare missionaries at the refugee camp, although they did not teach him anything about the Church. He joined after arriving in Salt Lake City.[30]

Examples of inspiration gained from experiences in Vietnam are numerous. At least twelve articles appeared in Church periodicals between 1979 and 1995.[31] There are also several books about prisoner-of-war experiences. Church periodical articles (and articles in magazines and journals with an LDS focus) that deal with escape from Vietnam, Laos, or Cambodia are just as numerous. The *Ensign* article about Sister Vy, "Out of the Tiger's Den," noted earlier, relates her difficult period of hiding in a cave for several years before leaving Vietnam to immigrate to North America. At least ten articles with related content have appeared since the late 1970s.

But a third category of articles manifests the impact of the war on members of the Church. Beginning in 1979, articles on refugees in the United States became more and more common. The Church had been helping LDS refugees since 1975, but now, as the number of refugees was rising (peaking in 1980), the First Presidency encouraged members to "support programs helping Southeast Asian refugees resettle."[32] Members were encouraged to become sponsors or to provide volunteer assistance. But most of the articles focused on Indochinese who were being baptized in growing numbers all over North America and who were forming branches of the Church. Hmongs, Laotians, Vietnamese, Khmers (Cambodians), and others were joining in Seattle, Oakland, Salt Lake City, Long Beach, Stockton, Elgin, Philadelphia, Chicago, Toronto, Vancouver, and elsewhere. The total number of Indochinese who have become Mormons outside of their home countries is not known to the author. But in 1994 a Church employee did a name-by-name count and found that there were about 6,000 Vietnamese Latter-day Saints, 4,500 of whom resided in the United States. Considering that there were only 250 Vietnamese members in the Saigon Branch in 1975, the growth among that people is amazing.[33]

The Veterans Association for Service Activities Abroad (actually the group's fourth name with the same acronym) has been particularly tenacious in its attempts to help Vietnamese members leave Vietnam, enter a temple for individual and family blessings, and find homes and work in the United States and Canada. VASAA was organized in 1982 in response to a letter from a member in Vietnam who asked for help. Seven years had passed since the fall of Saigon, and only then did the Communist government allow mail to begin flowing freely out of the country. Recognizing the needs of members in Ho Chi Minh City for financial assistance, clothing, and spiritual support, Dr. Virgil N. Kovalenko, a retired air force officer, contacted other veterans and civilian workers from the war era, returned missionaries from Vietnam, and Vietnamese members to consolidate their efforts to help the member families in Vietnam. From 1982 to this writing (1996), VASAA has continuously worked toward the goal of finding and "extracting" members from Vietnam and rendering other forms of assistance. Kovalenko and other VASAA members have raised money, collected clothing, gone to Vietnam and other Asian nations, cooperated with and kept Church authorities informed, made arrangements through various government and international relief and refugee organizations, guided members in correctly participating in the Orderly Departure Program, paid for airfare, collected life stories, reunited families, recovered Church membership records of the Saigon Branch, helped with the settlement of refugees in North America, and on and on. Every family was numbered. In 1996 the last of the families who were eligible or qualified, the Nguyen Ngoc Thach family, was brought out of Vietnam. (Some LDS families remain in Vietnam.) Brother Thach and his family cared for and held Church services in the Bien Hoa chapel after the American service people departed Vietnam. He was cruelly abused in prison for several years before being reunited with his family in Ho Chi Minh City. The Thach family had been listed as the number-one priority by VASAA, but ironically they were the last to come to America and the temple.[34]

THE 1990s: A PERIOD OF GROWING RELATIONSHIPS AND FRIENDSHIPS

Time is a great healer. It has allowed many bitter memories to be forgotten and has helped one-time enemies to bury their animosities. For several years before the U.S. government recognized the Socialist Republic of Vietnam in 1995, relations between the two nations had steadily improved. Questions of MIA accountability slowed the process, but finally reasonable assurances of good faith were recognized in Washington, D.C., and relationships were normalized.

By the 1990s the population of unified Vietnam was more than seventy million, and the total land area was slightly larger than New Mexico. Unfortunately for the people of Vietnam, the economy was among the weakest in Asia, and many features of the developed world were lacking. The infrastructure—transportation, electricity, water, and so on—was poorly developed and incapable of supporting much modern industry. Evidences of the constant warfare that had engulfed the country from the 1940s until 1975 stood as reminders of a painful and disrupted past. Nevertheless, visitors to Vietnam—academics and business people—reported a high level of friendliness and a warm openness among the people. Many nations were allowing their citizens to make investments in Vietnam or to carry on commerce and trade.

Since 1985 the Asia Area Presidency had looked toward the day when representatives of the Church, either humanitarian or proselyting missionaries, could move into Hanoi and other major Vietnamese cities. Following an earlier unsuccessful attempt to enter Vietnam through the help of VASAA, Elder Merlin R. Lybbert, Asia Area President, visited Hanoi from November 13 through 15, 1991. Accompanying him were Dr. J. Craig Merrell and a group of surgeons who were part of Operation Smile, a humanitarian organization of plastic and reconstructive surgeons who twice yearly visited Vietnam to perform reconstructive surgery. (Dr. Merrell had earlier done similar work in the Philippines.) They operated mostly on children with congenital deformities such as cleft lip or cleft palate, making it possible for them to smile (hence the name Operation Smile). Dr. Merrell was also president of Chesapeake Virginia Stake and helped with the Church's reentry into Vietnam.[35]

Elder Lybbert traveled with the Operation Smile people to present a state-of-the-art surgical microscope to medical professor Dr. Nguyen Huy Phan and the Tran Hung Dao Hospital on behalf of the Church. He was the first General Authority to enter the country since the Vietnam War ended in 1975. The gift made it possible for Vietnamese surgeons to perform microsurgery, a more complicated level of surgery than had been possible before in Vietnam. The Operation Smile team also taught local surgeons how to perform these difficult operations. "This training and the gift now opens the doors to these extremely talented Vietnamese surgeons to perform state-of-the-art surgery and life-transforming surgery to thousands of patients over the years," Dr. Merrell remarked.[36]

Elder Lybbert's visit made it possible to establish contact with the country's high-placed leaders. Friendly relations were established, top officials invited Elder Lybbert and his associates to return, and an invitation was extended to bring English teachers to Hanoi on a volunteer basis.

In June 1992 Elder Lybbert and Elder John K. Carmack, also of the Asia Area Presidency, traveled to Hanoi to build relationships and make arrangements to have English teachers enter the country. In the process of a number of meetings, they met with Mr. Vu Quang, head of the Government Board for Religious Affairs of the Socialist Republic of Vietnam. Dr. Phan, who had become a good friend, was a college classmate and dear friend of Quang. Although Vietnam had undergone fifteen years of religious repression after 1975, Mr. Quang informed Elders Lybbert and Carmack that religious liberty was now allowed and that "the official party has taken a position that religion is good for people, being the major source of instruction in moral and similar matters. People are free and even encouraged to practice their religions."[37] Vietnam's constitution of April 1992 allows freedom of religion.

Although there was much encouragement, Professor Phan cautioned Elders Lybbert and Carmack that any Church representatives who came to Vietnam should use great caution in teaching the gospel.

Before they left for Hong Kong, the Brethren received from local leaders at the hospital and at the Children's Palace—an enrichment center for Hanoi's schoolchildren—a firm invitation to send English teachers to Hanoi. During the next six months two qualified couples were selected and arrangements were made for their entry into Hanoi.

On January 6, 1993, Elder Carmack accompanied missionaries LaVar and Helen Bateman and Stanley and Mavis Steadman to Hanoi. They were the first LDS missionaries to serve in the northern part of Vietnam and the first missionaries to serve in Vietnam since 1975. Professor Phan and his colleagues at Operation Smile had made most of the visa and other arrangements. Their year in Hanoi was fruitful in many ways. They were extremely successful in teaching English to doctors from the Tran Hung Dao Hospital and to young people at the Children's Palace. The highlight of the year was their participation in a performance on October 28 and 29, 1993, of selections from George Frederic Handel's *The Messiah* with the National Vietnam Symphony Orchestra and a selected chorus of professional musicians. Although most of the musicians were Buddhists and unfamiliar with the music and score, they felt that they were performing important music. The director, Do Dung, said, "This is not just religious music; it is *great* music." Regarding his preparation to conduct the music, he said, "I have been far too busy and have no time—but I have received inspiration to interpret the music from your God."[38] Elder Steadman spearheaded the concert. Church Public Affairs made a significant financial contribution to underwrite the performance.

On August 28, 1993, the *Salt Lake Tribune* reported that the Church was planning to open a mission in Vietnam. Two days later, *The Daily Universe*, the Brigham Young University newspaper, headlined an article on the same topic and titled "LDS Missionaries to Enter Vietnam." Evidently the article was picked up by international wire services, for articles derived from it were printed in France and other countries. The problem was that neither article was true. Because couples were being prepared to enter Hanoi to replace the Batemans and the Steadmans, and also because six young elders were studying Vietnamese and English-teaching methods at the Missionary Training Center, a writer had concluded that a mission was planned. Church leaders in Hong Kong had received permission to bring more teachers, but they had no intention of creating a mission until all legal formalities had been completed to do so.

Within two weeks Elder Carmack was in Hanoi to meet with Vu Quang and other authorities. They were very gracious and expressed understanding of the awkward situation. But the matter did not go away. In January 1994 Elder Carmack again met with Vu Quang and others to discuss this and other matters. By this time a number of adversaries of the Church had called or written with complaints regarding the Church. Polygamy was again brought up, and its history had to be explained. Since this visit, the Church has not had further repercussions. Vu Quang has become a good friend of LDS leaders in Hong Kong and has handled matters fairly and with understanding.

Following the January 1994 meeting, Professor Phan advised Elder Carmack that the time was right to move ahead with an application for recognition of the Church. In February Elder David E. Sorensen of the Area Presidency, carried application materials to Hanoi. Although a number of meetings have been held with Vu Quang since that time, the application has not been acted upon by the prime minister.

Nevertheless, the Church's interest in helping Vietnam in humanitarian ways has grown. By the end of 1994, eight missionaries were serving in Hanoi and a number of humanitarian projects had been initiated. In 1995 the number of projects had grown to include English teaching, radiology training at two centers, neonatal training in modern techniques of newborn resuscitation (a budget of $50,000 supported this program for physicians and nurses throughout Vietnam), and training surgeons in improved oral and maxillofacial surgical techniques. In addition, the Church had sent several shipments of medical equipment for use in hospitals in Hanoi. When in late 1994 several villages in Vietnam suffered extensive damage from typhoons and floods, the Church donated $50,000 to rebuild schools and medical clinics in four villages. The humanitarian efforts that were pursued in the refugee camps in Thailand, Hong Kong, and the Philippines in the 1980s were being echoed in Vietnam in the 1990s. Many lives were being blessed through the services of humanitarian missionaries and the contributions of the Church.

"Once LaVar [Bateman] was walking down the street," wrote Louise Helps, "and a little old man came up who looked just like Ho Chi Minh, with a long beard. Grabbing both of LaVar's hands, he cried, 'Volunteer! Volunteer!' It was a simple moment, but one LaVar can never forget."[39]

Proselyting missionaries were not in Vietnam in 1996. When they would be allowed was not known. But the Church was making many friends and serving the needs of a great people in a truly Christian manner. Expatriate members of the Church were authorized to organize a branch in Hanoi in 1993. By late 1996 some thirty members were gathering regularly. An American banker, David K. Baggs, was the first branch president. And in September 1995 Neal Krautz, an Australian who works for a telecommunications company, was sustained as president of the newly reorganized Saigon/Ho Chi Minh City Branch. (President The was finally officially relieved of that responsibility.) At least three LDS Vietnamese families had been given permission to attend Church meetings, but for political reasons they usually met separately from the foreign members. In December 1996 two older sisters and one couple were serving as humanitarian missionaries in Ho Chi Minh City.

Undoubtedly, the most important moment in Church history in Vietnam since the 1970s was President Gordon B. Hinckley's visit to Ho Chi Minh City and Hanoi on May 29, 1996. As part of a seven-nation tour in conjunction with the dedication of the Hong Kong Temple, President Hinckley and his party met with twenty-six members of the Ho Chi Minh Branch at the home of President Krautz. Later that day President Hinckley flew to Hanoi, where he was welcomed by Professor Nguyen Huy Phan, who had been working with the Church and its representatives for several years. Professor Phan expressed gratitude for the many humanitarian acts that Church members had extended to the Vietnamese people.

While meeting with nineteen members of the Church at the home of President Baggs, President Hinckley spoke of an address he had given at BYU while the Vietnam War was raging. It was titled "A Silver Thread in the Dark Tapestry of War." The *Church News* reported that he talked "of how he felt that the Lord, in His own timetable and in His own way, would cause the gospel to be taught to the people of Vietnam. Then, in what he said was inspired by the Spirit, President Hinckley said he felt impressed to give what he described as an 'addendum' to the dedicatory prayer offered 30 years ago. He offered a prayer dedicating the entire land of Vietnam for the preaching of the restored gospel."[40]

President Hinckley has repeatedly expressed his faith, as he did in Ho Chi Minh City, that in "the due time of the Lord, this land will be opened, and many wonderful people will become beneficiaries of the gospel."[41] President Gordon B. Hinckley wrote the same message to the author in 1977: "Personally, I am satisfied that while there has been a distressing pause in the work in Vietnam, the day will come when it will be resumed and will again be fruitful."[42]

NOTES

1. Gordon B. Hinckley, "The Church in the Far East," *Improvement Era* 65 (June 1962): 440; see also Gordon B. Hinckley, "A Silver Thread in the Dark Tapestry of War," *Improvement Era* 73 (June 1968): 48–50.

2. See "First convert joins Church in South Vietnam," *Church News*, 24 November 1962, p. 7.

3. Vietnamese names, like Chinese, Japanese, and Korean names, are given with

the family name first. Confusion sometimes occurs because Vietnamese persons are "usually referred to—correctly and politely—by the last part of the given name" (*The Chicago Manual of Style,* 14th ed. [Chicago: University of Chicago Press, 1993], p. 747.)

4. See Vietnam Zone Historical Report, 1962 entry, LDS Church Archives; hereafter cited as VZHR.

5. "Unusual Sacrament Meeting," *Church News,* 30 July 1966, p. 4.

6. Richard C. Holloman Jr., "The Snap of the Silver Thread: The LDS Church in Vietnam," (research paper, Brigham Young University, 1977), p. 4; copy in LDS Church Archives. This paper should be consulted for a more complete bibliography of Brother Minh.

7. VZHR, 30 October 1966.

8. See Desmond L. Anderson, "Meeting the Challenges of the Latter-day Saints in Vietnam," *Brigham Young University Studies* 10 (winter 1970): 188 passim.

9. Spencer J. Palmer, *The Church Encounters Asia* (Salt Lake City: Deseret Book Co., 1970), pp. 141–43; Gordon B. Hinckley, Journals, 30 October 1966; in possession of President Hinckley; George L. Scott, "South Vietnam, Thailand Dedicated for Missionaries," *Church News,* 19 November 1966, p. 5.

10. Hinckley, "Silver Thread," pp. 48–50.

11. In JoAnn Jolley, "Blessed Are the Peacemakers: LDS in the Military," *This People* (June/July 1984): 68–69.

12. Marion D. Hanks Oral History, interviews by Gordon Irving, 1983, James Moyle Oral History Program, LDS Church Archives, typescript, p. 3.

13. Anderson, "Meeting the Challenges," p. 187.

14. Holloman, "LDS Church in Vietnam," p. 10; and R. Lanier Britsch and Richard C. Holloman, "The Church's Years in Vietnam," *Ensign* 10 (August 1980): 27.

15. William S. Bradshaw Oral History, interviews by R. Lanier Britsch, 1974, James Moyle Oral History Program, LDS Church Archives, typescript, p. 50.

16. Robert J. Lewis to the author, 17 December 1996, in possession of the author; also telephone interview on the same date.

17. Cong Ton Nu Tuong-Vy, "Out of the Tigers Den," *Ensign* 19 (June 1989): 44–45. Sister Vy's and Brother Lewis's memories differ on these events. Since they were both involved, it is difficult to discern which memory is more accurate.

18. Ibid., p. 46.

19. Bradshaw Oral History, p. 55.

20. Ibid., pp. 55–56.

21. See ibid., p. 59.

22. Jerry D. Wheat, Saigon Historical Report, April 1975, pp. 2–3; copy in possession of Richard C. Holloman Jr.; also Jerry D. Wheat, interview by the author, Hong Kong, 6 September 1995, tape recording.

23. Wheat interview.

24. Ibid.

25. See Dinh Van Thinh, "From an LDS Evacuee," unpublished article, 1975; in possession of Richard C. Holloman Jr.

26. Nguyen Van The, as told to David L. Hughes, "The Saigon Shepherd and the Scattered Flock," manuscript, p. 8; in possession of author.

27. Holloman, "LDS Church in Vietnam," p. 44.

28. The, "Saigon Shepherd," p. 75.

29. See David L. Hughes, "An End, a Beginning," *This People* (April 1985): 50–51.

30. "Laotian linguist, 20, helps other refugees," *Church News,* 4 August 1985, p. 4.

31. Each article that follows has Vietnam as its focus: William E. Phipps Jr., "In a Vietnam Helicopter," *Ensign* 9 (August 1979): 56–57; Lu Jones Waite, "The Day I Learned What It Means to Be a Gram," *Ensign* 11 (March 1981): 28–29; Kevin Stoker,

"Because of Snyder," *Church News*, 21 October 1984, p. 16; Gerry Avant, "Vietnam was 'land of opportunity' for gospel study," *Church News*, 23 November 1986, p. 6; Jon B. Fish, "Saved by Seminary," *New Era* 17 (March 1987): 18–19; Peter M. Hansen, "Seek Not after Your Own Heart," *New Era* 17 (May 1987): 8–11; Kevin Stoker, "One saved today," *Church News*, 30 May 1987, p. 16; Robert K. Hillman, "Peace amidst War," *Ensign* 19 (April 1989): 10–11; Larry S. Maloy, "The Army Nurse's Kindness," *Ensign* 20 (March 1990): 56–57; John L. Meisenbach, "Christmas in Vietnam," *Tambuli* 11 (December 1992): 24; Mark E. Hurst, "Airman in Vietnam survives pain of human unkindness," *Church News*, 29 January 1994, p. 12; and Robert K. Hillman, "I Knew It Wasn't Luck," *Ensign* 25 (September 1995): 62–63. This list is not complete.

32. "First Presidency Encourages Help for Refugees," *Ensign* 9 (October 1979): 79.

33. In addition to the articles in Church periodicals, studies document the immigration and adaptation of Indochinese Latter-day Saints. One example is: Robert G. Larsen and Sharyn H. Larsen, "Refugee Converts: One Stake's Experience," *Dialogue* 20 (1987): 37–55, which illustrates that the integration of Indochinese members has not always been an easy process. Another kind of study, recently undertaken by David H. Tanner and others at Brigham Young University, has been the Indochinese segment of the LDS Asian American Oral History Project of the Charles Redd Center for Western Studies.

34. Information for this section was gleaned from interviews with Kovalenko and from copies of "Lost and Found," the newsletter of VASAA; in possession of the author.

35. See Louise Helps, "Breaking New Ground in Hanoi," *Cameo: Latter-day Women in Profile* 2 (February 1994): 41.

36. Sheridan R. Sheffield, "Church donates medical gift to Vietnam," *Church News*, 11 January 1992, p. 3.

37. John K. Carmack, interview by the author, Salt Lake City, Utah, 30 November 1995.

38. As quoted in Helps, "Breaking New Ground," p. 48. See "Vietnamese performers share musical talent," *Church News*, 30 October 1993, p. 3; and "Vietnam: musicians perform 'Messiah,'" *Church News*, 4 December 1993, p. 5.

39. Helps, "Breaking New Ground," p. 51.

40. "Pres. Hinckley dedicates Cambodia, Gives 'addendum' to prayer during his visit to Vietnam," *Church News*, 8 June 1996, p. 5.

41. Ibid.

42. Gordon B. Hinckley to R. Lanier Britsch, 12 May 1977; in possession of the author.

17

SINGAPORE AND
MALAYSIA
1 9 6 8 – 1 9 9 6

Establishing the Church in the Hub of Southeast Asia

SINGAPORE: HUB FOR
SPREADING THE GOSPEL

Situated at the southern tip of the Malay Peninsula, a little above the equator, the small tropical island that is the Republic of Singapore is the hub of communications and economic activity in the islands of Southeast Asia. The name *Singapore* is derived from the Sanskrit words *Singa Pur,* meaning "city of the lion." Two-thirds of the nation's 2.7 million people live in the 37-square-mile city of Singapore, one of the most densely populated areas of Asia. The nation is stable and prosperous, and Singapore is among the cleanest, most modern cities in the world, with striking skyscrapers, beautiful parks, well-maintained roads, an efficient subway system, and an extremely attractive and well-planned airport. Eighty-eight percent of the populace is literate (generally the schools teach in two languages, English and Mandarin Chinese). The economy expanded rapidly during the 1970s and early 1980s (with an average annual growth rate of 9 percent), making Singaporeans wealthy by Southeast Asian standards (the per capita income by the early 1990s was more than $13,900 a year, and most Singaporeans own their own homes or condominium apartments).

The populace is ethnically diverse—truly a nation of immigrants—consisting of Chinese (76.4 percent), Malayan (14.9 percent), Indian (6.4 percent), and others, including Caucasians (2.3 percent). The principal religions of Asia are all represented: Chinese Buddhism, Daoism, Confucianism and animism, Hinduism, Sikhism, Islam, and Christianity. The Christian community is fairly large, with about 220,000 believers (8 percent of the nation's population). Singapore has no state religion, and religious freedom is allowed.

Opening the Work

Latter-day Saint interests in Singapore began in the late 1950s when Elder Mark E. Petersen planned to visit Singapore but canceled his trip because of political turmoil. Elder Spencer W. Kimball visited there in the early 1960s but found no members. In May 1963 Elder Gordon B. Hinckley found three members, all British, and held meetings with them. On December 10, 1964, Elder and Sister Hinckley and President and Sister Jay A. Quealy of the Southern Far East Mission met with three families who had been holding regular Sunday services since the previous September. At that time Elder Hinckley concluded that the Church should be fully established there, but four years passed before LDS missionaries entered the country, and only then did any native Singaporeans come into the Church. Elder Marion D. Hanks was also involved in the development of the Church programs in Singapore during these early years.

On March 19, 1968, about a month after President Keith E. Garner took the first six missionaries to Thailand, he sent Elders Todd Bake, Joel Richards III, Kim Shipley, and Melvin Shurtz to Singapore to begin proselyting work. Their efforts were soon rewarded when Alice Tan was baptized on May 4, 1968, and other local people joined the Church soon after.[1]

By October 1968 additional missionaries had joined the staff, new converts had joined the Church, and the Singapore government had recognized the Church as a legal corporation. On October 13, one day after the registration of the Church, President W. Brent Hardy, who had replaced President Garner, organized the Singapore Branch. He called a missionary, Elder John McSweeney, as branch president. Seventy-five people were in attendance at the organizational meeting, half of whom were investigators. Nearly forty people joined the Church between the arrival of the elders in March and the end of 1968.[2]

In April 1969 Elder Ezra Taft Benson, then supervisor of Asian missions, visited Singapore and, under authority from President David O. McKay, dedicated the nation for the preaching of the restored gospel. The service was held on the evening of April 14 on Mount Faber. Forty-five Saints, including President and Sister W. Brent Hardy, attended. In his address to the group, Elder Benson made two statements that he also reiterated in his prayer: "We expect confidently that thousands upon thousands of people in this choice country will hear the message and will accept the gospel, and that this may someday *become a center from which the gospel can be directed and sent into other countries which have not yet heard the message of the restored gospel.*" And again, "This will be a training ground for missionaries and others who will be able to *go out from here to carry the message to other nations in Asia.*"[3] In the decades that have followed, Singapore has played a much larger role in the growth of the Church than could have been foreseen when Elder Benson's words were uttered. Singapore has been the hub from which hundreds of missionaries have been sent to serve in various nations of South and Southeast Asia and from which the various programs of the Church have emanated.

Church leaders in Salt Lake City evidently had much more in mind for Singapore than Elder Benson was at liberty to discuss at the dedicatory service, for not long after that the First Presidency called G. Carlos Smith Jr. to preside over the soon-to-be-organized Southeast Asia Mission. This mission was to encompass Burma, Brunei, Cambodia, India, Indonesia, Laos, Malaysia, Singapore,

Southern Far East Mission president W. Brent Hardy (fourth from right), missionaries, members, and friends gathered atop Mount Faber overlooking Singapore to witness Elder Ezra Taft Benson dedicate that nation for the preaching of the restored gospel on 14 April 1969. (Courtesy Greg Gubler)

Sri Lanka, Thailand, and Vietnam, most of which were new to LDS efforts. When the Smiths arrived in Singapore on October 24, they had the pleasant experience of moving into an established branch where the missionaries and members had affairs well organized. Two days later, on October 26, Elders Ezra Taft Benson and Bruce R. McConkie met with the Smiths and the missionary force to officially initiate the mission. "Under the direction of President Smith," wrote Dale S. Cox, "the work was stepped up significantly, and the missionary force in Singapore was increased to 48 in the latter part of 1969. . . . Also during this period a comparatively large number of strong local men were baptized who were qualified to take responsible leadership positions." By the end of 1969, 118 people had entered the waters of baptism.[4] Many of the individuals and families who joined the Church in Singapore during the first several years have remained faithful and have provided strong leadership ever since.

Making the choice to become Latter-day Saints was usually not easy for Singaporeans. Long-held ideas and family traditions made accepting the gospel a challenge. A. C. and Helen Ho, who were baptized in 1969, described how they overcame these obstacles:

> The idea that there is such a thing as the "right church" hit us like a cannonball at first and left us several painful days to ponder over the matter. It was our belief that all churches belong to God and if a man would choose any church and worship God in all sincerity, he would be on the right path. It had never occurred to us that a particular church could be any "righter" than another until the missionaries introduced us to The Church of Jesus Christ of Latter-day Saints. . . .
>
> We had never heard of The Church of Jesus Christ of Latter-day Saints until the missionaries visited us one evening at home. At first we were skeptical. The introduction of the Book of Mormon hit us like a second cannonball—this time with greater impact than the first. We had to examine and handle the book physically before accepting it as scripture. It took us a while to read the

Book of Mormon and pray before we accepted the gospel. We are glad that we have received the gospel in its fullness. It has changed our lives. It has also helped us realize our duties in serving our brothers and sisters and setting the example by living according to the teachings of Christ.[5]

Expulsion of LDS Missionaries

Probably because the white-shirted Caucasian missionaries were so visible, and also because most (90 percent, President Smith estimated)[6] of their converts came from other Christian churches, newspaper editors and leaders of other Christian churches joined together in an effort to discredit the LDS Church. An article in the *Straits Times* of January 28, 1970, reported on the developing friction between the Church and the Inter-Religious Organization of Singapore: "One letter condemned the Mormon door-to-door campaign as an 'invasion,' describing the doctrines preached as 'naive fundamentalist medieval dogmatisms of the American Middle West.'" Although the polygamy issue had been a dead matter in many parts of the world for decades, newspapers headlined polygamy and the Church. One Protestant minister claimed the right of the Mormons to have the same privileges as all other religions, but at the same time he sharply criticized the Church for its intolerance because it claimed to have the true gospel. He suggested that the Latter-day Saints did not understand Singapore and the delicate balance that existed among the various religious communities, and he worried whether the Church's presence would create unwanted and unnecessary tensions within the relatively small community. Tensions among the ethnic groups in Singapore were an honest concern. Terrible riots and frictions had taken place as late as 1965, and few people wanted to see such problems arise again. A truce and balance had been established. Some people honestly feared that the peace would be eroded by the introduction of a new variable—the Mormons—in the equation.

The attacks against the Church caused strong feelings and eventually brought government action. Prime Minister Lee Kuan Yew and his government insisted on total stability and refused to allow even the possibility of religious upheaval. Without allowing the Church to defend its position, the government expelled twenty-nine LDS missionaries in March 1970. It also refused to grant any new visas or to renew old ones. When the announcement was made to the missionaries, it was a day of mourning. The mission secretary wrote, "The heavens quietly wept." By November 1970 the missionary force consisted of only the mission president, his wife, and three foreign elders. By 1973 the number of foreign elders had been reduced to only one, and this remained the size of the expatriate missionary force for a number of years. The unfavorable publicity generated a great deal of prejudice against the Church and caused the government to stop the remaining elders from tracting door-to-door during the few months before the last missionaries departed for home. To the present, such tracting has not been resumed. The missionaries have generally found it necessary to depend on the members for referrals.

Local Missionaries Rise to the Challenge

Of course, the expulsion of the missionaries set the Church back considerably. After 1970, when 124 people joined the Church, the number of converts dropped greatly: to 33 in 1971, 24 in 1972, 21 in 1973, and a low of 15 in 1974. But as has proved true elsewhere (in Tonga, for example), adversity has brought the Saints closer together and given them reason to manifest their commitment to the Church. Although the small membership base made it impossible for the two branches (the Singapore Second Branch was organized in June 1969) to produce a large number of local missionaries, they nevertheless provided a steady supply.

Elder Teo Thiam Chye was the first Singapore elder to receive a one-year missionary call. Until 1975 the Singapore missionaries received one-year calls from the mission president. But since then a number of young men and women have received calls from the prophet to serve as full-time, full-term missionaries. Serving a mission in Singapore is different from serving in most other places of the world. The missionaries simply leave home by driving to the mission office to begin their missions. Family and friends are still close at hand, and the sights and experiences of a lifetime are readily available. When release day comes, the missionaries still see their friends from their missions on the next Sunday at church. When Singaporeans attending school at BYU or BYU—Hawaii received their mission calls to Singapore, they returned home to a group of happy and eager family members to *start* their missions, whereas elsewhere in the world a mission call means separation from one's home and family. Only in 1985 did Singaporean missionaries begin going to the Manila Philippines Missionary Training Center to obtain their pre-mission training and to receive their endowments at the Manila temple.

These local elders and sisters were instrumental in greatly strengthening the branches and district in Singapore. Following their missions, many of them have gone on to school at BYU, BYU—Hawaii, and Ricks College, where they have distinguished themselves as scholars, student-body officers, and leaders in the Church. Upon returning to Singapore, they have served as branch and district leaders and now even as bishops in the Singapore stake. They have also taken work with various agencies of the Singapore government and helped to build their nation.

Although 1970 was a disappointing year, the Church in Singapore made some important strides forward. The branches moved into a remodeled Chinese mansion on Bukit Timah Road that served as a chapel until a new building was started on the same site in February 1972. Also in 1970, President Smith purchased a new mission home, and the government granted the Church a license to perform marriages. In 1971 the Church made further progress. On January 17 President Smith formed the Singapore District with Soren F. Cox as its first president. Dr. Cox, a professor of English from Brigham Young University, was teaching English at Nanyang University. Cox and his wife, Fern, who led the combined branch Relief Societies, made an important contribution to the Church at that time by helping other new leaders learn their assignments after the missionaries left so suddenly.

New Leaders Guide the Mission

In July 1972 Miller F. Shurtleff of Washington, D.C., replaced G. Carlos Smith as president of the mission. President Shurtleff was busy during his three years as president supervising missionary work in Thailand until the organization of the new Thailand Mission in 1973. He also led the work in Indonesia. (The new Indonesia Jakarta Mission was created on July 1, 1975, the day following Shurtleff's release.) The completion of the new chapel, mission office, and missionary quarters on the Bukit Timah Road property occurred under Shurtleff's leadership. He dedicated the new facilities, which had been started in February 1972, on May 23, 1975. Considering Singapore's role in the founding of the Thailand and Indonesia missions and the fact that the mission presidents in Singapore trained and supervised the missionaries who served in those areas, it can be said that Elder Benson's expressed hope and prayer that Singapore could be "a center from which the gospel can be directed and sent into other countries" was already in some measure being fulfilled.

Soren F. Cox returned to Singapore as mission president in July 1975. During his three years there, the number of convert baptisms grew from twenty-nine in 1975 to sixty-one in 1977. Ninety percent of the sixty-one converts were referred to the missionaries by members of the Church. By that time the missionary force had grown to include twelve full-time missionaries—ten Singaporeans, one Malaysian, and one American.

President Cox did much to consolidate the progress of the past. He called a six-member district council as well as counselors in the mission presidency and a clerk. With his support, but under the direction of A. C. Ho (Ho Ah Chuan) and then W. H. Lionel Walters, the seminary and institute program was instigated in

Southeast Asia. Singapore was also made the center for LDS genealogical efforts in Southeast Asia. Walters and the Church Genealogy Society representative were brought in from outside on professional visas, indicating that a better relationship had been developed with the government. During Cox's time both branches completed their auxiliary organizations, and the full program of the Church was offered to the Singapore members.[7]

In an effort to show their devotion and loyalty to their home government, members of the Church raised money to support a scholarship for a non-LDS Singapore student for study at BYU in Provo. Each year when this scholarship was granted, the mission president was invited to join with other contributors in a ceremony conducted by Prime Minister Lee Kuan Yew. The results were positive for the Church and for the Singaporean students who were blessed to receive the scholarship.

When President and Sister Cox returned home in July 1978, the Singapore Mission was made part of the Indonesia Jakarta Mission for the next eighteen months. Winfield Q. Cannon, counselor in the Indonesia Jakarta Mission presidency, and his wife, Wanda, were assigned to preside over missionary work in Singapore. Having served as a stake president in Los Angeles and as a mission president in Germany, Cannon was a man of considerable experience who was for all practical purposes the mission president. In fact, in a letter to J. Talmage Jones, who reopened the Singapore Mission, President Lester C. Hawthorne said: "Contrary to what you may have heard in Salt Lake City, we have nothing to do with the Singapore Mission. Winfield Cannon is the presiding authority, and in Singapore he is known as the president of the mission."[8]

Even though the mission was temporarily closed, Singapore's role remained important and missionary work continued. The band of about 550 Saints in 1978 grew to 660 when the mission was reopened in January 1980.

J. Talmage Jones and his wife, Vera Jean, were somewhat surprised to receive their call to Singapore. He had presided over a mission in Canada in the 1960s and as a Regional Representative for nine years following that. But his years of Church administration served him well as his responsibilities continually grew. His call was to preside over Singapore and Malaysia, but in April 1980 he received word from the First Presidency that India and Sri Lanka were being added to his areas of supervision, effective July 1, 1980.[9] He was just getting adjusted to this new charge when in December he received another letter from the First Presidency informing him that "the Indonesia Jakarta Mission will be discontinued as a separate entity and . . . will be attached to the Singapore Mission."[10] The change was to become effective as soon as proper arrangements could be made (officially it became effective on January 1, 1981). Fuller accounts of the work in India, Sri Lanka, and Indonesia are given later in this book, but it is important here to note the challenges President Jones faced in administering such a diverse mission. The distances were vast, the ethnic and religious differences were complex, the governmental restrictions on proselyting were difficult, the populations were enormous, and the languages were numerous. During the years since then, the Singapore Mission has had responsibility for various countries at different times. In 1996 it continued to guide Malaysia, Sri Lanka, and Pakistan as major undertakings. India was part of the Singapore Mission until January 1993, when the India Bangalore Mission was formed. The Singapore Mission also encompassed Indonesia during part of the 1980s and until July 1, 1995, when that nation again came under separate leadership.

A Boost from the Osmonds

In June 1980 the image of the Church in Singapore received positive support when Donny and Marie Osmond, popular musical performers and strong members of the Church, and their family visited Singapore. Press coverage was "very good to us," commented President Jones. The *Straits Times* printed several articles about the Church and gave the Osmonds considerable publicity. Thirty thousand people attended their show in the

National Stadium. But missionary work was helped most when the Osmonds spoke at a fireside sponsored by the Singapore District. The event was attended by 2,200 people—400 Latter-day Saints and 1,800 nonmembers. The long-term results included increased investigators for missionaries to teach, improved image and public recognition for the Church, and some baptisms.[11]

Growth continued until it was necessary to divide the Singapore First Branch in July 1980 into the Singapore and Clementi Branches. A little over a year later, in September 1981, the Singapore Second Branch was divided into the Toa Payoh and Bedok Branches. Two years after that, in June 1983, the Mandarin Branch was organized for those who spoke Mandarin. These remained the units of the Church until January 3, 1993, when the Philippines Branch was formed to serve the needs primarily of Filipino sisters who were in Singapore as domestic workers.

A Temple Closer to Home

The 1980s brought other significant blessings to the Saints in Singapore. A major development was the opening of the Manila Philippines Temple in 1984. Before that time it had been necessary for members to travel to distant places—Tokyo, New Zealand, Hawaii, or the U.S. mainland—to participate in temple worship and blessings. Of course, the cost was prohibitive for the Saints in Singapore. Nevertheless, some members did sacrifice and make the journey to one temple or another. Eddie Chew (the first Singaporean to serve as district president) and his family estimated it would cost them around $10,000 to travel to a temple and be sealed as a family. The cost seemed impossibly high. But then prospects brightened:

> One day, the mission president's wife told Sister Queenie Chew that the Lord will always find a way for his children to obey his commandments. With that encouragement . . . Sister Queenie Chew was determined to do all she could to save up money for the temple trip. Her

three daughters prayed every day that the Lord would help them to be sealed in the temple. They saved all the money which their grandmother gave them for their birthdays for the temple trip. Later, Sister Chew was blessed with a job in the hospital as a nurse at night. [Brother Chew also] began to make sacrifices he had not thought of before and added money to the temple trip savings. The Lord blessed them in many ways and in three years they had saved enough money to go to the Salt Lake Temple to be sealed as a family.[12]

Since 1984 the various branches (and now wards) took turns arranging an annual temple excursion to either the Manila Philippines Temple or the Taipei Taiwan Temple. These trips generally worked well, but occasionally problems arose. In 1995, because of tremendous anger directed at Singaporeans when their courts convicted a Filipino domestic worker of murder and carried out the sentence of hanging, the decision was made to take the excursion to Sydney, Australia, in order to assure the safety of the Singaporean members.

Continuing Governmental Relations

Singapore is a city-state, a very close society. The government was led from 1965, when Singapore separated from Malaysia and became a member of the Commonwealth of Nations, until 1990 by Prime Minister Lee Kuan Yew. He provided very strong leadership and created a society that allowed little deviation from a conservative path toward internal stability, multiethnic harmony, and economic progress. It was the quest for multiethnic harmony that brought the expulsion of foreign LDS missionaries in 1970. As late as 1988 the policy of allowing only two foreign missionaries (the mission president and one missionary, the president's wife being considered a dependent) into the country was still in force. Considering the loyal and steady service of the local missionaries following the events of 1970, one might question the need for the government to change its policy. However, there was a need to reinforce the local efforts, and in a remarkable meeting in early 1988 the policy was changed.

On March 18, 1988, Elder M. Russell Ballard, along with Jon M. Huntsman Sr., president of Huntsman Chemical Corporation, and Utah Senator Jake Garn met with Prime Minister Lee Kuan Yew. They were escorted to the meeting by U.S. Ambassador to Singapore Daryl Arnold. Sister Pang Beng Ling, local Church historian, described what transpired on this momentous occasion:

> They spent forty minutes with Prime Minister Lee, discussing government and business issues. The Prime Minister was interested in where Huntsman Chemical Corporation would expand in Southeast Asia. As they were about to leave, Prime Minister Lee asked how many children Brother Huntsman had. "[He] told him and then saw the opening to mention the Church and [its] emphasis on families. This naturally led to the issue of the ban on the number of missionaries. [Huntsman] came right out and asked if it could be lifted." The Prime Minister said, "Of course it can. I did not know there was a ban. This is no problem at all." President Lee then turned to his secretary [and said], "See that this is implemented. The Mormons are fine people. . . ." And so through his servants the Lord provided the way for the Church to grow in Singapore by opening the door for foreign missionaries to serve in Singapore again.[13]

From that time greater numbers—ten or twelve—foreign missionaries have been granted visas to live and serve in Singapore.

Jon M. Huntsman Jr. also had a positive influence on relations between the government and the Church. Although his appointment as U.S. Ambassador to Singapore was strictly a political matter, his membership in the Church was acknowledged. After he presented his credentials on September 21, 1992, thirty-two-year-old Huntsman met reporters' questions with answers in English and Mandarin Chinese, which he had learned as a missionary in Taiwan. He was the first Latter-day Saint to serve as an ambassador from any country to a nation in Asia.[14]

Church Values Versus Society's Values

Another problem that has resolved itself through changes in government policy is the issue of birth control and family planning. Because Singapore is small in size and the population density is considerable, the government early on created policies and negative incentives against large families. Family planning using all means of birth control, including abortion, was encouraged. Social pressure was also imposed by neighbors, friends, and employers. Families with more than two children were made to feel uncomfortable in many ways.

Members of the Church found themselves in a quandary: Should they openly oppose the government, which seemed to go against the twelfth article of faith ("We believe in being subject to kings, presidents, rulers, and magistrates, in obeying, honoring, and sustaining the law"), or follow the counsel of Church leaders, who encouraged having larger families if the health and well-being of the wife made it possible? Most of the members in Singapore were between the ages of eighteen and thirty, yet most of these young LDS families had no more than two children.

Church counsel on the matter was careful and wise, teaching correct principles but avoiding making statements that contravene local laws or regulations.

But to the joy of Church leaders and members alike, after more carefully studying the long-term implications of the two-child policy, government leaders in Singapore concluded that the general population was aging and there were too few children to grow up and handle the many jobs of a growing economy. By the 1990s, the policy had been reversed and the government had implemented financial incentives and tax breaks for families who would have more than two children.

Church Properties

Another matter that has brought the Church into regular inter-action with the government has been the need to increase and improve Church properties. Space limitations alone make land acquisition a difficult matter, but government policy regarding religious structures has created an even more difficult situation. Only four religions are recognized when land is sold for religious purposes: Buddhism, Islam, Hinduism, and Christianity. "The government," according to Talmage Jones, "allows each [religious] group to buy property for one building within each housing development. This presents no problem for the first three groups, but for the Christians, all denominations compete for the prize and the price goes sky-high."[15]

Over the years the Church has been able to purchase three properties for chapels: the first at Bukit Timah Road, the second in the Bedok area, and the third on Pasir Panjang Road. The building on Pasir Panjang is a large old mansion that has been remodeled for church use. At present the facilities are sufficient, but as growth comes the pressure of crowding will be felt.

Emphasis on Family Values

Wisely, the Church in Singapore has maintained a low profile. The difficulties of 1970 more or less mandated such a posture, but the sensitivity of many wise local leaders to the realities of life in Singapore has also led to a quiet, careful path regarding public relations. Gradually the Church has developed the trust and admiration of many in Singapore's close society. Evidence of this is most clear in the positive response that has come from the Church's efforts to encourage strong family values.

In October 1993 the Ministry of Community Development invited the Church, along with other churches and entities, to suggest ideas for a document on family values. Contributing was easy and natural for the Church leaders who participated in the discussions at public forums the ministry held on the topic. The Church's family home evening program gained the spotlight in several newspapers. A. C. Ho led out by writing a winning essay on the importance of family home evening. It was published in a national newspaper under the title "Building a Fortress." He and a friend also organized a family support group that met once a month for two and a half hours to discuss ways of teaching values to children.

The *Straits Times* featured the Ho family in its May 9, 1994, issue. The headline for the family section read "Every Monday is family night. Weekly ritual has been a Ho family tradition for over 15 years."

According to Pang Beng Ling, "More than 50,000 people attended the National Family Day exhibition on 19 June 1994. A *Family Home Evening Resource Book* was given to the Prime Minister, Mr. Goh Chok Tong, when he and his wife visited the Church booth that day. More than 80 Church members explained the Family Home Evening program and gave out fliers and book markers on that theme to the visitors at the exhibition."[16] It appears that participation in the National Family Day is becoming a tradition—the government invited the Latter-day Saints to take part again in 1995. Also, A. C. Ho was invited to serve on a national committee on family values.

The Creation of the Singapore Stake

Total number of members is clearly not the most important ingredient in the creation of a stake. The new Singapore Stake, created on February 26, 1995, by Elder Neal A. Maxwell with Area President John K. Carmack assisting, had only 1,650 members; but those who made the decision to create the stake knew that the leaders were mature and capable of taking on the added responsibility. The district presidency had discussed more than a year earlier the possibility of making the Singapore District the two thousandth stake of the Church. But they wisely knew that they were not quite prepared and did not push to become a stake before they were ready.

The new stake president was Leonard Woo, age thirty-nine, formerly the first counselor in the district presidency. He chose as his counselors Jacob Soh, also a former district president's counselor, and Michael T. Fisher, a young attorney engaged in international business. Tan Su Kiong, the last district president, was sustained as stake patriarch. Pang Beng Ling wrote: "Elder Maxwell remarked that it was an exhilarating and historic day for Singapore and all Southeast Asia, the feeling one might have when racing downhill on a bicycle. He reminded the members that very soon they would have to start peddling. He told them to be a large stake spiritually although the Singapore Stake is a small stake of 1600 members. He also told them to be a beacon to the other countries in Southeast Asia. . . . Elder Maxwell closed the meeting by giving an apostolic blessing to the Singapore Saints. He

Hoi Seng Leonard Woo, first president of Singapore Stake, was called to that office by Elder Neal A. Maxwell of the Quorum of the Twelve on 26 February 1995. (Photo by author)

blessed Singapore Stake that it will become more of a community of Saints, that the Saints would not go through the motions of membership but will go through the emotions of discipleship, and in the process of discipleship there will be a building of spiritual momentum in the stake, that it will be a light not only for Singapore but for other countries too."[17]

The new stake consisted of four wards and two branches, and an additional ward was organized in August 1995, bringing the number of units to seven.[18]

In conclusion, the Church in Singapore has truly come of age. With a stake to minister to members' needs in Singapore and the Singapore Mission to lead in missionary work there and in Malaysia, Sri Lanka, Pakistan, and other parts of Southeast Asia, the Church is well grounded to move forward in taking the restored gospel to the peoples of this vast realm. Elder Ezra Taft

The so-called Bukit Timah (road) chapel houses the Singapore Stake offices. The five-story building behind it (opened in January 1998) houses the mission office, temporal affairs, and other Church activities. (Photo by author)

Benson's words ring with prophetic clarity. Singapore has *"become a center from which the gospel [is being] directed and sent into other countries which have not yet heard the message of the restored gospel."*

GUARDED GROWTH IN MALAYSIA

The Federation of Malaysia was formed in July 1963. With a population of nineteen million in 1995, it presently consists of the Malay Peninsula (also known as West Malaysia) and the states of Sabah and Sarawak on the northwestern coast of the island of Borneo (East Malaysia). Eighty-two percent of the populous lives in West Malaysia. The governmental, religious, and ethnic situation is complex. The government consists of thirteen states under a constitutional monarchy, a bicameral parliament, and a prime minister. According to *The Statesman's Yearbook, 1992–93,* "The Constitution provides for one of the 9 rulers of the Malay States to be elected from among themselves to be the *Yang di-Pertuan Agong* (Supreme Head of the Federation). He holds the office for a period of 5 years." Because the nine rulers (sultans, rajas, and regents) are all Muslim, the king is always Muslim. Islam is the official religion, but there is freedom of religion. Unfortunately for Christians and other non-Muslims, considerable pressure has been applied to convert them to Islam, though it is strictly forbidden for Christians to proselytize Muslims. Fifty-five percent of the populace is Muslim, 25 percent are followers of Buddhist and Chinese religions, 8.6 percent are Christians (the percentage of Christians in Sabah and Sarawak is higher than in Western Malaysia), 8 percent are Hindus, and the remainder are animists, tribal, nonreligious, and so on. Ethnically the Malays are a majority at 52.5 percent. Chinese make up 30 percent, Indians 8.1 percent, and tribal peoples 8.9 percent. Bahasa Malaysia (Malay) is the official language, although most urban people speak English. A variety of Chinese, Indian, and tribal languages are also used. The urban centers are modern, boasting many high-tech industries. Per capita income in 1993 was U.S. $2,230.

The Introduction of the Church

Among this interesting variety of peoples and languages, the message of the restored gospel has taken root almost entirely among the Chinese and Indians of West Malaysia, although during 1995 Church representatives began working in Kuching, Sarawak (where a branch has been organized), and Kota Kinabalu, Sabah, both in East Malaysia.[19]

As is true for Singapore and many other countries of Asia, the first Mormons in Malaysia were expatriates. Beginning in the 1960s, LDS Americans who were working there and Australian military personnel carried on family or small group services in different cities and bases. The first Malaysian to join the Church there was Anthony T. K. Lim, who was baptized in 1972.[20] Today he serves as national director of public affairs for the Church. Other Malaysians were baptized earlier, but outside the country— Guan Chye Teh in Australia and Ivan Bee Ho in Taiwan, and perhaps others. Brother Ho served as a district president in Taiwan before returning to his home in the capital city of Kuala Lumpur (known simply as KL) to establish a business in 1973. After he arrived home, he found Latter-day Saints Bruce Knudson, an American entomologist, and Nicholas Jamba, a technical adviser. They formed a group and started meeting in one another's homes. They were active in spreading the gospel. "We'd bring personal friends," remembered Ivan Ho, "to weekday meetings and prepare food, show some slides and sing a few hymns." Anthony Lim and Rodney How were added to the small group, and before long they formed a branch that met in a rented hall.[21]

Under the guidance of the International Mission, Werner and Mercedes Kiepe were assigned to serve as Church representatives in Kuala Lumpur during 1978 and 1979. The Church received legal recognition in 1977, making it possible in 1979 for the Kiepes to purchase for the Church a two-level home that was large enough for meetings and social activities.[22] Other couples followed the Kiepes as Church representatives.

In January 1980 Malaysia was transferred to the Singapore Mission, which was reopened at that time. The following month President J. Talmage Jones called Church representative J. Floyd Stoker as the first president of the newly formed Malaysia District of the Singapore Mission. The following day, February 25, the Joneses traveled to Penang, a small but important island a short distance off the coast in the Strait of Malacca, and officially organized that branch in the city of Georgetown (formerly known as Prince of Wales Island, where Elder Elam Luddington had stopped and preached the gospel for five days in late February 1854). There were fifty active members in KL and twenty in Penang.[23] By July the Penang Branch had grown to forty-two members, half of them from Australia.

Obtaining Malaysian visas for representatives of the Church has been a difficult problem. In 1981 Chinese elders from Hong Kong and older couples from other British Commonwealth countries were allowed to enter without visas. But in early 1982 the Malaysian government became angry at the British government and reversed its open policy regarding Commonwealth visas. At that time three elders from Hong Kong and William S. and Laurel Redd from Canada were serving in Malaysia on Commonwealth passports. Since that time, a number of older couples have visited on tourist visas and helped with the development of the Church, but the government has never granted long-term visas. Missionaries are not allowed into Malaysia from any church.

Although much of the Church's growth is the result of temporary visits from elders and sisters from the Singapore Mission, much has been accomplished by local members who have served missions in their own country. As is true in India, Pakistan, Sri Lanka, and Singapore, citizens are free to propagate their religion among non-Muslims. In 1980 President Jones pondered deeply how he could legally increase the size of the missionary force. The answer came in a letter from a Malaysian student in London who had recently joined the Church. The writer, David Soon Ewe Seang, wanted to serve as a missionary in Malaysia. Jones wrote: "On Sunday . . . I spoke on the need for local members to become missionaries. Following the meeting a young Malaysian, Chong Sun Fu, introduced himself as a student from Australia, home for holidays. He had joined the Church in Melbourne. . . . He said, 'You have impressed me to go on a mission.' This will give us two very excited Malaysian native missionaries."[24]

The following June, the two elders, one converted in London and the other in Melbourne, commenced their missions in KL. They were the first full-time missionaries to be called to Malaysia. They were joined a year later by Elders Wu Yuk Choi and Yung Yik Wong, also from Malaysia. Two Malaysian sisters were called to serve about the same time.[25] Other Malaysian elders and sisters have followed to the present.

In May 1986, J. Alden Richins, area director for the Church Educational System, and Richard Ang, associate area director for Singapore and Malaysia, visited KL to initiate the seminary and institute program in Malaysia. A small group of potential institute students was already meeting twice a month. In January 1987 the institute program officially began in KL, Ipoh, and Penang.

During 1981 a small branch was established at Ipoh, a city between KL and Penang. Since then the work has progressed steadily—181 members in the country in 1983, 300 in 1987, 500 by the end of 1991, and 550 Latter-day Saints in Malaysia in 1995. And the number of branches has increased. In 1995, in addition to the branches in KL (110 members), Penang (60 members), and Ipoh (60 members),

Chong Sun Fu, with his wife, Geok Lee, has been a stalwart leader in Malaysia. Most recently he served for seven years as district president. Brother Chong was one of the first two LDS missionaries in Malaysia. (Photo by author)

there is a branch in Klang, near KL (70 to 80 members), and a singles branch of sixty young adults in Petaling Jaya, which was created to facilitate social interaction and marriages within the Church. The singles branch serves the entire KL metropolitan area. There is also a small group of three families in Melaka. The district president in 1995 was Chong Sun Fu, one of the first two missionaries to serve in his homeland. The Church owns meetinghouses in KL, Penang, and Ipoh. Activity is reported to be around 50 percent.[26]

In late 1994 eleven leaders of the Church from Malaysia and Singapore were invited to dine with the newly coronated tenth king of Malaysia, Tuanku Ja'afar, and his wife, Queen Tuanku Najiha, in the royal palace. The *Church News* reported this major event for the Church in Malaysia in these words:

> The meeting . . . was arranged by Brother and Sister [Vincent and Sandra] Gordacan, who are close personal friends of the king and queen. They met in Lagos, Nigeria, when Brother Gordacan was working for the U.S.

State Department and the future king was Malaysia's High Commissioner in Nigeria. . . .

After the meal, Brother Gordacan expressed the gratitude of the group to the king and queen for meeting with them. He said he admired the royal couple for their humility, generosity, and understanding toward their subjects.

"To be good Mormons," Brother Gordacan stressed, "members of the Church have to be good Malaysians." He explained that Church members uphold the law of the land, support the king and queen, and respect other faiths. "We respect the rights of all religions to worship God," he concluded.[27]

NOTES

1. See Dale S. Cox, "A Brief History of the LDS Church in Singapore," June 1978, mimeographed copy, p. 1. This item is found in Southeast Asia Mission, historical records and minutes, LDS Church Archives. Cox, the son of Soren F. and Fern Cox, a couple who served the Church in Singapore for five years, wrote this history from primary sources (letters, reports, minutes, mission publications, quarterly and yearly historical reports) and from personal interviews with his father and other Church members in the area.

2. See ibid., p. 3.

3. As quoted in Spencer J. Palmer, *The Church Encounters Asia* (Salt Lake City: Deseret Book Co., 1970), p. 158; emphasis mine.

4. See Cox, "LDS Church in Singapore," p. 4.

5. As quoted in Pang Beng Ling, *A History of The Church of Jesus Christ of Latter-day Saints in Singapore: Journey to Stakehood, 1964–1997* (Singapore: C. O. S. Printers Pte Ltd, 1997), pp. 64–65.

6. See G. Carlos Smith Jr. Oral History, interviews by William G. Hartley, Oral History Program, LDS Church Archives, 1972, typescript, p. 41.

7. See Cox, "LDS Church in Singapore," pp. 6–7.

8. Hawthorne to Jones, 30 November 1979, in Joseph Talmage Jones, Collection 1968–1982, LDS Church Archives.

9. First Presidency (Spencer W. Kimball, N. Eldon Tanner, Marion G. Romney) to J. Talmage Jones, 21 April 1980, Joseph Talmage Jones, Collection 1968–1982, LDS Church Archives.

10. Ibid., 3 December 1980.

11. See J. Talmage Jones, *In Singapore* (Salt Lake City: Publishers Press, 1984), pp. 29–30.

12. *Walk in His Ways: Basic Manual for Children, Part B* (Salt Lake City: The Church of Jesus Christ of Latter-day Saints, 1993), pp. 201–5; and Pang Beng Ling, *History of the Church . . . in Singapore*, p. 45.

13. In *History of the Church . . . in Singapore*, Pang lists the footnote for this account as follows: "Letter of 28 Oct 1993 to Pang Beng Ling from James N. Kimball on behalf of

Jon Huntsman." This quote appears only in a prepublication manuscript in possession of the author.

14. See "Ambassador's term brief, yet notable," *Church News*, 5 June 1993, p. 11.

15. Jones, *In Singapore*, p. 72.

16. Pang, *History of the Church . . . in Singapore*, p. 39.

17. Ibid., pp. 42–43.

18. The original wards were the Bedok Ward, the Singapore First Ward, the Toa Payoh Ward, the Clementi Ward, the Singapore Second Branch (Mandarin), and Singapore Third Branch (Philippines). The Ang Mo Kio Ward was organized on August 13, 1995.

19. Robert Hague to R. Lanier Britsch, 12 July 1995; copy in possession of the author.

20. See "Members dine with royalty," *Church News*, 17 December 1994, p. 12.

21. See "Malaysia converts see Church grow," *Church News*, 23 May 1981, p. 13.

22. See Joseph Walker, "Church in Malaysia is small but faithful," *Church News*, 14 March 1981, p. 12; and "Church acquires first property," *Church News*, 28 April 1979, p. 5.

23. See Jones, *In Singapore*, p. 9; and Jones to Carlos E. Asay and Jacob de Jager, 27 February 1980, Jones, Collection, LDS Church Archives.

24. Jones, *In Singapore*, p. 10.

25. See ibid., p. 112.

26. Robert and Delores Hague, interview by the author, Provo, Utah, 26 October 1995, tape recording. See also Robert Hague to R. Lanier Britsch.

27. See "Members dine with royalty," p. 12.

18

INDONESIA

1969 – 1996

Measured Progress in Indonesia

It is difficult for anyone who has not traveled in Southeast Asia to appreciate the vast territory that is encompassed there. Indonesia alone covers almost as much space on a map as the United States. Although much of this area is ocean, its size is tremendous all the same. Indonesians refer to their archipelago as *Tanah Air*—"land water." Indonesia consists of five large islands and 13,672 smaller ones (6,044 inhabited). Java, although not the largest island in size, has 107.6 million (60 percent) of the nation's 195 million people. The climate is tropical; the equator runs through several of Indonesia's main islands. The nation is large, diverse, beautiful, and generally fertile. The people speak many languages and form many cultural groups. Frank L. Cooley described Indonesia's complexity this way: "Geographical, ecological, geological and historical developments have combined to create conditions in which societies developed largely in isolation from one another for several hundreds, even thousands of years. This resulted in the formation of 200 to 300 distinct ethnic groups throughout the archipelago, each with its own language, social structure, customary law and folkways (*adat*), belief system, political system and sense of identity."[1]

Indonesia declared its independence from the Dutch on

August 17, 1945, but four years of wars and negotiations followed before the Dutch withdrew. When Indonesia became independent of Dutch control in 1949, the people agreed to share Bahasa Indonesia (closely related to Malay) as the common language. Today, most Indonesians are fluent in the national language, a blessing for LDS proselyting work. Taking the restored gospel to Indonesia through the use of 250 mutually unintelligible languages would be almost impossible. Eighty-five percent of the populous is literate. Local loyalties are still strong, but since the Indonesian Communist Party (PKI) was defeated in its attempt to take over the government in 1965, the people have had an increased sense of nationhood and a strong anti-Communist feeling in government.

The constitution of 1945 stipulates in Article 1 that "the State is based on the recognition of one all-powerful God" and in Article 2 that "the State guarantees to each citizen the freedom to embrace the religion of his choice and to fulfill the religious obligations which conform to his faith." Liberty to propagate religion is guaranteed "on condition that it does not disturb religious peace."[2] Because of its perceived "disturbing effect," open proselytizing is not allowed by the government; in fact, it discourages efforts by all religious groups to propagate their tenets. Hence, LDS missionary work has been limited to indirect methods such as radio broadcasts (used successfully during the early years of the mission), English-language instruction, speaking in worship services of other churches, and especially referrals from members. Over the years most of these methods have been limited or curtailed. Tracting and street contacting are not allowed.

Citizens are free to practice the religion of their choice, and some sense of religious toleration exists. But the choice has to be Islam, Protestantism, Catholicism, Buddhism-Hinduism, or since 1973, *Kebatinan*, or New Religions, of which national president Suharto was a member. Latter-day Saints have had trouble fitting into this limited list of religious options. For legal purposes in dealing with the Department of Religion, the Church has affiliated with the Protestants during the last few years. The influence of Islam is strong, and preference is often given to it by the Department of Religion, which is led by Muslims. Nevertheless, Islam is not the state religion. According to recent census figures, 87 percent of the populace is Muslim, but some observers believe a figure closer to 81 percent is more accurate. This figure includes many people who are only nominal Muslims. About 20 percent of all Muslims are devout, but the government lists as Muslims all persons who do not state a specific religious preference.

Indonesia is neither a religious state nor a secular state, as is the case in the United States, where there is separation of church and state. Indonesia calls itself a *pancasila* state—a state based on five principles: (1) belief in one all-powerful God, (2) humanitarianism based on justice and civility, (3) nationalism—the national unity of Indonesia, (4) rule by the people—democracy, and (5) social justice. The first principle, belief in one all-powerful God, was a compromise between nationalists who wanted a secular state and those who demanded an Islamic republic. For the most part, the government, particularly the military, has tried to treat all religions fairly. The military dominates state politics and has established policies to weaken Muslim activists who have sought greater control of government and politics. The result has been a state wherein the Muslim majority is more Indonesian than Muslim, more moderate than orthodox.

But not only the first principle has had a significant effect on missionary efforts; nationalism too has played a role. The government has consistently encouraged nationals to lead in every aspect of life. Foreign corporations and investments have been allowed and encouraged, but preference has been given to Indonesians. In the religious sphere as well, Indonesians have been encouraged to eliminate foreigners and to administer and staff their own organizations. As is true throughout this entire geographic realm, colonial powers are remembered and resented. The Muslim people of Indonesia, as well as elsewhere, remember and resent both the secularizing influence of the Western powers and the Christian missionizing of those nations. Most of the problems the Latter-day Saints have had with the government in Indonesia have not been directed specifically at the Church. The LDS Church has usually been lumped in with other Christian churches that have caught the attention of someone in government.

Christianity has grown rapidly since 1960 and is partly trace-able to the political upheavals of the mid-1960s. Close to 10 percent of the population (church statistics show 12.5 percent; government statistics, 9.6 percent) now claims to be Christian. This has, of course, helped the LDS mission a little, but only 2 percent of the people of Java are Christian, and Java, until recently, was the only island on which LDS missionaries had taught the restored gospel. Protestant and Roman Catholic mis-sionaries have been most successful working with animists. Few Indonesian Muslims have been converted. As a rule, Christianity has spread as a mass movement among the tribal peoples.

THE DEDICATION OF INDONESIA

For some time before Elder Ezra Taft Benson went to Indonesia in 1969 to dedicate that land for the preaching of the restored gospel, Church leaders in Hong Kong and Salt Lake City had considered opening this country as a mission field. Government instability before 1965 or 1966 had made Church leaders hesitant to move missionaries in, but by early 1967 E. M. ("Pete") and Maxine Grimm, who had a business friend named Jan Walandauw in Indonesia, suggested to Elder Gordon B. Hinckley that it would probably be possible to obtain visas for missionaries.[3] Three years passed, almost to the day, before arrangements could be completed for the missionaries to move in. Mr. Walandauw helped the Church on a number of occasions by explaining its intentions and purposes to government officials and by acting as a legal sponsor for many missionaries.

In October 1969, while President G. Carlos Smith Jr. was en route to Singapore to open the Southeast Asia Mission, he joined

Left to right: Elder Bruce R. McConkie and his wife, Amelia, and Elder Ezra Taft Benson and his wife, Flora, on a hilltop near Bogor, Island of Java, Indonesia, for the dedication of Indonesia for the preaching of the gospel, Sunday, October 26, 1969. Elder Benson offered the prayer. (Courtesy LDS Church Archives)

Elder Ezra Taft Benson of the Quorum of the Twelve, Elder Bruce R. McConkie of the First Council of the Seventy, and President W. Brent Hardy of the Southern Far East Mission (soon to be the Hong Kong–Taiwan Mission) in Manila for a mission presidents' seminar. Together they traveled with their wives to Jakarta, Indonesia, where they were met by a small band of Latter-day Saints, all but two of whom were Canadian, Dutch, or American. After discussing the advisability of dedicating Indonesia, Elder Benson determined that services should be held on the morning of Sunday, October 26, at a village known as Megamendung, near Bogor, about a ninety-minute ride from Jakarta. "As we stood on the hill, prior to the prayer," recalled Elder Benson, "we looked over the valley with its rice paddies, banana groves and corn-planted terraces and contemplated the gospel being preached to the millions in Indonesia."[4]

Twenty-three Saints and friends gathered as the Church leaders and others spoke. Elder McConkie explained why the Church dedicates lands for the preaching of the gospel: "When we perform a dedication in the Church, what we actually do is dedicate the people and the resources of the Church. . . .

"For all practical purposes, when we dedicate the Indonesian lands to the preaching of the gospel, we're both opening the door to the spread of truth in the nation involved and dedicating the resources of the Church and the talents and abilities of the members of the Church to spread the gospel in that nation."[5]

Elder Benson spoke with confidence about the spread of the gospel in Indonesia. Among other thoughtful and meaningful words, he said: "Father in Heaven, bless these humble people, many of them living almost in abject poverty. May the gospel reach them. May Thy servants come here in great numbers and carry this message to these Thy children. . . . Touch the hearts of the leaders of this great nation. . . .

"Let the love of the holy gospel spread throughout this land. May they receive a witness of the divine mission of Thy Beloved Son and the ministry of the Prophet Joseph. May they know Thee, Holy Father. They love Thee although they do not understand the nature of Thy divine personality."[6]

Following the dedication, the visitors left for other areas of Asia. G. Carlos Smith Jr., however, was left with the responsibility of getting missionaries into the country.[7]

THE EARLY MISSION YEARS IN INDONESIA

On January 5, 1970, President Smith sent six elders who were serving in Singapore to Jakarta. They were Greg Hawker, Larry Hunt, Ross Marchant, Robert K. Meier, Dale Storer, and Franklin Willard. Two days later, Smith himself flew to Jakarta, rented a missionary apartment that could double as a meeting place, and started making arrangements for the Church's legal recognition. The Minister of Religion had a difficult time understanding why the Church wanted to send representatives to Indonesia, considering there were so few Mormons there. With the exception of Brother Sutrisno, the first Indonesian convert, and a couple others, the only Latter-day Saints living there were expatriates. But the official eventually granted permission for the missionaries to continue entering the country on tourist visas. The Department of Religion (*Agama*) has never allowed LDS missionaries to have long-term visas that provide for open proselyting as the Church generally expects to do.

During the next two months, the missionaries participated in a number of firsts, such as tracting (it was still allowed at that time), holding a priesthood meeting, teaching the missionary lessons in the Indonesian language, organizing the first branch (the Jakarta Branch, organized on February 15 with Dennis B. Butler, an American who was working in Jakarta, as president), and finally, on March 29, baptizing the first two converts (that is, the first two baptized by full-time missionaries).[8]

Attending the first meeting was Mr. Siang Sililahih, who later became mayor of West Jakarta. Mr. Sililahih had become acquainted with the Church while attending Brigham Young University, where he received a master's degree in political science in the late 1950s. Although he was not a member of the Church, he had great respect for its members and teachings and desired that the people of Indonesia might have the gospel in their midst. He attended the first meeting of the Church to lend his influence and support. His friendship continued long after these early events.

The good beginning, notwithstanding, the work that President Smith had initiated to obtain recognition for the Church was not completed in time to satisfy the government. To the surprise of the missionaries, on April 11, 1970, the government stopped all LDS meetings and activities (such as door-to-door proselyting) until the Church was granted official recognition.

Fortunately, with the assistance of Briton McConkie, who represented the Church, and Siang Sililahih, who added his influence, on April 20 the Church received official recognition from the

Central Government's Department of Religion under the name The Foundation of The Church of Jesus Christ of Latter-day Saints, or Yayasan OSZA.[9] Under this legal organization the missionaries were allowed to continue teaching, and regular Church activities could be held. From then on, however, the elders were very careful in their proselyting methods. Of course, they were limited in what they could accomplish at that time because they spoke little Bahasa Indonesia. Until June they did not have an accurately translated version of the missionary discussions, and they had no literature to leave with interested individuals. It was not until April 1971, that the Church published its first literature in Bahasa Indonesia, a translation of *Joseph Smith's Testimony*.

THE BEGINNINGS OF TRANSLATION WORK

Everyone involved knew literature in the national language was essential to success, so translation projects were started early in the mission's history. On January 26, 1970, D'Monte W. Coombs, from the Salt Lake City headquarters of Translation Services, and Watanabe Kan of Tokyo, who directed all translation efforts in Asia, visited Jakarta to initiate the translation of Church books and materials into Bahasa Indonesia. One of the first translation assignments was given to Brother Sutrisno and Elder Larry Hunt, a missionary. They translated the name of the Church (Gereja Yesus Kristus dari Orang-orang Suci Zaman Akhir, abbreviated as Gereja OSZA) and the Articles of Faith.[10]

On that first visit Coombs and Watanabe contracted with a professional firm to translate the Book of Mormon into Bahasa Indonesia. What started as a standard project that should have taken only a year or two eventually took until March 1977, to complete. A number of missionaries and members of the Church were also involved, particularly Budi Darmawan, who eventually worked full-time on this and other translation projects and founded Church Translation Services in Indonesia. He was assisted by Han King Ishar and Wasito Bambang Kusamoyudo, each of whom spent a year working full-time reviewing the Book of Mormon translation. In the lengthy process of two full reviews, Darmawan discovered and hired Sister Irma Shalimar Wyude, a member who had unusual abilities as a rapid and accurate translator. She presently manages translation operations for the Church in Indonesia. While the Book of Mormon was under way, other projects were also completed, such as the missionary discussions (completed in June 1970), *Joseph Smith's Testimony* (mentioned above), and a selection of fifty hymns (January 1973). Tracts and lesson materials were also translated and printed during this time.

TRANSLATING THE *KITAB MORMON*
Alison Craig

From the beginning, the translation [of the Book of Mormon] was hampered by some unusual problems. Although Bahasa Indonesia, the official language of the Republic of Indonesia, is spoken by about seventy percent of the people [in 1977], only a few speak it as their native language. Most Indonesians grow up speaking one of the hundreds of other languages in the islands, and only learn the official national language in school.

It is a simple and regular language. Meanings of words are changed by adding prefixes or suffixes. Plurals are formed by repeating the word—for example, *orang* means "man," so "men" is *orang-orang*. But such simplicity does not make translation from English into Indonesian easy. Indonesian, like English, uses the roman alphabet, but there the similarity ends. There are few cognates—similar words that mean the same in both languages—and no similar sentence patterns. A word such as *consecration* causes problems. We use this one word to mean many things: ordaining someone, giving everything to the Lord, setting someone apart, and so on. There is no single Bahasa Indonesia word that means all these things—and for some of these meanings there is no word at all! Figures of speech such as "harrowing up" also cause this type of problem.

Another translation problem was the level of the language. Of course, it wouldn't be appropriate for scripture to be translated into street slang. And yet the Book of Mormon should not be translated into such formal language that no one but the most highly educated can understand it. The translators worked to set the Book of Mormon in simple, understandable language that was literate enough to convey the power and beauty of the scripture.

And to top off these problems, right in the middle of the translation the Indonesian government changed the system of spelling! The entire manuscript had to be corrected.

Brother Budi Darmawan, language coordinator for the Church Translation Services Department in Indonesia, was responsible for preparing the first draft of the translation. In June 1975 he sent it to Church Translation in Salt Lake City, where Americans like returned missionary Arne Hallam and staff experts on the Book of Mormon went over the translation word by word to make sure that the Indonesian version conveyed the exact meaning of the scripture. Then the manuscript was returned to Indonesia, where Brother Darmawan and others used the corrections and polished the language so that it would read smoothly in Bahasa Indonesia.

The translation made several more trips between Indonesia and the United States before it was at last ready for the printer. And now the Indonesian Saints are receiving a book . . . that has the power to change the life of anyone who reads it "with a sincere heart, with real intent, having faith in Christ." (Moro. 10:4.)[11]

By August 23, 1970, President Smith believed the elders were doing well enough in the language for them to train four new missionaries. He sent Elders Storer and Meier and two new missionaries to open the city of Bandung. It was in Bandung that the elders learned that by Indonesian law they would be required to gain permission to proselyte from the local government in every city where they desired to work. By September 4 they had received permission to proselyte there. Before the end of the year, more than sixty people attended a Christmas party in Bandung, and a few individuals had been baptized.

In November, Elders Frank Willard and Scott Cannon moved to Bogor, but they did not receive permission to proselyte until January 16, 1971. The first convert there was baptized on April 4.

The people of Jakarta, Bandung, and Bogor are called Sandanese. Missionaries from other Christian churches have had little success among them because they are generally strict Muslims. Nevertheless, the branches in all three cities grew steadily.

In late September 1971 G. Carlos Smith sent four elders to Jogjakarta, which lies close to the southern coast of central Java, to start working with the Javanese people. These people, although strongly Muslim, were more willing to listen to the missionaries. Through the help of a young couple named Moestadjab, who had friends in the Church in Jakarta, the elders found a home and began teaching the gospel. Two months later the Moestadjabs joined the Church, and within a year of the city's opening almost fifty people had been baptized. Over the next twenty-six months the elders opened five other major Javanese cities: Surakarta, Solo, Semarang, Surabaya, and Malang. The movement was ever eastward.[12]

In July 1972 Miller F. Shurtleff replaced G. Carlos Smith as mission president of the Southeast Asia Mission. Shurtleff, a man of many years of government service and one who knew bureaucracies well, fit the needs of the Church in Indonesia. Several serious problems arose regarding missionary visas and the status of the Church. In 1973 the government tightened its restrictions on all foreign missionaries. For most Christian organizations this was not as serious a problem as it was for the Latter-day Saints. Other churches sent professional ministers and missionaries who remained in the country for many years. Thus their rate of attrition was not as great in numbers or as rapid over time. The LDS way of doing missionary work was different; the government was reluctant to constantly grant a comparatively large number of missionary visas.[13] The missionaries all had to make expensive periodic trips to Singapore during their time in Indonesia to renew their visas. During this time the local government of Jakarta also made visits by Church authorities uncomfortable and less effective. When Elder A. Theodore Tuttle of the Seventy visited Indonesia, officials imposed a little-known law restricting foreigners from speaking in public.[14] But on the positive side, the new missionaries were arriving better prepared because they had been taught Bahasa Indonesia at the Language Training Mission. And the Church was still growing. By the end of 1974 there were 770 Indonesian Latter-day Saints and six organized branches.[15]

THE INDONESIA JAKARTA MISSION

Seeing the steady growth of the Church in Indonesia, the First Presidency and Council of the Twelve decided to make it a separate mission. In April 1975 President N. Eldon Tanner called Hendrik Gout (pronounced hōt), a retired major in the Dutch Royal Army, and his wife, Johanna Maria, to preside over the new mission. President Gout, who was born in Java, spoke the language fluently; his genealogy went back four generations in Indonesia. Following World War II, during which Gout spent three years as a prisoner in Japan, he returned to Celebes (Sulawesi) Island. In 1950 he and all other Dutch army officers were sent out of the country for a four-month furlough. However, the new government did not allow any of them to return to Indonesia.

In 1953 the Gouts joined the Church in the Netherlands, where he served as branch and district president as well as in many other ecclesiastical positions. His first wife died in 1962, and he married Johanna late that year. When President Gout retired from the military in 1969, he became head of Church translation operations in Holland, a position he held when he was called as mission president.

Because of his familiarity with Indonesia and its people, President Gout was well prepared to lead the mission; but because of his status as an ex-colonial military officer, the Indonesian government did not wish him to enter or stay in the country. Nevertheless, with faith that the problems would be worked out, the Gouts (including eight of their twelve children—five by the first wife, seven by the second) served their full mission.

Hendrik Gout described himself as one "who knows his way around Indonesia and loves and understands the Indonesian people." With the strong encouragement of Elder Adney Y. Komatsu, area supervisor, President Gout strengthened local leadership and improved proselyting methods. For example, he taught the missionaries to "ask not what you can do for the members but what the members can do for you." His objective was to get the members more involved in preparing new families to hear the gospel.[16] He also organized several new branches. Welfare services missionaries were integrated into the mission during this time.

THE FOUNDING OF THE LDS ELEMENTARY SCHOOL

President Gout's most important institutional contribution was the creation of an elementary school in Jakarta. Even before he came to Indonesia, Church leaders mentioned President Shurtleff's and their interest in establishing a school. By the fall of 1975 President Gout had informed CES leaders in Salt Lake

City that he was ready to push the project ahead if they thought it was time. On October 28 and 29 CES commissioner Neal A. Maxwell visited Jakarta and investigated the merits of the proposal. He was satisfied that an LDS school could help the people of Indonesia and also make the Church's desire to help its own people clear to government officials. On November 11 Alton L. Wade, supervisor of Church schools in the Pacific, visited Jakarta and gathered more information. When he returned home to make his report, he learned that the Church Board of Education had already approved the new school.[17]

During 1976 President Gout and other leaders gained government approval for the school, selected a site, and hired a faculty and two administrators. Mayor Siang Sililahih assisted the Church greatly in making introductions, cutting red tape, and helping to obtain approvals to open the school.

On January 6, 1977, the Church opened the doors of S.D. OSZA, the LDS Elementary or the Jakarta Elementary School, as it was often called. The school had only LDS Indonesians as teachers and administrators. Enrollment the first year was sixty-two, eleven of whom were members of the Church. Distance from the school and relatively high tuition evidently limited LDS participation. All students received daily gospel lessons and English instruction in addition to the normal Indonesian curriculum. The purpose of the school was to provide a service for the children of Indonesia (members and nonmembers), to build relationships with responsible citizens, and to further the image of the Church. Indonesian education officials soon recognized it as a school of "high standard."[18] The school maintained a steady enrollment of more than two hundred until 1987, when it was closed (a story that will be told later).

WELFARE SERVICES MISSIONARY WORK

By the end of 1978, fifty-two missionaries were working in Indonesia. Eight of these were local and foreign welfare services missionaries. Their services were somewhat different from those of typical missionaries. Possibly more than in any other Asian nation where the Church was well established at that time, the members suffered from poverty, malnutrition, disease, and other problems that relate to economic underdevelopment. The welfare services missionaries worked to help the Saints and others overcome these problems. Mary Ellen Edmunds, who started welfare services missionary work in the Philippines (and served in Hong Kong and Taiwan), also began that service in Indonesia in 1977. She reported that the members were eager to learn about health care and sanitation, as well as all other welfare concepts.

Sister Edmunds also reported concerning the tremendous impact the restored gospel has on new members of the Church. "We [Caucasian Americans] have no feeling for what goes on in the homes of the people who are struggling to become Latter-day Saints. We totally change people's lives." Before they become Mormons, typical Indonesians were almost totally uninvolved in their former religions. Now, as Latter-day Saints, they were expected to attend Sunday meetings two or more times each week. Women, who had been taught from childhood to be passive and submissive, were called, often soon after baptism, to work in the Relief Society and other auxiliaries and to become leaders and teachers.

According to Sister Edmunds's report at the time, the Indonesian Saints knew the principles of welfare services before they learned of the program. They helped each other and shared what they had. When asked how she found out who needed assistance, a Relief Society president in Solo responded: "Oh, Sister, in Solo we don't have telephones. We have to ask the Spirit if someone needs help." Regularly that Relief Society president rode her bicycle to the homes of members whom the Spirit prompted her to visit.[19] In many instances the Saints needed the welfare program only as a way to organize the acts of charity they already performed. As Elder Benson said in his dedicatory prayer, "They love Thee although they do not understand the nature of

Thy divine personality." They lived many of the principles even though they did not know the names of the programs.

PROBLEMS BEGIN TO SURFACE

In Gout's second year as president, the head of Protestant Christian Affairs called in his counselor in the mission presidency, Jules Taulu, and told him that his office had received complaints from Muslims regarding door-to-door proselyting by Mormon missionaries and Jehovah's Witnesses. He said this was not allowed. Actually, until that time there was no law against such activity, but a law was created to control it, and since then Latter-day Saints have not tracted.[20] This restriction caused some problems, but the missionaries have been innovative in the use of English-language classes, television and radio interviews, direct gospel discussions, and in meeting people in public places such as soccer games, barber shops, buses, and shops who were willing to invite them into their homes. The work was helped a great deal when the Book of Mormon, *Kitab Mormon*, was published in Bahasa Indonesia in early 1977.

The Church had grown considerably during its first nine years. By the end of 1978 there were almost sixteen hundred Indonesian Latter-day Saints, and the Church was established in all of the major cities on Java.

President Gout and his successor, President Lester C. Hawthorne, who took over in July 1978, were eager to expand the work beyond Java and into the pockets of Christians in the islands of Celebes, Kalimantan (Borneo), and Sumatra. But they were understaffed and unable to move beyond Java. At the end of 1978 only fifty-two missionaries were serving in the mission, and ten or twelve of them were local missionaries. Native Indonesian elders had initially been called as full-time missionaries in 1975. The first two were Tjan Hardjiono and Suharto (Indonesians frequently have only one name). These elders and other elders and sisters who were called later, such as Sister Aischa Meyer and Elder

Subandriyo, were among those who would assume the responsibility of leadership in the mission soon after this time. The missionary experience was among the most important developments for Indonesian Saints. Through it these young members learned gospel doctrine and developed the necessary faith and leadership skills to lead the Church during the coming difficult period of the Church's history in Indonesia.[21]

THE EXPULSION OF THE FOREIGN MISSIONARIES

The two and a half years of Lester C. Hawthorne's service as mission president were extremely stressful for him personally and for the Church, though the Church in Indonesia saw significant progress in several areas. On August 1, 1978, only a month after Hawthorne began his term as mission president, the Minister of Religion issued Ministerial Decree No. 70, which greatly curtailed LDS missionary work. The decree, which targeted all religious organizations, was intended to guarantee "the maintenance of national unity, security, and stability." As Garth Jones points out, it prohibited "religious proselyting when it:

"1. Directs its efforts towards a person or persons who already belong to another religious faith.

"2. Utilizes persuasion and/or material incentives (money, clothing, food/beverages, medicines) to attract persons of other religious faiths.

"3. Distributes pamphlets, bulletins, magazines, books and other materials in regions [communities] and at the homes where people with other religious faiths live.

"4. Involves visiting people who already adhere to other religious faiths in their homes for whatever reasons."[22]

Fifteen days later a further decree specifically restricted expatriate missionaries from religious training of Indonesian nationals. This decree would apply to the mission president and all of the foreign missionaries. Conservative Muslims felt that Christians were "poaching" and had unfair advantages technologically and financially that led to conversions to Christianity.

A year later, on September 1, 1979, President Suharto declared that "foreign missionaries should be replaced." The *Indonesian Times* article that reported his position began: "President Soeharto has asked that members of foreign missionaries [sic] working in Indonesia should be gradually replaced by Indonesian nationals. . . . Like in business field, expatriates in religious field should eventually be succeeded by Indonesian nationals."[23] The article stated that President Suharto thought a period of planning was required so that replacements could "run smoothly." But that which for other denominations was the beginning of a period of planning and perhaps a ten-to-twenty-year transition period was for the Latter-day Saints the beginning of a rapid end for foreign missionaries in Indonesia.

By late October, visa and other problems had become so severe that President Hawthorne predicted that a group of six departing missionaries would "be the last group of missionaries to serve a full two years in the Indonesia Jakarta Mission." He was almost right. The next day eleven missionaries were transferred to other missions because they could not renew their visas. This reduced missionary numbers to sixty, nine of whom were Indonesians.

The first few months following the August 1978 decree did not bring many changes, but in May 1979 pressure from the Department of Religion was stepped up. President Hawthorne's first indication that the mission was in real trouble came when he was told by the Minister of Religion that he could not preside as head of the Yayasan OSZA (the LDS Foundation) and that "all of the Church's activities in Indonesia would be stopped." The head of the Yayasan and the members were required to be Indonesian nationals. Since 1970 the officers of the Yayasan OSZA had been Indonesian members of the Church. They made up the board and took their responsibilities seriously. Shortly before this time, President Hawthorne thought that as president of the mission he should be the head of the Yayasan. He also reorganized the membership of the Yayasan by removing (he notified them by mail) the *bapaks,* the old-timers, and replacing them with younger men. Animosity developed toward the mission president. Feelings of nationalism were to arise in various branches of the Church during this time.[24] There were also problems between the old members of the Yayasan and the new. None of this sat well with the Department of Religion. President Hawthorne quickly reorganized the Yayasan with Indonesian members in charge, and it appeared for a moment that the serious threat had passed.

But beginning in July 1979 the Indonesian visa officer in Singapore would only issue to missionaries one-month tourist visas with a sticker or stamp attached saying "Cannot be renewed." On August 30 five missionaries were transferred to the Philippines, the first to be refused re-entry into Indonesia. They had been in Singapore for about a month and were not allowed to renew their visas. Three weeks later eight additional elders were sent to the Philippines to finish their missions. The only slightly consoling news was that other churches were suffering from the same problem.

During October 1979 Elder David M. Kennedy, Special Ambassador for the First Presidency of the Church, flew to Jakarta to use his influence with officials he knew in government. He was hosted warmly, but his efforts did not prove helpful. Adam Malik, vice president of Indonesia, agreed to "look into the matter further so as to ascertain the best possible cooperation in this matter," but his general agreement to help did not override the position and policies of the Department of Religion.[25] Later visits by Brother Kennedy, the last in 1983, did not bring the desired change. The lockout of new missionaries was enforced, but those who were already in the country in late 1979 were allowed to remain in the country until their normal missions were over. The last six foreign elders departed Indonesia in August 1981.

While all of this was happening, President Hawthorne saw the need to train local leadership. Consequently, he held numerous special leadership meetings. Knowing that local missionaries were going to be the salvation of the Church, he called more Indonesians to full-time service. He instituted a prospective missionary program in most branches for sixteen- to nineteen-year-old males. He also organized a Missionary Training Center (referred to as a mini-MTC) to better train the local missionaries when they entered the field. Mini-MTCs have continued to the present.

The Doctrine and Covenants was added to the list of translated works at the end of 1979. In addition to the Book of Mormon, fourteen tracts, some seminary materials, most priesthood handbooks, and some teaching manuals were available.[26]

In November 1980 President Hawthorne experienced a mild heart attack. He was released from his mission seven months early and flew to Salt Lake City for heart bypass surgery. J. Talmage Jones, who was already presiding over Singapore, Sri Lanka, India, and Malaysia, was asked to lead the Church in Indonesia as well. In December he received word from the First Presidency that "the Indonesian Mission will be discontinued as a separate entity and . . . will be attached to the Singapore Mission, effective immediately."[27]

THE CHURCH BECOMES AN "INDONESIAN CHURCH"

From the time of President Hawthorne's departure in December 1980, the Church has essentially been in the hands of local leaders. Expatriate members of the Church have helped along the way. For example, Terrill Hill of UNESCO served as a counselor under President Jones, but Jones's other counselor was Effian Kadarusman, who was the country director of the Church Educational System. Hill supervised the west part of Java, and Kadarusman handled the middle and eastern parts of the island. The missionary force since 1981, with the exception of humanitarian services missionaries and a few others who have entered on short-term visas in the 1990s, has been made up entirely of locals. Jones, like Hawthorne, had become converted to the value of local missionaries in Singapore and Malaysia and immediately saw the promise they offered in Indonesia. In early 1981 twenty-four Indonesians were serving in their homeland. That number increased to between thirty-five and forty-five over the next four or five years, and with the exception of a year or two at the end of the 1980s, the number remained quite steady.

Because of Indonesian visa policies, the Church has not been able to maintain a permanent foreign mission president in the country. Indonesia was part of the Singapore Mission from December 1980 until June 30, 1985. At that time Effian Kadarusman and his wife, Mary, became president of the reopened Indonesia Jakarta Mission. He served from 1985 to 1989, the final year being added to the normal term of three years because the person who had been recommended as Kadarusman's replacement needed to work another year before retiring. As it turned out, the Indonesian government would not allow the proposed president to remain in the country with a new religion visa category, so it was necessary to transfer Indonesia back to the Singapore Mission again.

This time, however, the Brethren called Piet Tandiman, an Indonesian member of long standing in the Church, to serve as full-time counselor to the mission president in Singapore. He lived in the mission president's home in Jakarta and was supported in the same manner as are other mission presidents. He was in charge of the Church in Indonesia, but he reported to President Warren R. Jones in Singapore. This arrangement was continued until July 1993, when Piet Tandiman's son, Juswan, was called as counselor in charge of missionary work and Dr. Dean Belnap, a child psychiatrist serving as a humanitarian services missionary at the University of Indonesia Medical Center, was called to assist with the members. In July 1994 Brother Subandriyo, country manager and physical facilities manager for the Church, was chosen to replace Juswan as counselor to Carl D. Warren in

The growth of the Church since 1980 has been dependent on the service of Indonesian elders and sisters. A mini–missionary training center has been in operation in Jakarta for many years. Shown here are missionaries in training in September 1995. (Photo by author)

Singapore. Juswan and his wife, Aischa, and later Subandriyo and his wife, Steffie, traveled to Provo, Utah, to participate in the Church's annual mission presidents' seminar at the MTC. They were responsible for operating the mini-MTC in Jakarta in a manner similar to the Provo MTC.

On July 1, 1995, Vern and Carol Tueller began service as humanitarian services missionaries at the University of Indonesia. Elder Tueller had taught dentistry at the University of California Medical Center in San Francisco for forty years and now turned these talents to the service of the Indonesian people.[28] The Church also asked him to spend part of his time directing affairs in Indonesia. Even with an invitation from the University of Indonesia in hand, the Tuellers had trouble getting more than a sixty-day visa. Subandriyo continued on as counselor in charge of missionary work.[29] He was the head of the Yayasan OSZA and was recognized by the government as the head of the Church in Indonesia. (In the 1980s the government required all churches to split the ecclesiastical and temporal parts of their organizations. The Yayasan OSZA was made responsible for the temporal parts of the Church, those that normally come under the director of temporal affairs or the country manager.

The Church continued to make progress on many fronts during the 1980s. Talmage Jones sought ways to build or buy more buildings for Church use. The Church owned only three buildings in 1981. A distribution center for Church materials was created, and publications in Bahasa Indonesian became more plentiful. In 1985 Subandriyo was hired to work full-time buying property and supervising the construction of chapels. By 1995 the Church owned ten chapels and leased two additional buildings for branch use. The most frustrating experience with property was the long-delayed completion of the Jakarta Selatan (South) chapel. After the elementary school's closure (see explanation in the section following this text), the decision was made to build a chapel on that property. The necessary approvals were obtained from the Church and the government, and construction commenced. However, when the foundation and pillars were up, opposition was raised by Muslim neighbors who did not want a competing religious structure in the neighborhood. Legal impediments stopped construction for five years. Finally, after working with the minister in charge of Protestant religions and completing some further clearances, the Church was allowed to proceed with construction and to complete the building in 1995. According to some members of the Church, the newly completed building has done much to enhance the image of the Church and to establish the Mormon presence in Jakarta.[30]

Under Subandriyo's guidance, membership and financial records were computerized during the mid-to-late 1980s and in the process became much more accurate.[31] Computers were also introduced in the translation process during this time, making that work easier to produce and correct. By 1995 electronic mail was in use between translators in Jakarta and the offices of the international magazines and the Translation Department in Salt Lake

City. Facsimile machines, too, have greatly increased the efficiency of translation and other operations in Indonesia.

Effian Kadarusman, country director of CES and former mission president, has provided years of service to the Church in Indonesia. (Photo by author)

The seminary and institute program was initiated in 1980 but moved forward slowly. Numbers of potential seminary students more than doubled between 1980 and 1987, but the percent enrolled dropped from 46 percent to 23 percent. Total numbers enrolled grew by only 23, making a total of 122 students. Institute figures are not clear for this same period. By 1987, 45 percent of the potential 125 students were attending institute classes. President William R. Bradford of the Asia Area Presidency was deeply concerned about the activity of Indonesian youth in seminary and institute as well as in all Church programs. Although mission president Effian Kadarusman had his responsibilities as associate area director of CES for Indonesia somewhat reduced, on February 9, 1987, his position was reemphasized by President Bradford. Two other men were also hired part-time as regional coordinators to help direct this work. Elder Bradford said, "The salvation of the Church in Indonesia rests on the CES program preparing our young people to be missionaries."[32]

The mission progressed as well as could be expected with the small number of missionaries. The local elders and sisters generally performed as well as their foreign counterparts had done, and membership continued to grow. By the end of 1987 membership stood at thirty-six hundred (up a couple thousand in six or seven years) in seventeen branches under three districts, the Jakarta

District in the west, the Surakarta District in central Java, and the Surabaya District in the east.

THE CLOSING OF THE
LDS ELEMENTARY SCHOOL

In addition to these manifestations of success, it appeared that the Jakarta Elementary School was serving the needs of the members as well as the nonmembers who were enrolled there. But for five years prior to 1987, when the school's closure was announced, CES leaders in Indonesia, Hong Kong, and Salt Lake City had been evaluating the effectiveness of the institution. For a time it had served the purposes of the Church quite well, but several things had changed. The student body was 90 percent non-Mormon, and most of those students were from families who could afford to enroll at other high-quality schools. The Church was paying 85 percent of the annual budget, but most of the children of the Church in Jakarta and throughout the island were not able to enroll because of distance and cost. Finally, the government issued a regulation against using the school as a proselyting tool.[33] When the school was first opened, missionaries had taught some of the religion classes at the school, set up displays there, met parents while they were waiting for their children, and so on.[34] These and other means of finding hearers of the gospel were closed off. President Kadarusman, who was also a CES director while serving as mission president, said: "We hardly baptized anyone from the Church school. If we baptized, we only baptized small children because it was an elementary school. Seldom did the parents join the Church because their children were baptized." He continued: "You can teach religion classes in that school, you can practice religion in that school, but you cannot persuade anyone to join the Church. So if they know you are doing religion activities to persuade people to join, your school will finally be closed down."[35]

The board of trustees of the Church Educational System

decided to close the school primarily because it was expensive, it was not serving the needs of enough Latter-day Saints, and Church funds could be reallocated to support other educational needs in Indonesia. Elder William R. Bradford, president of the Asia Area, was assigned to make the announcement in Jakarta. On February 9, 1987, he and other CES representatives met with the administrators and teachers at the school and announced the board's decision. Even though they had been forewarned that sooner or later the school would be closed, the closure caused great concern and upheaval in the lives of those employed by the school. The fallout from the announcement ultimately created great problems for the Church and personally for President Kadarusman.[36] Ultimately, after negotiations with the PTA and parents, the school was closed the next year. All of the students had found new schools to attend. The Church paid entry fees to other schools for most of the students and did what it reasonably could to cushion the blow caused by the closure.

Because of the school closure and other related matters, the Church in Jakarta suffered and unity was disrupted. Ultimately, after suffering more than two years of difficulty arising from the troubles brought about by the school closure, President Kadarusman completed the fourth year of his mission and was released. A month later, he and his family moved to Hawaii, where he continued his higher education. He was temporarily replaced by Eddie Harjono, who acted as CES director in Indonesia until Kadarusman returned in 1992.

Since the school's closure, observers have attempted to evaluate the decision. Was it the right thing to do? Kadarusman never questioned the decision in spite of the problems he suffered. He was convinced that the reallocation of part of the support funds for scholarships to support studies of young Indonesian members at colleges and universities was the wisest use of the money. Some moneys were used this way, but bickering over who was worthy to receive the help has somewhat limited this program. Nevertheless, with these scholarships LDS students have graduated in veterinary science, mechanics, economics, law, and in other fields.

On another side is the reality that the Church does not have a flagship, so to speak, to manifest its concern for the people and government of Indonesia. The school, though small, did make friends for the Church. The real tragedy of its closing, as was so often true in the early days of the Church, was the disunity that arose in the Church.

THE CHURCH IN INDONESIA TODAY

The Church has moved forward in an almost remarkable way considering the external and internal difficulties that have been placed in its path. There is not yet a stake in Indonesia, as there are in Bangkok and Singapore, but the circumstances are quite different in all three locations. Unlike Singapore, which is confined in size and has a totally different social and economic structure, and Bangkok, where the Church has had serious government problems but has nonetheless had steady support from foreign missionaries, the Church in Jakarta, which is probably the first candidate for stakehood, and in the remainder of the country has had to develop largely on its own. Almost as many people have been brought into the Church in Indonesia (4,600 members) as in Thailand (5,300 members), and far more than in Singapore (1,650 members), over the same period of time. The Church is actually most successful and active in central Java. Jakarta is strengthened by the faith and experience of Saints who have moved there from other districts. In the mid-1990s missionaries have been sent to other islands. Two elders were serving in Medan, Sumatra, and four were assigned to Manado, Sulawesi, in 1995.

According to Elder Tueller, Church members throughout Indonesia are striving to live in accordance with the counsel of President Howard W. Hunter, who encouraged all adult members to obtain a recommend to enter the temple even if they could not actually use it because they lived so far away from a temple. When asked what the most important Church development has been during the past fifteen years—the years since the foreign missionaries were expelled from the country—Brother Subandriyo answered: "The major development is that the teachings of the Church have made members into strong and valuable persons. I can see that if the gospel had not entered their lives, they may not be what they are now. This has benefited the member himself, his family, his community, and the country, because they have developed themselves."[37]

NOTES

1. Frank L. Cooley, "The Growing Seed: A Descriptive and Analytical Survey of the Church in Indonesia," *Occasional Bulletin of Missionary Research* 1 (October 1977): 3.

2. "Indonesia," in *Encyclopedia of Christianity*, ed. David B. Barrett (New York: Oxford University Press, 1982), p. 385.

3. Gordon B. Hinckley, Journals, 6 January 1967.

4. As quoted in "Indonesia Land Dedicated for Gospel Message," *Church News*, 29 November 1969, p. 3.

5. As quoted in Spencer J. Palmer, *The Church Encounters Asia* (Salt Lake City: Deseret Book Co., 1970), p. 161.

6. As quoted in ibid., pp. 171–72.

7. See G. Carlos Smith Jr. Oral History, interviews by William G. Hartley, Oral History Program, LDS Church Archives, 1972, typescript, pp. 2–4.

8. Southeast Asia Mission Historical Reports, 31 March 1970, LDS Church Archives.

9. See Jules L. L. Taulu, "Short History of the Church of Jesus Christ of Latter-day Saints in Indonesia," typescript in possession of the author. Taulu writes: "Gradually the LDS Church was organized and developed, and upon the request of the Foundation of the Church of Jesus Christ of Latter-day Saints, a permit was issued by R. I. Department of Religion, Dirjen Bimas KP No. Dd/P/VIII/25/294/70 dated 18 April 1970 in the name of the Foundation." This is the document that officially permitted the Church to move forward with its activities. See also Piet Tandiman, interview by the author, Jakarta, Indonesia, 13 September 1995, tape recording.

10. Effian Kadarusman, trans., "The History of the Translation of the Book of Mormon, according to the memory of and a few data from Han King Ishar," in possession of the author.

11. Alison Craig, "The Saints in Indonesia," *Ensign* 7 (January 1977): 88.

12. See Garth N. Jones, "Spreading the Gospel in Indonesia: Organizational Obstacles and Opportunities," *Dialogue* 15 (winter 1982): 79.

13. See Dale S. Cox, "The Church in the Third World: Singapore and Indonesia" (honors thesis, Brigham Young University, 1981), pp. 48–49.

14. See Southeast Asia Mission Historical Reports, by date, LDS Church Archives.

15. See Indonesia Jakarta Mission Historical Reports, 31 December 1975, LDS Church Archives.

16. See ibid.

17. See ibid.; and Alton L. Wade, interview by the author, Salt Lake City, Utah, 5 July 1979, tape recording.

18. Cox, "Church in the Third World," pp. 56–57.

19. Mary Ellen Edmunds, interview by Dale S. Cox, Provo, Utah, 27 February 1979, tape recording.

20. Jules L. L. Taulu, interview by the author, Jakarta, Indonesia, 13 September 1995, tape recording.

21. See Cynthia Collier, "The Church of Jesus Christ of Latter-day Saints in Indonesia," manuscript in typed and handwritten form, 1989; in possession of the author. The author expresses gratitude for Mrs. Collier's work.

22. Jones, "Spreading the Gospel," p. 80.

23. "President asks Catholic and Protestant leaders: Foreign missionaries should be replaced," *Indonesian Times*, 1 September 1979. This item is found in Indonesia Jakarta Mission History, 1979, LDS Church Archives.

24. Subandriyo, interview by the author, Jakarta, Indonesia, 12 September 1995, tape recording.

25. See Indonesia Jakarta Mission Historical Reports, 1979, LDS Church Archives.

26. See Cox, "Church in the Third World," pp. 61–62.

27. J. Talmage Jones, *In Singapore* (Salt Lake City: Publishers Press, 1984), pp. 61, 63.

28. Vern Tueller, interview by the author, Jakarta, Indonesia, 12 September 1995, tape recording.

29. Subandriyo, interview; Effian Kadarusman, Journal, by date, copy in possession of the author; Effian Kadarusman, interviews by the author, Laie, Hawaii, 30 May and 7 June 1990; Jakarta, Indonesia, 12 September 1995, tape recordings.

30. Taulu, interview; Joachim Ladjar, interview by the author, Jakarta, Indonesia, 13 September 1995, tape recording.

31. Subandriyo interview.

32. Bradford quote and statistics from J. Alden Richins, "1986–87 [CES] Historical Report for Southeast Asia," 15 October 1987; in possession of the author.

33. Kadarusman interview, 7 June 1990.

34. See Cox, "Church in the Third World," pp. 60–61.

35. Kadarusman interview, 7 June 1990.

36. Kadarusman, Journal, by date; and Kadarusman interview, 7 June 1990.

37. Subandriyo interview.

19

INDIA

1954 – 1982

Church Growth in South Asia

Frequently over the decades since the early East India Mission was closed in the 1850s, General Authorities of the Church have expressed their hope that the restored gospel could be established in India and other nations of South Asia. The local political, social, cultural, and religious frameworks, however, have made open, straightforward missionary work very difficult. With the exception of Pakistan, a Muslim nation that does not fear Christian missionaries, all of the countries of South Asia have laws or immigration policies that inhibit new missionary churches from entering their borders. (Pakistan allows proselyting among Christians only.) Such anti-missionary attitudes have restricted the work of spreading the restored gospel to the 1.28 billion people who live in this geographical realm.

Unlike Singapore and Hong Kong, which are small and somewhat describable, India is large, its land mass covering slightly more than one-third the size of the United States. A populous nation, India was home to more than 900 million people in 1995. India is also ethnically and linguistically diverse. Indo-Aryans in northern India represent 72 percent of the total population; Dravidians, mostly in southern India, 25 percent; and Mongoloids and others, 3 percent. Official languages include Hindi and

English, as well as fourteen other official languages: Bengali, Telugu, Marathi, Tamil, Urdu, Gujarati, Malayalam, Kannada, Oriya, Punjabi, Assamese, Kashmiri, Sindhi, and Sanskrit. Hindi is spoken by 30 percent of the populous. Throughout the country, English is the most important language for higher education, government, commerce, and communication. Literacy remains a problem, with an average rate of 48 percent (62 percent for males, 34 percent for females).[1] The Holy Bible has been translated into all of the primary languages of India—the entire Bible is available in forty-six languages, the New Testament in thirty-five, and portions of the Old and New Testaments in sixty.

The religious situation in India is more complex than in any other nation in the world, as the following figures for the distribution of religions in India indicate: Hinduism, 82 percent (78.8 percent if some tribal groups are not automatically included); Muslim, 12 percent (Muslims claim 14 percent); Sikhs, 1.92 percent (the majority lives in the Punjab); tribal religions, 1.5 percent; Buddhists, Jains, Baha'i, and Parsi combined, 1.39 percent. Christianity officially accounts for 2.61 percent of the total population, but the figure may be as high as 4 percent (Protestant, 1.91 percent; Roman Catholic, 1.76 percent; other Christian groups, 0.33 percent). Although these Protestant and Roman Catholic numbers appear small, they reflect as many as 16.2 million and 15 million adherents, respectively. The gross figures are not as useful as the statistics for each individual state. For example, in the south, where the Latter-day Saints have had the greatest success, the states of Andhra Pradesh (3.5 percent Christian), Tamil Nadu (6 percent Christian), and Kerala (20 percent Christian) have higher numbers of Christians than most of the northern Indian states.[2] Because the LDS Church has imposed voluntary restrictions on proselyting among Muslims, and because most Hindus are so tolerant of all religious beliefs that they see little need to restrict themselves by declaring one religion true among all the possibilities, the Christians are the most probable target population for successful teaching of the restored gospel. To date these three southern states have proved most hospitable to the Mormon message—Bangalore (in Karnataka state), where the mission is headquartered, being the exception.

India is a secular state. According to the constitution, this means "equal protection for all religions and non-interference by the state in purely religious concerns."[3] Unlike many countries, India does not have an office such as a ministry of religious affairs that deals specifically with religious matters. Several articles in the constitution of 1950 provide protection for religious individuals and organizations. Article 25 of the constitution provides "freedom of conscience and the right freely to profess, practise and propagate religion" to everyone, subject to "public order, morality and health" and to other fundamental rights. However, these legal protections have not limited intolerant Hindu factions from passing discriminatory laws that deprive individuals who convert to Islam or Christianity of their normal rights. Madhya Pradesh state, for example, has passed strong laws against conversions to Christianity.[4] In India (and in much of that part of the world), religious toleration and freedom of religion have taken on a different twist compared to what we are accustomed to in the Western world (which, incidentally, is the home of the concept of religious toleration and religious freedom). Whereas most Europeans and Americans interpret religious freedom to mean the right to practice one's religion without interference from any other individual, group, or the state and to have the right to influence others to accept, appreciate, and even affiliate with that religion (that is, convert), Indians generally do not accept these ideas.[5] America, of course, is the home of religious pluralism, and it is not surprising that Americans would find the Indian view of religious toleration curious and almost illogical. To most Indians, however, religious freedom means at the very least the right not to be bothered by missionaries or other groups who may desire to convince them to change their beliefs or religious practices. According to Charles W. Forman, "The real question in the Indian mind is whether such a thing as conversion has a place in India. . . . In other words, evangelistic work and conversions are . . . ruled out by the principle of religious freedom, for conversion implies the rightness of one belief or the wrongness of another, and so makes for intolerance." He goes on to write:

> This is indeed a form of tolerance, but it is a tolerance which makes room for all religions only on the basis of a prior agreement that God cannot be known in a final sense through any of them [that is, through any existing religious system]. The one thing which it will not allow is that God should ever make His very heart and essence manifest to man. If that were ever admitted as possible, the whole basis of this kind of tolerance would be destroyed. Here, then, is an interpretation of tolerance which is predicated on the impossibility of the Christian claim that God in relation to man is revealed in His very essence in Jesus Christ. It is predicated on the illegitimacy of any attempts at conversion, for conversion implies that the essential truth for man is to be found in one place and not in another.[6]

Such thinking has framed most government policies regarding Christian missionary work in India. The Hindu majority, for all its assertions of belief in toleration, is actually an unrelenting majority with little or no respect for the beliefs, practices, or opinions of others.[7] Into this setting the Church has found its way in the latter part of the twentieth century.

The difficult cultural and religious setting notwithstanding, by the mid-1990s significant progress had been made in India. The India Bangalore Mission was created in January 1993, and a foothold has been established in Sri Lanka, Pakistan, and Nepal. Every step forward has been carefully considered. Every move has been made with the best interests of the new or potential members at heart and the legal situation in mind. More than in any other part of Asia, the efforts of individuals, but mostly of older couple missionaries working almost alone, have accounted for the advances of the Church. As Indians, Nepalese, Sri Lankans (Sinhalese and Tamils), and Pakistanis have heard about the

Church and asked to be taught, these courageous couples have shared the principles of the gospel and even baptized the inquirers when they have sought that blessing in their lives. Just as the labors and sufferings of the early missionaries to this realm were the most heroic of that era, the labors and sufferings—but more frequently the joys and satisfactions—of the missionaries of our time have been of heroic proportions.

PIONEER EFFORTS IN SOUTH INDIA

The longest established community of Latter-day Saints in South Asia is the 250-plus members who live in and around the southern India city of Coimbatore. Most of these converts were brought into the Church as a result of the dedication and faith of S. Paul Thiruthuvadoss. Brother Paul, as he was known, was born into a Christian family, but he was not satisfied with the denominations he found and joined during the earlier years of his life. In 1954, when he was on the verge of turning to Hinduism, he found an LDS tract inside a used book. Impressed with its contents, he immediately wrote to Church headquarters in Salt Lake City for more information. During the following months and years, the Missionary Department sent Paul the standard works and many tracts, lessons, and books. In 1957 he requested baptism. At about the same time he started preaching the restored gospel as he understood it and even founded a Sunday School.[8]

Although he was visited by Elder Richard L. Evans of the Quorum of the Twelve in 1962, it was not until 1964, when Jay A. Quealey Jr., president of the Southern Far East Mission (which included India within its bounds), visited Paul for three days that matters started moving at a quicker pace. In December 1964 President Quealey returned again, this time with Elder Gordon B. Hinckley, who was responsible for all Church activity in Asia. Together with their wives, they spent two full days with Brother Paul and his people. They visited Paul's home and met his wife, his four children, and his aged father and mother. They visited a school that Paul built "with his own hands on a piece of ground he bought from his savings." Years later President Hinckley, as a member of the First Presidency, wrote: "It was a simple rough building; but studying there were some four hundred poor children, each being brought out of the darkness of illiteracy into the light of learning. What this act of love has meant and will mean in their lives is beyond calculation."[9] And they traveled into the countryside, to the villages "where the dust is thick and people are miserably poor."[10] Elder Hinckley described their meeting with Paul's rural friends:

> As we came into a little opening where there were a few trees, Paul's associates were playing the organ [probably a harmonium, a small reed instrument that is played while sitting on the floor or ground] and singing and beating a drum. . . . The people began to gather. Some two or three hundred gathered and sat on the ground. They had taken two cots and put rough blankets on them and we sat on these.
>
> A hymn was sung which we did not know. It was sung as the Indians sing with their particular type of musical arrangement. President Quealey then offered prayer and Brother Paul interpreted his prayer. I was then called on to speak and I did so for a few minutes with Paul interpreting. Paul then spoke to them in the Tamil language. . . . Some of the old men seated on the ground in front nodded their heads in approval. The congregation was very reverent.
>
> These were surely the poor of the earth. They appeared to have little or nothing. As we met with them, I thought of Jesus speaking to the multitudes.[11]

At the hotel Elder Hinckley spoke at length with Brother Paul regarding the doctrines of the Church. He and his companions also prayed for inspiration regarding how to proceed with the Church in India. "The task of working among the poor of India is so great," wrote Brother Hinckley, "that I do not know whether we should start. We certainly need the inspiration of the Lord in whatever action we take here."

The immediate question was whether or not to baptize Paul and his associates. Elder Hinckley in due time decided to recommend that two full-time missionaries be sent to India to baptize Paul and others and to teach the doctrines and order of the Church.[12]

Fewer than two months passed before Elder Hinckley's recommendations were to become reality. On February 5, 1965, President Quealey, along with Elders John Aki Jr. and Gilbert Mantano, arrived in India from Hong Kong. These elders were the first to serve in India in the contemporary era. Two days later President Quealey baptized Paul and his ninety-six-year-old father, Elder Mantano baptized Paul's wife, and Elder Aki baptized a schoolteacher named Stanley Ponraj. A few days later Paul was also ordained a priest in the Aaronic Priesthood, and his father and Stanley were later ordained deacons.

The events of the baptism were a minor miracle. A reservoir had been selected in which to perform the ordinance, but when the group arrived there they found it dry. Because the area was suffering from a drought, all along the way President Quealey had been silently praying that there would be enough water to perform the ordinance. Not far from the dry reservoir they found a young boy who said he knew of some water. He took them to a small stream that was dammed to create a pool of water large enough for the task. Before President Quealey could baptize Brother Paul, an irate farmer started yelling at the group. Paul talked to him and explained the nature of their presence. The farmer calmed down and explained his anger, telling Paul that he had attempted to harness his oxen to pull the stocks and drain the water onto his fields, but one of the animals had bolted and he had been trying to chase it down when he saw the group preparing for the baptism. Had he been able to harness his animals and pull the stocks, the baptisms could not have taken place that day.

The elders remained in India for six months. For the first month they did little else but study the language. They found the Tamil language very difficult, but with Paul's help and the tutoring of a professor from a local college, they were able to learn enough to be effective. When they rationally surveyed conditions, they soon concluded that they were in a difficult situation. They had expected to teach and baptize the teachers at Paul's school, but for various reasons they had all left. It was the elders' expectation to baptize perhaps a hundred people and establish a branch. But that was not to be. They rode their bicycles fifteen or twenty miles to the villages where Paul had taken Elder Hinckley and found the people "were pagans who have never heard the name Jesus Christ." Mantano went on to say that the villagers "are the lowest of all castes and they are only looking for the material aspects of the Church, although they are good people."[13] Events since then have proved this assessment to be a bit harsh, but building the Church in and around Coimbatore has been a struggle. Trying to use their time well, the elders visited with prospective members in Madukkarai (a subsection of Coimbatore where Paul lived), Summedu, Ettimadai, Chavadi Purdur, and other villages near Coimbatore. They ultimately baptized six other Indians. Most of their contacts were with extremely poor farmers, most of whom were illiterate. When the elders departed for home, Brother Paul was on his own as leader of the tiny band of Latter-day Saints.

Elder Mantano's reference to caste was significant. The caste system, although illegal since 1950, continues to dominate the social and economic fabric of India. People of all castes are theoretically protected and equal in the eyes of the law, but people are born into highly complex social and economic circumstances. Almost all occupations are determined by family tradition. Another aspect of caste, one of great importance to Indians, is the refusal of one caste to eat with another, thus maintaining ritual purity. This has serious implications for breaking the bread and the passing of the sacrament. Some members had difficulty making themselves take the sacrament from a low-caste elder. Only the Christian love of fellow members can overcome these kinds of traditions. When a person chooses to leave his native Hinduism

Members and friends from Chavadi Purdur and Ettimadai villages, along with missionaries and BYU student interns, gather in front of the Chavadi Purdur Branch meetinghouse following Sunday services. Most local members are field workers. Matthew (next to missionary sister at left of photo) and his father (below man with brass pot) have been the stalwarts of the branch. Matthew now works for the Church Educational System in India. (Courtesy Tricia Donaldson)

and become a Christian, he is choosing to leave his entire social and economic order as well as his religion. G. S. Gill further describes this challenge: "Hindu converts pay a high price for membership. Most often they lose their friends, family, inheritance, incentives and government reservations in education. The Christian converts tend to keep dual membership because of incentives such as subsidized education, marriage possibilities, and burial privileges given by their former church."[14]

Since the introduction of Protestant Christianity into India in the late eighteenth century, many, if not most, conversions to Christianity have been as mass movements. Few individuals have been able to survive such a move alone, but when the entire caste, extended family, or village converts, they are somewhat protected from the various kinds of wrath and reprisals that such a decision carries.

Even in Christian villages, such as those where LDS members reside near Coimbatore, much diplomacy and care must be exercised by local Church leaders to see that normal village relations continue and smooth interpersonal relationships go on. When a regular member of the community is suddenly elevated to the position of branch president, he is no longer a common person. He must meet with the village *panchayat* (council of elders), occasionally attend meetings with leaders of the other churches, and so on. Life in Indian villages consists of people interacting with people on the most basic human level. Friendships last a lifetime because most people never move from their natal villages.

Several missionaries and mission presidents have commented over the years since Paul came into the Church that "thousands" could be baptized in India. In most such instances a local preacher has approached a Church representative with the offer to join and bring "his people" or "his congregation" into the Church.[15] Such offers have been consistently refused because the burden on each person is to learn of Christ and develop faith in him, gain a testimony, repent, and be baptized. Mass movements, as they are called, portend too many problems and the almost certain fact that many or most of the "converts" will not truly be converted. Most mass movements into various Christian denominations have been by low-caste people or untouchables. Typically these people have been illiterate and extremely poor. Often they have expected some means of support or gifts from the church at Christmas or on other holy days. Generally they have lacked the leadership skills necessary to operate the LDS Church, particularly in its early stages. Since about 1980, Church leaders in India have followed a general policy of teaching people who are literate, generally in English as well as in local languages, and who are capable of building the Church and not being dependent upon it for support and sustenance. These facts notwithstanding, some members have noted the difficulty of living the gospel in the modern cities of India, where the literate who show leadership potential more frequently live. They have wondered if the meek of the earth may not be found most frequently among the simple, honest souls of the villages.

The dependent status of women in India also plays an important role in the development of the Church. Regarding the question of women's freedom to act independently in religious matters, Indian member Raj Kumar stresses that "it's socially impossible in India, because in Asia, and especially in India, the women are subdued by the menfolk. Before marriage they are under the strict law of their fathers and older brothers, the male members of the family. After marriage they are under the strict law of their husbands. And they don't treat them very kindly. . . . So they don't dare to take that step [join the Church] unless the whole family is involved."[16]

In other parts of the world it is common for women, single and married, to join the Church without family support. In India men join the Church alone, and if they are married their wives may follow at that time or afterward; but women in the Church as part-member families are much less common.

A new phase of closer contact, support, and supervision began in March 1970, when President G. Carlos Smith of the Southeast Asia Mission visited Paul and brought the Church in India under more constant care. Eighteen more Indian converts were baptized.[17] At the same time, President Smith ordained Paul an elder in the Melchizedek Priesthood and made Stanley a priest so they could conduct worship services in the village where the new converts had been baptized. Smith also encouraged Paul to register the Church as an official corporation within India. Paul found the task difficult but managed to register under the Societies Registration Act XI of 1860 on November 2, 1971. This made it possible for the Church to own property and to act as a corporate entity. Eleven years later, Church attorneys decided this early registration was insufficient for all of India, but for a time it served its purpose. In the same year, 1971, President Smith flew Paul to Singapore to observe the workings of the Church in fully functioning branches.

During the next eight years, mission presidents G. Carlos Smith, Miller F. Shurtleff, and Soren F. Cox made two or three trips to India each year. They often supervised baptisms, and eventually four groups were organized with a combined membership of 220 by 1978. Three of the groups had humble chapels[18] that were built with funds from the Southeast Asia or Singapore Missions. There were five local elders and thirteen Aaronic Priesthood holders, and the groups were gradually growing. Probably the greatest weaknesses within the Church in Coimbatore were the poverty and illiteracy of most of the members and the fact that Paul was forced to be a circuit rider, much like a nineteenth-century Protestant minister. In an effort to correct the latter problem, two pairs of elders were sent to Coimbatore during 1973 and again in 1974. These young men, George Groberg and Arne Hallam, and then Arne Hallam and Wayne A. Jones, worked under very restricted circumstances but were able to help the fledgling groups find their way and gain stability. Their work might have been easier if the members had not been situated in four different places, making it impossible to create one strong branch of the Church. All LDS worship services were conducted in Tamil.[19]

By 1979 there were more than two hundred baptized members of the Church in the Coimbatore area. Surprised members elsewhere have sometimes wondered how so many illiterate, low-caste farmers came into the Church. The answer is that it happened naturally, under the prayerful and watchful care of the mission presidents of that time. The following account, which comes from the oral history of mission president G. Carlos Smith, illuminates the situation:

I THOUGHT THAT THROUGH ALL NIGHT
G. Carlos Smith

When [we] got there [Coimbatore], it was on a Friday afternoon. [Myself, Sister Smith, and an American member named Dale Haws, who was working on a rice project] spent that afternoon with Brother Paul, and I asked him many questions. He speaks good English and he has a . . . degree in accounting. . . . He was most anxious for me to come and meet the people he'd been teaching the gospel to in this village about five miles from his home. I said, "Paul, I'd be very happy to meet them." He said, "They're ready for baptism, I've taught them a long time and they know as much about the Church as I do and they want to be baptized." I stayed awake most of the night worrying about it. What do you do when you baptize these people? What kind of situation do you put them in? The Lord has told us we're to teach everybody, they're all entitled to the gospel and if they ask for baptism, you can't deny them. So these thoughts were going through my mind. . . . Brother Haws took me out to Paul's home. This was a little humble home, a small concrete house. I said, "'Well, Paul, let's go out to your village and meet these people." This was Saturday. Dale drove us out on the narrow concrete road. When we got to their little lane, a dirt side road, we turned off and went up through the trees and across a dry stream. When we got up almost to the village, Paul said, "Stop your car here. The people are waiting for you." So we stopped the car and we got out.

Then we saw these people, a group of people dressed in their finest, which wasn't very good. They were poor Indian farmers. They were coming down the road to meet us and one man had a little instrument about eighteen inches long, two inches thick, and about six inches wide and he'd squeeze it, and it would make one sound, "oh oh oh oh." That was their organ and they were singing. They were singing to that music, "oh oh oh." They'd come to meet us. Paul had built them up. He was the representative of the Church there and he'd built them all up. . . . We followed the procession on up to one of the little adobe houses with a thatched roof. They'd built a bowery out over the front of a house, and they swept the floor. There are dirt floors in all the houses but they had swept it right clean with cow dung. When you want to clean anything real clean, you use cow dung in India. The natives do. They had two grass mats on the dirt floor, and a little bench at one end with a little bouquet of flowers and a bunch of bananas. That was a banana offering to me and Sister Smith. Then we sat on the bench and Brother Haws sat up there with us and the rest of them sat on the ground. I talked to the people. . . . They told Paul they wanted to be baptized. So I said, "All right, I'll interview you." One at a time I had them come up to me, and I asked them questions through Paul and got their answers. There was a wonderful spirit there, a fine feeling, so I said to Brother Haws, "Dale, I feel that we should baptize these people." He said, "Well, I have no objection." I said, 'Where can we baptize them, Paul?" There was a reservoir five miles away. . . . [T]hey rounded up a couple of taxis. . . . We hauled the people out to this reservoir. The water was extremely low but we walked down in a place deep enough and then we got the people together. I talked to them again, explained their obligations and so on. Then I said, "Now Paul, you're going to baptize these people." "Me?" he said. I said, "Yes. Do you know the baptismal prayer?" He said, "Yes." I had him repeat it to me so I knew he knew what he was saying. I said, "Now you're a priest in the Church, you have the authority to baptize." So I asked him to go down there in the water and baptize these people, and he did. I would read their names off and Dale and I were the witnesses. They'd go down in the water; Paul would baptize them and then they'd come out. Every time someone would come in (Paul was standing about up to his waist in the water), he'd brush the water vigorously with his hands. I said, "What are you doing, Paul?" He said, "There are snakes coming up and bothering me." He was chasing them away! As I recall there were eighteen people. The oldest was a lady in her sixties or seventies. The youngest was Paul's daughter who was twelve. He baptized these people, then brought them out on the bank again, where they changed their clothes—just held sheets up and changed their clothes, and put on their dry clothing. Then we talked to them again. I talked to them, and I had Brother Haws talk to them. Then he and I confirmed them members of the Church and then we got them in cabs and took them back to their village. By then it was dark. We went back to Dale's home and had dinner. I went to bed, but I didn't go to sleep. I started thinking this thing through again. I thought, "What have you done? Here you've baptized eighteen people. Where are you going to hold church? Who's going to be the leader? Who is going to help them or are you just going to baptize them and they'll flounder?" So, I thought that through all night.[20]

THE EDWINS ESTABLISH
THE CHURCH IN HYDERABAD

But the young twigs of the Church in Coimbatore were not the only fresh growth in India. In December 1977 Edwin and Elsie Dharmaraju,[21] who had recently been converted to the Church in Western Samoa, returned to their native India for the wedding of their daughter, Lata. While they were there, they spoke freely with their relatives concerning the restored gospel. It was fortunate that most of their family members were already Christians. The response to their newfound religion was warm and positive.

After the Edwins returned to Samoa—they traveled by way of Salt Lake City—they received letters from India asking for more information about the Church. There followed a series of discussions (which included a number of General Authorities) concerning who could go to India to teach the gospel. The International Mission presidency was then responsible for India, the Singapore Mission having been temporarily closed. The Brethren decided that the Edwins were the logical choice for that mission. On December 9, 1978, Brother and Sister Edwin departed for India having been set apart as short-term missionaries to teach the gospel, baptize and confirm, ordain men to the Aaronic Priesthood, and organize groups of the Church. They had previously sent almost five-hundred pounds of Church materials (books, tracts, sacrament trays and cups, Church tapes, and so on) that had been generously donated by Regional Representative Ralph G. Rodgers and other leaders of the Church in Samoa.

When the Edwins reached Hyderabad, family members gathered to hear the gospel message. They preached the gospel intensely and soon appointed December 27 as the day for baptisms. Brother Edwin baptized and confirmed eighteen people that day, including his father, mother, and a number of brothers and sisters. The next day the Edwins traveled to Vijayawada, a six-hour train ride away, and baptized four more members of Brother Edwin's family and organized a group of the Church. In all, twenty-two people were brought into the Church, and four men were ordained to offices in the Aaronic Priesthood. Brother Edwin described another important part of their mission:

> From Hyderabad we went to see my wife's parents, who live in a place called Bheemunipatnam, which is about 16 hours by train. Sister Edwin's father, [the] Reverend P. Sreenivasam, [was engaged] since the last 14

months, in the translation of the Book of Mormon into the local language of Hyderabad State called "Telugu." This language is spoken by nearly 50 million. Reverend Sreenivasam is an ordained Baptist minister.

Reverend Sreenivasam showed us more than 500 foolscap [13" x 16"] neatly handwritten sheets of the translation. We were taken aback by the amount of work he has already accomplished. He is now 82 years of age. He has been translating the Book of Mormon at the rate of a little more than a page per day.[22]

The Reverend Sreenivasam persisted in his translation project and completed the Book of Mormon in Telugu. Brother and Sister Edwin then typed the seven-hundred-page manuscript and carried it to President Spencer W. Kimball in March 1981. After review at the Translation Department in Salt Lake City, and typesetting at Osmania University Press in Hyderabad, India, Telugu *Selections of the Book of Mormon*[23] was published in Salt Lake City in 1982.[24]

Near the end of his report, Brother Edwin wrote that whatever he and his wife had accomplished on their mission was "just a minute droplet in the ocean." He was speaking of India's vast population then of nearly seven hundred million people and the many nations and kindreds and languages that coexist there. But they had created a beginning in Hyderabad, a beginning that was to grow in later years.

Before his release in June 1978 as president of the Singapore Mission, Soren F. Cox noted only six groups of the Church in India. There were no branches. The new converts in Hyderabad were only a group. In September 1980 the little units in Coimbatore were organized into branches. But by this time the Church in India was still hardly more than a glimmer of promise.

OTHER BEGINNINGS—THE PACE QUICKENS

Northern India, which encompasses the area from Pakistan on the west to Bangladesh in the east and from Kashmir in the north to the Deccan Plateau in the south, is as large as Western Europe and has a population as great as Latin America. The beginnings of the Church in northern India, particularly in and near Delhi, were similar in one aspect to what happened in Coimbatore and Hyderabad: a short time after the small group of people were baptized, they were left almost alone.

According to the account of Baldwin Das and Douglas Rose, "in 1968, Brother Charles Radford, an employee in the Office of the Defense Attache at the American Embassy [in New Delhi], befriended, taught, and baptized an Indian colleague in the Embassy, Brother Baldwin Das. Brother Das' family followed him into the Church, and they, in turn, introduced the gospel to the family of Mr. Roshan Juriel. The Juriels were also baptized by Brother Radford, and for the first time, the Church in North India had a permanent Indian presence."[25]

But Das and Rose went on to explain that "for several years, from 1969–1981, the Das and Juriel families survived on periodic meetings with Americans when they were present in Delhi, occasional visits from the mission presidents headquartered in Singapore [incidentally, the distance from Singapore to Delhi is almost as great as that from New York to San Francisco], Church ambassador David Kennedy, who helped establish the Genealogical Society of Utah (GSU) here, and [area] authorities."[26] Throughout those years mission presidents in Singapore and leaders in Salt Lake City struggled with the problems of caring for members of the Church in South Asia and establishing legitimate missionary work in the subcontinent. But as is true everywhere in the world, the Brethren refused to deviate from the principle of abiding by the laws of each country into which the Church enters. They were looking for a legitimate, legal means of expanding pastoral care in India.

For two years, from July 1978 until July 1980, India and South Asia were assigned to the International Mission in Salt Lake City. During that brief period, two couples were sent to Panjim, Goa, as representatives of the Church. They were not missionaries in the normal LDS sense. They were to make friends, answer questions, nurture members, minister as necessary, even baptize, but only when sought out by interested individuals or families. The first Church representatives were Tagg B. and Maria Hundrup, who went to Goa in 1978. They were hosted and watched over by Church member Bonnie Chowgule, who, with her husband, Ramesh, a wealthy Indian of considerable local prominence, lived there. Then in early 1980 Alma and Marie Heaton replaced the Hundrups. Their responsibility was to create a positive impression for the Church and to share their skills in recreation and dancing. Mingling of the genders through social dance has not found general acceptance in India, but Alma got almost everyone—even the Roman Catholic nuns from the convent next door—into dancing or acting. The Heatons also followed the pattern established by the Hundrups of riding the circuit (by airliner) from Goa to Delhi, to Coimbatore, to Hyderabad, to Bombay, and back to Goa to perform what they called "home teaching." This was important because it was the first effort the Church had made to minister to most of the clusters of Saints throughout the country.[27] Elders Hundrup and Heaton served successively as district president for India. Church activities were also important. Many friends met with the Hundrups, Heatons, and Chowgules for Sunday services, and a few people were baptized, most notably Michael Anthony, who later served a mission and has served in the building of the Church in Bangalore and the Church Educational System.

In July 1980 the First Presidency again assigned this vast area to the Singapore Mission, and President J. Talmage Jones began making several lengthy trips there each year. In February 1981 he wrote, "We have many dreams of what may be done in India—of course, we need about twenty couples." Then in April of that year President Jones noted a new possibility for getting representatives of the Church into India to build the members and support further growth. "We have 'discovered,'" he reported, "that it may be possible to have citizens of Commonwealth nations come to India without visas. Our visits to immigration offices have resulted in positive answers and we now have submitted the proposition to Salt Lake City, that we receive [British], Australian, New Zealand and Canadian couples and later elders."[28] In consultations with legal counselors, President Jones gained assurance that representatives of the Church could direct meetings, instruct and guide local Church members (couples who were sent to India were encouraged to put as much responsibility on local members as was possible), and even teach and baptize Indians who expressed an interest. But they could not proselyte, that is, seek out new investigators through tracting or other overt means. Indian citizens, on the other hand, were free to propagate their religion and teach whomever they wished. Young Indian elders and sister missionaries were clearly the answer to building the numbers in the Church, but for some reason, perhaps the belief that they were not experienced enough to serve in India without expatriate companions of greater experience in the Church, local missionaries were not called to serve in India until 1986. (However, at least fourteen Indians were called to missions outside India, beginning with Sister Maureen Das from Delhi, who served in the Philippines in 1972 and 1973.) Finances had been a serious worry, but Jones was told that Church representatives could receive contributions and the Church could own property and construct buildings.[29]

Jones's recommendations regarding British Commonwealth representatives were quickly accepted by Elder Marion D. Hanks, Executive Administrator over South and Southeast Asia, and Church leaders in Salt Lake City. Before the end of 1981, Horace and Edna Hayes from England had been sent to New Delhi to minister to the Das and Juriel families and other members, and additional couples, mostly from Commonwealth nations, had been called to Hyderabad, Goa, Bombay, and Bangalore. Others followed, and between 1978 and 1993, when the India Bangalore Mission was created, at least 120 couples served in India as representatives of the Church. American couples were allowed only six-

BYU performing groups such as the Young Ambassadors have done much to build friendships for the university and the Church. India's prime minister, Indira Gandhi, received the group in January 1982. Elder Horace Hayes (next to Mrs. Gandhi) arranged the visit. Author Lanny Britsch introduces artistic director Randy Booth and the young performers. (Photo by R. N. Khanna)

month visas, thus requiring expensive, time-consuming travel outside of India to renew visas. Young missionaries from Commonwealth countries were not called to India until the late 1980s because they were under the same proselyting restrictions as were the older couples.

The year 1982 brought several events and developments that furthered the growth of the Church in India: a tour by the BYU performance group the Young Ambassadors, incorporation of the Church as a legal entity, establishment of microfilming projects by the Genealogical Society of Utah, and the publication of the Book of Mormon in Hindi and selections in Telugu and Tamil. Actually, the 1982 tour of the Young Ambassadors was not the first to South Asia, nor the last. From December 26, 1979, to January 16, 1980, they toured India, Nepal, and Sri Lanka under the direction of Janie Thompson. In January and February 1982, Randy Boothe directed their performances in India and Sri Lanka. And in January and February 1986, under the direction of Mark Huffman, they again visited India, Nepal, and Sri Lanka. They made many friends for BYU, the Church, and the United States. On each tour the Young Ambassadors performed before packed halls of delighted viewers. "A cleansing sanity ran through the entire program," wrote Krishna Chaitanya of the *Times of India* in January 1980. "The numbers expressed a communion in delight, and a yearning for good fellowship with people all over the world. To these kids, a family of man does not at all seem an ideal difficult to realize, and their spontaneity and joy could infect old and disillusioned hearts too." In April 1982, as the cultural adviser for the group, I made the point that "through their love, smiles and example, the Young Ambassadors unlocked many hearts. The friends made and impressions left as a result of this tour will no doubt be of great value in establishing the restored gospel in that part of the world."[30] Highlights of the tours for the students included an audience with Prime Minister Indira Gandhi in 1982, and visits with Mother Theresa, Nobel Peace Prize winner, in 1980 and 1986.

Raj Kumar joined the Church following the Young Ambassadors tour of India in 1982. He subsequently served a full-time mission in California and returned to India as director of the Church's family history microfilming project. He now lives in Toronto, Canada, where he serves as bishop in his home ward. (Photo by author)

S. Paul Thiruthuvadoss had registered the Church in South India, but he had done so using his own name. Representatives of Kirton and McConkie, Church attorneys, advised incorporating the Church in Delhi. This would provide appropriate legal status for the holding of property and so on. Using local attorneys to assure proper procedure, Lee Ford Hunter took charge of most of the application procedures. Many months passed before the application was acted on, a normal occurrence when dealing with Indian bureaucracy. The registration was completed on January 25, 1982. The process created "The Indian Society of the Church of Jesus Christ of Latter-day Saints." Attorney Larry R. White guided the group through the final steps. Elder Hanks, President Jones, the Hayeses, the Dases, and others took part in the signing or participated in the first meeting of the new society.[31]

The Genealogical Society of Utah made arrangements in 1982 to begin microfilming Hindu pilgrimage records and Roman

Catholic church records. The Hindu records contain only names of births and deaths; the Catholic records include baptismal records, marriages, and death and burial records. Two microfilming cameras have been kept busy to the present. A variety of people have managed the operation, including couple missionaries and local Indians such as Raj Kumar, who was converted to the Church as a result of the Young Ambassadors' visit in 1982. Thousands of rolls of film, one thousand feet in length each, have been deposited in the Family History Archives in Salt Lake City. Copies have of course been given to the owners of the source documents.

INDIA FILLS GENEALOGY LINK
William B. Smart

Outside, a teeming mass of humanity filled the evil-smelling alleys and the broad promenades along the Ganges. Hawkers, fakirs, beggars, and pilgrims mingled with sacred cows and temple monkeys in an unending, noisy stream along the river.

But inside the monk-like cell was quiet and concentration. Sri Prasad Dixit leaned intently over the thick bundle of pages. "Had you gone to your father and brought the proper information, you would have saved us a great deal of trouble," he reproached as he flipped through the pages.

"But here. This name. Here is your father, recorded 40 years ago when he came to immerse the ashes of a son." Dixit's aged father, sitting quietly by, nodded confirmation.

More pages. Then a smile of triumph. "And here is your grandfather. He came here 70 years ago. Here is his father. And his father. And his father."

Five generations, each recorded in turn as faithful Hindus came to Hardwar to cast ashes of loved ones into the Ganges.

"I felt a shiver as he read those names of my ancestors," Raj Kumar declared later. "It was the spirit of Elijah."

The Dixits, father and son, are pandas, keepers of some of the oldest and most unique genealogical records in existence. It's a record the Utah Genealogical Society is undertaking to preserve on microfilm.

Hardwar, regarded by Hindus as the most holy place in India, lies just where the Ganges spills out of the foothills after its tumultuous passage down from the Himalayas. Here begin the vast Gangetic plains that stretch a thousand miles to Calcutta and the Bay of Bengal.

Hindus revere Hardwar as the "Door of Gods," the gateway to paradise, as well as the gateway to the Himalayas. They worship the Ganges as the "holy mother" who is the cleanser of all sins. . . .

To experience Hardwar is better to understand such fervor. With its many shrines and countless pilgrims and holy men, it comes close to the core of Hinduism and its 465 million adherents.

In the ancient temple of Śiva . . . worshipers, young and old, dip fingers in the fountain, anoint their foreheads, and cast marigold blossoms on the water.

Sacred cows wander past the temples and along the river. Monkeys clamber over the temple walls. Pitiable men, women, children, maimed, leprous, blind, rattle their begging cups. Fakirs with pythons coiling around their shoulders compete for coins. Stalls sell marigold blossoms or food offerings for worship. Long lines of hungry people queue up for food handouts.

Holy men, hair hanging in waist-long ropes, bathe in the Ganges morning and evening and emerge to smear bodies with cow-dung ashes.

"It's for beauty of the mind, beauty of the soul, and beauty of the skin," one of them explains.

Ghats for the burning of bodies loom above the river bank. At river's edge, small family groups cluster to cast into the holy waters the charred bones raked from the ashes.

A white-robed priest chants verses from the Veda. A son of the dead washes himself thoroughly. He and other family members sprinkle blossoms, then water from the river on the scarf-wrapped bone fragments. Reverently, the son places the bundle in the river. It sinks. The blossoms float downstream.

For yards out from the bank, the river bed is white with bone shards. . . .

At sunset, a great throng fills the amphitheater above the river for evening prayers. Over a loudspeaker comes a call. The crowd chants in response. Bells clang. Everyone stands. From 10,000 throats, in unison, comes a song:

"Oh mother Ganges, you are immortal. You make us happy. All Hindus worship you. You give eternal life, you cure their sickness. You give prosperity and happiness. Thank you."

. . . For thousands of years the pilgrims have come. For at least 1,000 years, pandas like the Dixits have recorded their passage.

Three thousand pandas operate at Hardwar today. Each represents a specific village or district of India. In most cases, the office passes from father to son; in the case of the Dixits, that has gone on for 15 generations.

Existing records go back some 500 years. None are found before that time because a conquering Mogul emperor, steeped in Islam, ordered the records destroyed.

The Dixits possess 32 such books reaching back 300 years. Many pandas have more and older books.

The system seems disorganized, but the way it works

is astonishing. A pilgrim hits town, coming from any of hundreds of places in India or abroad. He asks around for the panda representing his particular area. Somehow he is directed to the right place, as was Raj Kumar.

Once having found his particular panda and identified his family name, the pilgrim finds a mind that works like a computer. With amazing intergenerational memory, the panda pulls the right book out of his safe, thumbs through the pages, and produces the names.

These are the records the Utah Genealogical Society has been microfilming the past six years. Two operators under direction of [Raj] Kumar photograph some 8,000 pages a month, each page containing around 50 names.

So far [by 1988], records of about 40 pandas have been processed—something like 24 million names. Projecting these figures, one can figure there are 1.8 billion names yet to process on the records held by the remaining 2,960 pandas.

And that's only in Hardwar. There are at least three other pilgrimage destinations in India where pandas keep similar records.[32]

In addition to the Young Ambassador tour, the creation of the Indian Society of the Church, and the establishment of genealogical microfilming projects, the translation and publication of the Book of Mormon and other Church written materials were important in the development of the Church in India. The publication of Book of Mormon selections in Telugu has been noted earlier. In the same year, 1982, the entire Book of Mormon was published in Hindi, India's official language. (By 1995 the number of Hindi speakers had grown to 200,600,000; Telugu speakers to 69,623,000; and Tamil speakers to 58,547,000.) Most Latter-day Saints in India speak Telugu and Tamil. Fortunately, *Selections from the Book of Mormon* was also published in Tamil.

The Hindi translation project began in Fiji in 1975 under the direction of mission president Eb Davis. Many members of the Church in Fiji were of Indian ancestry, and many of the older people were fluent in Hindi but not in English. President Davis hired Vijendra Sharma, a nonmember linguist in Fiji, to do the initial translation. As is true with all contemporary scripture projects, the final product was published only after careful evaluation and revision by committees of specialists—ecclesiastical and professional.

The Tamil *Selections from the Book of Mormon* was done primarily under the hand of Daniel K. Shantakumar, a member originally from Coimbatore. He started the project in 1979; it was reviewed in 1980 and printed in Sri Lanka in 1982. At this writing (1995), completely new versions of the Book of Mormon are under way in Hindi, Tamil, and Telugu. Local Indian committees have been organized under the direction of the Asia Area Presidency. The Hindi version needed to be redone because it contains many usages that are peculiar to Fiji. The version in Telugu that was done by the Reverend P. Sreenivasam contains some interpretations that more closely approximate Baptist theology than LDS theology.[33] A variety of lesson materials, including *Gospel Principles* and a number of tracts, have been translated and printed in these languages as well as in Urdu, Bengali, and Kannada. Since 1989, approval has been given by the Translation Department to translate the Doctrine and Covenants and Pearl of Great Price into Hindi, Telugu, and Tamil, but those projects have been temporarily delayed until complete versions of the Book of Mormon in Telugu and Hindi are completed (they are under way) and the Hindi version of the Book of Mormon is revised (not yet under way).[34]

Written language materials are one thing, but spoken languages are another. During the foundation stages in India, leaders have consistently urged that English be used in Church services as well as in teaching prospective members. The economy of this policy is reasonable, but its application has been a problem. When an English-speaking man joins the Church, the first thing he desires to do is teach the gospel to his wife, to his parents, and to his close friends. Often these people have not understood English. And naturally the member has enthusiastically taught, through translation, those whom he or she loves. For this reason there is much simultaneous translating taking place in LDS church services in India. And the need for written materials in the languages of India continues to grow. It's a process that cannot be stopped.

NOTES

1. Central Intelligence Agency, *The World Factbook 1992* (Washington, D.C.: U.S. Government Printing Office), p. 155.

2. See Patrick Johnstone, *Operation World* (Grand Rapids, Michigan: Zondervan Publishing House, 1993), 273ff.

3. "India," in *World Christian Encyclopedia*, ed. David B. Barrett (New York: Oxford University Press, 1982), p. 375.

4. There is a long history of anti-conversion laws in India, dating back to the period of British occupancy. Since independence, many laws have been passed in various states that were intended to prevent or limit religious conversions. The purported reason for these laws was to prevent forced, fraudulent, or induced conversions, but the reality is that they made genuine conversions illegal and punishable. The law in Madhya Pradesh, which is ironically called the "Freedom of Religion Act, 1968," is probably the best known. When it was tested before the Supreme Court in 1977, the five-member panel held that "there is no fundamental rights to convert any persons to one's own religion." The court's opinion was that "what Article 25 (1) of the Indian Constitution grants is not the right to convert another person to one's own religion by an exposition of its tenets. It has to be remembered that Article 25 (1) guarantees 'freedom of conscience' to every citizen and not merely to the follower of one religion and that in turn postulated that there is no fundamental right to convert another person to one's own religion because if a person purposely undertakes the conversion of another person to his religion as distinguished from his effort to transmit or spread the tenets of his religion that would infringe on the 'freedom of conscience' guaranteed to all the citizens of the country alike." The court went on to state: "We find no justification for the view that Article 25 granted a fundamental right to convert persons to one's own religion. . . . What is freedom for one is freedom for others, in equal measure; and there can be no such things as fundamental right to convert any person to one's own religion."

This law still stands in spite of the strongly held opinion of many respected Indian jurists who believe the matter should be tested again. Among the strongest complaints against the decision is the observation that the decision contradicts Article 19, which guarantees freedom of speech. See Brojendra Nath Banerjee, *Religious Conversions in India* (New Delhi: Harneam Publications, 1982), pp. 247–53.

5. The words of the *Universal Declaration of Human Rights* generally ring true: "Everyone has the right to freedom of thought, conscience and religion; this right includes freedom to change his religion or belief, and freedom, either alone or in community with others and in public or private, to manifest his religion or belief in teaching, practice, worship and observance."

6. Charles W. Forman, "Freedom of Conversion—The Issue in India," *International Review of Missions* 45 (April 1956): 180–82.

7. Indian Christian writer Brojendra Nath Banerjee sharply condemns Hinduism, asserting: "Hinduism is a kind of totalitarianism. Its economic, cultural and social complex are undergirded by powerful religious sanctions. The Hindu system governs Hindu life from the cradle to the cremation; whether it is worship of God or Gods, social and ethical presumptions, legend or folklore—all are knit together to make that system. Although Hinduism is formless, it proves to be a successful force for religious, social and economic control. Anything that erodes this Hindu system will naturally be taken to be a threat and must be vehemently crushed down and not simply opposed" (*Religious Conversions in India*, p. 254).

8. Two documents are of considerable help in rebuilding Paul's history: "Report of The Church . . . in Coimbatore, India," by Paul Thiruthuvadoss, 30 December 1979; and "A Report about the L.D.S. Church in Coimbatore Area, December 17, 1979." Both reports are found in Joseph Talmage Jones, Collection 1968–1962, LDS Church Archives. (Paul was born on September 2, 1919, and died in February 1995.)

9. Gordon B. Hinckley, "'Whosoever Will Save His Life,'" *Ensign* 12 (August 1982): 4.

10. Gordon B. Hinckley, Journal, 12 December 1964; in possession of President Hinckley.

11. Ibid.

12. See ibid., 13 December 1964.

13. Gilbert Mantano, Journal, 23 April 1965.

14. Gurcharan S. Gill, India Bangalore Mission Report, September 1995.

15. J. Talmage Jones's reference to this problem in his book *In Singapore* (Salt Lake City: Publishers Press, 1984), pp.141–42) is probably the most available account. In March 1982 he wrote: "We all were made aware of the awful discrimination that exists in most of India. The caste system is illegal, but very much in effect. Many natives do not speak to their neighbors. If one family becomes interested in our activities, those in a higher caste immediately lose interest. I interviewed two potential missionaries and four leaders of a group of 200 people, all of whom desire to be baptized. . . . It is an awesome responsibility to determine how fast we should go with bringing large numbers into the Church. Indeed, on this trip alone we met fine people who are anxious to bring at least 1,000 followers to baptism."

In his oral history (1983) Elder Marion D. Hanks commented: "We could have baptized any number of people in India. We refused to do that." Elder Hanks explained that he had met several men who were intelligent, educated, and converted, but he did not allow their baptisms because the Church could not support them with the buildings, teachers, and missionaries that were necessary to get things going right (p. 57).

16. Raj Kumar Oral History, interview by Gordon Irving, 1987, James Moyle Oral History Program, LDS Church Archives, typescript, p. 75.

17. See G. Carlos Smith Jr. Oral History, interviews by William G. Hartley, Salt Lake City, Utah, 1972, LDS Church Archives, typescript, pp. 15–16.

18. Elder Marion D. Hanks, who supervised Asia as Executive Administrator from 1980 to 1983, described the chapels in these words: "They're little places, concrete floor, no riser, no nothing, just go in and sit on the floor—the men in the middle, the kids in the front, and the women at the back" (Marion D. Hanks Oral History, interviews by Gordon Irving, 1983, James Moyle Oral History Program, LDS Church Archives, typescript, p. 57.

19. This section is based on the testimony of S. Paul Thiruthuvadoss, LDS Church Archives; the journals of Gilbert Mantano and Wayne A. Jones, partial copies in posses-

sion of the author; and the author's interview with George Groberg, 12 June 1974, Provo, Utah.

20. Smith Oral History, pp. 15–16.

21. See Elizabeth S. VanDenBerghe, "Edwin Dharmaraju: Taking the Gospel Home to India," *Ensign* 20 (April 1990): 60–62.

22. Edwin Dharmaraju, "Mission to India," 14 February 1978, p. 5; typed copy in possession of the author. Several articles regarding this short-term mission have appeared in the *Church News* and the *Ensign*. Each was based on this report. An example is "Small branch established as converts return to India," *Church News*, 3 January 1981, p. 13.

23. "Book of Mormon Selections is a compilation of different parts of the book that have been approved by the Quorum of the Twelve. . . . The selections relate the basic story of the Book of Mormon and include chapters that deal with the Atonement and other major teachings of the Church" (Kerril Sue Rollins, "The Book of Mormon in Hindi, Tamil, and Telugu," *Ensign* 13 [February 1983]: 78).

24. See ibid., pp. 78–79. See also "3 India translations complete," *Church News*, 14 August 1982, p. 3.

25. Baldwin Das and Douglas Rose, "History in North India—The Church of Jesus Christ of Latter-day Saints," August 1987, typed report, p. 2, LDS Church Archives.

26. Ibid.

27. See Alma Heaton and Marie Heaton, *Behind the Taj Mahal: Spiritual Adventures in India* (Provo, Utah: n.p., 1992), p. 17 passim.

28. Jones, *In Singapore*, pp. 77, 89.

29. J. Talmage Jones to Marion D. Hanks, 24 November 1981, Joseph Talmage Jones, Collection 1968–1982, LDS Church Archives.

30. Dianna J. Greer, "Young Ambassadors 'unlock hearts' during tour of India," *Church News*, 24 April 1982, p. 13.

31. See Jones, *In Singapore*, p. 139.

32. William B. Smart, "India fills genealogy link," *Church News*, 9 January 1988, pp. 6, 12.

33. See notes 23 and 24.

34. See Jerry C. Garlock, comp. "A History of the Church in India" (Bangalore, India: n.p., 1995), pp. 71–76, 208–9. Garlock, a patriarch in the Church, was a senior missionary to India during 1994 and 1995. He was assigned to compile this history as part of his missionary duties. He has amassed considerable information, much of it of great value. He has not followed normal documentation procedures. There are no source notes, bibliography, or other markers to acknowledge author, copyright, rights to the information, and so on. He frequently quotes at length from published articles without attribution of author or quotation marks. When care is exercised in its use, this document is of great worth.

20

SOUTH ASIA

1982 – 1996

Church Growth in India Since 1982, and
Church Beginnings in Nepal, Sri Lanka, and Pakistan

RECENT PROGRESS IN INDIA

Once missionary couples started arriving in India, the Church there began to make significant progress. The *Deseret News 1983 Church Almanac* lists Church membership in India as totaling 198 in 1981. This figure was probably a bit low. Two years later the figure increased to 332. And by 1987 the number of members in India was seven hundred. New groups and branches were established in Erode and Rajahmundry in 1983 and in Bangalore in 1984.

Establishing Headquarters in Bangalore

The founding of the Church in Bangalore is instructive. When J. Talmage Jones first visited India in 1980, his impression was that he should establish a mission headquarters in Delhi, near the seat of government. But before his release in 1982, he felt that Bangalore was the better choice. Bangalore offered several advantages: a comfortable climate, smaller population (4.11 million versus 8.38 million in Delhi in 1991), considerable modernity (the city is called the "Silicon Valley" of India), and proximity to the

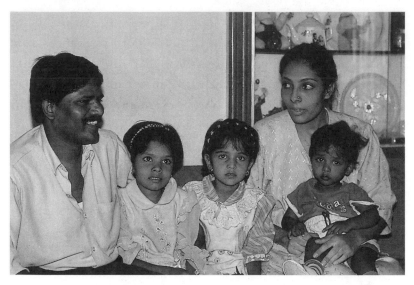

Michael Anthony and his wife, Christine, have contributed much to the growth of the Church in India. He was among the earlier converts. (Courtesy Michael Morris)

greatest number of Indian Latter-day Saints. But in early 1982 only one Mormon was in Bangalore, a young man named Michael Anthony.

Michael had been educated in an English-speaking school through the financial contributions of a Salt Lake City lawyer named Delvin Pond. During most of his early years, Michael did not know who his benefactor was, but Pond eventually supplied copies of the *Ensign* magazine, the Bible, and the Book of Mormon. Years passed and Michael gained a testimony that Joseph Smith was a prophet and that the Book of Mormon is true. A letter from Alma and Marie Heaton in Goa brought him in contact with the Church in India. He was baptized by Elder Heaton on May 1, 1980, in the Arabian Sea at Panaji (Panjim), Goa. But he returned to his home in Bangalore and didn't have much contact with the Church until President Jones looked him up in January 1982.

At the same time, President Jones decided that Bangalore was a good future site for a mission headquarters. All that was lacking was members of the Church and mission leaders, apartments for missionaries and a mission president, and officers and offices from which to administer the affairs of the Church. Anthony and Jones took the first step and found an apartment for a missionary couple. Those assigned to live there were Richard and Eunice Metcalf from Australia. With young Michael Anthony they held the first sacrament meeting in Bangalore. President Jones called Elder Metcalf as district president for all of India, a move that made Bangalore the administrative center for the country. The Metcalfs were put in charge of Church records and finances for the subcontinent. They were the first of thirteen couples to serve in Bangalore between 1982 and 1992.

In September 1982 Michael was sent by the Church to serve a mission in Utah. He served well, but before his normal release date he was sent back to India because his mother was critically ill. He arrived home too late to see her alive, but he attended her funeral. He had three months remaining in his mission and wanted to complete what he had started. He lived with a missionary couple in Bangalore, but he served without a companion. Although Elder Anthony talked with many people about the gospel, few adults would listen. Eventually he turned to children and youths and led them in what he called "social work" projects—pulling weeds, clearing stones, and so on. He also taught them the Articles of Faith and gospel-related songs such as "I Am a Child of God." The children learned and loved the gospel as he taught it. As a result of this service, twenty young people eventually joined the Church, and by 1995 two had served missions, four held leadership positions (Newton Samuel, for example, was president of Bangalore First Branch), and only one had become inactive. Michael's mission did not end with his official release, however. He continued as a member missionary. In addition to bringing youth into the Church, Michael also taught and baptized ten or twelve friends he had known from school and soccer games. One of them, Christina May, became his bride in 1986.[1] In 1995

Michael was serving as country director for the Church Educational System in India.

For Bangalore to make sense as the center of the Church in India, it needed a strong branch. In August 1984 President W. F. Lionel Walters from the Singapore Mission visited India and organized the Bangalore Branch. Elder Jack Humphreys, who was already serving as district president, was called as the first branch president. Michael Anthony was called as a counselor, Anthony Krishnan (a longtime friend of Michael) was called as clerk, and Ebenezer Solomon became executive secretary. Branch presidents were called from among the couple missionaries until 1986, when Brother Anthony was sustained as branch president. He selected Ebenezer Solomon as his counselor and Nixon Samuel (one of his young converts) as clerk.[2]

A competent financial and management team was needed in Bangalore. In 1983 Elder Metcalf contacted a local accounting firm to have a financial audit of the Church in India. The person assigned was Ebenezer Solomon, a young accountant who was nearing completion of his experiential training. He spent a good deal of time with the Metcalfs and, later, the Johnsons. In 1984 yet another couple worked with Ebenezer, and they asked him if he had any interest in learning about the gospel. He said he was interested; the time was right. He was baptized in June 1984.

Because he had served so well and faithfully as an accountant and auditor, the Church hired him as financial secretary in June 1985. He held this professional position for only a year when he accepted a mission call, which he filled from August 1986 until October 1988. His parents and brother joined the Church while he was serving elsewhere in India. Brother Solomon was again employed by the Church as an accountant following his mission. His responsibilities have steadily increased. In 1995 he was serving as country manager of temporal affairs for India, having responsibility for all financial, facilities, and materials management for the Church.

In 1985 Area President William R. Bradford formed the North

India District with headquarters in Delhi. Douglas Rose, who worked for the U.S. State Department, was the first district president. Three years later, in 1988, the Hyderabad District was created, bringing the number of districts to three.

Expanding the Missionary Force

Young Indian Saints, both elders and sisters, received mission calls steadily from the early 1980s onward. Most of the assignments were to the Philippines and the United States. An unfortunate result for the growth of the Church in India was that most of these missionaries—by count, 26 of 28—remained in the lands of their missions. About 1985 Church leaders in Singapore and Hong Kong decided to call Indian missionaries only to India. Between 1985 and 1992, the last year India was part of the Singapore Mission, thirty-five Indian elders served full-time missions in their home country. Considering the vastness of the subcontinent, there was plenty of room for assignments away from home. The results of this decision have been positive in several ways: native-born Indians know the languages, cultures, beliefs, problems, means of persuasion, and ways of discussion better than foreign missionaries do. They know how society works and how people interact. But most important is the legal right of Indians to proselyte the gospel among their own people.

But there were still never more than a few pairs of missionaries to teach more than four-fifths of a billion people. Between 1987 and 1991 membership grew from approximately seven hundred to close to nine hundred, an increase of fewer than fifty people per year. But the growth was real, and the couple missionaries continued to provide the foundation of gospel knowledge and experience in the branches. But if the couples were from America or other non-Commonwealth countries, they were granted only "tourist" visas and had to leave the country every six months. Usually they flew to Singapore, a costly and time-consuming undertaking. They did this despite their universal obedience to the non-proselyting regulations of the immigration authorities. In order to get the Church growing at a faster pace, leaders in Singapore and the Asia Area Presidency in Hong Kong felt the need to gain long-term visas for young elders to come into the country in significant numbers.

These efforts were undertaken in early 1988 by William Sheffield, Church attorney with Kirton and McConkie in Hong Kong. Sheffield had assisted Prime Minister Indira Gandhi with legal counsel during the 1970s and as a result knew her son, Rajiv, who was serving as prime minister following her assassination on October 31, 1984. Mr. Gandhi expressed willingness to assist with the Church's visa problem, but before he was able to bring influence on the Home Ministry, problems arose in the south Indian city of Erode that caused him to delay and then decline to do much to help. A missionary couple in Erode ordered a baptismal font, but because of disagreements with its builder, the missionary, a former lawyer, brought a lawsuit against him. Both sides took their cases before a judge. Unfortunately, the builder of the font also organized a campaign against the Church, encouraging citizens to write the prime minister posing the rhetorical question, "Why are Mormon missionaries allowed in the country?" He accused the missionaries of being CIA agents and created a major campaign against the Church. Finally, the mission president removed the missionaries from the area, but the damage had been done. This took place while William Sheffield was attempting to influence Prime Minister Gandhi. In February 1989 Gandhi informed Sheffield through the Indian Home Minister that "while the Church's missionaries were welcome 'as tourists,' they could not expect anything other than tourist visas."[3] In November 1989 Brother Sheffield left his employment with Kirton and McConkie, and at the same time Rajiv Gandhi was defeated in a national election. Sheffield feared that his best chances for obtaining change in the visa situation were ended with Gandhi's defeat, and he continued to worry about the visa problem. He determined to meet with Gandhi again, but before this could be accomplished the former prime minister was assassinated near Madras on May 21, 1991.

Since that time the Area Presidency and Church legal representatives have continued to nurture relationships with the prime minister's office, members of his government, and other individuals with important roles to carry out in government. For a few months, beginning in December 1995, missionaries were not allowed to renew their visas and were forced to leave the country permanently. Through successful negotiations, however, twenty-two two-year visas were approved by midyear in 1996. Among missionary couples, only the husband is counted as a missionary, the wives being numbered as dependents. Unfortunately, the twenty-two visas have not been easily forthcoming since the agreement was made. Gaining legal entry by our missionaries remains a problem.

The India Bangalore Mission

By 1992 the Brethren were satisfied that the time was right to move ahead with a mission in India. On November 7, 1992, the First Presidency announced the call of Gurcharan Singh Gill, native Indian and professor of mathematics at BYU, to serve as the first president of the new India Bangalore Mission. Brother Gill was uniquely qualified for his calling. Worldwide there were a fair number of Latter-day Saints of Indian ancestry, but few who had been stake presidents and held other responsible positions in the Church as he had.

G. S. Gill was born in northern India. He was raised on a farm, he recalled, "with chores of milking buffaloes; drying buffalo chips for fuel; extracting mustard for soap, lotion, and lamp fuel; grinding grain for the cattle and flour for the family; ploughing and watering the fields; and harvesting, threshing corn, hay, barley, sugar cane, and wheat." His people were Sikhs, and from them he gained much of his moral and spiritual character. Gill's father, although an uneducated man, insisted that his children obtain all the education they could. At age nineteen young Gill migrated to

Bangalore was selected by President J. Talmage Jones in 1982 to be the future mission headquarters. Although it has been well situated in relation to member populations, it has been inconvenient for church-state relationships in New Delhi. This is the mission office in Bangalore. (Courtesy G. S. and Vilo Gill)

the United States to study at Fresno State College, in California. Shortly before leaving India, he had lost to death an infant brother and a married sister. Being troubled by the question of their eternal fate, he began searching among the religions for answers. An LDS classmate named Shauna Atwood invited Gill to a stake conference meeting in Fresno.

In that session the stake president "explained the gospel plan from A to Z, the pre-existence, the plan of Jesus Christ, the justice of God, and the purpose of the temple and vicarious work for the dead. Ultimately, he said that those who died before the age of accountability do not need baptism." Gill's response to this good news was life changing. He later wrote: "I sat in my seat, awestruck at the very simple explanation of all things I had been haunted with since my sister and brother had passed away. I was glued to my chair, my bench, the whole time he was speaking, because within about 30 to 35 minutes, he had answered nearly every question that was raised in my mind before I came to the United States of America. The spirit of the Lord bore witness to me that the things that I was taught that day were true. I felt peace come to me, a heavy weight was lifted from my back and I was comforted."[4]

Gill had the feeling that this talk had been prepared just for him. He studied the gospel for eight months, during which he encountered ridicule from his Indian friends. Following his baptism, he transferred to BYU, where he graduated in 1958. While there he met and married Vilo Pratt, his Sunday School teacher. They are the parents of seven children. Shortly after the Gills arrived in India, Elder Monte J. Brough, president of the Asia Area, spoke to a fireside group in Bangalore and told those gathered that President Gill had been prepared by the Lord for his present calling.[5]

The Gills arrived in India on January 26, 1993, and the new mission was officially under way. Obviously, much had been accomplished before that time. The Church had been well established in the city of Bangalore in the previous decade, a residence had been procured for the mission president and his wife weeks before their arrival (Elder Tai Kwok Yuen had flown from Hong Kong to approve appropriate housing), and offices had been rented for various administrative purposes. But the missionary force was small and India was large. During the first year the number of young elders was increased from sixteen to forty-eight. By the end of 1994 the missionary force had grown to sixty-five young elders from outside India (at least fifteen of whom had Indian ancestry), fifteen Indian elders, five Indian sisters, and ten senior couples, including the first Indian couple, Luther and Mary Augustus Ravuri. The number of baptisms increased to 147 in 1993 and 269 in 1994. President Gill opened new cities—Calcutta and Cochin—or reopened former missionary areas such as Bombay (now called Mumbai). There were nine branches in early 1993 and twenty-one by mid-1995. He also divided the Hyderabad District and created the Rajahmundry District, bring-

ing the number of districts to
five. By mid-1995 there were
1,650 members of the Church
in India and Nepal.

THE OPENING OF MISSIONARY WORK IN NEPAL

Through all of these efforts
the various mission presidents
carried on with many missionaries who entered India on six-
month tourist visas. The
attitude of the Indian government was friendly as long as
the foreign elders maintained a
low profile. But leaving the
country three times during a
two-year mission was expensive, especially flying to
Singapore or Malaysia. In an
effort to save money and time,
President Gill investigated
using Kathmandu, Nepal, as a
destination for visa renewals.

*Missionaries to India have endured a
higher than average number of physical
problems while serving, but they have
loved the local people with the same
intensity that is typical throughout the
nations of the earth. (Courtesy Michael
Morris)*

He concluded that the savings would merit making this proce-
dural change. In fact, living costs in India were so inexpensive that
the full support cost of foreign missionaries, including flying them
to Nepal for visa renewals, was only U.S. $280 per month.

Not much had been done in Nepal by the Church before that
time. BYU's Young Ambassadors had performed there in 1980 and
1986, and other visitors from the Church had sojourned there.
The most significant visit had come in late February 1993, when
Elders John K. Carmack and Tai Kwok Yuen of the Asia Area

Presidency made an exploratory trip. They met with a few local Latter-day Saints and organized a group of the Church with Madhav Kumar Rimal as leader.[6] In early 1994 the mission rented an apartment in Kathmandu for missionaries to stay in while they were waiting two or three weeks for their visa applications to be processed. But because the elders were losing important work time, time when they could be teaching the gospel in Nepal, President Gill recommended to Church authorities that Nepal be assigned to the India Bangalore Mission. Furthermore, Gill asked that a missionary couple be assigned in Kathmandu to establish missionary work there and to supervise and care for the elders while they were in transit.[7]

President Gill's request was approved, and on June 2, 1994, Robert W. and Linda Houghton arrived in Kathmandu. Veterans in this part of the world, the Houghtons had previously served as couple missionaries in India (1986–1988), and Brother Houghton had also served as president of the Singapore Mission from 1988 to 1991. The Houghtons immediately rented a large home that would accommodate a number of sojourners. As they sought out the small group of Nepalese members of the Church, they found no interest among most of the supposed Mormons, but one or two families, the Rimals and Ram C. Baral, did want to be actively involved in the Church.

Because of Nepalese politics and religious laws, attempts to enter Nepal at an earlier date would have proven futile. Nepal (about the size of Wisconsin) is the world's only Hindu monarchy. Eighty-nine percent of the people are Hindu; 7 percent are Buddhist; and 3.5 percent are Muslim. In the 1990s Nepal was among the poorest and least-developed countries in the world.[8] Before 1951 Nepal was diplomatically closed to the outside world. In 1960 there were as few as twenty-five Nepalese Christians; by 1985 that number had grown to twenty-five thousand. Only since 1990 has the government allowed any significant degree of religious freedom, yet laws remain on the books making proselyting and conversion illegal. Current legal practice is vague regarding religious liberty, but estimates are that as many as fifty thousand of Nepal's population of 20.5 million are now Christian. Until this decade Christians have been persecuted and jailed for their beliefs.[9]

About six weeks into their mission, the Houghtons were joined in Kathmandu by Church members Dirk and Claudia Richards and their six children. Dirk was employed by the U.S. State Department. They added strength and numbers to the fledgling operation. Nepal officially became part of the India Bangalore Mission on August 25, and on October 25 the Kathmandu Branch was organized by President Gill with Dirk Richards as the first branch president. Richards's first counselor was Panna Lal Khadhi, who was the first Nepalese to be baptized in Nepal. The second counselor was Dhan Kumar Gurung. Interest in the Church increased, and by the end of 1994 some twenty-five members and investigators attended Church services each week. On December 1 two young elders, Joshua C. Chiles and David L. Pitcher, were transferred to Kathmandu, the first regular missionaries to be sent there as full-time missionaries. They were joined by two other elders in early 1995. By the time of President Gill's release in July 1995, he reported membership in Nepal of near fifty, a leased branch building, a leased residence for the missionaries, and an apartment for the couple. He was proud of the "strong branch there."[10]

The home-centered Church was an experiment directed by Elder Neal A. Maxwell to determine whether the Church could be established using homes for meetinghouses rather than building facilities for branches and wards. When it was implemented in India in 1992, there were initial increases in average sacrament meeting attendance among the fifty-one groups that were organized. Several families were assigned to meet together each Sunday except fast Sunday, when the entire branch would meet together. But by the time President Gill arrived, the initial excitement generated by the new program had worn off. He found that Indians, as with people everywhere, like to be together. They want to feel mutual support. Wherever there is persecution, members need to be together to sustain one another. Youth particularly needed the strength that comes from being integrated into a larger group. Two other problems worked against the success of the home-centered Church: first, the great number of distractions, such as noise, neighbors, nonmembers in the home, lack of sanitation, bugs, and animals such as pets and livestock; and second, and far more important, the lack of knowledge of the restored gospel among new members of the Church. There was too much residue from previous church experience. Gill found instances in which teachers were preaching Lutheran doctrine rather than LDS doctrine. Missionary work, too, was difficult with the home church. According to President Gill, "it is very, very difficult to bring an investigator to a home where there are not enough places to sit and have a sacrament meeting. . . . It is difficult to feel the Spirit in those kinds of circumstances."[11] So President Gill, having been charged by Elder Maxwell to build leadership and steer the Church in the right direction, stopped home groups in Bangalore in July 1993; and before long he did away with the home-centered Church all over the country. This change was not an easy thing to do, because all the branches, with the exception of those in Bangalore, were all meeting in the homes of the couple missionaries. Thus it was necessary to find larger and better meeting places all over the country. This was a daunting task, but suitable quarters were found.

Supervision of the Seminary and Institute Programs

One of the first assignments Vilo Gill received from President Monte J. Brough of the Asia Area was to guide the seminary and institute programs. On her initial tour of the mission, Sister Gill distributed teaching materials and under the direction of local priesthood leaders made assignments to teachers. Seminary classes had been held in several places, most consistently among the expatriate members in Delhi, since the early 1980s. But the goal now was to bring every young person of high school or college age into the program.

In August 1993 Murray and Donna Carver, couple missionaries, arrived in Bangalore with the assignment to direct the activities of the Church Educational System in India. During the next several months, they traveled widely, sometimes with the Gills, and did much to further the CES program. Unfortunately, Elder Carver suffered a massive heart attack on January 19, 1994, and passed away within minutes.

With the Carvers gone, the mission carried on its CES activities as well as possible until David Shuler, a veteran seminary and institute instructor whose in-country experience in India as an anthropology graduate student had begun in 1986, was assigned to serve as the first full-time CES director in India. Before assuming his post in June 1994, Shuler had supervised the field study and internships of more than twenty BYU anthropology students in various parts of India. The students had focused their work and studies on Bonnie Chowgule's orphanage in Goa and among the members of the Church in the villages near Coimbatore, where they concentrated on improving literacy and teaching English. By hiring an in-country director and providing a budget and full support for lesson and library materials, audiovisual equipment, and other needs, CES leaders were able to move the Church education program in India to a higher level. Working full-time, Shuler helped advance the program throughout the country. He placed special emphasis on institute classes because such a large percentage of new converts in India are single people between the ages of eighteen and thirty. Shuler encountered some problems with older married members who wanted to attend. It was concluded, however, to focus on the young people, married and single, who were between the ages of eighteen and thirty, because there remains such a strong tendency in India for young people to say little and participate less when their elders are present.[12]

Brother Shuler's assignment was for six months. Before he left India he selected and trained Michael Anthony to succeed him as

CES country director. Michael selected Daniel Matthew from Chavadi Purdur village near Coimbatore as his assistant. By mid-1995 seventeen seminary and institute classes had been organized in seven Indian cities, in addition to one institute class in Nepal.[13]

Life in India and Progress in the Church

Problems of many kinds exist in India and within the Church in India. Poverty is the most serious problem. Within the Church, with the exception of the mission office, only a few members own automobiles and small motorcycles, although such ownership places a person in the lower part of the middle class. Many of the members have not been well schooled in the arts of social interaction and the ways of mediating disagreements. Some express petty jealousies and engage in backbiting, faultfinding, and coveting. The latter is a significant problem. "Some people join the Church with the expectation of getting something from the Church," a member of the Area Presidency reportedly said.[14] Money is so scarce that some members have misappropriated Church funds. Church leaders frequently find themselves the target of criticisms and unkind accusations. President and Sister Gill devoted much of their time to the resolution of these kinds of problems. Their objective was to teach Christlike living, love, and mutual support and sustaining of one another.

Transportation and communications are another major problem. Traffic in Indian cities is usually extremely heavy, slow, inconvenient, and polluted. As inexpensive as it is by American standards, it is costly and very time-consuming for families to travel to Church meetings—sometimes changing buses two or three times—and to do home and visiting teaching. In most cases it is nearly impossible to do more than one visit per evening. Telephones are a rarity among Church members, making communications a difficult matter.

Other important but resolvable problems include (1) arranging burial places for Indian Latter-day Saints, (2) obtaining permission from the state and local governments to have a Church representative in each city authorized to perform weddings, and (3) maintaining good health. Concerning the latter, missionaries as well as local members have found themselves infected with malaria, typhoid, tuberculosis, or some kind of virus, bacteria, or parasite. As is true with all Indians, the missionaries have had to learn to boil their drinking water, soak their vegetables in disinfectant solutions, and take numerous other precautions.

Successes have also been satisfying during the first years of the mission. Obviously, the steady growth of Church members, branches, and districts has been encouraging. The Church has also been happy to be involved in providing relief to many who suffered in a devastating earthquake that killed between twenty and thirty thousand people and obliterated forty villages on September 30, 1993. On October 26 Elder Carmack traveled to New Delhi and presented to Mr. Ramu, the prime minister's personal secretary, $25,000 for the Prime Minister's Earthquake Relief Fund. The Church also contributed 160,000 pounds of clothing and other goods valued at $200,000. Another positive measure was the Church's contribution of money and equipment to Pathway, an educational and therapeutic institution in Madras for physically and mentally disabled children. It had been in operation since 1975, but through the support of William Sheffield, the Church, and a number of Indian benefactors, new facilities were built and dedicated on July 23, 1994. The founder and director of the organization, Dr. A. D. S. N. Prasad, was baptized a member of the Church the day before. Area President John K. Carmack was one of the distinguished guests at the dedication services.

On August 13, 1994, Ralph and Margaret Andersen and Raymond and Joan Rhead arrived in Madras to serve as the first Church-service missionaries in India. They were sent under the direction of Isaac Ferguson, director of Humanitarian Services for the Church (now LDS Charities). Their assignments related to assisting with vocational education in connection with the YMCA. Their first project was to upgrade the carpentry program at the YMCA Kottavakkam Boys Town. They soon became involved with a number of projects—a business education computer lab, guidance counseling, a placement center, and so on. They also gave talks to a number of civic and other organizations and participated in one or two international conferences. Elder Rhead, who had taught physical education and recreation at Weber State University in Utah, worked with schools, Pathway, and a Catholic school for the deaf and the blind. He was busily involved in teaching, coaching, and offering workshops on various sports.[15] Elder Rhead also helped the Church make many friends in Cochin when he directed a three-day basketball coaching workshop. The event was such a success that civic and other community leaders heralded the positive effects. Three local newspapers and two national newspapers, *The Hindu* and *Times of India*, published positive articles on the event.

Many foreign observers have noted the spirituality of the Indian people. This natural virtue is also evident within the membership of the Church. A missionary who served in Singapore, Malaysia, and India found the Indian people to be more spiritual than the people he encountered in the other countries where he served. This inclination is evident in the number of Indian members of the Church who have sought patriarchal blessings. A number of patriarchs have served as couple missionaries in India, and all of them have given many blessings. Elder Jerry C. Garlock gave more than one hundred blessings while serving during 1994 and 1995.

When Elder Neal A. Maxwell was in New Delhi in June 1992, "prophecies were given (conditional upon member sharing [the term used by Elder Maxwell to mean fellowshipping and teaching friends about the gospel]) that Delhi would have a [Latter-day Saint] temple and great expansion of the work."[16] With fewer than a thousand members in India at that time, the need for growth not only in total numbers but also in numbers of members who have attended the temple was clearly evident. Since then the Saints of India have made a start; they are beginning to go to the temple in spite of the great cost of traveling to Manila or Hong Kong, the

In June 1995, Sister Vilo Gill and President G. S. Gill (fourth from left on back row), along with Elder Tai's wife, Hui Hua, and Elder Tai Kwok Yuen, Area President for the Asia Area, met with young Indian Latter-day Saints in the first all-India youth conference. (Courtesy G. S. and Vilo Gill)

closest temple sites. President Gill had a goal to help more members become worthy of attending the temple. When asked if this goal was being achieved, he said: "Yes, it is. We had thirty-seven people go to the temple, and fifteen families were sealed together with their parents and children. . . . That has really been a spark.

Now the people know what being married forever means, what we have that other people don't have, how our temple marriages are so sacred and different than their marriages from the other churches, and so forth. . . . Those people have come back and really stirred the members into doing family history work, genealogy work, and beginning to pay tithes so they can go to the temple someday. It has really spurred a lot of enthusiasm."[17]

All but two of India's branch and district presidents were endowed in the temple by mid-1995. Clearly, the work of the Lord is moving forward in a solid, permanent manner in the great subcontinent of India.

THE CHURCH IN SRI LANKA

"One day in 1977," writes Douglas L. Vermillion, "President [Spencer W.] Kimball phoned his cousin Stanley C. Kimball in St. George, Utah, and said, 'Stan, the Lord wants you in Sri Lanka.' Stanley asked where that was and seemed to hesitate a bit. President Kimball said, 'Stan, there are people the Lord loves in Sri Lanka.' After a pause, Stanley answered, 'Then I'll go.' And so Stanley and Margaret Kimball accepted the call to initiate missionary work in Sri Lanka in 1977."[18]

A few Latter-day Saints had resided in Sri Lanka before that date, and two missionaries, Elders Chauncey W. West and Benjamin Franklin Dewey, had even spent several weeks there in 1853. But it was President Kimball's drive to take the restored gospel to all the world that prompted this move in 1977.

Sri Lanka seems to hang like an emerald pendant from the southern tip of the Indian subcontinent. Hot and humid, the tropical beauty of the island competes with Hawaii and other paradises to capture the eye of tourists and residents alike. Sri Lanka's population was 18.3 million in 1995, and its 24,800 square miles of land is almost twice the size of Taiwan (which, incidentally, has 20 million inhabitants). Like India, Nepal has considerable religious variety—69 percent Buddhist, 15.5 percent Hindu, 7.6 percent Muslim, and 7.5 percent Christian.

Unfortunately, during the years the Church has been in Sri Lanka, a bloody civil war between the Tamil people (who live mostly in the northeast and constitute 18 percent of the population) and the native Sinhalese (74 percent of the population) has disturbed this normally tranquil country. The main issue has been the nature of the minority status of the Tamils and whether they should have an independent state. India has been accused of supporting the Tamil autonomous groups, and relations between Sri Lanka and India have been strained. In recent years passage between India and Sri Lanka has been difficult if not impossible for LDS missionaries and leaders. For this reason, even though it would appear that Sri Lanka should be part of the India Bangalore Mission, it is not. It remains part of the Singapore Mission. This war, with its terrorist acts, has restricted LDS missionary efforts in the capital city of Colombo and has made Church work there precarious at times.

Among the very earliest investigators were Reginald A. and Easvary Rasiah. He is of Tamil ancestry, and his wife is Sinhalese. Concerning the problems surrounding their baptisms, the Kimballs wrote: "Satan was working . . . ; by the baptismal date of August 21, 1977, trouble had started between the Sinhalese and Tamil people. There was much looting, arson and killings. A curfew was slapped on the entire country by the prime minister from 5 P.M. August 20, to 6 A.M. August 22, and continued for ten days thereafter. On August 23, Brother Rasiah called early in the morning to say that the lives of him and his family were in danger and needed help. The Kimballs took them into their home and the Wilsons [a Canadian LDS family] took the four children and two grandchildren. After about ten days, conditions were brought under control, leaving thousands of Tamil people in refugee camps without homes or employment."[19]

In spite of the turmoil, five members of the Rasiah family were baptized on August 28, 1977. On the same day, the Colombo

Branch was organized with Elder Kimball as branch president. His first counselor was R. Bruce Wilson, who was attached to the Canadian High Commission. And Brother Rasiah also soon became a counselor. Two others, a young man named Sunil Arsecularatne and a sister named Gertrude Hettiarchchi, were baptized in the next two months. Only a year after his baptism, Brother Rasiah was called as president of the Colombo Branch. Brother Arsecularatne stands out as one of the pioneers: three times over the years he has served as president of the Colombo Branch.

During its first three years in Sri Lanka, the Church moved forward on several fronts. Elder David M. Kennedy, Special Ambassador for the First Presidency, arranged to have the Genealogical Society of Utah microfilm the vital records of Sri Lanka. This created the opportunity for a series of Church members to obtain long-term visas. While Harold Glenn and Mary Deane Clark served as Church representatives, they were instrumental in gaining, on March 2, 1979, official recognition for "The Church of Jesus Christ of Latter-day Saints (Ceylon) Ltd." from the Sri Lankan government.

During this time, Sri Lanka was dedicated for the preaching of the gospel. Sunil Arsecularatne described the dedication of Sri Lanka this way: "In 1979 Apostle James E. Faust visited Sri Lanka and dedicated the country for the preaching of the gospel. The dedication was held at Vihara Maha Devi Park (also known as Victoria Park) in Colombo and was attended by about 20 members. After Elder Faust completed his dedicatory prayer, he said, 'If the Prophet were present today he would have hugged the priesthood brethren present. Therefore, on behalf of the Prophet I would like to do the same.' So he hugged each of the brethren present. I was fortunate and blessed to be one of those present that day and to be one of the recipients of that warm embrace. It was indeed a great spiritual experience for all of those present on this important occasion."[20]

At the beginning of 1980 the Young Ambassadors made the

first of three visits to Sri Lanka. They also performed there in 1982 and 1986. "We have made good strides recently," Brother Rasiah commented. "The BYU Young Ambassadors came to Colombo and made a very good impression on people. People now know what you are talking about when you say you are a Mormon."[21]

During this early period the Church hired Mr. Alloy Perera, a nonmember Sri Lankan, to translate the *Gospel Principles* manual and the pamphlet *Joseph Smith's Testimony* into Sinhala. He also translated *Selections from the Book of Mormon*.

In February 1982 the Church, in conjunction with the Rotary Club, initiated a program for teaching English as a second language. During the period of the program, fifteen different sisters served in Colombo. Sri Lanka received single sisters, Indian missionaries, and couples to teach and strengthen the work. But six members of the branch also served missions in other countries. Upon returning home and marrying, they and their spouses have become firm contributors to the Church.

Church growth in Sri Lanka has been quite slow, fewer than ten new converts per year. And as is true everywhere, some have fallen away. Couple missionaries and young elders have never had long-term visas and have never had the right to do open proselyting. As is true elsewhere in South Asia, missionary work has been done only when investigators have come to the missionaries and asked to be taught the gospel. During some of the worst years of the civil war, it has been difficult to continue with regular Sunday services and other meetings. Conditions became so dangerous that couple missionaries were pulled out from 1988 to 1992. And after that they were removed from the country at least once because of bombs and other violence.[22] In 1995, however, couple missionaries, as well as young elders from the Singapore Mission, were serving in Colombo. At that date there were 125 members of the Church in the one branch. They were enjoying a new meeting place that had been procured in August 1995.

In the 1850s two LDS missionaries, Amos Milton Musser and Truman Leonard, taught the gospel in Karachi, Pakistan, and Leonard carried the gospel to Hyderabad, a hundred miles away (Hyderabad, Pakistan, is not to be confused with Hyderabad, India.) At that time the area now known as Pakistan was part of the province of Sind, which was ruled as part of British India. Elder Musser established a small branch and even constructed a little chapel, surely one of the first LDS chapels to be constructed on the continent of Asia. Musser and Leonard planted gospel seeds that bore fruit almost fifty years later, in 1903 (a story that has been told in chapter 2).

We have no clear record of how many Latter-day Saints since that time have resided as expatriates in Pakistan while serving in governments, international companies, or development agencies, but the number is probably many. Occasionally in the 1970s a reference appeared in the mission records that referred to members in Pakistan. The picture became somewhat clearer in the mid-1980s when groups in Lahore and Islamabad reported their activities to Church headquarters. Max and Barbara Williams reported holding sacrament and other meetings in their home in Lahore with "between 20 and 30 people" gathered. Pakistani Christians who were investigating the Church were among that number.[23] At the same time, Lee Wohlgemuth, who was employed by the U.S. State Department, wrote:

"There is a branch of the Church in Islamabad, the capital of Pakistan. We have three families who meet regularly every Sabbath (Friday), in the home of our branch president, Russell Backus, an irrigation engineer with USAID.

"We average over 20 people at our branch meetings, and sometimes, though not often, interested Pakistanis have attended our meetings."[24]

During the 1980s mission presidents and Area Presidency members periodically visited Pakistan to sense whether the time was right to begin doing missionary work there. By 1992 the Church was ready to move carefully into this Muslim nation.

The Islamic Republic of Pakistan is almost twice the size of California, with a population of 133 million. It came into being on August 14, 1947, when it and India gained their independence from British rule. Pakistan's sole reason for being was to create a homeland for the Muslims of the Indian empire. Heavily Muslim (96.7 percent of the total population), with only small Hindu (1.5 percent) and Christian (1.7 percent) communities, Pakistan has been influenced in recent years by extremist and fundamentalist forces that are determined to further Islamize the country by implementing the *shari'a* laws for any offenses against Islam. Minority groups, including Christians, have received rising levels of persecution since 1988. Although Pakistan has no caste system, Christians clearly belong to the lowest social and economic level. Christians who come from a Muslim background have especially come under constant threat, and some have even been martyred for their new beliefs. For these reasons the LDS Church has moved forward with extreme caution in Pakistan.

When Elders Monte J. Brough and John K. Carmack of the Asia Area Presidency visited Pakistan in November 1991, they observed that expatriate members in Karachi (a city of six million people), especially the Warren Anderson and James Hernandez families, were organized into a branch of eleven members and held regular Church services. In Islamabad, Pakistan's capital city of 204,000 people, a larger branch was organized which was made up of at least four American families and a number of Pakistani converts and investigators (about fifty people were regularly in attendance at Sabbath meetings). The number of Pakistani investigators indicated that the time might be right to begin missionary work with full-time missionaries.[25]

In February 1992 Elder Carmack was back in Pakistan. On this trip he met with the branches and branch leaders in Karachi and Islamabad. He participated in a wonderful fireside with the families of Robert and JuLynne Simmons, Roy and Janice Martin,

Ken and Joan Leahman, and Doug Bradshaw. These people were the ballast of the Church in Pakistan at that time. He also met with an attorney, Mr. Kahn, of the firm Kahn and Piracha, to discuss the legal status of the Church and limitations on religious activity. Elder Carmack was satisfied that legal matters could be worked out.

In June 1992 Elder and Sister Quaid Hansen arrived in Islamabad to commence full-time missionary service. They were the first full-time missionaries to serve since Elder Cooper formed the Karachi branch in 1903.

Later that month, on June 15, 16, and 17, the Pakistan Saints were blessed to receive a visit from two members of the Quorum of the Twelve, Elder Neal A. Maxwell and Elder Russell M. Nelson. They were accompanied by their wives, by President and Sister Warren Jones of the Singapore Mission, and by Elder Carmack. Pakistan was the last stop on a multination Asian tour by Elders Maxwell and Nelson. They maintained a tight and exhausting schedule in order to speak to the Saints, hold personal interviews, and survey the needs of the Church.

Among the many important things Elders Maxwell and Nelson accomplished was to meet with the new missionary couple and the Islamabad branch presidency to clarify issues relating to missionary procedures and baptisms.[26] The Area Presidency and President Jones had already agreed on a checklist to be followed before teaching any new contacts, but the importance of these rules was reemphasized by the Lord's chosen servants. The number-one rule was to teach the gospel to Christians only. A regimen of procedures was to be followed to gain assurance that all investigators were in fact Christians. There was to be no overt proselyting. Interested parties would be taught the gospel, but no one would be sought out by knocking on doors or street contacting.[27] These constraining rules notwithstanding, the Hansens had wonderful success from the beginning. They served in Islamabad for two months and had four baptisms. Then they moved to Lahore (a city of three million people), where they had sixteen

baptisms in November 1992, and still more followed. Church meetings were held in their rented home. By the end of the year, about seventy-five persons were attending sacrament meetings there.

The work has continued to expand. In August 1995 registration of the Church as "The Church of Jesus Christ of Latter-day Saints Pakistan" was completed. This did not mean the Church was recognized, for no Christian religion is recognized in Pakistan, but it did mean it could own property and carry on normal financial procedures. It also made the Church a more naturalized citizen of Pakistan, giving it and its members more recognized status.

The branches grew in number as more members joined the Church. The Pakistan District of the Church was organized with L. Niels Martin as the first president. Martin, who was very active in getting to know all of the members well, was a United Nations reclamation project worker. Other couples were called to Pakistan as missionaries, and in 1994 local Pakistani elders were called to labor in their own country. These elders were flown to Singapore, the mission headquarters for Pakistan, for a Missionary Training Center experience and actual on-the-street training with experienced missionaries. By mid-1994 couples were serving in Karachi, Islamabad, Lahore, and Faisalabad (the latter a city of 1.1 million people and the most recently opened city). More recently, Taxila, an ancient historical center near Islamabad, has been opened to missionary work. In 1995 there were more than four hundred members of the Church in Pakistan.

When the India Bangalore Mission was announced, it was anticipated that Sri Lanka and Pakistan would become part of that mission. However, because of his national origins as an Indian, President Gill was unable to obtain visas to either of these countries. Animosities between India and Pakistan run extremely deep. Disputes continue regarding control of Kashmir, water rights to the Indus River, and several borders. Since independence from British control in 1947, there have been three wars with India. Current internal strife caused the mission president,

Carl D. Warren, to remove missionaries from Karachi. Before President Gill even tried to make a trip to Pakistan, members there asked President Jones in Singapore not to let Gill come because they feared for his life and theirs. To even be associated with an Indian Christian could bring negative reprisals to Pakistani members. Pakistan was quickly assigned back to the Singapore Mission.

There are many challenges for the young Church in Pakistan, but those who have worked closely with the people there find them full of love for the restored gospel and eagerness to learn about the Church and how it should be organized and led. President Warren wrote that the Church was "making cautious progress. Our primary task in Pakistan . . . is to 'Perfect the Saints,' to put down deep roots and keep the growth in balance with the strength of these roots."[28]

NOTES

1. See Jerry C. Garlock, comp. "A History of the Church in India" (Bangalore, India: n.p., 1995), pp. 91–95.

2. See ibid., p. 97.

3. Ibid., p. 198. Garlock includes here a twelve-page recounting by Sheffield of his efforts to improve the visa situation. See also Vilo P. Gill, Journal, 30 October 1993; in her possession.

4. As quoted in Garlock, "Church in India," p. 53; see also "Y professor called to new mission," *Daily Universe* (BYU newspaper), 11 November 1992, p. 1.

5. See Vilo P. Gill, Journal, 4 February 1993.

6. John K. Carmack, interview by the author, Salt Lake City, Utah, 30 November 1995; notes in author's possession. See Sheridan R. Sheffield, "Asia Area: Welcome mat is out in several countries," *Church News*, 19 June 1993, p. 3.

7. See Gurcharan S. Gill, interview by the author, Provo, Utah, 24 October 1995; tape recording.

8. See "Nepal," in Central Intelligence Agency, *The World Factbook 1992* (Washington, D.C.: U.S. Government Printing Office), pp. 241–42.

9. See Johnstone, *Operation World*, p. 405.

10. Garlock, "Church in India," pp. 238–39; Gurcharan S. Gill, spoken and written texts of homecoming talk, 10 September 1995, Provo, Utah; copy in author's possession.

11. Gurcharan S. Gill interview.

12. David Shuler, interview by the author, Provo, Utah, 31 October 1995.

13. See Garlock, "Church in India," pp. 205–8.

14. See Vilo P. Gill, Journal, 7 November 1995.

15. See Garlock, "Church in India," pp. 218–20.

16. John K. Carmack interview.

17. Gurcharan S. Gill interview.

18. Douglas L. Vermillion, "There are people the Lord loves in Sri Lanka," draft article submitted to the *Ensign*, 24 January 1995. For this segment, I have drawn heavily on this draft, upon its published result, "Gospel Splendor in Sri Lanka," *Ensign* 25 (August 1995): 78–79; and Sunil Arsecularatne and Douglas L. Vermillion, "Pioneering Growth of the Church in Sri Lanka," August 1993, unpublished manuscript in author's possession.

19. Stanley C. and Margaret C. Kimball, "First Branch of the Church Established in Sri Lanka (Ceylon)." This undated item was found in the Joseph Talmage Jones Collection, LDS Church Archives.

20. As quoted in Arsecularatne and Vermillion, "Pioneering Growth," p. 2.

21. As quoted in Joseph Walker, "Sri Lanka native is branch president in own country," *Church News*, 1 November 1980, p. 7.

22. Warren R. and Becky Jones, interview by the author, Provo, Utah, 1 November 1995; tape recording in author's possession.

23. See "Loving the Lord in Lahore," *Church News*, 7 April 1985, p. 16.

24. Lee Wohlgemuth, "Correction: There's another branch meeting in Pakistan," *Church News*, 19 May 1985, p. 14.

25. See John K. Carmack interview.

26. See ibid.

27. See Warren R. and Becky Jones interview.

28. Carl D. Warren to Warren R. Jones, 12 September 1995; in possession of the author.

21

THE FUTURE
IS BRIGHT

"Go Forward with Faith"

In a way, the conclusion of any history book is but an introduction to the next. The Church is growing and changing so rapidly in Asia that only a few years will pass before a new edition or an entirely new book will be required to tell the entire story. Updating and new editions are especially needed for books like this one, which includes a journalistic effort to be current. How rapidly events have transpired and how great the changes have been in the development of the Church in Asia are illustrated well in my own writing. In 1979 I wrote:

> Since President Spencer W. Kimball delivered his monumental address to the Regional Representatives in April 1974,[1] the Church has entered a new era of missionary fervor. The Saints have "lengthened their stride" and "quickened their pace." Numbers of missionaries and new converts have increased. In March 1979, President Kimball again encouraged the Latter-day Saints to pray that the gospel might be taken to the nations and peoples in which the doors are not open to our missionaries. He emphasized the need to pray for entry into China and the need to study the Mandarin language.[2]
>
> President Kimball's urge to open China is not surprising. With its 958 million people (1979), China is the most populous country in the world. Approximately one-fourth

of the world's people speak Chinese. China is an ancient land with a magnificent history and a well-developed culture. As a rule the Chinese people are intelligent and able.

For more than a millennium Christian missionaries have considered China the "grand prize." But for various reasons, China has resisted Christianity. Historical circumstances, political intrigue, religious and philosophical disagreements, and cultural differences between missionaries and the Chinese people have thwarted the success of earlier Christian missionary groups.

Other great Asian nations are also within President Kimball's worldwide missionary vision. Although approximately 250 Indians near Coimbatore, India, are baptized Latter-day Saints, most of India's 675 million people are yet to be introduced to the restored gospel. The peoples of Pakistan, Bangladesh, Sri Lanka (Ceylon), Burma, Malaysia, Laos, Bhutan, Nepal, Tibet, Vietnam, and Mongolia too lie beyond the bounds of concentrated LDS missionary work. The small number of LDS missionaries in Indonesia is inconsequential in comparison with the 145 million people in that far-flung island nation. Obviously the major part of the Lord's children wait for messengers who can communicate the restored gospel to them.

When I read my own words, written eighteen years ago, I was struck by several points. First, that our beloved prophet, Spencer W. Kimball, has been gone from us for so long; and second, that the excitement he engendered within the Church to spread the gospel to the entire world has not faltered but increased under the leadership of President Ezra Taft Benson, President Howard W. Hunter, and President Gordon B. Hinckley. The approximately thirty thousand missionaries of President Kimball's time has expanded to more than fifty thousand in late 1996—and no limits are in sight for this growing army of the Lord.

Further, the desire of the Church to take the gospel to the Chinese people and others who have not yet received missionaries remains as sincere and as hopeful as ever. Some realities relating to China have changed dramatically since 1979. The population is well over 1.2 billion. The doors were opened to the outside world at about the time when I wrote the above passage, and the economy has grown tremendously. The decision for Hong Kong to revert to China in 1997 was not made until 1984.

From the standpoint of the Church, 1979 was the beginning of many wonderful relationships resulting from BYU performing arts groups, the David M. Kennedy Center's China Teachers Program, visits to the Polynesian Cultural Center by Chinese political leaders, and other people-to-people types of programs that flowered during the 1980s and 1990s. The Church of Jesus Christ of Latter-day Saints has no missionaries in China and will not have missionaries there until they are allowed to enter legally, but the Church has made thousands of good friends at all levels of society and throughout the country. Such relationships are valuable for their own sake.

In the years since 1979, India's population has grown from 675 million to more than 900 million, and Church membership there has grown from about 250 to close to 2,000. A small beginning, but an important one that will in time bear choice fruit.

In the quote above I listed a number of other nations in which the Church was either not established or was still in its infancy. These included Pakistan, Bangladesh, Bhutan, Nepal, Tibet, Sri Lanka, Burma, Malaysia, Cambodia, Laos, Vietnam, and Mongolia. By 1996, missionaries or non-proselyting representatives of the Church were working in Pakistan, Nepal, Sri Lanka, Malaysia, Cambodia, Vietnam, and Mongolia, seven of the twelve countries listed. During the eighteen years since 1979, the Church dedicated Burma and temporarily had a branch organized in Rangoon. Local political conditions have made missionary work there impossible. Bangladesh remains a difficult problem because of the poverty of the nation and the predominantly Muslim population and government. Unlike Pakistan, where our missionaries are allowed to teach Christians, Bangladesh has a Christian presence so small as to be negligible. Bhutan offers different prob-

lems. It is mostly Buddhist and has made missionary work difficult for all outsiders.

But we should not be confining ourselves to the years since
1979. Following the preamble periods in India in the 1850s and
Japan from 1901 to 1924, the main work of spreading the gospel
in Asia began with LDS servicemen in Japan in 1945. Since then
the Church has grown and prospered in Japan, Korea, Hong Kong,
Taiwan, the Philippines, Thailand, and Indonesia. The handful of
Latter-day Saints in Asia in 1945 has grown to more than 600,000,
and there are five temples, one hundred stakes, 1,690 wards and
branches, thirty-five missions, hundreds of chapels, well-developed CES programs, and many other evidences of the perma-
nence and continuing growth of the Church in this significant part
of the world.

President Gordon B. Hinckley referred to the undeveloped
state of the Church in Japan, Korea, Taiwan, Hong Kong, and the
Philippines when he first visited Asia in 1960. At that time I was
on my mission in Hawaii and met Elder Hinckley when he came
through on that first trip. I remember wondering what was happening in Japan and elsewhere in Asia and what he would find out
there. Being an unschooled youth and not having much vision of
the future, I had no idea that he would one day be President of
the Church. Nor could I imagine the wonderful growth of the
Church in Asia in future years. From time to time, returning missionaries from Japan stopped by the mission office and shared
their experiences with us. My main impression was that they were
pioneers, that they had gone to the ends of the earth, and that
their fledgling successes were happening in strange lands and
among strange people.

In May 1996, while returning from an assignment in the
People's Republic of China, I participated in the dedication of the
Hong Kong Temple. So much had happened in Asia since my first
introduction to it while in Hawaii in 1960 and my first visit there
in 1968; and I was struck by the reality that I was sitting in a
temple in Hong Kong. While I watched such events from the

sidelines, gained an education, and specialized in the history and religions of Asia, the Lord was guiding and directing one of his servants as he led the Church's efforts in that vast part of the earth. While I had been gathering information about Asian Church history, President Gordon B. Hinckley had been making it. His mark is upon the Church in Asia.

President Hinckley could not have more fittingly punctuated his relationship with the Saints in Asia than through his trip to Asia in May 1996. Taking advantage of his assignment to dedicate the Hong Kong Temple on May 26 and 27 during "a busy 18-day visit to seven countries and one territory in Asia, President Hinckley toured 13 cities, met with a number of government officials, answered numerous questions from reporters, [and] delivered 21 addresses to more than 75,000 people." Included in his itinerary was a visit to Shenzhen, China, making him the first President of the Church to visit China while in office; a visit to Cambodia, where he dedicated that land for the preaching of the gospel; and a visit to Vietnam, where in Hanoi he added an "addendum" to the dedicatory prayer he uttered in Saigon in 1966. Members of the Church in every country gathered in great numbers to hear him and his associates among the Brethren speak words of inspiration and encouragement. In Seoul he said, "In 1960 it was a different country. There was great poverty among the people. There was great suffering among the people.

"Now there is prosperity. There is peace. But I don't know that there is more faith than there was back then. I have had many wonderful, faithful, holy experiences in this land."[3]

"In Manila," Church News editor Gerry Avant reported, "President Hinckley spoke to more than 35,000 people, who crowded into the Amoranto Sports Complex for a fireside May 30. Twenty thousand had been expected. . . . Initially, hundreds were turned away from the doors. However, officials of the facility were so touched by the members' tears of disappointment that they relented and allowed them to enter." Upon hearing that the facility was full long before the scheduled meeting time, President Hinckley, his wife, Marjorie, and his associates went to the sports facility early. The gathering was probably the largest indoor congregation that a President of the Church had addressed in person.

President Hinckley spoke as true prophets always speak. He bore witness to the truth of the gospel and the divinity of Jesus Christ. And he gave counsel, counsel that might have been given in Los Angeles or Chicago or Provo. He was speaking to world-wide members of a worldwide Church. "We believe in being honest. We believe in rising above the morals of the world. You cannot be immoral. You cannot use filthy language. You cannot profane the name of God. We believe in being true, chaste, benevolent, virtuous, and if there is anything lovely, of good report, or praise-worthy, we seek after these things." And President Hinckley blessed the congregation, promising, "I bless you if you will walk in faith and live the gospel, you will have food on your table, clothes on your back, a roof over your head, and the blessings of heaven." In the Philippines this was a wonderful promise and a great blessing.

After ministering in Manila, meeting with the Saints in a large congregation in Cebu, and in a relatively small meeting with missionaries—saying he regarded them as "companions in this work"—he headed home. But his plane had to refuel on the Micronesian island of Saipan. During that brief stop he met with ten missionaries and sixty local members. President Hinckley never stopped. Neither does the spread of the restored gospel. Day by day the Lord's chosen sons and daughters are being gathered "from the East."

NOTES

    1. Spencer W. Kimball, "When the World Will Be Converted," *Ensign* 4 (October 1974): 2–14.
    2. Spencer W. Kimball, "'The Uttermost Parts of the Earth,'" *Ensign* 9 (July 1979): 2–9.

3. "President Hinckley Visits Asian Saints, Dedicates Hong Kong Temple," *Ensign* 26 (August 1996): 74–75. For further information on President Hinckley's May–June 1996 trip to Asia, see *Church News*, 1 June and 8 June 1996, and Sheri L. Dew, *Go Forward with Faith: The Biography of Gordon B. Hinckley* (Salt Lake City: Deseret Book Co., 1996).

M A P S

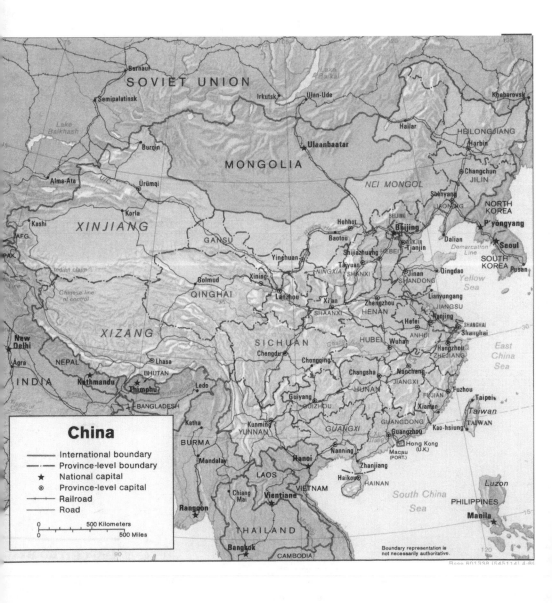

China

- ——— International boundary
- —·—·— Province-level boundary
- ★ National capital
- ⊙ Province-level capital
- ┼┼┼┼ Railroad
- ——— Road

0 ___ 500 Kilometers
0 ___ 500 Miles

Boundary representation is
not necessarily authoritative.

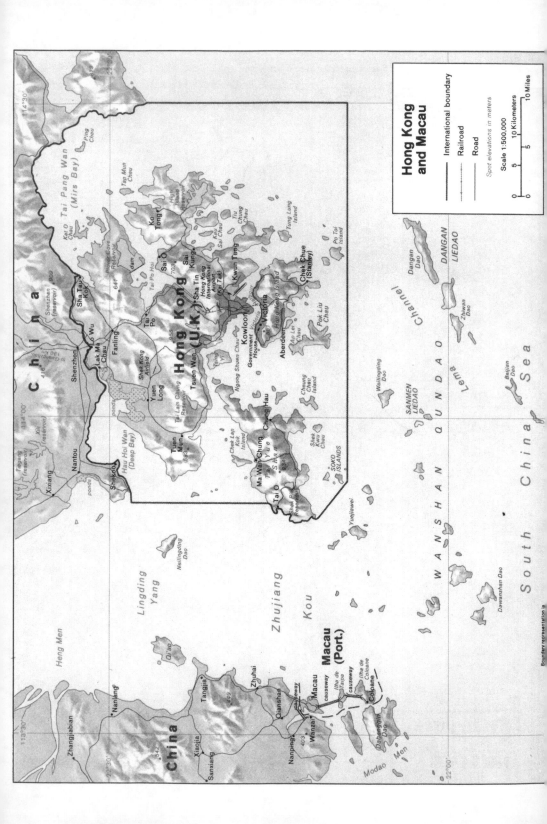

Hong Kong and Macau

International boundary
Railroad
Road

Spot elevations in meters

Scale 1:500,000

0 5 10 Kilometers
0 5 10 Miles

Boundary representation is
not necessarily authoritative.

China

Hong Kong (U.K.)

Macau (Port.)

South China Sea

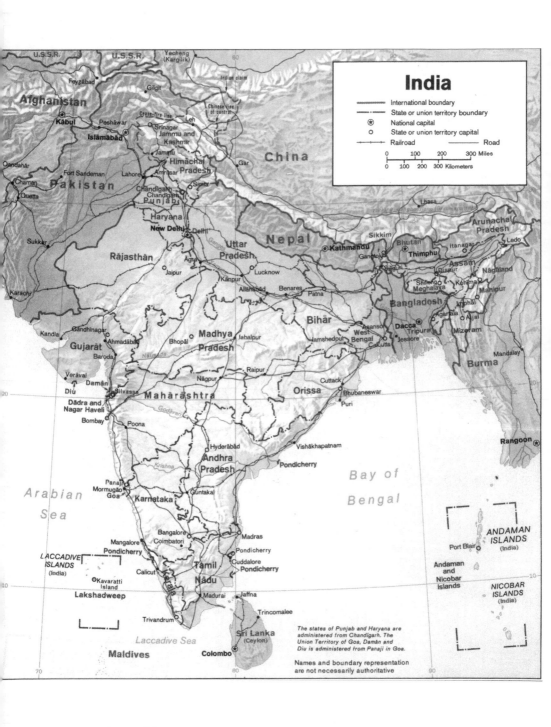

India

- International boundary
- State or union territory boundary
- ⊛ National capital
- ○ State or union territory capital
- Railroad
- Road

| 0 | 100 | 200 | 300 Miles |
| 0 | 100 | 200 | 300 Kilometers |

U.S.S.R.

U.S.S.R.

Yecheng (Kargilik)

Feyzābād

Gilgit

Indian claim

60

Afghanistan

Kābul

Peshāwar

Islāmābād

Srinagar

Jammu and Kashmir

Jammu

Chinese line of control

Leh

Gar

China

Qandahār

Fort Sandeman

Lahore

Amritsar

Himāchal Pradesh

Chaman

Pakistan

Chandigarh

Chandigarh

Simla

Lhasa

Quetta

Punjab

Haryana

New Delhi

Delhi

Sukkur

Rājasthān

Jaipur

Uttar Pradesh

Agra

Nepal

Kāthmāndu

Sikkim

Gangtok

Bhutan

Thimphu

Arunachal Pradesh

Itanagar

Ledo

Siliguri

Assam

Tezpur

Nagaland

Karāchy

Lucknow

Kānpur

Allahābād

Benares

Patna

Shillong

Meghālaya

Kohima

Imphāl

Manipur

Kandla

Gāndhinagar

Ahmadābād

Bhopāl

Madhya Pradesh

Jabalpur

Bihār

West Bengal

Asansol

Dacca

Agartala

Tripura

Ajal

Mizoram

Gujarāt

Baroda

Nārmada

Jamshedpur

Calcutta

Jessore

Bangladesh

Mandalay

Verāval

Damān

Silvassa

Mahārāshtra

Nāgpur

Raipur

Cuttack

Orissa

Bhubaneswar

Burma

Diu

Dādra and Nagar Haveli

Bombay

Poona

Godāvari

Puri

20

Krishna

Hyderābād

Andhra Pradesh

Vishākhapatnam

Rangoon

Panaji

Mormugāo

Goa

Karnataka

Guntakal

Pondicherry

Bay of Bengal

Arabian Sea

Bangalore

Coimbatori

Madras

ANDAMAN ISLANDS (India)

Mangalore

Pondicherry

Pondicherry

Cuddalore

Pondicherry

Port Blair

Andaman and Nicobar Islands

LACCADIVE ISLANDS (India)

Calicut

Tamil Nādu

Kerala

NICOBAR ISLANDS (India)

Kavaratti Island

Madurai

Jaffna

10

Lakshadweep

Trivandrum

Trincomalee

Laccadive Sea

Sri Lanka (Ceylon)

Maldives

Colombo

The states of Punjab and Haryana are administered from Chandigarh. The Union Territory of Goa, Damān and Diu is administered from Panaji in Goa.

Names and boundary representation are not necessarily authoritative

70

80

90

Japan

┿─┿─┿ Railroad
────── Road

North
Pacific
Ocean

Sea of
Japan

Yellow
Sea

East China
Sea

Philippine Sea

Boundary representation is
not necessarily authoritative.

Soviet Union: Harbin, Changchun, Jilin, Shenyang, Anshan, Mudanjiang, Vladivostok, Nakhodka

China

North Korea: P'YŎNGYANG, Sinŭiju, Hamhŭng, Wŏnson, Ch'ŏngjin

South Korea: SEOUL, Inch'ŏn, Taejŏn, Taegu, Kwangju, Mokp'o, Pusan

Demarcation Line

Ullŭng-do, Liancourt Rocks, OKI-GUNTŌ, Cheju-do, Tsushima, Korea Strait, Fukue-shima

Sakhalin, Soviet Union, La Perouse Strait, Wakkanai, Ostrov Iturup, Ostrov Kunashir, occupied by Soviet Union since 1945; claimed by Japan, Shikotan, Habomai Islands, Asahikawa, **Hokkaido**, Sapporo, Kushiro, Hakodate

Tsugaru-kaikyō, Aomori, Akita, Morioka, Sendai, Sado, Niigata, Iwaki, Utsunomiya, Kanazawa, Nagano, **Honshu**, TOKYO, Yokohama, Gifu, Nagoya, Shizuoka, Hamamatsu, Tottori, Okayama, Kōbe, Kyōto, Ōsaka, Takamatsu, Hiroshima, Tokushima, Matsuyama, **Shikoku**, Uwajima, Kitakyūshū, Fukuoka, Sasebo, Ōita, Nagasaki, Kumamoto, **Kyushu**, Kagoshima, ŌSUMI-SHOTŌ

North Pacific Ocean, IZU-SHOTŌ, NAMPO-SHOTŌ, Sumisu-jima, Tori-shima

TOKARA-RETTŌ

AMAMI-SHOTŌ, OKINAWA-SHOTŌ, Naha, RYUKYU ISLANDS, SENKAKU-SHOTŌ, SAKISHIMA-SHOTŌ, Daitō-jima, Okino-daitō-jima

BONIN ISLANDS (OGASAWARA-SHOTŌ), VOLCANO ISLANDS (KAZAN-RETTŌ), Iwo Jima

0		100		200 Miles
0	100		200 Kilometers	

South Korea

- —·—· Internal administrative boundary
- ★ National capital
- ⊙ Internal administrative capital
- +―+―+ Railroad
- ——— Expressway
- ——— Road

0   25   50 Kilometers
0   25   50 Miles

NORTH KOREA

Korea Bay

Yellow Sea

Sea of Japan

JAPAN
Kyushu

Yangdŏg-ŭp • Wŏnsan
Onch'ŏn • P'yŏngyang • Yŏnsan • T'ongch'ŏn
Namp'o • Songnim • Kosan
Sariwŏn • Ich'ŏn • Kuŭm-ni
Sinch'ŏn • P'yŏnggang • Demarcation Line and Demilitarized Zone
Changyŏn-ŭp • P'yŏngsan • Kansŏng
Haeju • Kaesŏng • Hwach'ŏn • Injeŭp • Yangyang
Ongjin • P'anmunjŏm • Yŏnch'ŏn • Kangnŭng
KYŎNGGI-DO • Munsan • Ch'unch'ŏn • **KANGWŎN-DO**
Kukch'ŏn • Kimp'o • Ŭijŏngbu • Kansŏng
INCH'ŎN-JIKHALSI • Hongch'ŏn • Pukp'yŏng-ni • Ullŭng-do
Inch'ŏn • Seoul • Yangp'yŏng • Yŏyang-ni
SEOUL-T'ŬKPYŎLSI • Wŏnju
Yŏju • Hwangji-ri
Suwŏn
P'yŏngt'aek • Ansŏng • Chungju • Chech'ŏn
Ch'ŏnan • Tanyang • Yŏngju
CH'UNGCH'ŎNG-BUKTO • Yŏngyang
Ch'ŏngju • Chŏmch'on • Yech'ŏn
Hongsŏng • **CH'UNGCH'ŎNG-NAMDO** • Andong
Kongju • Poŭn • Sangju • Ŭisŏng • Yŏngdŏk
Taech'ŏn • Taejŏn • **KYŎNGSANG-BUKTO** (Administrative center at Taegu)
Yŏngdong • Kimch'ŏn • P'ohang
Kunsan • Iri • Yŏngch'ŏn • Kyŏngju
Chŏnju • Taegu
Chinan • **TAEGU-JIKHALSI**
CHOLLA-BUKTO • Anŭi • Ulsan
Chŏngŭp • Hyŏpch'ŏn • Ŏnyang
Namwŏn • **KYŎNGSANG-NAMDO** (Administrative center at Pusan) • Namji • Yangsan
Yŏnggwang • Chinju • Masan • Chinhae • Pusan
Kwangju • **PUSAN-JIKHALSI**
Yŏngsanp'o • Sunch'ŏn • Samch'ŏnp'o • Kŏje-do
CHOLLA-NAMDO • Posŏng
Mokp'o • Yŏsu
Kangjin • Kohŭng • Shishi
Chindo • Tsushima
Chin-do • Wando
Western Channel
Korea Strait
Eastern Channel
Iki
HŬKSAN-CHEDO
Cheju-haehyŏp
Cheju • Fukuoka
CHEJU-DO • Cheju-do
Sasebo • Ōmuta

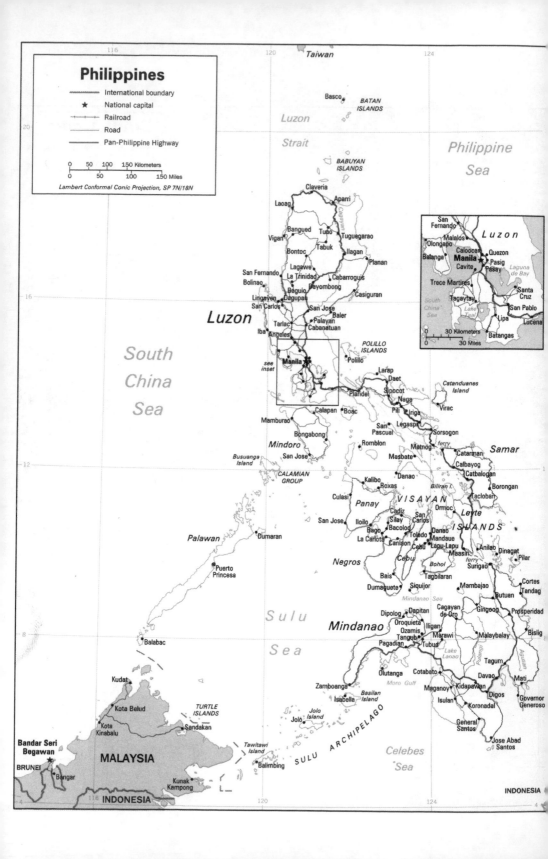

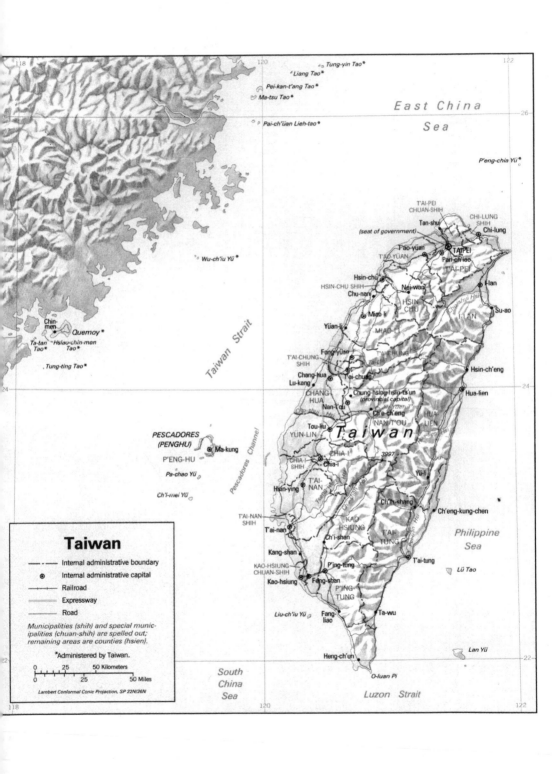

Taiwan

East China Sea

Tung-yin Tao*
Liang Tao*
Pei-kan-t'ang Tao*
Ma-tsu Tao*
Pai-ch'üan Lieh-tao*

P'eng-chia Yü*

T'AI-PEI
CHUAN-SHIH
CHI-LUNG
SHIH
Tan-shui
(seat of government)
Chi-lung
T'ao-yüan
TAIPEI
T'AO-YÜAN
Pan-ch'iao
T'AI-PEI
Wu-ch'iu Yü*
Hsin-chu
I-lan
HSIN-CHU SHIH
Nei-wan
Chu-nan
HSIN-
Su-ao
CHU
I-LAN
Miao-li
Yüan-li
MIAO-LI
Fong-yüan
Chin-
men
Quemoy*
T'AI-CHUNG
Ta-tan
Hsiao-chin-men
Chang-hua
T'ai-chung
Hsin-ch'eng
Tao*
Tao*
SHIH
Lu-kang
Tung-ting Tao*
CHANG
Chung-hsing-hsin-ts'un
Hua-lien
HUA
(provincial capital)
Nan-t'ou
HUA-
LIEN
Tou-liu
NAN T'OU
PESCADORES
YUN-LIN
Taiwan
(PENGHU)
Ma-kung
CHIA-I
3997
P'ENG-HU
SHIH
Chia-i
Pa-chao Yü*
Yü-li
T'AI-
Hsin-ying
NAN
Ch'i-mei Yü*
Ch'eng-kung-chen
Ch'ih-shang
T'AI-NAN
KAO
Philippine
SHIH
HSIUNG
T'AI-
Sea
T'ai-nan
Ch'i-shan
TUNG
Kang-shan
P'ing-tung
T'ai-tung
KAO-HSIUNG
Lü Tao
CHUAN-SHIH
Feng-shan
P'ING-
Kao-hsiung
TUNG
Ta-wu
Liu-ch'iu Yü*
Fang-
liao
Lan Yü

South
China
Sea
Heng-ch'un
O-luan Pi
Luzon Strait

Taiwan Strait

Pescadores Channel

Legend

- — · — Internal administrative boundary
- ⊙ Internal administrative capital
- ┼┼┼ Railroad
- Expressway
- Road

Municipalities (shih) and special munic-ipalities (chuan-shih) are spelled out; remaining areas are counties (hsien).

*Administered by Taiwan.

0   25   50 Kilometers
0   25   50 Miles

Lambert Conformal Conic Projection, SP 22N/26N

BIBLIOGRAPHY

BOOKS

Allen, James B., et al. *Hearts Turned to the Fathers*. Provo: BYU Studies, 1996.

Allen, James B., and Glen M. Leonard. *The Story of the Latter-day Saints*. 2nd edition. Salt Lake City: Deseret Book Co., 1992.

Banerjee, Brojendra Nath. *Religious Conversions in India*. New Delhi: Harnam Publications, 1982.

Barrett, David B., ed. *World Christian Encyclopedia*. New York: Oxford University Press, 1982.

Blumell, Bruce, and Garth Mangum. *The Mormons War on Poverty*. Salt Lake City: University of Utah Press, 1993.

Boardman, Eugene P. *Christian Influence Upon the Theology of the Taiping Rebellion*. Madison: University of Wisconsin Press, 1952.

Britsch, R. Lanier. *Unto the Islands of the Sea*. Salt Lake City: Deseret Book Co., 1986.

Brooks, Juanita, ed. *On the Mormon Frontier: The Diary of Hosea Stout*. 2 vol. Salt Lake City: University of Utah Press, 1964.

Brown, W. Norman. *The United States and India, Pakistan, Bangladesh*. 3d ed. Cambridge: Harvard University Press, 1972.

Central Intelligence Agency. *The World Factbook 1992*. Washington D.C.: U.S. Government Printing Office.

The Chicago Manual of Style, 14th ed. Chicago and London: The University of Chicago Press, 1993.

Culturgrams: The Nations Around Us. Vol. 2. Provo: Publications Division of the David M. Kennedy Center for International Studies, 1996.

Davis, Winston. *Japanese Religion and Society: Paradigms of Structure and Change*. Albany: State University of New York Press, 1992.

Dew, Sheri L. *Go Forward with Faith: The Biography of Gordon B. Hinckley*. Salt Lake City: Deseret Book Co., 1996.

Drummond, Richard H. *A History of Christianity in Japan*. Grand Rapids: William B. Eerdmans Publishing Co., 1971.

Fairbank, John K., Edwin O. Reischauer, and Albert M. Craig. *East Asia: Tradition and Transformation*. Boston: Houghton Mifflin Co., 1973.

Grant, Heber J. *A Japanese Journal*. Gordon A. Madsen, comp. N.p., n.d.

The Guide to the Scriptures. English Version. Salt Lake City: The Church of Jesus Christ of Latter-day Saints, 1993.

Hane, Mikiso. *Eastern Phoenix: Japan Since 1945*. Boulder, Colorado: Westview Press, 1996.

Heaton, Alma and Marie. *Behind the Taj Mahal, Spiritual Adventures in India*. N.p., 1992.

Hoke, Donald E. *The Church in Asia*. [Protestant.] Chicago: Moody Press, 1975.

Holtom, D. C. *Modern Japan and Shinto Nationalism*. Chicago: University of Chicago Press, 1943.

Jensen, Andrew. *Church Chronology*. Salt Lake City: Deseret Book Co., 1899.

Johnstone, Patrick. *Operation World*. Grand Rapids, Michigan: Zondervan Publishing House, 1993.

Jones, J. Talmage. *In Singapore*. Salt Lake City: Publishers Press, 1984.

Kane, J. Herbert. *A Global View of Christian Missions*, rev. ed. Grand Rapids: Baker Book House, 1975.

———. *Understanding Christian Missions*. Michigan: Baker Book House, 1974.

Latourette, Kenneth Scott. *A History of the Expansion of Christianity*. Vol. 6: *The Great Century: North America and Asia*, A.D. *1800*–A.D. 1914. Grand Rapids: Zondervan Publishing House, 1970.

Lim, Augusto A. "The Church in the Philippines." In *Mormonism: A Faith for All Cultures*, edited by F. LaMond Tullis. Provo: Brigham Young University Press, 1978.

Long, Lynellyn D. *Ban Binai, The Refugee Camp*. New York: Columbia University Press, 1993.

Marsh, Don W. *The Light of the Sun*. N.p., n.d. [probably 1969].

Neill, Stephen. *Colonialism and Christian Missions*. New York: McGraw-Hill, 1966.

———. *A History of Christian Missions*. London: Penguin Books, 1986. Rev. for second edition by Owen Chadwick.

Palmer, Spencer J. *The Church Encounters Asia*. Salt Lake City: Deseret Book Co., 1970.

———. *The Expanding Church*. Salt Lake City: Deseret Book Co., 1978.

———. *Korea and Christianity*. Seoul, Korea: Hollym Corporation Publishers, 1967.

Palmer, Spencer J. and Shirley H. Palmer, comps. and eds. *The Korean Saints: Personal Stories of Trial and Triumph, 1950–1980*. Provo: Religious Education, Brigham Young University, 1995.

Reischauer, Edwin O. *Japan, The Story of a Nation*. 4th ed. New York: McGraw-Hill Publishing Co., 1990.

———. *The Japanese*. Cambridge, Massachusetts: The Belknap Press of Harvard University Press, 1978.

———. *The United States and Japan*. New York: Viking Press, 1963.

Roberts, Brigham Henry. *A Comprehensive History of The Church of Jesus Christ of Latter-day Saints*. 6 vols. Salt Lake City: The Church of Jesus Christ of Latter-day Saints, 1930.

Smith, Ebbie C. *God's Miracles: Indonesian Church Growth*. Pasadena: William Carey Library, 1970.

Sonne, Conway B. *Knight of the Kingdom: The Story of Richard Ballantyne*. Salt Lake City: Deseret Book Co., 1949.

Spear, Percival. *India: A Modern History*. Ann Arbor: The University of Michigan Press, 1961.

Steinberg, David Joel, et al., eds. *In Search of Southeast Asia: A Modern History*. New York: Praeger Publishers, 1971.

Stout, Wayne. *Hosea Stout: Utah's Pioneer Statesman*. Salt Lake City: n.p., 1953.

Tate, Lucile C. *Boyd K. Packer: A Watchman on the Tower*. Salt Lake City: Bookcraft, 1995.

Tullis, F. LaMond, ed. *Mormonism: A Faith for All Cultures*. Provo: Brigham Young University Press, 1978.

Walk in His Ways: Basic Manual for Children, Part B. Salt Lake City: The Church of Jesus Christ of Latter-day Saints, 1993.

Whittaker, David J. "Richard Ballantyne and the Defense of Mormonism in India in the 1850s." In Donald Q. Cannon and David J. Whittaker, eds. *Supporting Saints: Life Stories of Nineteenth-Century Mormons*. Provo: BYU Religious Studies Center, 1985.

Wolpert, Stanley. *A New History of India*. 4th ed. New York: Oxford University Press, 1993.

Young, John M. L. *The Two Empires in Japan*. Tokyo: The Bible Times Press, 1958.

Younger, Shirley-Anne, et al. *For Those Who Dare to Dream*. Korea: s.n., ca. 1990.

ARTICLES, BOOKLETS, AND PAMPHLETS

"A Future Mission Field." *The Contributor* 16 (October 1895): 764–65.

Allen, James B. "First Excursion: A Church for all lands—Korea." *Church News*, April 7, 1979, 24.

"Ambassador's Term Brief, Yet Notable." *Church News*, June 5, 1993, 11.

"Anand Appointed Premier." *Bangkok Post*, June 11, 1992, 1.

Anderson, Desmond L. "Meeting the Challenges of the Latter-day Saints in Vietnam." *Brigham Young University Studies* 10 (Winter 1970): 186–96. Hereafter cited as *BYU Studies*.

"Area Conferences in Far East Planned." *Church News*, March 22, 1980, pp. 3, 11.

"Asia Area: Fifth Stake Organized." *Church News*, April 23, 1994, 12.

"A Temple in Japan." *Church News*, October 25, 1980, 16.

Avant, Gerry. "War's Tragedies Lead to Gospel." *Church News*, October 29, 1977, 5.

———. "First Temple in Chinese Realm." *Church News*, November 25, 1984, 3, 14.

———. "Korean is like a 'living treasure' among members" [on Han In Sang]. *Church News*, February 2, 1986, 6.

———. "'Land of Morning Calm' brightened by Korea temple." *Church News*, December 22, 1985, 6–7.

———. "LDS Leader Pays Visit to China's Mainland." *Deseret News*, May 28, 1996, A1–A2.

———. "Tears Flow, Faith Grows as Filipinos Greet Prophet." *Church News*, June 8, 1996, 4.

———. "Their prayers are answered, a temple in their midsts." *Church News*, April 11, 1981, 23.

———. "Vietnam was 'Land of Opportunity' for Gospel Study." *Church News*, November 23, 1986, 6.

Avant, Gerry, and John L. Hart. "His shoulders are used to heavy tasks" [regarding Han In Sang]. *Church News*, July 6, 1991, 6–7.

Bateman, Merrill J., Han In Sang, and Sam K. Shimabukuro. "Church Progress Continues in Japan and South Korea." *Ensign* 24 (May 1994): 111–12.

Beesley, Kenneth H. "The LDS Church and Higher Education in Mongolia." *Proceedings of the Fifth Annual Conference of the International Society.* (Provo: David M. Kennedy Center for International Studies, 1994): 32–4.

Benson, Ezra Taft. "The Future of the Church in Asia." *Improvement Era* 73 (March 1970): 14–15.

———. "A World Message." *Improvement Era* 73 (June 1970): 95–97.

Brady, Frederick R. "Two Meiji Scholars Introduce the Mormons to Japan." *BYU Studies* 23 (1983): 167ff.

Britsch, R. Lanier. "The Blossoming of the Church in Japan." *Ensign* 22 (October 1992): 32–38.

———. "Church Beginnings in China." *BYU Studies* 10 (1970): 159ff.

———. "The Closing of the Early Japan Mission." *BYU Studies* 15 (Winter 1975): 171–90.

———. "The Current Legal Status of Christianity in China." *Brigham Young University Law Review* Vol. 1995, Number 2: 347–99.

———. "The Early Missions to Burma and Siam." *Improvement Era* 73 (March 1970): 35–44.

———. "The Latter-day Saint Mission to India: 1851–1856." *BYU Studies* 12 (Spring 1972): 262–78.

———. "Mormon Missions: An Introduction to the Latter-day Saints' Missionary System." *Occasional Bulletin of Missionary Research* 3 (January 1979): 22–27.

Britsch, R. Lanier and Richard C. Holloman. "The Church's Years in Vietnam." *Ensign* 10 (August 1980): 24–30.

Britsch, R. Lanier, et al. "Problems and Opportunities of Missionary Work in Asia (A Symposium of Former Mission Presidents)." *BYU Studies* 12 (1971): 85ff.

Brockbank, Bernard P. "The Mormon Pavilion at Expo '70." *Improvement Era* 73 (December 1970): 121.

Brown, Hugh B. "Prophecies Regarding Japan." *BYU Studies* 10 (Winter 1970): 159–60.

Bushman, Claudia L. "Member wins Tchaikovsky prize." *Church News*, October 6, 1990, 13.

Cahill, Jerry P. "Times of Great Blessings: Witnessing the Miracles." *Ensign* 11 (January 1981): 70–75.

Calvert, S. "Our Trip to the Temple." *Tambuli* 18 (February 1994): Dateline Philippines, 3–4.

Campbell, Cherie. "Temple to Be Built in Tokyo." *Ensign* 5 (October 1975): 86–87.

Cannon, Hugh J. "The Chinese Realm Dedicated for the Preaching of the Gospel." *Improvement Era* 24 (March 1921): 443–46.

Carmack, John K., Kwok Yuen Tai, and John H. Groberg. "Conversation with the Asia Area Presidency." *Ensign* 25 (June 1995): 76–77.

Castel, Delmar. "Mabuhay-Deseret Foundation Conduct Screening, Clinic in Cebu." *Tambuli* 14 (September 1991): Dateline Philippines, 5.

"China: Two Apostles Visit, Assured that Religious Freedom Exists and People are Free to Worship as They Choose." *Church News*, January 28, 1989, 3–4.

"Chinese Ambassador Visits Utah." *Church News*, January 17, 1981, 5.

"Chinese Leader Visits Center." *Church News*, July 12, 1980, 9.

"Chinese Premier Visits BYU–Hawaii Campus, Polynesian Cultural Center." *Ensign* 14 (March 1984): 77–78.

Christensen, Craig B. "The Beginnings in Thailand." *Improvement Era* 73 (March 1970): 32–34.

Christensen, Duane and Jean. "Special Training and Counsel Given Manila Area Employment Specialists." *Tambuli* 16 (November 1993): Dateline Philippines, 1–3.

"Choir to Perform in Japan." *Church News*, December 30, 1978, 3

"Church Acquires First Property." *Church News*, April 28, 1979, 5.

"Church Donates Aid for Victims of Quake in China." *Ensign* 19 (May 1989): 109.

"Church Donates Funds for Filipino Relief." *Church News*, September 28, 1991, 4.

Church Educational System. *Overview 1978*. Salt Lake City, 1978.

"The Church Employment System." *Tambuli* 14 (June 1991): Dateline Philippines, 7–9.

"The Church Employment System Broadens Focus." *Tambuli* 16 (August 1993): Dateline Philippines, 4–6.

"Church Flourishes in Colony of Macao." *Church News*, September 23, 1978, 6.

"Church's Health Team Teaches Maternal Care." *Church News*, March 3, 1979, 13.

Clark Jr., J. Reuben. "The Outpost in Mid-Pacific." *Improvement Era* 38 (September 1935): 530–35.

"Conference in the Philippines." *Ensign* 5 (October 1975): 90–91.

Cong Ton Nu Tuong-Vy. "Out of the Tigers Den." *Ensign* 19 (June 1989): 44–47.

Conkling, J. Christopher. "Members Without a Church: Japanese Mormons in Japan from 1924 to 1948." *BYU Studies* 15 (1975): 191–214.

Cook, Joseph V., et al., comp. *A History of The Church of Jesus Christ of Latter-day Saints in the Philippines*. Pamphlet, 1965.

Cook, Mary Nielsen. "A Mighty Change in Mongolia." *Ensign* 26 (June 1996): 75–76.

Cooley, Frank L. "The Growing Seed: A Descriptive and Analytical Survey of the Church in Indonesia." *Occasional Bulletin of Missionary Research* 1 (October 1977): 3.

"Correction: There's Another Branch Meeting in Pakistan." *Church News*, May 19, 1985, 14.

Cowley, Matthew. "The Language of Sincerity." *Improvement Era* 52 (November 1949): 715.

Craig, Alison. "The Saints in Indonesia." *Ensign* 7 (January 1977): 86–90.

"Dedication Dates Set for Temples in Tokyo, Seattle." *Church News*, April 19, 1980, 4.

"Dedication Prayer for the [Tokyo] Temple." *Church News*, November 8, 1980, 12.

"Dedicatory Prayer of the Hong Kong Temple." *Church News*, June 1, 1996, 4.

"Dedicatory Prayer Recognizes Small Beginnings of Work." [Dedicatory prayer of Seoul Korea Temple.] *Church News*, December 22, 1985, 7.

"Donation to Help Flood Victims in China." *Church News*, August 17, 1991, 11.

Edmunds, Mary Ellen, et al. "International Health and the Church." *The Journal of Collegium Aesculapium* 1 (December 1983): 7–11.

"8 New Missions Formed." *Church News*, February 16, 1980, 3.

"Elder Nelson Is Named Honorary Professor by Chinese Medical College." *Church News*, September 29, 1985, 6.

"Elder Yoshihiko Kikuchi." *Ensign* 7 (November 1977): 101–2.

"Enterprise Development Programs Established in the Philippines." *Tambuli* 13 (March 1990): Dateline Philippines, 9.

"Expo '70 Ground Breaking." *Church News*, May 17, 1969, 4.

Fallows, James. "The World Beyond Salt Lake City: Mormons in Japan May Lose the Battle for Converts—but They Are Helping to Win the War for American Competitiveness." *U.S. News and World Report* 104 (May 2, 1988): 67.

Faust, James E. "Establishing the Church: Welfare Services Missionaries Are an Important Resource." *Ensign* 9 (November 1979): 91–93.

"First Convert Joins Church in South Vietnam." *Church News*, November 24, 1962, 7.

"First Presidency Encourages Help for Refugees." *Ensign* 9 (October 1979): 79.

Fish, Jon B. "Saved by Seminary." *New Era* 17 (March 1987): 18–19.

Ford, Joan Porter and LaRene Porter Gaunt. "The Gospel Dawning in Thailand." *Ensign* 25 (September 1995): 48–55.

Forman, Charles W. "Freedom of Conversion—The Issue in India." *International Review of Missions* 45 (April 1956): 180–93.

"Four New Areas will be Created Aug. 15, Bringing Total to 17." *Church News*, April 25, 1987, 3, 6.

"Funds Help Philippine Earthquake Victims." *Church News*, September 29, 1990, 5.

Gabriel, J. Antonio T. San. "Business and Job Fair." *Tambuli* 15 (December 1992): Dateline Philippines, 7–8.

Gardner, Marvin K. "Philippine Saints: A Believing People." *Ensign* 21 (July 1991): 32–39.

———. "Philippine Saints Recover from Earthquake." *Ensign* 20 (October 1990): 74–76.

"Gift to Help China Rebuild After Quake." *Church News*, February 25, 1989, 4

"Gospel Flourishes in the Refugee Camp." *Tambuli* 11 (March 1988): Dateline Philippines, 6.

Grant, Heber J. Conference Reports 1902 (April 5, 1902): 45–49.

———. Conference Reports 1903 (October 4, 1903): 6–13.

Greer, Dianna J. "Young Ambassadors 'Unlock Hearts' During Tour of India." *Church News*, April 24, 1982, 13.

Gulick, Sidney L. "American-Japanese Relations: The Logic of the Exclusionists." *The Annals of the American Academy of Political and Social Sciences* 127 (November 1925):181–87.

Han, In Sang. "Encounter: The Korean Mind and the Gospel." *Ensign* 5 (August 1975): 47.

"Han In Sang of the Seventy." *Ensign* 31 (August 1991): 75.

Hanks, Marion D. et al. "International Health and the Church." *The Journal of Collegium Aesculapium* 1 (December 1983): 13–17.

Hansen, Lynne Hollstein. "Membership Soaring in Asia." *Church News*, August 18, 1979, 3, 8.

———. "Y Students a Success in China." *Church News*, August 11, 1979, 10.

Hansen, Peter M. "Seek Not After Your Own Heart." *New Era* 17 (May 1987): 9–11.

Hart, John L. "Korean sings Italian opera: LDS baritone wins spot at Seoul Olympics." *Church News*, August 27, 1988, 14.

———. "Temple Moments: Great Is Their Joy." *Church News*, December 10, 1988, 16.

Hawkins, Victoria Varley. "Conference in Hong Kong." *Ensign* 5 (October 1975): 91–92.

Hayashi, Chikio. "The National Character in Transition." *Japan Echo* 15 (1988): 8–9.

Heal, Muriel Jenkins. "'We will Go': The Robertson Response." *Ensign* 12 (April 1982): 32–35.

Heaton, H. Grant. "Missionary System Set up in Hong Kong." *Church News*, October 29, 1955, 6.

"Helping Refugees Begin New Life." *Church News*, March 21, 1981, 7–10.

Helps, Louise. "Breaking New Ground in Hanoi." *Cameo: Latter-day Women in Profile* 2 (February 1994): 41, 48, 51.

Hill, John M., M. E. Woods, and Steven D. Dorsey. "A Human Development Intervention in the Philippines: Effect on Child Morbidity." *Social Science Medicine* 27, no. 11 (1988): 1,183–88.

Hillman, Robert K. "I Knew It Wasn't Luck." *Ensign* 25 (September 1995): 62–63.

———. "Peace Amidst War." *Ensign* 19 (April 1989): 10–11.

Hinckley, Gordon B. "The Church in the Far East." *Improvement Era* 65 (June 1962): 440–43.

———. "A Silver Thread in the Dark Tapestry of War." *Improvement Era* 71 (June 1968): 48–50.

———. "Whosoever Will Save His Life." *Ensign* 12 (August 1982): 3–6.

"Hong Kong Center Improves Attitudes Toward the Church, Baptisms Increase." *Church News*, September 10, 1977, 6.

Hong Kong Standard (September 1, 1957).

"Hong Kong Temple Visited by 13,000 During Open House." *Church News*, May 25, 1996, 4–5.

Hughes, David L. "The Saints in Saigon: An End, a Beginning." *This People* (April 1985): 46–51.

Hurst, Mark E. "Airman in Vietnam Survives Pain of Human Unkindness." *Church News*, January 29, 1994, 12.

"Indochinese Refugees" *Gist* (April 1983) Bureau of Public Affairs, Department of State, n.p.

Irving, Gordon. "Numerical Strength and Geographical Distribution of the LDS Missionary Force, 1830–1974." *Task Papers in LDS History*, 1975.

"Japan Area General Conference." *Church News*, August 16, 1975, 5.

Jenkins, Carri P. "Bridging Barriers." *BYU Today* 40 (August 1986): 18–22, 25, 34–35.

Jolley, JoAnn. "Blessed Are the Peacemakers: LDS in the Military." *This People* (June/July 1984): 67–73.

Jones, Garth N. "Spreading the Gospel in Indonesia: Organizational Obstacles and Opportunities." *Dialogue* 15 (Winter 1982): 79–90.

"Jubilance at Asian Temple Ceremonies." *Church News*, September 4, 1982, 3, 14.

Kimball, Spencer W. "The Uttermost Parts of the Earth." *Ensign* 9 (July 1979): 2–9.

———. "When the World Will Be Converted." *Ensign* 4 (October 1974): 2–14.

Konno, Yukiko. "Fujiya Nara: Twice a Pioneer." *Ensign* 23 (April 1993): 31–33.

Larsen, Robert G. and Sharyn H. "Refugee Converts: One Stake's Experience." *Dialogue* 20 No. 3 (1987): 37–55.

"LDS, Others Take Pride in Taiwan Temple at Open House." *Church News*, November 11, 1984, 12.

Lee, Harold B. "Miraculous Power of Divine Intervention Present in Orient." *Church News*, October 9, 1954, 8.

———. "Report on the Orient." *Improvement Era* 57 (December 1954): 926–30.

Lilly, Henry J. "From India's Coral Strand." *Improvement Era* 12, Number 6 (1908–1909): 423–34.

Liu, David C. H. "Taipei Taiwan Temple Dedicated." *Ensign* 15 (February 1985): 75–76.

Lofgreen, Charlotte D. "Mongolia: The Morning Breaks." *Cameo, Latter-day Women in Profile* 2 (February 1994): 23–24.

"Loving the Lord in Lahore." *Church News*, April 7, 1985, 16.

"Mabuhay-Deseret Foundation: Dedicated to Improve the Quality of Life." *Tambuli* 13 (March 1990): Dateline Philippines, 3–5.

"Mabuhay-Deseret Foundation Turns 2." *Tambuli* 13 (November 1990): Dateline Philippines, 6–7.

"Malaysia Converts See Church Grow." *Church News*, May 23, 1981, 13.

Maloy, Larry S. "The Army Nurse's Kindness." *Ensign* 20 (March 1990): 56–57.

Maquiran, Charrie R. "Seminary Classes Now Held in Bacolod City Public Schools." *Tambuli* 17 (August 1988): Dateline Philippines, 4.

"May Thy watch care be over it." [Dedicatory prayer of the Hong Kong Temple.] *Church News*, June 1, 1996, 4.

Meisenbach, John L. "Christmas in Vietnam." *Tambuli* 11 (December 1992): 24.

"Members Dine with Royalty." *Church News*, December 17, 1994, 12.

Mitchell, David. "Pornchai Juntratip, Spiritually Prepared." *Tambuli* 17 (February 1993): 42–45.

———. "The Saints of Thailand." *Tambuli* 17 (May 1993): 41–45.

"Mormon Missionaries now labor in Formosa." *Church News*, June 23, 1956, 19.

"Mongolia Dedicated for Preaching of the Gospel." *Church News*, June 19, 1993, 3.

Moss, Kevin. "Conference in Taiwan." *Ensign* 5 (October 1975): 92–93.

"New Missionary Training Center Dedicated." *Tambuli* 15 (November 1992): Dateline Philippines, 3–4.

"Open Minds, Hearts to People of China." *Church News*, March 16, 1991, 5.

Osumo, Rabai B. "The Church in the Philippines." *Tambuli* 5 (April 1991): Dateline Philippines, 12.

Parry, Jay A. "Hong Kong: Pearl of the Orient." *Ensign* 5 (August 1975): 51–54.

"Philippines: The Land of Joyous Service." *Ensign* 5 (August 1975): 58–61.

Phipps, Jr., William E. "In a Vietnam Helicopter." *Ensign* 9 (August 1979): 56–57.

"Plans announced for 9 new temples." *Church News*, April 4, 1981, 3–4.

"Polynesian Cultural Center Hosts Chinese President." *Ensign* 15 (October 1985): 78.

"Post Script: Para Sa Ating Kaalaman." *Liahona* 1 (November 1995): Dateline Philippines, 7.

"President Asks Catholic and Protestant Leaders: Foreign Missionaries Should Be Replaced." *Indonesian Times* (September 1, 1979). Found in Jakarta Indonesia Mission History, 1979. LDS Church Archives.

"President Benson visits Asian countries." *Church News*, June 10, 1978, 4.

President Hinckley Visits Asian Saints, Dedicates Hong Kong Temple." *Ensign* 26 (August 1996): 74–77.

"President Kimball Sees Missions in Communist China in Future." *The Herald*, Provo, Utah, April 1, 1979, 24.

Price, Harrison T. "A Cup of Tea." *Improvement Era* 65 (March 1962): 160–61.

"Prophet Testifies, Reaffirms Blessings." *Church News*, June 8, 1996, 7.

"Quake Jolts Philippines: 2 LDS Missing." *Church News*, July 28, 1990, 10.

Ricks, Kellene. "Korea: Land of the Morning Calm." *Ensign* 32 (July 1992): 32–37.

———. "Ng Kat Hing: Hong Kong Pioneer." *Ensign* 22 (August 1992): 50–52.

Robertson, Hilton A. Conference Report (October 1924):122–25.

———. Conference Report (April 1947): 53–56.

Rollins, Kerril Sue. "The Book of Mormon in Hindi, Tamil, and Telugu." *Ensign* 13 (February 1983): 78–79.

Roy, Denny. "Kim Ho Jik: Korean Pioneer." *Ensign* 18 (July 1988): 18–23. This article was reprinted in *Tambuli* 12 (February 1989): 8–13.

"The Saints in the Philippines." *Ensign* 5 (January 1975): 42–49.

Saunders, Shirleen Meek. "Whang Keun-Ok [Hwang Keun Ok]: Caring for Korea's Children." *Tambuli* 15 (October 1992): 32–41.

Scott, George L. "South Vietnam, Thailand Dedicated for Missionaries." *Church News*, November 19, 1966, 5.

Sheffield, Sheridan R. "Asia Area: Welcome Mat Is Out in Several Countries." *Church News*, June 19, 1993, 3.

———. "Church Donates Medical Gift to Vietnam." *Church News*, January 11, 1992, 3.

———. "From a Tiny Seed Comes Great Growth." *Church News*, May 11, 1991, 12.

———. "Gospel peace brings strength to opera singer." *Church News*, August 22, 1992, 5.

———. "Miracles Found in Philippines Quake." *Church News*, August 4, 1990, 3.

———. "Toll Continues to Rise in Philippines." *Church News*, July 28, 1990, 13.

"Six Missionary Couples to Help with Mongolia's Higher Education." *Church News*, September 19, 1992, 3–4.

Smart, William B. "India Fills Geneology Link." *Church News*, January 9, 1988, 6, 12.

Smith, G. Carlos. "Southeast Asia Mission." *Improvement Era* 73 (March 1970): 19.

Smith, Henry A. "Unusual Sacrament Meeting." *Church News*, July 30, 1966, 4.

Smith, Joseph Fielding. "Report on the Far East Missions." *Improvement Era* 58 (December 1955): 917–18.

Sorensen, David E., Rex D. Pinegar, and L. Edward Brown. "The Church in Japan, Korea, and Far-East Russia." *Ensign* 26 (November 1996): 110–12.

Stoker, Kevin. "Because of Snyder." *Church News*, October 21, 1984, 16.

———. "One Saved Today." *Church News*, May 30, 1987, 16.

Stowe, Dorothy. "Joy Spans the Pacific as Choir Visits Orient." *Church News*, September 22, 1979, 3, 8–9.

"Tagalog Selection from the Book of Mormon." *Tambuli* 11 (August 1988): Dateline Philippines, 6–7.

Taylor, Alma O. "About Japan and the Japanese Mission." *Improvement Era* 10 (November 1906): 6.

"Temple Brings Philippines All Blessings." *Church News*, September 30, 1984, 5, 10.

The, Grace May W. "Mabuhay-Deseret Foundation Is Still Around." *Tambuli* 17 (May 1994): Dateline Philippines, 4.

"Thousands Attend Temple Open Houses." *Church News*, September 30, 1984, 4.

"Thousands Visit Hong Kong Center." *Church News*, January 22, 1977, 3.

"3 India Translations Complete." *Church News*, August 14, 1982, 3.

"Three New Missions Formed." *Church News*, March 4, 1978, 3.

"3 Stakes formed from 1 in Philippines." *Church News*, July 9, 1977, 13.

"Top institute class graduate is Ph.D." *Church News*, January 29, 1977, 15.

"Translated Languages of the Book of Mormon." *Church News*, January 6, 1996, 7.

Tuason, Miles T. "From 17 La Salle to Temple Drive: 10 Years of the MTC." *Tambuli* 17 (October 1993): Dateline Philippines, 1–2.

———. "MTC Couples District Created." *Tambuli* 17 (March 1994): Dateline Philippines, 3.

"Two new General Authorities called" [includes biographical sketch of Han In Sang]. *Church News*, June 1, 1991, 3.

VanDenBerghe, Elizabeth S. "Edwin Dharmaraju: Taking the Gospel Home to India." *Ensign* 20 (April 1990): 60–62.

Van Orden, Dell. "Door to China May Be Opening." *Church News*, April 7, 1979, 3, 9.

———. "Emotional Rites Note 'Miracle of Philippines.'" *Church News*, October 7, 1984, 3, 10–11.

———. "Saints Throng to Area Meetings in the Far East." *Church News*, November 1, 1980, 3–4, 9.

———. "Tremendous Future for Church in Japan." *Church News*, November 8, 1980, 4, 10.

Vermillion, Douglas L. "Gospel Splendor in Sri Lanka." *Ensign* 25 (August 1995): 78–79.

"Vietnam: Musicians Perform 'Messiah.'" *Church News*, December 4, 1993, 5.

"Vietnamese Performers Share Musical Talent." *Church News*, October 30, 1993, 3.

Waite, Lu Jones. "The Day I Learned What It Means to Be a Gram." *Ensign* 11 (March 1981): 28–29.

Walker, Joseph. "Church in Malaysia Is Small but Faithful." *Church News*, March 14, 1981, 12.

———. "Sri Lanka Native Is Branch President in Own Country." *Church News*, November 1, 1980, 7.

Watabe, Masakazu. "Inner Unification and Outer Diversity." *Proceedings of the Sixth Annual Conference of the International Society*. (Provo: David M. Kennedy Center for International Studies, 1995): 66–70.

———. "The Unspoken Words." *Ensign* 10 (December 1980): 22–23.

Watanabe, Kan, et al. "Japan: Land of the Rising Sun." *Ensign* 5 (August 1975): 36–43.

Woodworth, Warner. "Third World Strategies Toward Zion." *Sunstone* 14 (October 1990): 13–23.

"Y Professor Called to New Mission." *Daily Universe* (November 11, 1992): 1.

Younger, Shirley-Anne. "Seoul Temple Dedicated." *Ensign* 16 (February 1986): 74–75.

THESES AND DISSERTATIONS

Britsch, R. Lanier. "Early Latter-day Saint Missions to South and East Asia." Ph.D. diss., Claremont Graduate School and University Center, 1967.

———. "A History of the Missionary Activities of the Church . . . in India, 1849–1856." Master's thesis, Brigham Young University, 1964.

Brooks, Karl. "The Life of Amos Milton Musser." Master's thesis, Brigham Young University, 1961.

Call, Lowell E. "Latter-day Saint Servicemen in the Philippine Islands: A Historical Study of Their Religious Activities and Influences Resulting in the Official Organizations of The Church of Jesus Christ of Latter-day Saints in the Philippines." Master's thesis, Brigham Young University, 1955.

Choi, Dong Sull. "A History of The Church of Jesus Christ of Latter-day Saints in Korea, 1950–1985." Ph.D. diss., Brigham Young University, 1990.

Cox, Dale S. "The Church in the Third World: Singapore and Indonesia." Honors thesis, Brigham Young University, 1981.

Groberg, Delbert H. "Toward a Synoptic Model of Instructional Productivity." Ph.D. diss., Brigham Young University, 1986.

Nelson, Terry G. "A History of The Church of Jesus Christ of Latter-day Saints in Japan from 1948 to 1980." Master's thesis, Brigham Young University, 1986.

Nichols, Murray L. "History of the Japan Mission of The Church of Jesus

Christ of Latter-day Saints, 1901–1924." Master's thesis, Brigham Young University, 1958.

Peterson, Gerald Joseph. "History of Mormon Exhibits in World Expositions." Master's thesis, Brigham Young University, 1974.

Suksabjarern, Manoth. "Roman Catholic, Protestant, and Latter-day Saints Missions in Thailand: An Historical Survey." Master's thesis, Brigham Young University, 1977.

Xi, Feng. "A History of Mormon-Chinese Relations: 1849–1993." Ph.D. diss., Brigham Young University, 1994.

MANUSCRIPTS, CHURCH RECORDS, AND LETTER COLLECTIONS

Beck, Calvin R. "History of the Seoul LDS Group, August 1953 to May 1954." LDS Church Archives.

CES Philippines: Personnel, Location, and Physical Facilities, 1995–1996. Friday, September 8, 1995. In possession of R. Lanier Britsch.

CES Philippines: Program Report on Seminary and Institute, 1995–1996. Wednesday, July 12, 1995. In possession of R. Lanier Britsch.

Chaichana, Suchat. "Church Educational System, Thailand Historical Report, 1993."

Chinese Mission Historical Reports. March 31, 1951. LDS Church Archives.

Fotheringham, William to Amos Milton Musser. October 19, 1853. LDS Church Archives.

Gill, Gurcharan S. India Bangalore Mission Report. LDS Church Archives.

Grant, Heber J. Letterbook, February 21, 1924–July 19, 1924. LDS Church Archives.

Hawthorne to Jones, November 30, 1979, in Joseph Talmage Jones, Collection 1968–1982. LDS Church Archives.

Indonesia Jakarta Mission, Historical Reports. By date, 1979. LDS Church Archives.

Japan Mission Journals, 1901–1924. LDS Church Archives.

Jenson, Andrew. "Manuscript History of the Japan Mission." 1918–1921. LDS Church Archives.

Jones, Joseph Talmage to Carlos E. Asay and Jacob de Jager. February 27, 1980. Joseph Talmage Jones, Collection, LDS Church Archives.

Jones, Joseph Talmage from First Presidency. April 21, 1980. Joseph Talmage Jones, Collection 1968–1982. LDS Church Archives.

Jones, Joseph Talmage to Marion D. Hanks. November 24, 1981. Joseph Talmage Jones, Collection 1968–1982. LDS Church Archives.

Kadarusman, Effian. "The History of the Translation of the Book of Mormon, According to the Memory of and a Few Data from Han King Ishar." In possession of R. Lanier Britsch.

Korea Mission, Historical Reports. LDS Church Archives.

Manuscript History of the East India Mission. LDS Church Archives.

Manuscript History of the Japan Mission, 1918–1921, 1948, 1951. LDS Church Archives.

Manuscript History of the Siam Mission. LDS Church Archives.

Missionary Department Annual Report. The Church of Jesus Christ of Latter-day Saints. 1978. LDS Church Archives.

Mission Financial and Statistical Reports. Central Pacific Mission. 1937–1948. LDS Church Archives.

Mission Financial and Statistical Reports. Chinese Mission. 1951. LDS Church Archives.

Mission Financial and Statistical Reports. Japan Mission, 1920–1924, 1948, 1951–1952, 1954–1955, 1958–1962. LDS Church Archives.

Mission Financial and Statistical Reports. Southern Far East Mission, 1955, 1958, 1959, 1962–1968. LDS Church Archives.

Palmer, Spencer J., R. Lanier Britsch, Ray C. Hillam, and Richard S. Beal. "Educational Needs of The Church of Jesus Christ of Latter-day Saints in Asia: Final Report." A report to the Church Commissioner of Education, 1972.

Pang, Beng Ling. "Singapore Church History." Manuscript, n.p.

Petersen, Mark E. to First Presidency. Tour of the Southern Far East Mission, general observations, July 6, 1959. LDS Church Archives.

Richey, Benjamin to George A. Smith. December 2, 1865. LDS Church Archives.

Richins, J. Alden. "1986–87 [CES] Historical Report for Southeast Asia." October 15, 1987.

Southeast Asia Mission, Historical Reports. March 31, 1970. LDS Church Archives.

Southern Far East Mission, Historical Reports. 1955. LDS Church Archives.

Stimpson, Joseph H. to David O. McKay. Copybook H., March 18, 1920. LDS Church Archives.

Stimpson to Alma O. Taylor. Copybook I., January 19, 1921. LDS Church Archives.

"Success Messenger." June 1966. LDS Church Archives.

Taiwan Taipei Mission, Historical Reports. March 31, 1976. LDS Church Archives.

Taulu, Jules L. L. "Short History of The Church of Jesus Christ of Latter-day Saints in Indonesia." Typescript in possession of R. Lanier Britsch.

Thiruthuvadoss, Paul. "Report of The Church of Jesus Christ of Latter-day Saints in Coimbatore, India." December 30, 1979. Joseph Talmage Jones Collection 1968–1982, LDS Church Archives.

———. A Report About the LDS Church in Coimbatore Area, December 17, 1979." Joseph Talmage Jones Collection 1968–1982, LDS Church Archives.

Vietnam Zone Historical Report. 1962, 1966. LDS Church Archives.

Wheat, Jerry D. Saigon Historical Report. April 1975. Copy in possession of Richard C. Holloman Jr.

White, Larry R. "A Short History of the Church in Thailand." Thailand Bangkok Mission Manual, 1993.

UNPUBLISHED AUTOBIOGRAPHIES, DIARIES, AND JOURNALS

Browning, Larry K. Diary. In possession of Browning.

Call, Willard. Diary. In possession of Adelaide W. Call, Spanish Fork, Utah.

Findlay, Ross and Linnie, compilers. *Missionary Journals of Hugh Findlay: India-Scotland.* Ephraim, Utah: n.p. 1973.

Gill, Vilo P. Journal. Copy in possession of its writer.

Hess, Alan H. Journal. LDS Church Archives.

Hinckley, Gordon B. Journals. In possession of President Hinckley, Salt Lake City, Utah.

Jones, Wayne A. Journal. Partial copy in possession of the author.

Kadarusman, Effian. Journal. Copy in possession of the author.

Montano, Gilbert. Journal. Partial copy in possession of the author.

Musser, Amos Milton. Journals. LDS Church Archives.

Robertson, Hilton A. Daily Diary, Japanese Mission 1954–1955. Copy in possession of the author.

———. Diary. 1949. LDS Church Archives.

———. Scrapbook. LDS Church Archives.

Taylor, Alma O. Journals; Papers. Special Collections, Harold B. Lee Library, Brigham Young University, Provo, Utah.

UNPUBLISHED ADDRESSES, ARTICLES, AND STUDIES

Arsecularatne, Sunil and Vermillion, Douglas L. "Pioneering Growth of the Church in Sri Lanka." Draft, August 1993.

Ashman, Peter. "Thailand: An Example of Mass Media Utilization in the Mission Field." Research Paper, Brigham Young University, 1980.

Benson, Ezra Taft. To All Stake and Mission Presidents in the Orient. April 8, 1975. Copy in possession of the author.

Browning, Diane E. "The Translation of Mormon Scriptures Into Chinese." Unpublished paper, Brigham Young University, 1977.

Carmack, John K. Temple Ground Breaking Remarks, Hong Kong Temple. January 22, 1994. Copy in possession of the author.

Collier, Cynthia. "The Church of Jesus Christ of Latter-day Saints in Indonesia." Manuscript. 1989. Copy in possession of the author.

Cook, Joseph V., Ruben Lancanienta, Clifford H. Huntington, and Augusto A. Lim. *A History of The Church of Jesus Christ of Latter-day Saints,* n.p. 1965.

Cox, Dale S. "A Brief History of the LDS Church in Singapore." Mimeographed copy, June 1978. Found in Southeast Asia Mission Historical records and minutes. LDS Church Archives.

Dharmaraju, Edwin. Mission to India, February 14, 1978, 5. Typed copy in possession of the author.

Das, Baldwin and Douglas Rose. "History in North India—The Church of Jesus Christ of Latter-day Saints." Typed report, August 1987. Copy in possession of the author.

Figuerres, Cyril I. A. "Demographic Study of Converts in Japan." A research report of the Research and Evaluation Division of The Church of Jesus Christ of Latter-day Saints, 1987.

———. "The Ammon Project: Establishing Real Growth and the First Generation Church in Japan." 1994. Copy in possession of the author.

Garlock, Jerry C., comp. "A History of the Church in India." Bangalore, India: n.p., 1995. LDS Church Archives.

Gill, Gurcharan S. Spoken and Written Texts of Homecoming Talk. Provo, Utah, September 10, 1995.

Heaton, H. Grant. Testimony, Ho Man Tin chapel, Kowloon-tong, Hong Kong, May 26, 1996. Tape recording in possession of the author.

Holloman, Richard C., Jr., "The Snap of the Silver Thread: The LDS Church in Vietnam." Research paper, Brigham Young University, 1977. LDS Church Archives.

Hyer, Paul V. "Preparations for a Mission in Postwar Japan: Paul Hyer's 'Mini-Mission Training Center.'" Unpublished paper. In possession of the author.

Kikuchi, Yoshihiko. "Increasing missionary productivity: Japan-Korea Area 1978–1982." n.p., n.d.

Kimball, Margaret C. and Stanley C. "First Branch of the Church Established in Sri Lanka (Ceylon)." n.d. Joseph Talmage Jones Collection, LDS Church Archives.

Larkin, Todd S. "The Tokyo South Mission Miracle: Experiences and Methods." Unpublished manuscript. In possession of the author.

Mason, James O. "The History of the Welfare Service Missionary Program." Address given August 12, 1979, Missionary Training Center, Provo, Utah. Typescript.

Nguyen Van The as told to David L. Hughes. "The Saigon Shepherd and the Scattered Flock." Manuscript.

Notes taken by the author at the temple dedication, May 27, 1996, Hong Kong.

Numano, Jiro. "Transition in the Reception of the Mormon Church in Japan: An Analysis in Terms of Newspaper and Magazine Articles." A paper presented to the Mormon History Association, Park City, Utah, May 20, 1994.

Patterson, Dale. "One Thoughtless Moment." Research paper, Brigham Young University, 1974.

Talbot, Steven N. "A History of the Chinese Mission of the Church of Jesus Christ of Latter-day Saints." Unpublished paper, Brigham Young University, 1977.

Thinh Dihn Van. "From an LDS Evacuee." Unpublished article, 1975. In possession of Richard C. Holloman Jr.

Vermillion, Douglas L. "There Are People the Lord Loves in Sri Lanka." Draft article submitted to the *Ensign*, January 24, 1995.

White, Larry R. "An Apostolic Blessing in Bangkok, June 1992." Typescript. In possession of the author.

———. "A Conversion Story: Srilaksana Gottsche." Bangkok, Thailand, September 1993. Copy in possession the author.

———. "The Opening of Cambodia." December 1994. Copy in possession of the author.

ORAL HISTORIES

Andersen, Dwayne N. Oral History. Interviews by R. Lanier Britsch. 1973. Typescript. The Oral History Program, Archives, Historical Department of The Church of Jesus Christ of Latter-day Saints, Salt Lake City, Utah.

Andrus, Paul C. Oral History. Interviews by R. Lanier Britsch. 1974. Typescript. The Oral History Program, Archives, Historical Department of The Church of Jesus Christ of Latter-day Saints, Salt Lake City, Utah.

Bradshaw, William S. Oral History. Interviews by R. Lanier Britsch. 1974. Typescript. The James Moyle Oral History Program, Archives, Historical Department of The Church of Jesus Christ of Latter-day Saints, Salt Lake City, Utah.

Christensen, Elwood L. Oral History. Interviews by R. Lanier Britsch. 1978. Typescript. The James Moyle Oral History Program, Archives, Historical Department of The Church of Jesus Christ of Latter-day Saints, Salt Lake City, Utah.

Clissold, Edward L. Oral History. Interviews by R. Lanier Britsch. 1976. Typescript. The James Moyle Oral History Program, Archives, Historical Department of The Church of Jesus Christ of Latter-day Saints, Salt Lake City, Utah.

Hanks, Marion D. Oral History. Interviews by Gordon Irving. 1983. Typescript. The James Moyle Oral History Program, Archives, Historical Department of The Church of Jesus Christ of Latter-day Saints, Salt Lake City, Utah.

Komatsu, Adney Y. Oral History. Interviews by R. Lanier Britsch. 1974. Typescript. The James Moyle Oral History Program, Archives, Historical Department of The Church of Jesus Christ of Latter-day Saints, Salt Lake City, Utah.

Kumar, Raj. Oral History. Interviews by Gordon Irving. 1987. Typescript. The James Moyle Oral History Program, Historical Department of The Church of Jesus Christ of Latter-day Saints, Salt Lake City, Utah.

Mauss, Armand L. Oral History. Interviews by William G. Hartley. 1974.
  Typescript. (Interview 2.) The James Moyle Oral History Program,
  Archives, Historical Department of The Church of Jesus Christ of Latter-
  day Saints, Salt Lake City, Utah.
Mauss, Vinal Grant. Oral History. Interviews by R. Lanier Britsch. 1975.
  Typescript. The James Moyle Oral History Program, Archives, Historical
  Department of The Church of Jesus Christ of Latter-day Saints, Salt Lake
  City, Utah.
Palmer, Spencer J. Oral History. Interviews by Brad Jenkins. 1977. Provo, Utah.
Slover, Robert H. Oral History. Interviews by R. Lanier Britsch. 1976.
  Typescript. The James Moyle Oral History Program, Archives, Historical
  Department of The Church of Jesus Christ of Latter-day Saints, Salt Lake
  City, Utah.
Smith Jr., G. Carlos. Oral History. Interviews by William G. Hartley. 1972.
  Typescript. The Oral History Program, Archives, Historical Department of
  The Church of Jesus Christ of Latter-day Saints, Salt Lake City, Utah.

INTERVIEWS

Arcansalin, Roland P. Interview with author, Manila, Philippines, September
  16, 1995.
Banks, Ben B. Interview with author, Manila, Philippines, September 16, 1995.
Brown, Lowell Edward. Telephone interview with author, Orem, Utah to
  Pocatello, Idaho, March 20, 1979.
Carlson, Monte. Interview by Feng Xi, Provo, Utah, February 18, 1994.
Carmack, John K. Interview with author. Salt Lake City, Utah. November 30,
  1995.
Clissold, Edward L. Interview by Kenneth Barnum and J. Christopher
  Conkling, Salt Lake City, November 8, 1973.
Corriveau, Troy. Interview with author, Bangkok, Thailand, September 7,
  1995.
Edmonds, Rita. Interview with author, Provo/Orem, Utah, December 28, 1995.
Edmunds, Mary Ellen. Interview by Dale S. Cox, Provo, Utah, February 27,
  1979.
Eldredge, Anan. Interview with author, Bangkok, Thailand, September 8,
  1995.
Gill, Gurchuran S. Interview with author, Provo, Utah, October 24, 1995.
Gottsche, Srilaksana Suntarahut. Interview with author, Bangkok, Thailand,
  September 8, 1995.
Groberg, George. Interview with author, Provo, Utah, June 12, 1974.
Hague, Delores and Robert. Interview with author, Provo, Utah, October 26,
  1995.
Hardy, W. Brent. Interview with author, Las Vegas, Nevada, June 2, 1975.
Iba, Stephen K. Interview with author, Provo, Utah, August 17, 1995.

Jones, Becky and Warren R. Interview with author, Provo, Utah, November 1, 1995.

Kadarusman, Effian. Interviews with author, Laie, Hawaii, May 30, 1990 and June 7, 1990; and Jakarta, Indonesia, September 12–13, 1995.

Kikuchi, Yoshihiko. Interview with author, Tokyo, Japan, September 21, 1995.

Kitamura, Eugene M. Interview with author, Tokyo, Japan, September 19, 1995.

Kovalenko, Virgil. Interview with author, Provo, Utah, November 12, 1995.

Ladjar, Joachim. Interview with author, Jakarta, Indonesia, September 13, 1995.

Larkin, Todd S. and Phillip J. Windley. Interview with author, Orem, Utah, July 9, 1996.

Lim, Augusto A. Interview with author, Manila, Philippines, September 16, 1995.

Mascardo, Emmanuel S. Interview with author, Orem, Utah, September 24, 1995.

Miller, J. Scott. Interview with author, Provo, Utah, October 3, 1996.

Niiyama, Yasuo. Interview with author, Orem, Utah, August 25, 1996.

Phelps, David N. Interview with author, Bangkok, Thailand, September 7, 1995.

Sakai, Kiyoshi. Interview with author, Tokyo, Japan, September 22, 1995.

Shuler, David. Interview with author, Provo, Utah, October 31, 1995.

Subandriyo. Interview with author, Jakarta, Indonesia, September 12, 1995.

Tandiman, Piet. Interview with author, Jakarta, Indonesia, September 13, 1995.

Till, Eugene P. Interview with S. Brad Jenkins, Provo, Utah, 1977.

Tueller, Carol and Vern. Interview with author, Jakarta, Indonesia, September 12, 1995.

Wade, Alton L. Interview with author, Salt Lake City, Utah, July 5, 1979.

Wheat, Jerry D. Interview with author, Hong Kong, September 6, 1995.

CORRESPONDENCE

Cook, Joseph V. to Keith E. Garner, September 1, 1965, LDS Church Archives.

Haugue, Robert to R. Lanier Britsch, July 12, 1995, in possession of author.

Hinckley, Gordon B. to R. Lanier Britsch, May 12, 1977, in possession of author.

Hyer, Paul V. to Richard B. Stamps, February 29, 1996, copy in possession of author.

Jones, "J" Stephen to R. Lanier Britsch, [CES Zone Administrators], October 25, 1996, in possession of author.

Warren, Carl D. to Warren R. Jones, September 12, 1995, in possession of author.

Woodworth, Warner to Dear Friends. Thanksgiving 1995, in possession of author.

HISTORY OF
ASIAN MISSIONS

Japanese Missions

*Name Changed

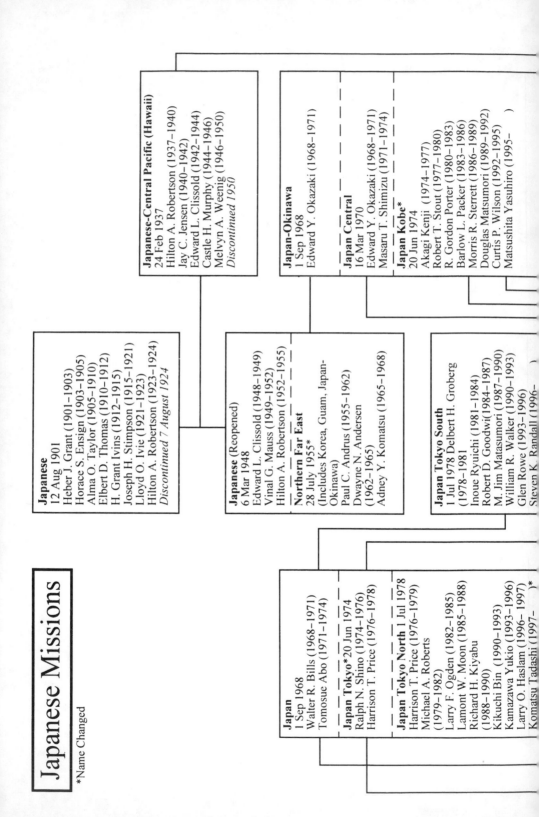

Japanese
12 Aug 1901
Heber J. Grant (1901–1903)
Horace S. Ensign (1903–1905)
Alma O. Taylor (1905–1910)
Elbert D. Thomas (1910–1912)
H. Grant Ivins (1912–1915)
Joseph H. Stimpson (1915–1921)
Lloyd O. Ivie (1921–1923)
Hilton A. Robertson (1923–1924)
Discontinued 7 August 1924

Japanese (Reopened)
6 Mar 1948
Edward L. Clissold (1948–1949)
Vinal G. Mauss (1949–1952)
Hilton A. Robertson (1952–1955)

Northern Far East
28 July 1955*
(Includes Korea, Guam, Japan-Okinawa)
Paul C. Andrus (1955–1962)
Dwayne N. Andersen (1962–1965)
Adney Y. Komatsu (1965–1968)

Japanese-Central Pacific (Hawaii)
24 Feb 1937
Hilton A. Robertson (1937–1940)
Jay C. Jensen (1940–1942)
Edward L. Clissold (1942–1944)
Castle H. Murphy (1944–1946)
Melvyn A. Weenig (1946–1950)
Discontinued 1950

Japan-Okinawa
1 Sep 1968
Edward Y. Okazaki (1968–1971)

Japan Central
16 Mar 1970
Edward Y. Okazaki (1968–1971)
Masaru T. Shimizu (1971–1974)

Japan Kobe*
20 Jun 1974
Akagi Kenji (1974–1977)
Robert T. Stout (1977–1980)
R. Gordon Porter (1980–1983)
Barlow L. Packer (1983–1986)
Morris R. Sterrett (1986–1989)
Douglas Matsumori (1989–1992)
Curtis P. Wilson (1992–1995)
Matsushita Yasuhiro (1995–   )

Japan
1 Sep 1968
Walter R. Bills (1968–1971)
Tomosue Abo (1971–1974)

Japan Tokyo*20 Jun 1974
Ralph N. Shino (1974–1976)
Harrison T. Price (1976–1978)

Japan Tokyo North 1 Jul 1978
Harrison T. Price (1976–1979)
Michael A. Roberts
(1979–1982)
Larry F. Ogden (1982–1985)
Lamont W. Moon (1985–1988)
Richard H. Kiyabu
(1988–1990)
Kikuchi Bin (1990–1993)
Kamazawa Yukio (1993–1996)
Larry O. Haslam (1996–1997)
Komatsu Tadashi (1997–   )*

Japan Tokyo South
1 Jul 1978 Delbert H. Groberg
(1978–1981)
Inoue Ryuichi (1981–1984)
Robert D. Goodwi (1984–1987)
M. Jim Matasumori (1987–1990)
William R. Walker (1990–1993)
Glen Rowe (1993–1996)
Steven K. Randall (1996–   )

Japan West
18 Mar 1970
Watanabe Kan (1970–1973)
Arthur K. Nishimoto (1973–1974)

Japan Fukuoka*
20 Jun 1974
Arthur K. Nishimoto (1974–1976)
Yamada Goro (1976–1979)
Roy I. Tsuya (1979–1982)
Takashi C. Shimizu (1982–1985)
John Sakamaki (1985–1988)
Raymond Y. Sasaki (1988–1991)
Cyril I. A. Figuerres (1991–1994)
Lorin D. Pinock (1994–1997)
James A. Mc Arthur (1997–   )

Japan Okayama
9 Jul 1976
William H. Nako (1976–1979)
Okomoto Ryo (1979–1982)
Yoshizawa Toshiro (1982–1985)
D. Glenn Hawkins (1985–1988)
Kitamura Masataka (1988–1990)
Utagawa Seiichiro (19990–1993)
Onda Yutaka (1993–1996)
Norman D. Shumway (1996–   )

Japan-Nagoya
1 Aug 1973
Sato Satoru (1973–1974)

Japan Nagoya*
20 Jun 1974
Sato Satoru (1974–1976)
Tanaka Kenji (1976–1979)
Sagara Kenichi (1979–1982)
Joe N. Ikeda (1982–1985)
David R. Broadhead (1985–1988)
W. Emery Smith (1988–1991)
Walter L. Ames (1991–1994)
James R. Mackley (1994– 1997)
Kent J. Diamond (1997–   )

Japan Osaka
1 Jul 1980
Ushio Shigeki (1980–1983)
Merrill L. Blalock (1983–1986)
Moriyama Shigeki (1986–1989)
Nishihara Satoshi (1989–1992)
C. Kent Peterson (1992–1995)
Discontinued 1 Jul 1995

Japan Okinawa
1 Jul 1990
Evan A. Larson (1990–1993)
Karl T. Pope (1993–1996)
Discontinued 30 Jun 1996

Japan East
5 Mar 1970
Russell N. Horiuchi (1970–1973)
Koizumi Kotaro (1973)

Japan Sapporo*
Koizumi Kotaro (1974–1976)
Suzuki Shozo (1976–1979)
David H. Hoki (1982–1985)
Rulon D. Munns (1985–1988)
Tsuchida Masaru (1988–1991)
Ned L. Christensen (1991–1994)
Paul H. Beckstrand (1994–   )

Japan Sendai
1 Jul 1974
Walter S. Teruya (1974–1977)
Richard D. S. Kwak (1977–1978)
Sakai Kiyoshi (1978–1981)
Sam K. Shimabukuro (1981–1984)
Aoyagi Koichi (1984–1987)
Niiyama Yasuo (1987–1990)
Fukuda Makoto (1990–1993)
Richard M. Austin (1993–1996)
Yoshino Kazuhiro (1996–   )

Chinese/Mongolian Missions

* Name Changed

Japanese
6 Mar 1948

Chinese (Hong Kong)
10 Jul 1949
Hilton A. Robertson (1949–1953)
Discontinued 9 Feb 1953

Southern Far East
28 Jul 1955
*Includes Hong Kong, Taiwan, Philippines, So. &
Southeast Asia*
H. Grant Heaton (1955–1959)
Robert S. Taylor (1959–1962)
Jay A. Quealey, Jr. (1962–1965)
Keith E. Garner (1965–1968)
W. Brent Hardy (1968–1969)

Hong Kong-Taiwan
1 Nov 1969
W. Brent Hardy (1969–1971)

Hong Kong
11 Jan 1971
W. Brent Hardy (1971)
William S. Bradshaw (1971–1974)
Jerry D. Wheat (1974–1977)
David H. H. Chen (1977–1980)
Garry P. Mitchell (1980–1983)
Brent R. Armstrong (1983–1986)
Charles W. H. Goo (1986–1989)
K. Y. Tai (1989–1992)
David L. Lowe (1992–1995)
John M. Aki, Jr. (1995–1997)
Tak Chung Stanley Wan (1997–   )

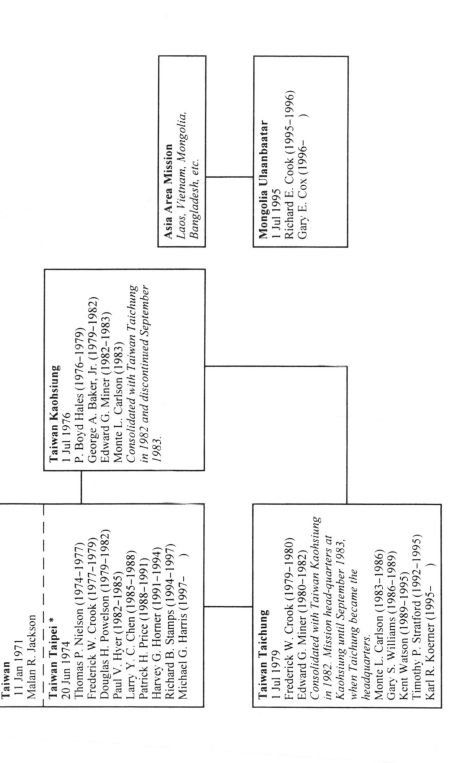

Taiwan
11 Jan 1971
Malan R. Jackson

Taiwan Taipei *
20 Jun 1974
Thomas P. Nielson (1974–1977)
Frederick W. Crook (1977–1979)
Douglas H. Powelson (1979–1982)
Paul V. Hyer (1982–1985)
Larry Y. C. Chen (1985–1988)
Patrick H. Price (1988–1991)
Harvey G. Horner (1991–1994)
Richard B. Stamps (1994–1997)
Michael G. Harris (1997–   )

Taiwan Kaohsiung
1 Jul 1976
P. Boyd Hales (1976–1979)
George A. Baker, Jr. (1979–1982)
Edward G. Miner (1982–1983)
Monte L. Carlson (1983)
Consolidated with Taiwan Taichung in 1982 and discontinued September 1983.

Taiwan Taichung
1 Jul 1979
Frederick W. Crook (1979–1980)
Edward G. Miner (1980–1982)
Consolidated with Taiwan Kaohsiung in 1982. Mission head-quarters at Kaohsiung until September 1983, when Taichung became the headquarters.
Monte L. Carlson (1983–1986)
Gary S. Williams (1986–1989)
Kent Watson (1989–1995)
Timothy P. Stratford (1992–1995)
Karl R. Koerner (1995–   )

Asia Area Mission
Laos, Vietnam, Mongolia, Bangladesh, etc.

Mongolia Ulaanbaatar
1 Jul 1995
Richard E. Cook (1995–1996)
Gary E. Cox (1996–   )

Philippines Missions

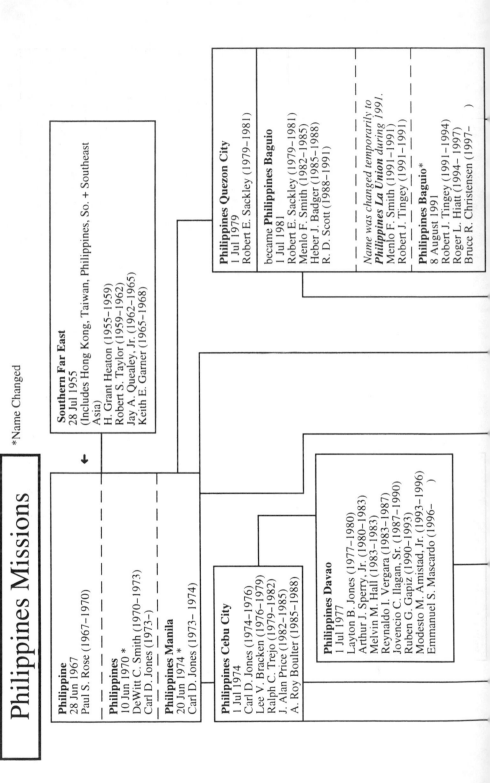

*Name Changed

Southern Far East
28 Jul 1955
(Includes Hong Kong, Taiwan, Philippines, So. + Southeast Asia)
H. Grant Heaton (1955–1959)
Robert S. Taylor (1959–1962)
Jay A. Quealey, Jr. (1962–1965)
Keith E. Garner (1965–1968)

Philippine
28 Jun 1967
Paul S. Rose (1967–1970)

Philippines
10 Jun 1970 *
DeWitt C. Smith (1970–1973)
Carl D. Jones (1973–)

Philippines Manila *
20 Jun 1974 *
Carl D. Jones (1973– 1974)

Philippines Cebu City
1 Jul 1974
Carl D. Jones (1974–1976)
Lee V. Bracken (1976–1979)
Ralph C. Trejo (1979–1982)
J. Alan Price (1982–1985)
A. Roy Boulter (1985–1988)

Philippines Davao
1 Jul 1977
Layton B. Jones (1977–1980)
Arthur J. Sperry, Jr. (1980–1983)
Melvin M. Hall (1983–1983)
Reynaldo I. Vergara (1983–1987)
Jovencio C. Ilagan, Sr. (1987–1990)
Ruben G. Gapiz (1990–1993)
Modesto M. Amistad, Jr. (1993–1996)
Emmanuel S. Mascardo (1996–)

Philippines Quezon City
1 Jul 1979
Robert E. Sackley (1979–1981)

became **Philippines Baguio**
1 Jul 1981
Robert E. Sackley (1979–1981)
Menlo F. Smith (1982–1985)
Heber J. Badger (1985–1988)
R. D. Scott (1988–1991)

Name was changed temporarily to **Philippines La Union** *during 1991.*
Menlo F. Smith (1991–1991)
Robert J. Tingey (1991–1991)

Philippines Baguio *
8 August 1991
Robert J. Tingey (1991–1994)
Roger L. Hiatt (1994–1997)
Bruce R. Christensen (1997–)

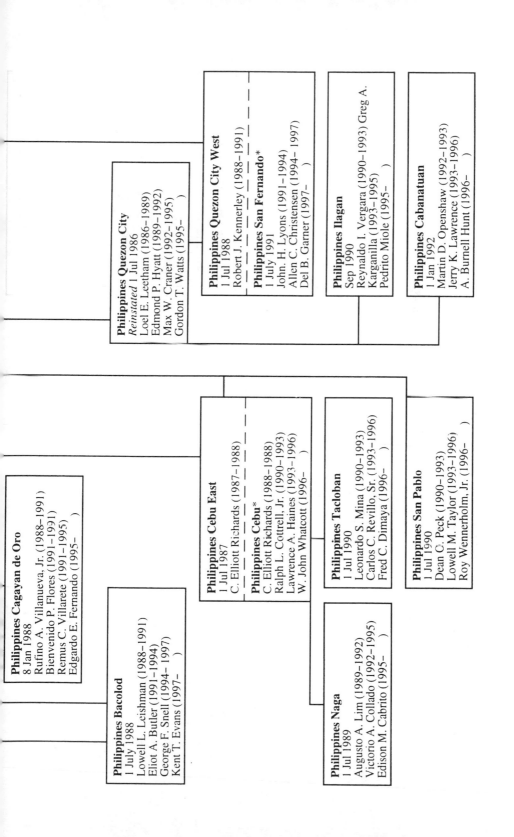

Philippines Cagayan de Oro
8 Jan 1988
Rufino A. Villanueva, Jr. (1988–1991)
Bienvenido P. Flores (1991–1991)
Remus C. Villarete (1991–1995)
Edgardo E. Fernando (1995–   )

Philippines Bacolod
1 July 1988
Lowell L. Leishman (1988–1991)
Eliot A. Butler (1991–1994)
George F. Snell (1994–1997)
Kent T. Evans (1997–   )

Philippines Cebu East
1 Jul 1987
C. Elliott Richards (1987–1988)

Philippines Cebu*
1 Jul 1987
C. Elliott Richards (1988–1988)
Ralph L. Cottrell, Jr. (1990–1993)
Lawrence A. Haines (1993–1996)
W. John Whatcott (1996–   )

Philippines Naga
1 Jul 1989
Augusto A. Lim (1989–1992)
Victorio A. Collado (1992–1995)
Edison M. Cabrito (1995–   )

Philippines Tacloban
1 Jul 1990
Leonardo S. Mina (1990–1993)
Carlos C. Revillo, Sr. (1993–1996)
Fred C. Dimaya (1996–   )

Philippines San Pablo
1 Jul 1990
Dean O. Peck (1990–1993)
Lowell M. Taylor (1993–1996)
Roy Wennerholm, Jr. (1996–   )

Philippines Quezon City
Reinstated 1 Jul 1986
Loel E. Leetham (1986–1989)
Edmond P. Hyatt (1989–1992)
Max W. Craner (1992–1995)
Gordon T. Watts (1995–   )

Philippines Quezon City West
1 Jul 1988
Robert J. Kennerley (1988–1991)

Philippines San Fernando*
1 July 1991
John. H. Lyons (1991–1994)
Allen C. Christensen (1994–1997)
Del B. Garner (1997–   )

Philippines Ilagan
Sep 1990
Reynaldo I. Vergara (1990–1993) Greg A. Karganilla (1993–1995)
Pedrito Miole (1995–   )

Philippines Cabanatuan
1 Jan 1992
Martin D. Openshaw (1992–1993)
Jerry K. Lawrence (1993–1996)
A. Burnell Hunt (1996–   )

Korean Missions

* Name Changed

Northern Far East
28 Jul 1955
Paul C. Andrus

Korean
8 Jul 1962
Gail E. Carr (1962–1965)
Spencer J. Palmer (1965–1968)
Robert H. Slover (1968–1970)

Korea*
10 Jun 1970
Robert H. Slover (1970–1971)
L. Edward Brown (1971–1974)

Korea Seoul*
20 Jul 1974
Eugene P. Till (1974–1977)
F. Ray Hawkins (1977–1980)
D. Brent Clement (1980–1982)
David C. Butler (1982–1985)
Lee Do Whan (1985–1988)
Paull H. Shin (1988–1991)
Michael E. Nichols (1991–1994)
Jun Jong Chul (1994–1997)
Darryl W. Harris (1997–   )

Korea Seoul West
1 Jul 1979
D. Brent Clement (1979–1980)
Kim Cha Bong (1980–1983)
Edwin H. Jenson (1983–1986)
Do Gil Whoe (1986–1989)
Bruce Snow (1989–1992)
Ronald K. Nielsen (1992–1995)
Earl S. Swain (1995–   )

Korea Pusan
1 Jul 1975
Han In Sang (1975–1978)
Rhee Honam (1978–1981)
Pak Byung Kyu (1981–1984)
James M. Harper (1984–1987)
Mark Peterson (1987–1990)
Seo Won (1990–1993)
W. Richard Herd (1993–1996)
Steven R. Leishman (1996–   )

Korea Taejon
1 Jul 1983
Hong Moo Kwang (1986–1989)
Ross H. Cole (1989–1992)
Lee Kang Woo (1992–1995)
Hong Byung Sik (1995–   )

South and Southeast Asia Missions

* Name Changed

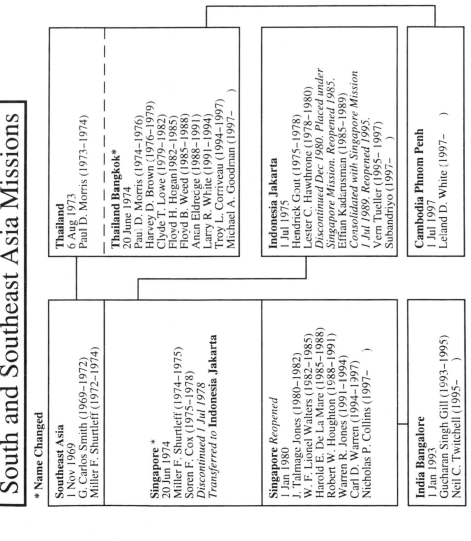

Southeast Asia
1 Nov 1969
G. Carlos Smith (1969–1972)
Miller F. Shurtleff (1972–1974)

Singapore *
20 Jun 1974
Miller F. Shurtleff (1974–1975)
Soren F. Cox (1975–1978)
Discontinued 1 Jul 1978
Transferred to **Indonesia Jakarta**

Singapore *Reopened*
1 Jan 1980
J. Talmage Jones (1980–1982)
W. F. Lionel Walters (1982–1985)
Harold E. De La Mare (1985–1988)
Robert W. Houghton (1988–1991)
Warren R. Jones (1991–1994)
Carl D. Warren (1994–1997)
Nicholas P. Collins (1997–   )

India Bangalore
1 Jan 1993
Gucharan Singh Gill (1993–1995)
Neil C. Twitchell (1995–   )

Thailand
6 Aug 1973
Paul D. Morris (1973–1974)

Thailand Bangkok*
20 June 1974
Paul D. Morris (1974–1976)
Harvey D. Brown (1976–1979)
Clyde T. Lowe (1979–1982)
Floyd H. Hogan1982–1985)
Floyd B. Weed (1985–1988)
Anan Eldredge (1988–1991)
Larry R. White (1991–1994)
Troy L. Corriveau (1994–1997)
Michael A. Goodman (1997–   )

Indonesia Jakarta
1 Jul 1975
Hendrick Gout (1975–1978)
Lester C. Hawthrone (1978–1980)
Discontinued Dec 1980. Placed under
Singapore Mission. Reopened 1985.
Effian Kadarusman (1985–1989)
Consolidated with Singapore Mission
1 Jul 1989. Reopened 1995.
Vern Tueller (1995– 1997)
Subandriyo (1997–   )

Cambodia Phnom Penh
1 Jul 1997
Leland D. White (1997–   )

INDEX

Aaronic Priesthood: in India, 11; in Japan, 118; in Hong Kong, 244; in Vietnam, 433

Adams, William, 30–31

Aki, Henry and SaiLang, 231–33

Aki, John, Jr., 512

Americans of Japanese Ancestry (AJA), 72, 74, 76–78

Anand Panyarachun, Thai prime minister, 401, 403–4

Andersen, Dwayne N. and Peggy, 111, 114–24, 145, 151

Andersen, Ralph and Margaret, 552

Anderson, Clarence LeRoy B., 108

Anderson, Richard Lloyd, 5

Anderson, Warren, 560

Andrus, Ed, 273

Andrus, Paul C. and Frances, 87–88, 100–101, 103–4, 106–7, 109–11, 115, 178–81

Andrus, W. Garth and Eloise, 344

Ang, Richard, 473

Animism: in Taiwan, 255; in the Philippines, 325; in Thailand, 375; in Vietnam, 424

Anthony, Michael and Christine, 524, 538–40, 550

Antonio, Emiliano, Jr., 334

Apostolic blessings: in the Philippines, 369; in Thailand, 402–3; in Singapore, 469

Arcansalin, Roland, 349

Area conferences: in Japan, 140–43; 152, 155; in Korea, 199; second series in Asian nations, including Korea, 204;

in Hong Kong and Taiwan, 261–62, 276–77; in the Philippines, 336–37

Arnold, Daryl, U.S. Ambassador, 465

Arnold, Mel, 89

Arsecularatne, Sunil, 557

Articles of Faith, The, 269, 405

Ashman, Peter, 388

Ashton, Marvin J., 142, 276; conducts ground breaking for Seoul Korea Temple, 208; participates in dedication of Manila Philippines Temple, 344

Asia: definition of, xi; purpose of missionary work in, 1, 3; significance of division of Japan Mission in, 100

Asia Educational Resources Project (AERP), 272

Asia North Area, 154, 168

Asian languages, xi–xiii; Bengali, 9, 507; Hindustani, 9, 27; Marathi, 13, 27, 507; Burmese, 27; Tamil, 27, 507; Telugu, 27, 507; Japanese, 47, 49; Cantonese, Mandarin, 236; Tagalog (Filipino), Ilocano, Cebuano, Hiligaynon (Ilonggo), Tag-English, 366; Pampango, Waray, 367; Thai, 379–81; Cambodian, 410; Bahasa Malaysia (Malay), 471; Bahasa Indonesia, 484; Hindi, 506; Urdu, Gujarati, Malayalam, Kannada, Oriya, Punjabi, Assamese, Kashmiri, Sindihi, Sanskrit, 507; Sinhala, 558

Asian names: characters used in, xii–xiii; Vietnamese (Chinese) characters, transliterated, 424

statement to Elder Hinckley, 128;
offers dedicatory prayer on Mormon
pavilion, 133; inspects property in
Korea as future temple site, 207;
dedicates chapel in the New
Territories, 270
Brown, L. Edward and Carol, 154,
184–87, 191, 193–98
Brown, Margaret, 399
Brown, Victor L., 128, 421
Browning, Diane E., 267–68
Browning, Elder and Sister F. Wallace, 67
Browning, Larry K., 266
Buddhism: in Japan, 81; in Taiwan, 255;
in the Philippines, 325; in Vietnam,
424
Bunker, Ellsworth, 428
Burma (Myanmar), 413–14
Burmese. *See* Burma
Bush, Lester, 432–33
Buying land and properties. *See* Chapels
and Church buildings; Property
BYU. *See* Brigham Young University

Caine, Fred A., 55–58
Calica, Virginia, 334
Call, Willard, 319
Cambodia: cautious approach to opening
missionary work in, 407–13; prince
and king of, 408; new constitution of,
408; becomes part of Thailand
Bangkok Mission, 411; buildings in,
413; political turmoil in, 413–14;
missionaries and mission president in
new Cambodia Phnom Penh Mission
forced to flee, 413
Cannon, George I., 154, 288–89; 341
Cannon, Hugh J., 220–31
Cannon, Scott, 487
Cannon, Winfield Q. and Wanda, 461
Cantonese. *See* China, languages spoken
in
Carlson, Gary and Barbara, 309
Carmack, John K., xiv, 283, 296, 407–9,
445–47, 468, 546–47, 552, 560–61
Carr, Gail E. and Gwyneth, 182–84, 187,
189
Carter, William F., 18–20
Carver, Murray and Donna, 550
Catholicism: early influences of, 1–3; in
Japan, 47, 81–83; in Korea, 171; in
China, 228; in the Philippines, 324–26

Cavender, Cecil L. "Bud" and Kay, 418
Cawit, Elder and Sister Carmelino, 350
Central National Library (Korea), 214
Central Pacific Mission (CPM). *See*
Japanese Central Pacific Mission
Ch'e Tsai Tien, 267–68
Ch'ing (Qing) Dynasty, 227
Ch'iu Hung-hsiang, 253–54
Cha Jong Hwan, 190
Chai Zemin, Chinese ambassador, 303
Chaitanya, Krishna, 527
Chang I-Ch'ing, 277
Chang Jae Hwan, 204
Chapels and Church buildings: first in
Asia, 18; in Japan, 85–86, 96, 109–10,
116–17; Japan Missionary Training
Center (JMTC), 152; in Korea, 182,
189–91, 207; in Hong Kong, 240,
270–71, 295; in Mongolia, 312; in the
Philippines, 330–33; in Thailand, 384;
in Vietnam, 420, 429; restrictions in
Singapore, 467. *See also* Property
Characters. *See* Asian names
Chau, Nguyen Hai, 439
Chen, David Hsiao Hsin, 251, 262
Cheney, Rex A., 182
Chesley, Larry, 431
Chew, Eddie and Queenie, 463–64
Chiang K'ai-shek, 227–29
Child, Sheldon F., 341
China: early missionary efforts in, 33–39;
historical perspective of, 227;
Protestant and Catholic inroads into,
227–29; languages spoken in, 236,
258–59; variety of sects present in,
238; publications translated in, 239;
Church buildings in, 239–42, 248–49;
economy in, 247; Church publications
for, 249–50; characteristics of Saints
in, 250–51; religious climate in, 284;
political leaders visit Salt Lake City
and Polynesian Cultural Center in
Hawaii, 303; language exchanges
between Xian Foreign Languages
University and BYU College of
Humanities, 304; Church contact
with and aid to, 300–306
Chiles, Joshua C., 548
Chinese Mission: officially opened, 231;
missionaries relocated from, 235;
organizational challenges of, 245
Chowgule, Ramesh and Bonnie, 524, 550

"Christian Boom," 83

Christianity: in Asia, 1; illegal in Japan, 6; repression of, in Japan, 46–48; growth of, in Japan, 83; introduced in Korea, 171–72; in China, 228–29; in lives of Chinese converts, 251; history and influence of, in Taiwan, 252

Choi Dong Heon, 209

Choi Hyun Soo, 221–22

Choi Wook Hwan, 190, 197, 203

Chong Sun Fu, 473–74

Chou Wen-tsung, 283

Christensen, Craig G., 378–79

Christensen, James L., 433

Christensen, Joe J., 193

Christiansen, Elder and Sister Elwood L., 68, 73

Chu Wan Yuen, 245

Chung Hee, 206

Chung Tai Pan, 183, 188

Church, Frank, senator from Idaho, 301

Church distribution center in Seoul, Korea, 217

Church Educational System (CES): in Japan, 140–41, 157–58; in Korea, 190–94, 220–21; in Hong Kong and Taiwan, 272–73, 294–95; in the Philippines, 335–36, 364–65; in Thailand, 397–98; in Malaysia, 473–74; in Indonesia, 489–90, 500; in Nepal, 549

Church growth, xii; concentrated in post-World War II era, 2–3; greatest period of, in Japan, 148

Church hymnal: translated into Japanese, 109; importance of, to Korean Saints and investigators, 188–89; translated into Korean, 189

Church Missionary Committee, proselyting plan announced by, 265

Church News, 206

Clark, Harold Glenn and Mary, 557

Clark, J. Reuben, Jr., 73

Clifford, John W., 294

Clissold, Edward L., 73, 77–78, 83–92, 101, 103, 111

Collado, Ambrosio, 342

Communism: Russian and Mongolian, 307, 313; in Vietnam, 424, 435–36

Confucianism: in Japanese life, 80–81; in Korea, 171, 180; in Taiwan, 255; "Three Bonds" and "Five Virtues" of, 287

Cong Ton Nu Tuong-Vy ("Sister Vy"), 429–31, 439–42

Conkling, J. Christopher, 74, 76

Conversion: to Christianity, 2; in Japan, 119–20; adjustments following, 162, 224, 491; ratios, in Korea, 180; in Mongolia, 313; in Singapore, 456; in Indonesia, 491; in India, 513–14

Cook, Joseph V., 327, 330, 334

Cook, Quentin L., 341

Cook, Richard E. and Mary, 314

Cooley, Frank L., 477

Coombs, D'Monte W., 381, 484

Cooper, John H., 29, 561

Corriveau, Troy L. and Lynn, 404–5, 411–12

Cowley, Matthew and Elva, 91, 231, 233

Cox, Dale S., 456

Cox, Gary E. and Joyce, 314

Cox, Soren F. and Fern, 459–61, 517, 522

Craig, Alison, 485–86

Craven, Rulon G., 299

Crook, Frederick W., 264–65

Cullimore, James A., 276, 428

Culture and customs: conflicts regarding, 5; in Japan, 52–53, 94–96, 116, 119–20, 138; examples of, 163; in Korea, 195; in Philippines, 323–26; in Singapore, 456; in Indonesia, 477–79; in India, 513–14

Daoism (Taoism): in Chinese realm, 285; in Philippines, 325; in Singapore, 453

Darmawan, Budi, 484–86

Das, Baldwin and Maureen, 523, 525, 528

Dashchoiliin Monastery, Mongolia, 313

David M. Kennedy Center for International Studies (BYU), China Teachers Program, 304

Davis, Eb, 533

Davis, Major L. B., 320

Davis, William E., 67

"Day of humiliation." *See* Johnson Act

de Jager, Jacob: supervises Philippines—Southeast Asia, 139, 154, 276; dedicates new visitors center in Hong Kong, 274, 276, 288; attends dedication of Burma, 414

Dedication of lands: Japan, 50; Asia (in general), 98–101; Korea, 177–78; Chinese realm, 229–31, 294; Mongolia, 311–12; Philippines, rededicated, 321–23; Thailand, 376–77; Cambodia, 412–13; Burma, 414; South Vietnam, 421–24; Indonesia, 480–82; reasons for dedicating lands, 482; Singapore, 454; Sri Lanka, 557

Dedication of temples: Tokyo Japan, 149–51; Seoul Korea, 204–12; Taipei Taiwan, 292–94; Hong Kong, 299–300; Manila Philippines, 342–46

Degn, Duane W., 237, 253

Deng Xiaoping, allows foreigners into People's Republic of China, 281, 300

Dereta, Nicholas, example of LDS servicemen holding sacrament services in Vietnam, 420

Derricott, Kent, 158–59

Deseret International Charities, 313

Detton, Richard L., 178

Dew, Sheri L., 204, 207

Dewey, Benjamin F., 18–30, 555

Dharmaraju, Edwin and Elsie, 520–21

Dharmaraju, Lata, 520

Do Dung, 446

Do Gil Whoe, 194

Dobson, Donald C., 409

Dobson, Sharlene, 409

Doctrine and Covenants: translation of, into Japanese, 100, 104–5; retranslation of, into Korean, 188; translation of, into Chinese, 267; translation of, into Vietnamese, 434. *See also* Standard works

Donomoto Tsutumo, 160

Dredge, Paul, 207

Drummond, Richard H., 82

Duncan, Chapman, 33–36

Dutch, influence of, in Indonesia, 477–78

Early missions: in 1800s, 5–7; in 1850s, 8–42; to India, 9–26; to Burma and Siam, 30–33; to China, 33–39; to Japan, 51–53

East India Mission, 19

Eastern Siberia. *See* Far-East Russia

Ebdalin, Franklin, Deputy Ambassador for the Philippines, 361

Economic conditions: in Japan, 94, 102, 153; in China, 247; in Taiwan, 252–54, 284; in Philippines, 335

Edmonds, Rita, 392–97

Edmunds, Mary Ellen, 273, 356–58, 491

Education: value of, to Koreans, 181; need for, in Asia, 272; offered through humanitarian organizations in Vietnam, 445–49

Eldredge, Anan, 379, 383, 398–400

Eldredge, Louis and June, 398, 436

English teaching in China. *See* David M. Kennedy Center

Ensign magazine, 360

Ensign, Horace S. and Mary, 49, 55–57

Esplin, Rulon, 68

Evans, Preston D., 74

Evans, Richard L., 510

Exclusion Act of 1924. *See* Johnson Act

Expo '70, the Japan World Exposition: Church announces participation in, 131; design and components of, 133–35; success of, 134–35

Fajardo, Aniceta, 319

Fallows, James, 158

Family names, xiii. *See also* Asian names

Far-East Russia, 166

Faust, James E., offers prayer in Beijing, 302; dedicates Sri Lanka for preaching of gospel, 557

Featherstone, Joseph E. and Marie, 55

Featherstone, Vaughn J., 350, 361–62

Fetzer, Emil B., 133, 144

Filial piety (*hsiao*), 285

Filipino. *See* Philippines

Filipino languages. *See* Philippines, languages spoken in; Asian languages

Findlay, Hugh, 9–14

Fish, Melvin C., 253

Fisher, Michael T., 468

Flammer, Gordon M., 376

Flandro, Royce P. and Jane, 309

Fong, Kenneth K. S., 237

Forman, Charles W., 508

Fort William, 17

Fotheringham, William, 18–22

Friends: to missionaries in India, 34; to early missionaries in Hong Kong, 34; to President Clissold in Japan, 86; to mission president in China, 240–42; of the Church in Mongolia, 313

Frost, Burr, 15

Fujiwara Takeo, 72

Funding of early missions, 16–17

Fyans, J. Thomas, 128

Fye, Rodney W., 177–78

Helps, Louise, 448
Henderson, Richard W., 411
Henstrom, Richard H., 175
Hernandez, James, 560
Hess, Alan H., 378
Hess, Jay, LDS prisoner of war, 431
Hettiarchchi, Gertrude, 557
Hill, George R., III, 341
Hill, John M., 358
Hill, Terrill, of UNESCO, 496
Hillam, Ray C., 304
Hinckley, Gordon B., xiv, 39, 136, 142–44,
    153, 157, 187, 214, 290, 348, 417, 480,
    566, 568–70; on entitlement of Asian
    peoples to hear the gospel, 3;
    supervises Asian missions, 103; on
    first tour of Asia, 109; role in
    purchasing property in Tokyo, 110;
    supervises Asian missions, 116;
    participates in Japanese Saints' visit
    to Hawaii Temple, 123; is assisted by
    Marion D. Hanks, 127; hears
    prophetic statement from Hugh B.
    Brown, 128; negotiates and plans for
    Mormon exhibit at Expo '70, 131;
    attends dedication of Mormon
    pavilion, 133; in Korea, 199, 204–5;
    assists with purchase of property in
    Korea, 207; is called as first counselor
    in the First Presidency, 210; dedicates
    Seoul Korea Temple, 210–12;
    encourages growth of Taiwan
    missionaries, 259; makes first tour of
    Asian missions, 260–61; presents first
    Chinese copy of Book of Mormon to
    President McKay, 267; dedicates
    chapel in Hong Kong, 270–72;
    influence of, in Asia missions, 275–76;
    creates Taipei Taiwan Stake, 277;
    creates stake in Hong Kong, 281;
    conducts ground-breaking ceremonies
    for Taipei Taiwan Temple, 292;
    involvement with Hong Kong
    Temple, 295–96, 299–300; visits Hong
    Kong Mission, 306; makes first visit to
    Philippines, 320; rededicates
    Philippines for preaching of gospel,
    321–23; assists in securing land, 330;
    visits American War Memorial
    Cemetery in Manila, 336–37; presides
    at ground breaking and dedication of
    Manila Philippines Temple, 342–46,

369; meets with Saints in Philippines,
    369–71; dedicates Thailand for
    preaching of gospel, 375–78; gives
    permission for using singing group in
    Thailand, 387; on fulfillment of
    dedicatory prayer in Thailand, 389;
    lends support for humanitarian efforts
    in Thailand, 390; dedicates Cambodia
    for preaching of gospel, 412–13;
    dedicates Burma for preaching of
    gospel, 414; dedicates Vietnam, with
    Elder Hanks, for preaching of gospel,
    417, 421–24; assists service personnel
    in Vietnam, 427; authorizes future
    Church building in Vietnam, 429;
    meets with Sister Vy of Vietnam, 431;
    finds and holds meetings with three
    Church members in Singapore, 453;
    visits earliest converts in South India,
    510–12
Hinckley, Marjorie, 210, 300, 376–77,
    412–14, 570
Hipwell, Jamie T., 411
Hirohito, Emperor, 82–83
Hiroi, Mr., 53
Ho, A. C. (Ho Ah Chuan), 456, 460,
    467–68
Ho Choi, 190
Ho, Helen, 456
Ho, Ivan Bee, 471–72
Ho Kam (Robert) Tong, Sir, 270
Ho Tung-hai, 281
Holloman, Richard C., Jr., 421, 427, 433
Hong Byung Sik, 188, 190
Hong Kong: missions in, 100, 228, 233,
    306; political climate in, 242;
    uncertainties surrounding reversion to
    People's Republic of China, 263;
    visitors center dedicated in, 274;
    living conditions in, 284
Hong Kong Saints, 97; self-sufficiency
    and welfare projects among, 246–47;
    outstanding missionaries among, 251;
    need for, to stay in Hong Kong and
    build leadership, 262–63
Hong Kong Temple: uncertainties
    surrounding property for, 295;
    inspiration of Lord through President
    Hinckley regarding, 294–95;
    announcement of and ground-
    breaking ceremonies for, 296; open

house and dedication of, 299–300; opens for regular sessions, 300

Hong Moo Kwang, 204

Hong Young Sook, 216

Hoopes, David C., 437

Hope, Bob, 302

Horiuchi, Russell N., 78, 135

Horner, John M., 17

Houghton, Robert W. and Linda, 547–48

How, Rodney, 472

Howard, Mario, 391

Hsiao (*xiao*), filial piety, 285

Hu Wei-I, 266, 269

Humanitarian services: by early Christian missionaries in Asia, 1–2; missionaries enter Mongolia, 281; provided in PRC, 303–4; in the Philippines, 352; through Mabuhay-Deseret Foundation, 359; in Thailand, 389–97; through Operation Smile, 444–45; medical and educational, offered in Vietnam, 445–49. *See also* Mabuhay-Deseret Foundation; Operation Smile; Welfare service missionaries

Humanitarian Services Department. *See* LDS Charities

Humphreys, Jack, 540

Hun Sen, 413

Hundrup, Tagg B. and Maria, 524

Hunt, Larry, 482, 484

Hunter, Howard W., conducts two sessions of Taipei Taiwan Temple dedication, 292; encouraged members to obtain temple recommend, 503, 566

Hunter, Lee Ford, 528

Huntsman, Jon M., Jr., 465

Huntsman, Jon M., Sr., 465

Huo Chea, biography of, 212–15

Hwang Keun-Ok, 198, 221–23. *See* Tender Apples Orphanage in Korea

Hyer, Paul V., 75, 87, 291, 294, 308–9

Hymns. *See* Church hymnal

Iami, Elder, 131

Iba, Stephen K., 335–36, 364

Ideographic characters, xii

Imai Kazuo, 94

India: early mission to, 8–9; included in Italian Mission, 9; early converts in, 10–13, 18; religious climate in, 11, 27; challenges of missionaries in, 26–28,

506–10; visit of Church representatives to, 258; India Bangalore Mission created in, 462, 543; official languages of, 506–7; discrimination against Christians in, 508–10; pioneering work in South, 510–20; challenges faced by converts in, 513–14; priesthood ordinations in, 516; Church registered in, 516; leadership and supervision of, 517–22; Book of Mormon translated into Telugu, 521–22; legal constraints in, 523–27; building reputation for Church in, 527–29; genealogy work in, 529–32; further translated materials available in, 532–34; local missionaries in, 541; problems with Church image in, 542; local leadership in, 543–45

Indonesia: Church in, 258; population and geography of, 477; missionary work in, 478–79; western influence on, 479; early Christianity in, 480; dedicated for preaching of gospel, 480–82; inherent spirituality of native people in, 482, 491–92; first missionaries in, 482, 487; legal recognition for Church in, 482–84; visa problems in, 483, 488; first missionary baptisms in, 483; earliest publications and translation work in, 484–86; first mission in, 488; mission and CES leadership in, 489–90; welfare services in, 490–92; government restrictions on tracting in, 492; first full-time Indonesian missionaries in, 492–93; foreign missionaries expelled from, 493–94; external pressures and internal strife in, 494–95; mini-MTC trains local missionaries in, 496; translations of standard works become available in, 496, 499–500; mission leadership, mission changes, and leadership training, 496–99; CES in, 500; closure of Church school, and aftermath, 501–3; future of Church in, 503–4

Indonesia, missions in: Indonesia Jakarta Mission, 460–61; attached to Singapore Mission, 462

Institute (of religion). *See* Church Educational System

Isune Nachie, 73
Italian Mission, India included in, 9
Ivie, Lloyd O. and Nora, 61
Iwakura Mission, 47

Jackson, Malan R., 237, 264–65, 267
Jackson, Dr. E. William, 359
Jamba, Nicholas, 472
Japan: victory of, in Sino-Japanese War, 44; discovery of, 45; Catholicism in, 46; dedicated for preaching of gospel, 50; missionaries' difficulty in learning language, 51–52; early converts in, 53–55, 71–74; obstacles to missionary work in, 60; mission statistics for, 63; religious history of, 81; pressure on and persecution against Christians in, 82–83; Church growth in, 83, 89, 92; calling of local missionaries to serve in, 94; cultural and religious traditions in, 95–96; society and economy since the war, 102; continuing missionary efforts in, 103–4; need for local leadership in, 117; becomes financially self-supporting, 120; divided into two missions, 127, 130–31; LDS Church membership in, 137–38; obstacles to Church growth in, 137–38; first area conference in, 140; great period of Church growth in, 148; conferences in, 152, 155; growth of economy and materialism in, 153
Japan, missions in, 44; Iwakura Mission, 47; early mission, 55; Japanese Mission reopened, 78; Japan East Mission, Japan West Mission created, 135; Tokyo South Mission, 140, 145; Nagoya Mission, 140; Japan Tokyo Mission, Japan Tokyo South Mission, Japan Tokyo North Mission, Japan Kobe Mission, Japan Osaka Mission, 145
Japan Mission: why opened, 44–45; why closed, 66–68; interim leadership in, 71–72; moved to Hawaii, 72; reopened, 78; post-war rebuilding of, 88; expanded, 93; divided into Northern Far East Mission (Japan, Korea, Okinawa) and Southern Far East Mission (Hong Kong, Taiwan, the Philippines, Guam), 98; includes Korea, 175; Northern Far East

Mission divided, renamed Japan Mission, 130–31. *See also* Japanese/Central Pacific Mission (CPM)
Japan Missionary Training Center (JMTC). *See* Missionary Training Centers
Japan World Exposition. *See* Expo '70
Japanese, The, 80
Japanese: persecution of Christians, 46; obstacle posed by the language, for American missionaries, 51; population in Hawaii, 72; language, 74–75; colonial period, 172
Japanese exclusion laws. *See* Oriental exclusion laws
Japanese/Central Pacific Mission (CPM) in Hawaii: opened, 73; missionaries to, 74; early Saints, 75–78; name changed, 77; combined with Hawaiian Mission, 79; language training for missionaries bound for Japan, 87; divided and renamed, 98; conversion of Adney Y. Komatsu through, 125
Japanese Mission. *See* Japan Mission
Japanese Saints: in Hawaii, 72; important tie with Japan(ese) Mission in Hawaii; traditions of, 116; social challenges and personal sacrifices of, 119–20; trip to Hawaii Temple, 120–24; in post–World War II Hawaii, 123
"Japanese Saints Sing" (recording), 121, 129
Jarvis, Erastus L., 55
Jensen, Jay C., 76–77
Jensen, Jay R., LDS prisoner of war, 431
Jesus Christ: acceptance of, 4; restored gospel of, 27; faithfulness of Korean Saints to gospel of, 224; basic lessons about, 243; previous knowledge of, almost essential to conversion, 251; Mongolian students ask to be taught about, 311; unknown by many in India, 513
Jesus the Christ, need for, 354
Johnson Act, 65
Johnson, Kenneth, 341
Jones, Carl D., 329
Jones, Garth, 493
Jones, J. Talmage and Vera Jean, 461–62, 472–73, 496–97, 499, 524–25, 528, 537–38

announced, 145; second tour of Japan, 159; "Spoken Word," 185; first Japanese and Korean tour, 204; "Music and the Spoken Word" aired over Thai radio, 384. *See also* Music

Morris, Harper K., 419

Morris, Paul D. and Betty, 386, 389

Mother Theresa, 527

Mount Pinatubo, eruption of, 361

Moyle, Henry D., 110

Mullennex, Captain John T., 418

Murphy, Castle H., 73, 77

Murphy, Dale, 159

Murray, Harry J., 323

Music: importance of, to Korean Saints, 188–89; New Horizons missionary quintet and Tender Apples choir in Korea, 198; BYU Young Ambassadors in PRC, 281, 301–2; as missionary tool in Thailand, 387–88; as missionary tool in Vietnam, 446; the Osmonds in Singapore, 462–63. *See also* Mormon Tabernacle Choir

Muslims, in Philippines, 354–55

Musser, Amos Milton, 15–29, 559

Mutual Improvement Association: started in Japan, 60–63; only Church meeting allowed in Japan during World War II, 71; foundations laid in post-war Japan, 89–90; organized in Thailand, 376

Myanmar. *See* Burma

Nagai Kimiko, 160

Nagoya, Japan, 89

Nakahigashi Mikio, 94

Nakamura Ayako, 108

Nakamura Nobu, 107–8

Nakazawa Hajime, 53

Nako, William, 78

Names, Asian. *See* Asian names

Nami Suzuki, 76, 88

Nangnoi Thitapoora, 376

Nara Fujiya: 71, 85, 88, 90, 94

National Family Day exhibition, in Singapore, 468

National Theater in Seoul, Korea, 204

Neill, Stephen, 172

Neilson, Thomas P., 264, 267, 277

Nelson, Russell M.: becomes proficient in Mandarin Chinese and teaches heart surgery in the PRC, 303, 305;

accompanies Elder Maxwell to Thailand, 402–4; visits Pakistan, 561

Nepal: opened for missionary work and assigned to India Bangalore Mission, 546–49; is world's only Hindu monarchy, 547; Church Educational System in, 549–51; challenges in, 551–52; welfare and humanitarian services in, 552–53; temple and genealogy work in, 553–55

Nestorian Christians, 1

New Home, A (refugee orientation video), 396

New Horizons: missionary quintet in Korea, 198. *See also* Music

Ng Kat Hing, 237, 244, 267, 299

Ngoc, Phan The, 428

Nghia, Dr., 439–40

Nhat, Dang Thong, 427, 433

Nielsen, Ronald K., 183

nisei (second-generation American of Japanese Ancestry), 87–88, 125; Church leaders in Japan, 135–36

Nishimoto, Arthur K., 78, 141

Nixon, Richard M., 427

Nora Koot, first Chinese female to serve as missionary, 244

Norodom Sihanonk, King of Cambodia, 408

Northern Far East Mission (Japan, Korea, Okinawa): created from Japan Mission, 98; rapid growth of Korea creates separate mission, 102; becomes fully self-supporting, 120; is divided, 130–31

Numano Jiro, 159, 160

Nunez, Maria Carmen, 368

Nutman, Molly, 273

Oaks, Dallin H., 305–6

Occupation forces in Japan, 78, 88

Oh Kehi, 175

Ohm Borin, first Cambodian branch president, 412

Okazaki, Chieko N.: joins Church and later serves in general presidency of the Relief Society, 78; serves with Ed in Japan-Okinawa Mission, 130–31

Okazaki, Edward: joins Church, 78; called to preside over part of divided Northern Far East Mission (Japan-Okinawa Mission), 130–31

Okinawa: included in Japanese Mission, 93; opened for missionary work, 105, 107

Ollis, Ronald R., 237

ōn (obligation), 96

Oniki, Ben, 104

Operation Smile, 444–45. *See also* Humanitarian services; Mabuhay-Deseret Foundation; Welfare service missionaries

Opie, Bruce, 390–95

Opposition: from Protestants in India, 11; hostile press in India, 13; in Japan, 43–49, 82–83, 137–38; from Korean government, 200; in Mongolia, 313; in Thailand, 391; in Singapore, 456–58, 464, 467; in Malaysia, 473; in Indonesia, 478, 488, 492–95; in India, 508–10; in Sri Lanka, 556–57; in Pakistan, 560

Oriental exclusion laws, 64

Osaka, 105–6

Osmond, Donny and Marie, 462–63

Osumo, Rabai B., 346

Our Search for Happiness, 157

Oviatt, Dee, 436

Owens, Robert, 18–22

Oya Shigeyuki, 411

Packer, Boyd K., 89

Pahl Mao (Sister), 410

Pak Byung Kyu, 194, 204, 215, 220

Pakistan: growth in, 559; persecution of Christians in, 560; full-time missionary service begins in, 561–62; progress in, 563

Palmer, Shirley, 215, 224

Palmer, Spencer J., 174–75, 184–85, 189–90, 194, 207, 215, 224

Pang Beng Ling (Sister), 465, 468–69

Pang Lai Har, 299

Park Byung Kyu, 201

Park Chung-Hee, president of the Republic of Korea, 201

Park Jae Am, 175, 195, 205, 212, 214

Park Nam Soo, 215

PCC. *See* Polynesian Cultural Center

Pearl of Great Price, translation of: into Japanese, 100, 104–5; into Korean, 188; into Chinese, 267–68; into Filipino languages, 367; into Thai,

383; into Vietnamese, 434. *See also* Standard works

Pedroche, Angel S., 328

Pelaez, Emmanuel, Philippines ambassador to the U.S., 361

People's Republic of China (PRC), 228, 297

Perera, Alloy, 558

Performing groups. *See* Brigham Young University; Music

Perry, L. Tom, 344

Perry, Commodore Matthew C., 6, 46

Petersen, Mark E., 248, 250, 255–56, 272, 320, 453

Pham, Tien Van, 441

Phan, Dr. Nguyen Huy, 445–49

Phan The Ngoc, 428

Phelps, David N., 402–3

Philippines: included in Japanese Mission, 93; Philippines/Micronesia area created, 154; the Church in, 258, 318, 320; success in, 323–26; high status of women in, 333; Filipino missionaries in, 334–35; local leadership in, 339; challenges in, 340; genealogy work in, 347–48; Missionary Training Center, 350; Church publications in, 360; scriptures translated into languages of, 366–68

Philippines Refugee Processing Center (PRPC), 351–53, 459

Philippines, languages spoken in: Tagalog, Ilocano, Hiligaynon (Ilonggo), and Cebuano, 325; Tagalog, Ilocano, Hiligaynon (Ilonggo), Cebuano, Pampango, and Waray, 367. *See also* Asian languages

Philippines, missions in: Southern Far East Mission, 320; Philippines Mission, 328; Philippines Cebu City Mission, Philippines Davao Mission, 329; Philippines Manila Mission, Cabanatuan Mission, 349; Philippines Quezon City Mission, 352; Philippines Naga Mission, 353

Pho family, 439

Phonetic characters, xii

Physical facilities. *See* Chapels and Church buildings; Property

Pierce, Thomas, 329